THE ḤANBALĪ SCHOOL OF LAW AND IBN TAYMIYYAH

The Ḥanbalī School of Law and Ibn Taymiyyah offers a valuable account of the development of Ḥanbalite jurisprudence, placing the theoretical and conceptual parameters of this tradition within the grasp of the interested reader.

This book studies the vibrant yet controversial interaction between Ibn Taymiyyah and the Ḥanbalī School of law to assess the extent to which this relationship was a conflict or reconciliation and provides a detailed exploration of the following issues:

- The strength of contributions made to this School by earlier paragons associated with Aḥmad Ibn Ḥanbal.
- The contextual constructs which shaped the tradition's development.
- The methodology and literature synonyms within the classical School.
- The manner in which Ibn Taymiyyah engaged with the Ḥanbalī tradition.
- The impact of his thought upon the later expression of the School's legal doctrines and its theoretical principles.
- The contribution made by this School in general to the synthesis of Islamic law.

The Ḥanbalī School of Law and Ibn Taymiyyah is a vital reference work for those with interests in Islamic law, the history of the Ḥanbalite tradition and its principal luminaries.

Abdul Hakim I. Al-Matroudi is a visiting senior lecturer in Arabic, Department of the Languages and Cultures of the Near and Middle East, SOAS. His research interests include Islamic law, Ḥanbalī law and Ibn Taymiyyah.

CULTURE AND CIVILIZATION IN THE MIDDLE EAST

Series Editor: Ian R. Netton

University of Leeds

This series studies the Middle East through the twin foci of its diverse cultures and civilisations. Comprising original monographs as well as scholarly surveys, it covers topics in the fields of Middle Eastern literature, archaeology, law, history, philosophy, science, folklore, art, architecture and language. Although there is a plurality of views, the series presents serious scholarship in a lucid and stimulating fashion.

ARAB REPRESENTATIONS OF THE OCCIDENT

East–West encounters in Arabic fiction

Rasheed El-Enany

THE ḤANBALĪ SCHOOL OF LAW AND IBN TAYMIYYAH

Conflict or conciliation

Abdul Hakim I. Al-Matroudi

ARABIC RHETORIC

A pragmatic analysis

Hussein Abdul-Raof

THE ḤANBALĪ SCHOOL OF LAW AND IBN TAYMIYYAH

Conflict or conciliation

Abdul Hakim I. Al-Matroudi

Routledge
Taylor & Francis Group
LONDON AND NEW YORK

First published 2006
by Routledge
2 Park Square, Milton Park, Abingdon, Oxon OX14 4RN

Simultaneously published in the USA and Canada
by Routledge
270 Madison Ave, New York, NY 10016

Routledge is an imprint of the Taylor & Francis Group

Typeset in Baskerville by
Newgen Imaging Systems (P) Ltd, Chennai, India
Printed and bound in Great Britain by
Biddles Ltd, King's Lynn

British Library Cataloguing in Publication Data
A catalogue record for this book is available
from the British Library

Library of Congress Cataloging in Publication Data
A catalog record for this book has been requested

ISBN 0–415–34156–6

CONTENTS

TABLES

PREFACE

The study of Ibn Taymiyyah's life and knowledge has attracted the attention of researchers. Yet the role of this scholar in the Ḥanbalī School of law has not been adequately researched and examined. Accordingly, this work seeks to study in depth some aspects of this role. After the Introduction, the work is divided into six chapters and a conclusion. Chapter 1 is divided into two sections: the first section studies and discusses several points related to Ibn Ḥanbal, after whom the Ḥanbalī School was named, and especially the question of whether he can be considered a jurist or just a traditionist (*muḥaddith*). The second section is devoted to the study of certain aspects of Ibn Taymiyyah, focusing on the most important of his works in the field of jurisprudence and its general principles. Chapter 2 is a comparison between the basic sources of law of both Aḥmad and Ibn Taymiyyah, which helps in deciding the rank of the latter's status in knowledge. Chapters 3 and 4 deal with Ibn Taymiyyah's role in clarifying and correcting certain issues in the principles of the Ḥanbalī School of law and Ḥanbalī jurisprudence respectively. The role of this scholar in influencing Ḥanbalī jurists is the subject of Chapter 5, where a detailed study and analysis of books of *ṭabaqāt* and *tarājum*, as well as treatises compiled by the scholars under study, is carried out. Chapter 6 discusses and studies Ibn Taymiyyah's position towards the triple divorce as a case study of the problematical *fatāwā* of Ibn Taymiyyah, which have been met with great opposition by Ḥanbalī scholars and surprisingly have left an influence on the School's position regarding this legal issue.

Although the subject of this work is the influence of a scholar who lived in the seventh–eighth/thirteenth–fourteenth centuries on the Ḥanbalī School of law, this is a subject of interest to today's scholars and the Muslim public because Ibn Taymiyyah is one of the scholars who has greatly influenced the Ḥanbalī School of law, which still exists as a school of law in various parts of the Islamic world. In addition, the various corrections and clarifications made by Ibn Taymiyyah to the Ḥanbalī School of law in both its jurisprudence and general principles may be applied to other schools of law, within which similar problems can be found.

ACKNOWLEDGEMENTS

I must express my appreciation to Professor Ian R. Netton, who has provided essential motivational force, insights, thought-provoking comments and valuable suggestions which have been vital to the completion of this work.

Sympathetic thanks are extended to my family, especially my parents, wife and children, for their general understanding, sympathy, encouragement and support throughout the years.

NOTE ON TRANSLITERATION

أ	a	ط	ṭ
ب	b	ظ	ẓ
ت	t	ع	ʿ
ث	th	غ	gh
ج	j	ف	f
ح	ḥ	ق	q
خ	kh	ك	k
د	d	ل	l
ذ	dh	م	m
ر	r	ن	n
ز	z	هـ	h
س	s	و	w
ش	sh	ي	y
ص	ṣ	ة	ah (in construct state -at)
ض	ḍ		

Vowels:

Short:		Long:				
ـَ	a	ـي	ī	يّ	iyy	final form: ī
ـُ	u	ـا	ā	وّ	uww	final form: ū
ـِ	i	ـو	ū			

Diphoongs:

ـَو	aw
ـَي	ay

INTRODUCTION

There has been a growing academic interest within both the Islamic and the Western worlds in *Sheikh al-Islam* Aḥmad b. ʿAbd al-Ḥalīm Ibn Taymiyyah (661–728/1263–1328), which covers a variety of subjects. This academic interest comes as a result of the fact that Ibn Taymiyyah is acknowledged to remain today to be one of the scholars who have had the greatest influence on contemporary Islam, particularly in Sunni circles.[1]

As far as Ibn Taymiyyah as a jurist is concerned, broadly speaking, there have been two points of view with regard to his status in knowledge. Some indicate that he was a Ḥanbalī scholar who at a later stage became an absolutely independent scholar; others assert that he can be considered as a Ḥanbalī scholar right up to the end of his life.[2] Insufficient consideration, however, has been paid to the nature of Ibn Taymiyyah's relationship with the Ḥanbalī School and his contribution to it. This work, therefore, is intended to concentrate on the role of Ibn Taymiyyah in the Ḥanbalī School of law.

The main role played by Ibn Taymiyyah in the Ḥanbalī School of law is his clarification and correction of various issues in jurisprudence and the general principles of jurisprudence of this School. Therefore, various issues which were clarified or corrected by Ibn Taymiyyah in jurisprudence and its general principles will be discussed and studied in this work. To illustrate this, jurisprudential examples will be provided and expounded when appropriate.

This research also seeks to study whether Ibn Taymiyyah has played a role in influencing Ḥanbalī jurists. This will be achieved through studying and tracing the opinions of this scholar and some aspects of his influence on representative scholars.

The purpose of the study

This work has been prepared and written with the following objectives.

- This work studies Ibn Taymiyyah's role in the Ḥanbalī School of law. Hence, an introductory chapter has been included in order to study and clarify the following two main points:

1 Some important issues concerning Ibn Ḥanbal, after whom the Ḥanbalī School of law is named.
2 Certain issues concerning Ibn Taymiyyah, in addition to a study of some of his written contributions to the sciences of jurisprudence and its general principles.

- To have a clear picture of the limitation of the role played by Ibn Taymiyyah in the Ḥanbalī School of law, a comparison will be made between the general principles of Aḥmad Ibn Ḥanbal and Ibn Taymiyyah. Furthermore, founded upon this comparison, an analytical study will be made of Ibn Taymiyyah's level of knowledge, that is, whether he was an imitator (*muqallid*), a restricted *mujtahid* or an absolute *mujtahid*.
- The role of Ibn Taymiyyah in clarifying and correcting certain issues in the principles of the Ḥanbalī School of law will be studied.
- The role of Ibn Taymiyyah in clarifying and correcting certain issues in Ḥanbalī jurisprudence will be considered.
- Whether or not Ibn Taymiyyah played an influential role in the jurisprudential thought of Ḥanbalī jurists during his time, and whether or not his influence has continued up to the present period, will be examined and illustrated by means of consulting the works of *tarājim* and selected Ḥanbalī scholars of various centuries.
- The issue of the validity of an intended triple divorce pronounced in one word or based upon three separate pronouncements before the revocation takes place will be examined, as a case study of the problematical *fatāwā* of Ibn Taymiyyah, which are claimed to be contrary to the position subscribed to by the Ḥanbalī School. In addition, a study will be conducted in order to determine whether Ibn Taymiyyah's position in relation to this issue has left an effect on the School.

Within these limitations, an attempt is made to formulate an understanding of Ibn Taymiyyah's role in the Ḥanbalī School of law.

The scope and method of the study

This investigation is restricted to the study and analysis of certain aspects of Ibn Taymiyyah's role in the Ḥanbalī School of law in the field of jurisprudence and its principles.

By reason of the fact that jurisprudence is founded upon the science of the principles of jurisprudence, I have opted to include several important issues in which Ibn Taymiyyah's role is evident within the Ḥanbalī principles of law. By contrast, only certain aspects of this scholar's role in Ḥanbalī jurisprudence will be examined in detail. Furthermore, amongst these selected areas, only particular representative examples will be discussed. This is due to the presence of a large number of issues included in this science which were corrected and clarified by Ibn Taymiyyah. Therefore, there is little benefit in making reference to a large number of these issues. Rather, an examination and analysis of a selected number will take place.

The chapter pertaining to Ibn Ḥanbal is based upon a vast number of references, particularly the sources of *ṭabaqāt* and biographical accounts of Ibn Ḥanbal.

The investigation of the issues related to the personal, educational and political life of Ibn Taymiyyah is founded upon a number of historical and contemporary sources, the majority of which are solely devoted to this scholar or contain information in reference to him, in addition to the books of *ṭabaqāt*.

In order to study and examine the general principles of these two scholars, and the role played by Ibn Taymiyyah in the general principles and jurisprudence of the Ḥanbalī school, a number of Ḥanbalī sources have been consulted. Ibn Taymiyyah's own works relating to these two sciences have been consulted, in addition to a selection of his other treatises. Furthermore, I have referred to various other recognised and authoritative sources belonging to other schools where required, in addition to source references in the science of *ḥadīth*.

In order to study Ibn Taymiyyah's influential role upon the Ḥanbalī jurists, books of *ṭabaqāt* and *tarājim* have been consulted. More important, selected jurisprudential treatises of leading scholars have been subjected to a careful study and examination. It ought to be noted that the study of this influence upon Ḥanbalī jurists will primarily be based upon examining Ibn Taymiyyah's opinions and preferences which are cited by these scholars.

The investigation and discussion concerning the case study of Ibn Taymiyyah's problematical *fatāwā*, which include his *fatwā* regarding triple divorce, is based upon a wide variety of Ḥanbalī sources, in addition to works from other schools' treatises where deemed appropriate. Ibn Taymiyyah's treatises in reference to this issue have also been consulted.

Despite the fact that numerous accounts have been written about Ibn Taymiyyah, the subject of this work has never received a thorough investigation by either former or contemporary scholars. Therefore, the primary objective of this work is to fill this gap by shedding light upon certain aspects of Ibn Taymiyyah's role in the Ḥanbalī School in reference to the science of jurisprudence and its principles.

1

IBN ḤANBAL AND IBN TAYMIYYAH

AḤMAD IBN ḤANBAL

Introduction

The Ḥanbalī School of law is acknowledged to be amongst the four canonical Sunni *madhāhib*.[1] It is named after Abū 'Abd Allah Aḥmad b. Muḥammad Ibn Ḥanbal (d. 241/855), a scholar who was born in Baghdad, in the year 164/780. His father died when he was a child, so his mother assumed responsibility for his upbringing from an early age. He was to become one of the most distinguished personalities of Islam, by virtue of his extensive studies of various Arabic and Islamic sciences in different parts of the Islamic world and his famed uncompromising stand against the inquisition instituted by the Abbasid al-Ma'mūn. He travelled to numerous places including Kufah, Baṣrah, Makkah, Madīnah, Yemen and Syria.[2] Even after he had become a famous scholar he did not cease to undertake these expeditions in pursuit of knowledge. When some of his contemporaries expressed their amazement at his frequent journeys, despite his considerable accomplishments and elevated station, he remarked: 'With the ink-pot to the grave-yard', that is, until the end of life![3] Aḥmad realised that knowledge was a bottomless sea, devoid of boundaries, and he was therefore obligated to pursue it to the end of his life. He knew also that he would be deemed ignorant if he was to rest on his laurels claiming mastery of everything. The era in which Aḥmad lived has become known amongst the scholars of the evolution of jurisprudence as the era of *mujtahids*,[4] owing to the great number of leading scholars who flourished at the time.

Aḥmad's teachers

There is scant reference to Ibn Ḥanbal and his teachers during his early steps upon the path of knowledge. It is known, however, that he started his education at a very early age in the institute called the *kuttāb*. Aḥmad mentioned: 'When I was a little boy I used to attend the *kuttāb*, and when I turned 14 I went to the *diwān*.'[5] It is known that students at the *kuttāb* in that period learned the basic elements of Arabic and Islamic studies in addition to other subjects.[6] Some of his teachers in the science of the Qur'an, for example, Ibn Abī Kathīr, are known us.[7]

A characteristic of Aḥmad at that stage which is abundantly clear from the sources is his ardent devotion and commitment to learning. In one narration, Aḥmad's mother is reported to have hidden his clothes in order to prevent him from going so early to study circles scheduled to take place after dawn. She would argue with her son and attempt to persuade him to wait until the call to the dawn prayer was announced.[8]

We are not aware of the exact time at which Aḥmad commenced his advanced study. In one report he said that he began his study and search for *ḥadīth* when he was 16 years old.[9] This would mean that he started in the year 179/795. This narration does not, however, necessarily mean that he did not study any of the sciences at an advanced level until he had attained 16 years of age. We can say this because of the following points:

- It is clear in this narration that Aḥmad was referring to the science of *ḥadīth* in particular and not to any other subject.
- Certain narrations in existence indicate that Ibn Ḥanbal studied under the guidance of some scholars before this date.[10]
- It is clear from Aḥmad's commitment to the acquisition of knowledge that he would not abandon an opportunity to attend the circles of the scholars, particularly as Baghdad was the centre of learning at that time.[11]

There are some sources which indicate that Ibn Ḥanbal attended the study circles of the leading Ḥanafī scholar Abū Yūsuf (d. 182/798).[12] This could have been possible for various reasons:

- Abū Yūsuf and Aḥmad were both residents in Baghdad.[13]
- Abū Yūsuf occupied a prominent station amongst his contemporaries. Furthermore, he was a scholar of jurisprudence who also had the knowledge of *ḥadīth*,[14] a science for which Aḥmad entertained a particular enthusiasm.

Does this, however, conflict with what is reported by the Ḥanbalī scholar al-Khallāl (d. 311/923), that Ibn Ḥanbal memorised the books of Ahl al-Ra'y and then abandoned them?[15] Does it also mean that he was referring to Aḥmad's studies with Abū Yūsuf? It appears that there is no contradiction between what has been mentioned previously and this narration, for Aḥmad's studies were conducted within the framework of Ahl al-Ḥadīth, and Abū Yūsuf in later years combined the methods of Ahl al-Ra'y and Ahl al-Ḥadīth, as Ibn Taymiyyah indicated.[16]

This suggests that Aḥmad did not leave Abū Yūsuf because of his affiliation to Ahl al-Ra'y. This argument is founded upon various premises, namely:

- As mentioned previously, Abū Yūsuf combined the methods of Ahl al-Ra'y and Ahl al-Ḥadīth. Therefore, his jurisprudence, particularly in its later stages, was an amalgamation of the two different methods.
- It seems that Ibn Ḥanbal only left the study circles of Abū Yūsuf on the death of the latter, who passed away in the year 182/798.[17] This means that Aḥmad studied for a period of three years under the supervision of Abū Yūsuf (179–182/795–798).
- The claim that he studied under Abū Yūsuf before affiliating himself with Ahl al-Ḥadīth appears unjustified. This is because Ibn Ḥanbal himself declared that he started studying *ḥadīth* when he was 16 years old, the same year in which he met Abū Yūsuf. He continued his studies under his supervision until the year 182/798.

It appears that Ibn Ḥanbal studied and committed to memory some of Ahl al-Ra'y's treatises, because the Ahl al-Ra'y method of studying Islamic law was widespread in Iraq. He thereafter abandoned these treatises by reason of his preference for the method of Ahl al-Ḥadīth. Ibn Taymiyyah says: 'Although Ibn Ḥanbal was from al-Baṣrah, he did not follow the method of this region in studying law; rather he studied according to the method of Ahl al-Ḥadīth.'[18]

It appears that Aḥmad studied two subjects under Abū Yūsuf. The first was *ḥadīth*. This is confirmed by Ibn al-Jawzī in his book *al-Manāqib*, where he related Ibn Ḥanbal's statement that Abū Yūsuf was the first scholar under whose authority he wrote down *ḥadīth*.[19] The second was jurisprudence; this is because Abū Yūsuf was one of the eminent jurists of his time and his fame as a jurist was greater than his status as a *muḥaddith*.[20]

His first well-known teacher in the science of *ḥadīth* was Hushaym (d. 183/799).[21] His studies with this scholar had a profound impact upon him, because Hushaym was one of the well-known scholars of Ahl al-Ḥadīth.[22] In one narration, Aḥmad is quoted by al-Aṣfahānī in *Ḥilyat al-'Awlyā'* as saying that he studied *ḥadīth* under Hushaym for the first time in 179/795.[23] Prior to 183/799, he concentrated his efforts on acquiring knowledge within Baghdad. It appears that an important factor in this was the presence of a large number of scholars in Baghdad, coupled with those who visited Baghdad from different parts of the Islamic world.[24] His engagement in the study of *ḥadīth* with Hushaym also seems to have kept him in Baghdad. This view is supported by the fact that Aḥmad's first journey to Kufah in 183/799[25] was after the death of his teacher.

After this period, Aḥmad started travelling in order to further his knowledge. During the course of his travels, he encountered several eminent scholars, such as Sufyān b. 'Uyaynah (d. 198/814).[26] He also employed his *ḥajj* journeys to gain knowledge in *hijāz*. It was on *ḥajj* that he first met his Sheikh, al-Shāfi'ī, in the year

187/803. He received a second opportunity to learn from Shāfiʿī when the latter journeyed in 198/814 to Baghdad, where he spent two years.[27]

Aḥmad's studies under Shāfiʿī, in addition to Abū Yūsuf, assisted him in developing his method of studying Islamic law by combining Prophetic tradition and jurisprudence.[28]

It seems that these two scholars enjoyed an excellent relationship. Aḥmad is reported to have said that he had not seen a scholar more excellent than his Sheikh, and al-Shāfiʿī commented in a similar manner concerning Aḥmad.[29] Al-Shāfiʿī also mentioned that Aḥmad was greater in the knowledge of *ḥadīth* than himself.[30] In other narrations it is related that al-Shāfiʿī asked Aḥmad to inform him of any authentic traditions of which he was aware, in order that he might establish his rulings based on them.[31] Moreover, Shāfiʿī advised the caliphs on two occasions to appoint Aḥmad as a judge, an offer Aḥmad is reported to have refused.[32]

Another scholar who taught Ibn Ḥanbal was ʿAbd al-Razzāq al-Ṣanʿānī (d. 211/826), who was one of the most knowledgeable scholars of *ḥadīth*.[33] The excellent reputation of this scholar had spread throughout the Islamic world. Aḥmad and his friend and fellow student Yaḥyā b. Maʿīn (d. 233/848) agreed to travel all the way to Ṣanʿāʾ in Yemen to study under this reputed scholar. On their way they went to Makkah to perform *Ḥajj*. There, they happened to meet ʿAbd al-Razzāq and attended his study circles in Makkah. After completing the *Ḥajj* they continued on their journey to Sanʿā', where they spent two years studying under the guidance of this Sheikh.[34]

It is worth mentioning that although Aḥmad did not meet imām Malik, he was certainly influenced by him. This can be observed through Aḥmad's reference to Malik's treatises, particularly his book *al-Muwaṭṭa*.[35] Aḥmad was also indirectly influenced by him through al-Shāfiʿī, who had been influenced by the Mālikī School to such an extent that he was known as a follower of that School during the first stage of the development of his jurisprudential thought (*al-ʿahd al-qadīm*), and it was during this time that Aḥmad met al-Shāfiʿī.[36]

Aḥmad passed away in Baghdad on Friday the twelfth of Rabīʿ al-Awwal 241/855 at the age of 77.[37]

Ibn Ḥanbal's *miḥnah* (inquisition)

Ibn Ḥanbal's suffered the *miḥnah* as a result of his outspoken rejection of the Muʿtazilite' concept of the created Qur'an. In the year 212/827, Caliph al-Ma'mūn decreed that this was the orthodox Muslim belief. At this point, however, the people were not forced to subscribe to this belief. In the year 218/833, al-Ma'mūn imposed his will on the Muslim community to accept the belief in the following manner:

- Positions in government were given only to those who declared that they believed in this doctrine.
- Testimony in courts was only accepted from those witnesses who believed in this Muʿtazilī doctrine.

- An inquisition was established whereby scholars were interrogated about their opinions concerning this issue. Those who rejected the Mu'tazilī doctrine were punished. Ahmad attained widespread respect and fame by refusing to accept the doctrine, despite receiving physical punishment.

This inquisition lasted from the time of al-Ma'mūn until the time of Caliph al-Wāthiq. When al-Mutawakil became caliph (232/846), he ended the inquisition and officially rejected this Mu'tazilī concept.[38]

Scholars' commendations of Aḥmad Ibn Ḥanbal

Praise for Aḥmad was widespread among his colleagues. For example,

- 'Abd al-Razzāq al-Ṣan'ānī (d. 211/826) said: 'I have never seen a more erudite and god fearing person than Aḥmad Ibn Ḥanbal.' He also said

  > Four men came to Yemen from Iraq who were amongst the leading *ḥadīth* scholars: Al-Shshādhakūnī (d. 234/849), who was the best in the memorisation of *ḥadīth*, Ibn al-Madīnī (d. 234/849), who was the most versed in *ḥadīth* differences, Yaḥyā Ibn Ma'īn, who was the most conversant about *rijāl* (narrators of *ḥadīth*) and Aḥmad Ibn Ḥanbal, who was the best of them in all the aforesaid qualities.[39]

- Wakī' (d. 197/813) the great *ḥadīth* scholar said: 'Nobody has come to Kufah who was equal to this young man' (i.e. Aḥmad Ibn Ḥanbal).[40]
- Al-Shāfi'ī said: 'When I left Baghdad, I left there no one more righteous, God fearing, or more knowledgeable than Aḥmad Ibn Ḥanbal.'[41]

The aforementioned quotations depict Aḥmad's rank amongst the most senior scholars, particularly scholars of *ḥadīth* and jurisprudence. Nevertheless, a controversial issue debated amongst some scholars was whether Aḥmad was both a scholar of *ḥadīth* (i.e. *muḥaddith*) and of jurisprudence (*faqīh*), or merely a *muḥaddith*.

Was Aḥmad a traditionist (*muḥaddith*) or a jurist?

Some scholars stated that Aḥmad was only a traditionist, not a jurist. By this, they meant that although he was a jurist, he could not be considered an imām in that field. Ibn Jarīr al-Tabarī (310/923) was amongst those who subscribed to this viewpoint; hence, he did not mention Aḥmad in his book *Ikhtilāf al-Fuqahā'* (Disagreements between Jurists), but rather affirmed that Aḥmad was only a man of *ḥadīth*. The leading Mālikī scholar Qāḍī 'Iyāḍ (d. 544/1149) also considered Aḥmad to be below the rank of *imāmah* (leadership) in jurisprudence.[42] It seems that this claim is grounded on several facts, some of which are as follows:

- Aḥmad was preoccupied with the studies of *ḥadīth* and made numerous scholarly journeys in pursuit of it.
- He did not author an independent treatise concerning the field of jurisprudence, whereas he wrote about *ḥadīth*.
- Aḥmad criticised '*ra'y*' in several places.[43]

A brief response to this claim

There are various points that can be made in rebuttal of this claim:

- As various leading scholars assert, familiarity with legal texts is one of the most important prerequisites for a scholar to assume before he is considered a *mujtahid*.[44] It ought not to be considered that mastery of the legal texts of the Qur'an and the *sunnah*, and understanding of their meanings, are easy to acquire. On the contrary, such a degree of excellence requires an effective system of learning and a long quest in search of knowledge. As we have observed from the accounts of the life of Aḥmad, he exhausted most of his time moving from one town or country to another in search of knowledge. He would meet narrators, listen to them, and distinguish between authentic and non-authentic traditions, accepting the former traditions and leaving the latter according to his criteria. Furthermore, Aḥmad did not underestimate the importance of jurisprudence and understanding the purport of *ḥadīth*. He was not merely a transmitter. Instead, Ibn Taymiyyah narrates that Aḥmad said he preferred one to understand these sciences as opposed to memorising them alone.[45] This is supported by the statement of Abū 'Āṣim that after Aḥmad there was no individual who had acquired a better understanding of jurisprudence than he.[46] Also, al-Nasā'ī (d. 302/914) mentions that Aḥmad combined knowledge pertaining to *ḥadīth* and jurisprudence.[47]
- It can be determined whether or not Aḥmad is deserving of occupying a position of leadership in the field of jurisprudence by studying his jurisprudential writings and opinions contained in the source works of the Ḥanbalī School. The juristic methodology of Aḥmad can be ascertained and evaluated by examining his juristic legacy as transmitted via his disciples. The leading Ḥanbalī scholar and one of the notable companions of Ibn Taymiyyah, Ibn al-Qayyim (d. 751/1350), affirmed this point when he remarked:

> those who adhere to different opinions from his School, whether by exercising independent reasoning or by imitating other imāms, respect and appreciate his texts and legal opinions for their accuracy and conformity with the Qur'anic texts, Prophetic traditions, and verdicts of the Companions of the Prophet. Whoever compares and contrasts his verdicts with

those of the Apostle's Companions will recognise the inherent agreement and harmony between them, as though they emanated from one and the same source. Even where the companions held two different opinions about one issue you will observe that Aḥmad has two opinions attributed to him.[48]

- The fact that Aḥmad authored no works on jurisprudence is probably due to the fact that he sought to imitate his contemporaries, whose practice was to neglect writing books on the science of jurisprudence.[49] This reticence may also derive from his belief that students and scholars should refer to the founding sources of legislation and not merely to the imāms' texts, as they are the products of personal reasoning.[50] Aḥmad's insistence that his jurisprudential opinions should not be recorded was based upon his belief that scholars and students of Islamic law ought to research legal issues by means of legal criteria. This, in turn, would enable them to practise freedom of thought based upon legal texts and render redundant the concept that they are obligated to follow a particular imām despite possessing their own ability to reason and investigate.

Ibn Ḥanbal's treatises

Several works have been attributed to Aḥmad. Some of these treatises are in the science of *ḥadīth*, such as his book *al-Musnad*.[51] This book of narrations constitutes a very important historical source for studying the origin and development of Islam, its institutions, and the life and teachings of the Prophet and his companions.[52] The collection contains a separate section for each companion who narrated traditions from the Prophet.[53]

In addition, Ibn Ḥanbal compiled a work entitled *Faḍā'il al-Ṣaḥābah*, which contains narrations concerning the features and merits of various companions of the Prophet.[54] Other treatises of *ḥadīth* concern *'ilm al-rijāl* (the science of narrators), for instance, *al-'ilal wa ma'rifat al-Rijāl*.[55]

He authored two types of work in the science of creed and tenets of faith: (1) treatises which contain Aḥmad's creed, such as *'Aqidat Aḥmad*, which has been transmitted by his student 'Abdūs;[56] (2) treatises which comprise Aḥmad's rebuttal of certain sects, particularly those which had emerged in his time, for example, *al-Radd 'Ala al-Jahmiyyah*. Some of his writings concern the science of Qur'an; an example of this is *Jawābāt al-Qur'an*.[57]

With reference to the sciences of *fiqh* and *uṣūl al-fiqh*, Ibn Ḥanbal did not write a complete treatise on this subject. Some treatises have, however, been attributed to him, including *Aḥkām al-Nisā'* and *Kitāb al-Ṣalāh* in *fiqh* and *al-Nāsikh wa 'l-Mansūkh* and *Ṭā'at al-Rasūl* in the science of *uṣūl al-fiqh*.[58] These books, however, concern specific subjects and do not discuss the various issues which are usually discussed by the jurists in their works in these fields.

It was mentioned earlier that Aḥmad did not grant permission for his disciples to record his opinions. This was because he believed that scholars and seekers of knowledge should derive their rulings from the sources directly and not by the imitation of other scholars.[59] Nevertheless, large numbers of his students did communicate his jurisprudential thought. It has been mentioned in various sources that more than 130 of his disciples narrated some issues of his jurisprudence.[60] Their works are known as *Masā'il al-Imām Aḥmad*. Several of these works have unfortunately been lost. For instance, al-Athram (d. 260/874) was one of Ibn Ḥanbal's most intelligent students, who in later years became a notable imām and Ḥāfiẓ. He was known for his extensive knowledge of Ibn Ḥanbal's *Masā'il*, which he used to narrate on his authority.[61] Sadly, however, Al-Athram's *Masā'il* can no longer be found, but some of these lost narrations can be found scattered in other Ḥanbalī sources.

In addition to this, al-Kawsaj (d. 251/865), who was a learned theologian, related a number of issues from Aḥmad. According to al-Khallāl, al-Kawsaj's jurisprudential *Masā'il* are substantial. Nevertheless, al-Khallāl mentioned the presence of oddity and strangeness in some of al-Kawsaj's *Masā'il*, in comparison with those of other narrators. The reason for that, as al-Khallāl explained, was the significant number of *Masā'il* narrated by him.[62] It appears that, by this, al-Khallāl meant that al-Kawsaj included in his large number of *Masā'il* some that cannot be found in the transmissions of other narrators.

There is another important point concerning these *Masā'il*. It was suggested amongst certain Ḥanbalis that these *Masā'il* had been recanted by Aḥmad. This opinion can be deduced from a narration of Ibn Ḥanbal, wherein he mentioned his disapproval of al-Kawsaj's transmission of his knowledge.[63] This claim, however, appears to be incorrect because well-known scholars such as Ibn Ḥāmid rejected this view and stated that this opinion was not known from any Ḥanbalī scholar.[64] It can also be said that Aḥmad's disapproval of al-Kawsaj's *Masā'il* was based on his well-known position of forbidding the writing down of his jurisprudence by his disciples. This is corroborated by the text of the same report. We find that al-Kawsaj explained to his Sheikh that he chose to transmit these *Masā'il* because of the people of Khurasān's need for knowledge. After Aḥmad had heard this explanation, he read al-Kawsaj's *Masā'il* and thereafter granted his permission to narrate them.[65]

It should be mentioned that al-Kawsaj mixed and contrasted Aḥmad's views with those of others, such as Ibn Rāhawiyh (d. 238/853) and al-Thawrī (d. 161/778). In some *Masā'il*, Aḥmad was asked to give his view on the opinions of other scholars.

Ḥanbal (d. 273/886) was another student of Aḥmad who narrated some *Masā'il* from him. He was a cousin of Aḥmad, and this appears to have given him the opportunity to narrate several *Masā'il* from him and to study *al-Musnad* under his guidance. Ḥanbal was known as reliable and authoritative.[66] According to al-Khallāl, Ḥanbal's narrations from Aḥmad were of a similar level of excellence and thoroughness to al-Athram's narrations. Al-Khallāl does, however, comment upon the presence of some unfamiliar *Masā'il* within his narrations.[67]

Some of Aḥmad's *Masā'il* were narrated by his two sons, Abū 'l-Faḍl Ṣāliḥ and 'Abd Allah. Abū 'l-Faḍl was Ibn Ḥanbal's eldest son and received traditions from

his father, narrated some of his *Masā'il* and became a judge during the lifetime of his father.[68]

Ṣāliḥ was charged with another task, which was to work as a secretary to his father. According to al-Khallāl, when Ṣāliḥ received letters containing questions, he would present them to his father, whose response he would thereafter write down and send back.[69]

Abū 'l-Faḍl's *Masā'il* are not systematically organised according to the regulations of *Abawāb al-Fiqh*; neither are they arranged according to different subjects such as creed, interpretation of the Qur'an and *ḥadīth*. The reason for this, according to some scholars, was that Ṣāliḥ used to attend his father's study circles and was accustomed to record whatever was discussed within those study circles, regardless of the subjects expounded upon.

Other *Masā'il* are narrated by al-Maymūnī (d. 276/889), who also heard traditions (*ḥadīths*) from Aḥmad. His *Masā'il* were divided into sixteen sections.[70] According to the Ḥanbalī scholar Abū Ya'la, al-Maymūnī stated that no other individual was present during the exposition of these *Masā'il* from Aḥmad.[71] Some of al-Maymūnī's *Masā'il* are mentioned in various places within Ḥanbalī sources. The content suggests that if the remainder could be located, it is likely that they would contain some useful and important *Masā'il*.

Muhannā b. Yaḥyā al-Shāmī was another narrator of Aḥmad's jurisprudence. This eminent scholar accompanied Aḥmad until his death.[72] Although he was considered amongst the well-known narrators of Aḥmad's knowledge, no treatise containing his narrations has been found. Some of his *Masā'il* have, however, been mentioned in various Ḥanbalī sources. The same can be said about Abū Ṭālib (d. 244/858), who was described by Abū Ya'la as an individual who displayed ardent enthusiasm in attending Aḥmad's classes and a person whom Aḥmad used to honour.[73]

Some *Masā'il* were written according to the systematic method of the jurists such as *Masā'il* 'Abd Allah, while others were not, such as *Masā'il* Ṣāliḥ.

The eminent Ḥanbalī scholar al-Khallāl performed an excellent task of editing Aḥmad's *Masā'il* from various narrations. According to al-Dhahabī, al-Khallāl obtained narrations from nearly 100 companions of Aḥmad.[74] He used these narrations to compile several books, such as *Al-'Ilm*, *al-'Ilal* and *al-Sunnah*. His greatest work is that of *al-Jāmi'*, which contains a vast number of Aḥmad's *Masā'il*, as narrated by the imām's students or their students.[75] This book comprised numerous volumes. According to al-Dhahabī, it consisted of approximately twenty or more volumes. Ibn al-Qayyim states that the number was *biḍ'at 'ashar* (the word *biḍ'at* can refer to a number between 3 and 9; therefore, here, the number denotes between 13 and 19) or more.[76] Some of these volumes have not reached us. This work of al-Khallāl was extremely important to the Ḥanbalī School. According to al-Dhahabī, there existed no independent school of law attributed to Aḥmad before the work of al-Khallāl.[77] Although *al-Jāmi'* was a large treatise, Ibn Taymiyyah states in his *Fatāwā* that al-Khallāl was not thoroughly conversant with all of Aḥmad's jurisprudential *Masā'il*.[78]

Narrators of Aḥmad's *Masā'il* agreed on a number of issues and differed about others. Their differences either stemmed from the principle that Aḥmad occasionally had more than one opinion concerning an individual issue, and as a consequence delivered different judgements, or from a misunderstanding or a mistake in the transmission of the *Masā'il* on the part of the narrator.[79]

The spread of this School

The Ḥanbalī School started in Baghdad, the birthplace of Aḥmad. His students and their students in turn succeeded in strengthening and promulgating this School until it became a leading School, competing with other *sunni* schools in Baghdad in the fourth century.[80] As mentioned earlier, the appointment to the judiciary of Abū Ya'la, together with some other Ḥanbalī scholars, was of great help in the expansion of this School. In the fourth century, the Ḥanbalī School established itself in al-Shām.[81] Then, in the sixth century, the School spread to Egypt.[82] This delay occurred because, as al-Suyūtī explains, Egypt was under the control of Ubaydis who were Shī'ah and suppressed the three Sunni Schools of law existing at the time in the country.[83] The presence of this School in Egypt was small, and it only started to spread after the appointment of the Ḥanbalī scholar al-Hajjāwī as a judge during the latter stage of the Ayyūbis (567–648/1171–1250).[84]

This School is now located in some of the above-mentioned areas but is neither so widespread nor so influential as it once was. Its failure to become as widespread as other schools of Islamic law is due to various factors, among them the fact that the Ḥanbalī School was never selected by the Caliphate as the State School and the fact that the three other schools of Islamic law (Ḥanafī, Mālikī, Shāfi'ī) had already become widespread.[85]

Some scholars, however, attribute the limited spread of the Ḥanbalī School to the fact that it does not encourage the use of independent reasoning.[86] Others claim that the reason for its limited influence is the strictness of this School.[87]

Nevertheless, the Ḥanbalī School has acquired a prominent position in the Arabian Peninsula, as a result of the successful vocation of Muḥammad b. 'Abd al-Wahhāb and the creation of the Kingdom of Saudi Arabia. This School is the official School of law in Saudi and Qatar today.[88]

IBN TAYMIYYAH AND HIS LEGACY IN THE SCIENCES OF JURISPRUDENCE AND ITS GENERAL PRINCIPLES

Ibn Taymiyyah's era

Ibn Taymiyyah's life extended over a period of 68 years (661–728/1263–1328), during the era of the first Mamluks (648–784H/1250–1382), or as it is commonly known 'The Era of the Baḥrite Mamluks'.[89] The history of this group originates from the time of King Najm al-Dīn Ayyūb (d. 648/1249), who brought them and settled them in Egypt in order to protect his throne.[90] After the death of King Najm al-Dīn in the year 648/1250, the group assassinated his son Turānshāh, who had succeeded him. Thereafter, one of the Mamluks, Aybeg (d. 655/1257), occupied the position of sultan himself. This marked the beginning of the era of the Baḥrī Mamluks.[91]

One of the most important events which occurred during that time was the unification of al-Shām and Egypt[92] after the defeat of the Mongols by Sultan Quṭuz in the famous battle of *'Ayn Jalūt* (658/1260).[93] Thereafter, the Mamluk government attempted to gain the support of the Muslims throughout the Islamic world by appointing an Abbasid as caliph in 659/1261. The caliph was granted the title of *'al-Mustanṣir bi Allah'*.[94] This caliph and those who succeeded him, however, were merely figureheads. They attended religious and political events, led their armies into battle against the Mongols and the one of them was referred to as *'Amīr al-Mu'minīn'*.[95] It is even recorded that on one occasion a caliph was sent to prison for being at variance with the throne.[96]

The Mamluk government headquarters were located in the city of Cairo, which became a political, cultural and educational centre.[97] The source of law during this era was neither contained in a clearly defined legal system nor bound by a written constitution.[98] Jurisprudence and justice were founded upon the Shāfi'ī School of law alone until Sultan al-Ẓāhir assumed control of the government and appointed a judge affiliated to each of the four main schools of law at the end of 663/1265.[99]

During this period, the political system was not based upon the *shurā*;[100] therefore, the public did not play a direct role in the political affairs of the state. Furthermore, heavy taxes were levied upon citizens. These were primarily used to fund the war effort against the Mongols, who had embarked on a wave of attacks in 617/1220, under their king, Ghengis Khan (d. 624/1227).[101] During their attacks, they committed massacres of both the armies and civilians. The atrocities were of such magnitude that it is recorded that the famous historian Ibn al-Athīr agreed to document the events only after considerable hesitation and insistence on the part of his contemporaries. In his account of the fate of Muslims, he referred to these tragic events as the worst disaster in the history of the Islamic world in which men, women and children and even pregnant women faced the same fate.[102] Another defeat of the Muslim army followed in 656/1258 at the hands of Hulegu, who led his forces into Iraq and al-Shām and abolished the caliphate.[103] Two years later, Quṭuz was finally able to defeat them in the famous battle of 'Ayn Jalūt 658/1260.[104]

The era of Ibn Taymiyyah also witnessed the struggle between the Mamluks and crusaders, whose presence in this area was finally ended following al-Ashraf Khalīl's military campaign, which began with the conquest of 'Akkā, after which other cities surrendered peacefully in the year 690/1291.[105]

Structurally, the society was divided into three strata:

1 The first category included the ruling class, that is, those people in positions of power such as the sultans, princes and high government officials. This

group assumed almost absolute power and control over government affairs and the citizens, including the caliphs themselves. On certain occasions, however, the ruling class was confronted by leading scholars on political and social issues.[106] This category was led by the most powerful amongst them.[107] The most famous of the Mamluk sultans were al-Ẓāhir and al-Nāṣir. It is said that no truly influential sultans assumed power after the demise of al-Ẓāhir except al-Nāṣir.[108]

2 The second category included the educated classes, namely, the scholars and intellectuals. Both the rulers and the ordinary people looked up to them for guidance and support and held them in high regard.[109]

3 The third category included the common people or lay public, consisting of the remainder of the population. All large towns in this period were occupied by many labourers, craftsmen, small shopkeepers, *fallaḥūn* (farmers, landtillers) and poor people. This portion of the population was the largest of all in number, but they were devoid of any form of direct participation in the political life of the country. In addition, the financial circumstances of this sector, particularly the *fallaḥūn*, was the most grievous, as they were subjected to heavy taxation.[110]

It appears that such rigid divisions of power, in conjunction with other factors, principally those outlined in the following points, contributed to creating social disharmony and disorder:

- The sudden demographic changes in society. This involved the immigration of people of different origins with diverse customs and traditions, to become part of the Mamluk society. For instance, after the Mongols' invasion of Iraq, many people emigrated from there and settled in Egypt and al-Shām.[111]
- The enduring political instability and power struggles resulting in a succession of sultans seizing power, usually by means of force.[112]
- A period of heavy taxation, primarily due to a state of perpetual war.[113]

Social and political unrest was undoubtedly accentuated by a prevailing ideological crisis too. Indeed, intolerance and conflict were common amongst the dominant religious schools of thought. Confusion and discord were also attributed to the widespread use of Greek philosophy, which had been translated into Arabic in the early period of Islam.[114] Netton, however, believes that the history of Islamic philosophy is not purely a history of 'influences' of a total legacy from Greece to the East and its intellectual milieu, undiluted by any home-grown thought at all.[115]

This period falls within the era of imitation (*taqlid*), wherein the majority of scholars were either making additions, explaining matters already known or gathering information connected with them, rather than developing novel theories and principles. The legal doctrines that they transmitted and propagated were mainly restricted to the four dominant schools of law.[116] Nevertheless, there were some eminent scholars who were recognised for their independent thought and their unique treatises. Ibn Taymiyyah was one such scholar.[117]

To say that Ibn Taymiyyah lived during both the best of times and the worst of times may not be too much of an exaggeration. Ibn Taymiyyah lived in a period of extremes. On the one hand, it developed a tradition of knowledge whose legacy is still regarded as a treasure by millions, not only in the Middle East but all around the world. On the other hand, it suffered the devastation and terror of the Mongol invasions and occupation.[118] Furthermore, for sixty years commencing in 657/1260, after the initial invasion and occupation, the Mamluks of Egypt and Syria were involved in a constant struggle with the Mongols.[119]

The emergence of Ibn Taymiyyah

Ibn Taymiyyah was born in the year 661/1263 in Ḥarrān,[120] from where his family migrated to Damascus after the Mongol conquest of Iraq. They abandoned all their property except their books, which constituted the most valuable possessions of this learned family, a family which provided the Ḥanbalī School with several eminent scholars, particularly Ibn Taymiyyah's grandfather, al-Majd, and his father, 'Abd al-Ḥalīm.[121]

Ibn Taymiyyah was renowned for his intelligence, which undoubtedly assisted him in his quest for knowledge at a very early age.[122] He was a particularly diligent and committed student, who memorised the Qur'an when he was just a small child. He then continued to study and memorise knowledge connected to jurisprudence, the Arabic language and some of the important sources of *ḥadīth*, until he attained proficiency in them.[123]

As a youth, Ibn Taymiyyah would frequent some of the most famous intellectual circles. He was educated by a large number of sheikhs. Certain sources claim that his teachers exceeded 200 in number.[124] They were well-known scholars throughout the Islamic world and specialists in various fields of the Arabic language and Islamic studies. Thus, he studied jurisprudence and its fundamentals under several leading scholars, for example his father, 'Abd al-Ḥalīm,[125] and Sharaf al-Dīn al-Maqdisī (d. 694/1295), the sheikh of the Shāfi'ī School and Mufti of Damascus.[126] He was instructed in the skills of *al-qirā'āt* by famous specialists such as al-Sa'dī (d. 676/1277) and Abū Isḥāq al-Ghusūlī (d. 684/1285).[127] In addition, he was taught history under the guidance of scholars such as Ibn al-Mujāwir (d. 690/1291).[128] Ibn Taymiyyah received instruction in the science of *ḥadīth* by leading scholars in the field, including Taqī al-Dīn al-Tunūkhī (d. 589/1193).[129]

Bearing in mind the large number of scholars from whom Ibn Taymiyyah received his education, and the diversity of their backgrounds, it is not surprising that his ideology was influenced by several doctrines of jurisprudence other than the Ḥanbalī, such as the Ḥanafī, Mālikī, Shāfi'ī and al-Ẓāhirī.[130] The reason for his comparative approach to study can therefore be appreciated.

In addition to his exemplary teachers, Ibn Taymiyyah had access to and is reputed to have absorbed a prodigious amount of knowledge from books and other sources.[131] Ibn 'Abd al-Hādī mentions that some of Ibn Taymiyyah's old contemporaries described him as 'raised in the best way, in the rooms of the scholars, drinking from the cups of understanding, cavorting in the field of learning and in the trees of books'.[132]

His father, who taught in al-Sukariyyah School, died in the year 682/1283, when his son was 22 years old. It was at this time that Ibn Taymiyyah was called to succeed his father as a lecturer. A group of eminent scholars from different Schools attended Ibn Taymiyyah's first lecture and were very impressed by his intellectual calibre and wit.[133] Thereafter, Ibn Taymiyyah established two types of lectures: the first comprised private lectures for his students, and the second consisted of public lectures in the form of sermons at the mosques on Fridays.[134]

It has been mentioned previously that the political situation of this time was characterised by chaos and disorder. It was during these difficult times that Ibn Taymiyyah found himself assuming the role of a political reformer working in several spheres. He studied and exposed the reason for the inherent weakness and chaos of the political system. He called the Muslim community towards unity, encouraging political leaders to govern with justice and fairness. He urged them to seek advice from sincere consultants in the different aspects of leadership and law.[135] Ibn Taymiyyah also called upon the leaders during that time to help create a strong and enlightened nation, beginning with the reform of the prevailing cultural and intellectual situation that tended to stifle the spirit of innovation and creativity. According to Ibn Taymiyyah, it was this deficiency that was largely responsible for the weakness of the Muslim world at that time.[136]

He campaigned tirelessly to put his theories into practice. He did not hesitate to involve himself in fighting against the Mongols and exhorted his people to do so.[137] It is said he travelled to Egypt in difficult circumstances in order to persuade the reigning sultan to come to the rescue of al-Shām with his army and protect it from being attacked by the Mongols.[138]

Ibn Taymiyyah's relationship with contemporary rulers was initially particularly good. He forged strong links with al-Nāṣir (d. 741/1341), who remained in power for a total of forty-four years.[139] As there were few formal or natural criteria for social classification at the time of Ibn Taymiyyah, one must be aware of status in the protocol of spatial arrangement in the ruler's court.[140] When Ibn Taymiyyah, who enjoyed Qalawūn's esteem, entered al-Nāṣir's court, the sultan broke with established practice and walked across the room, took Ibn Taymiyyah by the hand and walked with him before praising him to the group.[141] In addition, Ibn Taymiyyah was consulted in religious matters and other affairs and was able to exercise considerable influence over the government.[142] Decisions concerning appointments were influenced by him; for example, al-Nāṣir consulted him when he wanted to appoint a headmaster to Dār al-Ḥadīth al-Kāmiliyyah after the death of Ibn Daqīq al-'Īd.[143]

This excellent relationship proved, however, to be short lived and was undermined by fierce opponents who, apparently out of envy of him and his special status, sought to discredit the man and his religion. They succeeded in persuading the government to arrest him on several occasions.[144] Occasionally, controversies concerning Ibn Taymiyyah resulted in divisions within the government itself and even between the sultan and his deputy.[145]

Some sources argue that there was a political motive behind Ibn Taymiyyah's struggles and that he was emulating Ibn Tūmart (d. 524/1130),[146] but a comprehensive study of this scholar's life lends little credence to such a claim. My own research has found no evidence to suggest that this intellectual giant had, at any time during his life, aspired to occupy a position of political power. It is recorded that he had even refused the post of chief of justice, *mashyakhat al-shuyūkh* (the leader of scholars),[147] and the post of Amīr Ḥarrān.[148] We find he was once brought before the sultan and questioned about his political ambitions. Al-Bazzār, one of his disciples, recorded the following dialogue between Sultan al-Nāṣir and Ibn Taymiyyah:

> 'I was told that people obey you and that you intend to take over my position.' To which Ibn Taymiyyah replied: 'Would I do such a deed? By Allah, your realm and the Mongol's are not worth two *fils* to me.' Then, the sultan smiled with relief and concluded: 'By Allah, you are telling the truth and whoever informed on you uttered a falsehood.'[149]

Ibn Taymiyyah's detention

Ibn Taymiyyah was subjected to numerous bouts of persecution. He was repeatedly interrogated, prevented from issuing *fatāwā*, informed against to the sultans, exiled from his hometown and imprisoned. It all started in the year 693/1294, when Ibn Taymiyyah made a complaint against a Christian man who had censured the Prophet; Ibn Taymiyyah was imprisoned for a short time and then released.[150] In the year 698/1299 Ibn Taymiyyah was cross-examined about his creed after he authored a treatise entitled *al-Ḥamawiyyah*.[151] In essence, he declared that the opinions of *al-salaf* (the pious ancestors, the earliest generations) were the correct authority in matters of *aqīdah* (creed) and criticised the interpretations of later generations (*al-khalaf*).[152] Ibn Taymiyyah was ordered to appear before the Ḥanafī judge, b. Ḥusām al-Dīn, in court. Ibn Taymiyyah refused to do so, arguing that the function of a judge is to deal with worldly affairs and that he does not possess the authority to judge an individual's religious beliefs. The judge was angered by such a response and subsequently issued an open letter to be read in public denouncing Ibn Taymiyyah's creed as falsehood. This was, however, swiftly stopped by the sultan's deputy as soon as he was informed about it.[153]

Ibn Taymiyyah resumed his lectures briefly,[154] until he was again brought to court before the Shāfi'ī judge al-Gazuīnī, the Sultan's deputy and a group of scholars. After reading his treatise *al-Ḥamawiyyah*, he was questioned about the allegedly contentious issues it raised and was deemed innocent. The judge pronounced that whoever accused Ibn Taymiyyah of blasphemy was to be punished.[155]

Ibn Taymiyyah endured a similar ordeal again in the year 705/1305 at the hands of the deputy of the Sultan in al-Shām, in the presence of a committee of judges and scholars.[156] On this occasion, when he was asked about his creed, he declared that creed should not be sought from him or from whoever was more knowledgeable than he was. Rather, it should be sought from Allah and His Messenger, the Qur'an, and *sunnah* and the consensus of all eminent scholars throughout the Islamic world.[157] Ibn Taymiyyah meant by this that he had not invented a creed of his own. In other words, he wanted to clarify that his creed was based upon the Islamic sources of belief. Once his treatise *al-Wāsiṭiyyah*[158] was presented, Ibn Taymiyyah was found not guilty of the accusations levelled against him and his beliefs were recognised to be based upon those of the predecessors.[159]

Despite his acquittal, he was soon asked to appear before a committee in Egypt. On the day after his arrival, a meeting was held involving judges and governors, who questioned him concerning theological issues. Ibn Taymiyyah declined to answer the questions presented as he refused to acknowledge the authority of the judge Ibn Makhlūf (718/1318), as he was one of the instigators of the dispute. He objected, demanding, 'How can my opponent be the judge in our dispute?'[160] This outburst infuriated the judge, who thereupon sent him to prison and issued a letter to be read all over the country, branding Ibn Taymiyyah's creed as misleading and erroneous.[161]

One year later, he was offered a conditional release subject to agreeing to present himself before a committee of scholars in front of whom he would be asked to change some of his opinions. Ibn Taymiyyah rejected the offer and as a consequence remained in prison.[162] Eighteen months later, he was released by an oath from *Amīr al-Arab* Muhannā b. 'Īsā.[163] Ibn Taymiyyah chose to remain in Egypt, where he delivered lectures that attracted large numbers of students.[164] Some of these lectures touched on the very issues for which he had been tried and numerous complaints were made against him to the sultan,[165] as a result of which he was offered three alternatives by the government: return to Damascus; exile to Alexandria; or imprisonment. The first two choices were dependent upon the fulfilment of certain conditions. Ibn Taymiyyah elected to go to prison but was eventually persuaded by his students to accept the first choice. While he was en route to Damascus, however, the government altered its decision and recommended that he should be tried and sent to jail. The court judges were apprehensive about passing a judgement on Ibn Taymiyyah, so he chose to go to prison of his own accord. During the period of his detention he was allowed free visits, which included those by his own students.[166]

His opponents were not content with his being in jail and therefore pressed the Sultan for his exile to Alexandria.[167] When Ibn Taymiyyah arrived in Alexandria, he concentrated his efforts on discussions with high-ranking jurists and noble people who were granted easy access to him.[168] His opinions quickly gathered support and popularity.[169] Meanwhile, some of his adherents had decided to follow him there.[170]

In 709/1309, al-Nāṣir assumed control of the government again, ordered the release of Ibn Taymiyyah and requested his return to Cairo. He remained there until 712/1312.[171] Thereafter he returned to Damascus, where he spent two and a half years conducting research and delivering lectures and *fatāwā* without interference.[172] However, in 718/1318 there was a new inquisition awaiting Ibn Taymiyyah regarding his *fatwā* concerning the contentious issue of oaths invoking divorce. For example, a person might say, 'If I do such and such thing my wife is divorced.' The question was whether such an oath should have the effect of a direct divorce or not.[173] Ibn Taymiyyah subscribed to the opinion that it should not. He was subsequently advised by a Ḥanbalī judge not to issue this *fatwā* to the public.[174] Initially, he heeded the judge's advice. Despite a decree issued by the Sultan forbidding Ibn Taymiyyah from doing so, it was not long before he started pronouncing this *fatwā* again. As a consequence, a committee was established in order to question him. The trial concluded with his imprisonment. He was incarcerated for nearly six months, until he was released as a result of another decree issued by the Sultan.[175]

The final and most serious inquisition to which Ibn Taymiyyah was subjected involved the question of performing a journey in order to visit graves, which he considered a profanity in Islam. As a result, Ibn Taymiyyah was sent to prison again, where he stayed for over two years, until his death in 728/1328.[176]

At this stage, it would be prudent to consider the reasons behind Ibn Taymiyyah's persecution and detention. It is evident that certain aspects of his creed and jurisprudence and the issuing of controversial *fatāwā* had resulted in a direct conflict with the establishment. Equally serious, however, was his ideological clash with particular scholars, groups or sects and their leaders and followers.[177] Ibn Taymiyyah's intellectual stature, which was acknowledged by his followers and opponents alike, undoubtedly aroused a degree of envy and antagonism on the part of some of his contemporaries.[178] Al-Bukhārī al-Ḥanafī (d. 841/1437), for example, not only accused him of heresy, but went so far as to proclaim that whoever called him by the title *sheikh al-islam* should be considered as an unbeliever too.[179]

Ibn Taymiyyah's position among his contemporaries

Ibn Taymiyyah's contemporary scholars can be divided into three parties according to their attitude towards him:

1 those who supported and praised him;
2 those who opposed him and instigated his arrest and detention;
3 those who once constituted his admirers and then turned against him.

The overwhelming majority of his contemporaries fell within the first category.[180] This group included his disciples, those who were from different parts of the Islamic world and those who were affiliated to the various schools of law.[181] The first example of this group is Ibn 'Abd al-Hādī, one of Ibn Taymiyyah's students.

The status of this scholar amongst his contemporaries with regard to his knowledge of Ibn Taymiyyah appears to be particularly admirable. Ibn 'Abd al-Hādī was thoroughly conversant with his sheikh's treatises and knowledge. This may be evidenced through his discussion of several of his sheikh's opinions in his books. In addition, in his book *al-'Uqūd*, he mentioned a great number of Ibn Taymiyyah's treatises and promised that he would collect and classify the names of his sheikh's treatises according to the places where they were written and specify those books which were compiled in prison.[182] According to my knowledge, however, this promise does not appear to have been fulfilled by Ibn 'Abd al-Hādī. It seems that his familiarity with the opinions of Ibn Taymiyyah was the reason for the repeated requests made by Ibn Ḥāmid, a leading Shāfi'ī scholar, to Ibn 'Abd al-Hādī to write down an index of Ibn Taymiyyah's treatises.[183]

Ibn 'Abd al-Hādī demonstrated his admiration of his sheikh when he described him as 'the leader of the Imāms', 'the Mufti of the *Ummah*', 'the sea of sciences' and 'the unique scholar of the time'.[184] Ibn 'Abd al-Hādī's admiration of Ibn Taymiyyah may be observed through his book *al-'Uqūd*, wherein he gathered scholars' praises of his sheikh.[185] When he mentioned the treatises of his sheikh, he asserted that he was not aware of an individual amongst the earlier or later scholars who wrote as much as this scholar. This matter is of particular importance as he authored a large number of them in prison, basing them upon the information in his memory.[186]

The second example is Ibn Daqīq al-'Īd, a great Shāfi'ī scholar, who was once asked for his opinion concerning Ibn Taymiyyah. He responded by describing him as 'a man with a multitude of subjects of knowledge at his fingertips'.[187]

It ought to be noted that numerous scholars who can be categorised under this group were not merely *muqallids* of Ibn Taymiyyah; rather, they exercised their own independent reasoning on various issues. They admired his stature and intellect but did not agree with him on certain issues. For example, al-Dhahabī, who was one of Ibn Taymiyyah's disciples, differs from his sheikh on certain issues in both *al-furū'* and *al-uṣūl*. Despite these differences he readily conceded that Ibn Taymiyyah was indeed a *mujtahid* and that a *mujtahid*'s mistakes are excused.[188]

In addition, al-Dhahabī appears to have distanced himself from the more vociferous opponents of Ibn Taymiyyah. He pointed out that although Ibn Taymiyyah was mistaken in certain views in a number of his treatises, this should not affect his position as a great scholar and a free thinker. For he stated that the duty of a *mujtahid* in Islamic law is to practise independent reasoning which in certain instances may deviate from the correct judgement. Nevertheless, in the Hereafter, great thinkers are to be commended for their endeavours and forgiven for their mistakes.[189] Al-Dhahabī went on to declare that there was no individual at the time of Ibn Taymiyyah who was his equal or even similar to him. Furthermore, al-Dhahabī affirmed the exemplary status of Ibn Taymiyyah in various sciences, such as *Ḥadīth* and *rijāl*, interpretation of the Qur'an, philosophy and jurisprudence and its principles. Moreover, he stated that his sheikh had reached the rank of an absolute *mujtahid* in Islamic law.[190]

Such was al-Dhahabī's evident respect for the man that it is not possible to conceive that he wrote the letter attributed to him entitled '*al-Naṣiḥah al-Dhahabīyyah ilā Ibn Taymiyyah*' (Golden Advice to Ibn Taymiyyah, or An Advice from al-Dhahabī to Ibn Taymiyyah).[191] In addition, a careful study of this letter leads one to suggest that such a piece of work could not have been authored by al-Dhahabī himself. This premise is founded upon a number of factors, three of which are the following:

1 Al-Dhahabī's admiration and praise of Ibn Taymiyyah's work is undisguised in his treatises. He repeatedly referred to him as a *mujtahid* and favoured an approach of tolerance towards his mistakes.[192]
2 A number of scholars who attribute this letter to al-Dhahabī claim that it was written during the latter part of his acquaintance with Ibn Taymiyyah.[193] It appears that they do this to avoid the obvious contradiction between his praise of Ibn Taymiyyah in his other treatises and his criticism of him in this solitary letter. This claim seems, however, to be erroneous, because in his several biographical entries for Ibn Taymiyyah, al-Dhahabī mentioned the date of Ibn Taymiyyah's death,[194] which refutes the belief that there were two stages in his acquaintance with Ibn Taymiyyah.
3 The oldest sources for al-Dhahabī's biography do not mention this treatise amongst his legacy of knowledge.[195] Even al-Subkī, who was known for his opposition to Ibn Taymiyyah, did not mention it.[196] On the contrary, he was prepared to acknowledge Ibn Taymiyyah's extensive knowledge, as he did when he was reproached by al-Dhahabī for his attitude towards him.[197]

The second group was primarily composed of members of the political system of the time and those who had an influence upon it. For instance, Baibars (d. 709/1309), who was a Deputy Sultan of the Mamluks, was amongst Ibn Taymiyyah's opponents. The same can be said of his adviser, Naṣr al-Manbijī (d. 719/1319), who had a strong influence on his decisions.[198] Other opponents of Ibn Taymiyyah occupied prominent positions of power in the judicial system[199] or some religious organisations.[200] It was the efforts of this group against Ibn Taymiyyah that were primarily responsible for his persecution and tribulations. This point has been illustrated in the previous section, concerning Ibn Taymiyyah's detentions.

The third group differed in their opinion of Ibn Taymiyyah. In the beginning they supported him and approved of his work, and thereafter they turned against him. An example of this type of person was Abū Ḥayyān (d. 745/1344),[201] who was one of his erstwhile admirers. This individual used to write poetry in which he would praise Ibn Taymiyyah. Later, however, his poems became full of satire and vindictive abuse towards him. This dramatic shift appears to have been a direct retaliation against Ibn Taymiyyah's unflattering comments about Sībawayh and his book *al-Kitāb* (The Book) on the science of Arabic grammar.[202] Another example is al-Zamlikānī,[203] who was initially one of Ibn Taymiyyah's supporters and even lost his job due to his affiliation with him.[204] Later on, al-Zamlikānī opposed Ibn Taymiyyah on a number of issues, which ultimately resulted in his detention.[205]

Al-Dhahabī believed that it was Ibn Taymiyyah's harsh approach in dealing with his contemporaries, rather than fundamental ideological differences, that was the true cause of the reversal of attitudes towards him among his former sympathisers. He asserted that if Ibn Taymiyyah had coaxed his opponents, he would not have met with such a degree of opposition, for everyone knew and acknowledged his genius and the rarity of his faults.[206] He clarifies that he does not mean those scholars who plainly hated him or accused him of being an unbeliever; their judgements upon him were not based upon the content of his words, nor were they men of deep knowledge.[207]

Ibn Taymiyyah's alleged harshness in dealing with his opponents is an issue frequently mentioned by historians. I have traced the main source of this claim back to al-Dhahabī, who first made reference to it.[208] It appears likely that al-Dhahabī's very words were repeated in various sources, such as by Ibn Ḥajar in *al-Durar al-Kāminah*,[209] al-Ṣafadī in *al-Wāfī*,[210] al-Bazzār in *al-Aʿlām*,[211] Ibn Rajab in *al-Dhayl*[212] and al-Shawkānī in *al-Badr al-Ṭāliʿ*.[213]

Ibn Taymiyyah's own reaction to this accusation was as follows: 'What you have stated about the use of soft words is nothing but alien to me, as I am one of the people who use them most where they are deemed appropriate.'[214]

In other places, Ibn Taymiyyah explained his method in dealing with his opponents. He affirmed that even if his opponents were unjust towards him, he would not be unjust towards them,[215] for the only judge between them is the Book of Allah and the *sunnah* of His Messenger.[216]

Assuming this accusation was correct, was there any genetic influence on Ibn Taymiyyah's character from his family? Ibn Taymiyyah was quoted by al-Dawūdī as having admitted that harshness was one of his grandfather's characteristics.[217] Commenting upon this, al-Dhahabī stated: 'Our sheikh (i.e. Ibn Taymiyyah) had it, too.'[218] Others, such as al-Ṣafadī in *al-Wāfī*, took the view that Ibn Taymiyyah was influenced by Ibn Ḥazm's harshness.[219]

Ibn Taymiyyah's scholarly legacy in the sciences of *fiqh* and *uṣūl*

Introduction

Ibn Taymiyyah bequeathed a vast number of treatises dealing with various subjects in considerable detail. During the early stage of his scholarly life, he concentrated on matters of creed and the refutation of religious practices that he considered to be in conflict with the Qur'an and *sunnah* (innovations).[220] Later on, the attention he directed to other subjects (for example, jurisprudence and its fundamentals, *ḥadīth* and the interpretation of the Qur'an) was so profound that he became widely known as 'Sheikh al-Islam' and 'the interpreter of al-Qur'an', as an acknowledgement of his authority in these various disciplines.[221]

His disciples differed concerning the number of his treatises. Al-Dhahabī estimated them to be 4,000 *kurāsah* (booklets) or 500 *mujallad* (volumes).[222] Some scholars, such as Ibn 'Abd al-Hādī and al-Bazzār, disputed these figures, underlining the difficulty of specifying their number as some of them were never copied from the original manuscripts.[223] Others were written in prison and were taken away from him by the governors.[224]

A considerable amount of this heritage is devoted to the sciences of jurisprudence and its principles. It is evident, nevertheless, that he devoted considerable attention to the area of creed.

- When Ibn Taymiyyah was asked by his student al-Bazzār to write a complete and comprehensive treatise in the science of jurisprudence which would contain all of his jurisprudential opinions and preferences, and which would be used as a basis for *fatāwā*, Ibn Taymiyyah refused. He explained that the ruling in a jurisprudential issue is based upon independent reasoning; thus, there is no harm in a layman imitating one scholar or another. In matters concerning creed, however, conflicting opinions were usually based upon innovation (*bida'*) and invalid evidences. According to Ibn Taymiyyah, this led to a great deal of confusion amongst the public and he therefore devoted much of his time to attempting to address this problem.[225]
- Ibn Taymiyyah was sometimes forced to discuss issues of creed. This was because the majority of the accusations his opponents made against him were related to creed.

Despite Ibn Taymiyyah's emphasis on the science of creed, his competence as a jurist was recognised when he was only 18 years old.[226] After Ibn Taymiyyah's arrival in Damascus from Egypt in the year 712/1312, he concentrated on the science of jurisprudence.[227] In later years, and after his release from prison in the year 721/1321, he worked with some of his students on the correction of some of his earlier treatises.[228]

Muslims from all corners of the world sent him questions requesting *fatāwā*.[229] His published *fatāwā*, which comprised thirty-five volumes plus two indices, are sufficient proof for this. There is no doubt that his scholarly legacy concerning the science of jurisprudence and its principles has influenced the Ḥanbalī School of law to a significant extent.

It is beyond the scope of this work to embark upon a critique of all Ibn Taymiyyah's treatises, by reason of their large number. Nevertheless, a brief outline of some of his most important treatises follows and a whole section is devoted specifically to his treatises concerning jurisprudence and general principles of jurisprudence.

One of his most important treatises on creed is *Minhāj al-Sunnah al-Nabawiyyah.* In this work he used his knowledge of the *sharī'ah*, logic, philosophy and the

Arabic language to criticise the Shī'ī author Ibn Maṭahir. The book has now been published by al-Imām University and was edited by Muhammad Rashād Salīm.[230] Another book is *Kitāb al-Istiqāmah*, which concerns the obligation of the Muslim to adhere to the Qur'an and *sunnah* in matters of creed and practice.[231] In the first two chapters of this treatise, Ibn Taymiyyah discussed the Mutakallimūn's point of view that the pillars of faith (*uṣūl al-dīn*) can be determined through logical analogy and logical evidence, and not necessarily through the Qur'an and *sunnah*. He also refuted the claim made by some jurists that the *sharī'ah* required the use of analogy for its widespread application due to the lack of specific solutions to particular problems.[232]

Ibn al-Qayyim mentions only twenty of Ibn Taymiyyah's treaties on the subject of creed.[233] The actual figure is considerably higher when his shorter treatises are also taken into account. It appears that Ibn al-Qayyim chose to omit the smaller treatises in this field because if he had counted them, the number would have been very large.

Ibn Taymiyyah devoted a considerable part of his time to the interpretation of the Qur'an.[234] He is reported to have said that he would occasionally read up to 100 commentaries of the Qur'an before attempting to interpret a single verse of it.[235] Every Friday in the Grand Mosque of Damascus, Ibn Taymiyyah would chair study circles devoted to the interpretation of the Qur'an.[236] His legacy in this area is remarkable.[237] Consider, for example, *al-Tafsīr al-Kabīr*[238] and a set of volumes of *Majmū' al-Fatāwā* dealing entirely with this specialism.[239] Ibn al-Qayyim made reference to ninety-three of Ibn Taymiyyah's treatises in this field.[240]

Ibn Taymiyyah's treatises in fiqh *and* uṣūl

Here now follows a brief study of some of Ibn Taymiyyah's treatises in the science of jurisprudence and its principles.

Treatises in the sciences of Fiqh

Ta'līq 'Alā al-Muḥarrar In this work Ibn Taymiyyah commented on the treatise of his grandfather al-Majd entitled *al-Muḥarrar* in Ḥanbalī jurisprudence.[241]

Sharḥ al-'Umdah This is a commentary on the well-known book *al-'Umdah*, authored by the eminent Ḥanbalī scholar Ibn Qudāmah. Ibn Taymiyyah mentions in his introduction to this book that he was asked to compile it by a group of fellow Ḥanbalī scholars.[242]

Ibn Taymiyyah did not complete this work, for he only got as far as the book of *Ḥajj*. He analysed issues related to the subjects of purification, prayer, alms-tax, fasting and *Ḥajj*. Unfortunately, some parts of this book are yet to be discovered.[243] In this work, Ibn Taymiyyah demonstrates an extensive knowledge of the texts and statements of the companions. The book of fasting alone contains approximately 900 *ḥadīth* and *athar*. It provides considerable evidence of his knowledge of *Ḥadīth* combined with a comprehensive knowledge of the science of *Rijāl*.

Ibn Taymiyyah also demonstrates a great competence in the jurisprudence of the Ḥanbalī School of law. He possessed the ability to quote Ibn Ḥanbal and the opinions of the Ḥanbalī scholars at will. This work contains a study of conflicting opinions and narrations in the Ḥanbalī School, with Ibn Taymiyyah then mentioning his preferred opinion. In this book, Ibn Taymiyyah primarily restricted himself to the opinions of the School in stating his preference. He was to abandon some of these opinions at a later stage.[244]

The importance of this work stems from the fact that it is the only book written by Ibn Taymiyyah according to the method of jurists.[245] In addition, in certain instances, Ibn Taymiyyah even mentions some opinions of the Ḥanbalī scholars which cannot be found in any other source.[246] This treatise is also significant because it is the most comprehensive explanation available of the book *al-'Umdah*,[247] which is a recognised source in the Ḥanbalī School written by one of its most eminent scholars. Other commentaries on *al-'Umdah* contain various deficiencies.[248]

The fatāwā *of Ibn Taymiyyah* These *fatāwā* have been collected in various compilations, such as *Majmū' al-Fatāwā*, *al-Fatāwā al-Kubra*, *al-Fatāwā al-'Iraqiyyah* and *Majmū'at al-Rasā'il.*

These collections contain a large number of Ibn Taymiyyah's *fatāwā* in addition to smaller sections[249] and essays[250] on various subjects. Some of his other works, such as *al-Ḥisbah*, *al-Siyāsah al-Shar'iyyah*, *al-Jawāb al-Bāhir*, *al-Radd 'ala al-Akhnā'ī* and his *Mansak* in *al-Ḥajj*, are also incorporated within them.

By means of his *fatāwā*, Ibn Taymiyyah contributed to the expansion of the Ḥanbalī School of law in various ways. First, he helped the spread of the School by frequently mentioning in his answers the opinions of the Ḥanbalī School on the issues discussed. Second, he studied the opinions of the School and distinguished the correct from the incorrect, founding his judgement upon whether the opinion was based on authentic evidence or not. Third, Ibn Taymiyyah helped in the creation of a greater degree of tolerance amongst the Islamic schools of law by presenting in his *fatāwā*, in most instances, the opinions of other scholars. He would thereafter clarify their evidence.

Occasionally, we find that the same question has been repeatedly mentioned in the collections of *fatāwā*. This is probably because different questioners raised similar problems. These similar questions were all rehashed in these collections because each answer Ibn Taymiyyah gave usually contained some important and novel information.

One of the characteristic features of these collections is the smoothness and fluency of their style. This appears to be because the *fatāwā* contained in the collections were primarily related to questions raised by the lay public and his answers were consequently tailored to this audience.

Al-Qawā'id al-Nurāniyyah In this book, Ibn Taymiyyah studies jurisprudential disputes in the Islamic Schools of law regarding issues related to the prayer, alms-tax, fasting, *ḥajj*, various issues concerning transactions and contracts and finally vows and oaths.

Ibn Taymiyyah sought to demonstrate in this book the greater accuracy of the School of Ahl al-Ḥadīth, in particular the School of Aḥmad, in comparison to the other schools of Islamic law in the great majority of the disputed issues.

Al-Siyāsah al-Shar'iyyah Ibn Taymiyyah clarifies the topic of this book when he mentions that it is 'a short epistle on the principles of Divine law and Prophetic counsel which neither the ruler nor the ruled can go without'.[251] This book is divided into two parts; each part, in turn, is divided into several chapters and sections. The first part deals with public function and state revenues, whereas the second is devoted to the clarification of penalties concerning the violation of rights due to Allah and penalties and rights pertaining to individuals.

Al-Ḥisbah In this book Ibn Taymiyyah discusses various issues related to the institution of *al-ḥisbah*. This is a moral, as well as a socio-economic, institution in Islam, through which public life is regulated in such a manner that a high degree of public morality is attained. As a consequence, the community is protected from bad workmanship, fraud, extortion and exploitation.

This book can be divided into two parts. The first is devoted to the study and discussion of the concept, principles and mechanisms for the management of an Islamic economy. It highlights how different Islamic institutions play their respective roles in order to achieve the objectives of justice and freedom in society. It discusses several issues, including the basic principles of the *ḥisbah*, ethical guidelines for the regulation of business and economic life, collective good and state responsibility, price control and crime and punishment.[252]

In the second section, Ibn Taymiyyah not only clarified the philosophical foundations of the Islamic society but also presented a powerful exposition of the principal corrective mechanism at the heart of the Islamic scheme of life, that is, the act of commanding what is good and forbidding what is evil (*al-amr bi 'l-ma'rūf wa 'l-nahi 'an al-munkar*).[253]

Treatises in the principles of jurisprudence

Naqd Marātib al-Ijmā' Ibn Taymiyyah wrote this tract as a criticism and refutation of certain points made by Ibn Ḥazm in his book entitled *Marātib al-Ijmā'*. Ibn Ḥazm claimed that he had gathered together the issues, from diverse areas of the law, on which a consensus existed amongst the scholars as to their rulings.[254] Ibn Taymiyyah studied these alleged consensuses and found that a significant number of them were in part topics of known disputes amongst scholars. Furthermore, Ibn Taymiyyah observed that in some of the alleged instances of consensus, Ibn Ḥazm himself had preferred an opposing opinion and thus denied the existence of a consensus.[255]

The importance of this book stems from the fact that certain other scholars, including some affiliated to the Ḥanbalī School, had attested to the existence of consensus on some of these issues. Therefore, Ibn Taymiyyah's criticism is applicable to those scholars too. This book demonstrates that declarations of consensus should not be accepted at face value, without a careful analysis of the scholars' opinions.

Al-Musawwadah fī Uṣūl al-Fiqh This book was compiled by three scholars from the house of āl-Taymiyyah: al-Majd, the grandfather, the father, 'Abd al-Ḥalīm, and Ibn Taymiyyah. These eminent scholars left their contributions to this book in draft form until the Ḥanbalī scholar Ibn 'Abd al-Ghanī (d. 745/1344) collected, rewrote and arranged them.[256] From that point, this book has been an important source of Ḥanbalī *uṣūl*, cited by scholars affiliated to various schools. In certain instances, Ibn Taymiyyah criticised his grandfather's views, added to them and in various places introduced chapters and sections that had been left untreated by his father and grandfather. In relation to particular issues, Ibn Taymiyyah added important rules and maxims because he felt that there was a great need for them.

This book studies, comparatively and critically, issues arising from the general principles of Ḥanbalī jurisprudence and occasionally those of other schools and individual scholars. It illustrates the extensive knowledge of these three scholars concerning disagreement amongst the scholars of jurisprudence and its sources, in addition to other sciences such as the Arabic language.[257]

Risālah fī 'l-Qiyās This treatise was written by Ibn Taymiyyah in response to a question put to him concerning the correctness of the claim made by some scholars that certain rulings in Islamic law contradict analogy, even though these rulings are based upon either texts of the Qur'an and *sunnah*, analogy or the views of the companions.

Ibn Taymiyyah begins by explaining that analogy is divided into two kinds: valid and invalid analogy. He then goes on to define both terms.[258] According to Ibn Taymiyyah, this discussion is necessary because it is possible that legal rules can oppose an invalid analogy but not a valid one. This is followed by a comprehensive study of rulings which allegedly oppose analogy. Ibn Taymiyyah then shows that the rulings in those issues agree with valid analogy and the only contradictions are with reference to invalid analogy.[259]

Ibn Taymiyyah also studies several cases where a companion's ruling was alleged to be in contradiction to analogy. He revealed that when the companions were in agreement on a ruling, this ruling would invariably be consistent with valid analogy. It was possible, however, for a solitary companion's view to be inconsistent with such analogy.

Ibn Taymiyyah concludes that the real problem is not the apparent conflict between the rulings and analogy; rather, it is a misunderstanding of the distinction between valid and invalid analogies. This distinction can only be determined through an extensive study of the *sharī'ah* and its values. This treatise provides a strong rebuttal against Ḥanbalī scholars, among others, who claim the existence of a contradiction between text and analogy and use this as an excuse for departing from the implications of a text.[260]

Raf' al-Malām 'an al-A'immah al-A'lām The objective of this book is to explain the reasons for the existence of contradictions between certain scholars' opinions and authentic *ḥadīth*. Ibn Taymiyyah clarifies that none of the leading scholars intended deliberately to oppose the *sunnah* of the Prophet in any manner.

He provides three main reasons for these contradictions: First, the scholar did not believe that the Prophet uttered that particular *ḥadīth*. Second, the scholar believed that the *ḥadīth* in question was not of relevance to the issue at hand. Third, the scholar considered that particular *ḥadīth* to be abrogated. Ibn Taymiyyah elucidated upon these three main reasons and analysed the other issues which are associated with them.[261]

This treatise should be read in the context of the time in which Ibn Taymiyyah lived; this was an era of *taqlid*, in which fanaticism was also particularly widespread, not only amongst the lay public but also within the circles of the learned.

Ma'ārij al-Wuṣūl The primary objective of this book is to affirm that the Lawgiver clearly elucidated the sum total of the *uṣūl* and *furū'* of Islam in the Qur'an and *sunnah*. For the same purpose, Ibn Taymiyyah discussed several opposing opinions that were mainly presented by philosophers and Mutakallimūn and concluded that they were incorrect. This category of individuals included Avicenna (Ibn Sīnā') and Abū Ḥāmid al-Ghazālī. Ibn Taymiyyah argues that the problem is not that the sources of law do not contain sufficient evidence for various *furū'*. Rather, he is of the opinion that the real problem is that this evidence may be either unknown to some scholars or that its indicators are not manifest to them. Also, in certain instances, Ibn Taymiyyah observes that even when the evidence was known and the indicators were manifest, the evidence was not implemented due to their assumption that they were contradicted by other evidence.[262]

The contribution of this treatise to Islamic law in general and the Ḥanbalī School in particular is a significant one. This is because the issue concerning the sufficiency of the Qur'an and *sunnah* as sources of law has been hotly disputed among scholars over the centuries. It should be noted that when Ibn Taymiyyah asserts that these two sources are sufficient, it does not mean that he does not recognise the other sources of law, such as consensus and analogy. For he states that they are recognised sources whose authority is obtained only through the two main sources of law, the Qur'an and *sunnah*.

Iḍāḥ al-Dilālah fī 'Umūm al-Risālah li 'l-Thaqalayn This treatise deals with the universality of the mission of the Prophet Muhammad and the fact that he was sent as a messenger to mankind and the spiritual world. Most of this book is devoted to the discussion of topics related to the mission of the Prophet to the spiritual world and other related issues, such as spiritual possession, visions and exorcism.

This book occupies a special position, as it concerns the laws governing the relationship between mankind and the world of spirits. In addition, it deals with the question of whether or not these spirits are subject to the laws of the *sharī'ah*. Ibn Taymiyyah declares that spirits are indeed subject to these laws and states that the verses revealed to the Prophet address all created beings, both human and spiritual, as his message was directed to both worlds. Ibn Taymiyyah asserts that this remains the cardinal principle in relation to the Qur'an, even though the reason for the revelation of some of its verses may be related to certain incidents which occurred amongst the Arabs at that time. According to the consensus of

Muslim scholars, this is because none of the verses is restricted in its application to the specific reasons for its revelation.[263]

Qā'idah fī Tawaḥḥud al-Millah wa Ta'addud al-Sharā'i' This treatise studies the concept of the unity of creed amongst all Prophets and their diversity in relation to the laws. Ibn Taymiyyah affirms this concept by citing various pieces of textual evidence from the Qur'an and *sunnah.* He asserts that what has been approved by the Qur'an, *sunnah* or consensus in the field of Islamic creed is the same as that believed by all of the Prophets, and it is binding upon every Muslim. Whereas laws are miscellaneous, no particular law can be considered as binding on every Muslim; thus, various laws were brought by the different Prophets.

The significance of this work stems from the fact that it intended to combat intolerance and appeal for a greater degree of tolerance amongst the various schools of law. In the event of a dispute concerning jurisprudential issues, the different opinions of the scholars will be tolerated. Ibn Taymiyyah explains, however, that this tolerance does not mean that all the various opinions are correct and cannot therefore be criticised, unlike the situation with the various laws of the Prophets. This is simply because the Prophets are infallible. If they committed mistakes they would have been corrected by another revelation. No such divine correction exists for scholars' mistakes. Hence, criticism of scholars' opinions based upon their own independent reasoning is permitted, and no scholar has the right to impose his own opinion on other scholars as a binding principle of law.[264]

In addition to those mentioned, Ibn Taymiyyah authored other smaller treatises on this subject.[265]

Ibn Taymiyyah's death

After a lengthy journey in pursuit of knowledge and reform, and after being subjected to a series of detentions, Ibn Taymiyyah died on the eve of Monday the twentieth of Dhi al-Qi'dah 728/1328.[266] Amongst Ibn Taymiyyah's final words were his forgiveness to all those individuals who caused his detentions and persecutions, if they based their actions upon independent reasoning and were unaware that he was speaking the truth.[267] Ibn Rajab mentions that funeral prayers were performed for *sheikh al-Islam* Ibn Taymiyyah in most of the Islamic lands, far and near, and it was even reported that as far away as China, the prayer was performed for him and was described as a prayer for the interpreter of the Qur'an.[268]

2

A COMPARISON OF THE BASIC PRINCIPLES OF ISLAMIC LAW ACCORDING TO IBN ḤANBAL AND IBN TAYMIYYAH

Introduction

The sources of law which constitute part of the science of the principles of jurisprudence, termed '*uṣūl al-fiqh*', are discussed in this chapter. It is therefore appropriate to begin by defining this science. Several attempts to advance a suitable definition have been made, most of which have been criticised for being either too long, incomplete or containing unnecessary information. Nevertheless, some quite sufficient definitions have been advanced, including that suggested by Fakhr al-Dīn al-Rāzī. He states that

> *Uṣūl al-fiqh* is the aggregate, considered per se, of legal proofs and evidences that when studied correctly will lead either to certain knowledge of a *sharī'ah* ruling, or to at least a reasonable assumption concerning the source, the manner by which such proofs are adduced, and the status of the adducer.[1]

This definition establishes that the subject of *uṣūl al-fiqh* is concerned with the proofs within the *sharī'ah* source texts, considering them from the perspective of 'how' legal judgements are derived by means of independent reasoning from particular proofs and preference is given to one text over another where texts appear contradictory.[2]

This work studies the role of Ibn Taymiyyah in the jurisprudence and principles of the Ḥanbalī School of law. The objective of this chapter is to discover whether his role encompasses the general bases and principles of this School or is merely restricted to jurisprudential rulings. This is achieved through comparing the general principles of Aḥmad and Ibn Taymiyyah and highlighting the similarities and differences between them. If their principles were apparently identical, it would be assumed that Ibn Taymiyyah did not seek to influence the guiding principles of Ḥanbalī jurisprudence.

Aḥmad Ibn Ḥanbal's basic principles of jurisprudence

Ibn Ḥanbal was amongst those scholars who did not record their sources of law. This resulted in uncertainty and ambiguity concerning these sources, to the extent that some Ḥanbalī scholars were confused themselves. Some of his sources were nevertheless transmitted orally, and others could be inferred from his *fatāwā*. This section is devoted to tracing these sources, as found within his recorded statements and located in Ḥanbalī treatises.

Aḥmad's indications of the basic principles of jurisprudence

Certain indicators suggestive of his general principles of jurisprudence can be found in the words of Ibn Ḥanbal:

- Al-Athram narrates that Aḥmad says: 'It (the basis of jurisprudence) is the *sunnah* and *ittibā*ʿ (following).'[3]
- An explanation of what Aḥmad meant by *ittibā*ʿ can be found in another narration of Abū Dawūd. Aḥmad says: 'it is to follow what is reported from the Prophet and his companions, then one has the choice whether to follow the opinions of the followers (*tābiʿīn*)'.[4]
- Also, in a narration of Ibn Hāni', Aḥmad was asked what a scholar should do when he was asked about the legal ruling on an issue in which there is a disagreement among scholars. He clarifies that a scholar should give *fatāwā* which agree with the Book and *sunnah*, and whatever disagrees with them must be left aside.[5]
- Aḥmad's position in relation to the validity of analogy is somewhat ambiguous. It is not at first sight certain whether or not Ibn Ḥanbal implemented this source. This confusion is exacerbated by certain narrations of Aḥmad himself, in which he appears to refute the legitimacy of analogy. After studying the Ḥanbalī sources we find that Aḥmad's position regarding this issue can be better understood through the following:
    - Ibn al-Jawzī mentions that in the narration of al-Athram, he quotes Aḥmad as saying 'and (the correct) analogy is what is based on an original case'.[6]
    - This is further explained in another narration. Aḥmad clarifies what he meant by the correct analogy when he explains that the acceptable form of analogy is one wherein complete similarity is found between the 'root' and 'branch'. If these two cases accord with each other in some respects but differ in others, then the use of analogy is incorrect.[7]
    - Aḥmad, therefore, rejects analogy which does not agree with the conditions mentioned earlier for correct analogy. He states that if a ruling is based on an original case, and later on the original case becomes redundant,

the existence of analogy (in the branch case) can no longer be claimed.[8] According to this statement by Aḥmad, it will be unacceptable to consider it as correct analogy; the basis upon which this analogy was founded is no longer applicable.

– In order to eliminate the existence of incorrect analogy, Aḥmad in a narration asserts that the one who practises analogy must be an experienced scholar.[9]

These are some of the indications for Aḥmad's general principles of jurisprudence founded in his own statements. It is clear from them that Aḥmad was a scholar who had a tendency towards Ahl al-Ḥadīth, as we find him insisting on the *sunnah* and *ittiba*ʿ as the basis of jurisprudence. *Ittiba*ʿ in this context denotes adherence to the texts. This tendency can also be discerned from his cautious position towards analogy. These statements alone are, however, insufficient to depict a clear picture of the principles of jurisprudence used by this scholar. It is important also to study Ḥanbalī texts to see what they concluded to be his principles.

The general principles of Aḥmad's jurisprudence in the writings of Ḥanbalī scholars

The Ḥanbalī scholars who studied and made reference to Aḥmad's general principles can be classified into two categories:

1 Those individuals who were well-known scholars in the School but did not compile treatises devoted to the study of the general principles of the School.
2 Scholars who devoted some of their treatises to the study of the general principles of the School.

The first Ḥanbalī scholar whom we find to have tried to infer the general principles used by Aḥmad is al-Athram (d. 260/874), a well-known student of Aḥmad and narrator of his *Masāʾil*. He states that through his experience in narrating Aḥmad's *Masāʾil*, he found that the methodology employed by Ibn Ḥanbal in his legal rulings is

- That if there is a *ḥadīth* from the Prophet on the issue under discussion, Aḥmad will disregard the opinion of any of the companions and those who followed them.
- Where there are conflicting opinions of the companions on an issue, Aḥmad will choose some of them and will not consider the opinions of those who followed them.
- If these types of evidence (i.e. *ḥadīth*, opinions of companions) are not found, then he will select from the opinions of the followers (*tabiʿīn*).
- Finally, Aḥmad would use a *ḥadīth* whose chain has a defect as evidence, provided that there is no other evidence conflicting with it. Similarly, he uses

a *ḥadīth* which a successor has directly attributed to the Prophet without mentioning the last narrator, namely the companion (*mursal ḥadīth*), if there is no other contradicting evidence on the same issue.[10]

The leading Ḥanbalī judge and scholar Abū 'l-Ḥusayn Muḥammad b. Muḥammad Ibn al-Farrā', known as Ibn Abū Ya'la (526/1132), mentions in his book *Ṭabaqāt al-Ḥanābilah* that the four general principles of jurisprudence used by Aḥmad were the following:

1 The Qur'an
2 The *sunnah*
3 Opinions of companions
4 Analogy.[11]

Ibn Tamīm (d. 675/1276),[12] in his introduction to the book *'Aqidat al-Imām Aḥmad*, mentions that Aḥmad's general principles of law are five:

1 The Qur'an
2 The *sunnah*
3 The consensus of the scholars of the time
4 The opinion of a companion when it was widespread at his time without any sign of disapproval from the other companions. If jurisprudential dispute amongst the companions occurred, then Aḥmad would select one of these opinions
5 Analogy in the case of necessity only.[13]

The famous scholar Ibn Qayyim offers more clarifications and explanation on this point. He states that Ibn Ḥanbal based his method of deriving *fatāwā* on the following five sources:

1 Texts of the Qur'an and the *sunnah*. Therefore, if he found a text in the Qur'an or the *sunnah* concerning a particular issue, he would base his *fatwā* upon it, and would under no circumstances whatsoever consider other sources which might conflict with them. Ibn Qayyim states that Ibn Ḥanbal granted precedence to sound *ḥadīth* over practice (*'amal*), *ra'y*, analogy (*qiyās*), the opinion of the companions and silent consensus (*ijmā' sukūtī*).
2 The *fatāwā* issued by the companions in the absence of any contradictory opinion held by some of them. Whenever Ibn Ḥanbal found this type of evidence he would use it in preference to practice, *ra'y* and analogy.
3 When the companions held different opinions concerning an issue, Aḥmad would select from those opinions the one which was closest to the texts of the Qur'an and *sunnah*. Wherever it was not clear which opinion was closest, he would transmit the different opinions of the companions without demonstrating a preference. It ought to be mentioned that Aḥmad did not issue a new judgement at this stage.

4 For a ruling on an issue where none of the four sources of law mentioned earlier offered an immediate solution, Aḥmad would base his judgement upon a weak or *mursal ḥadīth* (a report of a saying of the Prophet which lacks a link in the chain going back to the Prophet).
5 Analogy. This source of law was used as a last resort by Aḥmad and was used only in the case of necessity.[14]

Other Ḥanbalī scholars who authored treatises on the general principles of Ḥanbalī law have presented these sources differently. They have added to those mentioned and classified them systematically. We shall now consider in more detail two selected Ḥanbalī references in the field of *uṣūl al-fiqh* which will be examined with reference to this point, that is, sources of jurisprudence in the Ḥanbalī School of law.

The first reference is *Kitāb al-Tamhīd*, authored by the eminent Ḥanbalī scholar Abū 'l-Khaṭṭāb. The importance of this book is founded upon the fact that it is the second complete Ḥanbalī treatise, after his sheikh Abū Ya'la's book *al-'Uddah*, in which we can find a comprehensive analysis of the principles of *fiqh*.

This scholar elected to divide the sources into the following three groups:[15]

1 Text (naṣṣ)

According to Abū 'l-Khaṭṭāb, the category 'text' is inclusive of the Qur'an, the *sunnah*, consensus and the views of the companions.

It might seem strange that Abū 'l-Khaṭṭāb included consensus and the views of the companions in the division of *naṣṣ*. It is probable that the reason for this inclusion is that consensus, as understood by most jurists, must be based upon the texts of the Qur'an and *sunnah*. Therefore, if consensus is founded upon a text, it can be considered as *naṣṣ* itself. The opinion of the companions, also, is not considered text in itself, but it seems that Abū 'l-Khaṭṭāb referred to the opinions of the companions as text for one of two reasons:

1 The opinion of one companion about which there is no known disagreement among the rest of the companions is considered to be a type of consensus, and consensus must be based upon a text of Qur'an or *sunnah* as cited previously. Therefore, it can be inferred that when Abū 'l-Khaṭṭāb referred to the opinion of the companions as text, he was taking into account the fact that the consensus of the companions is based upon a text.
2 It appears that Abū 'l-Khaṭṭāb follows the opinion of those scholars who gave great weight to the views of the companions. He said that the companions would not utter anything in matters pertaining to the *sharī'ah* except what they had heard from the Prophet himself.[16] These scholars also subscribed to the opinion that even if it was the companions' own view, then it ought to be granted precedence over rational evidence. This was founded upon two main arguments. First, the companions were present at the time of the revelation

and they would therefore understand the meaning of the text and the circumstances surrounding its revelation. Second, by reason of their pure Arabic origin, they would possess the ability to understand the texts in a manner more complete and perfect than later generations, for the texts were revealed in the highest and purest form of the Arabic language.

2 *The Implication of Texts* (ma'qūl al-naṣṣ)

Abū 'l-Khaṭṭāb divided this source into the following three categories:

1 Divergent meaning, *mafhūm al-mukhālafah*, or *dalīl al-khiṭāb*. *Mafhūm al-mukhālafah* may be defined as a meaning derived from the words of the text in such a way that it diverges from the explicit meaning thereof.[17]
2 Implicit meaning, *mafhūm al-Khiṭāb*, or *laḥn al-khiṭāb*. *Mafhūm al-Khiṭāb* is a rationally concomitant meaning that is obtained through further investigation of the signs that might be detectable therein.[18]
3 The meaning of the texts, *ma'nā al-khiṭāb*. Abū 'l-Khaṭṭāb included analogy in this category.

3 *Presumption of Continuity* (istiṣḥāb)

Abū 'l-Khaṭṭāb divided this source into two categories:

1 *Istiṣḥāb* of reason
2 *Istiṣḥāb* of consensus.

In *al-Rawḍah*, Ibn Qudāmah divides the sources of jurisprudence into two categories,[19] namely:

1 Agreed-upon sources:
   - Qur'an
   - *Sunnah*
   - Consensus
   - *Istiṣḥāb*.
2 Disputed sources, which include:
   - Laws of previously revealed religions
   - The opinions of the companions
   - *Istiḥsān*
   - *Istiṣḥāb*.

By means of a careful examination of the earlier contributions by Ḥanbalī scholars, it is clear that there are differences concerning Ibn Ḥanbal's sources of law amongst the scholars of his School. One such group includes al-Athram, Ibn Abū Ya'la, Ibn Tamīm, Ibn al-Qayyim and Ibn al-Jawzī, and the other comprises the rest of the Ḥanbalī scholars. It can be concluded, however, that the main sources of Aḥmad's principles are the Qur'an, *sunnah*, consensus and analogy.[20] This can be deduced from the following points:

- In the instances when mention is made of the opinion of a companion which was not known to be disapproved of by other companions, they are in fact referring to tacit consensus.
- In the instances when mention is made of the companions' disagreement regarding jurisprudential rulings, Aḥmad would choose the nearest of these opinions to the texts; this is in fact the act of Aḥmad returning to the sources of Qur'an and *sunnah*.
- The fact that some of these scholars do not refer directly to explicit consensus as one of Aḥmad's general principles of law does not necessarily mean that they believe that Aḥmad did not employ this principle. By accepting as one of the general principles of Aḥmad the undisputed opinion of a companion *a fortiori* they accept the consensus of the companions as a general principle. It may be also true that these scholars did not mention this principle because Aḥmad believed that explicit consensus after the time of the companions is very difficult to achieve (*muta'adhdhir*).
- Weak and *mursal ḥadīth* can be included under the source *sunnah*, but they would not be used by Aḥmad if he could find a stronger proof, namely, a clearly authenticated text, explicit or implicit consensus or an opinion of a companion which is closer to the Book and *sunnah*.
- Most of the additional sources mentioned by Ḥanbalī scholars can be included under the term 'analogy', for the term itself incorporates a wider meaning, it can also refer to 'independent reasoning', that is, *ijtihād*. The use of the term 'analogy' to denote *ijtihād* can be found in al-Shāfi'ī's book *al-Risālah*. When questioned whether analogy was the same as *ijtihād*, Shāfi'ī replied, 'These are two terms which have the same meaning.'[21]
- It can be argued that those scholars who did not mention some of the sources mentioned by other Ḥanbalī scholars failed to do so because most of them were either preferences (*ikhtiārāt*) between sources, for example, *istiḥsān*, or maxims for jurisprudence, such as *al-'urf* (custom).

In relation to the differences amongst the Ḥanbalī scholars in their act of identifying the Ḥanbalī sources of law, it appears that they occurred as a result of the following main factors:

- The *mujtahid*'s own independent reasoning has influenced the classification of the sources of law within the Ḥanbalī School. An example to illustrate this point is *istiṣḥāb*, as some scholars maintain that it is a source while others disagree.[22] Note also that Abū 'l-Khaṭṭāb in '*al-Tamhīd* discussed the issue of whether or not the laws of previously revealed religions were to be regarded as having authority in Islam.[23] He did not, however, include it in the category of 'text' in his classification. It appears that the reason for its exclusion was his conclusion that previously revealed laws (*shar' man qablanā*) were not to be considered as a source of law in Islam.[24] Thus, the apparent differences are partly the product of the differing methods of classification employed by the various scholars, rather than actual differences in the sources of law themselves.

- Some sources are inclusive of various sub-divisions. Hence, when a scholar declares his acceptance of a particular source, he may be referring to a specific branch of that source. Similarly, those who declare their rejection of a source may refer to the rejection of a particular branch of that source. This is clearly evident in *istiṣḥāb*, for those who accept it as a source refer to the acceptance of *istiṣḥāb al-'Adam* (presumption of original absence), whereas those who reject it refer to the rejection of *istiṣḥāb al-ḥāl* (continuity of attributes), though they do accept *istiṣḥāb al-'Adam* as a source.
- Some scholars were influenced by other scholars who preceded them in writing in the field of *uṣūl al-fiqh*. This resulted in the development of different approaches to the classification of the sources of law within the Ḥanbalī School. An example of this may be observed in the Ḥanbalī sources previously cited, namely, *al-Tamhīd* and *al-Rawḍah*. Abū 'l-Khaṭṭāb in his *al-Tamhīd* is influenced by his sheikh Abū Ya'la. This can be discerned by means of a comparison between *al-Tamhīd* and Abū Ya'la's *al-'Uddah*. In contrast, Ibn Qudāmah in his book *al-Rawḍah* was influenced by the eminent scholar al-Ghazālī and his book *al-Mustaṣfā*. For example, Ibn Qudāmah did not mention 'analogy' within his classification. He did, however, devote a lengthy chapter to the discussion of the issues relating to this source of jurisprudence at the end of his treatise, and it would appear that he did consider analogy to be a source of law. Al-Ṭūfī, a Ḥanbalī scholar, wrote a commentary on *Kitāb al-Rawḍah* in which he states that Ibn Qudāmah should have mentioned analogy with the agreed-upon sources at the beginning of his treatise, because analogy is one of these sources.[25] It is likely that the reason for Ibn Qudāmah's exclusion was founded upon his adherence to the structure of al-Ghazālī's book *al-Mustaṣfā*, which does not mention analogy with the agreed-upon sources at the beginning of his treatise.[26]

Although Aḥmad's principal sources of law were the Qur'an, *sunnah*, consensus and analogy, this does not mean that he did not adopt the other means and sources mentioned by Ḥanbalī scholars. He used them as a means of discerning preferences (*ikhtiyārāt*) between sources or employed them as maxims for jurisprudence but not as independent sources.

Ibn Taymiyyah's basic principles of jurisprudence

The researcher who studies Ibn Taymiyyah's jurisprudence and its principles encounters difficulty in identifying his sources of law. As a consequence, ascertaining whether he was a *mujtahid* or *muqallid* in this matter is problematic. This difficulty is further compounded by the fact that Ibn Taymiyyah did not author a complete treatise concerning *uṣūl al-fiqh* through which these sources could be readily identified.

Some contemporary writers have argued either that Ibn Taymiyyah's sources are the same as those of Ibn Ḥanbal[27] or that he was a Ḥanbalī scholar.[28] They have nevertheless disagreed in their identification of these sources. Abū Zahrah states that Ibn Taymiyyah's sources of law were the following:[29]

- *Naṣṣ* (text); according to him this includes the Qur'an and *sunnah*
- Consensus
- Analogy
- 'The remainder of the sources'; Abū Zahrah clarifies that this category includes the following sources of law:
  - Opinions of the companions
  - *Istiṣḥāb*
  - *Maṣlaḥah mursalah*; Abū Zahrah suggests that this source would include *istiḥsān*
  - *Sadd al-dharā'i'* (blocking the means, that is, preventing the use of lawful means to achieve unlawful ends).

These sources were also mentioned by al-'Uṭayshān,[30] who also expressed hesitation concerning whether or not to treat 'custom' as one of Ibn Taymiyyah's sources.[31]

This is different from al-Manṣūr, who states that Ibn Taymiyyah's sources of law were the following:[32]

- Qur'an
- *Sunnah*
- Consensus
- Opinions of the companions
- Analogy
- *Istiṣḥāb*
- *Maṣlaḥah mursalah*
- *Sadd al-Dharā'i'*
- Custom.

Finally, it is noted that Sulaymān considers the following to be Ibn Taymiyyah's sources of law:[33]

- Qur'an
- *Sunnah*

- Consensus
- Opinions of the companions
- Analogy
- *Sadd al-Dharāʾiʿ*.

By means of a careful analysis of the aforementioned studies, the following four conclusions can be drawn.

1 It would appear that most of those scholars who claim that Ibn Taymiyyah's sources of law were identical to those of Ibn Ḥanbal did not base their claim on a comprehensive study of Ibn Taymiyyah's treatises. Rather, this opinion appears to be founded on the premise that it was known that he was a Ḥanbalī scholar. Furthermore, it appears that some of them merely adopted the opinion of other scholars.
2 Despite the affirmation made by several scholars that Ibn Taymiyyah's sources were identical to those of Ibn Ḥanbal, they differed in their identification of those sources.
3 Some scholars who identified Ibn Taymiyyah's sources of law admit that certain sources were included in their list because the writers themselves felt that Ibn Taymiyyah had attached importance to them, and not because Ibn Taymiyyah had himself declared that they were his sources of law.[34]
4 The main reason accounting for the differing opinions amongst contemporary writers concerning Ibn Taymiyyah's sources of law is the absence of a complete treatise written by Ibn Taymiyyah on the subject.

We can therefore conclude that it is essential to trace Ibn Taymiyyah's sources by reference to his own treatises and jurisprudence. As a consequence, the remainder of this section is devoted to identifying these sources via two methods:

1 Identifying Ibn Taymiyyah's attitude towards the Ḥanbalī School of law in addition to the other schools. This will provide us with some indication as to his preferred principles.
2 Tracing the sources of Ibn Taymiyyah in his own treatises.

A section will thereafter follow in which a comparison will be made between the general basic principles of Ibn Taymiyyah and those of Ibn Ḥanbal.

Ibn Taymiyyah's attitudes towards the Ḥanbalī School and other Islamic schools of law

Before embarking upon this section's discussion, it should be pointed out that, certainly, my aim is not to reach a conclusion as to which Islamic school of law is the most accurate of the four well-known schools. Rather, my aim is solely to try to identify which school Ibn Taymiyyah demonstrated a tendency towards (and indeed whether or not he considered himself to be a follower of any particular school). It is not possible in this survey to compare the merits and demerits of each of the schools.

Ibn Taymiyyah praises Ibn Ḥanbal and his School on several occasions. He states that Ibn Ḥanbal's knowledge and that of his followers was commonly recognised by scholars.[35] In certain instances he mentions that the reason for his praise of the Ḥanbalī School was its strict adherence to the Qur'an and *sunnah*, and to the opinions of the companions and their followers.[36] Ibn Taymiyyah believes that this strict adherence to the texts results in Ibn Ḥanbal's views being devoid of any opinions which conflicted with the Qur'an and *sunnah*.[37]

As for weak opinions, Ibn Taymiyyah states that despite the existence of certain weak opinions within Ḥanbalī jurisprudence, there also usually exist other opinions which conform to the correct ruling on the same issues.[38]

Ibn Taymiyyah considers Ibn Ḥanbal to be a just scholar who judged every other scholar according to his merits.[39] He also praises the Ḥanbalīs for their unity and he describes their scholars as having fewer disagreements amongst themselves than those of any other school of law.[40]

Ibn Taymiyyah defends the existence of some *mufradāt* in the Ḥanbalī School. He says that the greater portion of Ibn Ḥanbal's *mufradāt*, on which there is no disagreement within the Ḥanbalī School, are the correct opinions. He goes on to say that what are termed *mufradāt* by some people, because Ibn Ḥanbal disagreed on these issues with Abū Ḥanifah and al-Shāfi'ī, are in fact not *mufradāt* at all. This is because Mālik either agrees with Ibn Ḥanbal concerning these issues or subscribes to an opinion which is very similar to his. Hence, it is not accurate to term them *mufradāt*. Ibn Taymiyyah also says that the opinion of Ibn Ḥanbal and Mālik concerning these issues is often the most correct one.[41]

This is Ibn Taymiyyah's attitude towards the Ḥanbalī School, but what is his opinion about the other schools of law?

It can be concluded from Ibn Taymiyyah's treatises that he was full of praise for those scholars who based their opinions on their independent reasoning, such as Abū Ḥanifah, Mālik, Shāfi'ī and al-Awazā'ī, and he refers to them as *mujtahids*. He believes that Mālik's *uṣūl* was the most accurate, while claiming that it was perfected by Aḥmad. In yet another statement he praises Shāfi'ī for his disagreement and correction of the Ahl al-Madīnah School.[42]

It would appear that these statements uttered by Ibn Taymiyyah contradict one another and do not clearly convey and demonstrate his jurisprudential inclination. Fortunately, we are able to consult his work *Ṣiḥḥat Uṣūl Madhhab Ahl al-Madīnah* (The Correctness of the Principles of the Madīnah School of Law) in seeking to reconcile these statements. He begins this treatise by declaring that the School of Madīnah was the most correct School, in relation to both its *uṣūl* and its *furū'*. This superiority was confined, however, to the time of the companions, their followers and the generation after them.[43]

Ibn Taymiyyah cited both textual and rational evidence to support this statement. He quotes the tradition of the Prophet, in which he states, 'the people of my generation are the best, then those who follow them, and then those who follow the latter'.[44] The rational evidence which is quoted concerns the fact that these generations lived either with the Prophet, or close to his time. One would expect them to have adhered closely to the *sunnah* of the Prophet, and their knowledge of the *sunnah* to have been more comprehensive than that of people who resided in other parts of the Islamic world and in later times.[45] This adherence to the *sunnah* was augmented by the fact that various forms of innovations had appeared in various parts of the Islamic world, but not in Madīnah.[46]

Ibn Taymiyyah analyses the historical roots of the School of Madīnah and states that this School of law founded its rulings upon the *sunnah* of the Prophet whenever a tradition could be found. They would adhere to the ruling of 'Umar in the event that no tradition of the Prophet was available. 'Umar was a companion who was known to have followed the Prophet in both the *uṣūl* and the *furū'*, and who was also known for consulting Ahl al-Shurā. It was even mentioned that Mālik narrated the greater portion of his *Muwaṭṭa'* from Rabī'ah, who narrated it from Sa'īd Ibn al-Musayyib, who transmitted it from 'Umar.[47]

After analysing the geographical location of the various schools of law at the time of Mālik, Ibn Taymiyyah states that the knowledge of Ahl al-Madīnah was praised and acknowledged by all parts of the Islamic world with the exception of Kufah. As a consequence, this School spread to Egypt, al-Shām and Iraq. Ibn Taymiyyah goes on to say that even the people of Kufah did not claim to be in possession of greater knowledge than the people of Madīnah before the assassination of 'Uthmān.[48]

It may appear therefore that Ibn Taymiyyah gave Mālik's School preference out of the various schools of law. It seems more likely, however, that in most cases Ibn Taymiyyah's comparison is actually between Ahl al-Madīnah and Ahl al-Ra'y, where he considers Ahl al-Madīnah to be more representative of Ahl al-Ḥadīth. Therefore, when Ibn Taymiyyah expresses a preference for the School of Ahl al-Madīnah over the School of Ahl al-Ra'y, he is in fact expressing his preference for the method of Ahl al-Ḥadīth over Ahl al-Ra'y, as opposed to the School of Mālik over the other schools of law. This can be supported by the following six points:

1. His praise of the people of Madīnah is restricted for the most part to a period before the existence of the Mālikī School of law.
2. Ibn Taymiyyah enumerated the most praiseworthy characteristics of this School in his treatise:

   - They adhered more strongly to the traditions of the Prophet in their method of deducing rulings.
   - They had an extensive knowledge of *sunnah*,[49] which meant that they did not need to consider *ra'y* in most cases.

   These are, of course, also the characteristic features of Ahl al-Ḥadīth.
3. Ibn Taymiyyah commends several scholars, such as al-Awzā'ī,[50] although they were not affiliated to the School of Mālik. Rather, they were eminent scholars who introduced independent schools or demonstrated a preference

for the method of Ahl al-Ḥadīth. Again, this lends weight to the submission that Ibn Taymiyyah's preference was for the Ahl al-Ḥadīth, rather than Mālik's School per se.

4 Ibn Taymiyyah states that Ibn Ḥanbal would deliver *fatāwā* founded upon the School of Madīnah, a school which he preferred to that of Ahl al-Irāq, but he also adds that it is common knowledge that Aḥmad based his *uṣūl* on the method of Ahl al-Ḥadīth because he was affiliated with his School.[51] This shows that, according to Ibn Taymiyyah, Ibn Ḥanbal considers the people of Madīnah as synonymous with Ahl al-Ḥadīth. This explanation is supported by Ibn Taymiyyah's own words when he states that Ibn Ḥanbal used to refer those who had questions to Ahl al-Ḥadīth and Ahl al-Madīnah.[52]

5 Ibn Taymiyyah mentions as being affiliated to this school scholars such as Isḥāq, Abū 'Ubayd and Abū Thawr. These individuals were not Mālikī scholars but rather from Ahl al-Ḥadīth. Ibn Taymiyyah continues by saying, 'and other scholars of Ahl al-Ḥadīth'.[53]

6 Ibn Taymiyyah states that one of the reasons for his preference for the School of Madīnah was the extensive knowledge of its exponents concerning the science of *ḥadīth* and the chains of narrators, as opposed to the School of Kufah, who possessed less knowledge concerning these matters. Furthermore, the fabrication of *ḥadīth* was widespread in that part of the world, particularly by the Shī'ah.[54] Ibn Taymiyyah's criticism of Ahl al-Kufah here is clearly a criticism of the tendencies of Ahl al-Ra'y.

Ibn Taymiyyah does mention on certain occasions that the School of Mālik (and not Ahl al-Madīnah, as was his habit in this treatise) was the most accurate in the matter of *uṣūl*. Nevertheless, he himself says that al-Shāfi'ī studied under Mālik and thereafter praises al-Shāfi'ī for the views he held that conflicted with those of Mālik. Furthermore, Ibn Taymiyyah goes so far as to say that some people included al-Shāfi'ī within the al-Ḥijāz School of law. He also added that al-Shāfi'ī, in the opinion of the followers of Mālik, was deemed one of them, but that al-Shāfi'ī disagreed with Mālik on certain issues. Ibn Taymiyyah attributes this disagreement to al-Shāfi'ī's status as a *mujtahid*.[55] Ibn Taymiyyah's categorisation of al-Shāfi'ī within the School of al-Ḥijāz can be considered an attempt by him to identify a broader school than that of Madīnah alone, again expressing his preference for Ahl al-Ḥadīth above all else.

Having accepted that Ibn Taymiyyah expressed a preference for the School of Madīnah, but only in the sense of it being representative at its time of Ahl al-Ḥadīth, it is necessary to delve further to ascertain which School Ibn Taymiyyah demonstrated a tendency towards. Beyond the fact that later scholars categorised him within the Ḥanbalī School, there are other pointers towards his preference for this School:

- Ibn Taymiyyah's initial instruction was primarily founded upon the Ḥanbalī School, and this must have exerted a great influence upon him.

- As mentioned previously, Ibn Taymiyyah praises the Ḥanbalī School and its sources of law. He expresses his admiration for Ibn Ḥanbal, emphasising that he based his sources on the texts of the Qur'an and *sunnah* and the *athār* of the companions.
- Although Ibn Taymiyyah praises Mālik's *uṣūl* in his work *Ṣiḥḥat Uṣūl Madhhab Ahl al-Madīnah*, he goes on to state that it was Ibn Ḥanbal who perfected this *uṣūl*.

When Ibn Ḥanbal himself was questioned in relation to who, out of Mālik or Sufiyān, was the most knowledgeable of the *sunnah* and the *athār* of the companions, he replied 'Mālik'.[56] Ibn Taymiyyah, however, asserts that Aḥmad's preference for the Mālikī School over Sufyān's School was, in fact, a preference for Ahl al-Madīnah over Ahl al-Irāq (i.e. Ahl al-Ra'y), because Sufyān was the leader of the scholars of Iraq.[57]

It is clear that by his expression of preference for Mālik's School, Ibn Taymiyyah is referring to the state of the School at the time of Mālik himself. This view can be supported by the following points:

- Ibn Taymiyyah restricted his praise of the School of Ahl al-Madīnah to the time of the companions, their followers and the generation who succeeded them. Mālik lived during the second Islamic century (93–179/711–795) and he is counted amongst the third generation. Al-Shāfi'ī (150–204/767–820) and Aḥmad (164–241/780–855) became famous independent scholars after the death of Mālik. Therefore, when Ibn Taymiyyah mentions that the School of Mālik was the most correct School in the third generation of Islam, this does not include a comparison with the Schools of Al-Shāfi'ī and Aḥmad.
- Ibn Taymiyyah stated elsewhere that following the death of Mālik, Baghdad became the leading centre of knowledge and no other region. It is known that Ibn Ḥanbal and other scholars of Ahl al-Ḥadīth were living there during that time.[58]
- Al-Shāfi'ī mentioned concerning the *Muwaṭṭa'*: 'It is the most authentic book after the book of Allah.'[59] Ibn Taymiyyah affirmed this opinion, saying: 'It is as he (i.e. al-Shāfi'ī), may Allah be pleased with him, said.' Despite the fact that it is generally agreed that *ṣaḥīḥ al-Bukhārī* and *Muslim* are the most authentic books after the book of Allah, Ibn Taymiyyah explains that 'it ought to be noted that at the time of Shāfi'ī's statement, this was correct because the two works of *ṣaḥīḥ ḥadīth* had yet to be compiled'.[60]
- When Ibn Taymiyyah compares the School of Ahl al-Ḥadīth with the School of Ahl al-Ra'y, it is clear that he prefers the School of Ahl al-Ḥadīth. This School comprises the Shāfi'ī and Ḥanbalī schools in addition to the School of Ahl al-Madīnah or Ḥijāz. When Ibn Taymiyyah compares and contrasts these three schools, however, we notice him commending the School of Aḥmad and stating that the opinions of this School are the most correct on

> numerous issues. This praise is only occasionally extended to the Shāfi'ī and Mālikī Schools. He asserts that the School of Aḥmad and occasionally Shāfi'ī occupies a moderate position between that of the School of Ahl al-Ra'y and the School of Ahl al-Madīnah or Hijāz.[61]

It is clear therefore that Ibn Taymiyyah admired the Ḥanbalī School. Did this admiration cause him to follow Ibn Ḥanbal's sources of law rigidly, or did he merely adapt these sources? Did he adapt them or did he have his own sources?

Ibn Taymiyyah's treatises clearly indicate that he possessed great respect for all the *mujtahid* scholars. In one of Ibn Taymiyyah's *fatāwā* he was asked whether or not Aḥmad was the greatest scholar. Ibn Taymiyyah responded that preference between scholars is not usually based upon clear decisive proofs, but rather on speculation and inclination. He goes on to state that this set of speculation leads to the fragmentation of the Muslim community, which is forbidden in Islam.[62]

He explains that an individual is required to respect all the *mujtahids*; for in Islam they will all be rewarded for their independent reasoning, even if they err in their judgement.[63]

Ibn Taymiyyah goes on to say that even if a person adheres to a particular School, he should not condemn other peoples' opinions outright.

In summary, he feels that it is not correct to provide a general answer to this question; the followers of each scholar will inevitably claim that their Imam is the best, whereas those who have extensive experience in the field know that every scholar has certain issues on which his opinions are the most correct. It is therefore not accurate to generalise when answering such questions.[64]

Ibn Taymiyyah's general principles of jurisprudence

Ibn Taymiyyah refers to the sources of law in various works. As mentioned earlier, in various places Ibn Taymiyyah states that the sources of law are four, namely, Qur'an, *sunnah*, consensus and analogy.[65] In the work *Qawā'id al-Karāmāt* (Maxims of Miracles), however, Ibn Taymiyyah refers to the following ways of deriving a *shar'ī* ruling:[66]

- Qur'an
- *Sunnah*. He divides the *sunnah* into categories:
  - the *mutawātir sunnah* that explains and elaborates on a Qur'anic text and does not conflict with the apparent meaning of the Qur'an;
  - the *mutawātir sunnah* that does not elaborate upon a text of the Qur'an and is even claimed to conflict with the apparent meaning of the Qur'an;

- the *mutawātir sunnah* that later scholars accepted because it had been generally accepted by former scholars or was narrated by trustworthy narrators.

- Consensus
- Analogy
- *Istiṣḥāb*
- *Maṣlaḥah Mursalah.*

The apparent contradiction between Ibn Taymiyyah's two citations of sources of law can perhaps be understood by recourse to another area in his treatises, where he explains that the sources of Islamic law are divided into two broad categories:[67]

1 What was conveyed by the Messengers and therefore leads to certainty. This includes the Qur'an, *sunnah* and consensus. Ibn Taymiyyah states that this type of source is pure, correct and not mixed with falsehood.
2 What was either not conveyed by the Messengers at all or was conveyed by them but neither allows certainty to be attained (*'ilm*), nor leads to doubt (i.e. it leads to conjecture). Ibn Taymiyyah says that this kind of source is a mixture of truth and falsehood. It can be explained through examples.

An example of a source of law not conveyed by the Messengers is inspiration (*ilhām*). This form of deduction can lead to both correct and incorrect conclusions. In another place in *al-Fatāwā*, Ibn Taymiyyah clarifies that this method occasionally gives the scholar who has an extensive knowledge of the Qur'an and *sunnah* and other sources of legal rulings the ability to choose correctly between conflicting opinions and proofs. Despite this, it cannot be claimed that inspiration is an infallible, independent method of deduction which always leads to a correct conclusion; this method cannot be used by scholars who do not have an extensive knowledge of the sources of Islamic law.[68]

An example of a source conveyed by Messengers but not leading to certain knowledge is analogy. It is clearly referred to in the Qur'an and was practised by the Prophet. It does not, however, always lead to correct and certain conclusions, but sometimes leads to conjecture. As a consequence, the results of analogy will not always be acceptable.[69]

This last method of classifying the sources of Islamic law sheds some light on why Ibn Taymiyyah refers to these sources in different ways. Whenever he mentions that the sources of law are the Qur'an, *sunnah* and *ijmā'*, he means the sources which contain certain knowledge.[70] Another explanation for the differences in his classifications of the sources of law is that the three aforementioned sources constitute the main sources from which others are derived. For example, the use of analogy and *istiṣḥāb* are based on the fact that they are used by and referred to in the main sources. Therefore, when Ibn Taymiyyah refers to these three alone as the sources of Islamic law, he is referring to the primary sources of Islamic law and not to all of the sources of Islamic law.

It could also be that Ibn Taymiyyah occasionally mentions these three sources because they are agreed upon, as opposed to others which are the subject of disagreement amongst scholars.

It is evident from the aforementioned statements that Ibn Taymiyyah does not refer to the opinions of the companions as a source of law. Nevertheless, it can be inferred from other statements of his that he does give weight to their opinions. Before citing some examples, it should be remembered that Ibn Ḥanbal divides the opinions of the companions into two types. The first type is where there is no disagreement amongst the companions; Aḥmad considers this to be a source of law. When disagreement occurred amongst the companions, Aḥmad would select the opinion he felt to be closest to the texts.

Ibn Taymiyyah appears to support Ibn Ḥanbal's approach towards the companions' opinions. He states that there is no doubt that when the first four caliphs enacted certain laws which provoked no disagreement amongst the remainder of the companions, this ought to be considered as a proof.[71] This type of opinion emanating from the companions is, in fact, a type of consensus known as the *istiqrā'ī* consensus. Ibn Taymiyyah also asserts that during the course of his lengthy journey on the path of knowledge, he did not come across any opinion agreed upon by the companions which conflicted with the sound analogy.[72] This indicates that Ibn Taymiyyah had come to the conclusion that the companions were infallible when they were in complete agreement.

If there was a disagreement amongst the companions regarding certain issues, Ibn Taymiyyah states that the solution is found by taking into consideration the general principles and spirit of the *sharī'ah* on that particular issue.[73]

Similarly, the categories of weak and *mursal ḥadīth* were included in Aḥmad's sources of law but are not mentioned by Ibn Taymiyyah as one of his sources of law. Once again, however, this does not mean that he did not implement these sources; he refers to them in other places and clarifies what is acceptable as a source of law from these categories. Ibn Taymiyyah admits that Ahmad accepted weak *ḥadīth* as a source of law, but he asserts that what Aḥmad intended by weak *ḥadīth* is not what the later generations understood by this term. He claims that weak *ḥadīth* in Aḥmad's terminology is comparable to the term *ḥadīth ḥasan*.[74] As for *mursal ḥadīth*, he accepts it as a source of law provided that it is a *mursal* emanating from one of the first three generations of Islam. He believes that this was the correct position of Ibn Ḥanbal on this issue.[75]

Ibn Taymiyyah's acceptance of weak *ḥadīths* and the opinions of companions further indicates his Ahl al-Ḥadīth tendency. He preferred to rely on tradition rather than develop new rulings, although always keeping a keen eye on the general principles of the *sharī'ah*.

Ibn Taymiyyah's basic principles of jurisprudence compared with those of Ibn Ḥanbal

By means of a careful comparison of the statements of Aḥmad and Ibn Taymiyyah, it appears that the principles upon which these two scholars based their jurisprudential thought were, to a considerable degree, identical. As we concluded earlier, Aḥmad's jurisprudential principles can be stripped down to four main sources, namely, the Qur'an, *sunnah*, consensus and analogy.

We saw earlier that Ibn Taymiyyah relies on several general principles: the Qur'an, the *sunnah*, consensus, analogy, *istiṣḥāb* and *maṣlaḥah mursalah.*

It is proposed that Ibn Taymiyyah's principles are in fact founded upon the same four foundations adopted by Aḥmad. The following points can be noted about Ibn Taymiyyah's views on these principles:

- Ibn Taymiyyah asserts that the Qur'an is accepted by all Sunni scholars as a source of law.
- Ibn Taymiyyah asserts that the three types of *mutawātir* mentioned by him are accepted as proofs in Islamic law without dispute among the scholars, with the exception of al-Khawārij, who denied the authority of the second type of *mutawātir* (i.e. that which is independent of a Qur'anic text and apparently conflicts with one), and some of Ahl al-Kalām and others who denied all or some of the last type of *mutawātir* (i.e. that which is accepted by later scholars because it had been generally accepted by former scholars or was narrated by trustworthy narrators). It seems that Ibn Taymiyyah merely intended by this categorisation of the *sunnah* to point out the existence of some dispute regarding their varying levels of authority among the scholars in Islamic law; he would have considered them as a single source.
- He accepts the authority of consensus as a source of law but feels that it is highly unlikely that explicit consensus can take place after the era of the companions.
- Ibn Taymiyyah mentions that analogy can be used as a source of law when there is no text available.[76]
- Although Ibn Taymiyyah apparently accepts sources other than those mentioned by Aḥmad, it can be argued that some of Ibn Taymiyyah's additional 'sources' are not really sources at all; for example, it is highly improbable that Ibn Taymiyyah considers *istiṣḥāb* as an independent source of law, it is in reality merely one of the methods of implementing the sources of law.[77] Ibn Taymiyyah also states that all real *maṣāliḥ* are in fact located within the *sharʿī* texts.[78] In other words, although *maṣlaḥah mursalah* relates to those items of common good for which there are no explicit texts, the principle of *maṣāliḥ* is derived from the Qur'an and *sunnah.*
- The assertion that Ibn Taymiyyah's principles are identical to those of Ibn Ḥanbal can also be supported by the fact that Ibn Taymiyyah does not criticise any of Aḥmad's general principles. On the contrary, he commends these general principles on various occasions.[79] Indeed, Ibn Taymiyyah expresses

his appreciation for the distinguished methodology which he regards as being based upon the amalgamation of an extensive knowledge of *ḥadīth* and jurisprudence. At the same time, Ibn Taymiyyah mentions that Aḥmad commanded a very good relationship with the scholars of these two sciences.[80]

- When a disagreement concerning certain issues within the general principles of jurisprudence does occur, we find that their disagreement is usually inconsequential. For instance, both Ibn Taymiyyah and Ibn Ḥanbal refer to the Qur'an and *sunnah* as the prime sources of law. According to Ibn Qayyim, however, Ibn Ḥanbal treats these two sources as essentially one source. This combined source occupies the first place in Ibn Ḥanbal's ranking of sources. In contrast, Ibn Taymiyyah treats these two sources separately. Nevertheless, these two opinions do not really conflict with one another. When Ibn Ḥanbal refers to the Qur'an and *sunnah* as a single source, he is taking into consideration the fact that, on the whole, the *sunnah* is an explanation of Qur'an and both are considered to be revelation. Hence, he believes they should be considered as one source. Ibn Ḥanbal's teacher, al-Shāfi'ī, influenced him on this point. Ibn Taymiyyah, on the other hand, considers that the *sunnah* is recognised as an independent source of law by the Qur'an itself and should therefore occupy a different rank.[81]
- The similarity between the general principles of these two scholars can be further evidenced through the considerable concordance in their jurisprudential rulings. Disagreement over general principles is one of the primary causes for disagreements in rulings among the scholars. In the instances where Ibn Taymiyyah's rulings differ from those of Ibn Ḥanbal, we find that this cannot usually be attributed to differences in their general principles. Rather, it was because Ibn Taymiyyah thought that there was a contradiction between the *fatwā* of Ibn Ḥanbal and his own general principles. On several occasions, Ibn Taymiyyah censures Ḥanbalī scholars for the existence of opinions within the School which contradict the general principles of Aḥmad and are yet attributed to him. He asserts that the scholars either narrated Aḥmad's opinion incorrectly or misunderstood his words.[82]

Ibn Taymiyyah's eagerness to measure the opinions in the School against Aḥmad's principles of jurisprudence indicates his great respect for these principles. Had he harboured misgivings about these principles, he would not have sought to 'purify' the School of opinions deviating from them. Ibn Taymiyyah's acceptance of Ibn Ḥanbal's principles would suggest that he was happy to consider himself a follower of Ibn Ḥanbal's School. There may yet, however, be scope to argue that he can be classified as an absolute *mujtahid*, independent of Ibn Ḥanbal's School.

To examine this point, the next section looks at:

- the nature of education in Ibn Taymiyyah's time;
- the classification of scholars in Islamic law;
- the opinions of some leading scholars regarding Ibn Taymiyyah's scholarly rank.

The nature of education in Ibn Taymiyyah's time

Ibn Taymiyyah's life is considered to fall within the stage of history known as the era of *taqlid*, according to writers who specialise in the evolution of jurisprudence. The majority of scholars were either adding to or explaining an area already known or gathering information connected to it, rather than developing new principles and disciplines. The legal doctrines that they transmitted and propagated were primarily restricted to the four dominant schools of law.[83] Nevertheless, most of these scholars and writers accept that during this era there were some eminent scholars who were recognised for their independent thought and their unique treatises.[84] A large number cite Ibn Taymiyyah as an example of the *mujtaihd* scholars who were found during the era of *taqlid*.[85]

Despite the restricted nature of scholarly activity, it appears that education flourished during the time of Ibn Taymiyyah, particularly in Egypt and al-Shām, for the following reasons:[86]

- the shift in the focal point for education from Baghdad to Egypt and al-Shām, following the fall of the Abbasid caliphate at the hands of the Mongols in 656/1258;
- the appearance of several distinguished scholars in various disciplines;
- the particular attention granted by the sultans of the time to knowledge and the learned;
- the existence and establishment of a large number of schools and institutes of learning, for instance, al-Jāmi' al-Azhar, Jāmi' al-'Aṭārin, al-Ṣāliḥiyyah School (641/1243), al-Manṣūriyyah (684/1285) and al-Nāṣiriyyah (703/1304) in Egypt[87] and Jāmi' Damascus and al-Ṣāliḥiyyah[88] in al-Shām. There were at least 200 schools teaching Arabic and Islamic sciences in Damascus alone.[89] Some of these were affiliated to one or more schools of law, while others taught all four schools.[90]
- Other than these centres of learning, there were several libraries that contained a large number of references covering many different branches of knowledge.[91]

The classification of scholars in Islamic law[92]

There are several classifications for scholars mentioned in treatises on *iftā'*, principles of jurisprudence and some of the books of *fiqh*. The classifications are often given in the context of who is entitled to give a legal opinion (*fatwā*) and what types of cases such a mufti can give opinions on. Ibn al-Qayyim, for example, in his treatise entitled *I'lām al-Muwaqqi'īn*, classifies Muftis into four categories:

The absolute independent mujtahid Those who possess a wide knowledge of the sources of law such as the sciences of the Qur'an, *sunnah* and the opinions of the companions. These scholars adhere to the evidence and not to other scholars' opinions. Ibn al-Qayyim recognises, however, that even these scholars may imitate others in certain issues, without negating their claim to be *mujtahids*; he argues that all the Imams imitated some scholars who were more knowledgeable than them on certain issues.

According to Ibn al-Qayyim, this category of scholars has the right to issue *fatāwā* and it is permissible to consult them concerning any legal rulings in Islamic law. Furthermore, these scholars are the ones to whom weight is given in novel issues of independent reasoning.

Affiliated mujtahid This type of *mujtahid* is well versed in both the *fatāwā* of an Imam and his general principles. These scholars are able to formulate an analogy and derive rulings for particular issues, founding their analogy and derivations on the previous *fatāwā* of that Imam. They support the School as well as the general principles of the Imams with whose opinions they are well acquainted. Furthermore, they organise the opinions of the Imam and support them with additional proofs.

Ibn al-Qayyim states that this category of *mujtahids* are not *muqallids* in relation to the ruling or the evidence of the Imam to whom they are affiliated. They will discard individual rulings of their Imam where they deem it appropriate. This is because, as Ibn al-Qayyim asserts, these scholars only followed these Imams in their methodology of independent reasoning and *fatwā*.

Restricted mujtahid Similar to the previous rank, this *mujtahid* is well versed in the fatāwā and opinions of an Imam and their legal evidence. Such scholars do not, however, question or disagree with these proofs. They believe that they do not need to obtain knowledge in the general principles of Islamic jurisprudence as the texts of their Imam are sufficient for them. This is founded upon the premise that the Imam arrived at this evidence after a deep study of the legal texts of the sharī'ah, and his conclusions should be sufficient for his followers.

This category includes a large number of scholars affiliated to the schools of law over the ages, most of whom have left scholarly works in the *fiqh* of their school. According to Ibn al-Qayyim, these scholars neither claimed to reach the status of independent reasoning nor acknowledged being *muqallids*.

Muqallids This category of scholars committed the *fatāwā* of their Imam to memory without taking into consideration his legal evidence. Hence, when they discover correct legal proofs that are apparently contrary to their Imam's position, they follow their Imam's opinions and ignore the contrary evidence. According to Ibn al-Qayyim, this group of scholars admits the fact that they are *muqallids* of their Imams in every respect.[93]

The rank of Ibn Taymiyyah among his contemporaries

According to al-Dhahabī, Ibn Taymiyyah started issuing *fatāwā* as early as when he was only 19 or even 17 years old;[94] his *fatāwā* at this stage and for a considerable period afterwards were based upon the Ḥanbalī School.[95] In later years, and after acquiring a vast amount of knowledge, he developed his own method of delivering legal verdicts. These edicts were founded directly on the original sources of law. Al-Dhahabī compares him with other scholars and Imams at the height of their knowledge when he describes him as 'a scholar who ladles his knowledge from a sea, whereas other scholars ladle from streamlets'.[96] Al-Birzālī, a student of Ibn Taymiyyah, asserts that his Sheikh had attained the status of *ijtihād* and that all of the conditions of the *mujtahid* were fulfilled by him.[97]

It is not clear, however, from al-Birzālī's statement what type of conditions stipulated by the rank of a *mujtihid* were fulfilled in Ibn Taymiyyah. Did he refer to the restricted *mujtahid* or the absolute *mujtahid*? This is all the more unclear because we do not have details of al-Birzālī's conditions for *ijtihād*. Scholars through the ages have differed on details of the ranks and requirements of *ijtihād*. Al-Dhahabī is more emphatic, claiming that Ibn Taymiyyah had attained the level of absolute *ijtihād*.[98] In his view, Ibn Taymiyyah superseded all others in the science of jurisprudence, disagreement within the schools of law and the *fatāwā* issued by the companions and their followers. Thus, when he delivered a *fatwā* he would not confine himself to a specific school of law; rather, he based his opinions exclusively on what he understood from the evidence.[99]

In general terms, the conditions required of an absolute *mujtihid* are that he has profound knowledge of the Qur'an, *ḥadīth* and principles of jurisprudence, an acquaintance with the essence and spirit of the *sharī'ah* and a proficiency in the Arabic language.[100] Ibn Taymiyyah's *fatāwā* clearly demonstrate that these conditions were fulfilled by him.[101] This is augmented by the testimony of several leading scholars who affirmed that Ibn Taymiyyah had attained an elevated status in several sciences. Ibn 'Abd al-Hādī states that Ibn Taymiyyah had mastered various sciences, including the interpretation of the Qur'an and the principles of jurisprudence.[102] Al-Mizzī, a leading scholar in *ḥadīth*, testifies that he had not encountered a scholar like Ibn Taymiyyah, and that he had not seen anyone more knowledgeable than him in the science of Qur'an and the *ḥadīth*.[103] Even al-Zamalkānī, one of Ibn Taymiyyah's opponents, concedes that when an individual asked Ibn Taymiyyah a question concerning a science, the comprehensive nature of his answers would lead him to believe that he was well acquainted with the subject of the question. After studying some of the *fatāwā* issued by Ibn Taymiyyah, al-Zamalkānī expresses his appreciation for them and affirms that the conditions of *ijtihād* were fulfilled by Ibn Taymiyyah.[104] His deep proficiency in the sciences of the Arabic language is also evident from a review of his various treatises. He was willing to challenge and reject certain accepted precepts in this science. Ibn Taymiyyah disaffirmed the concept of metaphor, opposing the later scholars of this science who subscribed to the opinion that metaphor exists in the language.[105] He disagreed with Sībawayh concerning seventy issues contained in his book *al-Kitāb*. This disagreement prompted Abū Ḥayyān, a scholar who honoured Sībawayh and his magnum opus *al-Kitāb*, to turn against Ibn Taymiyyah, having initially been amongst his admirers.[106]

It appears that Ibn Taymiyyah considered himself to be a *mujtihid* as well. This is illustrated by an incident which is mentioned by Ibn al-Qayyim in *I'lām al-Muwaqqi'īn*. He mentions that some Ḥanbalīs criticised Ibn Taymiyyah because he was teaching in a Ḥanbalī institute and receiving payment for it, whereas he could not be described as a Ḥanbalī scholar, by reason of his status as an absolute *mujtahid*. He responded to this criticism by arguing that the payment he received was a payment for his teaching and that he was deserving of it for his knowledge of the Ḥanbalī law and not because of his imitation of it.[107]

This discussion serves the purpose of establishing the status of Ibn Taymiyyah as a *mujtahid*. Evidence for his position within the various categories of *mujtahid* can be obtained from his jurisprudential writings. Ibn Taymiyyah's works in jurisprudence can be classified, generally speaking, into three types:

1 Works which were compiled at an early stage of his career. Ibn Taymiyyah indicates in his *fatāwā* that he imitated some scholars in the writing of a treatise dealing with *ḥajj*. He even admits that this book included incorrect opinions which he became aware of later on.[108]
2 Works written during an intermediate stage. Ibn Taymiyyah's work *Sharḥ al-'Umdah*[109] can be included under this category. Also, some opinions found in the collected *fatāwā* of Ibn Taymiyyah issued from this period.[110]
3 Works emanating from the third and final stage of Ibn Taymiyyah's scholarly life. There are several works which were written during this final stage, the most important of which is the greater portion of the collected *fatāwā* of Ibn Taymiyyah. These works display more circumspection in choosing between the opinions of other scholars. These works reflect an independent mind, willing to criticise popular opinions and to develop entirely new opinions, while also critically selecting from the opinions of all the schools.

This classification suggests that, by the final phase of his scholarly development, he had ceased to be a *muqallid* and could not even be said to have been a restricted *mujtahid*. Therefore, he must have been either an independent absolute *mujtahid* or an absolute *mujtahid* who chose to adopt another scholar's general principles of law and method of independent reasoning, having concluded that this scholar's method was correct.

Some Ḥanbalī scholars and others claimed that he was an independent absolute *mujtahid*,[111] whereas others considered him an absolute *mujtahid* who adopted Aḥmad's general principles of law and method of independent reasoning.[112] In order to arrive at a safe conclusion on this issue, the following important points ought to be considered:

- The independent absolute *mujtahid* and dependent absolute *mujtahid* occupy the same rank in knowledge. The only difference between them is that the independent absolute *mujtahid* uses his own sources of law as opposed to the dependent absolute *mujtahid*, who employs another scholar's general principles of law.[113] Therefore, the criterion used in order to differentiate between these two scholars is a question of whether or not they choose to employ their own sources of law. Both classes are equally capable of using their own sources, should they wish to do so.

- It has been concluded in this chapter that Ibn Taymiyyah used the same sources of law as Aḥmad. His additions to them were primarily clarifications of unclear points and corrections directed at Ḥanbalī scholars rather than Ibn Ḥanbal himself.

These two points taken together indicate that Ibn Taymiyyah was a dependent absolute *mujtahid*. This conclusion is supported by the statements of Ibn al-Qayyim in which he clarifies the status of his teacher's knowledge in Ḥanbalī law. He claims that his teacher's opinions enjoy a position not less, and may be even higher, than the opinions of leading scholars in the Ḥanbalī School, such as Ibn 'Aqīl, Abū 'l-Khaṭṭāb and even their teacher Abū Ya'la. Therefore, Ibn Taymiyyah's opinions can be used as the basis for *fatāwā* and rulings within the School.[114] In another statement, Ibn al-Qayyim asserts that the status of Ibn Taymiyyah was higher than that of leading Ḥanbalī scholars such as Abū Ya'la and Abū 'l-Khaṭṭāb.[115] It is clear that Ibn al-Qayyim thinks that Ibn Taymiyyah's rank of *ijtihād* is comparable to that of other leading Ḥanbalī scholars. To complete the analysis, it is necessary to become acquainted with the rank which Ibn al-Qayyim attributes to these other scholars. He says that scholars have two opinions with regard to whether these scholars, and others similar to them, were independent or dependent scholars. His own view is that whosoever studies and pondered over the opinions and *fatāwā* of these Ḥanbalī scholars would reach the conclusion that they were not *muqallids* of their Imams, for they disagreed with them on various issues. Nevertheless, he also thinks that they were below the rank of the Imams in terms of independent reasoning.[116] It can be said that when some scholars describe Ibn Taymiyyah as a *mujtahid muṭlaq*, they mean that he had obtained the proper requirements for a scholar to be considered as an absolute *mujtahid*, but this did not necessitate that he had developed his own general principles of jurisprudence.

The safest conclusion is that Ibn Taymiyyah ought to be considered an absolute *mujtahid* who at the same time chose to be dependent on Aḥmad's general principles of jurisprudence. It also seems that Donald Little was correct when he stated that Ibn Taymiyyah is probably the most prominent Ḥanbalī scholar after Aḥmad Ibn Ḥanbal himself.[117]

In this chapter, we have attempted to study and identify the general principles of jurisprudence adhered to by Ibn Ḥanbal and Ibn Taymiyyah. We saw that they were both scholars of Ahl al-Ḥadīth, preferring narrated texts whenever possible over novel opinions. At the same time, they shared a sceptical attitude towards the concept of consensus after the time of companions and, in their adherence to the Qur'an and *sunnah*, were willing to disregard the opinion of any solitary authority. It seems Ibn Taymiyyah adopted Ibn Ḥanbal's general principles after careful consideration, and certainly not out of mere allegiance to his School. We saw also that Ibn Taymiyyah's high rank in knowledge was acknowledged by his contemporaries, supporters and opponents alike.

In Chapter 3, an attempt is made to scrutinise his role in more detail and study some important issues related to Ibn Taymiyyah's role in the development of the general principles of jurisprudence.

3

RE-LAYING THE FOUNDATIONS

Ibn Taymiyyah and Ḥanbalī *uṣūl*

Introduction

Ibn Taymiyyah implements a critical method in the course of his discussion on Ḥanbalī jurisprudence and its general principles. He scrutinises the various contributions of the different Ḥanbalī scholars in these two fields and establishes that there are several opinions held by these scholars which are founded upon weak or incorrect evidence.[1] This will be elaborated upon in due course.

Even the founder of the Ḥanbalī School, Imam Aḥmad, is subjected to this form of critical study.[2] Ibn Taymiyyah's criticism of the Imam is, however, considerably less than his criticism of the Ḥanbalī scholars who succeeded him. In addition, Ibn Taymiyyah tends to find excuses for the Imam, vindicating him for his incorrect opinions. For instance, he would argue that Aḥmad was unaware of certain disagreements that existed among scholars because the root of the disagreement was not known at the time of the companions and only became known during the Imam's time.[3] Furthermore, Ibn Taymiyyah asserts that if one opinion of Aḥmad regarding a particular issue was weak, one would usually find another opinion in his jurisprudence which was in conformity with the correct one.[4]

Ibn Taymiyyah's criticism of some of the Ḥanbalī scholars who succeeded the Imam covers various issues of jurisprudence and general principles within the Ḥanbalī School. The first Ḥanbalī scholar after the Imam to be criticised by Ibn Taymiyyah was the eminent scholar al-Khallāl (d. 311/923). Ibn Taymiyyah states that al-Khallāl failed to mention in his book *al-Jāmi'* a considerable number of Aḥmad's *Masā'il*.[5] Al-Khiraqī (d. 334/945) also received criticism from Ibn Taymiyyah on a number of issues;[6] Ibn Taymiyyah held him responsible for several incorrect rulings within the Ḥanbalī School of law that, according to Ibn Taymiyyah, were subsequently attributed to Imam Aḥmad.[7]

Abū Ya'la (d. 458/1066), who was the leader of the Ḥanbalī School in his time, is the individual whose opinions were studied and discussed by Ibn Taymiyyah at the greatest length. On several points, Ibn Taymiyyah formed the conclusion that Abū Ya'la's opinions were either weak, incorrect, in need of re-examination, not comprehensive or simply not good.[8] In certain instances, Ibn Taymiyyah demonstrates how Abū Ya'la issued contradictory opinions on a single issue.[9] Occasionally, however, he would extrapolate from Abū Ya'la's views,[10] and on other occasions he even voiced his appreciation of them.[11]

Ibn Taymiyyah is also recorded to have commented upon other Ḥanbalī scholars, such as Abū 'l-Khaṭṭāb,[12] Ibn 'Aqīl[13] and Ibn Qudāmah.[14] He even commented, on occasions, on some of the opinions of his grandfather, al-Majd,[15] and others.[16]

Ibn Taymiyyah's critical study of the Ḥanbalī School of law, its jurisprudence, general principles and scholars exerted a significance influence on the School. This may be demonstrated clearly by considering the clarifications and corrections made by Ibn Taymiyyah to various issues covered within the School. In some of these matters, Ibn Taymiyyah clarifies that the predominant opinion of the School is in reality contrary to the words of Aḥmad. In others, he illustrates the existence of contradictory opinions in the words of the Ḥanbalī scholars. This chapter will demonstrate this point. We will explain in detail, the role of Ibn Taymiyyah in the correction and clarification of various important issues related to the principles of the Ḥanbalī School of law.

It was concluded in Chapter 2 that Ibn Taymiyyah concurs with Aḥmad on the general principles of law. Nevertheless, it can be shown that Ibn Taymiyyah played a strong role in developing the ruling principles of the Ḥanbalī School of law through various means. This was partly achieved through his clarification and correction of several important points related to the principles of the School. These corrections and clarifications were aimed at other Ḥanbalī scholars and not targeted at Ibn Ḥanbal's own words. Indeed, Ibn Taymiyyah often asserts that his opinions and views on these issues better reflected the real position of Aḥmad. In making these corrections, therefore, Ibn Taymiyyah demonstrated his respect for Ibn Ḥanbal's principles and sought to bring the School back in line with them. The following section illustrates some important corrections Ibn Taymiyyah sought to make to the principles of the Ḥanbalī School.

Ibn Ḥanbal and consensus (*ijma'*) as a source of law

Jurists have made various attempts to define the term *ijmā'*. Amongst the definitions available, we shall use the one offered by the leading scholar of *uṣūl al-fiqh*, al-Āmidī: 'The agreement of all recognised and qualified scholars who belong to the community of Muhammad (peace be upon him), in a certain period of time, on a ruling about a certain incident.'[17]

It appears that an accurate definition for this source of law ought to contain five important constituents:

1 unanimity
2 amongst the Muslim scholars

3 in any particular age
4 after the death of the Prophet
5 on a matter which can be included under independent reasoning.[18]

Various narrations emanating from Ibn Ḥanbal indicate his denial of consensus as a source of law. He states in several narrations that whosoever claims there is consensus amongst the scholars on any issue is lying, because some scholars may differ without his being aware of that. In another narration, Ibn Ḥanbal is reported to have said that the most that can be said is that there is no known disagreement amongst the scholars concerning a particular issue.[19] Nevertheless, Ibn Ḥanbal himself made reference to consensus on various occasions.[20] This apparent contradiction has caused uncertainty over Ibn Ḥanbal's actual position on consensus.

Scholars affiliated to the Ḥanbalī School do not deny the validity of consensus. Some of these individuals offer no explanation for contradiction present in the narrations from Aḥmad.[21] Others, however, have offered some interpretations. Abū Ya'la in *al-'Uddah* offers two possible explanations for Ibn Ḥanbal's apparently anti-consensus statements. First, when Aḥmad uttered these statements, he did so upon the platform of piety. This means that he preferred not to deliver a judgement concerning consensus because of his concern that he might commit a mistake. Therefore, he did not deny the authority of the consensus in real terms. Second, when Ibn Ḥanbal asserted that whosoever claims that there is a consensus on an issue is lying, he referred to those people who do not command an extensive knowledge of the disagreements and differing opinions amongst the scholars. This denotes that Ibn Ḥanbal did not reject the claims of consensus offered by those who command a wide knowledge of the differing opinions of the scholars.[22]

These two explanations were also affirmed by the Ḥanbalī scholar Abū 'l-Khaṭṭāb, Abū Ya'la's disciple.[23]

Ibn Taymiyyah, however, offers a different explanation. He says that consensus is of two types:

1 An explicit consensus
2 A tacit consensus.

The first type of consensus denotes an agreement amongst the scholars transmitted explicitly via a *mutawātir* chain of narrators, or by an action. The second type of consensus is similar to the first; it contains no confirmation of the absence of any opponents,[24] but only a statement of the narrator that no disagreement has become known to him.

According to Ibn Taymiyyah, it was Aḥmad's view that the first type of consensus was not valid after the period of the companions had elapsed, or after them and their followers, or these two generations and the third generation of Islam.[25] This means that Aḥmad restricted the acceptance of this type of consensus to these three generations at most and rejected the possibility of its existence thereafter. According to Ibn Taymiyyah, Aḥmad formed this opinion because it is very unlikely that the non-existence of opponents could be irrefutably proven in a ruling issued after the time of the first three generations of Islam. Ibn Taymiyyah explains that he arrived at this conclusion after he had thoroughly investigated the use of explicit consensus by Aḥmad.[26]

Ibn Taymiyyah asserts that Ibn Ḥanbal did not employ this type of consensus as a source of law, except where such consensus was attributed to the aforementioned generations.[27]

Although Ibn Taymiyyah does not clarify Aḥmad's position concerning the second type, he asserts that it is a proof whose establishment is not restricted to a specific period of time. According to Ibn Taymiyyah, this form of consensus does not lead to certainty but only to probability, which means that it can be set aside in favour of a stronger proof.[28]

The use of *ḍaʿīf* and *mursal ḥadīth* by Ibn Ḥanbal

The use of weak ḥadīth

It has been mentioned by several scholars that Aḥmad employed weak *ḥadīth* as a source of law. Amongst these scholars are Abū Yaʿla in his treatise *al-ʿUddah*, Abū 'l-Khaṭṭāb in his book *al-Tamhīd*, Ibn al-Jawzī in his book *al-Manāqib* and Ibn Qayyim in *al-Iʿlām*.[29]

Some Ḥanbalī scholars have attempted to explain the nature of the weak *ḥadīth* which were implemented by Aḥmad as a source of law. For instance, Abū Yaʿla states that the weak *ḥadīth* used by Aḥmad are deemed weak according to the classification of *ḥadīth* scholars, rather than that of jurists. He explains this statement by saying that *ḥadīth* scholars considered the *mursal ḥadīth*, *al-Tadlīs* and the transmission of additional information not given by other narrators as examples of weak *ḥadīth*. These types of *ḥadīth* are not, however, considered weak according to the method of classification employed by the jurists.[30] This assertion is corroborated by his disciple, Abū 'l-Khaṭṭāb, in his book *al-Tamhīd*.[31]

Ibn Taymiyyah disagrees with the explanation offered by Abū Yaʿla and Abū 'l-Khaṭṭāb concerning what is intended by weak *ḥadīth* as employed by Aḥmad as a source in Islamic law. Ibn Taymiyyah's interpretation of Aḥmad's position concerning this issue is based upon his thorough knowledge of the methodology of the science of *ḥadīth*, in addition to his investigation of Aḥmad's employment of weak *ḥadīth* in his jurisprudence.

In relation to the methodology of the science of *ḥadīth*, Ibn Taymiyyah states that the reference in every science should be sought amongst its people, that is, its specialists.[32] Therefore, the reference when determining the authenticity of a *ḥadīth* ought to be to scholars learned in the sciences of *ḥadīth* and *rijāl*.[33] He also asserts that the chains of narrations are of great importance, and whosoever cites a narration must be conversant with its chain before basing a ruling upon it. If he is not, his citation concerning even an unimportant matter will not be acceptable. This being the case, how can the citation of a narration on issues pertaining to matters as grave as *uṣūl* be accepted without evidence of the status of its chains?[34]

Ibn Taymiyyah asserts that the term 'weak *ḥadīth*' mentioned in Ibn Ḥanbal's sources of law does not carry the same meaning as that given by later scholars of *ḥadīth*. He bases this assertion on the fact that the division of *ḥadīth* into three categories, namely, *ṣaḥīḥ*, *ḥasan* and *ḍaʿīf*, only appeared when al-Tirmidhī (d. 279/892) introduced it. Before this period, scholars classified *ḥadīth* into only two categories: *ṣaḥīḥ*, and *ḍaʿīf*. The latter category itself includes two kinds of *ḥadīth*:

1 Those *ḥadīth* that contain a weakness but whose weakness is not so serious as to render the rulings contained therein invalid.
2 Those *ḥadīth* that contain a serious weakness to the extent that the rulings contained therein are invalidated and cannot be implemented in Islamic law.

This second category of weak *ḥadīth* is sometimes termed *al-wāhī* (feeble).[35] Ibn Taymiyyah goes on to assert that Aḥmad would not transmit a tradition from any narrator who was known to lie, but narrated only from those whom he considered to be trustworthy narrators.[36]

One can conclude from Ibn Taymiyyah's interpretation that the 'weak *ḥadīth*' that constituted one of Ibn Ḥanbal's sources, was not the *ḥadīth* classified as weak in the fully developed science of *ḥadīth* from after the time of al-Tirmidhī. Rather, it was classified as weak as opposed to being termed *ṣaḥīḥ*. It includes both *ḥasan ḥadīth* and weak *ḥadīth* without fatal defects *(al-wāhī)*. Ibn Taymiyyah also provides an explanation for Ibn Ḥanbal's oft-quoted statement that he refers weak *ḥadīth* to the use of reason. He emphasises that Aḥmad was referring here only to those *ḥadīth* classified as *ḥasan*, and not to *ḥadīth* which contained a serious weakness.[37]

The position of Ibn Taymiyyah in relation to the implementation of weak *ḥadīth* by Aḥmad in Islamic law was adopted by several later Ḥanbalī scholars, such as Ibn al-Qayyim, Ibn Badrān and al-Turkī.[38]

Ibn Taymiyyah also deals with the treatment of those weak traditions cited by Ibn Ḥanbal, particularly in what is known as *faḍāʾl al-aʿmāl* (virtuous actions).[39]

Ibn Taymiyyah states that no matter can be claimed to be meritorious or acceptable in Islamic law without a *sharʿī* evidence. Therefore, it is not acceptable to approve of an action founded upon a weak *ḥadīth*. Despite this, Ibn Taymiyyah defends Aḥmad's employment of weak *ḥadīth* in the field of 'virtuous actions', claiming that Aḥmad would cite only those *ḥadīth* when the general ruling itself was based upon an acceptable *ḥadīth*. The weak *ḥadīth* were cited only by reason of the additional information they supplied, such as the reward for a particular action. This is acceptable, according to Ibn Taymiyyah, provided that the scholar does not know that the *ḥadīth* is in fact fabricated.[40]

Having set out Ibn Taymiyyah's investigation for Aḥmad's use of weak *ḥadīth*, it should be noted that the word *ḥasan* was in fact used by a group of former scholars in the field of *ḥadīth*, such as Ibn al-Madīnī, al-Bukhārī (d. 256/870) and even Aḥmad himself. Does this, then, invalidate Ibn Taymiyyah's claim that the term *ḥasan* was first introduced to the science of *ḥadīth* by al-Tirmidhī? This point has been studied by al-Madkhalī, who, after considerable investigation, arrived at the following conclusion: the scholars who employed the term *ḥasan* before the era of al-Tirmidhī did not intend by its use what later became the alternative terminological meaning of this word. Rather, they intended various meanings which differed from one scholar to the next.[41] Thus, the earlier usage of the word does not invalidate Ibn Taymiyyah's argument.

The use of mursal ḥadīth *by Ibn Ḥanbal*

As mentioned previously, weak and *mursal ḥadīth* constituted the fourth category of Ibn Ḥanbal's sources of law.[42] Ibn Taymiyyah notes that scholars have differed concerning whether a *mursal ḥadīth* is acceptable as a proof or not. He believes that the correct opinion is that such *ḥadīth* can be accepted, rejected or set aside, depending on the type of *mursal* in question. The *mursal ḥadīth* that is acceptable as a proof in Islamic law is one reported by a narrator who is known for his narration of *mursal ḥadīth* from trustworthy narrators. The type of *mursal ḥadīth* that is rejected as a proof in Islamic law is the *ḥadīth* reported by a narrator who is known to contradict the narrations of trustworthy narrators. Judgement on the acceptability of a *mursal ḥadīth* from a narrator who occasionally narrates his *mursal ḥadīth* from trustworthy narrators and at other times from untrustworthy narrators is suspended.[43] Also, when *mursal ḥadīth* are narrated through so many chains that it cannot be supposed that any forgery has taken place, they are to be taken as authentic.[44]

Ibn Taymiyyah clarifies another important point related to the *mursal ḥadīth*. He states that some Ḥanbalī scholars, such as Abū Ya'la, Abū 'l-Khaṭṭāb and Ibn 'Aqīl, claim that there is no difference between the *mursal* of the earlier generations (the companions, their followers and their followers in turn) and subsequent generations, in their validity as a proof. Abū Ya'la states that this is the implicit meaning of Ibn Ḥanbal's words because he does not differentiate between the *mursal* of one generation and another.[45]

Ibn Taymiyyah argues that the acceptance of the *mursal* from all generations is not the true opinion of Ibn Ḥanbal. Ibn Taymiyyah supports his assertion by stating that Ibn Ḥanbal was known not to accept the *mursal* of his contemporaries and that he would always request the *isnād* ('chain') from them. Ibn Taymiyyah further supports his view by saying that he had traced the *mursal* used by Ibn Ḥanbal as a source of law and found that he did not use any *mursal* from after the first three generations.[46]

The existence of metaphor within the Arabic language

There exists a strong link between the Arabic language and the science of *uṣūl al-fiqh*, for this language is the means by which the texts of the Lawgiver can be understood and comprehended. Accordingly, agreement on the nature of the language has an important impact upon *uṣūl al-fiqh* and will have implications for jurists' understanding of the texts of the *sharī'ah*. Amongst the linguistic issues that have the most significant bearing upon *uṣūl al-fiqh* is the question of whether metaphor exists in Arabic. The scholars who have authored works on this subject claim that the Arabic language is divided into two parts: literal and metaphorical.[47] The greater portion of Ḥanbalī scholars were of this view,[48] which they support with certain proofs.[49] Indeed, it is said that the majority of scholars of *uṣūl* are of this opinion. Ibn Taymiyyah, however, insists that this is an inaccurate opinion and asserts that metaphor does not exist in Arabic. He studies and discusses this issue from two perspectives:

1 What is meant by the expression 'the majority of scholars,' and who is claimed to subscribe to the opinion that there is a division in the language?
2 What evidence is there that the Arabic language is divided into two parts, literal and metaphorical?

Who is included in the expression 'the majority of scholars'?

In discussing the identity of 'the majority of scholars,' to whom this opinion was attributed, Ibn Taymiyyah considers that the scholars of *uṣūl* may have meant

- Those individuals acquainted with the science of *uṣūl al-fiqh* from both the predecessors (*salaf*) and later generations (*khalaf*). Ibn Taymiyyah attests that this particular science was known in the earliest generations, long before al-Shāfi'ī set it down in writing.[50]

  Ibn Taymiyyah argues that if this is what is intended by 'the majority of the scholars' it is not correct to claim that the majority believe that metaphor exists in the language, but he seeks to show most of them do not subscribe to this opinion.[51]
- Those individuals who are aware of the sources of law in general, are able to differentiate between the *shar'ī* proofs and other types of evidence (e.g. rational evidence) and have the ability to demonstrate a preference between the various proofs. According to Ibn Taymiyyah, if this is what is intended by an *uṣūlī*, then it can be applied to every *mujtahid* in Islam. Ibn Taymiyyah implies that in this case, it cannot be claimed that the majority of *mujtahids* accepted the use of metaphor.[52]
- The renowned scholars, including the four well-known scholars after whom the four schools are named, in addition to al-Thawrī and al-Awzā'ī, whose opinions are often quoted in the books of *uṣūl al-fiqh*. Ibn Taymiyyah says that these scholars are the ones who are most well versed in this science. They used their knowledge of the subject to arrive at practical rulings. They did not, however, mention the term 'metaphor' as being part of the language,

and anyone who claims they did is displaying his ignorance.[53] Ibn Taymiyyah compares this group of scholars with later scholars who wrote about the subject but did not apply it in practice. Therefore, he says, the views of the latter group are either incorrect or are of little benefit in this area.[54]

- Those individuals who first authored works pertaining to this science, for example al-Shāfiʿī and Ibn Ḥanbal, among others.

  Ibn Taymiyyah mentions al-Shāfiʿī as a prime example of this early group, because Shāfiʿī was the first scholar to write about this subject in detail. Interestingly, he did not refer to the division of the language into literal and metaphorical. Furthermore, Ibn Taymiyyah states that although al-Shāfiʿī was well known for his extensive use of *uṣūl al-fiqh* in order to arrive at legal rulings, he did not make reference to the term 'metaphor' in any of his works.[55]
- Those individuals who wrote on the subject of the principles of jurisprudence amongst Ahl al-Kalām and Ahl al-Ra'y, such the Muʿtazilis, Ashʿaris and some of the followers of the four schools.

  If this is what is intended by the term 'the majority of the scholars', then Ibn Taymiyyah considers it would be correct to say that most of these scholars divided speech into the literal and the metaphorical.[56]

  He explains that this is due to the great influence exerted by the Muʿtazilah scholars upon the scholars in the science of *uṣūl al-fiqh*.[57]
- According to Ibn Taymiyyah, the final group of scholars to whom the term *uṣūliyyūn* may be applicable are those scholars who were affiliated to the Muʿtazilah, Ahl al-Kalām and those jurists who adhered to their methodology.

He emphasises that none of these scholars were Imams in any particular Islamic science; rather, they were merely followers of others.[58]

Ibn Taymiyyah argues, therefore, that the adoption of this division in the language differs depending on what classification of scholars is used. He accepts that the division between literal and metaphorical speech does exist in various sources of *uṣūl al-fiqh* within the Ḥanbalī School and others, but he believes the proponents of this view were affiliated to the Muʿtazili School or were writers influenced by their methods. Hence, when the greater portion of Ḥanbalī scholars, in addition to others, mentioned that this opinion was held by 'the majority of scholars', they ought to have clarified the group they were referring to.

In supporting his negation of this view, Ibn Taymiyyah returns to his principle that reference should be sought from the 'people of the science'. The leading scholars of the Arabic language, such as Khalīl, Sībawayh, al-Kisā'ī and al-Farrā', made no reference to a division of the language into the literal and the metaphorical.[59]

In a different place, Ibn Taymiyyah mentions a rather interesting point. He observes that occasionally scholars who were educated in and accustomed to using certain terminology would arrive at a stage where they assumed that the same terminology was used by previous scholars, without actually investigating this.[60]

What evidence is there for the existence of metaphor in Arabic?

The scholars who subscribed to the opinion that metaphor exists in the Arabic language cited various pieces of evidence.[61] This section comments on some of this evidence from Ibn Taymiyyah's point of view. It should be noted that Ibn Taymiyyah's main concern is whether metaphor is used in the Qur'an. The existence or absence of metaphor in the Arabic language will necessitate the same conclusion for the Qur'an.

1 Proponents of metaphor say that it is common knowledge that in the Arabic language certain words are used to denote certain alternative meanings. For example, the word 'lion' is used to describe a brave person, whereas the term 'donkey' is used to describe a dull or dim-witted person. This form of usage cannot be denied and it is left only to decide whether this usage is literal or metaphorical. To argue that the use of the term 'lion' for a brave person is literal is unacceptable, for when used in the literal sense, it refers to 'a large, strong animal of the cat family'. Furthermore, it cannot be claimed that both meanings are literal in form. If this was true it would result in equivalence (*ishtirāk*) between these words, and this would necessitate that neither meanings would predominate in the mind. In reality, however, when the word 'lion' is mentioned, the first meaning understood by the mind is that of a 'strong, brave animal'. It must therefore be concluded that the language is comprised of both literal and metaphoric aspects.[62]

Ibn Taymiyyah criticised this proof in various ways:

- The assertion that one word can have two different meanings is acceptable. The claim, however, that one of these two meanings must be literal and the other metaphorical is incorrect, except in the instance that this division is correct, and that is the point at issue. It cannot, therefore, be proved that speech is divided into two categories by the mere claim that there are two kinds. Ibn Taymiyyah asserts that this would be a circular argument, which is unacceptable as a proof in the science of *uṣūl al-fiqh*.[63]
- A group of those scholars who claimed that this kind of division exists in the Arabic language stated that part of Arabic speech is a combination of both literal and metaphorical language at the same time. These scholars divide speech into three kinds: literal, metaphorical and a combination of the two.[64]

  By raising this last point, Ibn Taymiyyah meant to show that these scholars could not agree amongst themselves that speech was divided into literal and metaphorical language, as a group amongst them felt compelled to accept the existence of a third category.
- Some of the scholars who assert the existence of metaphor claim that before words were used for the first time, they were neither literal nor metaphorical. These scholars also define a metaphor as 'a word which is used to mean something other than the meaning that was originally designated to it'.

Hence, it can be ascertained whether a word is being used literally or metaphorically by tracing the first meaning of the word. If it is later discovered that the word is now being used to mean something different, this means that it is being used metaphorically and not literally.[65]

This is a clear and logical method of classifying words in the Arabic language. Ibn Taymiyyah, however, objects to this approach on the basis that it is not feasible to determine with certainty the first intended meaning of all the words in the Arabic language by analysis of the narrations of the native Arabs who first articulated them.[66] So, for example, it could be (for argument's sake) that 'lion' was originally used for a brave person and than transferred to an animal with similar qualities!

Ibn Taymiyyah's criticism here is that it is difficult to formulate clear criteria by which speech can be classified as being either literal or metaphorical.

2 It is said that the Arabs use some words alone and in constructions, for example *al-ẓahr* (the back) and also *ẓahr al-insān* (the person's back), where both the solitary form and the construction denote same meaning. When *ẓahr* is used in a different construction, for example the expression *ẓahr al-ṭarīq* (the surface of the road), it is clear that *ẓahr* is metaphorical in nature.[67]

Ibn Taymiyyah rebuts this evidence by explaining that the use of annexation dictates the meaning of the words. Therefore, the adjunct does not have the same meaning as a single word. Furthermore, the meaning of the adjunct is dependent upon the possessive case. For example, the meaning of *ẓahr* in *ẓahr al-insān*, is clarified by the possessive case of *al-insān*, and the same can be said concerning the expression *ẓahr al-ṭarīq*.[68]

Ibn Taymiyyah presents another example of an alteration in meaning due to an annexation: the use of the word *khamsah* (five) and *khamsat 'ashar* (fifteen). The use of *khamsah* is literal when used for the number five, as it also is in *khamsat 'ashar*, meaning fifteen. Ibn Taymiyyah asserts that no individual can claim that the term *khamsah* in *khamsat 'ashar* is metaphorical.[69]

He also points out that according to the rules of the Arabic language it is impermissible to use words such as *ẓahr* (back) without the possessive case, because their meaning is dependent upon it.[70] They can also be used with the article *al* (the), and then the meaning will depend on what is known to either the speaker or the listener.[71]

3 It is claimed that scholars of succeeding generations have transmitted the notion that speech is divided into literal and metaphorical from the time of the earliest Arabs.[72]

Ibn Taymiyyah seeks to rebut this claim in the following ways:

- The claim that the term 'metaphor' is derived from earliest Arabs is incorrect for no one at all has transmitted this.[73] Furthermore, the companions who interpreted the Qur'an did not make reference to this division and did not refer to a single word of the Qur'an as being metaphorical.[74] Ibn Taymiyyah also asserts that the leading scholars, including the four Imams, did not mention this term. He admitted that the term had been mentioned by Ibn Ḥanbal and also by Abū 'Ubaidah (d. 209/824) but argued that when they used this term they intended a different meaning by it.[75] As mentioned earlier, he adds that it is not mentioned by the leading scholars of the Arabic language.[76]

- He declares that the original Arabs were unaware of the terms 'literal' and 'metaphorical'. How, therefore, can it be claimed that they ever articulated them? He goes on to note that no one claims that other linguistic terms commonly used by scholars of language, such as *maf'ūl* (object), *fā'il* (subject), *muta'adī* (transitive) and *lāzim* (intransitive), were ever mentioned by early Arabs, most likely because they were unknown to them. As a consequence, it is not feasible to claim that they were ever uttered by them and later transmitted to us, as is the case with 'literal' and 'metaphor'.

He continues that while such terms as *maf'ūl* and *fā'il* were unknown to the original Arabs, but were rather created by the scholars of the language, their meaning is nevertheless clear and logically acceptable. This cannot be said for the term 'metaphor'.[77] It would appear that Ibn Taymiyyah formulated this particular rebuttal in anticipation of a counter-argument, which can be summarised as follows: you (i.e. Ibn Taymiyyah and others) have declared that terms such as *maf'ūl* and *fā'il* were unknown amongst the Arabs but were created by the scholars of the language. These terms, however, have become acceptable to every individual; the same can be said of the term 'metaphor'. So even if we accept that the term was not used amongst the early Arabs, this does not invalidate its current use.

A group of Ibn Taymiyyah's opponents claimed that the issue upon which this dispute is founded is purely theoretical in nature and no real disagreement exists in practice.[78] This did not abate Ibn Taymiyyah's determination to refute it. Rather, he argued that this term 'metaphor' should not be used because it is incorrect according to logic, *sharī'ah* and language. Ibn Taymiyyah explains this by stating that according to logic, the term 'metaphor' is invalid because of the absence of clear correct criteria by which speech can be classified into literal and metaphorical. It is invalid according to language because it is an alteration in the language which procures no benefit. In reference to the *sharī'ah*, the use of this term leads to distortion and corruption. Ibn Taymiyyah enumerates two types of corruption:

1 It allows the greater portion of the Qur'an to be deemed metaphorical. It would appear that this is the primary reason for Ibn Taymiyyah's strong attack against the concept of metaphor. It is common knowledge that he was involved in serious disputes with a number of a group of theologians for their use of metaphor in relation to the names and attributes of Allah. Ibn Taymiyyah confirms this himself when he discusses the issue of metaphor.

He states that as a result of the use of metaphor, his opponents disaffirm that which Allah affirms for Himself concerning His Names and Attributes.

2 It allows for alterations to take place in Islamic law.[79]

Interpretations of correctness and error on the part of the *mujtahid*

Can it be assumed that every *mujtahid* is correct in his conclusions, or can there be only a single correct solution from amongst the several advanced for a particular problem, to the exclusion of all others? Furthermore, are there any guidelines for determining the correct opinion, if we say that only one of several opinions can be correct? Does this also mean that those scholars who arrived at an 'incorrect' judgement have committed a form of misdeed?

This problem is considered to be one of the most complicated issues in Islamic law. It is somewhat difficult to differentiate between the many opinions advanced on this problem. Thankfully, Ibn Taymiyyah sorts through these different opinions with a notable degree of clarity. In doing so, he also criticises the opinions of most of the Ḥanbalī scholars and clarifies his own opinion, which he believes is in conformity with the opinion of the Imams and the predecessors.

Ibn Taymiyyah states that the scholars have subscribed to the following opinions concerning this issue:[80]

1 Some scholars have maintained that the Lawgiver has established proofs that shall direct the *mujtahid* towards the correct opinion. Therefore, any *mujtahid* who strives to the best of his ability to ascertain these correct opinions will in due course obtain them. These scholars declared that anyone who did not arrive at the correct conclusion in any issue pertaining to the *uṣūl* or *furūʿ* had simply failed to exert himself sufficiently in this endeavour. It is therefore impossible to believe that a scholar did his best to ascertain the true opinion, yet was unable to arrive upon it. Such failure can occur only in the event of negligence on the part of the *mujtahid* in his method of applying independent reasoning. This is the general opinion of the majority of the scholars in this group, who did not differentiate between issues of creed and legal issues. This opinion was held by Bishr al-Marisī and the greater portion of the Muʿtazilite present in Baghdad.[81] Some scholars in this group, however, subscribed to this opinion only with regard to issues pertaining to dogma; in legal issues, they stated that the proofs for rulings could be both definite and indefinite. If the proof for a ruling is definite, the *mujtahid* must do his best to ascertain the correct opinion. If he fails to arrive at the correct opinion, it shows that he did not do his best and he will be considered to have committed a misdeed. If, on the other hand, the proofs concerning an issue are indefinite, it indicates that there is no specific opinion to be considered correct. Rather, the correct ruling for each scholar is that which he is able to ascertain by means of his independent reasoning. This opinion was held by

Abū al-Hudhayl al-'Allāf (d. 234/849) and those who followed him, such as Abū 'Alī al-Jubbā'ī (d. 302/915) and his son Abū Hāshim (d. 321/933). It is also the more recognised of the two opinions of al-Ash'arī (d. 324/936). This opinion was also favoured by al-Baqīllānī (d. 403/1013), al-Ghazālī (d. 505/1112) and Ibn al-'Arabī (d. 543/1148) and their followers.[82]

2 Al-Jahmiyyah, al-Ashā'irah and the majority of the jurists subscribed to the opinion that a *mujtahid* may sometimes ascertain the correct opinion and sometimes not. This is not necessarily because of negligence in attempting to determine the correct ruling, but rather because it sometimes cannot be attained. Having accepted that the correct ruling is sometimes unascertainable with absolute certainty, these scholars are still of the opinion that the *mujtahid* who fails to ascertain it may nevertheless be punished, not because he has committed a misdeed by erring in independent reasoning, but simply because the Lawgiver can exact punishment without reason. These scholars claim that it is understood from the revelation that every unbeliever will be punished in the Hell Fire; it makes no difference whether the unbeliever tried his best to ascertain the truth concerning Islam and did not succeed or whether he did not try at all.[83]

This group divided the disputes which occurred between the Muslim scholars into two kinds:

i Disputes concerning the *furū'*
ii Disputes concerning the *uṣūl.*

In relation to disputes concerning the *furū'*, most scholars affiliated to this group claim that if a *mujtahid* fails to ascertain the correct judgement, he will not be punished. As some of them state, this is because the Lawgiver pardons scholars who do not succeed in determining the correct ruling in relation to the *furū'*. They also cited the consensus of the predecessors that there is no sin upon those scholars who fail to ascertain the correct ruling. As for disputes in *uṣūl*, according to the majority among these scholars, the mistaken *mujtahid* commits a misdeed by his incorrect judgement. They assert that there ought to be sufficient evidence for the correct opinion in the revelation.

As indicated earlier, this second opinion is held by most jurists and the followers of the four Imams. This includes the greater portion of the followers of Imam Aḥmad. This can be seen clearly in *al-'Uddah* by Abū Ya'la, *al-Tamhīd* by Abū 'l-Khaṭṭāb and *al-Rawḍah* by Ibn Qudāmah.[84] However, Ibn Taymiyyah criticises this opinion and states that it is contrary to the view of the *salaf* and the four Imams. They believed that Muslim scholars do not incur sin because of their failure to determine the correct judgement in issues concerning either *uṣūl* or *furū'*.[85] Ibn Taymiyyah mentions that this opinion was held by Abū Ḥanifah, al-Shāfi'ī, al-Thawrī, Dawūd and others.[86] He states that it was not the practice of the companions and their followers to charge any individual with unbelief, provided they had exerted every possible effort in seeking to ascertain the correct ruling. The *salaf* did not even think that a *mujtahid* who had erred in his judgements committed sins.[87]

Ibn Taymiyyah supports this opinion. He states first that claims about the existence of a division of the *sharī'ah* into two parts (i.e. *uṣūl* and *furū'*) do not stand up to criticism.[88]

As an aside, Ibn Taymiyyah also criticises the claim that the content of the revelation requires that every unbeliever will be punished in the Hell Fire, whether or not the unbeliever tried his best to determine the truth about Islam; he argues that this is in fact contrary to the Qur'an, *sunnah* and reason. In rebutting this view, Ibn Taymiyyah cites different textual evidence, including the following:[89]

- He quotes part of a Qur'anic verse in which Allah says: 'We never punish until We have sent a Messenger (to give warning)' (Qur'an 17:15).
- He also quotes the verses 'Every time a group is cast therein, its keeper will ask: "Did no Warner come to you?" They will say: "Yes indeed, a Warner did come to us, but we belied him and said: 'Allah never sent down anything (of revelation), you are only in great error' " ' (Qur'an 67:8–9).

Ibn Taymiyyah believes that these are clear texts highlighting the principle that no group of people will be cast into the Hell Fire except after they have received a warning. According to Ibn Taymiyyah, those who were not able to ascertain the truth of Islam would not therefore be cast into the fire.[90]

Is the *sharī'ah* divided into two parts, *uṣūl* and *furū'*?

The majority of jurists subscribe to the opinion that the *sharī'ah* is divided into two sections, *uṣūl* (fundamentals) and *furū'* (subsidiary issues). It appears that all the scholars affiliated to the Ḥanbalī School are included in this category. This may be demonstrated by consulting the writings of both the early and later scholars.[91]

As mentioned earlier, Ibn Taymiyyah rejects this opinion and considers it an innovation introduced by the Mu'tazilah, Jahmiyyah and the Ahl al-Kalām. Ibn Taymiyyah suggests that this 'innovation' was transmitted to a number of scholars who authored works in *uṣūl al-fiqh*, and also therefore made reference to it in their treatises. Ibn Taymiyyah maintains that they were ignorant of the true nature of this view and its objective. Ibn Taymiyyah asserts that this opinion is not mentioned in the texts or by consensus, nor was it mentioned by any individual amongst the *salaf* or the Imams. It is therefore to be deemed invalid.[92] Ibn Taymiyyah demonstrates the invalidity of this division by mentioning that those who propagated this division did not establish appropriate criteria by which differentiation between the two divisions could be ascertained.[93] The three criteria employed by these scholars to differentiate between *uṣūl* and *furū'*, and criticised by Ibn Taymiyyah, are as follows:

1 He mentions that some scholars claimed that the issues of *uṣūl* comprise the theoretical issues of creed, as opposed to the issues of *furū'*, which concern practicalities.[94]

Ibn Taymiyyah criticises this view by describing it as unsystematic. He explains that the denial of certain practical issues, such as rejecting of the obligation of the five daily prayers, alms and fasting during the month of Ramaḍān, would result in a charge of unbelief against the perpetrator. In addition, denying the prohibition of adultery, usury, injustice and other comparable matters would result in a similar ruling, despite the fact that they are deemed practical issues within the *sharī'ah*. By contrast, certain theoretical issues have been the subject of disagreement, yet none of the disputing parties were considered to be transgressors. Ibn Taymiyyah cites examples of differences of opinion that occurred amongst the companions in relation to several issues. These included their difference of opinion as to whether the Prophet saw Allah or not, whether certain words were from the Qur'an or not, and concerning the meaning of some of the texts from the Qur'an and *sunnah*.[95]

Ibn Taymiyyah is asserting, by citing these disputes concerning theoretical issues that occurred amongst the companions, that they did not disapprove of such disputes. Nor did they charge one another with unbelief because of their uncertainty on these theoretical issues. Ibn Taymiyyah is attempting to illustrate through this that the division of *sharī'ah* into the *uṣūl* and *furū'* was not recognised by the companions, as there is nothing to indicate that they treated practical issues and theoretical issues differently.

Ibn Taymiyyah also makes the point that practical issues contain two aspects, namely, practice and theory. If errors committed in practical issues are pardonable, mistakes in theoretical issues, which are devoid of practical elements, are more deserving of being pardoned.[96]

2 The second criterion advanced for the differentiation between *uṣūl* and *furū'* is that issues of *uṣūl* are those which are founded upon definite evidence, whereas issues of *furū'* are based upon indefinite evidence.[97]

Ibn Taymiyyah refutes this assertion by stating that there are many issues considered to be *furū'* which are founded upon definite evidence. A portion of these are known by some scholars but not by others. A portion of the evidence is considered definite by consensus, such as the prohibition placed upon matters declared forbidden and the command placed upon those matters declared obligatory. Nevertheless, if an individual fails to comply with these rulings based upon definite evidence, because of his ignorance of them or due to the manner in which he interprets them, he will not be charged with unbelief or disobedience until he becomes aware of them.[98]

Ibn Taymiyyah supports his view by citing certain events which occurred during the time of the Prophet and his companions. He makes reference to a group of companions who drank after dawn during Ramaḍān because they misunderstood the meaning of a part of verse 187 in *surah al-Baqarah* wherein Allah says: 'eat and drink until the white thread appears distinct to you from the black thread.' They misunderstood this to mean that they were to wait until they could visually distinguish one thread from the other, whereas the verse is referring to the light of dawn and the darkness of night. Their mistake violated a definite proof, but they were neither charged with unbelief by the Prophet nor considered to be sinners. Another example cited by Ibn Taymiyyah is the case of a group of people during the time of the Caliph 'Umar who thought that consuming wine was permissible in Islam. These individuals were not accused of disobedience. Rather, they were made aware of this important ruling in Islam and sought repentance for their mistake. Ibn Taymiyyah also mentions that at the time of the Caliph 'Umar, a woman was accused of committing adultery. When the woman was questioned, she responded by saying that she was unaware that the act of adultery was forbidden in Islam. When her ignorance of the ruling became clear to the companions, she was not punished for her action.[99]

To further confirm the weakness of this second criterion, Ibn Taymiyyah cites the verse 'Our lord! Punish us not if we forget or fall into error' (Qur'an 2:286). It is related in the *Ṣaḥīḥ* that Allah said: 'I have done so.'[100]

Ibn Taymiyyah states that this text does not differentiate between mistakes in rulings based upon definite evidence and rulings based upon indefinite evidence.[101]

The citation of the Qur'anic verse also serves to affirm his view that an individual who commits a mistake in any issue, whether pertaining to the *uṣūl* or *furū'*, will not be committing a sin, for the verse declares in general terms that their mistake will be received with forgiveness. Hence, according to Ibn Taymiyyah, any individual who claims that errors of judgement are sins contradicts the evidence from the Qur'an, *sunnah* and consensus.[102]

Ibn Taymiyyah also criticises this criterion of differentiation from another perspective. He states that the nature of definite and indefinite evidence is connected more to the individual who analyses the evidence than to the evidence itself. For some types of evidence are considered by certain scholars to be definite, whereas other scholars consider the same types to be indefinite.[103]

As a result, it is unlikely that complete agreement could occur concerning the sum total of evidence claimed to be either definite or indefinite. Therefore, it would be inaccurate to employ this as a criterion in differentiating between the rulings of the *sharī'ah*.

3 The third criterion is that issues of *uṣūl* pertain to those rulings determined by the means of reason, such as the attributes of Allah, the divine decree and destiny. This is different from issues of *furū'*, whose rulings are known to us by means of revelation, such as the intercession (*shafā'ah*) and the removal of numerous individuals who committed major sins from the Fire.[104]

Ibn Taymiyyah responds to this opinion by stating that unbelief and transgression are *shar'ī* rulings which cannot be ascertained through the use of reason.[105]

It ought to be noted that Ibn Taymiyyah does not comment on the claim that the attributes of Allah, the divine decree and other comparable matters are determined only by the use of reason and not through revelation. This claim is, nevertheless, clearly unacceptable to Ibn Taymiyyah as he asserts in various places in his treatises that belief in matters of the unseen, such as the examples mentioned earlier, must be founded upon evidence from the Qur'an and *sunnah*, although sound reason will be found to agree with these two sources.[106]

Having stated that the division of the *sharī'ah* into the *uṣūl* and *furū'* is not correct, Ibn Taymiyyah himself adopts the same terms in various parts of his treatises. If this division is not correct, why then did Ibn Taymiyyah use it? The answer to this question is not entirely certain. It is possible that it was connected to a change in his independent reasoning. This explanation is applicable to certain sections of his treatises, evidently written at a later stage of his scholastic life but not others. Another plausible reason for the presence of these terms is that their use was ubiquitous amongst the scholars of his time. He therefore used them as means of communicating with other scholars. This explanation is vindicated by the fact that Ibn Taymiyyah himself affirms the permissibility of using the terminology of others if a need requires an individual to do so. This is on the condition that their meanings are correct. He mentioned that the *salaf* did not object to the use of certain terminology merely because it had not been used before, but only because it contained incorrect meanings.[107] Therefore, according to Ibn Taymiyyah, if it is possible that the meanings of these terms can be corrected by applying the Qur'an and *sunnah* to them, they can be used.[108]

The comprehension of texts and its contradiction of correct analogy

A group of scholars maintains that there is no clear provision in the texts of the Qur'an and *sunnah* for one-hundredth (*'ushr mi'shār*) of the issues of the *sharī'ah*.[109] Some scholars affiliated to the Ḥanbalī School, in addition to others, implemented this claim in practice by asserting that the rulings on many issues were determined by means of analogy and not by the text itself (*naṣṣ*). For example, they stated that the prohibition of all kinds of intoxicants with the exception of *khamr* is ascertained by recourse to analogy.[110]

Ibn Taymiyyah states that this opinion is incorrect. He says that the majority of scholars subscribe to the opinion that most rulings concerning obligations are founded upon textual evidence (*nuṣūṣ*). Other scholars went further and stated that the texts covered all rulings.[111]

According to Ibn Taymiyyah, this limitation of the scope of the *sharī'ah* texts occurred as a result of a misunderstanding of the general texts and their implications. He asserts that the texts contain all the rulings pertaining to obligation, whether by means of the explicit indication, inferred meaning or implied meaning of a given text. He explains this by making reference to the Lawgiver's use of general rulings that apply to many sub-categories, which are in turn applicable to innumerable branches.[112]

Ibn Taymiyyah refutes the opinion mentioned earlier that all intoxicants, with the exception of *khamr*, are prohibited by means of analogy and not by the texts themselves. He bases his objection on his principle that the Lawgiver uses a general, encompassing ruling that is applicable to various forms. He argues that the word *khamr* is applicable to all types of intoxicants. Therefore, their prohibition is actualised by means of the text itself. This principle dictates that all forms of intoxicants, regardless of whether they are liquids or solids, are prohibited by the texts.[113]

Ibn Taymiyyah stresses the need to use *taḥqīq al-manāṭ* (ascertaining the ruling's cause)[114] in order to determine whether a particular class is included under a general ruling or not.[115] He feels that the solution to most contested issues can be found within the texts by erudite scholars who possess a broad knowledge of the various legal pieces of evidence.[116] This does not mean that Ibn Taymiyyah denies the legal validity of analogy. On the contrary, he states that it is inaccurate to assert that the use of analogy is incorrect. At the same time he argues that a correct analogy cannot be in contradiction to a text (*naṣṣ*). If it does contradict the text, it is either incorrect or null and void.[117] His aim, therefore, is to place analogy firmly behind texts in priority.

Ibn Taymiyyah explains that there are two types of analogy, correct and incorrect (valid and invalid). Correct analogy is one that is introduced by the Lawgiver and either determines parallels between similar cases, a procedure known as *qiyās ṭard*, or differentiates between dissimilar ones, a procedure known as *qiyās 'aks* (*reductio ad absurdum*).[118]

Correct analogy is applicable when the cause upon which the original ruling is based is present in another case, without any distinguishing factor that would prevent the implementation of the ruling. Ibn Taymiyyah states that the *sharī'ah* is not opposed to this type of analogy.[119]

In addition, Ibn Taymiyyah mentions another type of analogy that is known as *qiyās bi al-ghā' al-fāriq* (isolating the cause). It is defined as an 'analogy based upon the absence of an effective disparity between two cases'.[120] Again, Ibn Taymiyyah maintains that the *sharī'ah* is not opposed to this type of analogy.[121]

He states that whenever the *sharī'ah* restricts certain rulings to specific cases, it denotes the presence of reasons for this act of particularisation. According to Ibn Taymiyyah, these reasons may be comprehended by some but not by others. For a specific analogy to be correct, it is not necessary that every scholar recognises it as correct.[122]

Ibn Taymiyyah clarifies that if a scholar discovers that certain Islamic rulings of law contradict analogy, it does not necessarily mean that those rulings contradict correct analogy, for the contradiction may in fact only be with an incorrect analogy which that scholar happened to consider correct. He argues that if we become aware of a text that contradicts analogy, then we must understand that the analogy is invalid in this particular case. It leads us to conclude that this particular case possesses its own distinguishing features which produce this particularisation. This is because there is no ruling present in the *sharīʿah* that contradicts correct analogy; the rulings may only be opposed by an invalid analogy.[123]

Ibn Taymiyyah does not invalidate any given analogy in all cases, but only in the particularised case. As a consequence, an analogy can be valid and invalid at the same time. It is invalid in the particularised case, by reason of the text, but valid in the remainder of cases.

Ibn Taymiyyah's insistence on the absence of contradiction between analogy and Islamic rulings of law seems to be an attack against a large number of Ḥanbalī scholars, as well as other scholars, who point out the presence of this contradiction in various legal rulings.[124]

Ibn Taymiyyah states that he came across no authentic *ḥadīth* that is not in accordance with the authentic general principles of Islam. He had examined what he could of the evidences of Islamic law and found no correct analogy contradicting an authentic *ḥadīth*. The converse is also true: clear rational evidence cannot contradict authentic narration. Rather, as Ibn Taymiyyah asserts, whenever an analogy is at odds with a narration, one of the two must be flawed. The ability to distinguish between correct and flawed analogy, however, escapes even distinguished scholars, let alone those who are less qualified. Indeed the ability to discern correctly those effective legal attributes that have an effect on rulings and to know the wisdom and meanings contained within Islamic law is one of the finest and subtlest types of knowledge. It includes the apparent, which many people know, and the subtle, which only the elite know. As a result, the analogy employed by many scholars contradicts textual evidence, because correct analogy is hidden from them, just as many subtle legal indications contained within textual evidence are hidden from them.[125]

Ibn Taymiyyah analysed certain cases in which it was claimed that there was a contradiction between analogy and textual rulings. Two examples are discussed in the following sections.

1 The contract of co-partnership: **muḍārabah**

It has been claimed that this form of contract contradicts correct analogy. According to Ibn Taymiyyah, this claim is based on the assumption that this contract is a type of hire, because it is work for a counter-value, and in a contract of hire, it is a condition that the work and counter-value are known. On account of this, because the work and the counter-value in a co-partnership contract are not known exactly, some scholars have argued that the permissibility of this form of contract contradicts analogy, which prohibits it.[126]

Ibn Taymiyyah criticises this view, arguing that this contract is a form of participation and not a type of hire. Therefore, there is no need to have precise knowledge of the work and counter-value.[127] Ibn Taymiyyah explains that according to Islamic law, work is of three types:

1 Where the work is stipulated by the contract and is also known and capable of being delivered. This type is the contract of hire, which is legally binding.
2 Where the work is stipulated by the contract but it is either completely or partially unknown, such as where an individual says, 'Whosoever finds such and such an item for me, I will give him such and such.' In Islamic law this form of contract is known as *ja'ālah* (reward, prize), which is a valid contract but not binding. If the two parties make this contract binding, rather than voluntary, then the contract is not valid.
3 Where the money and not the work are stipulated by the contract. This type is called the 'Contract of Co-Partnership' (*muḍārabah*). In this contract the giver of the money is not so much concerned with the actual work done as with the fruit of his labour, which is the profit.[128]

By means of this classification, Ibn Taymiyyah intends to rebut the claim that the contract of co-partnership is a type of hire, and to affirm that it is a type of participation. This may also be demonstrated by his statement concerning the frustration of a contract of co-partnership for any reason, such as the absence of a condition or the existence of an impediment. In this instance the worker ought to be given a fair part of the profit, rather than a fair wage.[129] Ibn Taymiyyah supports his opinion by giving the example of a worker who worked under an invalid contract of co-partnership. In the event that the individual worked for a long period of time, for instance ten years, and was thereafter paid a fair wage, he would receive more than the capital. This differs from a valid contract under which he would receive only a fair share of the profits.[130]

2 *A contract for the lease of a field with profit sharing* (muzāra'ah)

Ibn Taymiyyah observes that the claim of a contradiction in this case is based upon the assumption of certain scholars that *muzāra'ah* is a contract of hire for an unknown counter-value. As a consequence, a group of these scholars invalidated all of its forms, claiming that legal evidence indicates that this type of contract is prohibited. Others, however, accepted a portion of such contracts, based upon the people's need for them.[131]

Nevertheless, Ibn Taymiyyah criticises this view and asserts that if a scholar considers the matter carefully, he would conclude that the possibility of injustice and uncertainty occurring in a contract of *muzāra'ah* is more distant from the contract of hire for delayed payment. He explains that it is founded upon the contractual principle that the tenant on the land benefits from the harvest.[132]

Is it possible to make an analogy on rulings alleged to be in opposition to analogy?

Ibn Taymiyyah asserts that rulings said to be in opposition to analogy are of two types: agreed upon and disputed ones. According to Ibn Taymiyyah, agreed rulings can be used for the purpose of analogy with similar cases, for he explains that there is no ruling which contradicts a valid analogy. Furthermore, rulings are only claimed to contradict analogy because they include a special meaning (effective cause) by which they can be distinguished from other rulings. If this special meaning is present in another case, it can be given the same ruling by way of analogy. However, if the ruling claimed to oppose the analogy is one disputed amongst scholars, Ibn Taymiyyah demonstrates by recourse to a study of some of these cases that they are usually in agreement with analogy and not in opposition to it.[133]

Are there any rulings in Islamic law that are only for Arabs?

The Ḥanbalī School of law claims that there are certain rulings which are applicable to Arabs alone. Ibn Taymiyyah opposes this view because there are no texts in the Qur'an or *sunnah* to support it. He also states that the Lawgiver does not restrict any ruling to the Arabs, but rather employs general terms such as 'believer', 'unbeliever', 'hypocrite', 'pious person' and 'transgressor'.[134]

Ibn Taymiyyah mentions examples of rulings which have been claimed to be confined to the Arabs. Some scholars subscribe to the opinion that Arabs cannot be enslaved during a state of war.[135] Ibn Taymiyyah criticises this opinion and states that it opposes the opinion of the majority. He supports his view by citing certain historical events mentioned in the traditions. One example was the enslavement of Banī al-Muṣṭaliq by the Prophet. Furthermore, in the tradition concerning the tribe of Hawazān, the Prophet said, 'Select one of the two, enslavement or ransom.'[136] Ibn Taymiyyah even observes that most of those who were enslaved at the time of the Prophet were Arabs.[137]

His opponents make reference to the order issued by 'Umar in which he commanded that the Arab slaves be freed as a proof that their enslavement is impermissible. Ibn Taymiyyah responds that this order is not a legal ruling that must be followed. Rather, it was an order based on a *maṣlaḥah* existing at the time of 'Umar.[138]

Another ruling that was claimed to be restricted to the Arabs concerned their exemption from the poll tax (*jizyah*) if they did not accept Islam. The payment of this tax was said to be obligatory upon the People of the Book only.[139]

Ibn Taymiyyah mentions that according to the majority opinion, there is no difference between Arabs and non-Arabs in relation to this ruling. He supports this view by stating that all the texts pertinent to this issue are general. He also notes that this tax was levied upon the Zoroastrians of Bahrain and upon the

People of Yemen, who were a mixture of pagans and People of the Book. No differentiation was made between them in relation to the imposition of the tax. Ibn Taymiyyah therefore concludes that the poll tax can be levied upon the Arabs.[140]

It has also been argued that whatever the Arabs disliked ought to be prohibited for all Muslims and whatever they liked should be made permissible for all Muslims. This opinion was held by a number of Ḥanbalī scholars, such as al-Khiraqī, al-Hajjāwī and al-Buhūtī,[141] and according to al-Mardāwī this opinion is the correct opinion of the Ḥanbalī School.[142]

Ibn Taymiyyah states that this claim opposes the opinion of Aḥmad himself and those of the majority, including the early Ḥanbalī scholars. Ibn Taymiyyah cites two proofs to support his opinion. The first relates to the practice of the companions and their followers concerning that which was prohibited and that which was lawful. These rulings were not dependent upon what was liked or disliked amongst the Arabs. The second concerns the fact that the Arabs were fond of certain things that were later on prohibited in Islam, an example of this being the *maytah* (meat of an animal not slaughtered in accordance with *sharʿī* requirements). In addition, they had a disliking for matters which were made permissible in Islam, such as *al-ḍab* (a kind of lizard). The Prophet, who was an Arab, disliked this particular animal, he mentioned that his personal dislike for it did not render it prohibited. When the animal was eaten in his presence, he remarked, 'I do not eat it and I do not prohibit it.'[143]

Another example of this form of restriction concerns the precedence given to Arabs in assuming the position of Imam for prayers. Several Ḥanbalī scholars, such as al-Khiraqī, Ibn Ḥāmid and al-Qāḍī, have subscribed to this opinion.[144]

Ibn Taymiyyah responded by stating that this view opposes the opinion of the majority and no text exists to affirm it. Ibn Taymiyyah notes the tradition of the Prophet in which he states, 'The person who recites the Book of Allah in the most competent manner is to lead his people, and if two are equal in their ability to recite, then the one who has greater knowledge of the *sunnah*. If they are equal in relation to their knowledge of the *sunnah*, then the one who emigrated (to Madīnah) first. If they are equal in relation to the emigration, then the one who embraced Islam first.'[145]

Ibn Taymiyyah concludes that the tradition clearly makes no reference to a precedence in Imamate (leadership of the prayers) due to Arab origin.[146]

Ibn Taymiyyah's opponents cited the words of Salmān al-Fārisī as evidence to substantiate their opinion. He said, 'It is an obligation for us, with respect to you, that we do not lead you in prayers, nor do we marry your women.'[147]

Ibn Taymiyyah comments upon this statement by stating that this was Salmān's personal opinion and not a legal ruling that had to be followed, a matter which is different from the words of the Lawgiver.[148]

There is a dispute amongst the Ḥanbalī scholars, in addition to others, concerning the issue of whether a non-Arab is equal to an Arab in marriage.[149]

Ibn Taymiyyah comments upon this disagreement by stating that it is dependent upon independent reasoning. Hence, whichever of the differing opinions is supported by a text from the Qur'an or *sunnah* is the binding one. He also maintains that the words of an individual, whosoever he may be, are not a proof against these two sources. After highlighting this rule, Ibn Taymiyyah observes that there is no clear, correct text emanating from the Lawgiver dealing with this issue.[150]

After mentioning that the majority of scholars held the opinion that the Arab race and particularly the tribe of Quraysh was superior to other races of people, Ibn Taymiyyah states that this principle is not applicable in relation to individuals. He mentions that this is due to the presence of a large number of non-Arabs who are superior even to the greater portion of Arabs. Furthermore, in the later generations there were some non-Arabs who were superior to the Arabs who lived in the second and third centuries.[151]

Ibn Taymiyyah concludes that the Lawgiver only restricts the rulings to effective qualities and does not specify all Arabs in general by certain rulings. Nevertheless, Ibn Taymiyyah does accept that there are certain rulings that only apply to specific groups. For example, according to the opinion of some scholars, the ruler of the Muslim community must be from the tribe of the Quraysh. This, however, according to Ibn Taymiyyah, only applies if it is possible. He also stresses that leadership is not for all of Quraysh but only for the appointed leader in question.[152]

Another example of a ruling that is restricted to a specific group of people concerns the impermissibility of charity being donated to Banī Hāshim. Ibn Taymiyyah mentions that this is in order to prevent any accusation of favouritism being made against them and also because they are to be given their share from the *khumus* (the fifth taken from the booty, after which the remains are divided among the warriors) and *al-fa'ī* (that gained without any fighting).[153]

Maṣlaḥah **as a source of law**

The early Ḥanbalī scholars, such as Ibn Ḥāmid in his book *Tahdhīb al-Ajwibah*, Abū Ya'la in his treatise *al-'Uddah* and Abū 'l-Khaṭṭāb in his book *al-Tamhīd*, did not make reference to *maṣlaḥah* (benefit) as a source of law. The Ḥanbalī scholar al-Majd (d. 652/1254) asserts that the *maṣlaḥah* is not a source of law and attributes this opinion to the late Ḥanbalī scholars of general principles.[154] The eminent Ḥanbalī scholar Ibn Qudāmah (d. 620/1223) provides more information regarding *maṣlaḥah* and its status in Islamic law. He classifies *maṣlaḥah* into the following three categories:

1 A type the correctness of which is affirmed by the sources of law. This type is, in fact, the source of analogy.
2 A type the incorrectness of which is affirmed by the sources of law. This type cannot be employed as a foundation upon which a ruling may be established, for it would result in an alteration to Islamic law.

3 A type the correctness or incorrectness of which is not expressly affirmed by the sources of law.[155] This third type of *maṣlaḥah* is divided by Ibn Qudāmah into three kinds:

i Benefits deemed necessary (*ḍaruriyāt*). Ibn Qudāmah associated this type of *maṣlaḥah* with the five necessary interests in Islamic law (*al-ḍarūrāt al-khams*), namely, the preservation of religion, life, reason, offspring and material wealth. These are the five interests the scholars have concluded all rulings of Islamic law are geared towards protecting.
ii Complementary benefits (*ḥājiyāt*).
iii Luxurious benefits (*kamāliyāt*).[156]

In reference to the latter two types of benefits, Ibn Qudāmah mentions that he is not aware of a disagreement concerning the impermissibility of founding a ruling wholly upon these benefits, without the existence of other legal evidence to corroborate the accuracy and legitimacy of these benefits. As for *ḍaruriyāt*, he says there is disagreement amongst scholars concerning the acceptance of them as the sole basis for a legal ruling.[157] The position of Ibn Qudāmah with regard to the use of *maṣlaḥah* in Islamic law appears to be shared by the majority of Ḥanbalī scholars.[158]

This was the position of *maṣlaḥah* in the Ḥanbalī School of law before the time of Ibn Taymiyyah. Here now follows an analysis of *maṣlaḥah* and its validity according to the understanding of Ibn Taymiyyah.

Ibn Taymiyyah defines *maṣlaḥah* as 'That which is considered by a *mujtahid* to procure a benefit, while at the same time nothing exists within the rulings of Islamic law to oppose it'.[159]

We notice that in Ibn Taymiyyah's discussion of the sources of Islamic law, he demonstrates great caution in approving *maṣlaḥah* as a source. Ibn Taymiyyah states: 'The use of *maṣlaḥah mursalah* (in Islamic law) frequently results in the enactment of laws that are not permitted by Allah'[160] (i.e. they contradict the established rulings of Islamic law). He also observes that the majority of innovations (*bida'*) were erroneously justified by those who invented them as beneficial *maṣāliḥ* and therefore correct.[161]

Why was Ibn Taymiyyah so concerned about *maṣlaḥah*? The answer to this question can be determined by consulting Ibn Taymiyyah's own words. He felt that the use of what was deemed to be *maṣlaḥah* by certain leaders, scholars, and others was the source of great disorder within Islamic law. This occurred because some of the supposed *maṣāliḥ* claimed by individuals were, in fact, prohibited according to Islamic law, but those who implemented them were ignorant of their prohibition.[162] He reminds us that it is impermissible for scholars to declare certain matters lawful or unlawful based on their desires.[163] He explains that people often assume that these matters are of benefit to them in this life and in the hereafter, without appreciating that the claimed benefit is sometimes accompanied by harm that exceeds the benefit.[164]

From what has been mentioned, it may appear that Ibn Taymiyyah does not approve of the use of *maṣlaḥah* in Islamic law. Hence it might be assumed that he subscribes to the same opinion as the majority of Ḥanbalī scholars. This seems, however, not to be the case as we find Ibn Taymiyyah occasionally establishing rulings on the foundation of the *maṣlaḥah*.[165] Also, we find various references to *maṣlaḥah* in his writings. He asserts that the Messengers were entrusted by Allah to obtain *maṣāliḥ* and perfect the existing ones, in addition to preventing and eliminating the causes of corruption.[166] How, then, do we understand the statements that he made concerning the hazards of *maṣlaḥah?* Ibn Taymiyyah recognises that the divine law does not neglect the *maṣlaḥah* completely. He also affirms that the *sharī'ah* has been completed and there is no *maṣlaḥah* except that it has been mentioned in the *sharī'ah*.[167] This does not mean that every *maṣlaḥah* is expressly mentioned in a text of the Qur'an or *sunnah*; instead, it appears to mean that all correct *maṣāliḥ* are found within the general rulings and principles of the *sharī'ah*.

Ibn Taymiyyah maintains that if a *maṣlaḥah* is claimed to exist as a product of independent reasoning and not by reason of the *sharī'ah*, either this claimed *maṣlaḥah* is to be found in a text without the scholar being aware of it or it is not a valid *maṣlaḥah* at all.[168]

Ibn Taymiyyah also criticises those who restricted the use of *maṣlaḥah* to the preservation of the five necessary interests. He asserts that the preservation of the five necessary benefits, which is in fact a means of repelling harmful outcomes, is only a part of the scope of *maṣlaḥah*, for it is also comprised of other benefits.[169]

What is meant by *ra'y* in Islamic law?

This issue is a source of great confusion in the Ḥanbalī references, as well as those of other schools. Most of those who asserted the permissibility of employing *ra'y* neglected to clarify what they mean by the term. The ambiguity surrounding this issue appears to stem from a possible misunderstanding of certain Qur'anic verses. For example,

- 'But if they answer you not, then know that they only follow their own lusts. And who is more astray than one who follows his own lusts, without guidance from Allah' (28:50).

  This verse indicates that people may be divided into two categories: those individuals who adhere to the words of the Lawgiver and those who follow their own desires. Hence, those who adhere to their *ra'y* are not following the words of the Lawgiver; rather, they are following their own desires.
- 'Follow what has been sent down unto you from your Lord and do not follow any *auliyā'* beside him (Allah)' (7:3).
- '...Follow you that (Islam and its laws) and follow not the desires of those who are unaware' (45:18). This verse commands believers to adhere to the *sharī'ah* of Allah and prohibits them from following the desires of those who are ignorant.

In addition, the misunderstanding of certain narrations containing a condemnation of *ra'y* by the *salaf* contributed to certain scholars rejecting the role of *ra'y* in Islamic law. Some of these narrations are as follows:

- It has been narrated that the second caliph Abū Bakr said: 'what earth would give me support, and what sky would shelter me, if I explain a verse in the book of Allah using my own *ra'y*.'
- It has been narrated that 'Umar b. al-Khaṭṭāb said: 'The people of Ahl al-Ra'y are the enemies of the *sunnah*. This is because they could not understand it, nor could they memorize it, thus they put forward their *ra'y*.'
- Alī b. Abi Ṭālib said: 'If the religion was founded upon *ra'y*, then the bottom of the *khuff* would be more deserving of being wiped over than the top.'

Ibn Taymiyyah makes his position on this point clear. He attaches great importance to the texts of the Qur'an and *sunnah*, but acknowledges the role of *ra'y* in the process of determining a legal ruling. According to Ibn Taymiyyah, *ra'y* is divided into two different types: censured and praiseworthy. He explains that it is the censured form of *ra'y* that was criticised by the predecessors (*salaf*). Ibn Taymiyyah defines this *ra'y* as the one which opposes one or more of the following: the Qur'an, *sunnah* and the opinions of the predecessors and the general principles derived from them. Ibn Taymiyyah explains that this form of opposition to the sources can occur in the following ways:

- The opposition to one of these sources is founded upon no other sources. According to Ibn Taymiyyah, a *mujtahid* can only perpetrate this kind of opposition when he is unaware of those sources opposing his opinion.
- A scholar is aware of these sources, but does not implement them, because of some other consideration.[170]

Ibn Taymiyyah argues that the condemnation of *ra'y* is not applicable to independent reasoning by means of *ra'y*, which is founded upon established general principles in issues not mentioned explicitly in the Qur'an, *sunnah* and consensus.[171] According to Ibn Taymiyyah, the use of this form of *ra'y* is restricted to those scholars who are familiar with similar and dissimilar issues and who possess a great ability in the science of *fiqh al-ma'ānī* (textual implications).[172] Ibn Taymiyyah insists that whoever claims that the predecessors arrived at a consensus abandoning the use of *ra'y* in Islamic law is mistaken. Similarly, whoever claimed the companions founded some issues upon *ra'y* alone is also mistaken. Rather, Ibn Taymiyyah asserts that each scholar amongst the companions exerted his best efforts in independently determining a new issue, and every one of them presented the solution he arrived upon. These solutions often varied from one scholar to another. Some companions offered solutions based upon what they understood from the texts; others offered solutions based upon the use of *ra'y* and analogy.[173]

Ibn al-Qayyim, Ibn Taymiyyah's eminent student, argues for the presence of a grey area between the *ra'y* condemned by the companions and that praised by them. He refers to this as conclusively dubious *ra'y*, in which the decision to condemn or praise cannot be determined. According to Ibn al-Qayyim, the companions permitted the use of this third type of *ra'y* in practice, delivering *fatāwā* and determining a legal judgement. However, this usage was conditioned upon the existence of a state of necessity. In addition, the companions did not consider this type of *ra'y* as a binding source of law. Therefore, scholars may choose whether or not to establish their opinions and judgements upon it.[174]

Any acceptable *ra'y* comes within the category of rational knowledge. It ought to be asked then whether or not rational knowledge is considered as *shar'ī* knowledge.

According to Ibn Taymiyyah, the Ḥanbalī scholars' division of knowledge into *shar'ī* and rational is not accurate at all times. Rather, the terms 'revealed' *(naqlī)* and 'rational' *('aqlī)* should be used. Ibn Taymiyyah explains that this is because '*shar'ī* knowledge' can denote various meanings, including

- what the Lawgiver has ordered to be studied;
- what the Lawgiver has revealed.

Certain Ḥanbalī scholars preferred the first definition, and others the second. Nevertheless, Ibn Taymiyyah asserts that the term '*shar'ī* knowledge' can refer to these two meanings at the same time. Therefore, Ibn Taymiyyah concludes that the terms revealed and rational knowledge ought to be used, and these two types of knowledge can be included as sub-category under the term *shar'ī*.[175]

Ibn Taymiyyah also asserts that the presence of a contradiction between revealed and rational knowledge is impossible, for sound revealed knowledge is in conformity with clear rational knowledge.[176]

Postponing the clarification of the rulings of Islamic law

The Ḥanbalī scholars seem to agree on the impermissibility of postponing the act of giving an Islamic ruling of law whenever one is needed.[177] Some of the Ḥanbalī sources even made reference to an agreement amongst the scholars concerning this issue.[178]

Ibn Taymiyyah does not deny the existence of this consensus, but he states that it should not be understood incorrectly. He explains that just as the clarification of a legal ruling can become necessary, it can also occasionally become necessary to postpone the clarification. This necessity may be found on the part of the informant as well as the one subject to the ruling. The informant cannot notify all of the people at the same time, nor can he explain the sum total of legal rulings at once. This matter will be restricted to his ability and capacity. Similarly, anyone subject to a ruling cannot receive and completely understand the entire legal ruling at the same time; rather, he must do so gradually.[179]

Ibn Taymiyyah bases his recognition of the capacity and ability of the individual in the act of clarifying the Islamic rulings of law upon several pieces of textual evidence, an example of which is verse 16 from the chapter *al-Taghābun*, in which Allah says: 'So keep your duty to Allah (and fear Him) to the best of your ability.' In addition, verse 286 of *al-Baqarah*: 'Allah does not burden a person beyond his ability.' Furthermore, Ibn Taymiyyah quotes the Qura'nic verses referring to the removal of hardship (*rafʿ al-ḥaraj*). An example of such a verse is 2:185, 'Allah intends for you ease, and He does not want to make things difficult for you,' and verse 22:78, 'and has not laid upon you any hardship in the religion'.

Ibn Taymiyyah also connects the clarification of Islamic legal rulings to another concept in *uṣūl al-fiqh*, namely, the conflict between two advantages or disadvantages. In the event that two advantages conflict, the more advantageous of the two will be followed, even if this leads to the abandonment of the less advantageous. Similarly, in the event that one of two disadvantages must be selected, the one responsible is obliged to select the least disadvantageous one. In a situation where the disadvantages and advantages exist in a single action and cannot be separated from each other, the one responsible ought to weigh the possible benefit and injury arising from the act in question. If he discovers that the benefit does not outweigh the injury, he should abandon that course of action, and vice versa.[180]

It is interesting to note Ibn Taymiyyah's comment concerning an instance when one of two obligatory acts has been given priority by the one responsible. This would occur if it were deemed more important than the other act in a situation where the two acts cannot be practised at the same time. He states that the one that is not practised is, in fact, in that instance no longer obligatory (i.e. the person responsible will not be considered to have committed a sin). Similarly, an action is not deemed prohibited when it is considered the least serious of two prohibited acts and cannot therefore be avoided.[181]

Accordingly, Ibn Taymiyyah argues that before clarifying a legal ruling, scholars ought to consider the circumstances surrounding the one entrusted with giving a decision, and the consequence of clarifying the ruling. By contemplating the matter, the scholar will sometimes choose to go ahead with the clarification, but also sometimes avoid doing so, as it is said, 'the answer to some questions is that you do not answer them'.[182]

Ibn Taymiyyah supports this understanding of the procedure for clarifying jurisprudential rulings by citing several sets of evidence, such as the following:

- The Lawgiver did not reveal all jurisprudential rulings at once. Instead, the revelation of some rulings was postponed for certain reasons. Sometimes this delay was to enable the Muslims to become accustomed to the already revealed rulings. Certain other rulings were postponed until Islam had become widespread and secure.[183]

  On the strength of this, Ibn Taymiyyah concludes that scholars can also postpone the clarification of certain rulings until such time as the individual is able to practise them.[184]
- Allah said: 'We never punish until We have sent a Messenger' (Qur'an 1:15).

Ibn Taymiyyah says that there are two factors taken into consideration when determining whether the one responsible must implement a ruling or not:

1 whether it was possible for the individual to be aware of the ruling;
2 whether the individual had the ability to practise it.

Ibn Taymiyyah argues the need for these two conditions based upon the principle that an individual who is mentally insane is absolved from legal responsibility, because of his inability to understand the ruling. Therefore, Ibn Taymiyyah argues that those who are not aware of a given legal ruling ought to be dealt with in a similar manner. In addition, he mentions that the Lawgiver has pardoned those who are incapable of implementing certain rulings. For example, the sick are excused from fasting and the poor are not required to give *zakāt*. Therefore, Ibn Taymiyyah argues that anyone who is incapable of implementing certain rulings shall be pardoned in a similar manner.[185]

Ibn Taymiyyah also presents rational arguments for his position. He says that an individual studying Islamic law cannot possibly encompass all of the rulings within it at the very beginning of his education. If we agree that the laws he could not learn are not within his capacity, then they cannot in fact be obligatory for him at that stage. If these matters are not considered obligatory for him, the scholar should not order him to implement them at that stage, but should postpone the clarification of all of the obligatory and prohibited acts until the student becomes able to learn these Laws and practise them. Ibn Taymiyyah asserts that such a scholar will not be accused of condoning the practice of prohibited things or the neglect of obligatory acts.[186]

Ibn Taymiyyah concludes that scholars are not obliged to convey all the rulings within Islamic law at one go. The scholar ought to convey them periodically in a manner he believes is consistent with the understanding of the addressee and his ability to practise the rulings without the harm exceeding the benefit.[187]

Who is permitted to imitate others in *sharʿī* rulings?

Ḥanbalī sources mention that neither *mujtahids* nor imitators are permitted to imitate others in issues pertaining to *uṣūl*.[188] Some Ḥanbalī sources include the main pillars of Islam within the scope of this rule, in addition to the best known Islamic rulings, which are collectively described as 'necessary knowledge'.[189] They also appear to agree on allowing laymen to imitate scholars in relation to issues of *al-furūʿ*.[190] Most Ḥanbalī scholars also state that a *mujtahid* is not permitted to imitate another scholar.[191]

These opinions of the School, which are found within most Ḥanbalī sources concerning these questions, are problematic. According to these opinions, laymen are obliged to practise independent reasoning in spite of their inability to do so.

Similarly, according to some of these scholars, *mujtahids* are not permitted to imitate other scholars regardless of the prevailing circumstances.

One particular scholar has added further confusion on the issue of whether it is permissible for a scholar to imitate (*yuqallid*) another scholar. On this occasion, however, the individual in question is not a Ḥanbalī scholar, but a leading Shāfiʿī scholar Al-Shirāzī (d. 476/1083), who states that the opinion of Aḥmad's school is that it is permissible for a *mujtahid* to imitate another scholar, without restriction.[192]

Ibn Taymiyyah discusses these issues within the School and offers his own opinions. He identifies the existence of certain trends within the Ḥanbalī School on the subject of independent reasoning. First, there were those who declared that every Muslim, including laymen, was obliged to practise independent reasoning in issues pertaining to creed. Others held that the practice of independent reasoning is now prohibited and every individual must be an imitator in such matters. Ibn Taymiyyah supports a moderate view, according to which the practice of independent reasoning is obligatory upon those who have the ability to perform it.[193]

The practice of independent reasoning in issues of *furūʿ* proved a source of further disagreement amongst the scholars. One opinion was that it is obligatory for every individual, including laymen, to practise independent reasoning in issues concerning the *furūʿ*. Ibn Taymiyyah attributed this opinion to those he described as 'the extremists amongst the *Mutakallimūn* and jurists'. Ibn Taymiyyah considers this opinion as weak and supports his point of view by rational evidence. He agrees that the practice of independent reasoning is obligatory when the person responsible has the ability to practise it. This ability, however, is either deficient or absent in laymen, as it is clear that it is difficult for them to fulfil the conditions for the practice of independent reasoning. Therefore, it is not correct to create a general rule that all legally competent individuals must practise independent reasoning. A second view is the exact opposite: that is, all legally competent individuals must be imitators, regardless of their status in knowledge. This means that even scholars possessing the ability to practise independent reasoning must imitate the early Imams, rather than practise their own independent reasoning.[194]

Ibn Taymiyyah adopts the opinion that independent reasoning is obligatory for those scholars who have the ability to execute it. He does, however, acknowledge the occasional need for such scholars to imitate others where they are incapable of determining a ruling on a specific issue for some reason. For instance, they may not have found the necessary evidence, or they may believe that there is nothing to distinguish between the different evidence before them. Ibn Taymiyyah also acknowledges the need for scholars to practise *taqlīd* in certain instances, even when the necessary evidence is available; this would be the case, for instance, when there were constraints upon time.[195]

Ibn Taymiyyah supports his opinion by arguing that independent reasoning accepts the concept of divisibility and specialisation. He explains that certain scholars are able to practise independent reasoning on some issues but not on others. Therefore, it ought to be permissible for them to practise independent reasoning whenever they are able to do so.[196]

He argues that every individual is obliged to do that which he is able to do. The extent and scope of independent reasoning should therefore be founded strictly upon a person's ability. If a person studies an issue on which the scholars hold more than one opinion and discovers that one of the opinions is affirmed by textual proofs, which according to his knowledge do not conflict with any other texts, there are two options available to him:

1 to follow the opposing opinion solely on the basis that it is the opinion of his school of law. According to Ibn Taymiyyah, this is not an acceptable basis; rather, it is merely the practice of adhering to custom;
2 to follow the opinion that is supported by the evidence. According to Ibn Taymiyyah, this is the correct option, for there is no proof known to that person to override the evidence affirming his forwarded opinion.[197]

Those who consider following the opinion of one's school to be the legitimate option argue the possible existence of certain evidence vindicating the school's opinion which is unknown to the person who studied the issue.[198] Ibn Taymiyyah rejects this argument, repeating his view that every competent individual is obliged to do what he is able. He based this upon certain texts of the Qur'an and the *sunnah*, such as the Qur'anic verse in which Allah says: 'So keep your duty to Allah to the best of your ability' (64:16). Also, he cites the *ḥadīth* of the Prophet in which he states: 'when I enjoin a command upon you, do what you are able'.[199]

Ibn Taymiyyah concludes from these texts that a person who has exerted himself to the best of his ability in studying an issue has done as much as he is able. Having done this, he is obliged to follow that which he considers to be the correct opinion. If new evidence became apparent after that, he should adopt the opinion supported by it. Ibn Taymiyyah links this case with that of an absolute *mujtahid* who alters his opinion because of new evidence appearing before him. Ibn Taymiyyah stresses that when a person abandons an opinion for another because of the appearance of new evidence, he should be praised for doing so. This is different from the one who insists on following a particular view, despite becoming aware of the existence of evidence that invalidates his opinion and suggests the correctness of the opposing view; such a person would be censured.[200]

Those who consider it an obligation to follow the opinions of the imams rather than the apparent purport of the evidences also argue that the Imams were greater in knowledge, and therefore their opinions hold greater weight.

Ibn Taymiyyah put forward three points in response to this argument:

1 The Imams differed amongst themselves on various jurisprudential rulings. Therefore, according to the opponents' argument, none of their opinions can be followed, as the one who attempts to study these issues is not deemed more

knowledgeable than any of them and cannot possibly judge between their opinions.

2 Although the companions were not all of an equal rank in knowledge, they did not follow one another in jurisprudential issues. Rather, they would each base their opinions upon legal evidence. He presented an example in which some of 'Umar's opinions were abandoned by the companions in favour of the opinions of other companions who were less knowledgeable than 'Umar, because they had cited texts in support of their views.

3 He asserts that if people were obliged to follow the Imam as opposed to the legal evidence, it would result in a distortion of the *sharī'ah*, as appropriate evidence would be abandoned and the scholars' incorrect opinions would be followed.[201]

Ibn Taymiyyah asserts that what has been attributed by al-Shirāzī to Aḥmad concerning the unrestricted permissibility for a *mujtahid* to imitate another scholar is inaccurate.[202] In support of his rebuttal, he cites Aḥmad's well-known practice of requesting his more knowledgeable students (for example, Abū Dawūd, al-Ḥarbī, Muslim and Abū Zur'ah) not to imitate any other scholars. Instead, he would direct them towards practising their own independent reasoning based solely upon the general sources of Islamic law.[203]

According to Ibn Taymiyyah, the permissibility of *taqllid* amongst the *muqallids*, and occasionally the *mujtahids*, is conditional upon the *muqallids* not knowing of any conflict between the limited views and the texts. Otherwise, this *taqllid* is forbidden.[204] Ibn Taymiyyah encourages scholars who are able to practise independent reasoning to follow their own *ijtihād* based directly on the sources of law. This does not mean that they do not derive benefit from the views and independent reasoning of previous scholars. On the contrary, Ibn Taymiyyah emphasises that scholars ought to consider the treatises of previous scholars, particularly those from the first three generations.[205]

Ibn Taymiyyah's understanding is that it is innate in the nature of a human being to imitate others. He illustrates his point by presenting the example of a child who begins his life by following others in several different matters, one of which is religion. Upon attaining maturity, however, people are obliged to examine their actions and beliefs and determine whether they are in conformity with the sources of law. If they are incapable of doing that, they are permitted to imitate scholars, upon the condition that they do not know such scholars' opinions to be in opposition to the texts.[206]

Ibn Taymiyyah seeks to restrict the scope of imitation of a particular school by insisting that the most correct approach is that an individual with a question should ask a scholar, regardless of his jurisprudential school.[207] Ibn Taymiyyah's statement does not, however, entail a complete refusal to recognise the act of a layman imitating the rulings of a specific school. He argues that this form of imitation is permissible, but not obligatory.[208] He points out that adherence to a specific school must not be founded on worldly purposes, but should instead be established upon a good intention (i.e. to follow the truth).[209] Thus, whenever the truth becomes clear to an imitator, he should not hesitate to follow it, even if it opposes the views of his Imam.[210] This is because, as Ibn Taymiyyah explains, Muslim's duty is to obey Allah. He may only follow a school if this does not entail disobeying Allah's laws.[211] Indeed, the Imams themselves forbade people from adopting all of their opinions as a whole. Abū Ḥanifah described a ruling that he deduced by means of independent reasoning as follows: 'It is my opinion and it is to the best of my knowledge, but if someone offers a better one I will be willing to accept it.' Ibn Taymiyyah supports this with another statement from his most prominent student, Abū Yūsuf. When Abū Yūsuf visited Imam Mālik in Madīnah and the *sunnah* was clarified to him on certain issues, he immediately retracted his former views, because he became aware that they were in opposition to the texts and declared: 'If my Sheikh had known about these evidences he would have retracted as I did.' Similarly, Imam Mālik is reported to have said that he was only a human being; his opinions must therefore be examined in the light of the Qur'an and *sunnah*. Al-Shāfi'ī said that if a correct *ḥadīth* is found to be in opposition to a view of his, his opinion should be cast against the wall, that is, discarded. Ibn Taymiyyah also mentions the statement of Imam Aḥmad: 'Do not imitate me and do not imitate Mālik, Shāfi'ī or al-Thawrī, but learn as we did.'[212]

Ibn Taymiyyah discusses the statement of a leading Ḥanbalī scholar, Ibn Ḥamdān (d. 695/1296). He says: 'It is disapproved of for an individual who continuously followed a specific school to thereafter contradict it (not act upon it) without evidence, imitation or an alternative excuse.' Ibn Taymiyyah asserts that this does not contradict his view and says that two possible meanings can be inferred from Ibn Ḥamdān's statement:

1 Whosoever follows a specific school must not depart from any of its rulings without one of the three following reasons:

   i imitation of another *mujtahid*;
   ii a discovery of evidence supporting an opposing opinion in the school;
   iii a valid excuse permitting this departure.

2 The impermissibility of altering one's school. According to the second meaning, the statement declares that moving from one school to another is not allowed.

Ibn Taymiyyah considers these two possible interpretations of Ibn Ḥamdān's statement and concludes that the first meaning is what this scholar intended. In support of this, he quotes Ibn Ḥanbal as having said that it is impermissible for any Muslim to believe that a ruling on a point of Islamic law was obligatory and thereafter believe that it is not obligatory, without evidence and only upon the basis of whim and desire.[213]

Although Ibn Taymiyyah accepts that following a specific school is permissible (but not obligatory), he states that it is prohibited for imitators to use their schools as a criterion upon which they determine who will be granted their friendship and amity and vice versa.[214] He also recognises the possibly serious consequences of fanaticism, asserting that one of these consequences was the invasion of the Mongols into the heart of the Islamic world. He notes that fanaticism amongst the schools of law and their followers was clearly manifest at that time. Supporters of every school of law stood against one another. It is even reported that some of the adherents of the four schools of law would not follow, in prayer, an imam who was not affiliated to their school.[215]

Ibn Taymiyyah asserts that these fanatical followers were ignorant and had no knowledge of the evidence. They would quote incorrect and weak proofs and occasionally base their views, which they would fight for, on words narrated from certain scholars without being aware of the correctness and the authenticity of their chains.[216] Moreover, if they discovered some of their opponents adopting certain opinions which were in fact matters of jurisprudential dispute among the jurists, they would declare that this person should be abandoned and his act condemned. If the very same opinions were held by some of their affiliated members, however, they would ignore them and declare this issue as a matter of independent reasoning and dispute.[217] On account of this, division and disagreement predominated in the Islamic world.[218]

Corrections of misunderstandings of other schools of Islamic law by Ḥanbalī scholars: case study of the consensus of Ahl Al-Madīnah

Ibn Taymiyyah studied Ḥanbalī principles and jurisprudence and corrected some incorrect or generalised statements issued by certain Ḥanbalī scholars concerning other schools of law. One of these issues is the consensus of Ahl al-Madīnah.

The Ḥanbalī sources and the consensus of Ahl Al-Madīnah

All of the Ḥanbalī sources before Ibn Taymiyyah's time, and other sources compiled after his era, in the science of the principles of jurisprudence appear to be in agreement that the consensus of Ahl al-Madīnah is not considered to be a proof in Islamic law. This may be observed clearly in *al-'Uddah* by Abū Ya'la,[219] *al-Tamhid* by Abū 'l-Khaṭṭāb,[220] *al-Rawḍah* by Ibn Qudāmah,[221] *al-Musawwadah* by al-Majd,[222] *Uṣūl al-Fiqh* by Ibn Mufliḥ,[223] *al-Mukhtaṣar* by Ibn al-Laḥḥām,[224] *Sharḥ al-Kawkab* by Ibn al-Najjār[225] and *al-Madkhal* by Ibn Badran.[226]

These Ḥanbalī scholars have neglected to clarify what is to be understood by 'the consensus of Ahl al-Madīnah'. Only some of these scholars have mentioned some points in an attempt to clarify this concept. Ibn Qudāmah explains that there is an agreement amongst the scholars that the consensus of Ahl al-Madīnah was not considered a proof in his time.[227] The leading Ḥanbalī scholar Ibn 'Aqīl states that the consensus of Ahl al-Madīnah can be deemed a recognised proof in Islamic law, but would be dependent upon whether the consensus concerns an issue on which their opinion is in fact traceable to a *ḥadīth* from the Prophet. If their opinion was based merely upon their own independent reasoning, their consensus is not to be considered as a binding proof.[228]

Ibn Taymiyyah's clarification of this point

Ibn Taymiyyah clarifies that this consensus is divided into four categories:

1 The consensus of Ahl al-Madīnah that is considered to be a narration from the Prophet. An example of this type of consensus is their agreement on the quantity of *ṣāʿ* and *mudd* (two types of measurement).[229]

According to Ibn Taymiyyah, this type of consensus is agreed upon by the scholars. He mentions that it is the opinion of Abū Ḥanifah, Mālik, al-Shāfiʿī and Aḥmad, in addition to their followers.[230]

It appears that when Ibn Taymiyyah mentions Abū Ḥanifah as one of those scholars who subscribed to this opinion, he does so on the strength of two points:

i The general principles of Abū Ḥanifah grant priority to a correct text in favour of reason.

ii Abū Yūsuf, one of Abū Ḥanifah's most celebrated students, visited Mālik in al-Madīnah, where they discussed various issues, some of which concerned the narrations of Ahl al-Madīnah. During this discussion, it is reported that Abū Yūsuf accepted the validity of the opinion of Ahl al-Madīnah on certain issues. He also stated that if his companion (i.e. Abū Ḥanifah) had known what he knew, he would have retracted his previous opinions as he did.[231]

2 The practice of the people of Madīnah before the assassination of ʿUthmān. This type of consensus is considered as a proof in the School of Mālik and it is the opinion ascribed to al-Shāfiʿī. It is also the dominant opinion in Aḥmad's School.[232]

3 In the event that there are two conflicting traditions or analogies and we are not aware which of the two is to be preferred, but one of them was implemented by Ahl al-Madīnah, does the implementation of this *ḥadīth* by Ahl al-Madīnah grant preference to it or not?

According to Ibn Taymiyyah, scholars were divided into two groups on this question. The first were those who stated that the implementation of a *ḥadīth* or analogy by Ahl al-Madīnah grants preference to it. This opinion was held by Mālik and Shāfiʿī. Abū Ḥanifah, however, was of the opposite opinion. These two conflicting opinions are both found in the School of Imam Aḥmad. Ibn Taymiyyah asserts that the most determined opinion in the school is the one that is held by the majority of the scholars (i.e. Mālik and Shāfiʿī).[233]

4 Is the practice of the people of al-Madīnah during the later stage (i.e. after the assassination of 'Uthmān) a proof or not? Ibn Taymiyyah says that there are two opinions relating to this point. The first is that this practice is not deemed a proof. This is the opinion of Abū Ḥanifah, Shāfi'ī and Aḥmad.[234]

It is clear that the majority of Ḥanbalī scholars, in addition to others, do not recognise this last type of consensus. There are other scholars who claimed that such consensus is considered a proof within the Mālikī School. Nevertheless, Ibn Taymiyyah argues that this is not the case. He supports his argument as follows:

- Ibn Taymiyyah cites the leading Mālikī scholar 'Abd al-Wahhāb (d. 422/1031), who declared that this last type of consensus of Ahl al-Madīnah is not considered a proof amongst the leading Mālikī scholars. Furthermore, this scholar suspects that the opinion was created by a group of Mālikī scholars amongst the people of Maghrib, without any solid basis of evidence.
- Ibn Taymiyyah states that he could not find any indication in Mālik's words that he considered this type of consensus as a valid proof. He notes that if Mālik thought that this consensus was a proof, he would have recommended it to the people (as he did with the other sources, for example, the Qur'an and *sunnah*). The fact that he did not do so suggests that he did not think that it was a proof. On the contrary, Ibn Taymiyyah adds that when Mālik was presented with the opportunity to establish his *Muwaṭṭa* as the binding law of the state by Caliph Hārūn al-Rashīd, he refused and explained that he had only collected the knowledge of his town.[235]

It is evident from the discussions in this chapter that Ibn Taymiyyah played a notable role in the development of the general principles within the Ḥanbalī School. Part of this role was in the form of clarifications of ambiguous points and another was to correct misunderstandings of the general principles of the School. He exerted considerable effort in harmonising the principles the School had developed with what he considered to be the original principles of Aḥmad. In doing so, he wanted to rid the School of innovations and theoretical precepts introduced under the influence of groups such as the Mutazilis. He also sought to deal with certain possible ambiguities in Aḥmad's principles (such as the use of weak *ḥadīth*).

4

RECONSTRUCTION

Ibn Taymiyyah and Ḥanbalī jurisprudence

Introduction

As mentioned in Chapter 3, Ibn Taymiyyah employed a critical approach in his discussion of Ḥanbalī jurisprudence and its general principles. He found that the corpus of Ḥanbalī jurisprudence contained many rulings that were clearly based on explicit evidence, but there were many other rulings for which the source was unclear. He felt that this was due to a deficiency in the process of independent reasoning employed by the scholars who introduced these rulings into the School, or also due to a misinterpretation of the words of the Lawgiver or also of a precedent from Aḥmad. In Chapter 3, an attempt was made to show some of the corrections and clarifications made by Ibn Taymiyyah to issues concerning general principles of jurisprudence in the Ḥanbalī. This chapter contains a study and discussion of some of those corrections and clarifications made by Ibn Taymiyyah to the corpus of Ḥanbalī *fiqh*. This includes the following points within the School:

- innovation
- *ḥiyal*
- the use of precaution and piety
- incorrect opinions
- jurisprudential terminology
- jurisprudential rules
- narrations.

As the scope of these points is vast, this chapter will highlight a few examples in each area to reflect the general thrust of Ibn Taymiyyah's views and contribution to the development of the School.

Innovation in the Ḥanbalī *fiqh*

Ibn Taymiyyah was of the view that the Ḥanbalī School contained several rulings that could only be classified as *bidaʿ* (innovations). He was amongst those scholars who campaigned tirelessly against the presence of *bidaʿ* in Islamic law, in general, and in Ḥanbalī jurisprudence, in particular. He persevered in this struggle to such an extent that some of his eminent students, such as Ibn 'Abd al-Hādī and al-Bazzār, stated that one of the most important merits of their Sheikh was his effort in confronting innovation.[1]

Ibn Taymiyyah defines innovation as 'that which is not prescribed in the religion of Allah'.[2] He explains this general statement by stating that any action in Islam must be supported by evidence, either explicitly or implicitly, from the Qur'an, *sunnah* or consensus. He insists that the practice in certain places or, even the majority of them, and the opinion of certain scholars, or the majority of them, cannot be employed as evidence to justify innovation.[3] Ibn Taymiyyah traces the advent of innovation in Islam back to the assassination of 'Uthmān, for prior to this point, he believed that the Muslim community as a whole established its beliefs and practices upon two sources: textual proofs and reason that was in conformity to the texts.[4]

Ibn Taymiyyah connects the existence of innovation within Ḥanbalī *fiqh*, to various factors: First, he asserts that there is a link between innovation and the misuse of *maṣlaḥah* as a source of law. He states that many innovations were introduced as a result of some scholars and leaders considering these innovations to be *maṣāliḥ*.[5] Second, certain scholars based their rulings on what they incorrectly assumed to be a sound analogy and this meant that unsupported rulings were introduced into Islamic law.[6] Third, scholars would use the apparent meaning of a text to reach a ruling the without consulting the *sunnah* of the Prophet; Aḥmad considered this to be a matter practised by the people of innovation.[7] Fourth, Ibn Taymiyyah blames the method of writing adopted by most of the later Ḥanbalī scholars and others, who abandoned recourse to the Qur'an and *sunnah*, and instead relied on the opinions of their leaders and Imams in their treatises. As a consequence, the Qur'an and *sunnah* were judged according to whether they agreed with the words of their leaders and imams, and not vice versa.[8]

Ibn Taymiyyah occasionally blames outsiders for the deviation of some of the followers of Aḥmad, as it appears that some of the erroneous opinions in the School were wrongly attributed to the Imam or to some of his followers. These opinions were then transmitted from generation to generation as part of the School's body of law. He also indicates that some of the Imam's followers made additions to his words concerning particular points. Aḥmad's statements were also, on occasions, either misunderstood or conveyed incorrectly by some of his followers. Ibn Taymiyyah also argued that Aḥmad sometimes spoke about a specific point and his statement was then generalised by some of his followers. On some issues, according to Ibn Taymiyyah, Aḥmad's followers selected the less preferred (*marjūḥ*) of the two opinions attributed to the Imam.[9] Ibn Taymiyyah argued that imitation was partly responsible for the existence of some of these practices. Imitation and its negative consequences not only reduced the reality of the Lawgiver's sovereignty to mere theory and superstition, but also provided an escape for an individual from his responsibility to fulfil the Lawgiver's requirements.[10]

Finally, Ibn Taymiyyah also traces back the existence of particular types of innovation to the Mongol invasion. Greek philosophy and rational theology had of course been introduced to the Islamic world at a much earlier date, but the Mongol invasion, with its attendant destruction and confusion, appears to have helped it infiltrate Islamic doctrine to a greater extent. These external influences affected Ibn Taymiyyah greatly and fuelled his desire to purify Islamic society from innovations.[11]

Ibn Taymiyyah draws attention to the severity of the misdeeds committed by those learned people who legitimise some types of innovations and the public who imitate them. He asserts that a person, who pursues a matter with the belief of attaining divine nearness or by means of a word or deed renders a matter obligatory without these acts being prescribed by Allah, is guilty of claiming as religion that which Allah did not sanction. The individual who follows the innovator in this matter is guilty of ascribing a partner to Allah, a partner who authorised a religious practice for him without the sanction of Allah.[12] Nevertheless, Ibn Taymiyyah realises that a scholar may have his own interpretation to justify his ruling. The scholar will therefore be pardoned if he erred by reason of the exercise of independent reasoning. Indeed, he may even be rewarded for his efforts. This does not mean, however, that such a scholar may be imitated on this issue, as his rulings are inaccurate.[13]

Ibn Taymiyyah is an adamant opponent of certain scholars who classify innovation as good and bad. He argues that if a deed is considered good it must have the Lawgiver's implicit approval. If it appeared so, it is not acceptable to label it as a 'good' innovation; rather, it is deemed a *shar'ī* founded action.[14]

Ibn Taymiyyah himself classifies innovations that have been introduced into the *sharī'ah* into two types: innovations in statement and belief; innovations in actions and worship. An extensive knowledge of the Qur'an and *sunnah* should prevent a scholar from introducing these types of innovation.[15]

Ibn Taymiyyah also categorises innovations according to the intention of those who introduce them:

- Innovations introduced by scholars whose intention was to follow the textual legal evidences, but who misunderstood these texts in doing so.
- Innovations introduced by individuals who wanted to corrupt the *sharī'ah*.[16]

By means of a careful study of Ibn Taymiyyah's treatises, one discovers that he labels several rulings and practices in various subjects of jurisprudence as innovations. Ibn Taymiyyah notes that there is more innovation present in matters pertaining to worship than on issues of belief.[17] Ibn Taymiyyah believes that the presence of innovation in the Ḥanbalī School is far less than in the other schools. According to him, this is founded upon Aḥmad's teachings which include a detailed explanation of the *sunnah* and a severe condemnation of innovation. These principles are expressed in a more vociferous manner than in the statements of the other scholars.[18]

Here follows a study of some rulings and practices found in the Ḥanbalī *fiqh* that are considered by Ibn Taymiyyah to be innovations.

1 Ibn Taymiyyah and the ruling on the articulation of the intention for acts of worship

Scholars have agreed that the presence of correct intention is a condition for the validity of any act of worship.[19] This consensus is founded upon the *ḥadīth* of the Prophet in which he says: 'The reward for deeds is dependent upon the intention and every person will be rewarded according to what he intended.'[20] Scholars affiliated to the Ḥanbalī School, in addition to others, have disagreed on some details in relation to some acts of worship. They have differed concerning whether the intention is derived from the heart or whether it ought to be uttered upon the tongue in actions such as the performance of the prayer, the fast and *ḥajj*.[21] Certain Ḥanbalī scholars and others maintain that the intention should be uttered.[22] They state that the utterance of the intention confirms the action.[23]

Ibn Taymiyyah scrutinised this matter with reference to various acts of worship and concluded that the claim that it is recommended to utter the intention is incorrect. He labels it as an innovation.[24] Ibn Taymiyyah supports his position by citing the example of the Prophet and the rightly guided caliphs, for it has not been narrated that they uttered the intention in any act of worship.[25] For instance, an authentic *ḥadīth* mentions that the Prophet started the prayer with *al-takbīr*, that is, saying Allah *Akbar*. There is no mention of him uttering his intention to perform this action before commencing the prayer. Similarly, the Prophet is reported to have started the *ḥajj* with *al-talbiyah*, that is saying *labbayk Allahumma labbayk* and there is no narration suggesting that he uttered his intention.[26] The early scholars subscribed to the opinion that the intention should be performed silently. Ibn Taymiyyah asserts that the four Imams in addition to many other scholars were in agreement that the intention is derived from the heart.[27] He discusses the claim made by certain individuals affiliated to the Shāfiʿī School that there is an opinion in their School that the utterance of the intention for prayer is obligatory. They allege that this opinion is founded upon a statement of Shāfiʿī himself. Ibn Taymiyyah argues that this opinion is, in fact, based upon a misunderstanding of a statement by Shāfiʿī in which he says: 'The utterance is obligatory at its start, i.e. the start of prayer.' Some Shāfiʿī scholars understood this statement to mean that the utterance of the intention at the start of the prayer is obligatory. Ibn Taymiyyah, on the other hand, insists that Shāfiʿī was referring to the utterance of *takbīr* and not the utterance of the intention. The majority of scholars criticised the explanation of Shāfiʿī's statement given by some of his followers. Indeed, the majority of Shāfiʿī scholars agreed that their Imam was referring in his statement to the utterance of *takbīr*.[28] Interestingly, in seeking to show that the opinion of some Ḥanbalī scholars recommending the utterance of the intention in acts of worship is devoid of foundation, Ibn Taymiyyah makes use of the principle that a binding consensus cannot be overruled. He argues that this

Ḥanbalī opinion was issued after the scholars had reached a consensus that the intention should be preformed silently.[29]

2 *Ibn Taymiyyah and the issue of travelling to visit graves*

The act of visiting graves in Islam is a recommended action; this may be shown by consulting various *ḥadīths* of the Prophet in which he encouraged Muslims to visit cemeteries. In some of these *ḥadīths* he explains that graves are a means of reminding the Muslim of the Hereafter.[30] Therefore, we find that this action was practised amongst the early generations. In later years, the graves of righteous people were granted a special status by some people. Thus, people would set out on a journey for the sole objective of visiting these graves. This practice had become widespread by the time of Ibn Taymiyyah. As a consequence we find that he discusses this issue on numerous occasions. He issued a *fatwā* in which he stated that this was an innovated practice. It was this *fatwā* which resulted in one of the most serious periods of his detention that continued until his death in the year 728/1328.[31]

The opinion that it is permissible to undertake a journey solely in order to visit graves was held by both Ḥanbalī scholars and several leading scholars affiliated to other schools, both before and during Ibn Taymiyyah's time. Famous Ḥanbalī scholars who subscribed to this opinion included Abū Muhammad al-Maqdisī,[32] Ibn Ḥāmid and Ibn ʿAbdūs.[33] These scholars founded their opinion upon several proofs. First, the Prophet had said, 'visit graves'[34] which includes the act of travelling to visit them. Second, they cited *ḥadīths* in which the Prophet is reported to have encouraged people to visit his grave. Furthermore, in some of these *ḥadīths* he specified Paradise as being the reward for this deed. Abū Muhammad al-Maqdisī also pointed out that the Prophet would visit the Qubā' Mosque. He also commented upon the intended meaning of the Prophetic tradition in which he says, 'Do not travel except to three mosques, the Ḥaram mosque, the mosque of the Prophet and al-Aqṣā mosque.'[35] He claimed that although it is not recommended to travel on a journey for the purpose of worship except to these three places, this does not mean that it is impermissible.[36]

Ibn Taymiyyah criticises and refutes this opinion in various ways:

- He explains that this opinion opposes the aforementioned *ḥadīth* of the Prophet in which he states, 'Do not travel except to three mosques...' It is clear that this *ḥadīth* negates the validity of this act. There is nothing to suggest that it is merely disapproved of rather than prohibited. Therefore, this action is not permitted at all.[37]
- He asserts that all of the *ḥadīths* cited by his opponents in support of visiting graves are either unauthentic or fabricated. According to Ibn Taymiyyah, the people of innovation (*bidʿa*) who first endorsed this practice were responsible for fabricating these *ḥadīths*. Thereafter, some scholars of jurisprudence who possessed little knowledge of the science of *ḥadīth* cited them.[38]

- Ibn Taymiyyah argues that this practice was neither founded upon authentic *ḥadīth* nor was it known amongst the Prophet's companions and their followers. Similarly, it was not considered by any of the Imams to be a recommended deed. Therefore, whosoever performs this action as a *sharʿī* deed will be considered as practising an action that is contrary to the texts and the consensus of the Imams.[39] Ibn Taymiyyah argues in his book, *al-Jawāb al-Bāhir*, that whoever disagrees with this fact will be founding his opinions upon mere speculation and he challenges his opponents to cite any recognised source from any of the Imams to vindicate their position.[40]
- With reference to the evidence cited by Abū Muhammad al-Maqdisī, Ibn Taymiyyah presents the following criticism:
  - Abū Muhammad was not correct in citing the proof that the Prophet used to visit the Qubā' Mosque, for it is not necessary to saddle one's camel in order to reach Qubā' from Madīnah.[41] In other words, this could not be considered a journey.
  - He rebuts the claim of Abū Muhammad that the *ḥadīth* 'Do not travel except to three mosques' renders this act as not recommended but does not make it impermissible. Ibn Taymiyyah criticised Abū Muhammad in two ways:
    i Abū Muhammad's explanation of this *ḥadīth* implies that the act of travelling to visit graves is not a valid deed, whereas it is known that all those who travel to visit graves intend by it, and believe it to be, a good deed.
    ii A principle in *uṣūl al-fiqh* dictates that a text forbidding a deed results in its invalidity, unless there are other proof to lessen the degree of prohibition. According to Ibn Taymiyyah, this cannot be opposed by the *ḥadīths* cited by his opponents, because they are not authentic, as has been mentioned previously.[42]

Ibn Taymiyyah's *fatwā* was received with great opposition by some of his contemporaries. This was particularly so because his *fatwā* appears to include the act of undertaking a journey in order to visit the grave of the Prophet. He argues, however, that the *ḥadīths* cited by his opponents in favour of travelling for the purpose of visiting the grave of the Prophet are incorrect.[43]

Ibn Taymiyyah asserts that his opinion on the issue of travelling to visit graves was in fact the stance of all the earlier Ḥanbalī scholars in addition to others. It was only later that a disagreement developed on this point. Their disagreement concerned whether the act of undertaking a journey in order to visit graves was prohibited or not; none of them, however, considered it to be recommended.[44]

Ibn Taymiyyah's discourse with his opponents concerning this issue took the typical form of jurisprudential discussions. It appears Ibn Taymiyyah felt that there was a hidden motive behind the solid opposition to his opinion and he asserts that his words were twisted in several ways. He believed that the learned scholars did not regard his *fatwā* as being incorrect.[45] This belief is strengthened by the fact that his *fatwā* was issued seventeen years before the accusation in relation to this point was raised against him.[46]

3 Ibn Taymiyyah and the issue of increasing the rent in a hire contract

Certain Ḥanbalī scholars claim that it is permissible to increase the rent in a contract of hire before the time of its expiry, provided that the additional payment is less than a third of the original payment specified in the contract.[47]

Ibn Taymiyyah rebuts this opinion by stating that it is an innovation that was not known amongst any of the Imams of the Schools of law and that contradicted the consensus of the scholars.[48] According to Ibn Taymiyyah, the correct ruling in relation to this issue is that the owner has no right either to increase the original rent or to ask the hirer to return the hired object until the expiry date of the contract.[49]

Ibn Taymiyyah's opinion appears to be in agreement with a Ḥanbalī jurisprudential rule, which states that the owner of property has no right of disposal over it until the expiration of the lease period.[50] In addition, Ḥanbalī scholars have explained that if a tenant rents property for a specific period of time and thereafter vacates it before the expiry date of the hire contract, the tenant will be asked to pay the rent for the entire duration of the agreed term, as he is bound by the terms of the original contract.[51] Similarly, where the owner of the hired object increases the rent before the end of the contract, his action will be deemed invalid and the previous terms will remain legally binding.

Ḥiyal in Ḥanbalī *fiqh*

Ḥiyal (sing. *ḥīlah*) can be understood as the use of technical devices to circumvent prohibitions and obligations under the *sharīʿah*. Certain Ḥanbalī scholars, in addition to scholars from other schools, issued *fatāwā* and wrote treatises in which they affirmed the validity of particular types of *ḥiyal*. It is evident that the use of some of these *ḥiyal* was widespread amongst laymen and even amongst some scholars during Ibn Taymiyyah's time. Hence, we note that he devotes great attention to this problem and opposes it strongly.[52]

In this section, we will analyse Ibn Taymiyyah's position towards *ḥiyal* in Islamic law in general. This will also clarify his opinion concerning the legitimate use of *ḥiyal* as a *sharʿī* means by Ḥanbalī scholars. There then follows a case study of *ḥiyal* used by some Ḥanbalī scholars.

Ibn Taymiyyah defines *ḥiyal* as 'the means through which the legitimisation of prohibited acts or the invalidation of obligatory duties can be attained'.[53] He traces the emergence of the practice of certain *ḥiyal*, and the *fatāwā* validating them to the first century of Islam when the practice arose among a group of uninformed people. These people were severely criticised by the companions.

Ibn Taymiyyah says that the companions of the Prophet did not approve of any type of *ḥiyal*. On the contrary, whenever they were questioned about some of these *ḥiyal*, they would criticise them. Ibn Taymiyyah refers to the sources of *ḥadīth* and *athar* and mentions that they contain no *fatwā* from a companion validating the practice of *ḥiyal*. He discovers that the first *fatāwā* validating *ḥiyal* appeared during the era of the late followers (*sighār al-tābiʿīn*), a period after the first century of Islam.[54] The leading scholars of the time disapproved of these *fatāwā*.[55] Later on, however, the use of *ḥiyal* evolved and several scholars from different schools became involved in the act of issuing *fatāwā* and writing treatises in which they validated several types of *ḥiyal*.[56]

According to Ibn Taymiyyah, the use of *ḥiyal* is generally linked to certain scholars affiliated to Ahl al-Ra'y.[57] Nevertheless, the early scholars of this school criticised the use of *ḥiyal*.[58] He mentions that the *fatāwā* in this school supporting *ḥiyal* dated back to the generation of the teachers of Imam Aḥmad. Ibn Taymiyyah quotes Bishr al-Surī, one of his teachers, as saying that he had considered the knowledge during that time and determined that the method of learning was the proper and common method of Ahl al-Ḥadīth and the method of Ahl al-Ra'y. He commented upon the salient features of these two schools and mentioned that the use of *ḥiyal* was one of the characteristics of the school of Ahl al-Ra'y.[59]

Ibn Taymiyyah observes that even some of the followers of Ibn Ḥanbal were involved in this practice, regardless of the fact that their Imam was known for his severe opposition to it and is reported to have said: 'None of the *ḥiyal* are permissible.'[60]

Ibn Taymiyyah states that it is not possible to attribute the permission for *ḥiyal* to any of the Imams; to do so would be to censure them. Even if it has been narrated for one of them that he permitted a *ḥīlah*, the prohibition for which is agreed upon amongst the scholars, it means that either this narration is unauthentic or the narrator did not understand the Imam's objective in issuing the *fatwā*. In the event that the narration is sound, Ibn Taymiyyah insists that such *fatāwā* should still not be attributed to the Imams.[61] He explains that his position is based upon the premise that all of the Imams declared that if any of their views were in opposition to the correct opinion, the correct view ought to be followed and their views must be cast against the wall.[62]

It is interesting to note that Ibn Taymiyyah also finds the root for some of the *fatāwā* issued by the followers of the Imams in theological and not jurisprudential factors. There were certain adherents who affiliated themselves to an Imam in jurisprudential ramifications while at the same time disagreeing with them on theological issues. He presents the example of a group of Abū Ḥanifah's followers who were affiliated to the Muʿtazilites but nevertheless adopted Ḥanafī jurisprudence.[63]

Ibn Taymiyyah accepts that disputes concerning *al-furūʿ* are tolerated and that people are entitled to follow one Imam or another in these matters of disagreement, but he does not believe it is permissible for a person to resort to one of these *ḥiyal* by their act of following those scholars who declared them to be permissible. This is because Ibn Taymiyyah believes that the prohibition of *ḥiyal* is definite and not an issue of *ijtihād*.[64] He explains that the prohibition of *ḥiyal* can be located in the Qur'an, the *sunnah* and the consensus of the companions, in addition to other sources. In support, he mentions several verses from the Qur'an, one of which is verse 142 of *Surah al-Nisā'* in which Allah says: 'Verily, the hypocrites seek to deceive Allah, but it is He Who deceives them.' The argument Ibn Taymiyyah deduces from this verse may be summarised as follows: The action of deceiving Allah is prohibited, and *ḥiyal* is a form of deception; therefore, *ḥiyal* must be prohibited.[65]

Ibn Taymiyyah also cites verse 231 of *Surah al-Baqarah* in which Allah says: 'And treat not the Verses (Laws) of Allah as jest.' Ibn Taymiyyah explains his argument by stating that this verse comes after rulings for various issues, including divorce, marriage, saving the marriage and retracting a divorce. According to Ibn Taymiyyah, if this verse is read within context, it implies that any one who pronounces the relevant formulas in these situations without sincerely intending them would be mocking these rulings, and this verse prohibits ridiculing the rulings of Allah.[66]

Ibn Taymiyyah also mentions certain *ḥadīths* in support of his stance. He cites a *ḥadīth* (mentioned earlier), which he describes as primary evidence for the prohibition of *ḥiyal*, narrated by al-Bukhārī in which the Prophet states, 'The reward for deeds is dependent upon the intention and every person will be rewarded according to what he has intended.'[67]

The third category of evidence cited by Ibn Taymiyyah is the consensus of the companions. This occurred when some of the companions disapproved of certain *ḥiyal* and the remainder of the companions kept silent. In addition, it was common knowledge that they disapproved of the *ḥiyal* that were in existence during their time. It is evident that this type of consensus is a tacit consensus and not an explicit consensus.[68]

Furthermore, Ibn Taymiyyah refers to the juristic principle that intentions must be considered when judging actions, customs and acts of worship. The principle states that the validity of the intention determines the validity of the action. The conclusion sought by Ibn Taymiyyah through this process of logical deduction is that the intention in *ḥiyal* is invalid because the objective of any *ḥiyal* is to avoid the legal ruling. Therefore, the *ḥiyal* is also invalid.[69]

Ibn Taymiyyah also states that permitting *ḥiyal* contradicts the concept of *sadd al-dharā'i'* (blocking the means) because whereas the Lawgiver seals all the paths towards a prohibited act, the people supporting *ḥiyal* endeavour to obtain it by any possible means.[70]

Ibn Taymiyyah employs further logical arguments in support of his position. For example, he refers to *ḥiyal* as being a form of deceit, deceit is prohibited and therefore *ḥiyal* must be prohibited too.[71] Similarly, if it is prohibited for one person to deceive another, it must also be the case that an attempt to deceive the Creator by avoiding *shar'ī* rulings is prohibited.[72]

Let us consider the position of Ibn Taymiyyah on the contract of *nikāḥ al-taḥlīl* as an example of *ḥiyal* legitimised by some Ḥanbalī scholars.

Nikāḥ al-taḥlīl is a type of marriage performed by a person for the purpose of legitimising the remarriage of a man to his former wife, from whom she has been divorced thrice and thus irrevocably divorced.[73] Ibn Taymiyyah explains that this type of marriage can occur in various ways including the following:

- The *muḥallil* (the man who marries the divorcee) demonstrates that his intention in entering into a marriage contract is to legitimise the remarriage of the first husband and his ex-wife. This form of marriage is invalid.[74]
- The *muḥallil* conceals the truth that his intention in entering into this contract is to legitimise the remarriage of the divorced woman to her ex-husband. When this occurs there appears to be some confusion within the Ḥanbalī School. Although the early narration from Aḥmad prohibits this type of marriage, we find that certain Ḥanbalī scholars claimed the existence of two views (*wajhayn*) on this issue. Others claimed the existence of two narrations from Aḥmad: the first states that the contract is valid and the second states that it is invalid.[75]

Ibn Taymiyyah clarifies that the view of Aḥmad and the early Ḥanbalī scholars are that this form of contract is invalid. This is also the opinion of some of the later Ḥanbalī scholars such as Abū Ya'la in his late treatises, Abū 'l-Mawāhib and Ibn 'Aqīl (in his book *al-Tadhkirah*).[76] Another opinion attributed to Aḥmad states that despite this contract being valid, it is reprehensible.[77] This opinion is attributed to Ibn Ḥanbal as a *riwāyah* by some Ḥanbalī scholars such as al-Sharīf Abū Ja'far and Abū 'l-Khaṭṭāb, and is attributed to him as a *wajh* by other Ḥanbalī scholars such as Abū Ya'la in *al-Mujarrad* and Ibn 'Aqīl in *al-Fuṣūl*.[78] In addition, Ibn Taymiyyah states that this last opinion is the only *riwāyah* mentioned by Ibn al-Bannā.[79]

According to Ibn Taymiyyah, this last opinion within the Ḥanbalī School is based upon a narration from Aḥmad by his student Ḥarb (d. 280/893). In this statement Aḥmad is reported to have expressed his reprehension for this type of contract.[80] This extreme dislike is understood by some Ḥanbalī scholars to be equivalent to prohibition, whereas others understood it to be merely encouraging people to abstain from performing this act.[81]

Ibn Taymiyyah criticises the opinion that this type of contract is reprehensible and explains that Ḥarb's narration cannot be used as an evidence because the subject-matter of Ḥarb's narration is not *nikāḥ al-muḥallil*. He had in fact questioned Aḥmad concerning the ruling on a man who marries a woman whom he intends to divorce after a period of time. Therefore, Aḥmad's answer cannot be applied to the issue of *nikāḥ al-muḥallil*. Moreover, when answering the same question on another occasion, asked this time by 'Abd Allah b. Aḥmad, Ibn Ḥanbal declared this marriage to be reprehensible and that it is considered to be *mut'ah* (a temporary marriage whose limit is stated in the contract).[82]

Ibn Taymiyyah illustrates that if Aḥmad considers this type of contract to be *mut'ah*, then an analogous to the ruling on *mut'ah* must be applied to it. It is common knowledge that the contract of *mut'ah* is prohibited according to the opinion of the majority of the companions (excluding Ibn 'Abbās and some of his students) and all the jurists affiliated to the various schools of law. Therefore, Ibn Ḥanbal's declaration of reprehensibility must only be understood as a prohibition. Ibn Taymiyyah does affirm the presence of another narration on the same question, posed by Ibn Ḥanbal's disciple, Abū Dawūd. In this instance, Aḥmad is reported to have said that he reprehended this contract and that it is similar to the contract of *mut'ah*.[83]

Ibn Taymiyyah notes that this last narration may provide another explanation for the disagreement within the Ḥanbalī School concerning this contract. This is because Ibn Ḥanbal is reported in this narration to have said that this contract is similar to the contract of *mut'ah*, but not necessarily that it is identical to *mut'ah*.[84]

Ibn Taymiyyah's opponents cited other proofs in support of the permissibility of this type of contract. One is a *ḥadīth* attributed to the Prophet and reported by an unnamed companion. The narrator mentions that at the time of the Prophet a man married a woman, but the companions thought that he had not married her except in order for her to return to her ex-husband. When the news of this matter reached the Prophet, he asked 'Did he call witnesses?' They replied, 'Yes.' He asked if he had paid the dower and they replied, 'Yes.' Finally, he asked if sexual intercourse had taken place and they replied, 'Yes.' Thereafter, the Prophet said, 'The deceit has gone' (i.e. there is no *ḥīlah* in this contract and it is therefore valid).[85]

Ibn Taymiyyah objects to the citation of this *ḥadīth* by claiming that the tradition is void (*bāṭil*). He claims that one of the narrators of this *ḥadīth* is Mūsā b. Muṭayr,[86] who is described as *matrūk*, which can be literally translated as "abandoned". He was also described as *sāqiṭ*, which can be translated literally as 'falling' He was known for attributing unknown narrations to the renowned scholars of *ḥadīth*. Ibn Taymiyyah states that none of his narrations can be accepted.[87]

In support of his opinion, Ibn Taymiyyah quotes the opinions of several scholars of *ḥadīth* and *rijāl* who condemned Mūsā b. Muṭayr's narration. He quotes Ibn Ma'īn who describes this narrator as a liar[88] and Abū Ḥātim al-Rāzī who considers his *ḥadīth* as 'abandoned' and '*dhāhib*'.[89] He cites Abū Zur'ah who states that his *ḥadīth* is 'abandoned'[90] and 'Abd al-Raḥmān b. al-Ḥakam who declares that the people (i.e. of *ḥadīth*) abandoned his *ḥadīth*.[91] Ibn Taymiyyah also criticises an unnamed author who he describes as reckless for describing this narrator as reliable (*thiqah*).[92]

It is important to note that this disagreement concerns the situation where the *muḥallil* intends *taḥlīl* and does not disclose his intention. According to Ibn Taymiyyah, if the *muḥallil* (the new husband) and the *muḥallal lahu* (the former husband) agree upon the intention of *taḥlīl* before the contract, it is regarded as invalid by the majority of Ḥanbalī scholars.[93]

Furthermore, if this intention is expressed in the contract, it becomes invalidated by the vast majority of Ḥanbalī scholars,[94] although Abū Ya'la (in *al-Khilāf*) and Abū'l-Khaṭṭāb derived (*kharraja*) another opinion, from Ibn Ḥanbal's words. They made the express provision void but declared the remainder of contract valid.[95] Some Ḥanbalī scholars adopt this view in all cases.[96] Ibn Taymiyyah, however, considers this view to be wholly fallacious. He argues that it is not appropriate to describe this derivation (*takhrīj*) as an opinion of Imam Aḥmad.[97] He also points out that even those individuals who validate this type of contract regard it as reprehensible.[98]

The use of precaution (*iḥtiyāṭ*) and piety (*wara'*) in Ḥanbalī jurisprudence

From a review of treatises on *fiqh*, it will be seen that scholars sometimes express a preference for carrying out an action or refraining from one beyond the strict requirements of a text. The intention of the scholar is to ensure that, in the event of some doubts as to whether a ruling exists, the Muslim does not inadvertently fail to observe the law.

Although many scholars, including Ḥanbalīs, have made use of the concept of precaution, ambiguity continues to surround various aspects of it, such as the limitation on its use and its status in Islamic law. This section contains a study of these points from Ibn Taymiyyah's perspective and some practical examples illustrating Ibn Taymiyyah's role in Ḥanbalī jurisprudence.

We do not find Ibn Taymiyyah offering a definition of the term precaution in his treatises, but his student Ibn al-Qayyim defines it as 'an individual doing his best to follow the *shar'ī* rulings without exaggeration and extravagance nor omission'.[99]

Ibn Taymiyyah has made several references in his treatises to the status of precaution. Ibn Taymiyyah argues that all of the principles of the *sharī'ah* are indicative of the fact that precaution is neither obligatory nor prohibited.[100] In a different place, he explains that it can only be described as permissible.[101] According to Ibn Taymiyyah, this permissibility is confined to instances where the texts are not explicit in their rulings.[102] Ibn Taymiyyah asserts that if the permissibility of practicing precaution is not restricted to such grey areas in the texts, the criteria governing the implementation of precaution will be unclear and imprecise.[103]

Ibn Taymiyyah states that those scholars who arrived at opinions that are not in agreement with the texts are excused if these texts seemed ambiguous to them. As for those scholars for whom the implication of the texts was clear, they are not allowed to follow the opinions of the first group as a precautionary measure, because this is not within the proper scope of precaution.[104] In certain instances the Lawgiver has conveyed two methods for performing one deed. Examples are the mode of *adhān* (call to prayer), *ṣalāt al-khawf* (prayers under threat of attack) and *istiftāḥ* (post-*takbīr* words in the prayer). According to Ibn Taymiyyah, the correct position in such circumstances is that the individual should perform the action according to one form on one occasion and an alternative form on another. They should not apply precaution to the performance of this type of deed, as there is no scope for precaution where the texts are clear on an issue.[105] Despite the presence of a disagreement amongst the Ḥanbalī scholars in relation to the ruling concerning these issues, Ibn Taymiyyah asserts that the stance of Aḥmad with regard to these issues is comparable to his own deductions.[106]

In practice, there are several issues where Ḥanbalī scholars and others applied precaution to their rulings. It appears that this was due to the existence of disputes amongst the scholars on the rulings on these issues; therefore, the scholars applied precaution in order to err on the side of caution. Ibn Taymiyyah comments that precaution cannot be applied to issues merely because of the existence of differences of opinion. It is only permissible to exercise precaution in areas of dispute when we are unaware of the textual evidences pertinent to the issue.[107]

Scholars have explained that the objective in using precaution is to avoid committing a prohibited or disliked deed. Ibn Taymiyyah acknowledges this, but argues that there are exceptions to this general ruling. For instance, whenever a disliked action in the *sharī'ah* becomes necessary, it becomes obligatory to perform it and the reprehensibility disappears.[108] Similarly, if an action is prohibited in the *sharī'ah* as a way of blocking the means to another prohibited act, it can be permitted when a preponderant benefit exists.[109]

Ibn Taymiyyah's understanding of and approach towards precaution comes out clearly from his writings on Islamic law in general and the Ḥanbalī School in particular. For example, in certain jurisprudential issues, he states that al-Shāfi'ī exercised precaution in obligation, prohibition and permissibility to such an extent that it resulted in severe hardship on the part of the individual concerned (*al-mukallaf*).[110] Ibn Taymiyyah sometimes supports the use of precaution by Ḥanbalī School,[111] but in other cases he disagrees with its use. For instance, Ḥanbalī scholars have differed on the ruling when there are factors (e.g. clouds) that conceal the ability to sight the first appearance of the new moon after the setting of the sun on the twenty-ninth day of *Sha'bān*. A group of these scholars subscribe to the opinion that fasting in these circumstances is obligatory.[112] This opinion is based upon the use of precaution, as the next day could mark the first day of *Ramaḍān*. Other Ḥanbalī scholars hold the opinion that fasting on this day is forbidden, based on the *ḥadīth*, indicating that the commencement of *Ramaḍān* only occurs after the sighting of the new moon. Furthermore, they argue that an obligation cannot be based upon doubt.[113]

Ibn Taymiyyah takes a third position. He feels that most of Ibn Ḥanbal's words indicate that fasting on this day is neither obligatory nor prohibited, but rather that it is recommended. This is derived from a series of narrations from companions such as 'Umar, 'Ali and Mu'āwiyah, in which they were cited as fasting on that day.[114]

This case is an example of Ibn Taymiyyah's implementation of his aforementioned understanding of precaution. He sees no room for it in various situations. He does not accept that fasting on this day is obligatory, although this opinion is attributed to Aḥmad in one of two narrations and is the view held by the greater portion of later Ḥanbalī scholars (who claimed that it was also the position of the majority of earlier Ḥanbalī scholars).[115] Ibn Taymiyyah's rejection of this opinion is based upon several points, including the principle that precaution cannot be made obligatory. He states: 'Indeed, the doubtful and uncertain cannot be made obligatory nor prohibited, but can be made recommended. This is because the principles of the *sharī'ah* do not forbid precaution and yet do not render an act obligatory merely because of the presence of doubt.'[116]

One area in which Ḥanbalī scholars have extensively employed the concept of precaution is purification (e.g. ritual ablution). This has resulted in a significant degree of hardship upon individuals following this School. This difficultly did not go unnoticed by Ibn Taymiyyah. He states that applying precaution to water used in purification because of mere doubt about its ruling is impermissible in Islamic law. He asserts that all types of water are originally pure by themselves and cannot be claimed to be impure without evidence of impurity.[117]

The concept of precaution was well known within the Ḥanbalī School of law, particularly in matters pertaining to '*Ibādāt* (worship). Similarly, this School was described as the School of *wara'* (piety) in relation to worldly affairs, especially in issues of *mu'āmalāt* (transactions). In several Ḥanbalī sources there are narrations that Ibn Ḥanbal or other Ḥanbalī scholars practised or approved of certain types of *wara'*.[118] During the time of Ibn Taymiyyah, a statement was circulated amongst laymen and was even subscribed to by some scholars, to the effect that to consume the lawful was now an impossibility (*muta'dhdhr*). Those who propagated this claim supported their assertion with both textual and rational evidence. The core argument was that lawful and unlawful gains had become so mixed that they could no longer be distinguished from one another.[119]

Ibn Taymiyyah was presented with this statement and asked to respond to it. He began by tracing the origin of the statement. He explained that the statement was present during the time of the Imams, who agreed that whoever raised this claim was mistaken. Ibn Taymiyyah acknowledges that a similar claim circulated amongst the people of innovation, unqualified jurists and corrupted sections of the ascetics (Ahl al-Nusuk). This claim was received with strong disapproval by the Imams. Ibn Taymiyyah adds, that even Aḥmad, who was known for his exemplary piety, disapproved of this statement. In later years, serious deductions were made from this statement. Ibn Taymiyyah explains that this statement caused some scholars to go so far as to claim that certain *ḥudūd* punishments, such as the punishment for theft, could no longer be carried out because of the presence of doubt (*shubhah*), that is, the doubt occasioned by the mixing of lawful and unlawful money. According to Islamic justice, a *ḥadd* punishment is waived in cases of doubt.[120]

Ibn Taymiyyah notes that this argument was conveyed to some jurists who authored works on the subject of jurisprudence. These individuals consisted of two parties: those who subscribed to the opinion that the individual concerned must not consume in excess of what is necessary, and those who acknowledged the resultant hardship of this statement and therefore ignored the need to practice *wara'* (piety).[121]

According to Ibn Taymiyyah, some individuals derive their position of piety from narrations approving the use of this concept. Ibn Taymiyyah asserts that some of these narrations are either fabricated or misunderstood.[122]

Ibn Taymiyyah acknowledges that piety is one of the foundations of the religion (*qawāʿid al-dīn*). He supports this statement by several *ḥadīths*, including the authentic *ḥadīth* in which the Prophet says: 'what is lawful is evident and what is unlawful is evident, and in between them are things of a doubtful nature, which many people do not know. So he who guards against doubtful things keeps his religion and honour blameless, and he who indulges in a doubtful thing indulges in unlawful things'[123]

Ibn Taymiyyah explains, however, that *waraʿ*, which is defined by him as the avoidance of or refraining from doing something,[124] can be divided into two types. The first is the obligatory *waraʿ* which he defines as abstaining from whatever that would lead to the Lawgiver's censure and punishment. This type, according to Ibn Taymiyyah, includes doing the obligatory and refraining from committing the prohibited.[125] The second type of *waraʿ* is the recommended, which he defines as 'abstaining from whatever is feared to lead to the Lawgiver's censure and punishment without the existence of a contradicting preponderant benefit or injury that leads otherwise.' In this last category, according to Ibn Taymiyyah, are included deeds that have some similarity to either expressly obligatory or prohibited deeds in Islamic law.[126]

Ibn Taymiyyah clarifies what he means by 'the existence of a contradicting preponderant benefit or injury that leads otherwise', by stating that if there is a conflict between the practice of or the abstention from a deed that has some similarity to other obligatory or prohibited deeds, then the one that secures more benefits and that leads to lesser injury must be upheld.[127]

Ibn Taymiyyah asserts that whenever there is no doubt about the permissibility of something then abstaining from it is not correct *waraʿ* and whenever there is no doubt that an action is not ordered by the Lawgiver then doing it is not in fact correct *waraʿ*.[128]

In order to determine the correct understanding, implementation and implications of this concept, Ibn Taymiyyah suggests that the following principles must be taken into consideration:

- Not every matter considered by a jurist to be unlawful is prohibited. This is because prohibition is established by the Qur'an, *sunnah*, consensus or analogy. Therefore, whenever a disagreement occurs between scholars concerning whether a particular matter is prohibited or lawful, a decisive criterion will be the above-mentioned evidence.[129] Ibn Taymiyyah is of the view that part of the problem is that certain people have received *fatāwā* from certain scholars and then attempted to impose what they assumed to be the correct rulings upon all Muslims.[130]
- If a Muslim engages in certain types of transactions, which he considers to be lawful, it is permissible for other Muslims who do not agree with the permissibility of these transactions to engage in business with him. His fellow Muslims should accept the money that he made in his trade in disputed issues, even though they do not approve of their permissibility.[131]

- The mixing of prohibited substances with lawful ones is of two types:

  1. Matters prohibited due to their attributes, such as *maytah* (an animal not slaughtered in accordance with the *sharʿī* requirements), blood and pig. If this type is mixed with other lawful substances such as food or water, and this act of mixing results in a change in the lawful substance's taste, colour or smell, then the latter will be prohibited. If no change occurs, the scholars differ on whether or not the lawful substance becomes unlawful.[132]
  2. Matters prohibited due to the manner in which they were acquired, but which are in essence lawful, such as money taken by force or illegally. If this money is combined with money acquired legally, this process of mixing will not render the latter prohibited. Therefore, if a person usurped money and mixed it with his legally acquired money, the total sum of money would not be considered prohibited gain. Only the usurped part would be deemed prohibited gain. Therefore, the person whose money was usurped can take his money from the total sum of the usurper's money.[133]

  It is evident that Ibn Taymiyyah's intended objective from this point is to demonstrate the invalidity of the premise that whenever unlawfully acquired money is mixed with lawfully gained money, it becomes prohibited to transact with the whole sum of money.

- According to Islamic law, the unknown is almost equal to the non-existent; various rulings are founded upon this principle. For instance, when a valuable article is found and its owner is unknown, the finder is obliged to advertise the matter for the duration of a year. If, after this period elapses, no one has claimed the article, the finder can pursue one of two courses: he can either take possession of the item himself or donate it as a charitable gift. In either circumstance, if the owner of the valuable appears, the finder will be responsible for paying compensation to him. Another example of a ruling based upon this principle is that if a person dies leaving an estate in the absence of a known heir, this estate may be disposed off in a manner beneficial to the community. If an heir of the deceased appears later on, he will be compensated accordingly.[134]

In elucidating these principles, Ibn Taymiyyah intends to remove much of the hardship resulting from the incorrect application of precaution. For example, those who agree that no wealth or food is permissible, because there is doubt about the seller's actions or earnings, have no sound basis for their position.

Incorrect (*ghalaṭ*) rulings in Ḥanbalī *fiqh*

As mentioned previously, Ibn Taymiyyah started his jurisprudential career within the Ḥanbalī School. In later years, he familiarised himself with the other schools of law too. During this later stage, he developed a new approach to his study of *fiqh*, both Ḥanbalī and otherwise. It was a significantly more critical approach, in which he studied, analysed and compared the various opinions of the School. Ibn Taymiyyah's adoption of this new critical method of study resulted in several benefits for later scholars and students. Among his most important legacies is his analysis of a large number of weak opinions within the Ḥanbalī School. He expended his best efforts in detecting and attempting to rectify these opinions. This section is devoted to elucidating several issues pertaining to this subject. To begin, we shall clarify the most important causes for the existence of these opinions within this school from Ibn Taymiyyah's perspective. Thereafter, we shall examine some of the particular rulings that Ibn Taymiyyah considered to be incorrect. We shall concentrate only on a few examples, as the study of all of these issues is certainly beyond the scope of this work.

Ibn Taymiyyah occasionally specifies the reasons for the existence of these opinions and occasionally these reasons are implied in his discussions. He explains that the process of transmitting the opinions of the Imam or the School is practised by scholars in two ways. First, scholars transmit what they hear or observe from the Imam of the School or his School and obviously attribute this statement or action to him or to his School as appropriate. Second, scholars occasionally attribute opinions to an Imam or to his School because they assume these opinions to be in conformity with the general principles of the Imam or the School, without actually having heard the opinion. According to Ibn Taymiyyah, this second method has resulted in serious mistakes, because scholars have attributed various opinions to the Imams and their schools based upon their own inferences opinions have thus been ascribed to the Imam or School.[135] This is one of the main reasons why the sources of the Ḥanbalī School contain a large number of conflicting narrations and opinions attributed to Imam Aḥmad,[136] resulting in great confusion within the School. Ibn Taymiyyah determined that there are several instances where certain Ḥanbalī scholars have incorrectly attributed narrations and opinions to the Imam; this is one of the main causes behind the presence of dubious opinions in the School.

Ibn Taymiyyah laments that certain authors also zealously quote their Imam's opinion, regardless of what the Book of Allah and the *sunnah* of the Messenger dictate on these issues. It is clearly evident from this practice that these scholars place the statements of their Imams above the source texts in authority.[137] Ibn Taymiyyah mentions that another reason for conflicting and weak opinions is that scholars wrote some of their treatises at an early stage of their scholarly life, but later on wrote other treatises in which they retreated or revised their earlier views. Other scholars, however, cited the earlier treatises as representing the view of the school.

Ibn Taymiyyah also explains why particular treatises often contain more weak opinions attributed to the School than others, authored by the same scholar. For example, there are several opinions wrongly attributed to Aḥmad by al-Qāḍī Abū Ya'la. Ibn Taymiyyah states that Abū Ya'la authored some of his works, such as *al-Muḥarrar*, by founding them upon a treatise from another school. He would consider the issues mentioned in these sources and then mention the views of Aḥmad and his companions concerning them. Occasionally, he would formulate his own ruling upon the general principles of the School. Ibn Taymiyyah argues, however, that Abū Ya'la was often incapable of determining the correct opinion of the School. His views, including the weak ones, were later attributed to the School because he was one of its leading exponents. In addition, in later years some of his eminent students and leading scholars of the School, such as Ibn 'Aqīl, followed his opinions and conveyed them in their jurisprudential treatises.[138]

It appears that some Ḥanbalī scholars delivered rulings concerning particular issues and other scholars then applied these rulings to other issues, which they believed were similar to the original issues. In fact, there was a dissimilarity between the two issues. This resulted in confusion and mistakes in several issues within the Ḥanbalī School.[139] Ibn Taymiyyah provides several more factors for the existence of weak or conflicting opinions: certain views are claimed to be the opinions of Aḥmad, when they are in fact the views of some of the Ḥanbalīs.[140] Some Ḥanbalī scholars based certain rulings on statements by Aḥmad where in fact there are more statements by him in opposition to these opinions.[141] Other rulings are based on old opinions of Aḥmad, which he subsequently abandoned due to a change in his independent reasoning.[142]

In several cases two conflicting narrations have been related to Aḥmad by his followers. In closer analysis, Ibn Taymiyyah discovered that Aḥmad actually differentiated between the two situations. His followers were therefore mistaken in assuming that the two narrations were two different opinions of Aḥmad for one situation.[143] Sometimes, conflicting opinions attributed to either the School or its Imam were in reality the product of later stage in the Ḥanbalī School, as Ibn Taymiyyah asserts.[144] These, in summary, are the main factors that can be described as historical. Ibn Taymiyyah also claims that there are other errors, which arose from defective reasoning. Certain incorrect opinions were based upon a misunderstanding of the terminology used in particular *ḥadīths*.[145] On other occasions scholars had misunderstood Aḥmad's reference to source texts. For instance, Aḥmad may have referred to a specific text by mentioning only a portion of it, but this portion may in turn refer to more than one text. Some of these texts may be weak or fabricated. Thereafter, some of the Ḥanbalī scholars assumed that Aḥmad preferred one of these types of *ḥadīths* over an authentic *ḥadīth* on the same issue.[146]

Ibn Taymiyyah also states that incorrect rulings arose when Ibn Ḥanbal based them on *ḥadīth* that he incorrectly deemed to be correct. According to Ibn Taymiyyah, these *ḥadīths* were inauthentic because of particular types of defects in them of which Ibn Ḥanbal had no knowledge.[147] This, unlike the other factors, has less to do with procedure and interpretation by the scholars of the School and is in fact simply a criticism by Ibn Taymiyyah of some of Ibn Ḥanbal's *ḥadīth* analysis.

The existence of conflicting and incorrect opinions within the School in certain issues where there is no *naṣṣ* emanating from the Imam, resulted in the Ḥanbalī scholars getting divided into two parties.[148]

In most instances where there are two or more opinions derived from Aḥmad mentioned in certain Ḥanbalī sources, such as *al-Kāfi* and *al-Muqni'* by Ibn Qudāmah, *al-Muḥarrar* by al-Majd and *al-Ri'āyah* by Ibn Ḥamdān, there is a certain degree of ambiguity as to which is the correct opinion. It would appear that Ibn Taymiyyah was aware of this and we therefore observe him clarifying the means by which the correct opinion of the School can be ascertained. He believes that this can be attained by consulting certain other Ḥanbalī sources, for instance *al-Ta'līq* by Abū Ya'la, *al-Intiṣār* by Abū 'l-Khaṭṭāb and *'Umad al-Adillah* by Ibn 'Aqīl. Ibn Taymiyyah notes that these texts have been summarised by other scholars and the texts and their summaries provide a useful guide to the correct opinions within the School.[149]

Ibn Taymiyyah believes in any case that a scholar who possesses an extensive knowledge of the general principles of Aḥmad and his statements should have no difficulty in determining the correct opinion of the School. He also asserts that a scholar who has an extensive knowledge of the *sharī'ah* and its evidences can ascertain what is correct in the *sharī'ah.* This last point contains an acknowledgement by Ibn Taymiyyah that the correct opinion in the School may not be the correct according to the *sharī'ah.* In that case, a scholar who has the ability to determine proofs from the *sharī'ah* is obliged to follow what is correct according to the evidences of *sharī'ah* and not according to the criteria of the School.[150]

It is evident from Ibn Taymiyyah's explanation for the existence of incorrect opinions in the Ḥanbalī School that he was not content with merely pointing out what was incorrect. Rather, we observe him attempting to eradicate this problem by identifying the root causes for their existence. Much of this is admittedly subjective and it is not hard to imagine other scholars disagreeing with Ibn Taymiyyah's criticism of, say, Abū Ya'la's opinions based on the *uṣūl* of the School or Aḥmad's classification of certain *ḥadīth* as sound.

Here now follow a few examples of rulings within the Ḥanbalī jurisprudence deemed as incorrect by Ibn Taymiyyah.

1 Ibn Taymiyyah and the issue of praying in a cemetery

To perform the prayer in a cemetery is deemed impermissible, for its prohibition blocks of the means *(yasudd al-dharā'i')* to polytheism.[151] Nevertheless, several Ḥanbalī scholars claimed that it is permissible to offer the prayer in a place where only one or two graves are situated. According to this group of scholars, this is based upon the premise that the cemetery must consist of three graves or more for it to be considered a cemetery.[152]

Ibn Taymiyyah asserts that the differentiation between a cemetery containing three graves or more and a cemetery containing one or two is not to be found in the words of Aḥmad or those of the other early Ḥanbalī scholars. Furthermore, he asserts that what may be determined from their general statements and citations is a prohibition of performing the prayer in a place where a single grave exists. Ibn Taymiyyah supports this opinion by explaining that *maqbarah* (cemetery) is given this name because it is a place where dead bodies are buried, and not because it is the plural of the singular term *qabr* (grave). Therefore, there is not even a lexical proof for the divergent opinion and, thus, the number of graves has no effect upon the ruling prohibiting prayer in a cemetery.[153]

2 *The extent of the permissible use of silver by males*

Ḥanbalī scholars appear to be in agreement on the ruling that it is prohibited for males to use silver except in certain matters, such as wearing a silver ring.[154]

Ibn Taymiyyah's opposition to the stance of the Ḥanbalī scholars is based upon the following points:

1 The Lawgiver has permitted the use of small amounts of silver for the purpose of ornament. Hence, small amounts of silver should be permitted if there is a need for it.
2 He accepts the principle that if there was a general text prohibiting the wearing of silver, the opinion of Ḥanbalī scholars would be considered accurate, but he argues there is no single authentic general text to prohibit the wearing of silver. Accordingly, no individual may assume the right to prohibit any type of adornment by the use of silver except if that type has been specifically mentioned in a text.[155]

Despite the presence of a clear consensus amongst the Ḥanbalī scholars concerning this point, we observe that in his treatise *al-Furū'*, Ibn Mufliḥ adamantly supports his Sheikh, Ibn Taymiyyah. He states that neither the Ḥanbalīs cite (textual) evidences to support their position nor could he find a prohibition in the words of Aḥmad.[156]

3 *Ibn Taymiyyah and the issue of the timing of a contract of* **hudnah** *(truce)*

Ḥanbalī scholars subscribe to the opinion that the *hudnah* (truce) cannot be accepted as a valid contract unless the exact duration of the contract is known. As a consequence, we find that several Ḥanbalī scholars defined the term *hudnah* as 'an agreement contracted for the people of *ḥarb* (war) for the suspension of fighting, enduring for a certain period of time, with or without consideration of payment'.[157] They differed in relation to the duration of the contract; certain Ḥanbalī scholars held the opinion that it is impermissible for the contract to exceed ten years in duration. Others permitted this and rendered it a matter subject to the *ijtihād* of the leader.[158] The first opinion was described by Abū Ya'la as the well known (*ẓāhir*) opinion of Ibn Ḥanbal.[159]

The two different groups of Ḥanbalī scholars cited various proofs for their respective opinions. Those who held the opinion that the duration of the truce must not exceed ten years based their opinion on the truce negotiated between the Prophet and the unbelievers of the Quraysh in the year of al-Hudaybiyah.[160] They assert that the duration of the truce must not exceed the period of the truce of Hudaybiyah, as the Prophet himself negotiated it and therefore it is a binding example.[161] Those who claim that it can exceed ten years argued that if the contract is deemed permissible for ten years, then it must also be considered permissible for an additional period, similar to the contract of hire. In addition, they state that the permissibility of the contract of truce during the ten-year period is founded upon a reason – public interest (*maṣlaḥah*) – that continues to be applicable beyond ten years. This purpose is probably more appropriate to a period condition of *hudnah* than it is to a state of war.[162]

Numerous Ḥanbalī sources appear to suggest that it is the position of all scholars, Ḥanbalī and otherwise, that the exact duration of the truce must be known.[163] Al-Mardāwī also asserts that this is the opinion that was adopted by the scholars of the Ḥanbalī School.[164] This suggestion appears to be inaccurate. During the course of this study, we shall learn that Ibn Taymiyyah is in adamant opposition to it. In addition, Ibn al-Qayyim asserts that a group of Ḥanbalī scholars, one of whom was the leading Ḥanbalī scholar Ibn Ḥamdān, affirms the existence of *wajhayn* (two views) in the School concerning this point.[165]

Ibn Taymiyyah rebuts this opinion, that is, that the period of the contract of *hudnah* must be specified, arguing that this opinion contradicts Aḥmad's general principles and is also in opposition to the texts of the Qur'an and *sunnah*, in which the period of most *hudnah* contracts was not specified.[166] He further supports his argument by the observation that in the Qur'an and *sunnah* the Lawgiver has ordered the believers to fulfil their pledges, conditions, covenants and contracts, warning them at the same time about the serious consequences of treachery and the act of breaking a vow or promise.[167] There is no restriction in duration mentioned for such pledges and contracts.

4 *Ibn Taymiyyah and the conditions stipulated by the parties partners in a contract of marriage*

The Lawgiver has specified certain conditions that must be fulfilled in order to legitimise a marriage, including, for instance, payment of the dowry and the presence of witnesses.[168] Furthermore, the Lawgiver allows the two parties to stipulate their own conditions, provided that these conditions do not conflict with a *sharʿī* text. Ḥanbalī scholars studied a large number of conditions, which could be stipulated by either party, and clarified whether or not they are valid.[169] One particular condition discussed by Ḥanbalī scholars is where the husband or wife stipulates the existence of certain attributes in his or her spouse, such as wealth, beauty and virginity. Here, only the conditions stipulated by the man are considered binding.[170]

Ibn Taymiyyah criticises this opinion and observes that it is not established upon a correct legal foundation. Furthermore, he asserts that the conditions stipulated by the woman are in fact more binding than those of the man and claims that there is a consensus of (early) Ḥanbalī scholars in addition to others on this point.[171] Therefore, it cannot be possible that only the man's stipulations are binding.

The practical effect of the opposition's opinion is that if a man stipulates certain attributes that are found to be absent in his partner, he has the legal right to dissolve the contract of marriage. If, however, that stipulation came from the woman, she would have no right to dissolve the contract. According to Ibn Taymiyyah's opinion, which he attributes to all scholars, the two parties possess the same right to dissolve the marital contract whenever such conditions have not been fulfilled.

5 Ibn Taymiyyah and selling non-existent material

Several Ḥanbalī scholars have stipulated that in order for an object to be sold it must be in existence at the time of the sale. They based their ruling on a *ḥadīth* of the Prophet in which he states, 'Do not sell that which you do not have.'[172]

Ibn Taymiyyah studied the various texts and evidence related to this issue, and states that there are two possible inferences from the meaning of the Prophetic *ḥadīth* 'Do not sell that which you do not have.' The first meaning is that it is prohibited to sell an object that does not exist at the time of the contract. The second meaning is that it is prohibited to sell an item that cannot be handed over to the buyer at the time of delivery.[173] This second meaning allows for the object to be absent at the contract, so long as it is ready by the date of delivery. Ibn Taymiyyah observes that the Lawgiver has permitted some transactions where the object is not present at the time of the contract. Examples are the contract of hire and the contract of *bayʿ al-salam* (forward purchase). Therefore, Ibn Taymiyyah concludes that the first interpretation was clearly not intended. It can therefore be concluded that the only possible correct meaning of the *ḥadīth* is the second one. Ibn Taymiyyah supports this conclusion by noting the absence of a single text from the Qur'an and *sunnah*, or any narration from the companions, which suggest that the sale of a non-existent item is prohibited merely because of its non-existence. There is evidence, however, that the Lawgiver prohibited the sale of certain non-existent items when sold in conjunction with items already in existence. This prohibition is not based upon the existence or non-existence of the item, but rather on the fact that these types of sale contain a great element of *gharar* (risk and uncertainty). As a consequence, there is a risk in these types of sale that the item in question may not be handed over at the time of delivery.[174]

6 Ibn Taymiyyah and the sale and replacement of a type of waqf *(endowment) with another*

If an endowment becomes unfruitful, the predominant opinion within Ḥanbalī jurisprudence is that it is permissible to sell it or replace it with another endowment.[175] If, however, the sale or replacement of the endowment is based merely upon the expectation of a greater yield arising from the new one, the Ḥanbalī scholars appear to agree that the sale and replacement is invalid. This may be evidenced by *al-Muḥarrar*,[176] *al-'Uddah*,[177] *al-Mughnī*,[178] *Sharḥ al-Zarkashī*,[179] *al-Inṣāf*,[180] *al-Rawḍ*,[181] *Ḥāshiyat al-Rawḍ*[182] and *al-Furū'*.[183]

Ibn Taymiyyah, on the contrary, asserts that it is permissible to sell an endowment or replace one type by another, irrespective of whether or not the current endowment has stopped bearing fruit. In both circumstances, he founds the permissibility of the sale and replacement of an endowment on the expected benefit from doing so. He bases this ruling on an analogy with the permissibility of changing the sacrificial animal (*hadī*) in *al-ḥajj* with another based upon the expected benefit rising from this change.[184]

Ibn Taymiyyah's opinion has been followed by some Ḥanbalī scholars amongst whom was Ibn Qāḍī al-Jabal, one of Ibn Taymiyyah's disciples. He gave this opinion greater weight by endorsing it as a judgement while he was serving as a judge.[185] The judgement of Ibn Qāḍī al-Jabal was challenged by certain Ḥanbalī scholars, such as the judge Jamāl al-Dīn al-Mardāwī (d. 769/1367) who insisted that this judgement was in opposition to the general principles of the Ḥanbalī School.[186] Al-Mardāwī also wrote a treatise clarifying his opinion on this issue and included a criticism of his opponents. This book is entitled '*al-Wāḍiḥ al-Jalī fi naqd ḥukm Ibn Qāḍī al-Jabal al-Ḥanbalī*'.[187] Al-Mardāwī mentioned that Ibn Mufliḥ is in agreement with this criticism.[188] Ibn Qāḍī al-Jabal did not retreat as a result of this criticism. Instead, he compiled a treatise in which he clarified the opinions regarding this issue and affirmed the correctness of Ibn Taymiyyah's view. Ibn Qāḍī al-Jabal was supported by various other Ḥanbalī scholars such as Burhān al-Dīn Ibn al-Qayyim and Ibn Sheikh al-Sulāmiyyah.[189] After this period, certain Ḥanbalī sources began to mention that there are two opinions or even narrations in Ḥanbalī jurisprudence regarding this issue.[190] This is an example therefore of how an opinion of Ibn Taymiyyah, in defiance of all other Ḥanbalī authority, was eventually adopted as part of the corpus of the Ḥanbalī jurisprudence.

7 *Killing a free person for a slave*

Ḥanbalī sources appear to agree that there is no equality between a free person and a slave in relation to the issue of retaliation. This means that a free person cannot be sentenced to death for killing a slave.[191]

Ibn Taymiyyah adamantly opposes the stance of the Ḥanbalī School, asserting that there are no correct definite texts which can be used as a legal foundation upon which this opinion may be established.[192] On the contrary, Ibn Taymiyyah argues that the evidences of the *sharī'ah* are indicative of the accuracy of his opposite position.[193] He explains that this may be evidenced through various *ḥādīths* where the Prophet states that whosoever kills his slave will as a consequence be executed.[194] Ibn Taymiyyah elucidates upon a detailed explanation for this: when the master kills his slave, the right of retaliation will be placed upon the leader of the Muslim community and not upon the master. This is simply because a killer cannot be granted the right of retaliation for one whom he himself killed.[195] Ibn Taymiyyah draws an analogy based upon the ruling that a killer has no right to the inheritance of his victim if they are related to one another. Similarly, a master cannot inherit the right of retaliation of his victim slave.[196] Ibn Taymiyyah further supports his position by clarifying that according to the *sunnah*, if a slave was punished by his master with extreme cruelty, the slave would automatically be freed.[197] Ibn Taymiyyah states that the killing of a slave is the most severe and extreme act of cruelty. Therefore, the deceased slave has in fact died while he was a free person, which again means that the leader of the Muslim community assumes the right of retaliation.[198] Ibn Taymiyyah explains that this principle can also apply to any free person who kills a slave, and not merely to a master who kills his slave.[199]

Ibn Taymiyyah concludes by asking why it would not be allowed to apply the death sentence to a free person who killed a slave, when the Prophet declared: 'the blood of Muslims is equal'.[200]

Although the words of Aḥmad and the Ḥanbalī scholars appear not to make reference to this opinion, Ibn Taymiyyah claims that this view is the strongest according to the opinion of Aḥmad.[201] It appears Ibn Taymiyyah is stating that this opinion is the strongest according to the general principles of Aḥmad, rather than any of his actual words in relation to this point.

Jurisprudential terminology of the Ḥanbalī School

The science of terminology occupies a position of great importance in Islamic law, for a ruling is determined by reference to its definition. Ibn Taymiyyah scrutinises the terms used by the Ḥanbalī scholars and makes reference to several terms that were surrounded with confusion and uncertainty. It appears that Ibn Taymiyyah attributes this confusion and uncertainty to the absence of a clear, correct criterion by which suitable definitions to the various terms may be ascertained. Consequently, Ibn Taymiyyah presents his own preferred criterion. He clarifies that the meaning of terms attached to rulings in the Qur'an and *sunnah* may be determined in one of the three ways. The first is where terms are defined by the Lawgiver, for instance, the terms '*ṣalāh*,' '*zakāt*,' '*ṣawm*' and '*ḥajj*'. The second is where terms that can be defined by reference to the language such as 'sun', 'moon', 'sky' and 'earth'. The third is where the meaning of terms can be determined by reference to the custom and practice of the people. Examples of this category are the terms 'sale', 'marriage' and 'possession'. Ibn Taymiyyah explains that this last method is neither defined by the Lawgiver nor have the people of language agreed upon its definition; therefore, these terms may differ from one society to another based upon the premise that customs vary from one society to another and from one time to another.[202]

It is evident that the first two categories are not capable of being altered because either the Lawgiver defines them or they are understood by recourse to the use of language. According to Ibn Taymiyyah, the establishment of this criterion for defining terms in Islamic law leads to a correct understanding of the two main sources of the *sharīʿah*, the Qur'an and *sunnah*.[203]

The following section contains a study of some cases wherein the Lawgiver has defined terms and, thereafter, certain Ḥanbalī scholars have apparently redefined them, or where terms are mentioned in a general context in the texts and have been particularised by the School.

1 Ibn Taymiyyah and the term **khamr**

According to Islamic law, *Khamr* is prohibited and particular rulings have been attached to it. This term has been mentioned in several texts of the Qur'an and the *sunnah*. For instance, in the Qur'an Allah states: 'They ask you (O Muhammad) about *khamr* and gambling. Say: 'In them is a great sin, and some benefit for men, but the sin is greater than the benefit' (2:219). Also, in the chapter of *al-Māʾidah* verses 90–91, Allah orders believers to abstain strictly from the consumption of *khamr*. There are also several *ḥadīths* which concern the issue of *khamr*.[204] In order for these rulings to be applied in practice, the term *khamr* must first be defined. Certain Ḥanbalī scholars, for instance Ibrāhim al-Ḥarbī (d. 285/899) and Abū 'l-Khaṭṭāb, connected the term *khamr* to particular kinds of intoxicants.[205] Similarly, some later Ḥanbalī scholars hesitated as to whether the punishment for consuming *Khamr* can be administered to those who take the *ḥashīshah* (hemp).[206]

Ibn Taymiyyah criticises these opinions for their opposition to the texts of the Qur'an and the *sunnah* as well as in addition to the words of Imam Aḥmad. Ibn Taymiyyah's claim rests on the generality of the texts prohibiting the consumption of *khamr*. Therefore, when these scholars particularised the texts in the absence of evidence, they were in fact opposing the two sources of law. Ibn Taymiyyah asserts in any case that the Lawgiver has defined this term in the ḥadith, 'Every intoxicant is *khamr*'.[207]

In reply to one justification given for the opposing opinions, Ibn Taymiyyah asserts that the practice of the Arabs of the pre-Islamic era is of no consequence in the understanding of *khamr*, since the Prophet defined it. Therefore, this term cannot be restricted to denote a specific form of intoxicant.[208]

In reference to the issue of *ḥashīshah* specifically, Ibn Taymiyyah affirms that the punishment for consuming *khamr* is applicable to the taking of *ḥashīshah*. This is, first, because it comes within the purview of the ruling on *khamr* and, second, because of the presence of harm in this substance similar to that in *khamr*. Indeed, in certain circumstances its harm is greater than that of *khamr*. Furthermore, he argues, it is common knowledge that those who take it become addicted to it.[209]

Ibn Taymiyyah also mentions the fact that the absence of discussion of this issue by former scholars cannot be used as an evidence to denote its permissibility. Ibn Taymiyyah explains that this is because the substance in question was unknown in the Islamic world until the time of the appearance of the Mongols.[210]

2 Ibn Taymiyyah and the term ḥayḍ *(menstruation)*

The term '*ḥayḍ* is the subject of several rulings in the Ḥanbalī School of law. The duration of the menstruation is not specified in a text, nor is it known by recourse to language. Certain Ḥanbalī scholars attempted to determine a limit to the period of menstruation. A group amongst them specified the maximum and minimum durations of it, while others specified only the maximum.[211] Ibn Taymiyyah declares that the truth is that there is neither a maximum nor a minimum duration for menstruation. For the basis of this stipulation is empirical observation and it is difficult to determine limits for such matters by experience, because of the inherent differences amongst women.[212] There is much scope for uncertainty in these matters and it is not accurate for an individual to reject that which he does not know.[213]

Ibn Taymiyyah argues that the narration cited by certain Ḥanbalī scholars to support the existence of a minimum period for menstruation is false, as it is unknown amongst the scholars of *ḥadīth*.[214] Ibn Taymiyyah goes on to explain that the Lawgiver defined specific Islamic law terminology but did not define the term menstruation. It can therefore be concluded that this term, and other similar terms, can only be determined by experience if the definition can also not be ascertained through the language.[215] According to Ibn Taymiyyah, this principle is also applicable to the period of postnatal bleeding.[216] As mentioned, however, gathering conclusive evidence from experience is difficult in these matters.

3 Ibn Taymiyyah and the term safar *(travelling)*

The term '*safar*' is mentioned in the texts and several rulings have been connected to it. A definition for the term 'travelling' must first be determined in order to implement these rulings. The majority of Ḥanbalī scholars confined travelling to a certain destination and differentiated between long journeys and short ones. They claim that those rulings that are connected to this term are dependent upon the duration of the journey. They state that these rulings are divided into two types: first, those rulings which can be applied to lengthy journeys alone. These include the acts of shortening and combining prayers, breaking the fast and wiping over footwear for a period of three days and accompanying nights. Second, rulings that are applicable to both long and short journeys. This includes the act of performing ablution with clean sand (*tayammum*), praying on the *rāḥilah* (the means of transport) and eating carrion in a state of necessity.[217]

Ibn Taymiyyah believes that these restrictions and factors for differentiation are devoid of foundation, for they are not expressed by the Lawgiver, nor are they required by the language.[218] Ibn Taymiyyah also rejects the *ḥadīth* cited by a group of Ḥanbalī scholars in which the Prophet is reported to have said: 'O people of Makkah, do not shorten prayers in a journey that is less than four *barīds* from Makkah to 'Asafān'.[219] Ibn Taymiyyah demonstrates that this *ḥadīth* is unauthentic in two ways:

1 The chain of this *ḥadīth* is acknowledged amongst the leading scholars of *ḥadīth* to be undoubtedly fabricated.[220]
2 It is known that the Prophet emigrated to Madinah. He spent most of his life there after the emigration, residing in Makkah only for a short period of time. Why, therefore, did the Prophet instruct the people of Makkah and not do the same to the people of Madinah? In addition, what is the position of the remainder of the Muslim world in relation to this ruling?[221]

Ibn Taymiyyah concludes that the correct understanding of this term can be determined only by means of its general meaning in the language and custom during the time it is used. Accordingly, all rulings are applicable to any journey that is accepted by the people of the language to come within the meaning of 'travelling'.[222]

4 Ibn Taymiyyah and the issue of khulʿ *(dissolution of marriage)*

According to Islamic law, divorce has been prescribed in order to provide a means for the husband to terminate the marriage. If, however, the wife is unhappy or feels an aversion towards her husband, she may also release herself from the marriage by the procedure known as *khulʿ*. This procedure is initiated when the wife asks for the marriage to be dissolved. A request can thereafter be made for the dowry to be returned, and any other gifts she received from her husband. If the process is performed and accepted by both parties, the marriage is dissolved.[223]

The point of discussion here concerns whether there are special expressions to be used in order for the marital contract to be dissolved via *khulʿ*, or whether this can be achieved through the use of any expression, even those used for divorce. According to al-Mardāwī, in the opinion of the majority of Ḥanbalī scholars, the terms used in *khulʿ* must be specific and it is not allowed to use, for instance, the terms for divorce. Should terms other than those specified by the Ḥanbalī scholars be used, the *khulʿ* will not take place.[224]

Ibn Taymiyyah criticises the position of the Ḥanbalī scholars and asserts that whenever *khulʿ* is conditionally performed upon a payment from the wife, there is no restriction on the expressions that must be used, for the procedure of *khulʿ* is the only method of dissolving the marital contract with the condition of payment.[225] The intention of the wife should therefore be obvious from her actions and there is no need for her to use a specific formula.

5 Ibn Taymiyyah and the term ʿāqilah

According to Islamic criminal law, there is no right of retaliation against the person who causes the death of another unintentionally, although blood money is required from the *ʿāqilah* and not from the killer.[226]

The Ḥanbalī School of law contains several opinions for the identification of who is referred to by the *'āqilah*. The two opinions which are most frequently cited are the following:

The first opinion is that the *'āqilah* consists of the paternal uncles and their children, however distant they are in descent. According to this opinion, the father, sons and brothers are not included. The second opinion states that the *'āqilah* consists of the father, sons, brothers and every agnatic heir.[227]

Ibn Taymiyyah subscribes to an opinion different from these two. He states that the words of the Lawgiver provide no definition for the term *'āqilah*. Therefore, the correct definition of this term is that it includes 'every individual who helps and supports the person at the time and the place'.[228] Ibn Taymiyyah's definition is wider in scope than all the other definitions offered by Ḥanbalī scholars.

It may appear that Ibn Taymiyyah's definition is in opposition to the practice at the time of the Prophet, where the relatives alone were asked to pay the blood money. Ibn Taymiyyah explains, however, that the relatives of an individual were included in the term *'āqilah* at the time of the Prophet, simply because the relatives were the helpers of a person at that time. The definition of this term changed in the time of 'Umar, when he established an organised army in several towns, and the members of this army were considered as the *'āqilah* to one another.[229]

It appears that Ibn Taymiyyah's understanding of the term *'āqilah* has influenced the understanding and application of this term in the current law of Saudi Arabia, for we note that it has been defined as 'a group that may stand for two thirds of the payment of the *diyah* within three years of the unintentional killing of another person by one of its members, if they are able to do so.'[230]

Rules in Ḥanbalī jurisprudence

Generally in his writings and particularly in his jurisprudence, Ibn Taymiyyah employs general rules and maxims in order to regulate the vast number of jurisprudential ramifications. The most important feature of his maxims is the principle that they are founded upon textual evidences and not according to the practice of the Ḥanbalī School. He asserts that the Qur'an and the *sunnah* contain general words which are in fact general rules encompassing a number of different ramifications.[231] Ibn Taymiyyah clarifies that the Lawgiver differentiates between rulings concerning dissimilar issues, while the rulings for similar issues will be similar.[232] He also states that an individual's neglect to ascertain a ruling concerning an issue coming within the general rules of the *sharī'ah* leads to the conclusion that he did not understand those general rules.[233] Also, the Lawgiver's maxims are in agreement with the general *maqāṣid* (goals and objectives) of the *sharī'ah* and *maṣlaḥah*, for they afford ease to those subject to its rulings.[234]

There is no doubt that Ibn Taymiyyah's understanding of the general maxims of Islamic law affected his use of rules in jurisprudence as well as his position towards rules used by Ḥanbalī scholars. He employs some rules while also disputing the correctness of several rules and maxims employed in the Ḥanbalī School of law. The following sections examine some of the rules used by Ibn Taymiyyah, demonstrate certain aspects of their implications for Ḥanbalī jurisprudence and also discusses particular Ḥanbalī rules that were the subject of Ibn Taymiyyah's criticism.

1 Rules used by Ibn Taymiyyah and certain aspects of their implications for Ḥanbalī jurisprudence

1 Ibn Taymiyyah uses the rule, 'if the Lawgiver connected a ruling to a general noun, it will govern all the classes falling under that general noun without any restriction or exclusion, unless they were restricted or excluded by the Lawgiver Himself'.[235]

On application of this rule to Ḥanbalī jurisprudence, Ibn Taymiyyah discovers that several rulings were not applied by Ḥanbalī scholars to some classes included within the meaning of a general noun. According to Ibn Taymiyyah, these scholars did not found their opinions on legal or linguistic evidences, which would justify the exemption of these classes from the general rulings.[236]

There follows three examples of Ibn Taymiyyah's use of the aforementioned rule:[237]

i *Ibn Taymiyyah and types of water* *Tayammum* (sand ablution) is a substitute for water ablution in the event that water is not available or someone is unable to use it. Ibn Taymiyyah notes here that the word 'water' is general; therefore, it includes all types of water (excluding impure water).[238] As a result, Ibn Taymiyyah condemns the commonly accepted opinion within the Ḥanbalī School that water is divided into three types: impure water, completely clean water (*ṭahūr*) and clean water (*ṭāhir*).[239]

According to these scholars, there is a difference between the second and the third category. The second type refers to water that has not undergone any type of change, as compared to that which has been used previously for ablution, or water that has been mixed with other clean substances. This alteration may result in a change in the taste of the water, its colour or its smell. Water characterised by one of these changes can, however, still be treated as 'clean' (the third category).[240]

This classification is based upon one of two narrations from Aḥmad. Early leading Ḥanbalī scholars preferred this narration and it is the predominant opinion amongst the later Ḥanbalī scholars.[241]

Ibn Taymiyyah, on the other hand, asserts that the other narration from Aḥmad, which states that all types of water may be used for the ritual ablution, is supported by most of Ibn Ḥanbal's words on this subject.[242]

According to Ibn Taymiyyah, this last opinion is the correct one because the classification of clean water into two types is not founded upon correct evidence from either the Qur'an, *sunnah*, consensus or analogy. On the contrary, by means of the implementation of the aforementioned rule, it is clear that the texts of the

Qur'an and *sunnah* indicate the incorrectness of this classification; the texts are general and do not refer to any classification of water.[243] Those Ḥanbalī scholars who were in favour of the three-fold classification, were confused as to what could be considered as completely clean water (*ṭahūr*) or only clean water (*ṭāhīr*).[244]

Ibn Taymiyyah's opinion is consistent with his maxim and provides a clear basis for this ruling, as opposed to the view of most of the later Ḥanbalī scholars, which is ambiguous and results in confusion and inconsistency.

The end result of the classification adopted by the Ḥanbalī scholars is that ablution can be performed with *ṭahūr* water, but not *ṭāhir*. According to Ibn Taymiyyah, however, ablution may be performed by using either type of water, as there is no legal distinction between them.

ii *Ibn Taymiyyah and the issue of wiping over Khuffayn* Another issue Ibn Taymiyyah analysed by recourse to this rule is the wiping over the *khuffayn* (boots) or *jawrabayn* (socks) as part of ritual ablution.

The commonly accepted opinion within the Ḥanbalī School states that the permissibility of wiping over the boots and socks is dependent upon several conditions. For instance, the boots or socks (or other similar items) should not be torn and they must be capable of standing firmly by themselves without being supported by another object.[245]

Ibn Taymiyyah asserts that the correct opinion on this point is that it is permitted to wipe over the boots and socks providing that they can be described as boots and socks. It is of no consequence whether they are torn, nor whether they are capable of standing without support.[246]

Ibn Taymiyyah again bases his opinion upon the same aforementioned rule; the texts permitting the act of wiping over the *khuffayn* are general. It is, therefore, not accurate to differentiate between them in the absence of textual evidences. He supports his opinion by the fact that the companions' boots and socks were not devoid of tears; hence, if there had been a prohibition regarding this matter, it would have been established and transmitted from them.[247]

It ought to be noted that this opinion is not the view of Aḥmad, nor of most of his followers. Ibn Taymiyyah, however, asserts that if Aḥmad's general principles and words in analogous issues are studied and analysed, one can conclude that this opinion is a syllogism of Aḥmad's opinion on the act of wiping over the boots and socks.[248]

iii *Ibn Taymiyyah and the issue of ratifying contracts* There are several opinions in the Ḥanbalī School in relation to the issue of ratifying contracts. The first opinion states that contracts cannot be ratified without the use of certain expressions specified by the jurists. Therefore, no transaction will be legally accepted unless these particular forms are used. This entails that there must be an offer from one person with certain terms and a resultant acceptance from another with certain terms. For example, if a person wants to buy an item, for example, bread, he must articulate the words *ishtaraytu hādhā* (I would like to buy this) and the buyer must respond by saying *qabilt* (I have accepted). This procedure must be applied to any transaction, whether small or large.

The second opinion of the School states that such formulas must be used except in the case of transactions that are usually ratified through actions alone, such as purchasing small items. In this circumstance, the aforementioned procedure need not be applied, as is also the case for an endowment of a mosque and the giving of a gift.[249]

Ibn Taymiyyah subscribes to the opinion that there is no specific formula that must be adhered to in order to ratify transactions, as there are no textual evidences in support of any of these forms.[250] He also asserts that it was not the practice of the Prophet, his companions and their followers to adhere to certain words when ratifying a contract.[251] Furthermore, Ibn Taymiyyah also argues that Aḥmad's general principles are in opposition to this opinion. Therefore, a transaction can be ratified by any procedure that is commonly known in a society.[252] He also criticises the claim that certain Arabic words must be used in order to ratify every type of transaction, such as the words *zawajtuka* and *qabiltu* in a contract of marriage. Ibn Taymiyyah asserts that this cannot be correct, as it is not only Arabs that deal in transactions. It would be similarly incorrect to teach a person to utter words in Arabic, the exact meaning of which he may not know; rather, he should be allowed to ratify contracts in his own language.[253]

Ibn Taymiyyah concludes by stating that the general principles of the *sharīʿah* indicate that the correct rule governing contracts is: 'Contracts may be ratified by any word or action that identifies the intention of the two parties in the contract, provided that these words and acts do not conflict with the *sharīʿah*.'[254]

2 Legal rulings are not binding until the one entrusted with the responsibility becomes aware of them.

Ibn Taymiyyah uses this maxim to oppose certain rulings of Ḥanbalī jurisprudence. One of these concerns the consequences of the beginning of *Ramaḍān* being established during the daytime of one of its days. According to the Ḥanbalī scholars, the *mukallaf* must do two things: he must immediately stop performing any action that nullifies the fast; and after *Ramaḍān*, he must make up this day of fasting. According to Ibn Taymiyyah, the individual concerned is obliged to start fasting as soon as the proof for the start of *Ramaḍān* is established, but the individual does not have to make up that day at a later time. Ibn Taymiyyah's opinion is founded upon the rule mentioned earlier; the Muslim cannot be responsible to make up the fast when he was not aware of the coming of *Ramaḍān* until later in the day.[255]

2 *Ḥanbalī rules refuted by Ibn Taymiyyah*

Some of the Ḥanbalī School's rules are clearly established upon the correct foundation of the Qur'an, *sunnah*, consensus, analogy or some other recognised source of law. It may be argued, however, that other rules are established upon incorrect conclusions deduced by certain scholars. These rules were then used to derive rulings, which were necessarily incorrect.

Ibn Taymiyyah recognised this problem and studied those rules developed by Ḥanbalī scholars. He accepts some of these rules and rejects others. As always, the criterion he employs in determining which rules to accept and which to reject is the extent to which they are based on correct evidences.[256]

The following section studies certain rules subjected to criticism and refutation by Ibn Taymiyyah:

1 Ibn Taymiyyah and the Ḥanbalī rule 'prayer cannot be postponed beyond its time except in two situations...'

Certain Ḥanbalī scholars subscribed to the following rule: 'Prayer cannot be postponed beyond its time except if the postponement is coupled with the intention of combining two prayers or if the individual concerned is engaged in fulfilling a condition of the prayer.'[257]

Ibn Taymiyyah criticises this rule and refutes it in several ways. First, he says that this rule has not been mentioned by any previous scholar, except for certain Shāfi'ī scholars. Even then, they did not generalise the rule, but rather restricted it to particular issues only. This is contrary to the later Ḥanbalī scholars who generalise the application of the rule.[258] Second, Ibn Taymiyyah asserts that this rule opposes the consensus of scholars who prohibit the postponement of the prayer after its due time simply because the individual concerned is engaged in the preparation of some of its conditions. Therefore, according to the consensus, if the time for a prayer arrives and the individual does not have water in order to perform the ablution, but knows that he can find water after the time of the prayer, it is prohibited to delay the prayer even though the individual is preoccupied with fulfilling one of the conditions in searching for water.[259]

Ibn Taymiyyah presents another example to illustrate this point and to support the consensus. An illiterate person has the ability to learn *Surat al-Fātiḥah* in order to read it in his prayer, as it is one of the pillars of the prayer. If it becomes clear, however, that he will not complete learning it until the time of the prayer elapses, the ruling states that he performs the prayer without it.[260]

In further rebuttal of the Ḥanbalī scholars, Ibn Taymiyyah mentions certain established rulings of Islamic law that are in opposition to it. For example, a person who does not know the *takbīr* and *tashahud* or any other obligatory acts of the prayers and cannot learn them within the prescribed time of a prayer is asked to pray in time even before learning them. Similarly, the individual who performs the prayer of *khawf* (prayer under threat of attack), when he could have performed the prayer in its complete form out of its time, is correct in performing the prayer of *khawf* within the time. Finally, a person, who does not know the direction of the *qiblah* or is doubtful about it, is obliged to pray and not delay the prayer until he reaches a city where he can determine the exact direction of the *qiblah*.[261]

2 Ibn Taymiyyah and the Ḥanbalī rule 'the general rule is that all contracts and conditions are prohibited except those permitted by the Lawgiver'.

Certain Ḥanbalī scholars subscribed to the opinion that all contracts and conditions are prohibited except those permitted by the Lawgiver. Ibn Taymiyyah indicates that the existence of this opinion is based upon the presence of certain narrations wherein Ibn Ḥanbal justified the invalidity of particular types of contracts because they were neither referred to by texts nor by analogy.[262]

Ibn Taymiyyah states that the correct rule in relation to this issue is in fact as follows: 'All contracts and conditions are permitted except where otherwise stated by the Lawgiver.' He argues that the majority of Aḥmad's narrations are in agreement with this. Indeed, Aḥmad is considered as one of the scholars most recognised for his acceptance of new contracts and conditions.[263] Ibn Taymiyyah believes that Aḥmad's general principles suggest that stipulations in contracts are acceptable providing that they do not contradict with a *sharī'ah* text.[264] He does note that most of the conditions and contracts accepted by Aḥmad are found to have an origin in texts or analogy, but he argues that this cannot be used as evidence to suggest that he did not permit contracts and conditions other than those founded on these two sources. Ibn Taymiyyah explains that this is because Aḥmad possessed an extensive knowledge of *ḥadīth*; it is therefore only to be expected that his acceptance of a condition or a contract is in agreement with a text or analogy, but this should not exclude others not covered by these sources.[265]

In addition, Ibn Taymiyyah mentions a rational form of evidence to support his opinion. He states that there are several texts ordering Muslims to fulfil their contracts and conditions and other texts forbidding them from breach of an agreement or promise. Therefore, if the general rule states that contracts and conditions are prohibited except those permitted by the Lawgiver, it would not be correct to order believers to fulfil contracts and conditions in general, without clarification.[266]

3 Ibn Taymiyyah and the Ḥanbalī rule 'the *naṣṣ* (text) of the endower (the founder of an endowment) is as the *naṣṣ* of the Lawgiver'.

This rule is present in certain Ḥanbalī sources, but there is ambiguity surrounding the meaning and application of this rule. Ibn Taymiyyah presents a clear explanation when he states that the similarity between the text of the endower and that of the Lawgiver is that both refer to the intended meaning of the 'author'. Therefore, we understand the intended meaning of the endower by recourse to his text as we understand the intended meaning of the Lawgiver by recourse to his text. Ibn Taymiyyah asserts that understanding the text of the endower requires knowledge of the individual's custom in writing and speech, and whether this language is formal Arabic or colloquial. Beyond this, however, Ibn Taymiyyah sees similarity between the text of the endower and that of the Lawgiver, in that acting upon the text of the Lawgiver is obligatory, whereas acting upon the text of the endower is subject to it being approved by the Lawgiver. This is because the text of the endower can contain both valid and invalid conditions, and it is not lawful to fulfil the invalid conditions.[267]

As an application of this, Ibn Taymiyyah says that if the endower ordered a person who was not the best suited to be the Imam during the prayer, his order would be ignored. Instead, the order of Allah ought to be followed by selecting the individual who was granted precedence by the Lawgiver.[268]

Narrations in Ḥanbalī jurisprudence

In Ḥanbalī jurisprudence, there are often conflicting narrations related by Ḥanbalī scholars from Imam Aḥmad. It is clear that Ibn Taymiyyah was aware of this problem as we find him in various issues trying to solve the contradictions between these narrations. The following section analyses two methods that Ibn Taymiyyah used to resolve these problems. First, he showed that some narrations had been attributed to Ibn Ḥanbal incorrectly. Second, he tried to show that certain opinions of Aḥmad were simply incorrect. This second method is, of course, not so much about resolving conflicting narrations as it is about discarding certain opinions contained in the narrations entirely.

1 Narrations proved by Ibn Taymiyyah to be attributed to Ibn Ḥanbal incorrectly

The large number of conflicting narrations and opinions attributed to Imam Aḥmad has resulted in great confusion within the Ḥanbalī School. Ibn Taymiyyah studied Ḥanbalī jurisprudence and he presented numerous pieces of evidence to substantiate his claim that certain Ḥanbalī scholars have attributed narrations and opinions to the Imam incorrectly. Examples are

- *Ibn Taymiyyah's opinion with regard to the narrations in Ḥanbalī jurisprudence concerning the punishment for drinking khamr* Ḥanbalī sources make reference to two narrations in relation to the punishment for consuming *khamr*. The first states that the punishment is forty lashes and the second states that it is eighty lashes.[269]

  Ibn Taymiyyah asserts that Aḥmad's second narration on this issue is not as the Ḥanbalī scholars have mentioned. According to Ibn Taymiyyah, Aḥmad's correct position as set out in the second narration is that the forty lashes is a *ḥadd* (fixed) punishment, while the number between forty and eighty is neither obligatory nor prohibited. Rather, it is a discretionary penalty that is left to the exclusive discretion of the judge, dependent upon the expected benefit of the sentence.[270]

  The leading Ḥanbalī scholar al-Zarkashī mentioned the two narrations of Aḥmad according to the Ḥanbalī scholars, then he commented saying: 'be aware that the vast majority of Ḥanbalī scholars convey the narrations (of Aḥmad with regard to this issue) as mentioned earlier.' Thereafter, al-Zarkashī mentioned the opinion of Ibn Taymiyyah in relation to Aḥmad's correct position in the second narration. Al-Zarkashī then stated that there can be no doubt that Ibn Taymiyyah's explanation is the opinion that is supported by legal evidences.[271]

- *The delay in acceptance in a marriage contract* In the Ḥanbalī School, there are two narrations attributed to Aḥmad regarding whether it is permissible for one of the parties to a marriage contract to delay acceptance. In one of these two narrations, Aḥmad is said to have prohibited the delay and to have insisted on the requirement of simultaneous acceptance of both parties at the same sitting, but in another narration he is said to have permitted the delay.[272]

Ibn Taymiyyah asserts that what is narrated from Aḥmad is the first narration whereas the second narration is in fact based on a statement issued by Aḥmad permitting the delay in specific circumstances, that is, when the acceptance was made by the second party after the information reached him, because he was not present at the same sitting (*majlis*). This statement of Aḥmad, according to Ibn Taymiyyah, was misunderstood and generalised by some leading Ḥanbalī scholars, such as Abū 'l-Khaṭṭāb in his treatise *al-Hidāyah*, Ibn Qudāmah in his book *al-Muqni'* and al-Majd in his book *al-Muḥarrar*, who thought Aḥmad's statement permitting delay in the acceptance of the marriage applied to all cases.[273]

2 Narrations of Aḥmad proved by Ibn Taymiyyah to be incorrect

We find that Ibn Taymiyyah disagrees with opinions adopted by the Ḥanbalī School on various issues, which he insists are based on incorrect narrations. His disagreement with these opinions and his refutation of the narrations upon which these opinions were based are supported by various textual and rational evidences. This section contains study cases of this point:

- *The nullification of ablution when a man touches a woman* The predominant opinion within the Ḥanbalī School is that when a man touches a woman his ablution will be considered nullified. This means that he is obliged to perform the ablution another time.[274] This opinion is held and supported by several Ḥanbalī scholars, such as al-Mardāwī.[275] The view, in fact, is based upon a narration of Aḥmad.[276]

  Ibn Taymiyyah argues that this narration is contrary to the general principles of Islamic law. In addition, he asserts that there is no report that the companions would re-perform their ablution because they had touched their wives or others.[277]
- *Compulsion in marriage* The majority of Ḥanbalī scholars subscribe to the opinion that the guardian of a virgin mature (of age) female can give her in marriage without the need to seek her consent. This opinion is reported as being narrated from Ibn Ḥanbal and has been supported by various leading Ḥanbalī scholars, such as al-Khiraqī, Abū Ya'la, Ibn Abī Ya'la, Abū 'l-Khaṭṭāb, Ibn al-Bannā, Ibn Qudāmah, Ibn Abī Hubayrah.[278] Al-Mardāwī describes this opinion as 'the correct opinion in Ḥanbalī jurisprudence' and also claims that it is the position of the majority of Ḥanbalī scholars.[279]

  Ibn Taymiyyah states that this opinion is incorrect and argues that the guardian has no right to compel a woman to accept a marriage. He bases his opinion on the following arguments:

- He quotes the *ḥadīth* of the Prophet in which he states: 'A matron should not be given in marriage except after her consultation; a virgin should not be given in marriage except after her permission.'[280] In this *ḥadīth*, Ibn Taymiyyah establishes the point that the Lawgiver does not differentiate between whether the woman is a virgin or not for the purposes of consent. Rather, the consent of both individuals is required in order to ratify the contract of marriage. The differentiation mentioned by the Lawgiver concerns the manner in which this consent can be expressed and the amount of consultation required.[281]
- He expresses his surprise that his opponents do not permit the guardian to dispose off a mature woman's wealth without her consent, while they allow him to ratify the contract of marriage without her consent, even though her marriage is incomparably more important than her wealth. Furthermore, he questions why, given that it is not permissible for the guardian to force his child to eat, drink or wear what she does not like, the Lawgiver would thereafter allow a guardian to compel his child to marry an individual she does not like. Ibn Taymiyyah also argues that the Lawgiver declares that He creates love and affection between the two parties of a marriage, so it is therefore not possible that He would allow a woman to live with someone she dislikes.[282]
- In the event of a dispute occurring between the two parties, which they are incapable of solving privately, the final option available in order to keep the marriage functioning is to appoint two *ḥakamayn* (arbiters). These two individuals attempt to reach a solution that is advantageous to both parties. This option can include the dissolution of the marital contract so that a woman can escape from a life of difficulty and hardship. If this is the procedure prescribed by the Lawgiver at this stage of a family crisis, could it be possible that the Lawgiver would permit the guardian of a mature female to compel her to accept a marriage against her own volition?[283]
- Ibn Taymiyyah states that virginity is not a legitimate reason for *ḥajr* (interdiction), for we find that the words of the Lawgiver do not make reference to this. Therefore, when the majority of Ḥanbalī scholars establish the permissibility of a marriage of compulsion upon the existence of virginity in a mature female, it is contrary to the general principles of Islamic law.[284]

From the discussions in this chapter, we can conclude that several aspects of Ḥanbalī jurisprudence were affected by Ibn Taymiyyah's contributions to this science. It is also evident that, in most instances, he attributes the existence of certain deficiencies to the Ḥanbalī scholars rather than to Imam Aḥmad himself. Nevertheless, examples were given of instances where Ibn Taymiyyah criticises narrations from Aḥmad and also Aḥmad's authentication of certain hadiths. Although he does show considerable respect for Aḥmad, his aim is always to bring the School's opinions in line with the Qur'an and *sunnah*. Interestingly, Ibn Taymiyyah occasionally rejects words accurately attributed to Aḥmad and claims that such words do not truly reflect Aḥmad's opinion as they contradict his general principles. It is as if he is correcting Aḥmad and showing him where he inadvertently ignored his own principles. This is further proof that Ibn Taymiyyah's aim is to adhere to the Qur'an and *sunnah*, rather than simply to cause the School to adhere to its Imam's words.

5

THE LEGACY

The influence of Ibn Taymiyyah on Ḥanbalī jurists

Introduction

Ibn Taymiyyah was amongst those scholars who exerted a great influence upon scholars both of his generation and of following generations. There have been certain characteristic features of his influence and they have extended to various subjects and sciences. Ibn Taymiyyah commanded a very large number of followers from all sections of society including scholars, members of the lay public and even political leaders.[1] Many of these individuals were authorities in their own fields: traditionists, jurists, authors and reciters, which illustrates his versatility and ability to attract a wide interest in the many study-circles he conducted.[2] A group of his students, such as al-Amīr Zayn al-Dīn Katabagha al-ʿĀdilī (721/1321),[3] Sayf al-Dīn Burāq (757/1356)[4] and Ṣalāḥ al-Dīn al-Takrītī (744/1344), were from the ruling circles.[5] Others, such as Fakhr al-Dīn al-Ṣāʾigh (d. 742/1341), were judges.[6]

A significant number of students attended this scholar's lectures and study-circles, while others benefited from his stay in prison during his frequent incarcerations.[7] A complete survey of Ibn Taymiyyah's notable students is not available,[8] but it is generally recognised that they were prodigious in number, '*khalqun kathīr*'.[9] These students were affiliated to various schools of Islamic law, for example, al-Dhahabī and Ibn Kathīr (d. 774/1372) were Shafiʿīs, while Ibn al-Qayyim and Ibn Mufliḥ were Ḥanbalīs.[10] Others were affiliated to different Islamic sects, for example, al-Zarʿī (d. 741/1340),[11] was for the most part Ashʿarī,[12] while al-Ṭūfī (d. 716/1361) claimed to be influenced by the Shiʿite doctrine.[13]

Despite their diverse backgrounds, it is interesting to note that most of Ibn Taymiyyah's disciples were influenced by his creed. There may have been various factors contributing to this, but one was the clarity of his approach in discussing the issues of this science.[14] He exerted great effort in order to clarify what he believed to be the true methodology of the *salaf*.[15]

There can be no doubt that Ibn Taymiyyah also influenced scholars in the sciences of *fiqh* and *uṣūl al-fiqh*. This influence became manifest in his time and has continued up to the present and it has been witnessed and recognised in various parts of the Islamic world. It is even reported that his jurisprudential influence reached India during his lifetime through the efforts of some of his students, such as al-Ardabilī, 'Alim al-Dīn and Ibn al-Ḥarīrī.[16] This influence resulted in reformations taking place in various aspects of the life of that part of the Islamic world, including the political system. This has prompted certain contemporary writers to claim that the first state based upon the *da'wah* of Ibn Taymiyyah was the Tughlugids' (*Taghliqiyyah*) state.[17]

Many of his students followed his example in enjoining what is proper and forbidding what is improper. This resulted, on several occasions, in some of these scholars being interrogated and imprisoned. For instance, Ibn Marī al-Ba'libikī was lashed and exiled; he then escaped to the Arabian Peninsula.[18] Sharaf al-Dīn al-Ḥarānī, well known as Ibn Najīḥ (d. 723/1323),[19] was detained due to his support for Ibn Taymiyyah.[20] Others such as Ibn al-Qayyim received the same penalty because they issued jurisprudential *fatāwā* in agreement with their sheikh's opinions. These statements often dealt with the same issues that had resulted in their teacher's detention.[21]

Ibn Taymiyyah was well known as a leading *mufti* in his time. Therefore, several Ḥanbalī scholars sought permission from him to issue *fatāwā*. The books of *Ṭabaqāt* make reference to several scholars who were acknowledged by Ibn Taymiyyah as having the authority to issue *fatāwā*. One such example was Ibn Qāḍī al-Jabal, a brilliant disciple who studied various sciences under Ibn Taymiyyah. Several leading scholars, one of whom was Ibn Taymiyyah, granted him authority in *iftā'* (issuing *fatāwā*), although he was only a youth.[22]

There is no complete record available detailing all the disciples of Ibn Taymiyyah in the various sciences or even in the science of jurisprudence and its principles alone. They can, however, be found scattered throughout the books of *ṭabaqāt*. It is beyond the scope of this work to attempt to compile a record of these scholars or even to discuss some examples of the eminent non-Ḥanbalī scholars who were influenced by this scholar, since this chapter is concerned only with the Ḥanbalī scholars who were influenced by Ibn Taymiyyah. Even then, it is beyond the scope of this work to mention all of the Ḥanbalī scholars influenced by him, for countless Ḥanbalī scholars have encountered Ibn Taymiyyah or his scholarly legacy. There were great many Ḥanbalī scholars who benefited from him during his lifetime, primarily as his students. These include Ibn al-Qayyim (d. 751–1350), Ibn Mufliḥ (d. 763/1361), Ibn 'Abd al-Hādī (d. 744/1343),[23] al-Zar'ī (d. 741/1340),[24] al-Manbijī (d. 730/1330),[25] Ibn Qāḍī al-Jabal (d. 771/1369),[26] Ibn 'Abd al-Ghanī al-Ḥarānī (d. 745/1344),[27] al-Ṭūfī (d. 717/1317), Ibn al-Muḥib al-Maqdisī (d. 737/1336),[28] Ibn Najīḥ (d. 723/1323),[29] al-Dhabāhī (d. 711/1311)[30] and Ibn al-Munajjā (d. 724/1324).[31] Certain other leading Ḥanbalī scholars are mentioned in the books of *Ṭabaqāt*, although it is unclear whether or not they were students of Ibn Taymiyyah. One of these is al-Ḥarānī (d. 745/1344).[32]

The objective of this chapter is instead to identify whether or not Ibn Taymiyyah has had an enduring influence on Ḥanbalī scholars from his generation up to the present time. It is only appropriate that the Ḥanbalī School of law is the subject of this study, as Ibn Taymiyyah's contact with this School was significantly greater than with the other Schools of law. In addition, Ibn Taymiyyah spent most of his life in Damascus, which was at that time an established centre of the Ḥanbalī School.[33] In assessing the extent of his influence, the following section studies and analyses a representative sample of Ḥanbalī scholars.

A study of the influence of Ibn Taymiyyah on selected Ḥanbalī jurists

In order to obtain a clear illustration of this influence, two types of sources have been consulted. The first are biographical accounts written by Ḥanbalī scholars and others. The second are selected treatises written by those Ḥanbalī scholars who form the subject matter of the study. These case studies include examples of Ḥanbalī scholars selected from different eras: Ibn al-Qayyim and Ibn Mufliḥ were eminent students of Ibn Taymiyyah; al-Jurāʿī (d. 883/1478) and al-Mardāwī (d. 885/1480) were leading Ḥanbalī scholars of the ninth *hijri* century; al-Hajjāwī (d. 968/1561) and al-Futūḥī (d. 972/1564) were scholars of the tenth century; al-Karmī (d. 1033/1624) and al-Buhūtī (d. 1051/1641) were scholars of the eleventh century; Ibn ʿAbd al-Wahhāb (d. 1206/1791) was a scholar of the twelfth *hijri* century; al-Saʿdī (d. 1376/1956) lived in the fourteenth century; finally, Ibn ʿUthaymīn (b. 1347/1928) was a leading contemporary scholar.

It ought to be noted, again, that the vast scope of this field is such that it is not feasible to treat all the aspects of Ibn Taymiyyah's influence upon these Ḥanbalī jurists. It should be sufficient to make reference to some examples to show whether or not Ibn Taymiyyah exerts an influence upon these jurists. Furthermore, this chapter is primarily restricted to the issues on which these scholars have made explicit references to Ibn Taymiyyah's opinions and preferences, rather than seeking to extract Ibn Taymiyyah's underlying influence from their general writings.

Ibn al-Qayyim (691–751/1292–1350)

This scholar's lineage (*nasab*) was Muhammad b. Abi Bakr b. Ayyūb b. Saʿd b. Ḥariz al-Zarʿī. He was known variously as Ibn al-Qayyim, Ibn Qayyim, Ibn Qayyim al-Jawziyyah, Shams al-Dīn and was also known by the *kunyah* Abū ʿAbd Allah.[34]

Ibn Qayyim attended the study-circles of various scholars in Damascus, the city in which he was born. Some of his teachers, such as his father and Ibn Taymiyyah, were authorities in various disciplines and so he studied more than one subject with them.[35] On the whole, however, it appears that he studied individual branches of knowledge under the supervision of specialist scholars. For instance, he received tuition in the science of inheritance and jurisprudence from Sheikh al-Majd al-Ḥarānī,[36] and he studied the science of *ḥadīth* and *rijāl* under the eminent scholar al-Mizzī.[37]

His biography suggests that he acquired the bulk of his knowledge in his birthplace, Damascus. It is probable that he did not feel the need to travel much to other parts of the Islamic world in order to seek knowledge, because this city was an important centre of knowledge at his time.[38]

Ibn al-Qayyim became a famous sheikh in his own right after completing his studies, and due to his scholarly reputation, he attracted many students.[39] His time was occupied in teaching, issuing *fatāwā* and composing several important treatises on various sciences. Amongst his most famous books in the science of jurisprudence and its principles are *Zād al-Maʿād fi hadi khair al-ʿIbād* and *Iʿlām al-Muwaqqiʿīn ʿan Rabb al-ʿAlamīn.*[40]

He has been referred to in certain sources as a Ḥanbalī scholar.[41] Nevertheless, one specialist in Ibn al-Qayyim's treatises and jurisprudence declared, after a comprehensive study of his works, that he was an absolute *mujtahid*.[42] Indeed, he became recognised as one of the *mujtahids* revivers of the religion of the fourteenth century.[43]

The influence of Ibn Taymiyyah on Ibn al-Qayyim

Ibn al-Qayyim was described as 'one of the notable companions of Ibn Taymiyyah'.[44] Several scholars mention that he was inseparable from (*lazama*) his sheikh and studied under his supervision and guidance (*akhadha ʿanhu*).[45] His companionship of Ibn Taymiyyah lasted for a lengthy period of time, spanning from the return of the latter from Egypt in 712/1312 until his death in 728/1328.[46] He was exceedingly familiar with the opinions and words of his sheikh; on various issues he narrates from him directly (*samiʿtu*),[47] or he mentions acts that he personally saw his sheikh performing (*shāhddtu*).[48]

Ibn al-Qayyim clarified the status of his sheikh's knowledge of Ḥanbalī law. He asserts that the position of his sheikh's preferences (for one opinion over another) are at the least not inferior, if not superior, to the preferences of leading scholars in the Ḥanbalī School of law, such as Ibn ʿAqīl and Abū 'l-Khaṭṭāb, and even their sheikh Abū Yaʿla. Therefore, Ibn Taymiyyah's preferences can be employed for the support of *fatāwā* and rulings.[49]

Ibn al-Qayyim's jurisprudential treatises, as well as his other treatises, are indicative of the great impact Ibn Taymiyyah made on this scholar. He was particularly influenced by the methodology implemented by his sheikh in delivering *fatāwā*, as well as by his personal characteristics.[50] The great similarity between the opinions of these two scholars on various issues is a testament to the extent to which Ibn al-Qayyim was influenced by him. This influence is further evidenced through his allusions to and lengthy citations of the opinions and preferences of his teacher.[51] It is also abundantly clear that Ibn al-Qayyim was very familiar with Ibn Taymiyyah's works, as he left a great document entitled *Asmāʾ muʾallafāt Ibn Taymiyyah* in which he listed on an extensive number of his sheikh's treatises. Another proof of his familiarity with the opinions and preferences of his sheikh is his ability to differentiate between the earlier (subsequently retracted) and later opinions of Ibn Taymiyyah.[52]

It is clear that Ibn al-Qayyim attaches great importance to these opinions and preferences. He often cites Ibn Taymiyyah when consolidating various opinions in the School,[53] and when labelling various rulings in the School as incorrect (*ghalaṭ*).[54]

There is clear similarity between Ibn Taymiyyah's position towards the leading scholars and Imams and that of Ibn al-Qayyim. Ibn al-Qayyim asserts that the superiority of scholars in the level of their knowledge does not necessitate the acceptance of all of their opinions. Similarly, the existence of some incorrect opinions within their rulings does not render all of their opinions invalid or mean that these scholars can be censured because of their adherence to these incorrect opinions. According to Ibn al-Qayyim, the correct stance is that we should believe that these *mujtahids*, in holding these incorrect opinions, were not in fact committing a misdeed. Conversely, we should not consider them to be infallible. This method, in fact, according to Ibn al-Qayyim, was the same method employed by these Imams themselves and other leading scholars towards the opinions held by the companions of the Prophet. Ibn al-Qayyim asserts that this method of dealing with the Imams cannot be rejected except by two types of persons, either those who do not know the excellent characteristics of the scholar in Islam or those who are ignorant of the *sharī'ah*. This, as Ibn al-Qayyim explains, is because an individual who possesses knowledge of the *sharī'ah* and is acquainted with real life situations can see clearly that a great renowned scholar can err sometimes and that he is forgiven for his mistakes and rewarded for his independent reasoning. He must not be, however, followed in these mistaken rulings nor should he be attacked for holding these opinions.[55]

It is interesting to note that Ibn al-Qayyim's understanding of the correct position to take towards the opinions of leading scholars seems to contribute to his critical approach in studying the Ḥanbalī law, in which he also seems to be influenced by his sheikh. Therefore, for instance, he sometimes rejects some opinions found in the School and at other times accepts opinions after making certain modifications.[56] Occasionally, Ibn al-Qayyim states that Aḥmad's opinion is incorrect and further supports his claim by comparing Aḥmad's ruling to the general principles of Aḥmad himself.[57] In order to solve an existing conflict between scholars, he occasionally cites the position of his sheikh.[58] In addition, he describes certain opinions of his sheikh as 'opinions that suit the general principles of Imam Aḥmad',[59] 'what the correct evidences bear witness to',[60] 'what was endorsed by the majority of the Predecessors',[61] 'what is nearer to the implementation of the *ḥadīth* and the general principles of the *sharī'ah*',[62] 'the undoubtedly correct opinion necessitated by the words and general principles of Aḥmad'.[63] On occasion, he praises his sheikh by stating that he has not read any other previous scholar making a certain beneficial point made by Ibn Taymiyyah.[64] In various rulings, he defends the opinions of his sheikh, although they were in opposition to the predominant opinion of the School. These opinions include those that resulted in some of his detentions, such as the ruling concerning the triple divorce and giving an oath for a divorce. Ibn al-Qayyim devotes particular sections of his treatises to assert the correctness and accuracy of his sheikh's positions, which he affirms through the use of various textual and rational evidences.[65] Concerning some of these issues, Ibn al-Qayyim declares that his sheikh was able to refute his opponents' evidence, but his opponents succeeded in altering the argument concerning the disputed issues from one whose foundation was jurisprudential in nature to one which was political. Hence, they would lodge their complaints in political circles. According to Ibn al-Qayyim, this was the most potent 'evidence' for his opponents, one to which his sheikh was incapable of responding. As a consequence, Ibn Taymiyyah was detained for long periods of time.[66]

Despite the opposition Ibn Taymiyyah received, Ibn al-Qayyim asserts that his sheikh's position regarding these jurisprudential issues exerted a great influence upon the society of his time. According to Ibn al-Qayyim, this influence took various forms, such as the suspension of innovations and the increased use of texts and sayings of the companions as evidence.[67]

It seems also that Ibn al-Qayyim benefited from his sheikh's knowledge in the science of *ḥadīth*. He cites him in various places in this regard.[68] Sometimes he refutes certain *ḥadīths* and he backs his opinion with statements issued by Ibn Taymiyyah rebutting the same *ḥadīths*,[69] and sometimes he cites his sheikh's clarification of certain terms or phrases mentioned in some *ḥadīths*.[70] On other occasions, he outlines opposing opinions to those of his sheikh with regard to some *ḥadīths* and then he gives preference to Ibn Taymiyyah's opinions.[71] It is interesting, however, that where Ibn Taymiyyah seems to find certain statements in some *ḥadīths* problematic, as they seem to him to be in opposition to general rulings, we find Ibn al-Qayyim asserting that the alleged conflict is non-existent.[72] This appears to indicate that both Ibn Taymiyyah and Ibn al-Qayyim had a critical and analytical approach towards the textual content of *ḥadīths*.

It is important to note that Ibn Taymiyyah's influence upon this scholar also extended to theology. Ibn al-Qayyim declares in his poem entitled '*al-Nuniyyah*' that prior to his contact with Ibn Taymiyyah, he had subscribed to a number of incorrect opinions concerning creed. Once he had met Ibn Taymiyyah, however, he altered these opinions.[73]

Due to the strong connection between Ibn al-Qayyim and his sheikh, he shared in some of the interrogations experienced by his sheikh. He was occasionally interrogated for issuing a *fatwā* in agreement with the *fatwā* of his sheikh. For instance, he was imprisoned after he issued a *fatwā* concerning the issue of undertaking a journey in order to visit the grave of the Prophet and concerning the triple divorce, on which he agreed with his sheikh.[74]

This close relationship between Ibn Taymiyyah and Ibn al-Qayyim appears to be the cause for the claim made by some individuals that Ibn al-Qayyim was only an emulator of Ibn Taymiyyah.[75] Ibn Ḥajar, while testifying to the extensive knowledge of this scholar in various sciences, observes that Ibn al-Qayyim was very fond of his sheikh Ibn Taymiyyah, and this caused him to defend his sheikh and to follow him in all of his opinions.[76]

Ibn Taymiyyah's clear influence upon Ibn al-Qayyim must be accepted. It appears, however, that the allegation that Ibn al-Qayyim was only emulating his sheikh is incorrect, as a careful study of his treatises reveals that he occasionally asserted opinions of his own.[77] On certain issues, he discloses an inclination towards opinions that are in opposition to his sheikh's point of view.[78] Sometimes, he states that his sheikh was unaware of the existence of some opinions held by other scholars.[79] In fact, Ibn al-Qayyim openly disagreed with Ibn Taymiyyah in relation to some issues.[80]

Ibn al-Qayyim was known for his prodigious studies in various Islamic sciences.[81] The treatises produced by him were in fact founded upon a large number of sources, besides the teachings of Ibn Taymiyyah.[82] Both Ibn Rajab and Ibn Kathīr state that he had acquired a large number of books that were not available to most scholars.[83] Furthermore, Ibn al-Qayyim was educated under several other leading scholars of his time,[84] which suggests that Ibn Taymiyyah was not the only intellectual influence upon him.

It is more correct to say that Ibn al-Qayyim followed his teacher's method of studying jurisprudence in a comparative and analytical manner. He would thereafter formulate his own opinion on the basis of its proximity to the texts of the Qur'an and *Sunnah*.[85] When we observe Ibn al-Qayyim to be in agreement with his sheikh, it is clearly apparent that he was not merely influenced by him, but that his agreement is based upon a comprehensive analysis of the evidence.[86] It appears that his vast encyclopaedic knowledge assisted him in this process of investigation.[87] In fact, it would not be incorrect to say that Ibn al-Qayyim both conveyed and revised his sheikh's knowledge.[88]

An examination of Ibn al-Qayyim's treatises has revealed the fact that, in comparison with other Ḥanbalī scholars, he has not in fact made many direct references to the opinions and preferences of Ibn Taymiyyah.[89] This clearly does not mean that Ibn Taymiyyah did not influence him, for we find a great similarity between the jurisprudential rulings of these two scholars. The influence went to the core of Ibn al-Qayyim's approach to jurisprudence. Al-Shawkānī noted that this agreement was founded upon the fact that Ibn al-Qayyim primarily based his opinions upon legal evidences, just as Ibn Taymiyyah did. Al-Shawkānī does not dispute the fact that the lengthy period of association between these scholars left an influence upon the jurisprudential opinions of Ibn al-Qayyim.[90] It is probable therefore that Ibn al-Qayyim sometimes related an opinion shared by him and Ibn Taymiyyah, without seeing the need to make reference to his teacher.

In closing, it is useful to mention two concise statements made by two leading scholars. The first is that of Ibn Ḥajar al-'Asqalānī, who says: 'If there was no virtue of Ibn Taymiyyah except his famous disciple, al-Sheikh Shams al-Dīn Ibn Qayyim al-Jawziyyah, the writer of the great beneficial treatises that benefit his followers as well as his opponents, this would be more than sufficient to illustrate the excellence of his (Ibn Taymiyyah's) rank.'[91] The second statement is from al-Sa'dī who describes Ibn al-Qayyim as 'the one student who benefited the most from his sheikh, and the one was most proficient in his scholarly legacy (*aqwamuhum bi 'ulūmih*), and the most knowledgeable in the sciences of revelation and reason amongst Ibn Taymiyyah's students' (Tables 1 and 2).[92]

Table 1 The extent to which Ibn al-Qayyim in his book *Ẓād al-Maʿād* cites the jurisprudential opinions and preferences of Ibn Taymiyyah

Volume 1	57, 61, 62, 71, 131, 136, 199, 222, 237, 264, 276, 304, 311, 316, 319, 324, 360, 375, 378, 407, 434, 439, 440, 448, 456, 464, 465, 472, 480, 495, 499, 505, 518, 520
Volume 2	21, 22, 53, 88, 118–122, 127, 141, 148–150, 209–210, 218, 231, 333
Volume 3	37, 138, 152, 309, 454, 492
Volume 4	358
Volume 5	9, 86, 155, 197, 215, 248, 306, 312, 353, 406, 415, 438, 450, 475, 557, 593, 606, 658, 673, 717, 730, 749, 781, 783, 807, 809, 811, 823, 833

Table 2 Ibn al-Qayyim's citation of Ibn Taymiyyah's jurisprudential opinions and preferences in his book *Iʿlām al-Muaqqiʿīn*

Volume 1	137, 473, 479, 498, 508 twice, 519, 520
Volume 2	5, 8, 9, 14, 15, 16, 20, 33, 35, 36, 60, 111, 132, 164, 239, 365, 412
Volume 3	7, 42, 96, 118, 120 twice, 123, 125 twice, 150, 223, 224, 274, 279, 283, 298 twice, 301, 352, 360, 367, 448
Volume 4	7, 12, 27, 78, 99, 111, 144 twice, 203, 215, 219, 223, 226, 233, 243, 264, 272, 295, 319, 322, 334

Ibn Mufliḥ (708–763/1308–1362)

Ibn Mufliḥ's full name was Muhammad b. Mufliḥ b. Muhammad b. Mufrij al-Maqdisī al-Ṣāliḥī. He was born in Damascus,[93] and it was in this city that he commenced his education. Ibn Taymiyyah was the most eminent teacher of Ibn Mufliḥ. Amongst his other famous teachers were the judge Jamāl al-Dīn al-Mardāwī (d. 769/1367), Ibn al-Musallam (d. 726/1326), al-Mizzī and al-Dhahabī. Under the tutelage of these scholars, Ibn Mufliḥ studied various sciences, such as jurisprudence and its principles, *ḥadīth* and syntax.[94] He was primarily recognised as an authority in the science of *al-Furūʿ* (jurisprudence). He appears to have been recognised by scholars as a master of this subject as early as when he was only 21 or 22 years old. This can be understood from a narration referred to in several books of *Ṭabaqāt*, in which Ibn al-Qayyim is quoted as saying, in the year 731/1331, that 'there is no one more knowledgeable in the world regarding the Ḥanbalī School of law than Ibn Mufliḥ'.[95]

After completing his studies and developing his own approach, Ibn Mufliḥ was appointed as a teacher. He instructed students in several schools, such as al-Ṣāḥibah, Sheikh Abī ʿUmar and al-Salāmiyyah.[96] Ibn Mufliḥ was not only a teacher of jurisprudence but also a *muftī*,[97] and, for a certain period of time, a judge.[98]

Ibn Mufliḥ was also a respected author, particularly in the science of jurisprudence and its principles, which was his specialist field. He compiled the book *al-Furūʿ*, which concerns the science of jurisprudence. This treatise has become very well known and a recognised source within the School. Several Ḥanbalī scholars have expressed their appreciation of this work and described it as one of the greatest, most precious and most comprehensive treatises.[99] Another important treatise by Ibn Mufliḥ is his book *uṣūl al-fiqh*, which (as the name suggests) concerns the science of the principles of jurisprudence. It has been claimed that there is no other Ḥanbalī treatise in this science that is comparable to this book.[100]

The influence of Ibn Taymiyyah on Ibn Mufliḥ

Ibn Taymiyyah was astonished by the extensive knowledge of Ibn Mufliḥ and he would often remark: 'you are not Ibn Mufliḥ (the son of the successful), you are Mufliḥ (the successful)'.[101]

Ibn Mufliḥ attached himself to Ibn Taymiyyah and absorbed a large amount of his knowledge. This companionship continued until he became the most knowledgeable of Ibn Taymiyyah's students in relation to his sheikh's opinions and preferences. It is even reported that Ibn al-Qayyim would consult him in this matter.[102] This can be further supported by Ibn al-Mubrrid, who reported that it was said that the foremost amongst Ibn Taymiyyah's students in jurisprudence was Ibn Mufliḥ, in *ḥadīth* it was Ibn 'Abd al-Hādī and in creed and sects and in the renunciation of worldly pleasures (*azhadahum*) it was Ibn al-Qayyim, who also achieved a balance between (*al-mutawassiṭ bayn*) the two sciences of *ḥadīth* and jurisprudence.[103]

The Ḥanbalī sources and biographical accounts do not contain much clarification of Ibn Taymiyyah's influence upon his student, Ibn Mufliḥ. Therefore, the most relevant treatise concerning this point is Ibn Mufliḥ's aforementioned book *al-Furū'*. According to al-Mardāwī, it is one of the most important treatises written in the Ḥanbalī jurisprudence.[104]

It is evident from a reading of *al-Furū'* that Ibn Mufliḥ commands an extensive knowledge of his sheikh's opinions and preferences. These opinions and preferences are primarily related to the various issues of jurisprudence, although he does occasionally cite his sheikh's opinions regarding issues of creed.

It is also apparent that, through his lengthy association with him, he was able to acquire most of his sheikh's jurisprudential knowledge. He would also frequently consult several treatises of his sheikh in compiling his own work, for we find him quoting numerous treatises, such as *Sharḥ al-'Umdah, Iqtiḍā' al-Ṣirāṭ al-Mustaqīm, al-Ajwibah al-Miṣriyyah, al-Ṣārim al-Maslūl, Minhāj Ahl al-Sunnah* and *al-Fatāwā al-Miṣriyyah.*[105]

This long and close association with Ibn Taymiyyah and his treatises appears to have conferred upon Ibn Mufliḥ the ability to predict Ibn Taymiyyah's position on certain issues in the absence of an explicit text from him. On occasions, he makes reference to 'what the words of Ibn Taymiyyah indicate would be his opinions'.[106] He mentions various rulings on which Ibn Taymiyyah clearly had a preference, and those about which he entertained a reservation or hesitation.[107] On various issues, Ibn Mufliḥ attempts to clarify the intended meaning of his sheikh's words.[108]

All the aforementioned points affirm the fact that this scholar commanded a great familiarity with his sheikh's opinions and treatises.

It goes without saying that Ibn Mufliḥ attaches great importance to the opinions of Ibn Taymiyyah; he cites his opinions in various places in his book,[109] and on several occasions, he expounds the opinions of Ibn Taymiyyah complete with his evidence. Such citations occasionally run to several pages.[110] Ibn Mufliḥ sometimes supports his opinions by citing the position of his sheikh.[111]

It is important to note that Ibn Mufliḥ considered Ibn Taymiyyah's narrations as a source through which even conventional Ḥanbalī jurisprudence can be determined. On occasions, Ibn Mufliḥ appears to mean Ibn Taymiyyah when he says '*ba'ḍ aṣḥābina*' (some of our fellow Ḥanbalīs) without mentioning Ibn Taymiyyah by name.[112] On various issues, he attributes some rulings to the Ḥanbalī School as narrations (*riwayāt*), *wajh* or *qawl* (opinions) and occasionally attributes opinions to some scholars via the narrations of Ibn Taymiyyah.[113] Ibn Taymiyyah's classification of opinions within the Ḥanbalī School is also cited by Ibn Mufliḥ.[114] On certain issues, he affirms the existence of an agreement between his sheikh and the Ḥanbalī School.[115]

On the other hand, certain opinions attributed by Ibn Taymiyyah to the Ḥanbalī School are questioned by Ibn Mufliḥ. On several issues, he describes the attribution of opinions by his sheikh to the School as 'strange'. He suggests that Ibn Taymiyyah's 'strange opinions' are caused by a misunderstanding of general statements uttered by either Ibn Ḥanbal or some of the leading Ḥanbalī scholars.[116] Occasionally, Ibn Mufliḥ appears to reject Ibn Taymiyyah's claim concerning the existence of certain opinions in the Ḥanbalī School. He studies the possible legal ground upon which this claim is founded. Thereafter, he cites clarifications made by Ḥanbalī scholars of those grounds, in a manner that does not support the claim of his sheikh.[117] On other issues, also, he declares clearly that what Ibn Taymiyyah mentioned as *ẓāhir al-madhhab* (the predominant opinion within the School) he himself had not found to be mentioned as such by Ḥanbalīs.[118] Indeed Ibn Mufliḥ sometimes asserts that the opinions found in the School on a certain issue do not include those Ibn Taymiyyah claims the existence of.[119]

Despite the critical approach adopted by Ibn Mufliḥ in studying the attribution of opinions by Ibn Taymiyyah to the Ḥanbalī School, some Ḥanbalī scholars have questioned the correctness of the attribution of some of these opinions by Ibn Taymiyyah to the School which Ibn Mufliḥ narrates from him. They asserted that some of these opinions were only attributed to the School by Ibn Taymiyyah and denied the existence of these opinions within the School.[120]

This critical approach does not detract from the general respect Ibn Mufliḥ felt for Ibn Taymiyyah. Ibn Mufliḥ considers his sheikh as an authority not only on the Ḥanbalī School but also on the opinions of the other schools of law, he attributes various opinions to these schools, basing them upon the words of Ibn Taymiyyah.[121] Furthermore, Ibn Mufliḥ occasionally accepts the existence of a consensus amongst scholars or the fact that a ruling originates from the opinion of the predecessors based upon Ibn Taymiyyah's narration of it.[122] There are occasions, however, where Ibn Mufliḥ disputes the accuracy of Ibn Taymiyyah's narration of a consensus of the scholars. He cites some Ḥanbalī scholars who assert the existence of conflicting opinions within the School regarding the issues in question.[123] Clearly, therefore, Ibn Mufliḥ's knowledge of Ḥanbalī *fiqh* was vast enough to use it as a measure against such claims of consensus.

As with Ibn al-Qayyim, Ibn Taymiyyah also influenced Ibn Mufliḥ in his general approach towards the study and analysis of Ḥanbalī jurisprudence. Ibn Mufliḥ cites his sheikh's opinions when they are in opposition to the Ḥanbalī School, or at least to the opinions of some of its leading scholars.[124] On several occasions, he also cites his sheikh's thoroughgoing discussion of the opinions of Ḥanbalī scholars and their evidences.[125] Similar to Ibn al-Qayyim, Ibn Mufliḥ conducts his own corrections of Ḥanbalī jurisprudence and some of his counter-arguments for this purpose are based upon the words of his sheikh.[126]

Ibn Mufliḥ was also impressed by Ibn Taymiyyah's campaign against innovation. We find him classifying several practices and rulings as innovations; in doing so, he occasionally cites the words of Ibn Taymiyyah in support.[127]

Considering Ibn Mufliḥ's long association with Ibn Taymiyyah, it is to be expected that he would have been influenced by him to a considerable degree, but it would be incorrect to consider him a blind follower of his sheikh. For the most part, his interest was in transmitting, rather than supporting, the jurisprudential rulings of Ibn Taymiyyah. On certain occasions, he demonstrates his support for his sheikh's jurisprudential rulings,[128] but on other occasions he criticises his sheikh's opinions and disputes his evidence.[129] In some places, Ibn Mufliḥ even states that his sheikh's opinions are 'disorderly' or that his sheikh seems to hesitate in his rulings.[130] In other places, he calls Ibn Taymiyyah's opinions regarding some jurisprudential issues 'strange' and goes on to suggest reasons for the existence of these strange rulings.[131] He sometimes considers Ibn Taymiyyah's ruling to be 'questionable' (*fīhi naẓar*),[132] or he argues that the opinion of certain Ḥanbalī scholars is more likely to be correct than that of his sheikh.[133] On other occasions, although Ibn Mufliḥ does not expressly state his view on the opinion of his sheikh, it is nevertheless clear that he is not in agreement with him. This can be deduced from his citation without criticism of various evidences that are contrary to his sheikh's opinions.[134] Ibn Mufliḥ occasionally observes that although the evidence seems to suggest certain conclusions, Ibn Taymiyyah does not hold them.[135] On certain issues, Ibn Mufliḥ considers some of the legal evidence cited by Ibn Taymiyyah to be weak and he occasionally quotes Ibn Ḥanbal in support of the view that some *ḥadīths* employed by Ibn Taymiyyah are unsound.[136] Ibn Mufliḥ is not afraid to point out where Ibn Taymiyyah is alone in subscribing to certain opinions.[137] As other times, Ibn Mufliḥ attempts to find an accommodation between the opinion of his sheikh and other Ḥanbalī scholars by weighing up the evidence carefully.[138]

It is evident that Ibn Mufliḥ was well versed in his sheikh's opinions, to the extent that he was able to dispute claims by other scholars that Ibn Taymiyyah subscribed to certain opinions by reference to what he knew of Ibn Taymiyyah's opinions on such matters.[139] Despite Ibn Mufliḥ's considerable familiarity with Ibn Taymiyyah's knowledge, however, he was prepared to admit when he was unsure about his sheikh's opinion on any particular issue.[140] Despite this, there are occasions where Ibn Mufliḥ narrates what he considers to be Ibn Taymiyyah's opinions but the narration appears to be incomplete. In such situations further clarification is needed as the ruling is problematic without it.[141]

The study of *al-Furūʿ* not only provides us with the information necessary to determine the extent of Ibn Taymiyyah's influence upon Ibn Mufliḥ but also helps us to collect a considerable number of Ibn Taymiyyah's opinions. The Table 3 shows the volumes and page numbers of *al-Furūʿ* wherein Ibn Mufliḥ has cited the opinions and preferences of his sheikh.

Table 3 References to Ibn Taymiyyah's opinions and preferences made by Ibn Mufliḥ in his book *al-Furūʿ*

Volume 1	72, 73 twice, 77–78 twice, 78, 79 twice, 85, 87, 93, 97, 100, 101, 103, 106, 107, 118, 119, 123, 124, 125, 128 thrice, 129–130, 133, 134, 139, 148, 151, 153, 154, 155, 157 twice, 160, 163 thrice, 165 twice, 167, 173, 176, 179,181 twice, 183 twice, 184, 193 twice, 196, 197, 198, 199 twice, 201, 203 thrice, 205, 206 thrice, 208, 209, 213, 217, 219, 220 twice, 222 twice, 224, 227 thrice, 229, 231, 234, 235, 238, 241 twice, 242, 244, 245 thrice, 246, 255, 256, 258, 259, 261 twice, 262, 263, 267 thrice, 269 twice, 272, 281, 287 thrice, 289, 291, 293, 294 twice, 295 twice, 304, 306 thrice, 308, 319, 324, 325, 330, 333, 334, 336, 345, 346, 347 twice, 352, 353, 354, 355, 356 twice, 357, 358, 360, 379, 375, 393, 397, 400 twice, 408, 410, 413 four, 414, 415 thrice, 418, 421 twice, 423 twice, 425, 427, 428, 430, 431, 433, 442, 444 twice, 452, 454 thrice, 456, 457 thrice, 458, 459, 460 thrice, 467, 485, 491 twice, 492, 493, 494, 496 four, 505 twice, 513, 516, 517, 518, 520, 522, 524, 526 twice, 528, 531 twice, 534, 538, 539, 542, 544, 546, 547, 548 thrice, 553, 554 twice, 556, 558, 560, 562, 567, 568 twice, 569, 572, 573 twice, 576 twice, 577 twice, 578, 584, 585, 587, 590, 591, 597, 599, 604, 607
Volume 2	8, 11, 13, 17, 22, 25, 27, 28 twice, 30, 33, 38, 47, 51, 54, 57, 58 thrice, 64, 69, 71, 72, 74, 89, 91, 99, 105, 109 twice, 110, 118, 125, 129, 130 four times, 131, 136, 137 twice, 142, 150 twice, 155, 156, 159, 160, 167, 175, 177, 179, 184–185, 210, 216, 217, 221, 223, 243, 248 twice, 249, 251 twice, 252, 260, 263, 264, 273, 274, 276 twice, 277, 286, 287 twice, 289, 290, 291 twice, 298, 299, 302, 304, 305, 307, 310, 311, 312, 313 twice, 314,315, 316, 323, 327, 336, 338, 348, 351, 399, 403, 404, 407, 437, 440 twice, 443, 464 twice, 445 twice, 467, 474, 477, 498, 500, 534, 537, 540, 557–558, 576, 587, 588, 589, 591 twice, 592 twice, 602, 603, 610, 619, 620, 629 twice, 637, 639, 641, 651, 654, 658, 661, 665, 667
Volume 3	4, 7, 9, 13, 19, 24, 41, 42, 48 twice, 50, 65 twice, 66, 74, 75 twice, 76, 100, 108, 112, 113, 115 twice, 118, 124, 125, 137, 138, 143, 144, 145 thrice, 167, 168, 194, 204, 206, 225, 226, 227, 232 twice, 237 twice, 239 twice, 272, 293, 297, 300 twice, 301, 340, 344, 350, 356, 357, 374, 390, 440, 454 496, 497, 499, 500, 502, 503, 508, 509, 513, 514, 515, 516, 519, 520, 521, 523 twice, 524, 528, 529, 531 twice, 534, 539 twice, 541, 545, 546, 554, 555, 564, 565

Table 3 Continued

Volume 4	5, 6, 9, 22, 23, 25, 27 twice, 36, 38, 41, 42, 50, 51 twice, 54 twice, 60, 62 twice, 64, 74, 77, 79 twice, 84, 86, 92, 94, 97, 98, 102 twice, 105, 126, 131, 134, 135 twice, 137 twice, 138, 139 twice, 145, 147, 148, 149, 153, 154 155, 157, 159, 160 twice, 162, 164, 167, 168, 170, 171 twice, 179, 185, 186, 187, 196 thrice, 197, 202, 207, 225, 237, 238, 242, 244 twice, 250, 262, 264 twice, 265 twice, 275, 283, 285 twice, 286 twice, 288 twice, 289, 291, 292, 293, 298, 307, 316, 317, 322, 335, 343, 345, 346, 349, 353, 375, 377, 384 thrice, 393, 396, 397, 399, 400, 402, 404, 405 twice, 406 twice, 411 thrice, 415, 416, 417 thrice, 418 twice, 423, 426, 428, 435 twice, 436, 439 twice, 440 twice, 441, 446, 448, 458, 460, 461, 463, 465, 474 twice, 477, 478, 482 twice, 500, 503, 508, 510, 511, 514, 516, 517, 520, 523, 524, 526, 527, 529 thrice, 531, 538, 555, 558, 559, 568, 581 twice, 585, 587, 588, 589, 593, 594, 595 four times, 596, 599 four times, 600 five times, 601, 602, 603 twice, 608, 609, 610, 612 twice, 615, 618 twice, 619 twice, 621, 622, 623, 625, 630, 631, 635, 636, 638, 639, 645, 649, 652, 655, 661, 662, 668, 712, 716,717
Volume 5	3 thrice, 8, 9, 11, 44, 47, 50, 51, 52, 53 twice, 77, 81, 85, 100, 132, 133, 136, 145, 147, 155 twice, 160, 162, 163, 169, 172, 176, 178 twice, 188, 189, 192, 193, 194, 195, 199, 207, 210, 211, 212, 215, 216, 217 thrice, 218, 200 twice, 224 twice, 225 twice, 234, 247, 268, 272, 285, 288, 293, 300, 302 thrice, 304, 308, 310, 322, 329, 339, 342, 343 twice, 346, 352, 354, 356,361, 362, 363 twice, 364, 365, 367 thrice, 368, 370, 371, 378, 409, 414, 424 twice, 425, 426, 432, 440, 442, 452, 464, 466, 474, 492, 500, 506 twice, 507,515, 518 twice, 519, 524, 526 twice, 530, 545, 546, 548, 550 twice, 555, 558 wice, 570, 574, 587, 589, 596, 599 twice, 601, 603, 604, 606, 614, 635, 640,642, 650, 660, 662, 663,668, 669
Volume 6	12 twice, 46, 54 twice, 55 twice, 56, 61, 64, 68, 71, 73, 75 twice, 76 twice, 83, 89, 95, 106, 107 twice, 109, 115 twice, 118, 120, 123, 126, 136, 139, 142 twice, 143 twice, 144, 147 twice, 150, 152 twice, 153 twice, 156, 157, 159, 160, 161, 164 twice, 165 twice, 167, 172, 175, 178, 182, 183, 184, 185, 188, 194, 195, 196, 202, 204, 205, 213, 217, 218, 223, 228, 229, 230, 237, 243, 246, 250, 253, 255, 256 twice, 257, 259, 260, 265 twice, 267, 269 twice, 270 twice, 271, 272 twice, 273, 274 twice, 275 twice, 276, 279, 280 twice, 284, 287, 288 twice, 290 thrice, 291, 292, 293, 294, 295, 296 twice, 297 twice, 303 twice, 304, 313, 315, 319, 320, 321, 335, 338, 339, 340 thrice, 341, 342, 344, 345, 347 thrice, 350, 352, 353, 365, 367, 386, 389, 390, 398, 402, 404 twice, 408, 414, 415, 417, 420, 422, 423 twice, 424, 425, 428, 429, 436, 437, 440, 454, 457, 462, 463, 467, 473, 475, 475, 479, 480 twice, 487, 489 twice, 492, 494, 497 twice, 498 twice, 499 twice, 500, 501, 502, 504, 505 twice, 511, 513, 514, 516, 519, 525, 527 twice, 533 twice, 549, 550, 551 twice, 553, 555, 562, 564, 565, 567, 570, 572, 573, 576, 578, 581, 582, 584, 588, 589, 594, 595, 599, 601, 605, 615, 617, 625, 629, 633

Al-Jurāʿī (d. 883/1478)

Al-Jurāʿī's full name was Abū Bakr b. Zayd b. Abī Bakr b. Zayd b. ʿUmar b. Maḥmūd al-Ḥasanī. He was born in Jurāʿ, one of the areas in Nāblis, in 825/1422.[142] The Jarakisah Mamluks governed Egypt and al-Shām during this period.[143]

Al-Jurā'ī's journey for the acquisition of knowledge can be divided into three main phases. The first phase was at his birthplace in Jurā' where he studied the fundamentals of various Arabic and Islamic sciences, such as the Qur'an and its interpretation, jurisprudence and syntax. The second phase started when he moved to Damascus in the year 842/1438,[144] where he attended the classes of various leading scholars such as Ibn Qundus (d. 861/1457), a well known Ḥanbalī scholar, under whom he studied such sciences as jurisprudence, principles of jurisprudence, inheritance, Arabic language and rhetoric.[145] He also studied under the supervision of Abū Sha'r (d. 844/1440), who was a leading scholar in various sciences, such as *ḥadīth, tafsīr, fiqh* and *usūl*.[146]

The year 861/1457 marks the beginning of the third phase of al-Jura'ī's quest for knowledge. In that year, he travelled to Egypt where he studied under several leading scholars, such as al-Balqīnī (d. 868/1464), al-Jalāl al-Maḥalī (d. 864/1459), al-Ḥiṣnī (d. 881/1476), the judge 'Izz al-Dīn al-Kinānī (d. 876/1471), Ibn al-Humām al-Ḥanafī (d. 861/1457) and al-Sakhāwī (d. 902/1497).[147]

A careful study of the biographies of al-Jurā'ī's teachers indicates that during the first phase he was engaged in the study of the fundamentals of various sciences, such as Qur'an, *ḥadīth, Tafsīr* and *fiqh*. He progressed during the second stage to a more detailed study of a number of Islamic and Arabic sciences but was still primarily taught by Ḥanbalī scholars. During the third stage, it is evident that the majority of his teachers were from a non-Ḥanbalī background. After a lengthy period of time travelling and having expended considerable effort in his quest for knowledge, al-Jurā'ī became a teacher, judge and *mufti*. He also composed several treatises, most of which concerned the science of jurisprudence and its principles.

The influence of Ibn Taymiyyah on al-Jurā'ī

A study of some of the treatises al-Jurā'ī composed reveals that he was familiar with the opinions and preferences of Ibn Taymiyyah. This may be evidenced in a number of ways: he describes some of Ibn Taymiyyah's jurisprudential preferences as being contradictory;[148] he comments upon Ibn Taymiyyah's indecision on certain rulings;[149] he mentions that Ibn Taymiyyah holds two conflicting opinions concerning a single issue in different places in his treatises;[150] he highlights the fact that Ibn Taymiyyah occasionally mentions two of Aḥmad's narrations without indicating a preference for one of them.[151]

The opinions and preferences of Ibn Taymiyyah appear to command the respect of al-Jurā'ī. He cites Ibn Taymiyyah's classification of the opinions of the Ḥanbalī School,[152] and some of his legal derivations.[153] He quotes Ibn Taymiyyah's explanation of the causes behind the existence of jurisprudential disputes.[154] He occasionally explicitly mentions Ibn Taymiyyah's criticism of some of the narrations related from Ibn Ḥanbal or the opinions of the Ḥanbalī scholars.[155] Furthermore, it is reported that he wrote a treatise in which he defended Ibn Taymiyyah against the claim advanced by the leading Shāfi'ī scholar, Ibn al-Hā'im, that Ibn Taymiyyah issued sixty problematic rulings.[156]

The influence of Ibn Taymiyyah's opinions upon al-Jurāʿī also manifested itself through his introduction of new meanings for existing terms in the Ḥanbalī School. This can be observed in his book *Ghāyat al-Maṭlab*, in which he presents several terms in relation to Ibn Taymiyyah. These terms are as follows:

- *ʿAla al-Ashhar*: This term is used by al-Jurāʿī to refer to the presence of a narration from Aḥmad in the Ḥanbalī School, which was preferred by Ibn Taymiyyah and which is opposed by another narration in the School.
- *Fī al-Ashhar*: Al-Jurāʿī uses this term to denote the existence of a *wajh* in the Ḥanbalī School, which was preferred by Ibn Taymiyyah and which is opposed by another opinion in the School.
- *Fī Ashhar*: This term is used by al-Jurāʿī to refer to the existence of an opinion held by Ibn Taymiyyah, which opposes the opinion subscribed to by other Ḥanbalī scholars.[157]

By use of these terms, al-Jurāʿī has systematically categorised Ibn Taymiyyah's opinions concerning jurisprudential issues into the following categories:

- Opinions preferred by Ibn Taymiyyah, which are in fact narrations from Aḥmad.
- Opinions preferred by Ibn Taymiyyah, which are in fact *wujūh* (opinions) in the Ḥanbalī School of law.
- Ibn Taymiyyah's opinions, which are in opposition to the predominant opinion of the Ḥanbalī School of law.

The opinions and preferences mentioned by al-Jurāʿī in his book *Ghāyat al-Maṭlab* can be divided into four types, as follows:

1 Narrations preferred by Ibn Taymiyyah (the opposite of those opinions labelled by al-Jurāʿī in his book *Ghāyat al-Maṭlab* as *ʿala al-Ashhar*) (Table 4);
2 a *wajh* preferred by Ibn Taymiyyah (the opposite of those opinions labelled by al-Jurāʿī in his book *Ghāyat al-Maṭlab* as *fī al-Ashhar*) (Table 5);
3 Ibn Taymiyyah's preferences only (the opposite of those opinions labelled by al-Jurāʿī in his book *Ghāyat al-Maṭlab* as *fī ashhar*) (Table 6);
4 miscellaneous opinions and preferences of Ibn Taymiyyah attributed to him by al-Jurāʿī in his book *Ghāyat al-Maṭlab* using the name 'Abū 'l-ʿAbbās' or '*sheikh al-islam*' (Table 7).

Table 4 Narrations preferred by Ibn Taymiyyah (the opposite of those opinions labelled by al-Jurāʿī in his book *Ghāyat al-Maṭlab* as *ʿala al-Ashhar*)

7b, 16b, 22b, 24b, 25b, 26a, 26b, 29b, 31a, 32a, 32b twice, 39b, 43b, 46a, 47a, 49b, 57a, 58a, 79b, 87a, 95a, 103a, 116a, 138b, 190a, 192a

Table 5 A *wajh* preferred by Ibn Taymiyyah (the opposite of those opinions labelled by al-Jurāʿī in his book *Ghāyat al-Maṭlab* as *fi al-Ashhar*)

3a, 5a, 7b, 11a, 12b, 13b, 14b, 15a, 17b, 21a, 23b, 24a, 24b, 26a, 27a, 29b, 31b twice, 39b, 40a, 42a, 68a, 72a, 139a, 167b, 198b, 201

Table 6 Ibn Taymiyyah's preferences only (the opposite of those opinions labelled by al-Jurāʿī in his book *Ghāyat al-Maṭlab* as *fi al-Ashhar*)

10a, 12b, 26a, 29a, 34b, 41a, 41b, 43a, 142b

Table 7 Miscellaneous opinions and preferences of Ibn Taymiyyah attributed to him by al-Jurāʿī in his book *Ghāyat al-Maṭlab* using the name 'Abū 'l-'Abbās' or '*sheikh al-islam*'

3a, 4b, 6a twice, 7a twice, 8a twice, 10a twice, 10b, 11a twice, 12a, 13a, 15 thrice, 17a, 20a, 21a, 22b, 24b, 26a twice, 27a twice, 32a twice, 34b, 38a twice, 40a twice, 40b, 41a thrice, 42a, 42b, 44a thrice, 46a twice, 47b, 49a, 53a, 55a, 56a, 56b twice, 58a twice, 58b, 60a, 60b, 61a twice, 62b thrice, 63a, 64b, 65a, 65b twice, 66a thrice, 66b, 67a, 67b thrice, 68b thrice, 70a, 71a twice, 72a, 74a, 76a, 77a twice, 78b, 79a thrice, 80b, 81a, 82b twice, 83a, 85a, 86a, 87b, 89a twice, 90a thrice, 90b, 91a, 91b thrice, 93a, 94b, 96a twice, 97b, 98a, 99b, 102b twice, 103a, 103b, 104a twice, 104b, 105a twice, 105b twice, 109a, 110b, 111a twice, 111b, 112a four times, 112b thrice, 113b, 114a, 114b thrice, 115a, 121a twice, 121b twice, 124b, 125a twice, 126b twice, 127a four times, 128a, 128b twice, 129b, 130b twice, 131a, 131b four, 135b, 137a four times, 138a, 138b thrice, 139a, 140a twice, 141a, 142a, 143a twice, 142b five times, 144a twice, 147 twice, 155a, 159b twice, 160b, 163a, 163b, 166a, 166b, 167b, 175b twice, 176a, 176b, 178a, 178b, 179a twice, 180b, 181a, 184a thrice, 185a, 185b, 186a thrice, 186b thrice, 187b, 189a, 189b, 189a, 191b, 192a, 192b, 193a, 193b twice, 194a, 194b, 195b, 197b twice, 198a twice, 199a, 199a, 200a twice, 201b, 205a twice, 205 twice, 206a, 206b, 207a, 207b twice, 209a five times, 213a, 213b, 214a, 214b twice, 215b, 219b, 220a twice, 222a twice, 223a

Ibn Taymiyyah's influence on the writings of this scholar can be attributed to various factors.

- It has been mentioned previously that al-Jurāʿī spent a long time acquiring knowledge in the city of Damascus. Here, Ibn Taymiyyah's legacy was still very much alive through the activities of his followers.
- The treatises of this scholar are indicative of the fact that he must have consulted Ibn Taymiyyah's jurisprudential treatises and *fatāwā*.
- He consults the treatises of Ibn al-Qayyim and Ibn Mufliḥ, they are two of the most important sources of Ibn Taymiyyah's opinions and preferences.[158]
- As mentioned previously, al-Jurāʿī studied under Abū Shaʿr, who was well known for his comprehensive understanding of Ibn Taymiyyah's knowledge.[159]

This did not prevent al-Jurāʿī from criticising some of Ibn Taymiyyah's opinions. On certain issues, he argued that Aḥmad's scholarly legacy did not support what Ibn Taymiyyah claimed to be the opinion of the School.[160] He even states that Ibn Taymiyyah's opinion on some issues is contrary to the consensus of the Ḥanbalī scholars.[161]

Al-Mardāwī (d. 885/1480)

His full name was Abū 'l-Ḥasan 'Alī b. Sulaymān b. Aḥmad b. Muhammad al-Mardāwī. He was born in the year 817/1414.[162] This scholar served the Ḥanbalī School of law in various ways:

- As a jurist: After studying under the guidance and supervision of several great scholars, al-Mardāwī became a well-known jurist in the School, to the extent that he was awarded with the title 'the *muṣaḥḥiḥ* (corrector) and *munaqqiḥ* (reviewer) of Ḥanbalī jurisprudence'. At a later stage in his life, he was widely regarded as the leader of the School.[163]
- As a judge.[164]
- As a writer: Al-Mardāwī bequeathed a great scholarly legacy in the science of Ḥanbalī jurisprudence. The most important works amongst this collection are *al-Inṣāf* and *Taṣḥīḥ al-Furū'*.[165] These books are composed in a unique manner, for they are not written according to the normal method employed by Ḥanbalī scholars. Rather, they scrutinise previous Ḥanbalī works and then advance various corrections to the original works.

Ibn Taymiyyah's influence on al-Mardāwī

It is clear that al-Mardāwī commanded a wide knowledge of Ibn Taymiyyah's opinions and preferences. This can be evidenced in a number of ways:

- A vast number of Ibn Taymiyyah's opinions and jurisprudential preferences are to be found in the work *al-Inṣāf*.[166] He also quotes at length from the treatises of Ibn Taymiyyah.[167]
- Al-Mardāwī occasionally mentions certain opinions as 'most probably the opinion of Ibn Taymiyyah'.[168] This expression suggests that al-Mardāwī has an understanding of what can be attributed to this scholar. In addition, where some Ḥanbalī scholars mention certain rulings and attribute them to 'some former Ḥanbalī scholars', we find al-Mardāwī asserting that the scholar to whom they are referring is Ibn Taymiyyah.[169]
- He speculates on what Ibn Taymiyyah's opinion would be on certain issues, either by drawing an analogy with Ibn Taymiyyah's opinions on other issues[170] or according to Ibn Taymiyyah's general principles.[171]
- He is familiar enough with Ibn Taymiyyah's views to point out where he retracted an opinion,[172] or where he abstained from giving a legal ruling.[173]

The significance of Ibn Taymiyyah's influence on al-Mardāwī can be clearly noticed in the methodology he employs in his book *al-Inṣāf*. He mentions that his approach in this book is to convey jurisprudential opinions from Aḥmad and the Ḥanbalī scholars. He offers a precise and systematic methodology for discovering the opinion of the School. If the predominant opinion within the School is clear or well known or was preferred by the vast majority of the scholars, then he would support it in spite of the existence of another opinion claimed by a minority of Ḥanbalī scholars to be the predominant opinion. If, on the other hand, there is a distinct dispute among the Ḥanbalī scholars about what is the predominant opinion, then he would rely on the position of particular Ḥanbalī scholars, including Ibn Qudāmah, al-Majd, Ibn Mufliḥ and Ibn Taymiyyah. He explains the importance of these scholars in Ḥanbalī jurisprudence when he states that they reviewed the contribution of former Ḥanbalī scholars and they explained clearly and masterfully the general rules of the School. If these scholars also disagreed on what is the predominant opinion in the School, then he would follow in most cases what Ibn Mufliḥ preferred in his book *al-Furūʿ*. If for some reasons al-Mardāwī disagrees with Ibn Mufliḥ's preference or when Ibn Mufliḥ himself does not offer any preference, al-Mardāwī mentions that in most cases the predominant opinion will be that agreed upon by Ibn Qudāmah and al-Majd. In the event of a disagreement occurring between these two scholars, al-Mardāwī states that the predominant opinion will be that which was supported by either Ibn Rajab or Ibn Taymiyyah. If no support can be found from these two scholars then the predominant opinion will be that which is held by Ibn Qudāmah rather than al-Majd.[174] Al-Mardāwī asserts that this methodology employed by him is in agreement with the methodology specified by Ibn Taymiyyah to solve the existence of disputes about the predominant opinion within the School.[175]

Al-Mardāwī utilises the statements of Ibn Taymiyyah in various ways. He mentions various rulings present in Ḥanbalī jurisprudence and considered by Ibn Taymiyyah to be innovations,[176] problematic,[177] irregular,[178] very weak[179] or incorrect.[180] He cites Ibn Taymiyyah's opinion regarding the authenticity of some *ḥadīths*, [181] and he also cites his explanations for some *ḥadīths* and certain jurisprudential terminology and statements.[182] On various occasions, he conveys opinions within the Ḥanbalī School[183] or those which were agreed upon among scholars[184] through the narrations of Ibn Taymiyyah, even if they are not found in other Ḥanbalī sources.[185] He cites Ibn Taymiyyah on various issues in relation to the classification of opinions within the Ḥanbalī School.[186] In various issues, he uses Ibn Taymiyyah's opinion to indicate what is more correct from the opinions within the Ḥanbalī School,[187] or what Ḥanbalī scholars support.[188] Al-Mardāwī mentions the rulings that Ibn Taymiyyah determined through the use of analogy with,[189] or derivation from,[190] the predominant opinions in the School concerning other issues. Also, we find that al-Mardāwī in *al-Inṣāf* mentions various points from Ibn Taymiyyah under the heading of 'beneficial knowledge'.[191]

A careful analysis of al-Mardāwī's comments and his manner of narrating Ibn Taymiyyah's opinions and preferences provides us with a clear picture of his position towards these opinions, which can be summarised as follows:

- He occasionally supports Ibn Taymiyyah's stance, where it reflects an opinion within the Ḥanbalī School,[192] and sometimes even where it is not an opinion found within the School.[193] Even where Ibn Taymiyyah states that certain rulings pronounced by some Ḥanbalī scholars cannot exist in reality, we find that al-Mardāwī occasionally supports Ibn Taymiyyah's position. He states that reason testifies to its correctness and requires it. He labels it as the exact, correct opinion about which there can be no doubt.[194] Indeed, al-Mardāwī uses a rich variety of expressions to show his agreement with Ibn Taymiyyah's positions. On some occasions, he asserts that the adoption of Ibn Taymiyyah's opinion is, in fact, itself an implementation of all of the legal evidences on these issues.[195] On other similar issues, he states that he finds himself leaning towards Ibn Taymiyyah's opinion.[196] He asserts that Ibn Taymiyyah's opinion in relation to some issues is supported by the authentic *Sunnah*.[197] In other cases, he asserts that Ibn Taymiyyah's opinion reflects the practice of all Islamic generations.[198] Al-Mardāwī mentions that great hardship will result from implementing the opinion opposing that held by Ibn Taymiyyah.[199] He occasionally asserts that the general principles of the Ḥanbalī School of law necessitate the correctness of Ibn Taymiyyah's opinion.[200] Al-Mardāwī even describes some of Ibn Taymiyyah's rulings as being the correct opinions and people have no choice but to follow them.[201] Al-Mardāwī also asserts, with reference to certain issues, that a large number of leading Ḥanbalī scholars are in agreement with the opinion of his sheikh.[202] He cites some Ḥanbalī scholars supporting Ibn Taymiyyah's position on some issues,[203] and on other issues, in contrast, we find that al-Mardāwī cites Ibn Taymiyyah criticising opinions within Ḥanbalī jurisprudence that were sometimes adopted by leading Ḥanbalī scholars such as al-Khiraqī, Abū Ya'la, Abū 'l-Khaṭṭāb, Ibn 'Aqīl, Ibn al-Jawzī, al-Majd, Ibn Ḥamdān and Ibn Qudāmah.[204] Of course, al-Mardāwī also supports his own opinions by citing statements of Ibn Taymiyyah.[205]

- Al-Mardāwī describes some of Ibn Taymiyyah's rulings as strong, without actually disclosing his own opinion.[206] Al-Mardāwī occasionally mentions that Ibn Taymiyyah's opinion is the closest to what is correct.[207]
- Al-Mardāwī occasionally declares Ibn Taymiyyah's opinion to be incorrect,[208] or problematic (*fīhi naẓar*).[209] He cites scholars who criticise some of Ibn Taymiyyah's opinions,[210] and agrees with the criticism in a number of these cases.[211] Sometimes, after refuting Ibn Taymiyyah's opinion, al-Mardāwī asserts that Ibn Taymiyyah would not reject his (i.e. al-Mardāwī's) opinion if he had heard it.[212] He describes some of Ibn Taymiyyah's opinions as being contrary to the widely recognised opinion of the Ḥanbalī School.[213] Concerning some of these issues, al-Mardāwī says that Ibn Taymiyyah's statements regarding certain issues go beyond what is known from Aḥmad,[214] or that Ibn Taymiyyah is unsystematic when conveying certain Ḥanbalī opinions. For he sometimes describes an opinion in the School as a 'narration' and sometimes as an 'opinion'.[215]
- On some issues, al-Mardāwī neither supports nor opposes Ibn Taymiyyah's opinions, but points out the existence of conflict between a number of Ibn Taymiyyah's opinions.[216] For instance, he notes that Ibn Taymiyyah describes

an issue in one part of his treatise as being 'not obligatory', whereas in a different part he declares: 'there is no dispute amongst the scholars concerning its obligation'.[217] Al-Mardāwī notices that Ibn Taymiyyah's rulings are occasionally in opposition to some of his own general rules.[218] In other places, al-Mardāwī suggests the presence of hesitation emanating from Ibn Taymiyyah regarding certain issues.[219] On some occasions, we find that al-Mardāwī tries to find an accommodation between the position of the School and that of Ibn Taymiyyah.[220]

This analysis of al-Mardāwī's attitude towards Ibn Taymiyyah's opinions and preferences indicates that, for the most part, he was a conveyer of Ibn Taymiyyah's opinions rather than a staunch supporter of these views.

Al-Mardāwī's familiarity with the opinions and preferences of Ibn Taymiyyah is derived from various sources, some of which are the following:

- Al-Mardāwī's consultation of various treatises authored by Ibn Taymiyyah, such as *Sharḥ al-'Umdah*,[221] *al-Qawā'id*,[222] *Iqtiḍā' al-Ṣirāṭ al-Mustaqīm*[223] and *al-Fatāwā al-Maṣriyyah*,[224] *al-Siyāsah al-Shar'iyyah*,[225] *Sharḥ al-Muḥarrar*,[226] *Minhāj al-Sunnah*.[227] These sources, in addition to others, are mentioned by al-Mardāwī as being references for his book, *al-Inṣāf*.[228]
- Al-Mardāwī uses the narration of Ibn Mufliḥ as a source of Ibn Taymiyyah's opinions;[229] it was from this scholar that he sought an explanation for some of Ibn Taymiyyah's statements.[230]
- He consults other sources containing Ibn Taymiyyah's opinions, such *al-Ikhtiyārāt* by al-Ba'lī,[231] *Tajrīd al-'Ināyah fī Taḥrīr al-Nihāyah* by Ibn al-Laḥḥām,[232] *al-Fā'iq* by Ibn Qāḍī al-Jabal,[233] *al-Ṭabaqāt* by Ibn Rajab[234] and al-Zarkashī.[235]
- Al-Mardāwī studied under the leading scholar Abū Sha'r,[236] who, as mentioned earlier, was well-versed in Ibn Taymiyyah's opinions (Table 8).

Table 8 The extent of al-Mardāwī's citation of Ibn Taymiyyah's opinions and preferences in his book *al-Inṣāf*

Volume 1	22, 24 twice, 27, 32, 33 twice, 36 thrice, 38, 43, 47 twice, 56, 57, 59 twice, 60, 62, 67,73, 77, 79, 81, 82 four, 83 four, 84, 86 twice, 87 thrice, 88 four, 89, 92 twice, 95 twice,100, 101, 102 thrice, 110 thrice, 111, 114, 118, 121 twice, 124 twice, 128 twice, 130,135 twice, 140, 142, 147, 158, 159, 162 twice, 167, 168, 169, 172 twice, 173 twice,176, 177, 179 twice, 182 twice, 183 twice, 186 twice, 187, 190, 191, 192, 194, 198,199, 200 twice, 201 thrice, 202, 211 twice, 215, 228,232, 234, 237, 243, 244, 247, 250 twice, 251, 253, 259, 260 twice, 261 twice, 262, 216 thrice, 217, 218, 219, 222, 263 thrice, 265, 270, 271 twice, 272, 279, 281, 282, 283 twice, 284 twice, 285, 293 thrice,296 twice, 298, 300, 303, 304 twice, 307, 309 twice, 310, 312, 313, 314, 317, 318 five, 320, 322, 324, 325 twice, 327, 328, 330, 332, 334 twice, 335 four, 338, 342, 344, 347,348, 352?, 354 twice, 351, 355, 357 twice, 358 twice, 359, 361 twice, 372, 376 thrice,377, 383 twice, 386, 389 four, 393, 394, 396, 397, 399, 402,

	405 twice, 408, 409, 415, 417, 422, 423 thrice, 424 twice, 426 thrice, 428 twice, 429–430, 435, 437, 440, 441 thrice, 442, 443 twice, 448, 450, 452 twice, 459 twice, 469, 472, 473 twice, 474, 475,476, 479, 480, 481, 482, 483, 486 twice, 490, 495, 496, 498
Volume 2	8, 11, 23, 24, 26, 29, 30 twice, 39, 43, 44, 47 twice, 49, 55, 57, 58, 64, 74,78, 79 thrice,80 twice, 88, 98, 107, 108, 112, 118, 134, 137, 138 twice, 146, 154, 155, 156, 159, 161,162 twice, 164, 165 thrice, 167, 170 twice, 172, 175, 176, 178 twice, 180, 181 twice,184, 189, 190, 192, 193 twice, 198, 202, 206 twice, 208, 209, 210 twice, 212 twice,214, 218 twice, 219, 222, 229, 230 thrice, 231, 233 thrice, 234, 240, 245, 246, 247, 252,253, 260, 263, 267, 272, 273, 274, 276, 277 twice, 278 thrice, 280 twice, 288, 289 thrice, 290, 291, 308, 309, 316, 318 twice, 320, 321, 322, 325, 330, 335, 337 twice, 339, 340, 341 twice, 342, 343, 362, 365 twice, 368, 378 thrice, 387, 389, 396, 398, 399, 400, 406 four times, 407, 411, 412, 414, 415, 420, 422, 426, 427, 430, 436, 439, 441, 449, 451, 456, 458 twice, 462 twice, 463, 464, 505, 509, 524, 525, 531, 533 thrice, 534, 543, 548, 549, 550, 551, 557, 558, 560, 562 twice, 567, 569 thrice, 570
Volume 3	19, 22 twice, 28, 35, 39 twice, 65 twice, 84, 85 twice, 90, 100, 114, 115 twice, 130, 131, 132, 139, 145, 147, 149 twice, 150, 153, 165, 177, 179, 181, 182, 186, 192, 195, 196, 201, 212, 217, 218, 221, 234 twice, 237, 239, 251, 254 thrice, 255, 257, 261, 262, 266, 268 twice, 269 thrice, 270, 273 twice, 277 twice, 278 twice, 282, 285, 286, 287, 294, 295, 297, 299 twice, 300, 301, 302, 303 five times, 311 twice, 312, 313, 315, 318twice, 322, 329, 332, 335 twice, 337, 342, 343, 344, 346 thrice, 347 thrice, 349, 354, 357 thrice, 366, 367, 368 twice., 383, 385, 386, 387 twice, 400 twice, 405, 407 twice, 411, 413 thrice, 425, 431, 433, 434 twice, 435, 447, 453, 460, 465, 467, 488, 489, 495, 500 twice, 503, 506, 508, 562, 563 thrice
Volume 4	4, 5, 6, 7, 11 twice, 15, 16, 29 twice, 31, 38, 40, 43, 44, 49, 52 twice, 53, 57 twice, 66 twice, 71, 73, 74 twice, 80 twice, 82, 87, 89, 107, 110 twice, 111, 114, 115, 116 twice, 119 four, 124, 125, 135, 143, 144, 149, 160, 167, 169, 176, 185, 189, 190, 191, 196, 198, 199 twice, 200, 202, 205, 207, 209, 212, 213, 215, 217, 221, 222 twice, 223, 232, 233, 234 thrice, 235 twice, 236 twice, 237, 238, 240, 249, 252, 256, 257, 258 twice, 264 twice, 265 twice, 266, 275, 277, 278, 282, 283, 286, 287, 289 twice, 290, 291, 295 twice, 296, 299 twice, 301, 302, 308 twice, 309, 310 thrice, 319, 321, 327, 330, 332, 333, 335, 337 twice, 338, 339 thrice, 348, 351, 353 thrice, 355, 356 twice, 357, 359, 367, 373, 374, 375, 378, 397, 398 twice, 399, 405, 407, 410, 414, 415, 417, 426, 427, 428, 449, 459, 461 twice, 462, 463 four, 464 thrice, 466, 467, 468 thrice, 469, 473, 474, 475, 481
Volume 5	12, 14 twice, 16 twice, 23, 32, 33 thrice, 34, 41, 43, 44, 47, 48, 53, 60, 65, 68 twice, 69, 76 twice, 80 twice, 98, 108, 109, 112, 125, 130, 131, 134, 143, 148, 149, 154, 167, 168, 177, 190 twice, 196, 203, 205, 210, 215 twice, 216, 234, 236, 237, 238, 249, 250, 254, 255 twice, 256, 261 twice, 264, 269, 271, 274, 276 thrice, 281, 282, 285, 303, 322, 324 twice, 327, 332, 339, 340, 344, 347, 348, 368, 372, 373 four, 375, 404, 420 thrice, 421, 422, 425 twice, 426 twice, 427, 437, 440, 446, 452, 454 twice, 461 thrice, 462, 463 twice, 468, 469, 471 twice, 472, 473, 478, 481, 482 twice, 483 twice, 484, 485
Volume 6	3, 4, 5, 8, 13, 16, 21, 27, 29, 30 thrice, 36 twice, 37 twice, 38, 39, 40, 41 twice, 42 twice, 43, 44 thrice, 46, 47 twice, 51, 63, 67 twice, 68, 82, 84, 90 twice, 91,

(Table 8 continued)

Table 8 Continued

	93 twice, 94, 102, 112, 113, 117, 119, 122 twice, 130 twice, 131, 132, 144, 146, 155, 168, 174, 179, 193, 196, 202, 213, 215 twice, 219, 225 twice, 228, 236, 238, 241, 255, 257, 272 twice, 286, 326, 371, 376, 377, 414, 429, 446
Volume 7	3, 9 twice, 10, 11 twice, 12, 17, 21, 22, 23 twice, 25, 27, 28, 29, 31, 46 twice, 47 twice, 49 four, 50, 51 twice, 52 twice, 53, 54 twice, 55 twice, 56 twice, 57 twice, 58, 61, 63 four, 64 four, 65, 66 twice, 68 four, 69 twice, 72 thrice, 77, 78, 80, 84 twice, 88 twice, 94, 96, 97, 99 twice, 100 twice, 101 twice, 102 twice, 104, 112, 115, 116, 117, 130, 131, 133 thrice, 134, 135, 137 twice, 141 twice, 146 twice, 148, 155 twice, 156 twice, 157, 161, 201, 202, 208, 209, 231 twice, 235, 237, 245, 270, 287, 298, 303, 304 twice, 306 twice, 308, 309, 311, 323, 326, 340, 345, 348, 349, 352 twice, 354, 358, 370, 371, 379 twice, 382, 386, 394, 403 twice, 405, 407, 408, 415, 423, 437, 446, 475, 494, 495 twice
Volume 8	3, 6 twice, 8 twice, 10, 11 twice, 12, 18, 25, 26, 28, 29 twice, 30 thrice, 32, 37 twice, 40, 45 twice, 46, 48, 51 twice, 55 twice, 57, 58 twice, 59, 64 twice, 66, 68, 69 twice, 71, 74, 75, 77, 80, 86, 87, 90 twice, 94, 99 twice, 100, 101 thrice, 102, 107 twice, 108 twice, 109, 110, 114, 115, 117, 120 twice, 122 twice, 125, 126, 127, 128, 134, 136, 137 twice, 144 twice, 145, 152, 153, 154 twice, 155 twice, 156 twice, 158 thrice, 160, 161, 163, 164 thrice, 165, 166 twice, 168 twice, 172, 173, 176, 177, 180, 181, 188, 198, 200 twice, 201 twice, 202 twice, 206, 207, 210, 213 twice, 214, 216, 217, 218, 221, 222, 229, 230 twice, 231, 238 twice, 241 twice, 244, 247, 248, 249, 251, 252 twice, 255, 258, 270, 271, 278, 284, 289, 296, 298, 302 twice, 303, 306, 307, 310, 315, 317, 318, 319, 320, 325 thrice, 326 twice, 330 thrice, 332, 333, 336, 338, 340, 347 twice, 354, 355, 360, 362, 364, 371, 373, 381, 382 twice, 383 twice, 384, 387, 393 twice, 396, 398, 410 twice, 412 twice, 419, 423, 424 twice, 426, 427, 431, 432, 433, 436, 437, 438, 439, 441, 444, 446, 448 twice, 449 twice, 451, 452, 453 twice, 463, 467, 479
Volume 9	5, 7, 22, 27, 28, 35, 55, 59, 60 twice, 61 twice, 64, 65, 71, 79, 80, 87, 88, 105, 107, 114, 116, 120, 121, 138, 145 twice, 150, 154 twice, 168, 170, 202, 220, 233, 249, 258, 267 twice, 268, 269 twice, 276, 279, 284, 288, 289, 292 twice, 295 twice, 312, 314, 316, 317, 334, 341, 342, 343, 357, 365, 365, 371, 383, 395, 403, 406 twice, 412, 419, 440, 442, 444, 447, 469, 483, 487, 491
Volume 10	3 twice, 6, 7, 16, 34, 67, 140, 150, 151, 154, 156, 168, 169, 171, 177, 183, 185, 199, 201, 203, 215, 217, 222, 225, 226 twice, 228 twice, 230 twice, 231, 234, 239, 241, 243, 244, 247, 249 twice, 250 thrice, 277, 285, 286, 292, 295, 299, 301, 303, 306, 312, 313 twice, 319, 322, 323, 325, 326, 327 twice, 333, 334, 342, 345, 348, 349, 351, 355, 356, 357, 358 twice, 359, 370, 371, 374, 382, 383, 386, 387, 388, 393, 397 twice, 398, 404 twice, 408, 440
Volume 11	12, 14, 15 twice, 18, 19 four, 25, 27 twice, 28, 29, 31, 32, 34, 38, 39, 45 twice, 47, 53, 94, 117, 120 twice, 121, 123, 125, 128, 133, 135, 147, 150, 152, 165, 169, 170, 171 twice, 172, 175, 179 twice, 180, 181 twice, 187, 190, 192, 195, 198 twice, 213, 220, 221 twice, 222, 225, 231, 233 twice, 237, 242, 246 thrice, 248 thrice, 249–250, 253, 255, 260 twice, 261 twice, 271, 272, 274, 284, 286, 288, 297, 301, 305 twice, 311 twice, 313, 314, 315, 316 twice, 317, 322, 323 twice, 324, 325, 327, 328 twice, 330,332, 333, 335 twice, 340, 341 five, 346 thrice, 348, 355, 358, 363, 368, 379, 396, 407
Volume 12	6, 7 twice, 8, 9 twice, 13, 18, 20, 38, 39, 41 twice, 44, 45, 46 thrice, 48, 49 twice, 50 twice, 53 twice, 62, 71, 73, 81, 83, 86, 92, 98, 104, 108, 109, 111, 113, 120 twice, 122 four, 124, 127, 129, 130, 131, 144, 145 thrice, 151, 152, 161, 171, 195, 197, 198, 211, 222 twice, 224 twice, 225, 230, 236

Al-Ḥajjāwī (d. 968/1561)

His name was Mūsā b. Aḥmad b. Mūsā b. Sālim b. 'Īsa b. Sālim al-Ḥajjāwī. He was born in Palestine in the year 895/1490, where he started his basic studies. He then moved to Damascus where he continued his studies until he assumed the position of *muftī* of the Ḥanbalī School in Damascus. He was also an erudite teacher who himself exerted a considerable influence upon various later Ḥanbalī scholars. This scholar authored and left various important treatises, such as *al-Iqnā'* and *Zād al-Mustaqni'*.[237]

Ibn Taymiyyah's influence on al-Ḥajjāwī

Al-Ḥajjāwī cited Ibn Taymiyyah's opinions on various jurisprudential issues in his treatise *al-Iqnā'*.[238] The source works of these opinions are Ibn Taymiyyah's treatises, such as *Sharḥ al-'Umdah*[239] and *al-Fatāwā al-Miṣriyyah*,[240] and the treatises of his students such as Ibn Qāḍī al-Jabal in his book *al-Fā'iq* [241] and Ibn al-Qayyim.[242]

Ibn Taymiyyah is referred to by the use of the term '*al-sheikh*' in *al-Iqnā'*. This is clarified in the introduction when al-Ḥajjāwī states that whenever this term has been used, he means '*sheikh al-Islam*, the sea of sciences, Abū 'l-'Abbās, Aḥmad Ibn Taymiyyah'.[243] In the Ḥanbalī School of law, this term had been commonly used to refer to the leading Ḥanbalī scholar, Ibn Qudāmah. Since the appearance of Ibn Taymiyyah, however, Ḥanbalī scholars began to associate this term with Ibn Taymiyyah as well. Later on, particularly in the time of al-Ḥajjāwī and the following period, the Ḥanbalī scholars have employed this term to denote Ibn Taymiyyah exclusively.[244]

Ibn Taymiyyah's opinions and preferences cited and mentioned by al-Ḥajjāwī in *al-Iqnā'* can be primarily classified as follows:

- Al-Ḥajjāwī refers to various rulings and practices labelled by Ibn Taymiyyah as 'innovations'.[245] In the majority of instances, it is not clear whether al-Ḥajjāwī agrees with Ibn Taymiyyah's position in relation to these issues or not, as he does not comment on them.
- On occasions, al-Ḥajjāwī mentions the opinion of Ibn Taymiyyah as the opinion of the School.[246] On other issues, he bases some rulings on no more than the words of Ibn Taymiyyah.[247]
- Occasionally, al-Ḥajjāwī mentions an opinion of Ibn Taymiyyah's that is contrary to the recognised opinion within the Ḥanbalī School,[248] and on certain issues, al-Ḥajjāwī mentions Ibn Taymiyyah's rejection and refutation of opinions held by certain Ḥanbalī scholars.[249]
- Al-Ḥajjāwī cites Ibn Taymiyyah's explanations and definitions of certain words, terms and rules.[250]
- Some of Ibn Taymiyyah's opinions and preferences mentioned by al-Ḥajjāwī contain information beyond what is known in the School.[251] Al-Ḥajjāwī also

points out exceptions made by Ibn Taymiyyah to a general ruling held by the School.[252]

- Al-Ḥajjāwī occasionally mentions opinions held by Ibn Taymiyyah in which he accepts the opinion of the School in certain forms and rejects it in others.[253]
- He also cites Ibn Taymiyyah attributing opinions to 'most of the scholars',[254] 'all of the Imams',[255] 'possibly all of the scholars'[256] or 'all of the scholars'.[257]
- Al-Ḥajjāwī occasionally cites Ibn Taymiyyah classifying[258] or supporting some opinions within the Ḥanbalī School.[259]

In most instances, it is evident that al-Ḥajjāwī adopts a passive approach towards the opinions and preferences of Ibn Taymiyyah as cited in *al-Iqnāʿ*. Only in a few cases does he express his agreement with Ibn Taymiyyah's rulings.[260] On certain issues, he prefers an opinion of Ibn Taymiyyah that is in opposition to the recognised opinion within the Ḥanbalī School.[261] In addition, al-Ḥajjāwī sometimes cites Ibn Taymiyyah attributing opinions to 'most of the scholars' whereas the School in fact holds the opposite opinion.[262]

It appears that al-Ḥajjāwī's agreement with Ibn Taymiyyah on some issues is based on the fact that the same opinions had been approved by previous leading Ḥanbalī scholars. For instance, the words of approval used by al-Ḥajjāwī to support Ibn Taymiyyah are occasionally the very words used by al-Mardāwī.[263] It ought to be mentioned that, to the best of our knowledge, al-Ḥajjāwī did not directly criticise or refute any of Ibn Taymiyyah's opinions and preferences cited in *al-Iqnāʿ*, even if he did not often expressly support them either.

It can be concluded that the level of influence Ibn Taymiyyah exerted upon this scholar was apparently limited.[264] This can also be supported by the fact that the rulings in *al-Iqnāʿ* are, generally speaking, in agreement with the predominant opinions of the Ḥanbalī School. On several issues, these rulings are contrary to Ibn Taymiyyah's position.[265]

This relatively minor influence can be attributed to the methodology employed by al-Ḥajjāwī in *al-Iqnāʿ*. He states that his book is based upon only one opinion in the School, that is, the opinion of the leading Ḥanbalī scholar al-Mardāwī in his books *al-Inṣāf*, *Taṣḥīḥ al-Furūʿ* and *al-Tanqīḥ*.[266] The leading Ḥanbalī scholar al-Karmī who compiled a treatise in which he amalgamated *al-Iqnāʿ* and *al-Muntahā*, asserts that the authors of these two books generally followed the opinions of al-Mardāwī.[267] It is not surprising, therefore, that Ibn Taymiyyah has a relatively minor influence on the treatise.

Nevertheless, al-Ḥajjāwī's citation of Ibn Taymiyyah's opinions demonstrates the importance given to Ibn Taymiyyah and his knowledge in the tenth century. *Al-Iqnāʿ*, which is among al-Ḥajjāwī's most important treatises, has become one of the main sources upon which *iftāʾ* and judgement are based in the Ḥanbalī School of law. The importance of the work has continued to be recognised from the tenth century up to the present time, amongst the Muftis in the Ḥanbalī School

Table 9 The extent to which al-Ḥajjāwī cited Ibn Taymiyyah's opinions and legal preferences in his book *al-Iqnāʿ*

Volume 1	3, 4, 19 twice, 27, 32, 42, 43, 55, 59, 74–75, 77, 78, 79, 80, 103 twice, 111, 114, 119, 126, 129, 136, 144 twice, 147, 149 thrice, 153, 154, 157, 159, 160, 165, 169, 170, 184, 189, 195, 198, 199, 205, 231, 232, 233 twice, 237 twice, 291, 300, 304 twice, 316, 318, 321, 323, 328, 333, 334, 341, 346, 368, 382, 387, 396 twice, 398 twice, 402, 409 twice, 411
Volume 2	15, 24, 35, 39, 44, 47, 48, 51 twice, 52, 54, 55 thrice, 58 thrice, 64, 76, 72, 92, 123–124, 163, 175, 184, 185 twice, 201, 202, 204, 207, 208, 209, 223, 273 thrice, 275, 278, 281, 287, 297, 301, 319, 337, 357, 361, 363, 389, 397
Volume 3	4, 5 twice, 11, 38, 60, 132, 157, 159, 161, 163, 167 twice, 182, 186, 189, 190, 192, 200, 201, 220, 221 thrice, 229 twice, 231, 232 twice, 240, 241, 242, 243, 248, 254 twice, 262
Volume 4	2, 3, 4, 5, 9, 10, 21 twice, 47 twice, 72, 112, 133, 136, 141, 144, 153–154, 158, 162, 168, 246, 265–266, 269, 270–271, 271 twice, 272, 273, 292, 297, 306, 308, 315, 316, 317, 320, 332, 334, 354, 357, 359, 360, 364, 367–368, 369–370 five, 376–377, 381, 384, 389, 390 twice, 391, 392, 400, 428, 437 twice, 441, 453, 454, 455

in various parts of the Islamic world, and indeed amongst the judges in the Saudi courts of law (Table 9).[268]

Ibn al-Najjār (d. 972/1564)

This scholar's name was Muḥammad b. Aḥmad b. Abd al-'Aziz al-Futūḥī, though he was well known as Ibn al-Najjar. He was born in Cairo in the year 898/1493. He studied under various scholars, one of whom was his father, the chief judge al-Futūḥī.[269] Later on, he became a leading teacher and judge. He compiled several important treatises pertaining to Ḥanbalī jurisprudence and its principles, such as *Muntahā al-Irādāt* and *al-Kawkab al-Munīr*. Al-Shaʿrānī mentions the people's agreement that the death of this sheikh would occasion the death of Aḥmad's *fiqh* in Egypt.[270] He died in the year 972/1564.[271]

Ibn Taymiyyah's influence on Ibn al-Najjār

The vast majority of this scholar's opinions, mentioned in his jurisprudential treatises, are in agreement with the predominant opinions of the Ḥanbalī School of law.[272] Ibn al-Najjār quotes Ibn Taymiyyah's opinion on a jurisprudential opinion in *al-Muntahā* on only one issue. This can be attributed to various factors. The point is that *al-Muntahā* is written according to the method of *mukhtaṣarāt* (short treatises) which necessitates brevity. The second reason involves the methodology employed by Ibn al-Najjār in this treatise. Ibn al-Najjār mentions in the introduction to this book that he combined two books, the first being *al-Muqniʿ* by Ibn Qudāmah and the second *al-Tanqīḥ al-Mushbiʿ* by al-Mardāwī.[273] He then added some important issues that are not mentioned in these two books.[274] In addition, he excised various things found in the original works, some of which are the following:[275]

- He omitted words and phrases that he considered unnecessary.
- He omitted the *marjūḥ* (the less preferred) opinions and all the divergent branches that the two scholars founded upon them.
- He mentions in his book only those opinions preferred by al-Mardāwī in his book *al-Tanqīḥ*, even if the other Ḥanbalī scholars held otherwise. He occasionally made exceptions to this general rule in certain circumstances:
  - When Ḥanbalī scholars practice the opinion preferred by other Ḥanbalī scholars.
  - When the opinion is described by certain Ḥanbalī scholars as being *'ashhar'* (the more predominant opinion) as compared to the one mentioned by al-Mardāwī in his book *al-Tanqīḥ*.

The argument that the scant citation of Ibn Taymiyyah in *al-Muntahā* is because it is a *mukhtaṣar* and the methodology employed by Ibn al-Najjār can be further supported by the fact that Ibn al-Najjār does cite Ibn Taymiyyah's opinions in his treatise *Ma'ūnat ūlī al-Nuhā*, which is a commentary on *al-Muntahā*.[276] The opinions of Ibn Taymiyyah mentioned by Ibn al-Najjār in this treatise can be classified into the following categories:

- Ibn Taymiyyah's jurisprudential preferences.[277]
- Rulings and actions regarded by Ibn Taymiyyah as innovations.[278]
- Ibn Taymiyyah's own classification of opinions within the Ḥanbalī School.[279]
- Refutation and criticism of some rulings within the School.[280]
- Beneficial points.[281]
- Explanations by Ibn Taymiyyah of the real intended meaning of some statements issued by Aḥmad or other Ḥanbalī scholars.[282]
- Additional points added by Ibn Taymiyyah to existing rulings in the Ḥanbalī School.[283]

It is interesting that in *Ma'ūnat ūlī al-Nuhā*, Ibn al-Najjār used the narration of Ibn Mufliḥ,[284] and occasionally the narration of al-Mardāwī,[285] as a source for Ibn Taymiyyah's opinions.[286] Ibn al-Najjār also cites these two scholars in some issues endorsing and supporting the position taken by Ibn Taymiyyah,[287] and in others

Table 10 Opinions of Ibn Taymiyyah cited by Ibn al-Najjār in his book *Ma'unat ūlī al-Nuhā* (Volume 1)

177, 183, 199, 201, 203, 204, 205, 208, 223, 224, 231, 237, 240, 245, 246, 247, 249, 250, 281, 282, 294, 306, 315, 316, 317, 318, 320, 326, 344, 357, 364, 374, 378, 382, 387, 409, 413, 432, 433, 492, 502, 587, 608, 680, 686, 693, 701, 711, 715, 716, 752, 769, 772

he cites Ibn Mufliḥ expressing some reservations about some of Ibn Taymiyyah's opinions.[288] Also, where some leading Ḥanbalī scholars find some narrations in the School strange and unlikely, Ibn al-Najjār quotes al-Mardāwī asserting that Ibn Taymiyyah was in favour of the narration in question (Table 10).[289]

Al-Karmī (d. 1033/1623)

His full name was Mar'ī b.Yūsuf b. Abi Bakr b. Aḥmad al-Karmī. He was born in Palestine, where he acquired knowledge from the leading Ḥanbalī scholars, such as Muhammad al-Mardāwī and Yaḥyā b. Mūsā al-Ḥajjāwī.[290] Thereafter, he moved to Cairo where he completed his studies.[291] Later on, he assumed the position of the sheikh of the School, and divided his time between teaching, issuing *fatāwā* and compiling various important sources. Several of these works, for example, *Ghāyat al-Muntahā* and *Dalīl al-Ṭālib*, concern the science of jurisprudence.[292]

Ibn Taymiyyah's influence on al-Karmī

It is evident that this individual had knowledge of Ibn Taymiyyah's opinions and was sympathetic towards his cause. This may be evidenced by his biography of Ibn Taymiyyah, which is an abridgement of the works of the two Ḥanbalī scholars, *al-'Uqūd* by Ibn 'Abd al-Hādī and *al-A'lām* by al-Bazzār.[293] In addition, Ibn Taymiyyah's opinions and preferences have been cited by al-Karmī on various issues, where he refers to him as '*al-sheikh*'.[294] It is evident that this scholar commanded a particular knowledge of Ibn Taymiyyah's opinions and preferences, for we find him identifying some of his opinions which were cited by some Ḥanbalī scholars without attributing them to Ibn Taymiyyah.[295]

This scholar refers to various rulings and practices considered by Ibn Taymiyyah to be agreed upon among scholars,[296] and others which are considered by him as innovations.[297] On certain issues, al-Karmī makes reference to Ibn Taymiyyah's opposition to opinions of the Ḥanbalī School,[298] Ibn Taymiyyah's criticism of some Ḥanbalī rulings,[299] in addition to his explanation and classification of some Ḥanbalī statements.[300] He sometimes attributes to Ibn Taymiyyah extrapolations made to statements in the Ḥanbalī scholars.[301] In some instances, he expressly supports Ibn Taymiyyah's position.[302]

Various sources are mentioned by this scholar when he makes reference to Ibn Taymiyyah's opinions. These include Ibn Taymiyyah's own treatises, such as *Sharḥ al-'Umdah*,[303] and *Minhāj al-Sunnah*,[304] and the treatises of his students, such as *al-Ikhtiyārāt* by al-Ba'lī[305] and *al-Ādab al-Shar'iyyah* by Ibn Mufliḥ.[306] Needless to say, al-Karmī's acquaintance with al-Ḥajjāwī and Ibn al-Najjār must be a primary cause for Ibn Taymiyyah's influence upon him (Table 11).

Table 11 The extent to which al-Karmī cited Ibn Taymiyyah's opinions and preferences in his book *Ghāyat al-Muntahā*

Volume 1	19, 15, 22, 29–30, 51,63, 77–78, 93, 96, 97, 113, 132, 144, 163, 170, 172, 175, 177/2, 178, 180, 183, 189, 196, 227, 230, 243, 244, 254, 264, 269, 270, 277, 279, 301, 302, 331, 332, 333, 343, 345, 356, 360/2, 362, 381, 386, 387, 404, 442, 443, 453, 459, 462, 464, 473, 475, 487, 488, 489, 493, 494, 501, 504, 505, 506, 507/2, 509
Volume 2	1, 11, 19, 21 twice, 26, 30, 31, 33, 34, 43, 46, 52, 61, 82, 83, 93, 101, 103, 107, 109–110, 121 thrice, 122, 124, 127, 139, 141, 190, 208, 212, 241, 245, 250, 270–271, 290, 291, 295 twice, 299, 300 four, 301, 302, 305, 306, 307, 310, 316 twice, 318, 324–325, 327, 368
Volume 3	2, 5 thrice, 15, 28, 29, 33, 63, 64, 66, 84 twice, 105, 107, 122, 130, 131, 134, 158, 223, 236, 269, 300, 316, 317 twice, 334, 337, 338, 339 twice, 345, 349, 369, 373, 393, 394, 395, 400, 401, 403 twice, 409, 414, 435, 439, 449, 487, 489

Al-Buhūtī (d. 1051/1641)

His name was Manṣūr b. Yūnis b. Ṣalāḥ al-Dīn b. Ḥasan b. Aḥmad though he was commonly well known as 'al-Buhūtī'. Certain Ḥanbalī scholars awarded him with the title 'the sheikh of the Ḥanbalīs in Egypt'.[307] The majority of his treatises are devoted to the study and explanation of existing Ḥanbalī source works, such as *al-Iqnāʿ*, *al-Muntahā* and *al-Zād.*[308]

Ibn Taymiyyah's influence on al-Buhūtī

Al-Buhūtī apparently possessed an acute knowledge of Ibn Taymiyyah's views, for he is able to identify an opinion of Ibn Taymiyyah even when it is cited by Ḥanbalī scholars without they attributing it to him.[309] Al-Buhūtī himself cites Ibn Taymiyyah's opinions and preferences on various issues referring to him as '*al-sheikh*'.[310] Various sources were referred to by this scholar when conveying the opinions of Ibn Taymiyyah. These included Ibn Taymiyyah's own treatises, such as *Sharḥ al-ʿUmdah*[311] and *Minhāj al-Sunnah*,[312] in addition to the treatises of his students such as *al-Ikhtiyārāt* by al-Baʿlī,[313] *al-Ādab al-Sharʿiyyah* and *al-Furūʿ* by Ibn Mufliḥ[314] and *al-Fāʾiq* by Ibn Qāḍī al-Jabal.[315] Furthermore, it can be argued that the presence of Ibn Taymiyyah's opinions in the treatises of this scholar is a direct consequence of his acquaintance with the legacy of the two leading Ḥanbalī scholars al-Ḥajjāwī and Ibn al-Najjār.

As with some of the other scholars examined earlier, this scholar makes reference to Ibn Taymiyyah's opposition towards the opinions of the Ḥanbalī School,[316] his criticism of certain Ḥanbalī rulings[317] as well as his additions to[318] explanation[319] and classification[320] of some Ḥanbalī statements. Al-Buhūtī also mentions various rulings and practices considered by Ibn Taymiyyah to be innovations.[321]

In some issues, he supports the position of Ibn Taymiyyah,[322] and on one occasion, where Ibn Mufliḥ states that what Ibn Taymiyyah declares to be the opinion of the Ḥanbalī School is, in fact, only a *wajh* in the School, al-Buhūtī asserts that Ibn Taymiyyah's view is indeed the predominant opinion within the School and is also the opinion determined by Ibn al-Najjār in *al-Iqnā'*.[323]

Sometimes, al-Buhūtī derives an analogy based upon Ibn Taymiyyah's opinions.[324] Occasionally, he conveys the existence of consensus regarding some issues from the treatises of Ibn Taymiyyah such as *Sharḥ al-'Umdah*.[325]

Al-Buhūtī mentions rulings in the School and points out that Ibn Taymiyyah restricted their application to particular situations.[326] Similarly, al-Buhūtī also mentions existing rulings in the School, which were generalised by Ibn Taymiyyah.[327]

This scholar cites Ibn Taymiyyah's practice on certain issues, such as his practice in relation to exorcism.[328]

Al-Buhūtī disagrees with or does not fully accept some of the opinions held by Ibn Taymiyyah. This can be noticed through al-Buhūtī's citation of statements issued by some leading Ḥanbalī scholars in which they seem to disagree with Ibn Taymiyyah.[329] He also cites other leading Ḥanbalī scholars clarifying that some opinions within the School which were supported by Ibn Taymiyyah, were in fact old statements of Aḥmad, who had replaced them with new opinions (Tables 12–14).[330]

During this period (i.e. the time of al-Karmī and al-Buhūtī), it is evident that the citation of Ibn Taymiyyah's opinions by Ḥanbalī scholars was an established practice. Note that these two scholars even cite Ibn Taymiyyah's arguments that certain

Table 12 The extent to which al-Buhūtī cited Ibn Taymiyyah in his book *al-Rawḍ al-Murbi'*

25, 52, 138, 210, 294

Table 13 The extent of al-Buhūtī's citation of the opinions and preferences of Ibn Taymiyyah in his book *Kashshāf al-Qinā'* (Volume 1)

21, 24, 32, 35, 54, 55, 64, 67, 75, 110, 120, 149, 157, 158 twice, 159, 176, 183, 187, 201, 212, 222 twice, 232, 244, 245, 256, 257, 270, 279, 284, 287, 294, 299, 300, 308, 309, 314, 332, 335, 337, 345, 359, 363, 411 thrice, 413, 414, 437, 468, 470 twice, 478, 506

Table 14 The extent to which al-Buhūtī cited Ibn Taymiyyah's opinions and legal preferences in his book *Sharḥ al-Muntahā*

Volume 1	13, 19–20, 26, 27, 39, 40, 44, 49, 53, 61–62, 73, 74 Twice, 78, 92, 155, 158 172, 174, 181, 195, twice, 234, 237, 252, 253–254 twice, 268, 299, 332, 351–352, 358, 359, 363, 425, 437, 439, 455, 477, 465, 466
Volume 2	52, 69, 70, 71 twice, 72, 94, 129, 142, 159, 173, 176, 204–205, 232, 275, 277, 291, 332, 342, 347, 351, 354, 374, 423, 427, 457 twice, 495, 501, 503 four, 506, 507, twice, 511, 516–517, 522, 524, 525, 577, 625, 683
Volume 3	18, 39, 56, 79, 86, 89, 91 twice, 96, 97, 114, 120, 121, 128, 131, 135, 245, 272, 351, 355, 356, 360, 362, 385, 395, 400, 404, 418, 422, 446, 465 twice 467, 479, 480, 493–494, 501, 547, 564, 566, 571, 579, 584–585

rulings in Ḥanbalī jurisprudence are innovations, even though they are mentioned in the treatises of the two main Ḥanbalī sources, *al-Iqnāʿ* and *al-Muntahā*.[331]

Despite the references to Ibn Taymiyyah's opinions in the treatises of these two scholars, it seems that Ibn Taymiyyah exerted only a limited influence upon their views. This can be concluded through the following:

- Several rulings in the Ḥanbalī School that have been termed innovations by Ibn Taymiyyah are nevertheless found in the treatises of these scholars.[332]
- Various rulings in the Ḥanbalī School that have been declared incorrect by Ibn Taymiyyah are to be found in the treatises of these scholars.[333]
- In certain instances, we find the two scholars citing some leading scholars who refute opinions in the School that were subscribed to by Ibn Taymiyyah.[334]

One can therefore conclude that the Ḥanbalī scholars of this era (i.e. the eleventh century) and the one preceding it (i.e. the tenth century) founded their opinions, in the main, on the existing opinions within the School. This reliance on existing opinions meant that there was little discussion of the legal evidences. This is the essence of Ibn 'Abd al-Wahhāb's criticism of *al-Iqnāʿ* and *al-Muntahā*. These two sources have remained the two most important Ḥanbalī works from the time they were compiled. Despite this, Ibn 'Abd al-Wahhāb states that the majority of the rulings present in these two sources are opposed to the words of Aḥmad and even to the texts of the *sharīʿah*.[335] It seems reasonable to suggest that a greater emphasis on Ibn Taymiyyah might have encouraged the discussion of legal evidences.

It ought to be noted that, since both of al-Karmī and al-Buhūtī confined themselves to the clarification of the writings of Ibn al-Najjār and al-Futūḥī,[336] it was inevitable that their works would be affected by the two latter scholars' methodology which limited the influence of Ibn Taymiyyah.

Ibn 'Abd al-Wahhāb (d. 1206/1791)

This scholar's full name was Muhammad b. 'Abd al-Wahhāb b. Sulaymān b. 'Alī al-Wahaybī. He was born in the year 1115/1703 in a town called al-'Uyayynah where he studied, from an early age, under several scholars. One of those entrusted with this task was his father, who was a jurist and a judge. Thereafter, he embarked upon various journeys in order to seek knowledge in the Ḥijāz, Iraq and al-Aḥsā'. He was later to become the leading scholar and reformer of his time. In addition, he bequeathed several treatises in various subjects. Ibn 'Abd al-Wahhāb did not leave a great number of works in the field of jurisprudence. His authorship on this subject is contained in two medium-sized volumes that were collected and published by the Imam University in Saudi Arabia. The two volumes are composed of the following:

- *Mukhtaṣar al-Inṣāf wa 'l-Sharḥ al-Kabīr.*
- *Mukhtaṣar al-Hadī.*

- *Adab al-Mashī ilā al-Ṣalāh.*
- *Aḥkām al-Ṭahārah.*
- *Shurūṭ al-Ṭahārah wa arkānuhā wa wajibātuhā.*
- *Arba' Qawā'id.*
- *Mabḥath al-Ijtihād wa 'l-khilāf.*

It appears possible that Ibn 'Abd al-Wahhāb wrote little on the science of jurisprudence because he was preoccupied with the re-establishment of basic Islamic beliefs, which had been almost forgotten by the society of his time.[337]

After undertaking lengthy journeys for knowledge, teaching and reforming, Ibn 'Abd al-Wahhāb died in the year 1206/1791, following a short period of illness.[338]

Ibn Taymiyyah's influence on Ibn 'Abd al-Wahhāb

Scholars have mentioned that Ibn Taymiyyah exerted an important influence on Ibn 'Abd al-Wahhāb. He sought encouragement from his example in the development of his determination to denounce rigid imitation of medieval commentaries and to utilise independent reasoning.[339] It is said that the Ḥanbalī scholar 'Abd Allah Ibn Ibrāhim al-Najdī was the first person who introduced him to the works of Ibn Taymiyyah.[340] Later on, it appears that he became known amongst his contemporaries for his acquaintance with Ibn Taymiyyah's words. On one occasion, he was approached by some of his contemporaries and requested to explain some of Ibn Taymiyyah's statements.[341] Ibn 'Abd al-Wahhāb also became known for his citation of Ibn Taymiyyah, to the extent that the extensive citation of Ibn Taymiyyah's opinions is a characteristic by which some scholars identified some of Ibn 'Abd al-Wahhāb's treatises.[342]

Ibn Taymiyyah's influence upon Ibn 'Abd al-Wahhāb can be evidenced through various aspects, some of which are the following:

- There is a clear similarity between the jurisprudential rules employed by Ibn 'Abd al-Wahhāb and those of Ibn Taymiyyah. Occasionally, he attributes these rules to Ibn Taymiyyah,[343] and sometimes he does not.[344]
- Ibn 'Abd al-Wahhāb is in agreement with Ibn Taymiyyah concerning various important issues, such as the refutation of Greek logic and the veneration of saints, tombs and shrines.[345] Like Ibn Taymiyyah before him, 'Abd al-Wahhāb fell foul of the financial beneficiaries of the local shrine establishments.[346]
- There is a clear similarity between the various jurisprudential opinions of these two scholars.[347] Nevertheless, we find that Ibn 'Abd al-Wahhāb subscribes to certain opinions in the School which Ibn Taymiyyah criticised.[348] This may be because of one of three reasons: either he believed that they are the correct ruling despite Ibn Taymiyyah's disagreement, or he was unaware of Ibn Taymiyyah's criticism of them, or he was simply reporting the opinions

adopted by the Ḥanbalī School rather than expressing his own position with regard to these issues.

- He occasionally mentions the opinion of the School and then makes reference to a conflicting opinion of Ibn Taymiyyah, without expressing a preference.[349] On certain occasions, he cites two conflicting opinions narrated from Ibn Taymiyyah regarding a single issue.[350]
- It appears that he was influenced by the critical approach adopted by Ibn Taymiyyah towards the study of Ḥanbalī jurisprudence. Therefore, we notice that he declares most of the rulings mentioned in the treatises *al-Iqnāʿ* and *al-Muntahā*, which have long been the two main reference works for Ḥanbalī scholars, to be in opposition not only to the words of Aḥmad but also to the words of the Lawgiver.[351]
- His position on the concept of imitation reflects that of Ibn Taymiyyah; both Ibn Taymiyyah and Ibn ʿAbd al-Wahhāb were strongly attacked by scholars in their time, who claimed that they were in opposition to the entire works of earlier schools. Both of these two scholars lived in the era of *taqlid*. This period started at the end of the tenth century. During this period, scholars were no longer considered capable of exercising, or permitted to exercise, independent reasoning. This state of affairs continued for a considerable period of time and few social forces or individuals dared to challenge the authority of imitation or some of the medieval legal manuals. Amongst the noteworthy exceptions were these two leading scholars.[352]
- He was influenced by Ibn Taymiyyah's zero-tolerance of innovations. He labels various practices and rulings in the Ḥanbalī School as innovations. In the majority of these issues, he explains that he based his judgements upon Ibn Taymiyyah's opinions.[353]

It was shown earlier that the extensive citation by Ḥanbalī scholars in the tenth and eleventh centuries of the opinions of Ibn Taymiyyah did not necessarily mean that he exerted a noticeable influence upon the opinions of these scholars; on the contrary, these individuals were usually in agreement with the stance of the early Ḥanbalī scholars. This changed after the call of Ibn ʿAbd al-Wahhāb. We notice that the opinions of Ibn Taymiyyah have considerably influenced the opinions of Ḥanbalī scholars since the time of Ibn ʿAbd al-Wahhāb up to the present time, particularly after the publication of a large number of Ibn Taymiyyah's treatises.[354]

The effect of this influence is also apparent within the ruling circles. In the twentieth century, King ʿAbd al-ʿAziz of Saudi Arabia declared his intention to formulate a code of law embodying the teaching of Ibn Taymiyyah.[355] In addition, the resolution of the Ministry of Justice number 3/1253 dated 2/3/1381H states that the legal preferences of Ibn Taymiyyah are considered as one of the sources of judgement.[356] Furthermore, although Ḥanbalī jurisprudence in its entirety forms the predominant School of law in Saudi Arabia, and its jurisprudence is taught in all educational institutions in the country, particular emphasis has been placed on the opinions and preferences of Ibn Taymiyyah on those issues on which he disagrees with the School.[357]

Ibn 'Abd al-Wahhāb possessed various treatises of Ibn Taymiyyah and it was known that he honoured his works.[358] He also abridged some of Ibn Taymiyyah's works, such as *Minhāj al-Sunnah.*[359] He also gave due importance to the work of some of his students, most notably Ibn al-Qayyim. He cites the opinions of Ibn al-Qayyim on various issues[360] and he also abridged some of his works. For instance, Ibn 'Abd al-Wahhāb's work entitled *Mabḥath al-Ijtihād wa 'l-Khilāf* (section on jurisprudential disagreement and independent reasoning) is in fact an abridgement of a portion of Ibn al-Qayyim's book, *I'lām al-Muaqqi'īn.* He also abridged the work of al-Mardāwī entitled *al-Inṣāf.* It was concluded earlier that this book is amongst the most comprehensive sources of Ibn Taymiyyah's opinions and preferences. In this abridgement, Ibn 'Abd al-Wahhāb refers to those opinions and legal preferences of Ibn Taymiyyah mentioned in the original work *al-Inṣāf.* In his *Mukhtaṣar*, this scholar refers to Ibn Taymiyyah as '*al-Sheikh*' (Tables 15 and 16).[361]

Table 15 The extent of Ibn 'Abd al-Wahhāb's citation of Ibn Taymiyyah's opinions and preferences in his book *al-Ṭahārah*, which is comprised of 43 sheets

6 six times, 7 twice, 9 thrice, 10 twice, 12, 13 thrice, 14, 15, 16 twice, 18, 20, 21 twice, 22 twice, 23 twice, 24, 25, 27, 28, 9, 30, 31, 32, 33 twice, 34 thrice, 35 twice, 37, 38, 39, 40, 41, 42, 43

Table 16 The references made by Ibn 'Abd al-Wahhāb to Ibn Taymiyyah's opinions and preferences in his book *Mukhtaṣar al-Inṣāf,* referring to him as '*al-sheikh*'

15 nine times, 20 seven times, 21 thrice, 25 twice, 26 nine, 32 four, 40 thrice, 47 six, 48 six, 54 ten, 63 six, 64 six, 73 once, 74 eleven, 75 once, 80 nine, 81 eight, 87 thrice, 88 five, 89 thrice, 90 six, 97 thrice, 98 thrice, 104 four, 108 twelve, 110 five, 113 four, 139 five, 140 nine, 150 eight, 162 five, 163 ten, 164 twice, 171 sixteen, 185 eleven, 186 six, 198 sixteen, 204 seven, 208 twice, 224 eleven, 225 four, 230 seven, 235 four, 237 twice, 257 five, 258 eight, 260 once, 261 six, 263 five, 265 twice, 266 nine, 268 five, 271 five, 272 four, 284 four, 298 four, 299 five, 321 eight, 341 four, 342 eight, 345 once, 346 twice, 357 eight, 358 once, 369 six, 388 thrice, 389 four, 403 six mistake?, 404 seven, 405 nine, 428 six, 429 eight, 430 five, 436 five, 437 thrice, 465 thrice, 466 twelve, 467 thrice, 486 once, 487 six, 488 four, 489 six, 502 twice, 504 twice, 515 six, 520 twice, 521 five, 533 seven, 534 six, 550 twice, 551 nine, 552 four 554 once, 560 nine, 561 ten, 565 five, 566 eight, 576 twice, 577 four, 578 six, 579 four, 580 four, 585 thrice, 586 thrice, 588 thrice, 592 once, 593 twelve, 594 thrice, 598 five, 600 once, 606 once, 612 once, 616 nine, 617 nine, 626 twice, 627 eleven, 632 thrice, 633 thrice, 636 twice, 642 four, 643 twice, 658 eleven, 659 six, 660 six, 663 thrice, 664 nine, 666 once, 668 once, 669 once, 674 four, 675 five, 679 five, 682 four, 684 once, 685 nine, 686 twice, 687 thrice, 689 four, 692 once, 693 twice, 699 five, 704 twice, 715 thrice, 716 seven, 717 thrice, 723 four, eleven, 725 eight, 730 six, 731 thrice, 736 six, 751 once, 752 ten, 753 seven, 754 thrice, 776 five, 777 nine, 778 seven, 779 eight, 780 ten, 781 nine, 782 twelve, 783 twice

Al-Sa'dī (d. 1376/1956)

This scholar's full name was 'Abd al-Raḥmān b. Nāṣir b. 'Abd Allah b. Nāṣir b. Ḥamad al-Sa'dī. He was born in the year 1307/1889. His mother and father died in the years 1310/1892 and 1313/1895 respectively.[362] He acquired knowledge in various Arabic and Islamic sciences under the guidance and supervision of several scholars in his time.[363] In addition, he possessed or had access to a large number of references and source works that he used in his personal studies.[364]

Later on, this scholar became the sheikh, mufti and Imam of the city of 'Unayzah's Grand Mosque (in Saudi Arabia) and its Friday preacher. He supervised al-Ma'had al-'Ilmī, the institute of Arabic and Islamic studies in his town.[365] He was also offered the position of judge on various occasions, these offers were rejected, an action which appears to have been motivated by piety.[366]

This scholar bequeathed a significant scholarly legacy in various sciences. His works concerning the sciences of jurisprudence and its sources are of considerable importance in relation to the contemporary sources of the Ḥanbalī School. Amongst the most important of these treatises are:

- *Al-Mukhtārāt al-Jaliyyah min al-Masā'il al-Fiqhiyyah*: In this book, al-Sa'dī mentions his preferences in relation to many jurisprudential issues. He states that the sole criterion applied by this scholar in his selection of his preferred views is the correctness of the evidence upon which these opinions are based. This is so, even if they are contrary to the recognised opinion of the Ḥanbalī School.[367]
- *Al-Fatāwā al-Sa'diyyah*: This treatise comprises the *fatāwā* issued by this scholar during his life.
- *Ṭarīq al-Wuṣūl*: This book contains various rules and maxims concerning different sciences, amongst which are the two sciences of jurisprudence and its principles. Another reference to this treatise will be made later on in this section.
- *Al-Qawā'id wa al-Uṣūl al-Jāmi'ah wa 'l-Furūq wa 'l-Taqāsim al-Badī'ah al-Nāfi'ah*: This treatise is divided into two sections: the first contains rules that apply equally to various similar sets of circumstances; the second part deals with issues that have some aspects of similarity but have different rulings in Islamic law.

Ibn Taymiyyah's influence on Al-Sa'dī

Several biographers who have written accounts of this scholar believe that al-Sa'dī benefited greatly from Ibn Taymiyyah and Ibn al-Qayyim. Al-Bassām, who was one of al-Sa'dī's students, mentions that the treatises of Ibn Taymiyyah and Ibn al-Qayyim enabled al-Sa'dī to comprehend issues in their true light.[368] Another student of al-Sa'dī, al-Qāḍī, states that his sheikh was wholeheartedly engaged throughout his entire life in the consultation of the books of jurisprudence and *ḥadīth* and those written by Ibn Taymiyyah and Ibn al-Qayyim, for they were his 'staple diet' (*sabūḥ* and *ghabūq*).[369] The testimonies of these two students of al-Sa'dī are corroborated by al-Sa'dī's own son, 'Abd Allah. He testifies that the most oft-consulted and the most beneficial sources for his father were those of these two scholars. He asserts that they had a significant influence upon al-Sa‘dī.[370] In addition, Ibn Bāz, the former Mufti of Saudi Arabia, encountered al-Sa‘dī on various occasions. He testifies to the presence of a great link between this scholar and Ibn Taymiyyah and Ibn al-Qayyim, explaining that al-Sa‘dī used to pay great care and attention to the works of these two scholars.[371] Some of al-Sa‘dī's treatises are either abridgements or explanations of the works of these two scholars. Furthermore, Ibn Salīm (d. 1323/1905), one of al-Sa‘dī's teachers, was an admirer of the treatises of these two scholars.[372]

Al-Sa‘dī reveals his opinion of Ibn Taymiyyah's treatises when he states that the treatises of 'the great Imam, the sheikh of Islam and Muslims, Taqī al-Dīn Aḥmad b. 'Abd al-Ḥalīm b. 'Abd al-Salām b. Taymiyyah, may Allah sanctify his soul, contain all the beneficial and correct sciences'.[373] He also asserts that these treatises contain the sciences of narration and reason, morals and manners. Similarly, they combine the objectives of the *sharī‘ah*, the legal means, jurisprudential issues and their evidence from the *sharī‘ah* in addition to the philosophy behind these rulings. Al-Sa‘dī, asserts that Ibn Taymiyyah's treatises are characterised by a detailed, clear explanation of the correct opinions, in addition to a criticism of the incorrect views. He also states that Ibn Taymiyyah's books contain a considerable degree of authenticity. On account of what has been mentioned, al-Sa‘dī asserts that whosoever commands an extensive knowledge of both Ibn Taymiyyah's treatises and the works of other scholars would reach the conclusion that there are no treatises which are equal, or even similar, to those of Ibn Taymiyyah's.[374]

Al-Sa‘dī describes the influence exerted by Ibn Taymiyyah upon his time and the following generations. He states that it is obvious that 'the existence of *sheikh al-islam* Ibn Taymiyyah and his students in the centuries of this *ummah* is by the grace of the Creator'.[375] He states that they 'have performed a significant role in the clarification and conveyance of great knowledge as well as in their struggle against the people of innovation and disbelief'.[376] Al-Sa‘dī affirms the importance of Ibn Taymiyyah's treatises which had become widespread by the fourteenth Islamic century, by pointing out that there is great benefit to be acquired from their existence.[377]

It is clear that al-Sa‘dī was well known among his contemporaries as being well versed in Ibn Taymiyyah's scholarly heritage, as we find that he was approached several times to explain and clarify the position of Ibn Taymiyyah regarding certain questions.[378] In defending Ibn Taymiyyah against his detractors, al-Sa‘dī also points out that some of Ibn Taymiyyah's opinions have been gravely misunderstood.[379]

Ibn Taymiyyah's scholarly works have left a considerable impression on al-Sa‘dī's writings on various sciences such as creed, interpretation of the Qur'an, jurisprudence and its principles.[380] One of the most important manifestations of Ibn Taymiyyah's influence upon this scholar is the strong connection between his jurisprudence and the general principles of jurisprudence.[381] Al-Sa‘dī asserts that the sources and maxims of sciences are as important as the foundations of houses and roots of trees, for just as the house and tree cannot stand upright without their foundations and roots, similarly, legal rulings must be derived from the general principles of Islamic law.[382] Al-Sa'dī acquired a significant number of the general rules and maxims of the *sharī'ah* from Ibn Taymiyyah and his disciple Ibn al-Qayyim. It ought to be noted that he compiled a treatise in which he gathered more than one thousand general principles and rules related to several sciences from the treatises and *fatāwā* of these two scholars.[383]

An obvious element of Ibn Taymiyyah's influence upon this scholar can be noticed through the concordance between al-Sa'dī's legal preferences and the opinions of Ibn Taymiyyah on many jurisprudential issues. Al-Sa'dī made his own legal preferences in jurisprudence, some of which are contrary to the position of the Ḥanbalī School. His preferences are generally in agreement with the opinions of Ibn Taymiyyah and Ibn al-Qayyim.[384] In several instances, he indicates that the preferred opinion is that of Ibn Taymiyyah.[385] Occasionally, he mentions only the opinion that he prefers, without referring to Ibn Taymiyyah.[386] On certain issues, he mentions the opinion of the School and his sheikh, without expressing a preference,[387] while at other times he refers to views of his sheikh as very strong opinions and proceeds to set out in detail the basis for these opinions.[388]

A study of the *fatāwā* issued by al-Sa'dī in his treatise *al-Fatāwā al-Sa'diyyah* shows that he cites Ibn Taymiyyah's jurisprudential opinions over forty times. On only one occasion do we find that al-Sa'dī disagrees with Ibn Taymiyyah,[389] and on three issues he does not reveal his own opinion.[390] On two other occasions, he admits his inability to reach a conclusion regarding what is the most correct opinion.[391] On the remaining issues, we find that al-Sa'dī offers his support to Ibn Taymiyyah's opinions describing them as 'very strong',[392] 'what agrees with the general principles and foundations of the *sharī'ah*',[393] or 'the moderate opinion'.[394]

Although this scholar's citations of Ibn Taymiyyah's jurisprudential opinions and legal preferences are not particularly numerous, he does subscribe to the same opinions as Ibn Taymiyyah on a large number of other jurisprudential issues, without explicitly referring to Ibn Taymiyyah's position on these issues.[395] This approach adopted by al-Sa'dī, in addition to his student Ibn Uthaymīn, as will be explained later on, is reminiscent of the approach adopted by Ibn al-Qayyim.

It is also evident that Ibn Taymiyyah influenced al-Sa'dī in his approach towards Ḥanbalī jurisprudence as we find him employing a critical method in his study of the School's rulings. Al-Sa'dī wrote a treatise in which he objected to various Ḥanbalī rulings which he believed were in opposition to the correct evidences.[396] He states that it is obligatory upon the one who seeks knowledge to have a firm determination to give precedence to the words of Allah and His Messenger above the words of any one else. Therefore, those seeking knowledge should practice independent reasoning in relation to understanding the words of the Lawgiver; if they commit mistakes they will be forgiven.[397]

It appears that Ibn Taymiyyah's influence spread through al-Sa'dī' to various parts of Saudi Arabia, due to the widespread distribution of al-Sa'dī's works.[398] This has been complemented by a significant number of al-Sa'dī's students assuming positions as teachers, judges, leading scholars and muftis. They have collectively conveyed the methodology of their teacher to the current generation (Tables 17–19).[399]

Table 17 The extent of al-Sa'dī's citation of Ibn Taymiyyah's opinions and preferences in *al-Mukhtārāt al-Jaliyyah*

15, 27, 41, 46, 60, 69, 108, 109, 114, 115, 116, 118, 119, 126 twice, 127

Table 18 The agreement of al-Sa'dī's legal preferences with those of Ibn Taymiyyah in *al-Mukhtārāt al-Jaliyyah*

7 twice, 8twice, 9, 10, 11, 12, twice, 13, 14, 15 twice, 16 thrice, 18 thrice, 19, 22, 24–26, 27, 29, 32, 35, 37, 40–41, 45 twice, 47, 48, 49, 50, 52, 53, 54 twice, 57 twice, 59 twice, 62, 63 twice, 68, 90, 101, 103 twice

Table 19 The extent of al- Sa'dī's citation of Ibn Taymiyyah's opinions and preferences in *al-Fatāwā al-Sa'diyyah*

129, 144, 155, 182, 183, 194, 208, 221, 241, 241–242, 243, 286, 293, 295, 298, 329, 343, 438, 450, 472–474, 476–478, 482, 499, 500, 512, 517, 519, 526, 528 twice, 532, 534, 537, 553, 556, 561, 564, 566, 570, 576, 581, 596, 598, 599

Ibn 'Uthaymīn (d. 1421/2000)

Muhammad b. Ṣāliḥ Ibn 'Uthaymīn was one of the most eminent students of al-Sa'dī. This sheikh was born in the town of 'Unayzah on the 27th of Ramaḍān in the year 1347/1929. He graduated from *al-Sharī'ah* college and then became a teacher of Islamic sciences at an institute affiliated to the Imam University. Later on, he was appointed as a professor in *al-Sharī'ah* college in the Imam University. In addition, he was also a member of the Body of Senior Scholars in Saudi Arabia. Various works containing the *fatāwā* issued by this scholar have been published. He also compiled various treatises on miscellaneous subjects. Twenty works accredited to this scholar have been published to date. One particular treatise is in the science of jurisprudence and is entitled '*al-Sharḥ al-Mumti' 'Ala Zād al-Mustaqni'*'.[400]

Ibn Taymiyyah's influence on Ibn 'Uthaymīn

It is evident that Ibn 'Uthaymīn attaches great importance to Ibn Taymiyyah's views and preferences, as he is in agreement with him concerning numerous issues. His praise for him indicates that this scholar appears to have great admiration for Ibn Taymiyyah. His lucid explanations indicate that Ibn 'Uthaymīn is well versed in the terminology employed by Ibn Taymiyyah.[401] He also conveys the wisdom behind certain rulings in Islamic law from Ibn Taymiyyah's perspective.[402]

Ibn Taymiyyah's influence on Ibn 'Uthaymīn can be evidenced through several points, one of which is Ibn 'Uthaymīn's use of the opinions of Ibn Taymiyyah. This section briefly analyses the explicit and implicit references he makes to the work of Ibn Taymiyyah. In some instances Ibn 'Uthaymīn mentions Ibn

Taymiyyah's preferences without expressing an opinion himself.[403] Sometimes he refrains from giving his view, while describing Ibn Taymiyyah's opinion as strong or very strong.[404] Ibn 'Uthaymīn often prefers Ibn Taymiyyah's opinion to the predominant opinion of the Ḥanbalī School.[405] He conveys his praise for Ibn Taymiyyah's opinions using a variety of expressions: he mentions that the evidence affirm the accuracy of Ibn Taymiyyah's opinions;[406] he says that Ibn Taymiyyah's opinion is the one that deserves to be followed;[407] he describes Ibn Taymiyyah's opinion as the best opinion amongst the various conflicting opinions;[408] he states that Ibn Taymiyyah's opinion is correct according to the general rules of the School[409] and he states that Ibn Taymiyyah's ruling is most in conformity with the needs of the people.[410] At other times, however, Ibn 'Uthaymīn is not so forthcoming in his support for Ibn Taymiyyah. On occasions, he mentions, with evident hesitancy, that it can be said that the opinion of Ibn Taymiyyah is accurate.[411] On certain issues he accepts Ibn Taymiyyah's opinion but with slight modification.[412] Sometimes he mentions that Ibn Taymiyyah is in opposition to the opinions of the Ḥanbalī School, but does not reveal his own opinion; the implication, however, is that he is not entirely convinced by Ibn Taymiyyah's arguments. Indeed, there are other times where Ibn 'Uthaymīn openly disagrees with Ibn Taymiyyah.[413] After preferring the opinion of the School and supporting it by various evidences, he refers sometimes to the existence of a conflicting opinion held by Ibn Taymiyyah.[414] In addition, on certain occasions, he explains that he has followed the opinion of the School rather than that of Ibn Taymiyyah as a means of precaution.[415] In one particular case, he even states that Ibn Taymiyyah's ruling is problematic as it is contradicted by the practice of some of the companions.[416] He sometimes describes an opinion within the Ḥanbalī School as more likely to be correct than Ibn Taymiyyah's opinion,[417] or he states that the legal evidence supports his position, rather than that of Ibn Taymiyyah.[418] There are certain rulings which Ibn Taymiyyah restricted to certain people; Ibn 'Uthaymīn responds that he 'finds something in his heart' against the ruling, as he feels that the *sharī'ah*'s evidences affirm the generality of the rulings.[419] In certain rulings where Ibn Taymiyyah insists on the prohibition of some acts, Ibn 'Uthaymīn believes that they are permissible provided that particular conditions are fulfilled.[420] In one case, he argues that a ruling given by Ibn Taymiyyah was inaccurate, and that he believes that Ibn Taymiyyah was influenced by the predominant opinion of other jurists. He asserts that Ibn Taymiyyah's opinion and that of the other jurists contradict various authentic evidences.[421]

Interestingly, Ibn 'Uthaymīn occasionally gives unusual reasons for adopting Ibn Taymiyyah's views. In one issue, he states that he imitated Ibn Taymiyyah's opinion, owing to the absence of correct evidence pertaining to that issue.[422] He also suggests that following some of the *fatāwā* of Ibn Taymiyyah is occasionally a necessity as the opposing opinion causes unnecessary and unwanted hardship.[423]

As mentioned previously, there are various jurisprudential rulings on which these two scholars agree. Ibn 'Uthaymīn does not necessarily refer to Ibn Taymiyyah's position on the issue in question (Tables 20).[424]

Ibn 'Uthaymīn also adopts some of Ibn Taymiyyah's strategies in resolving the conflict between two jurisprudential opinions. In *al-Sharḥ al-Mumti'*, for example, he sometimes opts for opinions which take a median position between the conflicting rulings of other jurists. He justifies this approach by stating that Ibn Taymiyyah sometimes utilised this methodology.[425]

Another area where Ibn Taymiyyah's influence on this scholar can be witnessed is Ibn 'Uthaymīn's citation of Ibn Taymiyyah's criticism of certain Ḥanbalī opinions and narrations.[426] As is the case with Ibn Taymiyyah, Ibn 'Uthaymīn does not appear to have any difficulty with rejecting opinions in the School if they conflict with his view of what the correct evidence is. This reflects Ibn Taymiyyah's critical approach to the body of Ḥanbalī law.[427] He also labels several rulings within the School as innovations and it is clear that on many of these, he takes his inspiration from Ibn Taymiyyah[428] Ibn 'Uthaymīn was also influenced by various rules and maxims employed by Ibn Taymiyyah.[429]

There appear to have been several causes for the emphatic influence of Ibn Taymiyyah upon Ibn 'Uthaymīn, the most important of which are the following:

- This scholar was influenced to a considerable degree by his sheikh al-Sa'dī, who was also, as mentioned earlier, considerably influenced by Ibn Taymiyyah. Ibn 'Uthaymīn studied various subjects under al-Sa'dī, such as creed, interpretation of the Qur'an, *ḥadīth* and jurisprudence and its general principles.[430] Ibn 'Uthaymīn was highly regarded by al-Sa'dī, as evidenced by his response when Ibn 'Uthaymīn's father transferred his residence to Riyadh and expressed a desire that his son should do likewise. Al-Sa'dī wrote to him: 'this is not possible, rather we hope that Muhammad will remain with us and benefit'.[431] The sheikh desired that Ibn 'Uthaymīn continue his classes and thus derive benefit from his tuition. Ibn 'Uthaymīn describes the impact upon him of his relationship with this sheikh when he comments: 'I was greatly influenced by him in his manner of teaching and presenting knowledge and making it understandable to the students by use of examples and explanations. I was also greatly influenced by his good manners. Indeed Sheikh 'Abd al-Raḥmān [i.e. al-Sa'dī] had excellent manners and character in addition to an abundance of knowledge and worship.'[432]
- Ibn 'Uthaymīn studied certain works pertaining to the sciences of *ḥadīth* and jurisprudence under Ibn Bāz, the former *mufti* of Saudi Arabia. This included some of the works of Ibn Taymiyyah.[433]
- The mass publication and circulation of Ibn Taymiyyah's works, and in particular his *Fatāwā*, commenced during this period. A large number were first published after 1380/1960, that is, after the death of al-Sa'dī.
- Ibn 'Uthaymīn also abridged some of the works of Ibn Taymiyyah and Ibn al-Qayyim. Although it could be said that his desire to abridge the works came from his existing respect for those two scholars, it is also likely that the net of abridgement brought him into contact with their ideas on a more intimate level.

Table 20 Various issues in *al-Sharḥ al-Mumtiʿ* (Volume 1–8)[434] where Ibn ʿUthaymīn refers to Ibn Taymiyyah's opinions and is in agreement with him

The issue	*The predominant opinion in the Ḥanbalī School*	*Ibn Taymiyyah*	*Ibn ʿUthaymīn*
How many division of water are there?	Three[435]	Two[436]	Two[437]
Does the quantity of the water have an effect on its purity if it is infiltrated by an impurity?	If the water is less than two *qullah*, it becomes impure as soon as it encounters dirt[438]	The quantity of water has no effect: the real consideration is whether a change has occurred or not[439]	The same opinion as Ibn Taymiyyah[440]
Is the *siwāk* permitted for a fasting person in the afternoon?	No[441]	Yes[442]	Yes[443]
Should the intention be uttered in acts of worship?	This is recommended and the worshipper says it silently[444]	This is not allowed and it is an innovation[445]	The same opinion as Ibn Taymiyyah[446]
Is the permissibility of wiping over the *khuffayn* conditional upon other matters?	Yes[447]	No[448]	No[449]
Is wiping over the *lufāfah* (cloth wrapping) permissible?	No[450]	Yes[451]	Yes[452]
Can a woman perform *ṭawāf* during her period?	No[453]	Yes, in a case of necessity[454]	The same opinion as Ibn Taymiyyah[455]
When a person has a bath is it sufficient that he intended to remove the major impurity?	No[456]	Yes[457]	Yes[458]
Is there a time limit for menstruation?	Yes[459]	No[460]	No[461]
May trees be rented for their fruits?	No[462]	Yes[463]	Yes[464]
Does *ḥuqnah* break the fast?	Yes[465]	No[466]	No[467]
Does cupping break the fast of the cupper even if he does not have contact with the blood?	Yes[468]	No[469]	No[470]

Conclusion

In conclusion, the following points can be deduced from this chapter:

- Ibn Taymiyyah's opinions and preferences have been cited by Ḥanbalī scholars from his time up to the present time. The level of citation and Ibn Taymiyyah's influence upon these scholars has differed from one scholar to the next. Indeed, copious citation of Ibn Taymiyyah's opinions by some of these scholars does not necessarily entail that they were influenced by Ibn Taymiyyah in most rulings. Some Ḥanbalī scholars such as Ibn al-Qayyim and al-Sa'dī, do not cite a great deal of Ibn Taymiyyah's opinions, but it is clear that they were greatly influenced by him. On the other hand, other scholars such as Ibn Mufliḥ and al-Mardāwī cite a great number of Ibn Taymiyyah's opinions without there being much apparent impact on their jurisprudential opinions. Like all great scholars, Ibn Taymiyyah, gave wings to his students and enabled them to soar. Some therefore were more profoundly influenced by his overall methodology, even if they did not agree with many of his conclusions. Others saw him as an important teacher and authority in the School, possessing an independent mind. They would like his opinions perhaps as counter-arguments to the School's predominant opinion, without necessarily agreeing with him.
- It is also evident that those scholars who were influenced by him to a significant degree support Ibn Taymiyyah's position because they consider that the evidence of the *sharī'ah* testify to their correctness, and in this they follow his method. This is also further stressed by 'Abd Allah Ibn 'Abd Wahhāb (d. 1242/1826), who discusses a jurisprudential issue in which Ibn Taymiyyah's position seems to oppose the opinion of possibly all scholars. According to him, the near-unanimous opinion is supported by correct textual evidences. 'Abd Allah Ibn 'Abd Wahhāb asserts that those who oppose the position of most of the scholars have no legal ground for their opinion apart from the fact that it was supported by Ibn Taymiyyah, who based his ruling on a narration from Ibn 'Abbās. He states that what was cited by Ibn Taymiyyah to support his position cannot be used in opposition to the correct legal evidence narrated from the Prophet. 'Abd Allah Ibn 'Abd Wahhāb adds that although Ibn Taymiyyah was one of the *mujtahid* scholars, if his ruling contradicts with the correct evidence then his opinion has to be rejected. He asserts it is not permissible to imitate the opinion of the sheikh without knowing the correctness and accuracy of the evidences adduced by him and his understanding and interpretation of the opposing evidences. 'Abd Allah Ibn 'Abd Wahhāb says that the correct position in dealing with the opinions of scholars is to compare them to what is in the book of Allah and the *Sunnah* of his Messenger. He also states that it is not permitted to imitate the opinion of a scholar simply because they were more knowledgeable in the meanings of these legal evidence. He asserts that such practice was denounced by Ibn Taymiyyah and labelled as a censured imitation.[471]

- During the tenth and eleventh centuries, the citation of Ibn Taymiyyah's opinions and his influence upon Ḥanbalī scholars appears to be very limited. There may be various factors behind this; the methodology adopted by these scholars in the writing of their treatises is a major factor.
- From the twelfth century up to the present time the citation of Ibn Taymiyyah's opinions and his influence upon Ḥanbalī scholars appears to have gradually regained its importance. This can be attributed to various factors amongst which are the following:

  – The call of Muhammad Ibn Abd al-Wahhāb.
  – The widespread presence of students of the leading scholar al-Sa'dī, who was greatly influenced by Ibn Taymiyyah.
  – The considerable attention devoted to the treatises written by Ibn Taymiyyah and his disciple Ibn al-Qayyim. This resulted in the editing and publication of a large number of them.

In this chapter, a number of important points have been elaborated upon with reference to Ibn Taymiyyah's influence upon Ḥanbalī scholars. There is no doubt that he has became a major reference for Ḥanbalī scholars down the ages, either in challenging predominant opinions in the School or as a source for unusual opinions or as an inspiration for employing a critical methodology in analysing the School's body of law. It seems also that his influence has grown in the past century through the efforts of certain followers amongst the scholars and the widespread dissemination of his writings.

Chapter 6 offers a more detailed study of one particular jurisprudential ruling issued by Ibn Taymiyyah, which gives an example of the way that he has influenced the Ḥanbalī School.

6

A CASE OF CONFLICT?

The intended triple divorce revisited

Introduction

Several issues in Ibn Taymiyyah's jurisprudence proved to be a source of confrontation between him and other scholars within the Ḥanbalī School. This chapter is devoted to an analysis of one of the most significant jurisprudential issues in Ibn Taymiyyah's life. His opinion on this issue was a catalyst for some of his interrogations and also left an indelible influence upon Ḥanbalī jurisprudence.[1] This matter concerns the intended triple divorce. Does it have the effect of the third and final repudiation or is it treated as a single pronouncement with the stated number having no effect?[2]

Great confusion has been caused by the alleged existence of consensus opposing Ibn Taymiyyah's opinion in relation to this point. Furthermore, Ibn Taymiyyah's position is not clearly presented in some of the sources. The discussion in this chapter will therefore focus on the following points:

- A clarification of the position of the Ḥanbalī School of law concerning this point according to Ibn Taymiyyah and the Ḥanbalī sources.
- A clarification of the position of Ibn Taymiyyah on this issue.
- A presentation of Ibn Taymiyyah's evidences on this point and his criticism of the opposition's evidences.
- An examination of whether or not Ibn Taymiyyah's opinion regarding this point is contrary to a consensus of Muslim scholars.

Types of divorce in Islamic law

It can be said that Islamic law categorises divorce into two types: *sunni* and *bidʿī*. *Sunni* (i.e. in accordance with the *sunnah*) divorce occurs when a man divorces his wife through a single pronouncement during a stage of her purity from menstruation in which he has not had sexual intercourse with her. *Bidʿī* divorce takes place if a man pronounces divorce during the stage of menstruation or in a period of purity during which sexual intercourse has occurred.[3]

Valid divorces are in turn classified in Islamic law into two kinds: *rajʿī* (revocable) and *bāʾin* (irrevocable).[4]

The position of the Ḥanbalī School of law concerning the 'triple divorce'

A certain degree of confusion exists concerning this issue. The difficulty arises from: what is actually meant by triple divorce? Is this type of divorce permissible or not? Is it binding? What was the actual opinion of Ibn Ḥanbal himself? This section seeks to clarify these points.

1 What is actually meant by triple divorce?

The dispute amongst the Ḥanbalī scholars does not relate to the situation where the divorce is pronounced three times, each pronouncement taking place after a period of waiting *('iddah)*. This point is 'agreed upon' as permissible amongst the Ḥanbalī scholars, a stance which is also accepted by Ibn Taymiyyah.[5]

The most important forms of the triple divorce which form the subject-matter of the controversy within the Ḥanbalī scholars:

- Where the divorce is pronounced thrice in one sitting within one phrase (i.e. *anti ṭāliq thalāthan*).
- Where the divorce is uttered in three phrases in one sitting (*anti ṭāliq anti ṭāliq anti ṭāliq* or *anti ṭāliq wa ṭāliq wa ṭāliq* or *anti ṭāliq fa ṭāliq fa ṭāliq*).
- Where the divorce is uttered at three different times, once on every occasion until the completion of the three pronouncements before *raj'ah* (revocation).

In all three forms, the Ḥanbalī scholars discuss two separate points:

1 whether this type of divorce is permissible or not;
2 if it is permissible, what is its resultant effect? Does it have the effect of the third and final irrevocable repudiation or a single revocable divorce?

2 Triple divorce, permissible or prohibited?

There is a disagreement amongst the Ḥanbalī scholars as to whether or not the triple divorce is considered a permissible form of divorce.[6] Their disagreement was founded upon conflicting narrations emanating from Ibn Ḥanbal himself.[7] According to several Ḥanbalī scholars, the correct narration of Ibn Ḥanbal concerning this issue states that it is prohibited.[8] Ibn Taymiyyah, who also believes that this type of divorce is prohibited,[9] clarifies the reason for the existence of these conflicting narrations. He mentions that initially Ibn Ḥanbal held the opinion that this type of divorce was permissible, but later on he altered his opinion. Ibn Taymiyyah quotes Ibn Ḥanbal as stating that he pondered over the Qur'anic verses specifically concerning divorce and determined that the only form of permissible divorce is the revocable type.[10]

According to Ibn Taymiyyah, after this alteration in Ibn Ḥanbal's opinion, this view became the predominant opinion in the Ḥanbalī School.[11]

According to Ibn Taymiyyah, the vast majority of Ḥanbalī scholars are in agreement with him that this type of divorce is an innovation and that its performance is prohibited. If this type of divorce begins to be performed, however, the Ḥanbalī scholars consider it as a valid divorce. Ibn Taymiyyah opposes this stance; he believes that it is prohibited and that it cannot have a legal effect.

3 The legal effect of triple divorce

If the divorce is pronounced triply in one phrase at once (i.e. *anti ṭāliq thalāthan*) or repeated three times in one sitting (*anti ṭāliq anti ṭāliq anti ṭāliq*); or the divorce is uttered at three different times within one period without *raj'ah* taking place (revocation), several leading Ḥanbalī scholars say that the opinion within the Ḥanbalī School is that this form of divorce has the effect of the final repudiation.[12]

4 Ibn Taymiyyah's position on the legal effect of triple divorce

Ibn Taymiyyah's opinion is that a triple divorce has the same ruling as a single pronouncement and the number mentioned has no effect.[13] According to him, there is no distinction between the utterance of three divorces in one phrase (such as *ṭalaqtuki thalāthan* – I have divorced you thrice), or in three separate phrases (such as *anti ṭāliq, anti ṭāliq, anti ṭāliq* – you are divorced, you are divorced, you are divorced).[14]

Ibn Taymiyyah's evidence

Ibn Taymiyyah cites several types of evidences to support his opinion, three of which are the following:

1 He cites several pieces of textual evidence, including the following:

- Muslim narrates that Ibn 'Abbās said: 'Divorce in the period of the Messenger of Allah (peace and blessing be upon him), Abū Bakr and in the first two years of the caliphate of 'Umar, if pronounced thrice at once was counted as one, but 'Umar gave it effect against them.'[15]
- Ibn 'Abbās also said: 'Rukānah divorced his wife thrice in a single session and was greatly saddened in his longing for her. The Messenger of Allah questioned him, 'how did you divorce her?' He replied, 'I divorced her thrice in a single session.' The Prophet said 'that is a single divorce, return to her by revocation if you want'.[16]

2 Ibn Taymiyyah argues that no one during the time of the Prophet who divorced his wife triply was considered by the Prophet to have performed a legally valid divorce. He asserts that there is no authentic or sound *ḥadīth* that suggests otherwise. He acknowledges the existence of certain narrations

mentioned in some of the collections of *ḥadīth*, such as a *ḥadīth* narrated by 'Ali, another by 'Ubādah and another by al-Ḥasan, but he declares that they are either weak or fabricated.[17]

3 Ibn Taymiyyah makes reference to rational evidences, examples of which are:

- He asks how the majority of Ḥanbalī scholars can consider this divorce to be impermissible and yet also claim that it is binding? He states that the texts necessitate that only the Sunni divorce can be binding. He supports his argument by referring to a maxim that was, according to him, implemented by the *salaf* and the leading jurists, including the four Imams. This maxim states: 'Every contract, which is permitted in certain forms and prohibited in others, such as sale and marriage, if performed in the prohibited form, will not be considered binding, and vice versa in the instance of the permitted form.'[18] Ibn Taymiyyah appears to imply that it is clear that this rule applies to the triple divorce because it is a prohibited form of divorce. Therefore, the jurists must consider it as non-binding and accept only the permitted forms of divorce.
- He also argues that if this divorce is considered by the Lawgiver to be impermissible but this does not result in its invalidity, what purpose is served by the division of divorce into two types, permissible and impermissible?[19] What difference does it make to the Muslim?
- Ibn Taymiyyah argues that the Lawgiver prohibits certain matters because they contain absolute or preponderant corruption (*mafsadah*). The purpose behind the prohibition is to prevent that corruption. If, however, an act is prohibited, yet at the same time its consequences are binding, what is the purpose of the prohibition? According to Ibn Taymiyyah, if this were true it would lead to the existence of a contradiction in the legal rulings, but the Lawgiver is far removed from making contradictory rulings.[20]
- Ibn Taymiyyah explained why some leading scholars, such as 'Umar, had ruled that the triple divorce takes the effect of a total of three separate divorces. He argues that 'Umar had seen that the people of his time were using this form of divorce widely, despite it being prohibited by the Lawgiver. He felt that therefore there was a need for strict action to prevent them from doing so and hoped that the best way was to bind these people to the consequences of their actions.[21]

According to Ibn Taymiyyah, this type of action can be included under the class of 'discretionary punishments', which can be used when it is needed. He acknowledges the existence of certain rulings where a separation between a couple is enforced by either the Lawgiver or the leader of the Muslim community.[22] Ibn Taymiyyah stresses, however, that 'Umar's ruling concerning the triple divorce met with considerable opposition amongst the companions. According to

Ibn Taymiyyah, this opposition was based on the following reasons:

- 'Umar's opponents amongst the companions deemed this type of discretionary punishment impermissible;
- they thought that the Lawgiver did not impose this type of punishment;
- they believed that the ruling issued by 'Umar and other scholars did not differentiate between those who deserved punishment because they perform an act deliberately, while aware of its consequences, and those who were unaware of its prohibition in the *Sharī'ah* or performed some form of interpretation (*ta'wīl*) of it.[23]

Ibn Taymiyyah's rebuttal of the evidences of his opponents

Ibn Taymiyyah's opponents cited several evidences, some of which are the following:

- The companion Fāṭimah bint Qays was divorced by her husband triply.[24]
- Rifā'ah also divorced his wife triply.[25]
- 'Uwaymir, who was an imprecator (*mulā'in*) of his wife, divorced her thrice.[26]

In their argumentation, the opposition declared that all three events occurred during the lifetime of the Prophet, who was not reported to have voiced his objection. The opposition concluded that these proofs suggest that the triple divorce is permissible and takes the effect of three separate divorces.[27]

Ibn Taymiyyah studied the various evidences and then reached the following conclusions:

- Fāṭimah and Rifā'ah's husbands made three pronouncements of divorce, and then the divorce took legal effect after their period of waiting had expired. Therefore, the opposition cannot cite these *ḥadīths* as proofs, as the divorces in question were conducted according to the Sunni divorce. He supports his claim by citing a narration in the *Ṣaḥīḥ* wherein it is mentioned that the divorce that took place was in fact the third divorce pronouncement, which therefore completed three divorces.
- According to Ibn Taymiyyah, when the narrators of the first two *ḥadīths* mention that the divorces were '*thalāthan*' (triple divorce), it does not necessarily mean that the divorces were in the triple form. The same term can also apply to three divorces which take place separately after their waiting periods or revocability. In fact, Ibn Taymiyyah asserts that the latter meaning of '*thalāthan*' is the one most likely to be intended. This is because this type of divorce is agreed upon amongst the Imams as a binding form of divorce in accordance with the *sunnah*. In addition, Ibn Taymiyyah states that this type of divorce was common practice during the time of the Prophet whereas the triple pronouncement of divorce, on the few occasions that it occurred, was

disapproved of by that generation. According to Ibn Taymiyyah, the logical conclusion is that this word '*thalāthan*' should be understood according to the commonly practised meaning of the word during that time. This is because it is impermissible to link a word of general impact to a practice which is disapproved of and not to the commonly practised meaning.[28]

- In relation to the citation of the *ḥadīth* of 'Uwaymir, Ibn Taymiyyah presents the following criticism:

  - The triple divorce performed by 'Uwaymir took place after a permanent separation had occurred between him and his wife (or at least the obligation of separation) by reason of the *li'ān* (imprecation). Furthermore, it can be said that the divorce pronounced by 'Uwaymir only affirmed the permanent separation caused by the *li'ān*. The dispute at hand, however, concerns whether or not a separation can be initiated by the triple divorce. It is clear from Ibn Taymiyyah's textual and logical discussion of the *ḥadīth* of *li'ān* that he intends to clarify that the citation of this *ḥadīth* by the opposition is inaccurate, as it is irrelevant to the dispute amongst the scholars.
  - If the separation was caused as a result of the triple divorce, its legal consequences must become manifest. One such consequence is that the divorce becomes revocable if a new marriage takes place between the wife and a second husband, and thereafter the second marriage ends. This cannot be the case with *li'ān*, which confirms the fact that the separation in the *ḥadīth* of 'Uwaymir was caused by means of the *li'an* and not by a triple divorce.
  - The transmitter mentioned in this narration that 'Uwaymir divorced his wife triply. He then states that the Prophet validated this form of divorce. Ibn Taymiyyah argues that if this divorce is valid and was practised during the time of the Prophet as a valid form of divorce, there would have been no need for it to be validated by the Prophet.[29] The narration therefore contains inconsistency or the facts have been misunderstood.

Ibn Taymiyyah then points out some of the serious consequences of affirming the validity and legal effect of a triple divorce:

- The scholars who subscribe to the opinion that it is valid are also of the opinion that the *taḥlīl* marriage is prohibited. In this ruling, they were following the Prophet and his companions. As for the triple divorce, there is no evidence from the Lawgiver that it is binding and equal to three divorces. A combination of these two rulings resulted in great hardship and also led to the appearance of several types of corruption. Some people apostatised from Islam, because they were legally compelled to be separated from one another due to the utterance of the triple divorce. This resulted in hatred between people and, more importantly, it led to a reduction in the prestige of Islamic law.

- Conversely, some of these scholars attempted to ameliorate the hardship arising from the combination of the two rulings by permitting the *taḥlīl* marriage. This opinion, however, was widely disapproved of by the majority of the early scholars, including the Imams.[30]

Was this ruling of Ibn Taymiyyah in opposition to the consensus of the Ḥanbalī scholars before his era?

The Ḥanbalī sources appear to suggest that there was no disagreement regarding this issue in the School.[31] Ibn Taymiyyah retorts that there were some Ḥanbalī scholars who held the opinion that a triple divorce does not have the effect of three separate divorces,[32] but he does not identify who these Ḥanbalīs were.

The following section contains a study of two types of selected Ḥanbalī sources: the first type predates Ibn Taymiyyah and the second group of sources were written after the appearance of this scholar. This system has been adopted in order to provide a clear picture of the issue as related in the Ḥanbalī sources. In addition, it will also help to identify Ibn Taymiyyah's influence upon the Ḥanbalī sources and the School with regard to this issue.

Some of the books of *masā'il*, which were the first sources collected in the Ḥanbalī School, contain references made by Aḥmad on this topic. In every instance, Aḥmad maintains that the intended triple divorce has the effect of three separate divorces, which occur after the required periods of waiting.[33]

Al-Khiraqī (d. 334/945) in his *Mukhtaṣar*, the oldest Ḥanbalī jurisprudential *Mukhtaṣar*, states that this type of divorce is a divorce in accordance with the *sunnah* but declares that it is preferable to divorce according to the agreed upon form.[34] As mentioned earlier, the agreed form is that one divorces his wife through a single pronouncement during a period of her purity from menstruation in which he has not had sexual intercourse with her.

Ibn al-Bannā (d. 471/1078) in his commentary on al-Khiraqī's *Mukhtaṣar*, points out the existence of a dispute within the School regarding the issue of whether the triple divorce is a Sunni or *bidʿī* divorce. He does not, however, suggest any sign of disagreement in the School on its legal effect, that is, that it has the effect of the third repudiation.[35]

Ibn Qudāmah (d. 620/1223) in his book *al-ʿUmdah* does not mention any disagreement in the Ḥanbalī School about the effect of the triple divorce, but it is interesting to note that he classifies this type of divorce as prohibited rather than Sunni.[36] Bahā' al-Dīn al-Maqdisī (d. 624/1227), in his commentary on *al-ʿUmdah* entitled *al-ʿUddah Sharḥ al-ʿUmdah*, also does not refer to a division within the School in relation to the effect of this type of divorce, and he supports the stance taken by Ibn Qudāmah in which he considers this type of divorce to be *bidʿī*.[37]

Al-Majd Abū 'l-Barakāt (d. 652/1254), Ibn Taymiyyah's grandfather, in his book *al-Muḥarrar* asserts the existence of a dispute amongst the Ḥanbalī scholars as to the status of a triple divorce, but he does not mention a dispute about its legal effect.[38]

As for the source works of Ḥanbalī jurisprudence compiled after Ibn Taymiyyah's time, we find that the situation has altered. The following section contains a study of two of these sources: *al-Inṣāf* by al-Mardāwī and *al-Furū‘* by Ibn Mufliḥ. The importance of these two sources stems from the fact that their authors were considered leading scholars of the Ḥanbalī School. The first was recognised as the leader of the School during his time,[39] while the second was considered the most knowledgeable individual in the School.[40]

Al-Mardāwī states that the correct opinion within the Ḥanbalī School is that the triple divorce has the effect of three separate divorces. He says that this was Aḥmad's view and was subscribed to by the *al-aṣḥāb* (the followers of Aḥmad).[41] Al-Mardāwī's statement implies the existence of consensus regarding this issue amongst the followers of Aḥmad. At the same time, al-Mardāwī's statement that this ruling was 'the correct opinion in the School' implies that there was a difference of opinion within the Ḥanbalī School; someone must have held 'the other opinion'. Al-Mardāwī does not identify the opponents of the predominant view of the School, although he does attribute it to Ibn Taymiyyah. It is possible that he therefore believes that there was an agreement amongst Ḥanbalī scholars concerning this ruling up to the time of Ibn Taymiyyah. Although he does mention that al-Majd, Ibn Taymiyyah's grandfather, was said to hold the opposing opinion and secretly issued *fatāwā* in support of it, al-Mardāwī clarifies that this was made known to him by Ibn Taymiyyah himself.[42] It seems that even if al-Majd did hold this opinion, there was no public disagreement in the School before Ibn Taymiyyah.

A similar analysis is found in '*al-Furū‘*', a treatise written by Ibn Mufliḥ, who was of course one of Ibn Taymiyyah's students. He refers to the opposing opinion, attributes it to Ibn Taymiyyah and cites his words at length in order to explain his view. Again, Ibn Mufliḥ does not attribute this opinion to any of the other Ḥanbalī scholars.[43]

Does this mean that there were no Ḥanbalī scholars who publicly subscribed to this view before Ibn Taymiyyah? If so, what of Ibn Taymiyyah's statement claiming that certain Ḥanbalī scholars held this opinion?

This is a problematic issue to which the Ḥanbalī sources, according to my knowledge, do not present an answer. It is possible that Ibn Taymiyyah was alluding to his grandfather by the statement 'some Ḥanbalī scholars', for Ibn Taymiyyah himself mentions that his grandfather subscribed to this opinion. It is also plausible to assume that Ibn Taymiyyah did not mean that Ḥanbalī scholars held this opinion,[44] but rather that it conforms to the methodology employed by particular Ḥanbalī scholars. As we saw earlier, it was the practice of several Ḥanbalī scholars to attribute opinions to the School based upon their agreement with the general principles of Ibn Ḥanbal. Therefore, this attribution was based upon mere inference and deduction and not by a clear narration. There are two possible methods Ibn Taymiyyah could have used in order to draw this conclusion.

First, Ibn Taymiyyah believes that the notion that the triple divorce is considered impermissible by Ibn Ḥanbal, yet at the same time is legally binding, is against

Ibn Ḥanbal's own principles. Ibn Taymiyyah makes several points in support of his argument:

- Ibn Ḥanbal himself relates two *ḥadīths* showing that the triple divorce is considered as a single divorce.
- There are no correct *ḥadīths* from the Prophet opposing this view. In addition, the Qur'an is in complete agreement with the *sunnah*, as there is no verse supporting the opposing view.
- According to Ibn Ḥanbal, a prohibition in the words of the Lawgiver necessitates the invalidity of the prohibited act, if it is committed.

According to Ibn Taymiyyah, a combination of these three points leads to the following conclusion: Ibn Ḥanbal's opinion, according to the principles on which he based his jurisprudence, must be that the triple divorce is considered a single divorce and cannot have the effort of more than that number.[45]

Ibn Taymiyyah asserts that Aḥmad's ruling that triple divorce is prohibited and at the same time legally effective is contrary to Aḥmad's own general principles.

The second manner in which Ibn Taymiyyah attributed this opinion to some Ḥanbalī scholars is again an inference from the methodology of particular scholars. He discusses Ibn Ḥanbal's reasons for not acting upon *ḥadīths*, such as the *ḥadīth* of Rukānah, which declare that the triple divorce takes the effect of only a single divorce. He explains that Ibn Ḥanbal abandoned these *ḥadīths* because he initially understood from other texts that this type of divorce is permissible. Ibn Taymiyyah deduces that Ibn Ḥanbal used the principle of abrogation in order to harmonise the apparent contradiction between the texts, so that he believed the *ḥadīth* giving full effect to it abrogated those treating it as single divorce. According to Ibn Taymiyyah, it became clear to Ibn Ḥanbal later on that there is no contradiction between the correct *ḥadīths* and he declared that this type of divorce could not have the effect of more than a single divorce. However, Ibn Ḥanbal maintains his view that this form of divorce is binding as three separate divorces. According to Ibn Taymiyyah, this is primarily attributed to Ibn 'Abbās. He is the narrator of the *ḥadīth* which states the triple divorce has the effect of a single divorce, but, he also used to issue a *fatwā* in support of the opposite opinion. According to one of two opinions from Ibn Ḥanbal, the practice of the narrator issuing a *fatwā* that is contrary to his narration is a defect that weakens the implementation of that narrator's transmission, as it suggests that an abrogation has occurred. Ibn Taymiyyah argues that the apparent opinion of the School, which he asserts is the final opinion held by the majority of Ḥanbalī scholars, is that this is not a defect. Ibn Taymiyyah supports this by stating that Ibn 'Abbās revealed that he did not implement his narration because he found that this type of divorce was widely practised by the people of his time and thus there was a need for drastic measures to prevent this abuse.[46] Therefore, he felt that the best way to check this abuse was to leave people to face the consequences of their rashness.

It appears that Ibn Taymiyyah's purpose is to prove that Ibn 'Abbās did not think that his narration of the *ḥadīth* was abrogated. Ibn Taymiyyah also gave another narration from Ibn 'Abbās in which he issued a *fatwā* stating that a triple divorce pronounced at once is considered to be a single divorce.[47] It is possible that Ibn 'Abbās issued this *fatwā* before he became concerned about the abuse of this form of divorce.

Ibn Taymiyyah refers to the presence of Ḥanbalī scholars who did not think that a narrator acting contrary to his narration is a defect which weakens his narration. Therefore, it is possible that when he said that some Ḥanbalī scholars held that the triple divorce is equivalent to a single divorce, he was referring to those Ḥanbalī scholars who do not think that there is a defect in a narrator acting in a manner contrary to his narration. The main ruling in the School was based primarily on the contradiction in Ibn 'Abbās's stance. Ibn Taymiyyah may have felt, therefore, that if the problem with Ibn 'Abbās's narration could be resolved; there would have been nothing to stop some scholars accepting the single-divorce opinion.

Ibn al-Qayyim had some difficulty with Ibn Taymiyyah's claim. He mentions that he attempted at length to identify the scholars who subscribed to this opinion but failed to do so.[48] He then advanced possible meanings for Ibn Taymiyyah's claim that this opinion was held by earlier Ḥanbalī scholars:

- By 'some Ḥanbalī scholars' Ibn Taymiyyah means his grandfather al-Majd. As mentioned earlier, Ibn Taymiyyah claimed that his grandfather used to hold this opinion and would secretly issue *Fatāwā* in accordance with it.
- A second possible explanation is based upon a disputed issue in the field of *uṣūl al-fiqh* and was discussed by Ibn Taymiyyah earlier: When the narrator of a *ḥadīth* issues a *fatwā* in conflict with a *ḥadīth* he narrated, is it the correct position to follow the *ḥadīth* and ignore the *fatwā* of its narrator? Or is it to suspend the *ḥadīth* and to follow the *fatwā* of its narrator, as it is possible that he was aware of another text that abrogates the *ḥadīth* that he narrated? There are two opinions on this issue and both from Aḥmad. In the matter at hand, Aḥmad did not implement the *ḥadīth* of Ibn 'Abbās (in which he narrated that the triple divorce was considered as a single divorce during the time of the Prophet, Abū Bakr and a period of the caliphate of 'Umar), because Ibn 'Abbās used to issue *fatwā* in opposition to his narration. This accords with one of Aḥmad's opinions, which gives preference to the *fatwā* over the *ḥadīth*. According to Aḥmad's second opinion, the narration is to be preferred. Ibn al-Qayyim effectively concludes that if Aḥmad were to rule according to this second opinion, he would have said that the triple divorce has the effect of only a single divorce.[49]
- The final point Ibn al-Qayyim advances in order to solve this problem is that even if there was no earlier Ḥanbalī scholar who held this opinion, the fact of Ibn Taymiyyah's preferring this ruling gives it the standing of a *qawl* (opinion) in the School. According to Ibn al-Qayyim, if Ibn Taymiyyah is to be considered of a similar rank to the leading Ḥanbalī scholars, such as al-Qāḍī and Abū 'l-Khaṭṭāb, his opinion should be considered one that can be

attributed to the School. Indeed, Ibn al-Qayyim asserts that Ibn Taymiyyah was of a higher status than these scholars. Therefore, his view is accepted and can be attributed to the School as an opinion.[50]

It is clear from the previous discussion that Ḥanbalī sources after Ibn Taymiyyah's time began to refer to the existence of another opinion in the School on the subject of the triple divorce and attributed this opinion to Ibn Taymiyyah. This contrasts with the Ḥanbalī sources before Ibn Taymiyyah which do not refer to any disagreement within the School regarding the effect of the triple divorce. This leads us to the conclusion that Ibn Taymiyyah's opinion was contrary to that of the Ḥanbalī scholars before his era, unless he was correct in attributing this opinion to his grandfather or to certain other Ḥanbalī scholars. The next section will analyse whether Ibn Taymiyyah's opinion was in opposition to the consensus of the scholars of the *ummah*?

Is Ibn Taymiyyah's opinion on triple divorce in opposition to an existing consensus amongst the scholars?

Ḥanbalī sources before Ibn Taymiyyah appear to suggest that there was a consensus amongst the Ḥanbalī scholars on this issue, for they do not make reference to any opposing opinions. The other three schools of law also appear to share this position.[51]

There are many scholars, before and after Ibn Taymiyyah's time, who maintain the existence of a consensus amongst the scholars that the triple divorce, pronounced once, has the effect of a third and final repudiation. This claim was made by al-Shāfi'ī,[52] Abū Bakr al-Marwazī,[53] Abū Bakr al-Rāzī,[54] Ibn al-'Arabī,[55] al-Bājī,[56] Ibn Rajab,[57] Ibn 'Abd al-Barr,[58] Ibn al-Tīn,[59] al-Subkī,[60] Ibn Ḥajar al-Haythamī[61] and al-Dusūqī.[62] Certain other scholars claimed that the existence of such consensus can be understood from a statement made by Ibn al-Mundhir in his book, *al-Ijmā'*.[63] Also, some scholars, such as al-Sarkhasī in his book *al-Mabsūṭ*, attribute the opinion that triple divorce takes the effect of only one divorce to the Shī'ah. This implies that the Sunni scholars were in agreement on giving the triple divorce the effect of three separate divorces carried out in accordance with the *sunni* divorce.[64] Indeed, Ibn Taymiyyah himself mentions that some scholars argued that his opinion was in opposition to the consensus of the scholars at the time of 'Umar.[65]

1 Ibn Taymiyyah's rebuttal of the existence of a consensus amongst Muslim scholars regarding the triple divorce

Ibn Taymiyyah refutes the claim that the scholars agreed that the triple divorce has the effect of the third repudiation. His refutation of this alleged consensus is based upon several proofs, including the following:

- Ibn Taymiyyah explains that his opposing view was held by some of the companions, such as Abū Bakr, 'Umar in the first two years of his caliphate, 'Alī, Ibn Mas'ūd, Ibn 'Abbās (in one of his views), al-Zubayr and Ibn 'Awf. Similarly, many of the followers subscribed to the same view. Ibn Taymiyyah asserts that the existence of a dispute amongst the predecessors concerning this issue is a fact that cannot be denied.[66]
- As mentioned earlier, he asserts that his grandfather, al-Majd, used to hold the opinion that the triple divorce counts only as a single pronouncement. At other times, however, he declared that it has the effect of three separate Sunni divorces. According to Ibn Taymiyyah, these conflicting positions were based on an alteration in his independent reasoning or on the use of *maṣlaḥah* in particular cases.[67]
- Ibn Taymiyyah cites Ibn Mughīth in *al-Muqni'* where he attributed Ibn Taymiyyah's opinion to some of the Mālikī scholars of Cordoba (Qurṭubah), such as Ibn Zinbā', al-Ḥusaynī, Ibn Mukhlid and Ibn al-Ḥabāb. In addition, Ibn Mughīth attributed this opinion to approximately twenty Mālikī scholars from Toledo (Ṭulayṭilah).[68] Ibn Taymiyyah also mentions that there is a narration from Malik supporting this opinion.[69]
- Ibn Taymiyyah claims that this opinion was held by Muhammad b. Muqātil al-Rāzī, who was a leading Ḥanafī scholar.[70]
- The majority of the Ẓahirites state that the triple divorce has the effect of a single pronouncement.[71]
- Ibn Taymiyyah criticises the inconsistency of his opponents who claim to follow the ruling of 'Umar on this issue, while they did not follow him on other issues, in which consensus could more safely be claimed and which also appear to be supported by evidences from the Qur'an and *sunnah*. He presents the example of the *taḥlīl* marriage. Some scholars permitted this form of contract, despite 'Umar's ruling to the contrary and despite the evidence of the Qur'an and *sunnah* opposing their view. Another example is their disagreement with 'Umar's ruling concerning the issue of land conquered by the Muslims by means of force. They subscribed to the opinion that the land must be, or can be, divided amongst the soldiers, whereas 'Umar preferred otherwise.[72]
- He argues that those who claimed that this ruling was agreed upon by the companions were simply unaware of the opposite view.
- He suspects that another reason which assisted in the creation of the alleged consensus is that some Shi'ites followed the opinion that the triple divorce has the effect of a single one.[73] Certain Sunni scholars perhaps felt the need to disassociate from the Shi'ites on this issue.
- Ibn Taymiyyah draws attention to the point that not every ruling issued by 'Umar was accurate and a matter of consensus, for some of them were based upon his own independent reasoning. He supports this by refering to the opposition of some of the companions to particular rulings. For instance,

> on the issue of providing residence and maintenance to a woman divorced irrevocably, 'Umar had the opinion that she is legally entitled to assistance. The majority of the companions disagreed with him. Some of them were of the opinion that she is entitled to residence only and others were of the opinion that she is not entitled to any form of assistance at all, neither residence nor maintenance.[74]

There are in fact several leading scholars who agree with Ibn Taymiyyah in affirming the existence of a dispute amongst the scholars regarding the ruling on triple divorce.

These include Ibn Ḥazm,[75] Ibn Rushd,[76] al-Nawawī,[77] Ibn Qudāmah,[78] al-Lakhmī,[79] al-Ṭaḥāwī,[80] al-Nasafī,[81] Abū 'l-Walīd al-Qurṭubī,[82] Ibn al-Qayyim,[83] Ibn Ḥajar,[84] al-Shawkānī,[85] Ibn Bāz[86] and most of the members of the body of senior scholars in Saudi Arabia.[87] It is interesting to note that some of those who claim the existence of consensus regarding this point were zealous opponents of Ibn Taymiyyah,[88] and it is possible that they were influenced by a desire to refute him in making this claim.

2 *Has the ruling of the Prophet been abrogated by the consensus of the companions at the time of 'Umar?*

Ibn Taymiyyah asserts that a binding ruling issued by the Lawgiver cannot be altered. This is because a ruling cannot be abrogated after the death of the Prophet, due to the termination of revelation. He points out that rulings issued by companions which are contrary to the texts were not based upon an assumption that their consensus could abrogate the text of the Lawgiver. It was, rather, an example of independent reasoning for which they will be rewarded. Ibn Taymiyyah states that he initially believed that the view of some of the Mu'tazilites, Ḥanafīs and Mālikīs that consensus can abrogate a text of the Lawgiver was based on the idea that consensus must be based upon a text in the first place. It is indisputable that one text can be abrogated by another text. Later on, however, he discovered that their intention was to claim that consensus by itself can abrogate a text. According to Ibn Taymiyyah, this opinion is very dangerous as it leads to alteration in the *sharī'ah*.[89]

3 *Is this issue a matter for independent reasoning?*

When there is a disagreement amongst the companions on a ruling (as is the case with triple divorce), a method is required by which one or another opinion can be given preference. According to Ibn Taymiyyah, the correct method is to undertake a careful study of the evidence concerning the disputed issue in the sources of the Qur'an and *sunnah*, as these two sources have been mentioned by the Lawgiver as references to be consulted in order to rectify disputes concerning religious and legal issues.[90]

After consulting these sources, Ibn Taymiyyah asserts that there is nothing whatsoever in the Qur'an or in the *sunnah*, which can be considered as evidence for those who claim that the triple divorce has the effect of three separate divorces. He also states that the use of analogy and contemplation upon the general principles of Islamic law support this conclusion. He reiterates the rule that: 'if there is a contract or type of worship which is occasionally permissible and occasionally prohibited, it will not be binding when it is performed in its prohibited form, and vice versa.'[91]

Ibn Taymiyyah argues that when the evidence of the *Sharī'ah* suggests the accuracy of an opinion, it cannot be considered irregular (*shādhdh*), even if it was held by only a minority of scholars. This is because the scholars are in agreement that the number of scholars who hold a particular opinion has no bearing on its correctness and accuracy.[92]

After explaining this point, Ibn Taymiyyah goes on to say that those who hold the opinion that triple divorce has the effect of three separate divorces will be rewarded for their independent reasoning, despite the fact that they are mistaken. This is because they exercised their best efforts in seeking to determine the correct ruling. In support of his argument, Ibn Taymiyyah calls upon several points, including:

- The verse in chapter *al-Baqarah* 'Our Lord! Punish us not if we forget or fall into error' (Qur'an 2:286). It has been narrated from the Prophet that Allah said: 'I have done so.'[93]
- The authentic *ḥadīth* narrated by al-Bukhārī and Muslim in which the Prophet says, 'When a judge exercises *ijtihād* and issues a correct judgement, he will have two rewards. If [however] he errs in his judgement, he will be conferred with one reward.'[94]

In addition, Ibn Taymiyyah asserts that when a *mujtahid* issues a *fatwā* on a *shar'ī* matter on which opinions already exist, and he bases his *fatwā* on evidence that he believes affirm the correctness of his position, no one has the right to compel him to follow an opposing opinion.[95] This does not mean that his opponent's opinion will be considered to be part of the *sharī'ah* brought by the Prophet. This is particularly so if those opinions are known to be in opposition to the Qur'an and *sunnah*. He supports this assertion by what is narrated of some of the companions that when they issued a ruling by use of independent reasoning, they would declare that the *sharī'ah* is far removed from their mistakes.[96]

There may be another interesting reason for Ibn Taymiyyah's continuous declaration that his opponents are excused for those incorrect rulings that they assumed to be based on correct evidence. It appears that when Ibn Taymiyyah excused his opponents, despite his belief that they were mistaken in their legal rulings, he hoped to be the recipient of similar treatment from his opponents, particularly as Ibn Taymiyyah believed that he was in possession of the correct proof. Ibn Taymiyyah must have felt particularly aggrieved about the treatment he received for opposing the majority, having been prevented from issuing a *fatwā* concerning this issue and having been imprisoned for the same reason.

As mentioned previously, there is no Ḥanbalī scholar before Ibn Taymiyyah's time known to have held the opinion that the triple divorce is equivalent in effect to a single divorce, excluding his grandfather al-Majd, as Ibn Taymiyyah himself mentions. It is therefore interesting to note that various scholars and organisations after his time have adopted Ibn Taymiyyah's opinion, such as al-Ḥarīrī (d. 803/1400),[97] Jamāl al-Dīn al-Imam (d. 798/1396),[98] and al-Dawālibī (d. 862/1458).[99] Ibn al-Mubarrid also states that it appeared to him that the scholars who came from the families of Mufliḥ and al-Mardāwī in the time of Ibn Rajab agreed with Ibn Taymiyyah's opinion.[100] Furthermore, it is now the codified law in various Islamic countries, such as Egypt,[101] Sudan,[102] Syria, Jordan, Morocco[103] and Libya.[104] This opinion was also held by several leading contemporary scholars, such as al-Sa'dī,[105] Ibn 'Uthaymīn and Ibn Bāz, the former *mufti* of Saudi Arabia.[106]

It can be concluded that the claim that Ibn Taymiyyah's opinion on triple divorce violated the consensus of the scholars is simply not true, as disagreement on the issue was mentioned by various other scholars. It should be pointed out that no proof could be found during the course of the current study that could support Ibn Taymiyyah's claim that his ruling was also held by his grandfather al-Majd, in addition to other earlier Ḥanbalī scholars. It does appear, however, that there is some truth to Ibn Taymiyyah's argument that the ruling within the School is in opposition to Aḥmad's general principles. It is also evident that Ibn Taymiyyah's ruling has left a long lasting influence on Ḥanbalī scholars. The Ḥanbalī sources appear to agree on the principle that the triple divorce amounts to an irrevocable divorce. Nevertheless, as a result of Ibn Taymiyyah's efforts in connection with this matter, certain Ḥanbalī sources started referring to the existence of another view within the School and usually attributed it to Ibn Taymiyyah and those who supported his position.

CONCLUSIONS

The following conclusions can be deduced from this research:

- The study of Ibn Ḥanbal's life and works proves that he was a jurist as well as a traditionist (*muḥaddith*).
- Ibn Taymiyyah lived in an era known for its political and social upheaval and one that has become known as the era of imitation. He was subjected to various detentions and persecutions but nevertheless succeeded in attaining an elevated status amongst his contemporaries.
- A comparison of the general principles and sources of Ibn Ḥanbal and Ibn Taymiyyah based upon their words and their approaches suggests no vital differences between them. These sources are the Qur'an, *sunnah*, consensus and analogy. They also used several methods in ruling legal preferences, such as *Istiḥsān*, *Istiṣḥāb* and *Istiṣlāḥ*. A study of the educational environment during Ibn Taymiyyah's time, the opinions of some of his contemporaries with regard to his status in knowledge and the jurisprudential treatises of this scholar supports the view that he was an absolute affiliated *mujtahid* (*mujtahid muntasib*). It appears that, despite being capable of forming his own School, he chose to affiliate himself to an existing one and work to correct some of its aberrations.
- Ibn Taymiyyah played a noticeable role in developing and refining principles and rulings within the Ḥanbalī School of law. His influence has been detected in several issues and important findings have been noted, some of which are:

  - Ibn Taymiyyah asserts that consensus can be of two types: explicit and tacit. The first type concerns an explicit agreement amongst scholars, narrated through a *mutawātir* chain of narrators. In the second type there is no affirmation of the non-existence of opponents, but it cannot be said that all scholars have expressed their view. Ibn Taymiyyah asserts that, contrary to the claim of some scholars, Aḥmad did not completely reject the concept of consensus. Rather, he used the first type of consensus as a source of law but he confined the authority of this type of consensus to the first three generations, for the creation of this type of consensus after this period is particularly difficult. Tacit consensus, on the other hand, is a proof that the establishment of which is not confined to a specific time, but at the same time does not lead to certainty but merely to probability. Therefore, this type of consensus can be rejected in favour of a stronger proof.

- Ibn Taymiyyah resolves the problematical issue regarding weak *ḥadīth* being one of Aḥmad's sources of law. He clarifies that the classification of *ḥadīth* during Aḥmad's time was different from the one that appeared later during the time of al-Tirmidhī. He concludes that the weak *ḥadīth* used by Aḥmad were in fact equivalent to the *ḥasan ḥadīth* according to the new classification of *ḥadīth*.
- It has been traditionally accepted that the Arabic language is divided into two categories: literal and metaphorical. This view is mentioned and approved of in most Ḥanbalī sources. Ibn Taymiyyah rejects the existence of this division. His rejection is based upon a critical study of the evidences for the existence of the term metaphor in Islamic terminology and the Arabic language, in addition to a critique of the identity of the alleged majority subscribing to the division of the language.
- Another complicated issue in the principles of jurisprudence is the correctness of and errors made by the *mujtahid* scholars. The opinions on this point appear to be unclear and occasionally contradictory. Ibn Taymiyyah analyses the various opinions of the jurists and concludes that the most accurate viewpoint regarding this issue is that only one of the various opinions offered by scholars on any single issue can be correct. This does not mean, however, that those scholars who erred are sinful and liable for punishment in the Hereafter. Rather, in accordance with a sound *ḥadīth*, they are *mujtahids* who will be rewarded for their independent reasoning. He rejects the distinction made between *uṣūl* and *furū*, so that a scholar who errs in the *uṣūl* of Islam is liable for punishment, whereas he will be excused if the error concerns the *furu*ʿ. He argues that this claim is based on the false claim that the *sharīʿah* is divided into two essential categories: *uṣūl* and *furū*ʿ.
- Ibn Taymiyyah's rejection of the claim that the *sharīʿah* is divided into two types: *uṣūl* and *furū*ʿ is based upon the non-existence of any *sharʿī* evidence supporting this division. He further supports his opinion by analysing the criteria presented by certain scholars through which differentiation between the two types can be achieved. He concludes that none of the criteria advanced can lead to a clear cut division; rather, they lead to ambiguity and uncertainty.
- Particular Ḥanbalī scholars followed the views of others who claimed that the texts of the Qur'an and *sunnah* cover only a small percentage of the issues of the *sharīʿah*. Ibn Taymiyyah firmly opposes this view and insists that the texts cover most of the issues of *sharīʿah* by themselves,

without the need for recourse to analogy. He attributes the opposing opinion to a misunderstanding of the general texts and their implications.

- He also asserts that there is no contradiction between correct texts and correct analogy, as they are always in agreement with one another. Where there is an apparent contradiction, this is only because a scholar has employed an incorrect analogy or utilised an unsound text.
- Another interesting point studied by Ibn Taymiyyah is the claim made by the Ḥanbalī scholars that certain rulings are only applicable to Arabs. Ibn Taymiyyah concludes that the Lawgiver only bases these rulings on effective qualities and does not distinguish all Arabs in general by certain rulings.
- It is commonly believed that *maṣlaḥah* is one of the general sources of law in the Ḥanbalī School, but a careful study of the sources and references in the general principles of the School suggests otherwise. In fact, most Ḥanbalī scholars are of the opinion that *maṣlaḥah* is not a source of law. Nevertheless, it is clear that *maṣlaḥah* was used by Ibn Taymiyyah and other Ḥanbalī scholars. There is, however, a difference between Ibn Taymiyyah's method in using *maṣlaḥah* and that of most of the Ḥanbalī scholars. We find that Ibn Taymiyyah was very cautious in his use of it, due to his belief that it frequently results in the enactment of laws contrary to the general rulings of Islamic law. He also notes that most innovations that had cropped up were justified as beneficial *maṣāliḥ* by those who innovated them. Ibn Taymiyyah also rejects the restriction of *maṣlaḥah* to the preservation of the five necessary benefits (*al-Ḍarūrāt al-Khams*). Rather, he believes that the preservation of the five necessary benefits is only a part of the scope of the *maṣlaḥah* as it also pertains to all other benefits that the *sharī'ah* seeks to preserve and procure.
- The Ḥanbalī scholars have permitted the use of *ra'y* when deciding certain jurisprudential rulings, the Ḥanbalī sources are unclear as to what is meant by the term *ra'y*. Ibn Taymiyyah asserts that the only permitted type of *ra'y* is the one based upon general principles derived from the Qur'an, *sunnah* and consensus. He also asserts that it is incorrect to divide knowledge into rational and *shar'ī*. The correct division is to divide knowledge into textual and rational, which are both considered to be *shar'ī*.
- The Ḥanbalī sources mention that neither *mujtahids* nor imitators are permitted to imitate in issues concerning *uṣūl*. Certain Ḥanbalī sources include within this the main pillars of Islam as well as those well-known Islamic rulings that are described as 'necessary knowledge'. They appear to permit laymen to imitate scholars in relation to issues of *al-furū'*. In addition, the majority of Ḥanbalī scholars state that a *mujtahid* is not permitted to imitate another scholar. Ibn Taymiyyah subscribes to a moderate view. He states that the practice of independent reasoning is obligatory upon those who have the ability to undertake it. He also

accepts the need to imitate by those qualified to practice independent reasoning if they are incapable of determining a particular ruling.

- Ḥanbalī sources have often examined particular issues concerning the other schools of law. The consensus of Ahl al-Madinah was selected as a case study for the purpose of this research. The Ḥanbalī scholars do not consider this consensus as a proof in Islamic law, and yet do not advance a suitable explanation of what is intended by this consensus. Ibn Taymiyyah's clarification presents a clear explanation and classification of this concept and its legitimacy. This is an example of Ibn Taymiyyah's efforts in refining the Ḥanbalī School, while also advocating a just approach to the tools used by other schools.

• Ibn Taymiyyah's role in developing Ḥanbalī jurisprudence has been notable. The following points are worthy of note:

  - Ibn Taymiyyah believes that the presence of innovation in the Ḥanbalī School is considerably less than in the other schools. This is rooted in the detailed explanation of the *sunnah* given by Aḥmad and his severe condemnation of innovation. Nevertheless, Ibn Taymiyyah finds various rulings and practices in the Ḥanbalī School that he considers to be innovations. He also notes that more innovations are to be found in issues of worship than those of belief. He links the existence of innovation in Ḥanbalī jurisprudence to various factors, for instance: the misuse of *maṣlaḥah* in Islamic law; rulings based on invalid analogy; the method of writing adopted by most of the later Ḥanbalī scholars. This research studied certain rulings labelled by Ibn Taymiyyah as innovations. It can be concluded that these innovations do indeed have no foundation in the *sharī'ah*, nor in the words of Aḥmad.
  - The *fatāwā* permitting certain types of *ḥiyal* in Islamic law have traditionally been linked to the School of Abū Ḥanifah. Ibn Taymiyyah observes that some leading Ḥanbalī scholars also engaged in issuing *fatāwā* permitting certain types of *ḥiyal*, despite the fact that their Imam was known for his strong disapproval of *ḥiyal*. The issue of the *taḥlīl* marriage was examined as a case study of a ruling in the School that was considered by Ibn Taymiyyah to be a form of *ḥiyal*. He argues that rulings issued by certain Ḥanbalīs permitting some forms of this marriage were based on incorrect evidences and a misunderstanding of Aḥmad's words.
  - The use of precaution and piety by Ḥanbalī scholars in jurisprudential rulings has led in some instances to great hardship and difficulty. Ibn Taymiyyah argues that all of the principles of the *sharī'ah* are indicative of the principle that precaution is neither obligatory nor prohibited. He asserts that it can only be described as permissible and this permissibility is confined to areas where the legal texts are not explicit on certain rulings. Ibn Taymiyyah asserts that if the permissibility of practising

precaution is not restricted to the implicit meaning of the texts, the criteria governing the implementation of precaution will become unclear and imprecise. Ibn Taymiyyah notes that several Ḥanbalī sources contain narrations in which Ibn Ḥanbal or other Ḥanbalī scholars are said to have practised or approved of certain types of *wara'*. Ibn Taymiyyah acknowledges that piety is one of the foundations of the religion (*Qawā'id al-Dīn*), but insists that in order to determine the correct understanding and implementation of this foundation, several important principles must be taken into consideration.

- Ibn Taymiyyah seeks to prove that Ḥanbalī jurisprudence contains various rulings that are incorrect. He determines this by comparing these rulings with the general sources of Islamic law in addition to the statements and general principles of the Imam of the School.
- Various forms of terminology in the Ḥanbalī School of law were subjected to Ibn Taymiyyah's scrutiny. He connects the existence of an incorrect definition of various terms in Islamic law to the absence of clear criteria by which a correct understanding of these terms can be attained. Ibn Taymiyyah proposes such criteria when he divides terminology used and attached to rulings in the Qur'an and *sunnah* into three types: terms defined by the Lawgiver; terms defined by the language and terms whose definitions can be determined by considering the custom and practice of the people. He asserts that these criteria lead to a correct understanding of the two main sources of the *sharī'ah*, the Qur'an and *sunnah*. Ibn Taymiyyah proves that certain terms defined by the Lawgiver have been redefined by some Ḥanbalī scholars. Other terms that are general in the texts have been erroneously particularised by the School.
- An important feature of Ibn Taymiyyah's jurisprudential maxims is that they are based upon textual evidences and not on the practice of the Ḥanbalī School. He asserts that the Qur'an and *sunnah* contain general words which are, in fact, general rules covering a number of different occurrences. He also states that scholars who could not determine a ruling within the general rules of the *sharī'ah* did not understand those general rulings. He also noted that Ḥanbalī scholars did not apply several rulings to particular kinds that are included under general nouns. These scholars did not base their opinions on legal or linguistic evidences which dictate the exclusion of these types from the general rulings.
- Ibn Taymiyyah critically studied the narrations in Ḥanbalī jurisprudence. He suggests that certain narrations have been attributed to Ibn Ḥanbal incorrectly or attributed to him or to other leading scholars by inference only.

• A study of selected Ḥanbalī sources proves that the citation of Ibn Taymiyyah's opinions and preferences amongst the Ḥanbalī scholars has continued, in differing degrees since his era up to the present time. It was noted, however, that the numerous citations of his opinions by some scholars do not mean that they were particularly influenced by him. Those scholars who were influenced by him appear to support Ibn Taymiyyah's position because they believe that the evidences of the *sharīʿah* affirm their correctness. From the twelfth Islamic century up to the present time, the citation and influence of Ibn Taymiyyah on Ḥanbalī scholars appears to have gradually increased in momentum. This can be associated with various factors, some of which are: the call of Ibn ʿAbd al-Wahhāb; the widespread presence of al-Saʿdī's students; the increased level of editing and publication of Ibn Taymiyyah's works as well as the works of some of his students, especially those of Ibn al-Qayyim.

- Various jurisprudential rulings issued by Ibn Taymiyyah have been severely criticised by Ḥanbalī scholars but at the same time have left an influence on the School. Some of these opinions are claimed to be in opposition to the consensus of Ḥanbalī scholars or even the consensus of all Muslim scholars. The intended triple divorce was selected as a case study. A careful study of Ḥanbalī references, Ibn Taymiyyah's treatises and recognised sources of the other Schools of law affirms that Ibn Taymiyyah's *fatwā* on this issue does in fact find support in the opinion of some other scholars. Therefore, the claim that Ibn Taymiyyah's opinion was in opposition to the consensus of all Muslim scholars is inaccurate. It seems, however, to be correct that Ibn Taymiyyah's position on this issue was in opposition to the stance of all former Ḥanbalī scholars. Nevertheless, it is clear that Ibn Taymiyyah's opinion on this issue has left a long lasting effect on the position of the School. We find that, since the time of Ibn Taymiyyah, the Ḥanbalī sources have started referring to the existence of dispute among Ḥanbalī scholars with regard to this issue. Indeed, several reputed scholars have since held the same opinion as Ibn Taymiyyah.

It may therefore be concluded that Ibn Taymiyyah's contribution to the sciences of jurisprudence and its general principles has undoubtedly left an indelible mark in Islamic law in general and the Ḥanbalī School of law in particular, a mark that can be observed up to the present time. Indeed, it appears that in the past century his influence has increased dramatically. He is used as an inspiration and a reference for the critical review of traditional opinions in both the Ḥanbalī School and other schools. Scholars and governments alike have found that particular rulings that Ibn Taymiyyah made, in opposition to the majority of scholars, better serve the interests the *sharīʿah* seeks to protect. He also serves as an example for those who argue that the door of *ijtihad* was never closed. There is no doubt that his work was dynamic and free from the strictures of *taqlid*.

NOTES

INTRODUCTION

1 *EI*, vol. iii pp. 954–955.
2 See a discussion of this issue in Chapter 2 of this work.

1 IBN ḤANBAL AND IBN TAYMIYYAH

1 Most western scholars translate *madhhab* as 'school', Makdisi, on the other hand, asserts that *madhhab* cannot be translated as school of law except in the pre-classical period, before the tenth century, but rather it should be translated as 'guild'. See, Melchert, *the formation*, pp. xiv–xvii, Makdisi, *Religion*, pp. 233–252. In this work *madhhab* has been translated as school of law because it appears to be the closest meaning to the term *madhhab* and because the reference to schools of law by the term *madhhab* has become problematic, as it is a word which can refer to *madhhab* in creed and or, *madhhab* in jurisprudence.
2 Ibn al-'Imād, *Shadharāt*, vol. 2 p. 86, Ismā'il, *al-Tashrī'*, p. 342.
3 Ibn al-Jawzī, *Manāqib*, p. 37. There is a similar narration in the *Musawwadah* p. 514.
4 This era spanned from 132/749 to the middle of the fourth century of Islam. At the very start of this period the Umayyad Dynasty declined and was supplanted by the Abbasids. See, Sharaf al-Dīn, *Tārīkh*, p. 143, 'Abd al-Qādir, *Naẓrah*, p. 191, al-Suyūṭī, *Tārīkh*, p. 273, Philips, *The Evolution*, p. 52. In this era, Islamic law developed rapidly, especially under the influence of the eponyms for the four major *sunni* schools: Abū Ḥanifah, Mālik, al-Shāfi'ī and Ibn Ḥanbal. Another element of this era was the composition of several important references in jurisprudence and *ḥadīth*. This era is known as 'the golden era of Islamic law', 'the era of the flowering of Islamic law', 'the era of Composition' and 'the era of the *mujtahiddīn* Scholars'. See, al-Sāhī, *al-Madkhal*, pp. 86–87. This flowering was facilitated by several important factors: The importance attached, generally speaking, by the Abbasid caliphs to knowledge and to the scholars of that time; the discovery of papyrus (*al-kaghid*) in the time of the Umayyad which facilitated the copying of the sources of the different sciences, and the appearance of several famous scholars. Al-Ibrāhīm, *al-Madkhal*, pp. 153–154, al-Ṭurayfī, *Tārīkh*, pp. 86–99. In addition to the four schools of law, there were many other schools of law in this period, such as those of al-Zahiris, al-Awzā'ī, al-Layth and others. See, al-Ddībānī, *al-Madkhal*, pp. 281–285, al-Zarqā, *al-Fiqh*, pp. 77–78, al-Dr'ān, *al-Madkhal*, p. 127, Shalabī, *al-Madkhal*, pp. 204–207, Zaydān, *al-Madkhal*, pp. 148–151, Ḥassān, *al-Madkhal*, p. 90, Madkūr, *al-Madkhal*, pp. 163–166. Contemporary scholars are of the opinion that these schools died out. However, Ibn Taymiyyah states that several of these schools in fact amalgamated with the surviving schools. He gives the example of Ibn 'Uyayynah whose

school was incorporated within the schools of Shāfi'ī and Aḥmad, and also mentions that al-Layth's opinions are usually in agreement with those of Mālik or al-Thawrī. Ibn Taymiyyah, *Fatāwā*, vol. 4 p. 177. Ibn Taymiyyah mentions that at his time the school of al-Thawrī was still in existence in Khurasān. Ibn Taymiyyah, *Fatāwā*, vol. 20 p. 583. This opinion of Ibn Taymiyyah does not appear to have been commonly known by his contemporaries. This could be why he said: 'If it was said: Where did you find this explanation?' then he explained that it is found in the book of the Shāfi'ī scholar Abū Ḥāmid al-Aṣfarā'inī entitled '*Diwān al-Sharāi*''. Ibn Taymiyyah, *Fatāwā*, vol. 4 pp. 177–178. There has been a growing interest among contemporary scholars and researchers in collecting and studying the jurisprudential opinions of old eminent scholars. Sometimes whole treatises (consisting often of several volumes) have been devoted to these scholars.

5 Ibn al-Jawzī, *Manāqib*, p. 23.
6 Makdisi, *The Rise*, p. 19.
7 Ibn Sa'd, *al-Ṭabaqāt*, vol. 7 p. 237, al-Nashratī, *al-Imām*, p. 27.
8 Ibn al-Jawzī, *al-Manāqib*, p. 31.
9 Ṣāliḥ, Sirat, p. 31.
10 Al-Aṣbahanī, *Ḥilyat*, vol. 9 p. 164.
11 Al-Nashratī, *al-Imām*, p. 29.
12 Ibn al-Jawzī, *Manāqib*, p. 65, Ibn Taymiyyah, *Minhāj*, vol. 7 p. 530, Ibn 'Abd al-Hādī, *Manāqib*, p. 127, al-Dhahabī, *Tadhkirat*, vol. 1 p. 292.
13 Al-Dhahabī, *Tadhkirat*, vol. 1 p. 292, vol. 2 pp. 431–432.
14 Ibn Taymiyyah clarifies Abū Yūsuf's status when he describes him as being more knowledgeable than Zufar (d. 158/775), another student of Abū Ḥanifah. In addition, he states that when Abū Yūsuf disagreed with Abū Ḥanifah and Muḥammad followed him, the correct opinion will be found with Abū Yūsuf. Ibn Taymiyyah attributes this to the fact that Abū Yūsuf travelled to al-Ḥijāz where he studied traditions, which were not known in his region. He was therefore reported to have said: 'If my companion (i.e. Abū Hanifah) knew what I know (i.e. of traditions) he would change his ruling as I did.' Hence, it is clear that Abū Yūsuf was a scholar of jurisprudence who possessed knowledge of the science of *ḥadīth*. Ibn Taymiyyah, *Fatāwā*, vol. 20 p. 304. Also, al-Muzanī described Abū Yūsuf as demonstrating the greatest attachment to tradition amongst *Ahl al-Ra'y*. Ibn Ma'īn says: 'There is none more knowledgeable and trustworthy (*athbat*) than Abū Yūsuf (amongst *Ahl al-Ra'y*).' Al-Dhahabī, *Tadhkirat*, vol. 1 p. 293.
15 Al-Dhahabī, *Siyar*, vol. 11 p. 188.
16 Ibn Taymiyyah, *Fatāwā*, vol. 20 p. 304.
17 Al-Dhahabī, *Tadhkirat*, vol. 1 p. 293.
18 Ibn Taymiyyah, *Fatāwā*, vol. 10 p. 362, vol. 20 p. 40.
19 Ibn al-Jawzī, *Manāqib*, p. 26.
20 Al-Dhahabī, *Tadhkirat*, vol. 1 p. 293.
21 In one narration on the authority of Ḥanbal, Aḥmad says: 'I memorised all that I heard from Hushaym during his life.' Al-Dhahabī, *Tadhkirat*, vol. 2 p. 431, al-Aṣfahānī, *Ḥilyat*, vol. 9 p. 164.
22 Al-Dhahabī, *Tadhkirat*, vol. 2 p. 431. In *al-Ṭabaqāt* by Ibn Sa'd, Hushaym was alleged to have used some types of *tadlīs*. Ibn Sa'd, *Ṭabaqāt*, vol. 7 p. 227. *Tadlīs* is defined by Burton as:

> dissembling by giving the impression of being able to report from a person whom one has not however met, or if having met him, not heard from him what one purports to transmit as being his words. It is also used for disguising the name of an informant, with the probable intent to mislead. One who practises *tadlīs* is a *mudallis*.
>
> (Burton, *An Introduction*, p. 201)

23 This is according to some narrations of Ibn Ḥanbal. In others, however, he states that he first heard from this scholar in the year 177/793. Al-Aṣbahānī, *Ḥilyat*, vol. 9 pp. 162–164, al-Dhahabī, *Siyar*, vol. 11 p. 183. It seems that this difference is not related to narrators; rather, it is related to Aḥmad himself. This is because he states in another narration that he studied under Hushaym in the year 177/793 and that he did not understand (*ya'qil*) all that he narrated. Thereafter, he states that he joined Hushaym's circles later on in the year 179–180/795–796.

24 Al-Aṣbahānī, *Ḥilyat*, vol. 9 pp. 162–163, al-Dhahabī, *Siyar*, vol. 11 p. 183.

25 Ibn al-Jawzī, *Manāqib*, p. 29.

26 Ṣāliḥ, *Sirat*, p. 32, Ibn al-Jawzī, *Manāqib*, p. 29, Ibn al-'Imād, *Shadharāt*, vol. 3 p. 186.

27 Ibn al-Jawzī, *Manāqib*, p. 144. Abū Zahrah, *Ibn Ḥanbal*, p. 27. Ibn Taymiyyah suggests that the first meeting between these two scholars was the one which took place around the year 198/814. See, *Minhāj*, vol. 7 p. 533.

28 Abū Zahrah, *Ibn Ḥanbal*, p. 31–33. Ibn Taymiyyah, in his book *Minhāj*, vol. 7 p. 530, 533, asserts that Aḥmad studied under Abū Yūsuf, but he does not believe that Aḥmad was a student of al-Shāfi'ī. He asserts, rather, that these two scholars were contemporaries who met (*jalasā*) and benefited (*istafādā*) from each other.

29 Al-Aṣbahānī, *Ḥilyat*, vol. 9 p. 170, Ibn Abū Ya'la, *Ṭabaqāt*, vol. 1 pp. 6, 18, al-Dhahabī, *Siyar*, vol. 11 pp. 195–196, Al-'Ulaymī, *al-Manhaj*, vol. 1 p. 130.

30 Ibn Abū Ya'la, *Ṭabaqāt*, vol. 1 p. 6.

31 Al-Aṣbahānī, *Ḥilyat*, vol. 9 p. 170, Ibn Abū Ya'la, *Ṭabaqāt*, vol. 1 p. 6, al-Dhahabī, *Siyar*, vol. 11 p. 213.

32 Ibn al-Jawzī, *Manāqib*, pp. 360–362, al-Dhahabī, *Siyar*, vol. 11 p. 224. Aḥmad was also asked during the latter part of his life to narrate *ḥadīth* to the Caliph of that time and to his son. Aḥmad, however, vowed not to narrate any *ḥadīth* with its chain to any one, because of his fears of temptations. Ibn Taymiyyah, *Minhāj*, vol. 7 pp. 97–98, Ibn Abū Ya'la, *Ṭabaqāt*, vol. 1 p. 12.

33 Ibn Sa'd, *Ṭabaqāt*, vol. 6 p. 74, Ibn Ḥajar, *Tahdhīb*, vol. 6 pp. 310–315. This scholar was said to have some characteristics of Shi'ism. When Ibn Ḥanbal was asked about this, he stated that he had not heard from him anything to support this, Ibn Ḥajar, *Tahdhīb*, vol. 6 p. 313.

34 Al-Aṣbahānī, *Ḥilyat*, vol. 9 pp. 174–175.

35 Ṣāliḥ, *Masā'il*, vol. 1 p. 96.

36 Ibn Taymiyyah, *Fatāwā*, vol. 20 p. 331.

37 Ṣāliḥ, *Sirat*, p. 121, Ibn al-Jawzī, *Manāqib*, p. 549, Ibn Abū Ya'la, *Ṭabaqāt*, vol. 1 p. 16, Ibn Mufliḥ, *al-Maqṣad*, vol. 1 p. 70.

38 Ṣāliḥ, *Sirat*, pp. 48–65, al-Suyūṭī, *Tārīkh*, pp. 328–332, Ibn al- Mufliḥ, *al-Maqṣad*, vol. 1 p. 69, Al-Shaṭī, *Mukhtaṣar*, pp. 11–13, al-Aṣbahānī, *Ḥilyat*, vol. 9 pp. 193–207, al-Dhahabī, *Siyar*, vol. 11 pp. 232–265, Nimrod, *Aḥmad*, pp. 198–287, Haque, '*Aḥmad Ibn Ḥanbal*', pp. 72–83. There are some treatises which deal with the *Miḥnah*, for instance *Miḥnat Aḥmad* by al-Ḥāfiẓ 'Abd al-Ghanī al-Maqdisī.

39 Ibn al-Jawzī, *Manāqib*, pp. 87–88.

40 Ibid., p. 90.

41 Al-Dhahabī, *Tadhkirat*, vol. 2 p. 432. Ibn 'Abd al-Hādī, in his book entitled *Manāqib*, (pp. 130–148) mentions a large number of statements articulated by scholars in praise of Ibn Ḥanbal.

42 Introduction of *Ikhtilāf al-Fuqahā'* by al-Ṭabarī, pp. 10–16, Abū Zahrah, *Ibn Ḥanbal*, pp. 163–181, Al-Turkī, *Uṣūl*, pp. 81–93, Shalabī, *al-Madkhal*, pp. 200–201, Madkūr, *al-Madkhal*, pp. 156–157, 'Abd al-Qādir, *Naẓrah*, p. 288, Schacht, *An Introduction*, p. 63 Some contemporary writers repeated the same accusation against Aḥmad. See, for instance, Safiullah, '*Wahhabism*', p. 80. Schacht remarks: 'for some time Ibn Ḥanbal and his adherents were regarded by the followers of the other schools not as real 'lawyers' but as mere specialists in traditions. Nevertheless, the Ḥanbalīs became one

of the recognised schools, and although they were never numerous, they counted among their adherents a surprisingly high proportion of first-class scholars in all branches of Islamic learning'. Schacht, having consulted the books of *Masā'il*, reached the conclusion that Aḥmad was in fact both a jurist and a traditionist. Moreover, Schacht considers Aḥmad's treatise *al-Musnad* as the real basis of his school of law. Schacht, *Thalāthat Muḥāḍarāt*, p. 107, quoted by al-Hāj, *al-Ẓāhirah*, vol. 2 p. 375.

43 Al-Buhūtī, *Kashshāf*, vol. 1 p. 21, *Sharḥ Muntahā*, vol. 1p. 9, al-Turkī, *Uṣūl*, pp. 83–84, Ḥassān, *al-Madkhal*, p. 112, Shalabī, *al-Madkhal*, pp. 200–201.
44 Abū Ya'la, *al-'Uddah*, vol. 5 pp. 1594–1600. al-Mardāwī, *al-Taḥbīr*, part 3 vol. 2 pp. 630–636, al-Ṭūfī, *Sharḥ*, vol. 3 pp. 577–580.
45 Ibn Taymiyyah, *Minhāj*, vol. 7 p. 428, al-Ba'lī, al-*Ikhtiyārāt*, p. 64. Also, Ibn Mufliḥ mentions this narration of Aḥmad in his book *al-Furū'*, vol. 1 p. 534. According to Ibn Taymiyyah, Aḥmad combined knowledge in the sciences of *ḥadīth* and jurisprudence. See, Ibn Taymiyyah, *Minhāj*, vol. 7 p. 429.
46 Ibn Ḥajar, *Tahdhīb al-Tahdhāb*, vol. 1 p. 73.
47 Ibn 'Abd al-Hādī, *Manāqib*, p. 144. Similar statements are narrated also from other leading scholars, see, Ibid., p. 144, 146.
48 Ibn al-Qayyim, *I'lām*, vol. 1 p. 58.
49 Ibn Abū Ya'la, *Tabaqāt*, vol. 1 pp. 6–7, Ibn Mufliḥ, *al-Maqṣad*, vol. 1 p. 66. Al-Dhahabī and al-Ṭūfī mention that Aḥmad did not believe in composition. See, al-Dhahabī, *Siyar*, vol. 13 p. 522, al-Ṭūfī, *Sharḥ*, vol. 3 p. 626.
50 See, Ibn Taymiyyah, *Fatāwā*, vol. 20 pp. 211–212.
51 It is clear that there are narrations in the *Musnad* inserted by 'Abd Allah, Aḥmad's son. It is also widely believed that al-Qaṭī'ī added some narrations to the *Musnad*. This, however, has been proved inaccurate. See for details, al-Faryawā'ī, *Sheikh al-Islam*, vol. 1 p. 545.
52 Haque, *Aḥmad Ibn Ḥanbal*, p. 68.
53 This system of arrangement has its own advantages and disadvantages. One of its most serious drawbacks is that it is usually difficult to find a tradition under its subject. Ibn al-Bannā tried to solve this defect by compiling his book '*Al-Fatḥ al-Rabbānī*' in which he rearranged *al-Musnad* according to subjects. Nevertheless, *al-Musnad*'s system affords the researcher the opportunity to find in one section the sum-total of narrations transmitted by a single companion.
54 According to Ibn Taymiyyah, Aḥmad did not mean to narrate only what he thought to be authentic. Rather, he wanted to collect what his sheikhs narrated on this issue. Therefore, it is clear that this book contains correct as well as weak *ḥadīths*. Later on, 'Abd Allah b. Aḥmad b. Ḥanbal and al-Qaṭī'ī added to the narrations narrated by Aḥmad in this book. Most of the narrations added by al-Qaṭī'ī are lies and fabrications. See, Ibn Taymiyyah, *Minhāj*, vol. 5 p. 23, vol. 7 pp. 97–99, 223.
55 Abū Zayd, *al-Madkhal*, vol. 1 p. 352.
56 This book has been referred to by several scholars such as Ibn Abū Ya'la in his *Ṭabaqāt* vol. 1 p. 311. Recently, this work has been translated into English.
57 The book '*al-Radd*' has been published, and the second book '*Jawābāt*' is mentioned in several sources, such as Ibn al-Jawzī in his *Manāqib* p. 261 and Ibn Abū Ya'la in his *Ṭabaqāt* vol. 1 p. 8.
58 The first two books have been published and the last two have been mentioned in several sources, such as Ibn Abū Ya'la, *Ṭabaqāt*, vol. 1 p. 8, Ibn al-Jawzī, *Manāqib*, p. 261, and Ibn al-Qayyim cited the book of *Ṭā'at al-Rasūl* on several occasions in his book *I'lām*; see for example vol. 2 pp. 300–304. Al-Dhahabī asserts that the book entitled *Kitāb al-Ṣalāh* was not written by Aḥmad. Al-Dhahabī *Siyar*, vol. 11 p. 287. This, however, has been called into question by the contemporary Ḥanbalī scholar Abū Zayd. For details see, Abū Zayd, *al-Madkhal*, vol. 2 pp. 617–618.

59 Ibn al-Jawzī, *Manāqib*, p. 263.
60 Ibn Abū Ya'la, *Ṭabaqāt*, vol. 1 p. 7. Al-Dhahabī in his *Siyar* mentioned a narration which states that there were about 5000 people who attended Ibn Ḥanbal's study circles and only less than 500 who were known to write down his lessons. Abū Zayd in his book *al-Madkhal al-Mufaṣṣal*, vol. 2 p. 1211 mentions that the narrators of Aḥmad's *fiqh* numbered 200.
61 Ibn Abū Ya'la, *Ṭabaqāt*, vol. 1 p. 66.
62 Al-Thaqafī, *Mafātīḥ*, vol. 2 pp. 353–354.
63 Ibn Abū Ya'la, *Ṭabaqāt*, vol. 1 p. 114, vol. 2 p. 174.
64 Ibid., vol. 2 p. 174.
65 Ibid., al-Thaqafī, *Mafātīḥ*, vol. 2 pp. 353–354. In another narration, Aḥmad's disapproval was not because al-Kawsaj used to narrate Aḥmad's *masā'il*, but due to his taking money for narrating them. Ibn Abū Ya'la, *Ṭabaqāt*, vol. 2 p. 174.
66 Ibn Abū Ya'la, *Ṭabaqāt*, vol. 1 p. 143, Ibn Mufliḥ, *al-Maqṣad*, vol. 1 p. 366, al-'Ulaymī, *al-Manhaj*, vol. 1 p. 245.
67 Ibn Abū Ya'la, *Ṭabaqāt*, vol. 1 p. 143.
68 Ibn Rajab, *al-Dhayl*, vol. 1 pp. 173–176, Ibn Mufliḥ, *al-Maqṣad*, vol. 1 pp. 444–445.
69 Ibn Rajab, *al-Dhayl*, vol. 1 p. 173, Ibn Mufliḥ, *al-Maqṣad*, vol. 1 p. 444.
70 Ibn Abū Ya'la, *Ṭabaqāt*, vol. 1 p. 212, al-Dhahabī, *Siyar*, vol. 13 p. 89.
71 Ibn Abū Ya'la, *Ṭabaqāt*, vol. 1 p. 213.
72 Ibid., p. 345.
73 Ibid., vol. 1 p. 39, Ibn al-Jawzī, *Manāqib*, p. 673.
74 Al-Dhahabī, *Siyar*, vol. 11 p. 331.
75 Ibid.
76 Ibid. and Ibn al-Qayyim, *I'lām*, vol. 1 p. 58.
77 Al-Dhahabī, *Siyar*, vol. 14 p. 298.
78 Ibn Taymiyyah, *Fatāwā*, vol. 34 pp. 111–112.
79 This point will be further elaborated in Chapter 4 when discussing the issue of the existence of incorrect opinions within the Ḥanbalī School.
80 Abū Zayd, *al-Madkhal*, vol. 1 p. 498, 'Abd al-Qādir, *Naẓrah*, p. 300.
81 Abū Zayd, *al-Madkhal*, vol. 1 p. 498, 502.
82 Al-Suyūṭī, *Ḥusn al-Muḥaḍarh*, vol. 1 p. 480, Abū Zayd, *al-Madkhal*, pp. 498, 504, al-Dusūqī, *Muqadimah*, p. 210.
83 Al-Suyūṭī, *Ḥusn al-Muḥaḍarh*, vol. 1 p. 480.
84 Ibid., p. 506.
85 Mūsa, *al-Madkhal*, p. 163, Abū Zahrah, *Ibn Ḥanbal*, pp. 406–416, al-Ṭurayfī, *Tārīkh*, pp. 131–134, al-Hazāymh, *al-Madkhal*, pp. 89–90, al-Ṭanṭāwī, *al-Madkhal*, p. 207, Ismā'īl, *al-Tashrī'*, pp. 344–345, Abū Zahrah, *Tārīkh*, pp. 542–543, 'Abd al-Qādir, *Naẓrah*, p. 300, al-Dusūqī, *Muqadimah*, p. 210, Madkūr, *al-Madkhal*, p. 156.
86 It seems that this claim was first raised by Ibn Khaldūn. See: Ibn Khaldūn, *al-'Ibar*, vol. 1 p. 803, Abū Zahrah, *Ibn Ḥanbal*, p. 407. Also, this same accusation has been raised by some contemporary writers, such as Madkūr, in his work *al-Madkhal*, pp. 156–157. Several scholars have, however, asserted that this claim does not stand on solid ground, as the books of Ḥanbalī jurisprudence are full of the use of independent reasoning. Also, Abū Zahrah asserts that it is not an accurate explanation for the narrow expansion of the Ḥanbalī School. Abū Zahrah explains that it was this School after all which declared that the door of independent reasoning cannot be closed. Abū Zahrah, *Ibn Ḥanbal*, p. 407. Also, see: al-Dr'ān, *al-Madkhal*, pp. 166–168, Ḥassān, *al-Madkhal*, p. 112.
87 This accusation is levelled against the school of Aḥmad: 'It is a strict school', or that it is 'the strictest of the four juristic Schools'. Al-Dr'ān, *al-Madkhal*, pp. 163–164, Ḥassān, *al-Madkhal*, p. 112, Madkūr, *al-Madkhal*, p. 156, Abū Zahrah, *Tārīkh*, p. 505, Sha'bān, *al-Tashrī'*, p. 344. Other scholars assert that there is no real basis for this

accusation and it was only made because of certain facts, the main four of which are: the personal life of Aḥmad which was characterised by piety and *wara'*; various followers of this School participated in *ḥisbah*; their disputes with their opponents regarding issues of creed; the existence of some fanatics among the followers of this School who were involved in attacks on some of their opponents. Al-Dr'ān, *al-Madkhal*, pp. 164–166, Ḥassān, *al-Madkhal*, p. 112, Abū Zahrah, *Tārīkh*, p. 505. Some of those who describe the Ḥanbalī School as strict refer to the strictness in the adherence to textual evidences when delivering juristic verdicts. See, for instance, Sha'bān, *al-Tashrī'*, p. 344. This, however, is problematic as, if a researcher goes back to the definition of jurisprudence in relevant terminology, they find that it has been defined in several ways, one of which is: 'the derivation of practical legal rulings from their detailed evidence'. Detailed evidence consists of textual and rational evidences. If no text can be found, then other sources of Islamic law will be implemented, and this was employed by Aḥmad. Some people base their claim concerning the strictness of the Ḥanbalī School on certain juristic verdicts on some minor questions. A number of those questions are, however, not limited to the Ḥanbalī School. Yet, there is no doubt that there are scattered questions in which the Ḥanbalī School is, in my opinion, strict. Such strictness is not, however, attributable to the Ḥanbalī juristic sources and principles; rather it is by virtue of the School granting precedence to caution and prudence in those questions.

88 Abū Zayd, *al-Madkhal*, vol. 1 p. 509, al-Dusūqī, *Muqaddimah*, pp. 210–211, al-Ṭanṭawī, *al-Madkhal*, p. 207, Philips, *The Evolution of Fiqh*, pp. 86–87, Schacht, *An Introduction to Islamic Law*, pp. 66–67, Mūsā, *al-Madkhal*, p. 163, Badrān, *al-Sharī'ah*, p. 212.

89 Scholars are in general agreement as to why they were called '*Mamālik*', which was a reference to their original status as slaves. Opinions differ however concerning the reason why they were called 'Al-Baḥriyyah'. Some scholars attribute it to the fact that they were transported to the Ayyūbi's Kingdom over the sea (*Baḥr*). Another view is that they lived in an area of land bordering the river Nile which was known as '*al-baḥr*'. The first opinion was adopted by al-Dhahabī, though the majority of writers have mentioned the second. See: Al-Maḥmūd, *Mauqif*, vol. 1 p. 104, Lane-Poole, *The Mohammadan Dynasties*, p. 80, Islahi, *Economic*, p. 23, Irwin, *the Middle East in the Middle Ages*, pp. 3–4, 18, Ashtor, *A Social and Economic History of the Near East*, p. 280, al-'Abbādī, *fi Tārīkh*, p. 82.

90 Al-Nadwī, *al-Ḥāfiẓ*, p. 20, Lane-Pool, *The Mohammadan Dynasties*, p. 80. Ibn Kathīr in *al-Bidāyah* vol. 13 p. 201, describes al-Ṣāliḥ Ayyūb as the *istādh* (teacher) of the Mamluks. There are occasional references to the employment of Mamluks, apparently of Iranian origin, under the Umayyads and early Abbasids in the eighth century. The employment of the Mamluks by the caliphs and by provincial dynasties only really became widespread in the ninth century. By this time the overwhelming majority of such troops were clearly Turkish in origin. They were playing an increasingly important and ultimately a dominant role in the affairs of the Caliphate and the states which succeeded it or seceded from it. At the time of the last of the great Ayyūbid princes, al-Ṣāliḥ Ayyūb, ruler of Egypt from 1240 and of Damascus from 1245 until his death in 1249, the reliance on Turkish Mamluks increased markedly. Most of the Mamluks purchased by al-Ṣāliḥ Ayyūb were descendants from a Turkish tribe, the Kipchak. It is said that they had not been employed in significant numbers by any previous ruler of Syria or Egypt. Al-Ṣāliḥ Ayyūb also created a new elite corps, the Baḥriyyah, who were numbered between 800 and 1,000 and were composed predominantly of Kipchak Turks. See: Irwin, *the Middle East*, pp. 3–5, 12, 18. Also, Ashtor, *Asocial and Economic history*, p. 280, Amital-Preiss, *Mongol*, p. 18, al-'Abbādī, *fi Tārīkh*, pp. 77–78. It is because of this connection between al-Ṣāliḥ and Mamluks that some sources named this group after him, see Holt, *The Age*, p. 83.

91 Ibn Kathīr, *al-Bidāyah*, vol. 13 p. 202 and cf. to Irwin, *the Middle East*, p. 26, Holt, *The Age*, p. 83. Some researchers debated the point that the Baḥrī Mamluk's era started

from the year 1250 as they mentioned that not one of the five rulers who held the Sultanate between 1250 and 1260 was a Baḥrī Mamluk and two of those rulers openly opposed the Baḥrī faction. Furthermore, for the first two years at least, there was a widespread reluctance amongst the former emirs and slaves of al-Ṣāliḥ Ayyūb to acknowledge that the Ayyūbid Sultanate over Egypt had really ended with the murder of Turānshah. See: Irwin, *The Middle East in the Middle Ages*, p. 26, Amital-Preiss, *Mongol*, p. 17.

92 Ibn Kathīr, *al-Bidāyah*, vol. 13 p. 251.

93 Ibid., p. 248. Also, Ibn al-'Imād, *Shadharāt*, vol. 7 p. 508 and Amital-Preiss, *Mongols*, pp. 26–48.

94 Ibn Kathīr, *al-Bidāyah*, vol. 13 p. 261, Ibn al-'Imād, *Shadharāt*, vol. 7 p. 513, Sourdel, *Medieval Islam*, p. 131, al-'Abbādī, *fī Tārīkh*, pp. 156–157, Amitai-Preiss, *Mongols*, p. 56. There are two interesting points about this caliph discussed in some sources. First, some sources doubted the relationship of this caliph to the Abbasids. For further details see: Al-'Abbādī, *fi Tārīkh*, pp. 157–158. The second is that several weeks after the installation of this caliph, he was sent with a relatively small army to free Iraq from the hands of the Mongols. There have been several attempts to unveil the sultan's motivation behind this dispatch. For a critical study of this point see Amitai-Preiss, *Mongols*, pp. 58–60, al-'Abbādī, *fī Tārīkh*, pp. 159–160.

95 Ibn al-'Imād, *Shadharāt*, vol. 7 p. 513, Amital-Preiss, *Mongols*, p. 63, al-'Abbādī, *fi Tārīkh*, pp. 161–162, Holt, *The Age*, p. 112, Louist, *Nazariyyāt*, pp. 174–176.

96 This was the caliph al-Mustakfī, who was at first imprisoned then placed under house arrest and at the end exiled to Qūṣ, a city in Egypt, till his death 740/1339. Ibn Kathīr, *al-Bidāyah*, vol. 14 p. 191, 204.

97 For further details of this point see Berkey, *The Transmission of Knowledge in Medieval Cairo*. This does not mean that the great city of Damascus at that time lost its importance as a cultural and educational centre. For more details see Chamberlain, *Knowledge and Social Practice in Medieval Damascus 119–1350*.

98 Abū Zahrah, *Ibn Taymiyyah*, p. 120.

99 Ibn Kathīr, *al-Bidāyah*, vol. 13 p. 274.

100 *Shurā* in Islamic law here denotes that the head of state should consult those of sound judgement concerning problematic issues and have recourse to the people in order to resolve cases of difficulty, so as to be safe from mistakes and free of errors. See: Al-Māwardī, *al-Aḥkām al-Sulṭaniyyah*, p. 68. The Prophet was ordered by Allah to follow this procedure, as Allah says in The Qur'an: 'And consult them in the matter, and if you have come to a decision, then place your trust in Allah' (3:153).

101 These taxes were of extreme importance to the Mamluks, and at the same time they were very costly and burdensome to the public. This was because the war between the Mamluks and Mongols lasted for approximately sixty years. For further details of the events of this era see Ibn Kathīr, *al-Bidāyah*, from vol. 13 p. 102 to vol. 14 p. 29. Amitai-Preiss, *Mongols and Mamluks*, al-'Abbādī, *Tārīkh* pp. 107–252.

102 Ibn Kathīr, *al-Bidāyah*, vol. 13 pp. 102–103, Ibn al-Athīr, *al-Kāmil*, vol. 12 pp. 358–359.

103 Ibn Kathīr, *al-Bidāyah*, vol. 13 pp. 226–230, Amitai-Preiss, *Mongols*, pp. 15–16.

104 Ibn Kathīr, *al-Bidāyah*, vol. 13 pp. 248–249, Ibn al-'Imād, *Shadharāt*, vol. 7 p. 508, Amitai-Preiss, *Mongols*, pp. 26–48. The Mongols unintentionally and indirectly helped create the force which was to stop them at 'Ain Jālūt and was to frustrate their plans to conquer Syria in the succeeding years. This occurred as the Mongols attacked the steppes of southern Russia, the Mamluks's land of origin, and brought upon most of them death, slavery and captivity. Then they were bought by the Ayyūb Sultans, especially by al-Ṣāliḥ, and later on they became the rulers who were able to stop the Mongols. Amitai-Preiss, *Mongols*, p. 18.

105 Ibn Kathīr, *al-Bidāyah*, vol. 13 p. 356.

106 As it happened between Ibn Taymiyyah and some of the sultans of his time and between al-Nawawī and sultan al-Ẓāhir. See: Al-Karmī, *al-Kawākib*, pp. 93–96, al-Bazzār, *al-A'lām*, pp. 74–75, Abū Zahrah, *Ibn Taymiyyah*, pp. 120–123.
107 Al-'Abbādī, *fī Tārīkh*, pp. 119–125, Abū Zahrah, *Ibn Taymiyyah*, pp. 119–120, al-Nadwī, *al-Ḥāfiẓ*, pp. 24–25.
108 Abū Zahrah, *Ibn Taymiyyah*, p. 123, al-Nadwī, *al-Ḥāfiẓ*, p. 23. For further details of the era of these two rulers, see: Holt, *The Age*, pp. 90–98, 107–119, Amitai-Preiss, *Mongols*, pp. 49–235, al-'Abbādī, *Tārīkh*, pp. 145–208, 223–233.
109 Mūsa, *Ibn Taymiyyah*, p. 35, Abū Zahrah, *Ibn Taymiyyah*, pp. 121–122, 124.
110 Islahi, *Economic*, p. 29, Abū Zahrah, *Ibn Taymiyyah*, p. 124. Maqrizī and some others assert that the year 806/1403–1404 was the one which marked a turning point for the worse, with regard to the economic situation of the Mamluk Sultanate. David Ayalon counters that this event should be regarded as only one of the important milestones in the process of decline. He also asserts that the visible roots of this decline were evident considerably earlier than at the end of the eighth/fourteenth centuries to the beginning of the ninth/fifteenth centuries and this decline is also clearly noticeable in the third reign of Sultan al-Nāṣir Muhammad b. Qalaūn (709–741/1309–1340). For further details of this point see Ayalon, 'Some Remarks on the Economic Decline of the Mamluk Sultanate' pp. 108–124 *in Jerusalem Studies in Arabic and Islam*, 1993 (16).
111 Ibn Kathīr, *al-Bidāyah*, vol. 13 p. 243.
112 For a clear picture of the political situation of this era, see: Al-Ṣafadī, *al-Wāfī*, vol. 7, *al-Manhal*, vol. 1, Ibn Kathīr, *al-Bidāyah*, vol. 13 and 14, Ibn Ḥajar, *al-Durar*, vol. 1, Ibn Barada, *al-Nujūm*, vol. 9 and Amital-Preiss, *Mongol*, al-'Abbādī, *fī Tārīkh*, pp. 77–237. During this era, a succession of different sultans ruled the country. Ibn Kathīr, *al-Bidāyah*, vol. 13 pp. 353–394, vol. 14 pp. 3–61, al-Nadwī, *al-Ḥāfiẓ*, pp. 22–23.
113 Islahi, *Economic*, p. 29.
114 Ibn Taymiyyah, *Fatāwā*, vol. 9 pp. 9–10, Muhammad, *Sheikh al-Islam*, pp. 39–42. Ibn Taymiyyah in his book *al-Manṭiq* attributes responsibility to Muslim philosophers for the existence of some problems in the Islamic sciences, including the science of the general principles of jurisprudence. Ibn Taymiyyah *Fatāwā*, vol. 9 pp. 23–24. He asserts that the leading Imāms in the Arabic and Islamic sciences, who compiled treatises on these subjects before the translation of Greek philosophy, did not pay any attention to philosophy. *Fatāwā*, vol. 9 p. 23. He concedes nonetheless that the approach adopted by the Muslim philosophers is clearer than other philosophers. *Fatāwā*, vol. 9 p. 15. Furthermore, he mentions that although some Muslim philosophers produced certain innovations, they did contribute to the criticism of philosophy. *Fatāwā*, vol. 9 pp. 9–10.
115 Netton, *Allah Transcendent*, p. 6.
116 Ibn Khuldūn, *al-'Ibar*, vol. 1 pp. 802–803, 806.
117 Al-Mardāwī mentions that there were some scholars who reached the status of *mujtahid* during this era and he gives Ibn Taymiyyah as an example. Ibn al-Najjār, *Sharḥ al-Kawkab al-Munīr* vol. 4 pp. 569–570.
118 A similar statement is made by Ridgeon in his unpublished PhD thesis 'Nothing but the Truth', p. 16, in describing the time of 'Azīz Nasafī, who lived in the thirteenth century.
119 Amital-Preiss, *Mongol*, pp. 1–2.
120 Ibn Kathīr, *al-Bidāyah*, vol. 13 p. 270, Ibn al-'Imād, *Shadharāt*, vol. 8 p. 143. There are two views concerning the reason why Ibn Taymiyyah was called by this name. The first: Abū 'l-Barakāt b. al- Mustanfī, the author of the history of *Arbela*, questioned Fakhr al-Dīn, Ibn Taymiyyah's uncle, about it. He replied:

> My father, or my grandfather, I am not sure which, made the pilgrimage to Makkah, leaving his wife in a state of pregnancy. On arriving at Taima, a little girl who came out of a tent attracted his attention, and on his return

> to Ḥarrān he found that his wife had lain in of a daughter [*sic*]. When the child was presented to him, he exclaimed: ya Taimiya! ya Taimiya! (O the girl of Taima! The girl of Taima!) Being struck by her resemblance to the little girl he saw there. The child was, therefore, named Taimiya
>
> (*Ibn Khallikan's Biographical Dictionary*, vol. III p. 97 and Ibn 'Abd al-Hādī, *al-'Uqūd*, p. 2)

The second opinion was that his mother or grandmother was called Taymiyyah and that he was named after her. Al-Karmī, *al-Kawākib*, p. 52, Ibn 'Abd al-Hādī, *al-'Uqūd*, p. 2. Grammatically, the attribute to Taima is Tymawayi because the masculine form of the relative adjective derived from Tayma is Taimaui. *Ibn Khallikan's Biographical Dictionary*, vol. III pp. 97–98. There were four places known by the name Ḥarrān, as Yāqūt al-Ḥamawī mentioned in his book *Mu'jam al-Buldān*: the first, a village in Ḥalab, the second, an area in Damascus, the third, Ḥarrān al-Kubra and al-Sughra two villages in Bahrain, the fourth, a place between al-Raḥa and al-raqah. The last one was the birthplace of Ibn Taymiyyah. It is claimed that this city was named after Ḥaran, the Prophet Ibrahim's brother, who first built it. This city was a famous centre of the Sabians. At the time of the Tartars' invasion, this town was destroyed. See: Al-Hamadhānī, *al-Buldān*, p. 179, Yaqūt, *Mu'jam*, pp. 271–273, al-Bazzār, *al-I'lām*, p. 73.

121 Ibn Rajab, *Dhayl*, vol. 2 p. 387.
122 Al-Bazzār, *al-I'lām*, pp. 18–19.
123 Ibn al-'Imād, *Shadharāt*, vol. 8 p. 143.
124 Ibn 'Abd al-Hādī, *al-'Uqūd*, p. 3, al-Karmī, *al-Kawākib*, p. 54 and Ṣafi al-Dīn, *al-Qawl*, pp. 5–6. Following the custom of the time, Ibn Taymiyyah compiled a mashyakhah that included forty-one sheikhs and four *sheikhāt.* This mashyakhah is narrated by al-Dhahabī see Ibn Taymiyyah, *al-Arba'ūn*, p. 61.
125 Ibn Rajab, *Dhayl*, vol. 2 p. 388.
126 Ibn Kathīr, *al-Bidāyah*, vol. 13 p. 380.
127 Ibn Taymiyyah, *al-Arba'ūn*, pp. 101,127.
128 Ibid., p. 121.
129 Ibid., p. 73.
130 Ibn Rajab, *Dhayl*, vol. 2 p. 54, al-Karmī, *al-Kawākib*, p. 54.
131 Al-Karmī, *al-Kawākib*, pp. 54, 78.
132 Ibn 'Abd al-Hādī, *al-'Uqūd*, p. 5, and the same statement is quoted by Chamberlain, *Knowledge*, p. 125.
133 Ibn Abd al-Hādī, *al-'Uqūd*, Ibn Kathīr, *al-Bidāyah*, vol. 13 p. 338, Ibn al-'Imād, *Shadharāt*, vol. 8 p. 143.
134 Ḥarbī, *Ibn Taymiyyah*, pp. 31–32, Abū Zahrah, *Ibn Taymiyyah*, p. 437. The subject of Ibn Taymiyyah's disciples will be studied in some detail in the chapter dealing with the influence of this scholar upon Ḥanbalī jurists. This has been done in order to avoid repetition.
135 Ibn Taymiyyah, *Fatāwā*, vol. 28 pp. 67–68, 180.
136 Ibid., pp. 65–66, 80–81, 126, 241–243, 306–307.
137 Al-Bazzār, *al-I'lām*, pp. 69–70, al-Karmī, *al-Kawākib*, pp. 91–99, Ibn Taymiyyah, *Fatāwā*, vol. 28 pp. 410–423.
138 Ibn Kathīr, *al-Bidāyah*, vol. 14 p. 17, al-Karmī, *al-Kawākib*, p. 95.
139 Al-Ṣafadī, *al-Wāfī*, vol. 7 p. 19.
140 Chamberlain, *Knowledge*, p. 159.
141 Ibn Kathīr, *al-Bidāyah*, vol. 14 p. 58, Chamberlain, *Knowledge*, p. 161.
142 Al-Bazzār, *al-I'lām*, p. 70, Ibn Kathīr, *al-Bidāyah*, vol. 14 pp. 41, 85.
143 Ibn Kathīr, *al-Bidāyah*, vol. 14 p. 31. See another example where Ibn Taymiyyah was consulted about an appointment of a headmaster in *Knowledge* by Chamberlain p. 97.
144 Al-Bazzār, *al-I'lām*, pp. 75–76.

145 Al-Shawkānī, *al-Badr*, vol. 1 pp. 66, 68, al-Ṣafadī, *al-Wāfī*, vol. 7 p. 22.
146 Ibn Ḥajar, *al-Durar*, vol. 1 p. 166, al-Bazzār, *al-I'lām*, p. 74, Little, the Historical, p. 322. Al-Shawkānī stated that this alleged accusation was behind his long lasting imprisonment. See: Al-Shawkānī, *al-Badr*, vol. 1 p. 71.
147 Ibn Rajab mentioned that he saw in Ibn Taymiyyah's writing that he was offered these positions before the year 690/1291. See: Ibn Rajab, *Dhayl*, vol. 2 p. 390.
148 Al-Bazzār, *al-I'lām*, p. 73.
149 Ibid., pp. 74–75. Another example is when the deputy of al-Shām was asked to send Ibn Taymiyyah to Egypt and he refused. The messenger tried to threaten the deputy by claiming that it had come to the knowledge of the political circles in Egypt that Ibn Taymiyyah had prepared to take the deputy's position. As a consequence, the deputy agreed to send him to Egypt. Al-Karmī, *al-Kawākib*, p. 128. This same accusation is said to have been started by Naṣr al-Manbijī who mentioned it to the ruling circles in Egypt and encouraged them to take action against Ibn Taymiyyah (ibid.).
150 Ibn Kathīr, *al-Bidāyah*, vol. 13 p. 374. This event was behind Ibn Taymiyyah's writing of *al-Ṣārim al-Maslūl 'Alā shātim al-Rasūl* (ibid.).
151 *Al-Ḥamawiyyah* is one of Ibn Taymiyyah's treatises on creed. It was written as an answer to a question sent to him from Ḥamāh, a town in Syria. See: Al-Karmī, *al-Kawākib*, p. 102. This book has been published with *Majmū' al-Fatāwā* in addition to a separate issue.
152 This is the main issue upon which this treatise was based. As a consequence various parts of it contain an affirmation of the creed of *al-Salaf* and criticism of *al-Khalaf*. See: Ibn Taymiyyah, *al-Ḥamawiyyah*, with *Fatāwā*, vol. 5 pp. 5–120.
153 Al-Karmī, *al-Kawākib*, pp. 113–114, Ibn Kathīr, *al-Bidāyah*, vol. 14 pp. 4–5.
154 Ibn Kathīr, *al-Bidāyah*, vol. 14 p. 5.
155 Ibid., pp. 40–42, al-Karmī, *al-Kawākib*, p. 114.
156 Ibid., pp. 114–115.
157 Al-Karmī, *al-Kawākib*, p. 117.
158 *Al-Wāsiṭiyyah* is another treatise of Ibn Taymiyyah's concerning creed. It was written as a response to a request by a judge from the town of *Wāsiṭ* pertaining to the belief of the predecessors. See: Al-Karmī, *al-Kawākib*, p. 118. The treatise was published in two forms, with *Fatāwā* and in separate issues.
159 Al-Karmī, *al-Kawākib*, pp. 117–125.
160 Ibn 'Abd al-Hādī, *al-'Uqūd*, p. 266, Ibn Kathīr, *al-Bidāyah*, vol. 14 p. 42, and al-Karmī, *al-Kawākib*, p. 130.
161 Ibid.
162 Al-Karmī, *al-Kawākib*, p. 130. Also: Ibn 'Abd al-Hādī, *al-'Uqūd*, pp. 266–267, and Ibn Kathīr, *al- Bidāyah*, vol. 14 p. 46.
163 Al-Karmī, *al-Kawākib*, p. 131, Ibn Kathīr, *al-Bidāyah*, vol. 14 p. 49.
164 Ibn Taymiyyah was asked by the sultan's deputy to stay in Egypt for a while in order to benefit the people by his knowledge, according to Ibn Kathīr in *al-Bidāyah*, vol. 14 p. 50, Ibn 'Abd al-Hādī in *al-'Uqūd*, p. 269 and al-Karmī in *al-Kawākib*, p. 131. It appears that Ibn Taymiyyah himself wanted to stay longer after he recognised the advantages of it. This can be understood from the letter Ibn Taymiyyah wrote to his mother (Ibn 'Abd al-Hādī, *al-'Uqūd*, pp. 273–275) in Damascus in which he apologised for being away from her and in which he explained that this was for the sake of the greater good.
165 Ibn Kathīr, *al-Bidāyah*, vol. 14 p. 50, and al-Karmī, *al-Kawākib*, p. 133.
166 Ibid. pp. 133–135.
167 Ibn Kathīr, *al-Bidāyah*, vol. 14 pp. 54–55. There were rumours spread abroad that Ibn Taymiyyah was killed while he was in Alexandria, according to al-Karmī in *al-Kawākib*, p. 135.
168 Ibid.
169 Ibid.

170 Al-Nadwī, *al-Ḥāfiẓ*, p. 94.
171 Al-Karmī, *al-Kawākib*, p. 130. Also: Ibn 'Abd al-Hādī, *al-'Uqūd*, pp. 266–267, and Ibn Kathīr, *al-Bidāyah*, vol. 14 p. 46.
172 Ibn Kathīr, *al-Bidāyah*, vol. 14 p. 74, Ibn 'Abd al-Hādī, *al-'Uqūd*, pp. 337–341 and Ibn Rajab, *Dhayl*, vol. 2 p. 401.
173 Ibn Kathīr, *al-Bidāyah*, vol. 14 p. 95, 106, Ibn 'Abd al-Hādī, *al-'Uqūd*, pp. 325–326, Ibn Rajab, *Dhayl*, vol. 2 p. 401.
174 Ibn Kathīr, *al-Bidāyah*, vol. 14 p. 95.
175 Ibid.
176 Ibid., pp. 135–136, 148–153, and al-Karmī, *al-Kawākib*, pp. 148–158, 174.
177 Al-Shawkānī, *al-Badr*, p. 68, al-Maḥmūd, *Mauqif*, vol. 1 p. 174. It appears that Naṣr al-Manbijī was also responsible for some of Ibn Taymiyyah's detentions, especially those in the year 705/1305. Furthermore, Naṣr al-Manbijī seems to have succeeded in convincing some scholars, such as the judge Ibn Makhlūf, to join his campaign against Ibn Taymiyyah. See: Ibn Kathīr in *al-Bidāyah* vol. 14 p. 41, and al-Karmī in *al-Kawākib*, pp. 114–115, 127–128, Ibn 'Abd al-Hādī in *al-'Uqūd* p. 204.
178 Al-Dhahabī, *Dhayl Tārīkh*, p. 24.
179 Ṣafī al-Dīn al-Ḥanafī, *al-Qawl*, p. 8. Ibn Nāṣir al-Shāfi'ī wrote a treatise entitled '*al-Radd al-Wāfir*' in which he criticised and refuted this claim. He quoted eighty-seven scholars who referred to Ibn Taymiyyah as '*sheikh al-islam*'. See: Ibn Nāṣir, *al-Radd al-Wāfir*, pp. 57–222.
180 Ibn Nāṣir, *al-Radd al-Wāfir*, pp. 57–265, al-Karmī, *al-Kawākib*, pp. 159–173. Also, al-Nadwī, *al-Ḥāfiẓ*, p. 110.
181 Ibid., al-Bazzār, *al-I'lām*, p. 31, Ibn al-'Imād, *Shadharāt*, vol. 8 p. 146.
182 Ibid., p. 64.
183 Ibn Ḥāmid, *Risālah*, p. 15, Ibn 'Abd al-Hādī, *al-'Uqūd*, p. 505.
184 Ibn 'Abd al-Hādī, *al-'Uqūd*, p. 2.
185 Ibid., pp. 4–26.
186 Ibid., p. 26.
187 Al-Bukharī, *al-Qawl*, p. 7.
188 Al-Shawkānī, *al-Badr*, vol. 1 pp. 64–65.
189 Al-Dhahabī, *Dhayl*, pp. 23–26.
190 Ibn 'Abd al-Hādī, *al-'Uqūd*, pp. 23–25.
191 Shaysānī, *al-Ḥāfiẓ*, p. 61, al-Munajjid in his introduction to Siyar *A'lām al-Nubalā'*, vol. 1 p. 21.
192 Al-Dhahabī, *Dhayl*, p. 25, *Tadhkirah*, pp. 1496–1497, al-Dawūdī, *Ṭabaqāt*, p. 48.
193 Shaysānī, *al-Ḥāfiẓ*, pp. 61–63, al-Munjjid in his introduction to Siyar *A'lām al-Nubalā'*, vol. 1 pp. 20–21.
194 See, for instance, al-Dhahabī, *Dhayl*, p. 27, *Tadhkirat*, p. 1497.
195 Ibn al-'Imād, *Shadharāt*, vol. 8 pp. 267–268, al-Ḥusaynī, *Dhayl al-'Ibar*, p. 148, al-Suyūtī, *Dhayl Tadhkirat*, pp. 347–348, Ibn Kathīr, *al-Bidāyah*, vol. 14 p. 243, al-Asnawī, *Ṭabaqāt*, vol. 1 pp. 558–559, al-Shawkānī, *al-Badr*, vol. 2 pp. 110–112, al-Nu'aymī, *Tārīkh al-Madāris*, vol. 1 pp. 78–80, Ibn Ḥajar, al-Durar, vol. 3 pp. 426–427, al-Katbī, *Fawāt al-Wāfīyyāt*, vol. 3 pp. 315–316, *al-Wāfī*, vol. 2 pp. 163–168, Ibn Nāṣir, *al-Radd*, pp. 65–73, al-Zaraklī, al-A'lām, vol. 6 pp. 222–223, Kaḥālah, *Mu'jam*, pp. 289–290.
196 Al-Subkī, *Ṭabaqāt*, vol. 9 pp. 100–124.
197 Ibn Rajab, *Dhayl*, vol. 2 pp. 392–393. Also, Ibn Nāṣir, *al-Radd*, p. 96. Furthermore, the style of this letter is poor and does not reflect al-Dhahabī's method of writing nor his knowledge of the Arabic language and Rhetoric. Also, it should be pointed out that some writers stated that al-Dhahabī's writing was an easy target for counterfeits and that this treatise might be one such example. See: Ibn Nāṣir, *al-Radd*, p. 69 (footnote).

It is interesting to note however that al-Wāsiṭī (d. 711/1311), who was considered to be one of Ibn Taymiyyah's students and followers, refers to the existence of a treatise in which the writer defamed Ibn Taymiyyah. Al-Wāsiṭī, *al-Tadhkirat*, p. 40. The identity of the writer is not revealed by al-Wāsiṭī, but through an analytical study of al-Wāsiṭī's book '*al-Tadhkirah*', one is able to conclude certain facts about the possible author. When al-Wāsiṭī attempted to explain the motive behind the compilation of this treatise, he mentioned that one of the reasons could be that the writer of this treatise was influenced by his old age (ibid., p. 41). In another place, al-Wāsiṭī indicates that this treatise was written to criticise Ibn Taymiyyah, a scholar who devoted his time to defending Islam at the end of the seventh century (ibid., pp. 30, 40). It can be deduced from these last two points that this treatise was written at the end of the seventh century by a writer who was old at that time. We can therefore conclude from this that the author could not have been al-Dhahabī; al-Dhahabī was 28 years old at the end of the seventh century as he was born in 673/1274. In addition, even if we considered the time of al-Wāsiṭī's death in the year 711/1311 as the time of the compilation of this treatise, he still could not have been the writer of this treatise as he was only 38 years old at that time. More clues are available through following the discussion of al-Wāsiṭī on this point. He points out that people of innovation will be gratified when they know that 'one of our followers has traduced Ibn Taymiyyah' (ibid., p. 41). It is clear from this statement that the writer was not one of those who were considered to be 'the people of innovation', but was rather one of those scholars who adopted the same line as that of Ibn Taymiyyah. If this is true, why did he write the treatise? Al-Wāsiṭī surmises that the writer was influenced by either his old age or by covetousness (ibid., p. 41).

198 Al-Karmī, *al-Kawākib*, p. 114, Little, *Ibn Taymiyyah*, p. 324.

199 For instance, Judge Jalāl al-Dīn al-Ḥanafī (see: al-Karmī, *al-Kawākib*, p. 113), Judge Ibn Makhlūf al-Mālikī (see: al-Karmī, *al-Kawākib*, pp. 115, 129) and al-Shāfi'ī judge. See: al-Karmī, *al-Kawākib*, p. 149. Also, one of his most serious opponents was al-Subkī. See: Ibn 'Abd al-Hādī, *al-Ṣārim*, pp. 18–19.

200 An example of this group is Karīm al-Dīn al-Ayākī who was the head of mashyakhat Sa'īd al-Su'adā' in Cairo. This Sheikh used to attack Ibn Taymiyyah. See: Ibn Kathīr, *al-Bidāyah*, vol. 14 p. 55.

201 Abū Hayyān was a famous scholar in the science of Arabic Language. See: Ibn Nāṣir, *al-Radd*, pp. 113–114. Al-Ḥadīthī obtained her PhD from Cairo University in the year 1964 in a study of this scholar as a grammarian and this work was published in 1966.

202 Ibn al-'Imād, *Shadharāt*, vol. 8 p. 146.

203 Al-Zamlikānī was a famous Shāfi'ī scholar and judge who died in 727/1327. See: Ibn al-'Imād, *Shadharāt*, vol. 8 p. 140.

204 Ibn Kathīr, *al-Bidāyah*, vol. 14 p. 55.

205 Ibn Nāṣir, *al-Radd*, p. 103. Al-Zamlikānī wrote two treatises criticising Ibn Taymiyyah. The first, '*Al-Radd 'alā Ibn Taymiyyah fī Mas'alat al-Ziyārah*' (criticism of Ibn Taymiyyah about the issue of visiting graves). The second, '*Al-Radd 'alā Ibn Taymiyyah fī Mas'alat al-Ṭalāq* (criticism of Ibn Taymiyyah about the issue of divorce) see: Ibn al-'Imād, *Shadharāt*, vol. 8 p. 140.

206 Al-Dhahabī, *Dhayl*, p. 24.

207 Ibid., p. 24.

208 Al-Dhahabī, *Dhayl Tārīkh*, p. 24.

209 Ibn Ḥajar, *al-Durar*, vol. 1 pp. 156, 161–162.

210 Al-Ṣafadī, *al-Wāfī*, vol. 7 p. 18.

211 Al-Bazzār, *al-I'lām*, p. 77.

212 Ibn Rajab, *Dhayl*, vol. 2 p. 395.

213 Al-Shawkānī, *al-Badr*, vol. 1 pp. 64, 70.

214 Ibn Taymiyyah, *Fatāwā*, vol. 3 p. 233.
215 Ibid., p. 245.
216 Ibid., pp. 245–246.
217 Al-Shaybānī, *Awrāq*, p. 11.
218 Ibid.
219 Al-Ṣafadī, al-*Wāfī*, vol. 7 p. 18.
220 Al-Bazzār, *al-A'lām*, pp. 35–37.
221 Al-Shawkānī, *al-Badr*, vol. 1 p. 64, al-Ṣafadī, *al-Wāfī*, vol. p. 20, Ibn Rajab, *Dhayl*, vol. 2 p. 391, al-Karmī, *al-Kawākib*, pp. 64–72, and al-Nadwī, *al-Ḥāfiẓ*, p. 284.
222 Al-Karmī, *al-Kawākib*, p. 78. It seems that al-Dhahabī intended to point out the large number of Ibn Taymiyyah's treatises without being specific about their exact number. It appears that he was not certain himself as he mentioned differing figures in other places, such as in *Dhayl Tārīkh al-Islam* and *Dhayl Tadhkirat*, where he mentioned the number of 300 volumes or more, and in *Dhayl al-'Ibar* where he mentioned the number of 200. See: al-Dhahabī, *Dhayl Tārīkh al-Islam*, p. 23 *Dhayl al-'Ibar*, p. 84, *Dhayl Tadhkirat*, p. 1497.
223 Ibn 'Abd al-Hādī, *al-'Uqūd*, pp. 64–66, al-Bazzār, *al-I'lām*, pp. 25–28. Ibn al-Qayyim in his book *Asmā'* mentions that he did not have knowledge of the exact number of his sheikh's treatises. Ibn al-Qayyim, *Asmā'*, p. 8. Abū 'Abd Allah, Ibn Rushayyiq or most likely Ibn Taymiyyah's brother, asserts that even if Ibn Taymiyyah himself wanted to specify the exact number of his treatises, he could not have done so. Ibn 'Abd al-Hādī, *al-'Uqūd*, p. 64. It should be pointed out the ascription of the book Asmāz to Ibn al-Qayyim has been questioned by the editors of *al-Jāmi'*. They assert that the author of this work was Ibn Rushayyiq, Ibn Taymiyyah's secretary. This is, also, confirmed by the contemporary Ḥanbalī scholar Abū Zayd, for details see Shams and al-'Imran, *al-Jāmi'*, pp. 10, 56–61.
224 Ibn 'Abd al-Hādī, *al-'Uqūd*, pp. 28, 368, al-Karmī, *al-Kawākib*, p. 174, and al-Ṣafadī, *al-Wāfī*, vol. 7 p. 23. In *al-Bidāyah*, we find al-Birzālī specified the amount of these treatises as 60 volumes and 14 bundles of *kurasāt* (booklets). See: Ibn Kathīr, *al-Bidāyah*, vol. 14 p. 146. Meanwhile, Ibn 'Abd al-Hādī narrated from Ibn Rushayq that these treatises were 14 packets (*ruzmah*). See: Ibn 'Abd al-Hādī, *al-'Uqūd*, p. 28. These treatises were taken to *Khizānat al-Kutub al-'Ādiliyyah* (*al-'Ādiliyyah* library), according to Ibn Kathīr in *al-Bidāyah*, vol. 14 p. 146. This was not however the abiding place of these books as al-Birzālī stated that the judges and jurists divided them amongst themselves (ibid.). It appears that either all of these books or at least some of them were taken back from the scholars mentioned earlier and were kept with al-Qazwinī, the Shāfi'ī judge of the time. Then they were handed to the next Shāfi'ī judge al-Subkī (one of Ibn Taymiyyah's opponents). In the year 742/1341, this judge was ordered by al-Fakhrī, the sultan's deputy of the time, to return the treatises. After much hesitation, the judge handed them to the deputy who in turn handed them to Zain al-Dīn 'Abd al-Raḥmān, Ibn Taymiyyah's brother, and Ibn al-Qayyim. Ibn Kathīr, *al-Bidāyah*, vol. 14 p. 215. This account differs from what Ibn 'Abd al-Hādī related in his book *al-'Uqūd* (p. 44) from Ibn Rushayq (d. 749/1348), that these books were not returned presumably. Ibn Rushayq was not aware of the recovery of these books. Perhaps Ibn Rushayq's statement was made before the restoration of these treatises. This is probable, since Ibn 'Abd al-Hādī, the author of *al-'Uqūd*, died in 744/1343 and his book must have been written before this date.
225 Al-Bazzār, *al-A 'lām*, pp. 35–37.
226 Ibn Taymiyyah was given the *ijāzah* (permission) to issue *fatāwā* by Sharaf al-Dīn al-Maqdisī, who used to pride himself in this. See: Ibn Kathīr, *al-Bidayah*, vol. 13 p. 380.
227 Ibn 'Abd al-Hādī, *al-'Uqūd*, p. 321, al-Karmī, *al-Kawākib*, p. 141.
228 Ibn 'Abd al-Hādī, *al-'Uqūd*, p. 327.
229 Ibid., pp. 223–224. It seems that Ibn Taymiyyah was well known outside al-Shām to such an extent that al-Ṣafadī in *al-Wāfī* declared that Ibn Taymiyyah's fame outside al-Shām was more than his fame in it. See: al-Ṣafadī, *al-Wāfī*, vol. 7 p. 19.

230 This book was published in 1986.
231 Ibn Taymiyyah, *al-Istiqāmah*, vol. 1 p. 3.
232 Ibid., pp. 6–24. Most of the remaining part of the book is devoted to a critique of *al-Risālah al-Qushairiyyah* by al-Qushairī. Ibid., pp. 81–473, vol. 2 pp. 3–198. The last section of this treatise is devoted to the issue of '*ḥisbah*' (a term that refers to the act of commanding what is good when it is being neglected, and forbidding what is bad if it is being practised) vol. 2 pp. 198–348.
233 Ibn al-Qayyim, *Asmā'*, pp. 19–20.
234 Ibn al-'Imād, *Shadharāt*, vol. 8 pp. 144, 145–150. Also: al-Shawkānī, *al-Badr*, vol. 1 p. 64. Al-Ṣafadī asked him various questions pertaining to *Tafsīr* and recognised that he had acquired beneficial knowledge which he had heard from no other scholar nor read in any book. See: al-Ṣafadī, *al-Wāfi*, vol. 7 pp. 20–22. Ibn Rajab explained that because of Ibn Taymiyyah's extensive knowledge on this subject, he was able to criticise other interpreters, and on occasions refuted some of their opinions. See: Ibn Rajab, *Dhayl*, vol. 2 p. 391. Ibn Taymiyyah's treatises include various examples where this scholar criticised the interpreters see, for instance, *Fatāwā*, vol. 14 pp. 48–50,68–69,455,495, vol. 16 pp. 18–32,72–73, vol. 15 pp. 30–31. It is worth remembering that Ibn Taymiyyah did not write a complete treatise in interpreting the whole of the Qur'an. See: Barakah, *juhūd*, p. 181. When Ibn Taymiyyah was urged to do so by some of his followers, he replied that there was no real need for this because some Qur'anic verses were either so clear that they required no further interpretation or they had already been adequately explained by other interpreters before him. Instead Ibn Taymiyyah agreed to target those verses which were problematic to interpreters of al-Qur'an, who therefore encountered difficulties and disagreed in their interpretations of them. Ibn Taymiyyah admitted that it was not necessary for him to cover every single verse which may be included in this category as it was possible for the readers to understand the remainder by using analogy. See: Ibn 'Abd al-Hādī, *al-'Uqūd*, pp. 43–44. In 1995, an MA thesis was submitted to al-Imām University which was an edited version of a treatise entitled (*Tafsīr Ayāt ashkalat 'alā kathir min al-'Ulamā' ḥattā lā yūjad fi ṭā'ifah min kutub al-tafsīr fīhā alqawl alṣawab bal lā yūjad fīhā illā mā huwā khaṭa'*) (Interpretation of verses were problematic to some of the interpreters to the extent that the correct interpretation of some verses were not found in some commentaries of al-Qur'an. Even worse is the presence of mistakes and inaccuracies). This book was published in 1997.
235 This is according to Ibn Taymiyyah's disciples Ibn 'Abd al-Hādī, in *al-'Uqūd*, p. 42 and al-Karmī in *al-Kawākib*, p. 78. Al-Ṣafadī, in his book *al-Wāfī* (vol. 7 p. 16), quotes a trustworthy person who heard Ibn Taymiyyah declaring that he had studied 120 Qur'anic interpretations. It appears that there is no conflict between these two narrations because in Ibn 'Abd al-Hādī's narration, Ibn Taymiyyah stated that he *may* have read about 100 books of *tafsīr*.
236 Al-Karmī, *al-Kawākib*, p. 59.
237 In his biography of Ibn Taymiyyah, al-Bazzār mentioned that he was told that Ibn Taymiyyah started writing a tafsīr, which had it been completed would have constituted fifty volumes. See: al-Bazzār, *al-I'lām*, p. 23.
238 This *Tafsīr* has been published in ten volumes.
239 This book '*Majmū' al-Fatāwā*' is a collection of various treatises and *fatāwā* by Ibn Taymiyyah. This remarkable work was created by the contemporary Ḥanbalī scholar, Ibn al-Qāsim, with the assistance of his son Muhammad. In this treatise there are five volumes (13–17) devoted to the Interpretation of the Qur'an. Furthermore, various issues of this science were mentioned in different parts of this treatise.
240 Ibn al-Qayyim, *Asmā'*, pp. 8–18.
241 Ibn 'Abd al-Hādī, *al-'Uqūd*, p. 37 and Ibn Rajab in *al-Dhayl*, vol. 2 p. 404, mention that this book of Ibn Taymiyyah was in several volumes. This book was used by

several Ḥanbalī scholars, such as al-Mardāwī in *al-Inṣāf* and Ibn al-Laḥḥām in *al-Qawā'id*. See: al-Mardāwī, *al-Inṣāf*, vol. 1 p. 15, Ibn al-Laḥḥām, *al-Qawā'id*, p. 45.

242 Ibn Taymiyyah, *Sharḥ*, book of purification, vol. 1 p. 59.

243 Al-Ḥasan, Introduction to *Sharḥ al-'Umdah*, book of *al-Ḥajj*, vol. 1 pp. 49–50.

244 For instance, see: *Sharḥ al-'Umdah*, The book of Purification, pp. 62–64.

245 Al-Ḥasan, Introduction to *Sharḥ al-'Umdah*, p. 54. Most of the parts of *Sharḥ al-'Umdah* by Ibn Taymiyyah have been edited and published and their information is as follows:

- The book of Purification was edited and submitted as a PhD thesis to the Islamic University of al-Madinah by al-'Uṭayshān in the Academic year 1403/1983 and was published by Maktabat al-'Ubaykān, Riyadh in the year 1412/1991.
- Part of the book of *Ṣalāh* was edited by al-Mushayqiḥ and published by Dar al-'Āṣimah in the year 1997.
- The book of Fasting was edited by al-Nushayrī and published by Dar al-'Ānṣārī in the year 1996.
- The book of *Ḥajj* was edited and submitted as a PhD thesis to the University of al-Imām, Riyadh and was published by Maktabat al-Ḥaramīn in the year 1988.

246 Al-Ḥasan, Introduction to *Sharḥ al-'Umdah*, book of *al-Ḥajj*, vol. 1 p. 67.

247 Ibid., p. 5.

248 The commentary by al-Maqdisī (d. 624/1227), which was the first known commentary on *al-'Umdah*, discusses the topics of the original book briefly and the commentary of Ibn 'Abd al-Mu'min (d. 739/1338) is not known to have survived. The first commentary (written by al-Maqdisī) has been published several times and the second commentary is mentioned by some Ḥanbalī scholars, such as Ibn Rajab in his treatise *al-Dhayl*, vol. 2 p. 429.

249 See for instance, *Fatāwā*, vol. 21 pp. 68–70, 74–77, vol. 22 pp. 95–98, 100–104, 132–134, 282, 288, 327–328, 342–351, 370–373, vol. 23 pp. 30–33, 177–187, vol. 25 pp. 41–47, 49, 54–55, 295–297, 320–328, vol. 26 pp. 13, 14–17, 97, 304–305, 307, vol. 27 pp. 29–35, 491–494, 502–504, 505–511, vol. 28 pp. 26, 179–180, 181–189, 210–213, 216, 236–238, 656–657, 658.

250 See for instance, *Fatāwā*, vol. 22 pp. 77–92, 335–356, 376–403, 526–601, vol. 23 pp. 5–52, 69–84, 136–173, 178–209, 209–218, 288–309, 309–327, vol. 24 pp. 33–163, 223–253, vol. 25 pp. 5–41, 103–114, 126–202, 216–259, vol. 26 pp. 160–175, vol. 27 pp. 5–19 vol. 28 pp. 121–179, 190–202.

251 Ibn Taymiyyah, *Public Policy*, p. 11.

252 Aḥmad in his introduction to Ibn Taymiyyah *al-Ḥisbah* (*Public duties in Islam*) p. 17.

253 Ibid., p. 71.

254 Ibn Ḥazm, *Marātib*, pp. 19–20. Two examples can be given: the first is an alleged consensus which is disputed by Ibn Taymiyyah, whereas the second example is proven by Ibn Taymiyyah to have been disputed by Ibn Ḥazm himself. The first concerns the issue of appointing two rulers to the Muslim Community. Ibn Ḥazm states that the scholars agreed that it is forbidden to appoint two rulers to the Muslim Community in the world, there being no difference if this was in one place or in different parts. *Marātib* p. 144. Ibn Taymiyyah states that the dispute concerning this point is well known amongst the *mutakallimūn*. He points out that the Karāmiyyah and others adopted the view that it is permissible to do so. In addition, Ibn Taymiyyah noted that the position of the leading scholars is that the Muslim Community is either to be in agreement or disagreement. In a state of agreement amongst the Muslim Community the appointment of two rulers is not allowed. If, however, the Muslim Community is divided, every part of the Islamic world appoints only one ruler. Thereafter, these different parts of the Muslim Community either live in peace with each other or fight each other (for the purpose of affirming the concept that there can be no two rulers for the Muslim Community at the same time). Ibn Taymiyyah concluded that the advantages of living

in peace preponderate over warfare which results in serious disadvantages. *Naqd* p. 216. The second example concerns the issue where a man divorced his wife and did not have witnesses for that. Ibn Ḥazm declared that there is no known disagreement amongst the scholars that the divorce is binding. *Marātib* p. 83. Ibn Taymiyyah pointed out that Ibn Ḥazm in his book entitled *al-Muḥalla* preferred the opposing viewpoint to this opinion and denied the existence of a consensus on this point. *Naqd*, p. 213.

255 Ibn Taymiyyah, *Naqd*, pp. 205–206. Ibn Taymiyyah denied the existence of an agreement amongst the scholars concerning the point that whoever contradicts a consensus is considered an unbeliever. Even al-Naẓẓām (d. 131/748), Ibn Taymiyyah adds, was not pronounced an unbeliever, although he declared that consensus is not a source of law (ibid., p. 204).

256 The contribution of every scholar can be identified through the indications left by the writer of the manuscript. If the section starts with the word *shaykhunā* (our sheikh), this means that the following section is written by Ibn Taymiyyah, and if the section starts with the words *wālid shaykhinā* (our shaykh's father), it refers to Ibn Taymiyyah's father ʿAbd al-Ḥalīm. If there is no sign at all at the beginning of a section, it means that it is written by al-Majd, Ibn Taymiyyah's grandfather. The greater portion of this book is written by the grandfather and the son.

257 Furthermore, in different parts of this treatise, the writers demonstrate a great ability to measure issues by the *uṣūl* of the Ḥanbalī School and they command an extensive knowledge of the different narrations of Imām Aḥmad. In the event of contradiction, obscurity and ambiguity among these narrations, the three scholars, and particularly the grandfather and the son, demonstrate a great ability to solve them which occasionally results in the criticism of some leading Ḥanbalī scholars. It is interesting to note that the opinions of al-Qāḍī Abū Yaʿla were cited in the bulk of the treatise's issues. It is likely that this is related to Abū Yaʿla's high status in the Ḥanbalī School; he was known as the sheikh of the School and was the first Ḥanbalī scholar who is known to have written a complete comprehensive treatise in the science of *uṣūl al-fiqh*. Accordingly, his views were granted great weight and cited in the sources compiled after that. In *al-Musawwadah*, however, the opinions of Abū Yaʿla were primarily cited for the purpose of study, criticism, refutation and occasionally for extrapolation.

258 Ibn Taymiyyah's act of starting with the classification of the two types of analogy indicates the importance of precision when dealing with legal terminology.

259 In this book, Ibn Taymiyyah, as was his custom, studied other viewpoints and determined the sources upon which they based their opinions. Thereafter, he clarified the invalidity of these sources and evidences.

260 This book also provides an interesting discussion concerning the permissibility of founding an analogy from a ruling claimed to be in opposition to analogy. Finally, the fact that this book assumes a moderate position towards the issue of analogy is another point of importance. This is because the Ẓāhiris oppose analogy, while the others accept it in addition to accepting the possibility of the existence of a conflict between text and analogy. Ibn Taymiyyah's position assumes a middle course as he accepts analogy and proves that correct analogy cannot be in opposition to text. In the event that this is found, it will necessitate that the conflicting analogy is incorrect.

261 Ibn Taymiyyah, *Fatāwā*, vol. 20 p. 231.

262 This is not a rejection by Ibn Taymiyyah of the permissibility of using *ra'y* in legal ruling. See pages 127–129 of this work.

263 See this treatise in Ibn Taymiyyah, *Fatāwā*, vol. 19 pp. 9–65.

264 Ibn Taymiyyah, *Fatāwā*, vol. 19 pp. 106–128.

265 For instance:

- *Qāʿidah fi Taṣwīb*: This essay by Ibn Taymiyyah deals with the issue of whether or not it is possible for every scholar to determine the correct ruling through the use of his own independent reasoning. Furthermore, if it is not possible and the scholar tries his best to determine the correct ruling but does not, is it possible for the scholar to commit a sin by rendering an erroneous independent reasoning? Ibn Taymiyyah, *Fatāwā*, vol. 19 pp. 203–227.

- *Qā'idah fi 'l-'Ulūm wa 'l-I'tiqādāt.* Ibn Taymiyyah, *Fatāwā*, vol. 19 pp. 129–152.
- *Qā'idah fi ajnās,* A section on the sources of law without a title. Ibn Taymiyyah *Fatāwā*, vol. 19 pp. 5–9.
- Section dealing with the sufficiency of the message of the Prophet Muhammad in the law. This essay also has no title. Ibn Taymiyyah, *Fatāwā*, vol. 19 pp. 66–76. Another similar essay in vol. 19 pp. 280–289.
- Section concerning the obligation to follow the Qur'ān and the *sunnah.* Again this essay has no title.
- Section with a similar subject to the last treatise with some other details concerning the people's need for the message. Ibn Taymiyyah, *Fatāwā*, vol. 19 pp. 93–105.
- Section dealing with what is meant by *Shar'ī* knowledge and whether or not it includes rational evidences. Ibn Taymiyyah, *Fatāwā*, vol. 19 pp. 228–235.
- Section studying legal terminology and whether they can be understood through revelation languages or the custom of the people. Ibn Taymiyyah, *Fatāwā*, vol. 19 pp. 235–260.
- Section dealing with imitation and contradiction of texts by alleged consensus or the saying of leading scholars. Ibn Taymiyyah, *Fatāwā*, vol. 19 pp. 260–276.
- Section dealing with the meaning of the *shar'ī* knowledge (*'ilm shar'ī*). Ibn Taymiyyah, *Fatāwā*, vol. 19 pp. 306–311.

266 Al-Bazzār, *al-A'lām*, p. 84, al-Karmī, *al-Kawākib*, pp. 174–175.
267 Ibid.
268 Ibn Rajab, *Dhayl*, vol. 2 p. 407.

2 A COMPARISON OF THE BASIC PRINCIPLES OF ISLAMIC LAW ACCORDING TO IBN ḤANBAL AND IBN TAYMIYYAH

1 Al-Rāzī, *al-Maḥṣūl*, vol. 1 p. 94. The translation of this definition is in *Uṣūl al-Fiqh al-Islami* by al-'Alwānī, p. 1.
2 Al-'Alwānī, *Uṣūl*, p. 1. *Uṣūl al fiqh* is similar to *uṣūl al-qānūn* of secular law in that both are concerned with the methodology of the law and rules of deduction and interpretation. Kamāli, *Principles*, p. 6.
3 Ibn al-Jawzī, *al-Manāqib*, p. 244. In the *Masā'il* of 'Abd Allah, vol. 3 p. 1355, there is a narration in which Aḥmad states that Allah mentions the obedience of the Prophet in upwards of thirty (*nayyf wa thalāthīn*) places in the Qur'an.
4 Abū Dawūd, *Masā'il*, p. 276, Abū 'l-Khaṭṭāb, *al-Tamhīd*, vol. 3 pp. 256–257.
5 Ibn al-Qayyim, *I'lām*, vol. 1 p. 61.
6 Ibn al-Jawzī, *Manāqib*, p. 244.
7 Ibn al-Qayyim, *I'lām*, vol. 1 p. 340.
8 Ibn al-Jawzī, *Manāqib*, p. 244.
9 Ibid., Ibn Badrān, *al-Madkhal*, p. 85.
10 Ibn al-Jawzī, *al-Manāqib*, p. 244. Ibn Badrān in his book *al-Madkhal*, p. 85, mentions this methodology as a narration by al-Athram from Aḥmad. This, however, seems to be inaccurate as Ibn Badrān clarifies that the reference from which he took this narration is *al-Manāqib* by Ibn al-Jawzī. Having referred to the published edition of *al-Manāqib*, it is clear that Ibn al-Jawzī narrated from al-Athram and then separately cited al-Athram mentioning his own experience with regard to the methodology employed by Aḥmad in legal rulings.

11 Ibn Abū Ya'la, *Ṭabaqāt*, vol. 1 p. 6.

12 See the biography of this scholar in the following sources: Ibn Rajab, *Dhayl*, vol. 2 p. 290, Ibn Mufliḥ, *al-Maqṣad*, vol. 2 p. 386, Ibn Badrān, *al-Madkhal*, p. 417.

13 Ibn Tamīm, *Muqaddimah*, with Ibn Abū Ya'la, *Ṭabaqāt*, vol. 2 pp. 283–285.

14 Ibn al-Qayyim, *I'lām*, vol. 1 pp. 59–64. Ibn Badrān in his book, *al-Madkhal* pp. 113–119, mentions these same general principles and it is clear, as is attested to by the book's editor, that he based his discussion of this issue on Ibn al-Qayyim's discussion in *I'lām*. Also, most contemporary writers when they mention Aḥmad's general principles of jurisprudence, they rely on the study of Ibn al-Qayyim on this issue. For examples, see Mūsā, *al-Madkhal*, p. 161, Abū Zahrah, *Ibn Ḥanbal*, pp. 215–217, al-Hazāymah, *al-Madkhal*, p. 89, al-Ṭanṭāwī, *al-Madkhal*, pp. 203–204, Ismā'īl, *al-Tashrī'*, pp. 343–344, Abū Zahrah, *Tārīkh*, pp. 491–493, Madkūr, *al-Madkhal*, p. 157, Abū Zayd, *al-Madkhal*, vol. 1 pp. 152–156, al-Ddībānī, *al-Madkhal*, pp. 268–269, al-Dar'ān, *al-Madkhal*, pp. 161–163, Shalabī, *al-Madkhal*, pp. 202–203, Sharf al-Dīn, *Tārīkh*, p. 194, Ḥassān, *al-Madkhal*, pp. 109–111, Philips, *The Evolution of Fiqh*, pp. 85–86.

15 Abū 'l-Khaṭṭāb, *al-Tamhīd*, vol. 1 p. 6.

16 Abū Ya'la (in his book *al-'Uddah* vol. 2 p. 582) seems to agree with this view as he comments on a narration from Aḥmad in which he says: 'knowledge is found in the words of the Prophet and then his companions and then their followers'. Abū Ya'la comments that Aḥmad said this because he felt that most of their opinions are based on revelation.

17 Kamali, Principles of Islamic Jurisprudence, p. 176.

18 Ibid., p. 169.

19 Ibn Qudāmah, *al-Rawḍah*, vol. 1 pp. 145–146, al-Ṭūfī, *Sharḥ al-Rawḍah*, vol. 2 p. 8.

20 Abū Zahrah, in his treatise *Tārīkh al-Tashrī'*, p. 493, concludes that Aḥmad's sources, as mentioned by some Ḥanbalī scholars such as Ibn al-Qayyim, go back to the following main sources: texts, opinions of companions (and possibly opinions of the followers), and analogy.

21 Al-Shāfi'ī, *al-Risālah*, p. 288. This also has been mentioned by Abū Zahrah, *Tārīkh*, p. 493. This view, however, has been criticised by several eminent scholars, such as al-Ghazālī, al-Ṭūfī and al-'Umarī. See: al-Ghazālī, *al-Mustaṣfā*, vol. 2 pp. 279–280, al-Ṭūfī, *Sharḥ*, vol. 3 p. 224, al-'Umarī, *al-Ijtihād*, pp. 29–33. Having said that, it can be suggested that this word '*qiyās*' came through two stages. At first, it was used as a broad term to include analogy and other sources based on the use of independent reasoning. Later, it was used solely for the source of analogy.

22 For the position of the Ḥanbalī scholars with regard to *istiṣḥāb*, see: Abū Ya'la, *al-'Uddah*, vol. 4 pp. 1262–1272, *al-Masā'il*, pp. 84–85, Abū 'l-Khaṭṭāb, *al-Tamhīd*, vol. 4 pp. 251–294, Ibn Qudāmah, *al-Rawḍah*, vol. 1 pp. 320–324, āl-Taymiyyah, *al-Musawwadah*, pp. 488–490, al-Ṭūfī, *Sharḥ*, vol. 3 pp. 147–168, Ibn Badrān, *al-Madkhal*, pp. 286–287.

23 Abū 'l-Khaṭṭāb, *al-Tamhīd*, vol. 2 pp. 411–425.

24 Ibid., vol. 1 p. 100, vol. 2 pp. 411–412.

25 Al-Ṭūfī, *Sharḥ al-Rawḍah*, vol. 2 p. 8.

26 Another possible reason why Ibn Qudāmah did not mention analogy among the agreed upon sources, is that there is disagreement among scholars with regard to the nature of analogy; is it literal in *al-tamthīl* (cast in the form of analogy) and metaphorical in *al-shumūl* (categorical syllogism) or vice versa or literal in both. The opinion of the majority of scholars is the last. The second opinion is held by Ibn Ḥazm. The first opinion is held by two leading scholars, namely: al-Ghazālī and Ibn Qudāmah. For further details of this disagreement among scholars, see Ibn Taymiyyah, *Fatāwā*, vol. 9 p. 259.

27 For the sources indicating that Ibn Taymiyyah implemented the same sources as those of Ibn Ḥanbal, see for instance, Abū Zahrah, *Ibn Taymiyyah*, pp. 376, 378, 411,

al-Manṣūr, *Uṣūl al-Fiqh*, vol. 2 p. 669, al-'Uṭayshān, *Manhaj Ibn Taymiyyah*, pp. 51, Mūsā, *Ibn Taymiyyah*, p. 165.
28 For the sources that labelled Ibn Taymiyyah as Ḥanbalī see, for instance, Laoust, *Naẓariyyāt*, p. 122, Schacht, *An Introduction*, pp. 63, 66, 72, 81.
29 Abū Zahrah, *Ibn Taymiyyah*, pp. 380, 383, 394, 411–424.
30 Al-'Uṭayshān, *Manhaj*, pp. 51–74.
31 Ibid., pp. 89–91.
32 Al-Manṣūr, *Uṣūl al-Fiqh*, vol. 1 pp. 190–200.
33 Sulaiman, *al-Fikr al-Fiqhī*, p. 22.
34 Ibid.
35 Ibn Taymiyyah, *Fatāwā*, vol. 4 p. 170.
36 Ibid., vol. 20 p. 29. Ibn Taymiyyah, *al-Qawā'id*, p. 7, *Fatāwā*, vol. 10, pp. 263–264, *Mukhtārāt*, p. 3, *Rasā'il*, vol. 3 pp. 336–337, 401.
37 Ibn Taymiyyah, *Fatāwā*, vol. 20 p. 229.
38 Ibid., vol. 20 p. 29.
39 Ibid., vol. 20 p. 330.
40 Ibid., vol. 4 p. 166.
41 Ibid., vol. 20 pp. 229–230.
42 Ibid., vol. 20 pp. 328, 331, 332.
43 Ibid., vol. 20 p. 294.
44 Ibn Taymiyyah, *Fatāwā*, vol. 20 pp. 294–295. See this *ḥadīth* in al-Bukhārī, *Ṣaḥīḥ*, vol. iii pp. 497–498, Muslim, *Ṣaḥīḥ*, vol. iv pp. 1345–1347.
45 Ibn Taymiyyah, *Fatāwā*, vol. 20 p. 299.
46 Ibid., pp. 301–302.
47 Ibid., vol. 20 pp. 312–313.
48 Ibid., pp. 314–315.
49 Ibid., vol. 20 p. 330.
50 Ibn Taymiyyah, *Fatāwā*, vol. 23 p. 398, vol. 4 pp. 177–178.
51 Ibid., pp. 309–310.
52 Ibid., p. 310.
53 Ibid.
54 Ibid., pp. 316–317.
55 Ibid., p. 332.
56 Ibid., p. 329. This narration is also mentioned by 'Abd Allah b. Aḥmad in his *Masā'il*, p. 275.
57 Ibid., p. 330.
58 Ibid., p. 319.
59 Ibid., p. 320.
60 Ibid., pp. 320–321.
61 This can be seen throughout Ibn Taymiyyah's book, *al-Qawā'id*.
62 Ibid., p. 291.
63 Ibid., p. 292.
64 Ibid., p. 293.
65 Ibn Taymiyyah, *Fatāwā*, vol. 20 p. 9.
66 Ibid., vol. 11, pp. 339–344.
67 Ibid., vol. 19 p. 5.
68 Ibid., vol. 10, p. 473, vol. 13 pp. 68–70, vol. 19 pp. 271–272.
69 Ibid., vol. 19 p. 7.
70 Ibid., vol. 20 p. 164.
71 Ibid., vol. 20 p. 573.
72 Ibid., p. 583.
73 Ibn Taymiyyah, *Kubrā*, vol. 3 p. 285.

74 For further clarification and discussion of this issue, see the section entitled 'The use of *ḍaʿīf* and *mursal ḥadīth* by Ibn Ḥanbal' in Chapter 3 of this work.
75 For further details, see ibid.
76 Ibn Taymiyyah, *Fatāwā*, vol. 20 p. 351.
77 Al-Turkī, in his book *Uṣūl Madhhab Aḥmad* (p. 428), asserts that *istiṣḥāb* is one of the various ways through which the sources of law can be implemented. Also, Ibn Salāmah in his book *al-Ta'sīs* (vol. 2 p. 145) states that to consider *istiṣḥāb* as an independent source of law, exceeds the bounds of what is acceptable *(tajāwuz ʿAẓīm)* as *istiṣḥāb* in fact is dependent on textual evidences.
78 Ibn Taymiyyah, *Fatāwā*, vol. 11 pp. 344–345.
79 Ibn Taymiyyah, *al-Qawāʿid*, p. 7, *Fatāwā*, vol. 10 pp. 263–264, *Mukhtārāt*, p. 3, *Rasā'il*, vol. 3 pp. 336–337, 401.
80 Ibn Taymiyyah, *Minhāj*, vol. 7 pp. 428–429.
81 Abū Zahrah, *Ibn Taymiyyah*, pp. 379–384, al-Manṣūr, *Uṣūl*, vol. 1 pp. 242–243.
82 For further elaboration on the reasons for the existence of incorrect opinions within the Ḥanbalī School from Ibn Taymiyyah's perspective, see the section entitled 'Incorrect *(ghalat)* Rulings in Ḥanbalī *fiqh*' in Chapter 4 of this work.
83 Ibn Khuldūn, *al-ʿIbar*, vol. 1 pp. 802–803, 806, al-Sāhī, *al-Madkhal*, p. 118, al-Hazāymah, *al-Madkhal*, pp. 100–101, Ghanāym, *fī 'l-Tashrīʿ*, p. 47, al-Ḥuṣarī, *Tārīkh*, pp. 225–226, Shalabī, *al-Madkhal*, pp. 138–139, al-Ibrahīm, *al-Madkhal*, p. 179, Zaydān, *al-Madkhal*, p. 126.
84 Al-Sāhī, *al-Madkhal*, p. 119, al-Hazāymah, *al-Madkhal*, p. 101, Ghanāym, *fī 'l-Tashrīʿ*, p. 49, al-Ḥuṣarī, *Tārīkh*, p. 226, Shalabī, *al-Madkhal*, p. 141, al-Ibrāhīm, *al-Madkhal*, p. 179, Zaydān, *al-Madkhal*, p. 126, Ibn al-Najjār, *Sharḥ al-Kawkab al-Munīr*, vol. 4 pp. 569–570.
85 Al-Sāhī, *al-Madkhal*, p. 118, al-Hazāymah, *al-Madkhal*, p. 101, Ghanāym, *fī 'l-Tashrīʿ*, p. 47, al-Ḥuṣarī, *Tārīkh*, p. 226, Shalabī, *al-Madkhal*, p. 141, al-Ibrāhīm, *al-Madkhal*, p. 179, Zaydān, *al-Madkhal*, p. 144.
86 Muhammad, *Shiekh al-Islam*, pp. 42–43.
87 For further details on educational life in Cairo in the Baḥrite Mamluk era see, Berkley, *Transmission of Knowledge in Medieval Cairo*.
88 Al-Ṣāliḥiyyah was part of Damascus, then it became a separate town after the immigration of al-Maqādisah to it. This town had a huge number of learning centres, which were affiliated to the four schools of law. Some of these centres specialised in various subjects of knowledge, such as Dūr al-Qur'an for teaching the science of Qur'an, and Dūr al-Ḥadīth for teaching the science of *Ḥadīth*. For more details of the history of al-Ṣaliḥiyyah, its schools and its scholars, see: Ibn Ṭūlūn, *Tārīkh al-Ṣāliḥiyyah*.
89 Al-Nuʿaymī, *Tārīkh al-Madāris*, vol. 1 p. 129 to vol. 2 pp. 29–126. It is worth mentioning that it has been the custom amongst contemporary writers to refer to this book by this name and to attribute it to al-Nuʿaymī. This appears to be inaccurate, however, as al-Nuʿaymī did not write his own *Tārīkh* but gave permission to one of his students to write down this treatise as mentioned in the preface of the book (vol. 1 p. 3, and also see the editor's introduction to *Tārīkh al-Madāris*). Only an abridged form of the sheikh's book was eventually issued. The author is anonymous, but from the preface of the book it appears that he had a Shāfiʿī background. See al-Nuʿaymī, *Tārīkh al-Madāris*, vol. 1 p. 3.
90 For more details on the institutions affiliated to the four schools of law, see al-Nuʿaymī, *Tārīkh al-Madāris* (Shāfiʿī, vol. 1 pp. 129–472, Ḥanafī, vol. 1 pp. 473–650, Mālikī, vol. 2 pp. 3–28 and Ḥanbalī, vol. 2 pp. 29–126).
91 In this era great attention was given to libraries, within the political circles. For instance, it was reported that king al-Mua'yyad collected more than 100,000 books in his own library. Ibn Barada, *al-Nujūm*, vol. 9 p. 253.

92 For sources on the classification of scholars, see āl-Taymiyyah, *al-Musawwdah*, pp. 546–550, Ibn al-Salāḥ, *Adab*, pp. 21–38, al-Mardāwī, *al-Inṣāf*, vol. 12 pp. 258–265, Ibn al-Najjār, *Sharḥ al-Kawkab*, vol. 4 pp. 468–471, al-Nawawī, *al-Majmū'*, vol. 1 pp. 75–77.

93 Ibn al-Qayyim, *al-I'lām*, vol. 4 pp. 266–268. Ibn al-Qayyim's classification of *mujtahids* has been used here for several reasons, one of which is that he was the student of Ibn Taymiyyah and, therefore, his classification represents the time of Ibn Taymiyyah.

94 Ibn 'Abd al-Hādī, *al-'Uqūd*, pp. 4, 24.

95 This can be supported by the fact that Ibn Taymiyyah himself in his treatise *al-Fatāwā* (vol. 26 p. 98) mentions that he wrote a book on *ḥajj*, in which he admitted following and imitating other scholars, which he subsequently rejected because it came to his knowledge that these opinions were in contradiction with the *sunnah* of the Prophet.

96 Ibn 'Abd al-Hādī, *al-'Uqūd*, p. 25.

97 Ibid., p. 12, Ibn al-'Imad, *Shadharāt*, vol. 8 p. 147. There were various scholars who agreed with this description of Ibn Taymiyyah as a *mujtahid*. For further details see, Ibid.

98 Ibn 'Abd al-Hādī, *al-'Uqūd*, p. 24.

99 Ibn Rajab, *Dhayl*, vol. 2 p. 389, Ibn al-'Imād, *Shadharāt*, vol. 8 p. 144.

100 The scholars have differed about the extent of knowledge needed for an absolute *mujtahid*. The scholars have agreed that the absolute *mujtahid* must be knowledgeable of the Qur'an and its sciences. This comprised several points, including the ability to interpret the legal verses of the Qur'an, the reasons for their revelation, knowing the abrogating and abrogated verses, their general and specific meanings. They, however, disagreed about other details related to this condition, such as whether a *mujtahid* must have knowledge of the entire Qur'an or not. Some were of the opinion that a *mujtahid* needs only to have knowledge of the legal verses, while others assert that he should have knowledge of the meaning of the entire Qur'an. They also disagreed over whether he is required to memorise the entire Qur'an or not. With regard to the knowledge of *ḥadīth*, this includes several points such as knowing the meanings of *ḥadīth*, their terminology and the authenticity of their chains. Hethlain, *Iftā'*, pp. 164–169. Also see, al-Ṭūfī, *Sharḥ*, vol. 3 pp. 577–584, Ibn Qudāmah, *Rawḍah*, vol. 2 pp. 345–349, Abū Ya'la, *al-'Uddah*, vol. 5 pp. 1594–1600, Abū 'l-Khaṭṭāb, *al-Tamhīd*, vol. 4 pp. 390–393, al-'Umarī, *al-Ijtihād*, pp. 57–117.

101 This statement will be further elaborated on and supported by examples later on in this chapter.

102 Ibn 'Abd al-Hādī, *al-'Uqūd*, p. 3.

103 Ibid., p. 7.

104 Ibid., pp. 7–8.

105 See the section entitled 'The existence of metaphor within the Arabic Language' in Chapter 3 of this work.

106 Ibn al-'Imād, *Shadharāt*, vol. 8 p. 146.

107 Ibn al-Qayyim, *I'lām*, vol. 2 p. 239. Compare this with Schacht who states that Ibn Taymiyyah did not claim *ijtihād* for himself. Schacht, *An Introduction*, p. 72. It seems that Ibn Taymiyyah was acting as a *muḥtasib* upon those who gave legal rulings without having the legal tools for *ijtihād*. They would ask indignantly whether it was the government that had placed him as a *muḥtasib* over them. He would retort that, seeing there were *muḥtasibs* for bakers and food supplies, it was only appropriate that there be one for the issuing of *Fatāwā*. See: Ibn al-Qayyim, *I'lām*, vol. 4 p. 272.

108 Ibn Taymiyyah, *Fatāwā*, vol. 26 p. 98.

109 See pp. 46–47. It should be pointed out here that Ibn Taymiyyah mentioned opinions in this book which he later on retracted. See, for instance, *Kitāb al-Ṭahārah*, pp. 62, 77, 84–85, 114, 221, 516.

110 The majority of Ibn Taymiyyah's surviving *fatāwā* are products of the final stage in his career. Although some *fatāwā* issued in the middle stage are clearly extant. This may be observed by the contradictory nature of some of the *fatāwā* found in the treatises devoted to this field. See, for instance, Ibn Taymiyyah, *Fatāwā*, vol. 21 pp. 41–43 and compare to *Fatāwā*, vol. 21 p. 35.
111 See, for instance, al-Mardāwī, *al-Inṣāf*, vol. 12 p. 259, Abū Zayd, *al-Madkhal*, vol. 1 p. 479. Al-Mardāwī asserts that the *fatāwā* and treatises of Ibn Taymiyyah testify to the correctness of the claim that he was an absolute *mujtahid.*
112 Several scholars and writers mention that Ibn Taymiyyah was an absolute dependent *mujtahid* while some describe him as an affiliated *mujtahid.* See, for example, al-Sāhī, *al-Madkhal*, 205, Zaydān, *al-Madkhal*, p. 144, Muāfī, *Taysīr*, vol. 1 p. 117.
113 Ibn Taymiyyah, *al-Musawwadah*, p. 547, al-Mardāwī, *al-Inṣāf*, vol. 12 p. 260, al-'Amrī, *al-Ijtihād*, p. 176, Abū Zayd, *al-Madkhal*, vol. 1 p. 480.
114 Ibn al-Qayyim, *I'lām*, vol. 4 pp. 147–148.
115 Ibid., p. 436. Ibn Ḥamdān mentions that Abū Ya'la declared himself to be an absolute dependent *mujtahid.* See al-Mardāwī, *al-Inṣāf*, vol. 12 p. 260.
116 Ibn al-Qayyim, *I'lām*, vol. 4 p. 267.
117 Little, Donald, 'The historical and historiographical significance of the detention of Ibn Taymiyya', p. 317.

3 RE-LAYING THE FOUNDATIONS: IBN TAYMIYYAH AND ḤANBALI *UṢŪL*

1 Ibn Taymiyyah asserts that the *sunnah* was stronger and clearer before the building of schools in the Islamic world, an activity which started during the fourth–fifth centuries. See, Ibn Taymiyyah, *Minhāj*, vol. 4 p. 129, *Fatāwā*, vol. 35 p. 41.
2 Ibn Taymiyyah in *Fatāwā*, vol. 20 p. 186.
3 Ibid., vol. 32 p. 135. In addition, on certain issues Ibn Taymiyyah mentions that the reason for Ibn Hanbal's inaccurate rulings is that he based them upon incorrect *ḥadīths*, which he assumed were authentic, whereas in fact they were not. See Ibn Taymiyyah, *Fatāwā*, vol. 21 p. 497.
4 Ibn Taymiyyah, *Fatāwā*, vol. 20 p. 229.
5 Ibid., vol. 34 pp. 111–112.
6 For instance, see Ibid., vol. 34 p. 111.
7 Ibid., vol. 24 pp. 50, 104.
8 For examples, see *al-Musawwadah*, pp. 181, 183, 188, 236, 264, 268, 327, 421.
9 For examples, see ibid., pp. 195.
10 For examples, see ibid., pp. 243–244.
11 For examples, see ibid., pp. 9, 232, *Fatāwā*, vol. 20 p. 453, *Majmū'at*, vol. 2 p. 412.
12 For examples of Ibn Taymiyyah's criticism of Abū 'l-Khaṭṭāb, see: Ibn al-Najjār, *Sharḥ*, vol. 4 p. 673, āl-Taymiyyah, *al-Musawwadah*, p. 191.
13 For examples of Ibn Taymiyyah's criticism of Ibn 'Aqīl see: āl-Taymiyyah, *al-Musawwadah*, pp. 201–202, *Majmū'at*, vol. 2 p. 412, *Fatāwā*, vol. 17 pp. 59, 513.
14 For examples, see *al-Musawwadah*, p. 408.
15 See, for examples, Ibn al-Qayyim, *Zād*, vol. 1 pp. 434–435, al-Mardāwī, *al-Inṣāf*, vol. 7 p. 270, vol. 8 pp. 88, 200, 303, 382.
16 See for example, *Fatāwā*, vol. 22 pp. 292, 621, vol. 23 p. 281.
17 Al-Āmidī, *al-Iḥkām*, vol. 1 p. 168.
18 For references to the discussions and disagreements of the scholars on these points, see, for example, Abd Rahim, *The concept of ijmā'*, p. 92, al-Ibrāhim, *al-Madkhal*, pp. 50–52, Badrān, *Uṣūl*, pp. 111–113, Zaydān, *al-Wajīz*, pp. 179–182, Salāmah, *al-Ta'sīs*, vol. 1 p. 131, al-Turkī, *Uṣūl*, pp. 347–348, al-Ṭūfī, *Sharḥ*, vol. 3 pp. 6–7, Abū Ya'la, *al-'Uddah*, vol. 4 pp. 1057–1058, Abū 'l-Khaṭṭāb, *al-Tamhīd*, vol. 3 pp. 224–357.

19 See these narrations in the following sources, Abū Ya'la, *al-'Uddah*, vol. 4 pp. 1059–1060, āl-Taymiyyah, *al-Musawwadah*, pp. 315–316, Ibn Taymiyyah, *Kubrā*, vol. 6 p. 286, 'Abd Allah, *al-Masā'il*, pp. 438–439, Abū 'l-Khaṭṭāb, *al-Tamhīd*, vol. 3 p. 247, al-Jurā'ī, *Sharḥ Mukhtaṣar*, vol. 2 pp. 460–461, al-Mardāwī, *al-Taḥbīr*, part 3 vol. 1 p. 8, Ibn al-Najjār, *Sharḥ al-Kawkab*, vol. 2 p. 213.

20 For examples, see: āl-Taymiyyah, *al-Musawwadah*, p. 316, *Fatāwā* vol. 23 p. 284, Abū Ya'la, *al-'Uddah*, pp. 1060–1061, Abū 'l-Khaṭṭāb, *al-'Uddah*, vol. 3 p. 249.

21 Ibn Qudāmah, *al-Rawḍah*, p. 276.

22 Abū Ya'la, *al-'Uddah*, vol. 4 p. 1060.

23 Abū 'l-Khaṭṭāb, *al-Tamhīd*, vol. 3 pp. 248–249.

24 Ibn Taymiyyah, *Fatāwā*, vol. 19 pp. 267–268. With Ibn Taymiyyah's clear division of consensus as a source of law into two types, it is surprising that some writers (see, for instance, Safiullah, *Wahhabism*, p. 73) referred to only one of these two types.

25 Ibn Taymiyyah, *al-Musawwadah*, p. 316. Al-Turkī, in *Uṣūl al-Imam Aḥmad* p. 359, thinks that this understanding of Ibn Taymiyyah to Aḥmad's position is weakened by the fact that the evidences testifying to the authority of consensus are applicable to all time, in the absence of evidence confining this authority to the time of the companions.

26 Ibn Taymiyyah, *al-Musawwadah*, p. 316.

27 Ibn Taymiyyah, *al-Musawwadah*, p. 316. Al-Jurā'ī, *Sharḥ Mukhtaṣar*, vol. 2 p. 462.

28 Ibn Taymiyyah, *Fatāwā*, vol. 19, p. 268. Ibn al-Qayyim asserts that Aḥmad rejects tacit consensus when it is claimed by those who have no knowledge of the agreement and disagreement of the scholars. See *I'lām*, vol. 2 pp. 245–246.

29 Abū Ya'la, *al-'Uddah*, vol. 3 pp. 938–944, Abū 'l-Khaṭṭāb, *al-Tamhīd*, vol. 3 p. 123, Ibn al-Jawzī, *al-Manāqib*, p. 244, Ibn al-Qayyim, *I'lām*, vol. 1 p. 61.

30 Abū Ya'la, *al-'Uddah*, vol. 3 p. 941.

31 Abū 'l-Khaṭṭāb, vol. 3 p. 123. It appears that Abū 'l-Khaṭṭāb is following the opinion of his Sheikh Abū Ya'la in this issue. See *al-'Uddah* vol. 3 p. 941.

32 Ibn Taymiyyah, *Minhāj*, vol. 7 pp. 34, 196.

33 Ibid., vol. 7 p. 195.

34 Ibid., vol. 8 p. 110.

35 Ibn Taymiyyah, *Fatāwā*, vol. 18 pp. 23–25, *Minhāj*, vol. 4 pp. 341–342.

36 Ibn Taymiyyah, *Minhāj*, vol. 7 p. 52. As Ibn Taymiyyah observes (*Minhāj*, vol. 7 p. 223), this does not mean that there are no weak *ḥadīth* in Aḥmad's narrations within the *Musnad*. According to Ibn Taymiyyah (*Minhāj*, vol. 7 p. 53) Aḥmad occasionally narrated weak *ḥadīths* because there are other narrations which corroborate their correctness or weakness.

37 Ibn Taymiyyah, *Minhāj*, vol. 4 p. 341.

38 Ibn al-Qayyim, *I'lām*, vol. 1 p. 61, Ibn Badrān, *al-Madkhal*, p. 116, al-Turkī, *Uṣūl*, pp. 295–296. Ibn al-Qayyim (*I'lām*, vol. 1 p. 61) asserts that generally speaking, the Imams agree with Aḥmad in giving precedence to the weak *ḥadīth* over analogy. For examples of issues where Abū Ḥanifah, Malik and al-Shāfi'ī gave precedence to weak *ḥadīth* over the use of analogy, see Ibn al-Qayyim, *I'lām*, vol. 1 pp. 61–62.

39 Ibn Taymiyyah, *Fatāwā*, vol. 10 pp. 408–409.

40 Ibid., this stance of Ibn Taymiyyah has also been cited by some Ḥanbalī scholars, such as Ibn Mufliḥ in *al-Furū'* vol. 1 pp. 568–569.

41 Al-Madkhalī, *Taqsim al-Hadith ila ṣaḥīḥ wa ḥasan wa ḍa'īf*. For further details of the grading of *Ḥadīth* see Azami, *Studies in Ḥadīth Methodology and Literature*, pp. 61–67.

42 The Ḥanbalī sources mention that there are two narrations from Ibn Ḥanbal on the use of the *mursal ḥadīth* as a source of law. The first is that it is a source of law. In the second Aḥmad accepts *mursal ḥadīth* if it is supported by the opinion of the majority of scholars and the apparent meaning of the Qur'anic text. Abū Ḥanifah and Malik agree with the first narration whereas all other scholars agree with the second. See, Abū 'l-Khaṭṭāb, *al-Tamhīd*, vol. 3 pp. 131–146, Ibn Qudāmah, *al-Rawḍah*, vol. 1

pp. 267–269, Ibn Badrān, *Nuzhat*, vol. 1 pp. 267–268, Ibn Taymiyyah, *Fatāwā*, vol. 32, p. 189. Some Ḥanbalī scholars, such as Ibn Mufliḥ in his book *Uṣūl*, vol. 2 p. 636, and Ibn al-Najjār in *Sharḥ al-Kawkab*, vol. 2 p. 577, mentions that one of the two narrations of Aḥmad on this issue is that he rejects the *mursal ḥadīth*.

43 Ibn Taymiyyah, *Minhāj*, vol. 7 p. 435. Ibn Taymiyyah mentions that one type of *mursal ḥadīth* that is definitely acceptable is the *mursal ḥadīth* which is narrated through so many chains of narrators that they could not reasonably have conspired to tell a lie. Ibn Taymiyyah, *Fatāwā*, vol. 13 pp. 347–348.

44 Ibn Taymiyyah, *al-Tafsīr al-Kabīr*, vol. 2 p. 213.

45 Abū Ya'la, *al-'Uddah*, vol. 3 pp. 917–920, Abū 'l-Khaṭṭāb, *al-Tamhīd*, vol. 4 pp. 143–144, āl-Taymiyyah, *al-Musawwadah*, p. 251, Ibn Mufliḥ, *Uṣūl*, vol. 2 pp. 633–634.

46 Ibn Taymiyyah, *al-Musawwadah*, pp. 251–252. Ibn Mufliḥ in his book *Uṣūl al-Fiqh*, vol. 2 pp. 634–635, mentions this criticism of Ibn Taymiyyah to Ḥanbalī scholars.

47 Al-Ghazālī, *al-Mustaṣfā*, vol. 1 pp. 677–680, al-Ansārī, *Fawātiḥ*, vol. 1 pp. 270–278, al-Bukharī, *Kashf*, vol. 1 pp. 61–65, Ibn Ḥabīb, *Mukhtaṣar*, p. 11, al-Juwaynī, *al-Waraqāt*, p. 29, al-Qarāfī, *Mukhtaṣar Tanqīḥ*, p. 43, *Sharḥ Tanqiḥ*, pp. 42–50, al-Shirāzī, *al-Luma'*, p. 9, al-Zarkashī, *Salāsil*, pp. 173–192, Ibn Juzayy, *Taqrīb*, p. 73, Ibn 'Abd al-Salām, *al-Imām*, pp. 235–273, al-Aṣfahānī, *Sharḥ al-Minhāj*, vol. 1 pp. 225–227, al-Khabbāzī, *al-Mughnī*, p. 131, al-Sarkhasī, *Uṣūl*, vol. 1 pp. 170–171, al-Zarkashī, *al-Baḥr al-Muḥīt*, vol. 2 pp. 178, 184–189, al-Shāshī, *Uṣūl*, p. 42. For some other works on majāz: B.G. Weiss, 'Medieval Muslim Discussions of the Origin of Language', Zeitschrift der deutschen morgenlndischen Gesellschaft. Wiesbaden (1974: 125), pp. 33–41; H. Loucel, 'L'Origine du langage d'après les grammairiens arabes', Arabica (1963: 10) pp. 188–208 and pp. 253–281; Arabica 11 (1964), pp. 57–72 and pp. 157–187, M. Shah, 'The Philological Endeavours of the Early Arabic Linguists: Theological Implications of the tawqif-istilah Antithesis and the majaz Controversy (Parts I and II)', Journal of Quranic Studies, 1:1 (1999), pp. 27–46, and 2:1 (2000), pp. 44–66, R. Arnaldez, *Grammaire et théologie chez Ibn Hazm de Cordoue* (Paris, 1956); W. Heinrichs, 'On the Genesis of the Haqıqa-Majaz Dichotomy', Studia Islamica (1984:59), pp. 111–140, W. Heinrichs, 'Contacts between scriptural hermeneutics and literary theory in Islam: the case of majaz', Zeitschrift fuer Geschichte der Arabisch-Islamischen Wissenschaften/Majallat Tarikh al-'Ulum al-'Arabiya wa 'l-Islamiya, no. 7, pp. 253–284, 1992.

48 Ibn 'Aqīl, *al-Wāḍiḥ*, vol. 1 p. 112, Abū Ya'la, *al-'Uddah*, vol. 1 pp. 172–174, *al-Masā'il*, p. 48, Abū 'l-Khaṭṭāb, *al-Tamhīd*, vol. 1 p. 249, Ibn Qudāmah, *al-Rawḍah*, vol. 1 p. 150, āl-Taymiyyah, *al-Musawwadah*, pp. 164–170, 173, Ibn Mufliḥ, *Uṣūl*, vol. 1 p. 100, al-Jurā'ī, *Sharḥ Mukhtaṣar*, vol. 1 p. 163, al-Mardāwī, *al-Taḥbīr*, part 1 vol. 1 p. 341, Ibn al-Najjār, *Sharḥ al-Kawkab*, vol. 1 pp. 149–156, 191, al-Ṭūfī, *Sharḥ*, vol. 1 p. 484, Ṣafī al-Dīn, *Qawā'id*, p. 36, Ibn Badrān, *al-Madkhal*, pp. 173–174.

49 Some individuals said that the majority of the scholars divided the language into two parts. See, for examples: Ibn Mufliḥ, *Uṣūl*, vol. 1 p. 100, al-Mardāwī, *al-Taḥbīr*, part 1 vol. 1 p. 341, Ibn al-Najjār, *Sharḥ al-Kawkab*, vol. 1 p. 191, al-Ṭūfī, *Sharḥ*, vol. 1 p. 532. Others, such as Abū Ya'la, seem to claim the existence of consensus among scholars on this issue. āl-Taymiyyah, *al-Musawwadah*, p. 170.

50 Ibn Taymiyyah, *Fatāwā*, vol. 7 p. 88, vol. 20 pp. 400–401. When Ibn Taymiyyah makes reference to the Predecessors and their acquaintance with the science of *uṣūl*, he does not mean that they were aware of the details of this science as it later became understood, nor as it later became systemised in the treatises pertaining to the principles of jurisprudence. It would appear that he is referring to their practise of issuing *fatāwā* and *ijtihād* according to the sources of Islamic law and not to any adoption of the technical terms of this science. Similarly, many rules and regulations of the Arabic language found in reference books are not known by the greater portion of native

speakers. On the whole, however, these rules and details were derived from the speech of these people.

There have been several claims in relation to the identity of the first scholar to write on the subject of *uṣūl al-fiqh.* The Ḥanafis claim that Abū Ḥanifah, Abū Yūsuf, and Ibn al-Ḥasan were the first to write on this subject. The Shāfi'īs' claim that their Imam was first. It appears that the Shāfi'īs' claim is the correct one for several reasons, two of which are the following: First, the treatise of al-Shāfi'ī is extant, unlike the alleged treatises of the three Ḥanafī scholars. Second, some scholars assert that Abū Yūsuf and Ibn al-Ḥasan wrote treatises concerning the issues on which Abū Ḥanifah gave rulings, which were then mistakenly assumed by some Ḥanafī scholars to be the books of *uṣūl.* The fact that al-Shāfi'ī was the first individual to write on this subject does not mean that scholars prior to him did not use this science. See: Abū Sulayman, *al-Fikr*, pp. 60–66, Ismā'īl, *Uṣūl*, pp. 20–30, al-Ibrāhīm, *al-Madkhal*, pp. 18–21.

51 Ibn Taymiyyah, *Fatāwā*, vol. 20 pp. 400–401.
52 Ibid., vol. 20, pp. 403–404.
53 Ibn Taymiyyah, *al-Imān*, p. 84, *Fatāwā*, vol. 7 p. 88, vol. 20 p. 403.
54 Ibn Taymiyyah, vol. 20 p. 402.
55 Ibn Taymiyyah, *al-Imān*, p. 84, *Fatāwā*, vol. 20 pp. 75, 402–403.
56 Ibn Taymiyyah, *Fatāwā*, vol. 7 p. 88, vol. 20 pp. 403–404.
57 Ibid., vol. 20 p. 404.
58 Ibn Taymiyyah, *al-Imān*, p. 84, *Fatāwā*, vol. 20 p. 404.
59 Ibid.
60 Ibn Taymiyyah, *Iqtiḍā'*, vol. 2 p. 583, *Fatāwā*, vol. 20 p. 453.
61 Abū Ya'la, *al-'Uddah*, vol. 2 pp. 695–706, *al-Masa'il*, pp. 48–49, Abū 'l-Khaṭṭāb, *al-Tamhīd*, vol. 2 p. 273, Ibn Qudāmah, *al-Rawḍah*, vol. 1 p. 150, āl-Taymiyyah, *al-Musawwadah*, pp. 164–174, al-Ghazālī, *al-Mustaṣfā*, vol. 1 pp. 677–680, Ibn Mufliḥ, *Uṣūl*, vol. 1 p. 102, al-Ṭūfī, *Sharḥ*, vol. 1 pp. 532–537, al-Jurā'ī, *Sharḥ Mukhtaṣar*, vol. 1 p. 166, Ibn Badrān, *al-Madkhal*, pp. 173–186.
62 Abū 'l-Khaṭṭāb, *al-Tamhīd*, vol. 2 pp. 239–240, Ibn Mufliḥ, *Uṣūl*, vol. 1 p. 103, al-Ṭūfī, *Sharḥ*, vol. 1 pp. 517–518, Ibn Taymiyyah, *Fatāwā*, vol. 20 pp. 405–407, Ibn al-Najjār, *Sharḥ al-Kawkab*, vol. 1 p. 191.
63 Ibn Taymiyyah, *Fatāwā*, vol. 20 pp. 407–408.
64 Ibid., p. 408.
65 Ibn Taymiyyah, *al-Imān*, p. 86, *Fatāwā*, vol. 20 p. 408.
66 Ibn Taymiyyah, *al-Imān*, p. 87, *Fatāwā*, vol. 20 pp. 408–409.
67 Ibn Taymiyyah, *Fatāwā*, vol. 20 p. 409.
68 Ibn Taymiyyah, *al-Imān*, p. 95, *Fatāwā*, vol. 20 pp. 409–410.
69 Ibn Taymiyyah, *Fatāwā*, vol. 20 pp. 409–410.
70 Ibid., vol. 20 p. 431.
71 Ibid., p. 449.
72 Abū 'l-Khaṭṭāb, *al-Tamhīd*, vol. 2 p. 265, Ibn Taymiyyah, *Fatāwā*, p. 451.
73 Ibn Taymiyyah, *al-Imān*, p. 84, *Fatāwā*, vol. 20 p. 451.
74 Ibn Taymiyyah, *Fatāwā*, vol. 20 p. 451.
75 Aḥmad did mention the term 'metaphor' in his book *al-Radd 'ala al-Jahmiyyah*, when he mentioned the use of *naḥnū* (we) by a single important person instead of *anā* (I): '*hādhā min majāz al-lughah*'. Ibn Taymiyyah was aware of this statement and relates it in his treatise *al-Imān* (p. 84). His explanation of this statement has, however, varied; in his *Fatāwā* (vol. 20 p. 451) he states that Aḥmad did not explain what he meant by that term, and Ibn Taymiyyah offers no explanation of his own; in *al-Imān* (p. 85), he states that some scholars declare that what Aḥmad meant by the word *majāz* is that the use of 'we' instead of 'I' by a single important person is *jā'iz* (permissible) and not strictly speaking 'metaphor.' Also, Abū Ya'la in *al-Masā'il* (p. 48) refers to two incidents

where Aḥmad was reported to refer to the existence of metaphor in the language. It should be pointed out that whereas Aḥmad is reported to have said '*hādhā min majāz al-lughah*', in another narration, however, he uses the phrase '*hādhā min jāaz al-lughah*'. This last statement supports Ibn Taymiyyah's explanation that what Aḥmad meant is that these linguistic usages are permitted in the language as literal usage and not as a metaphor.

76 Ibn Taymiyyah, *Fatāwā*, vol. 20 pp. 451–452, *al-Imān*, p. 84.

77 Ibn Taymiyyah, *Fatāwā*, vol. 20 p. 452, *al-Imān*, p. 92.

78 Ibn Badrān, *al-Madkhal*, p. 184, Ibn Taymiyyah, *Fatāwā*, vol. 20 p. 454, *al-Imān*, p. 85.

79 Ibn Taymiyyah, *Fatāwā*, vol. 20 pp. 437–438, 454–462. We find that some Ḥanbalī scholars allude briefly to Ibn Taymiyyah's position on metaphor. See, for instance. al-Jurā'ī, *Sharḥ Mukhtaṣar*, vol. 1 pp. 164–166, al-Mardāwī, *al-Taḥbīr*, part 1 vol. 1 pp. 341–342.

80 Ibn Taymiyyah, *Fatāwā*, vol. 19 pp. 204–211. The scholars of *uṣūl* hold various opinions on this issue. For examples, see al-Shāfi'ī, *al-Risālah*, pp. 299–303, al-Ghazālī, *al-Mustaṣfā*, vol. 2 pp. 533–587, al-Aṣfahānī, *Sharḥ al-Minhāj*, vol. 2 pp. 836–840, al-Asnawī, *Nihāyat al-Sū'l*, vol. 4 pp. 556–573, al-Shirāzī, *al-Wṣūl*, vol. 2 pp. 433–452, al-Zarkashī, *al-Baḥr*, vol. 6 pp. 235–264, al-Juwaynī, *al-Burhān*, vol. 2 pp. 1316–1324, al-Badkhashī, *Sharḥ*, vol. 3 pp. 276–284, al-Ṭūfī, *Sharḥ*, vol. 3 pp. 602–604, Ibn al-Najjār, *Sharḥ*, vol. 4 pp. 488–492, al-Shawkānī, *Irshād*, pp. 434–440, Kamali, *Principles*, pp. 383–386, al-'Amrī, *al-Ijtihād*, pp. 124–163.

81 Ibn Qudāmah, *al-Rawḍah*, vol. 2 p. 359, Ibn Taymiyyah, *Fatāwā*, vol. 19 p. 204, al-Ṭūfī, *Sharḥ*, vol. 3 p. 603.

82 Al-Ghazālī, *al-Mustaṣfā*, vol. 2 pp. 533–538, Ibn Taymiyyah, *Fatāwā*, vol. 19 p. 205.

83 Ibid., vol. 19 p. 206. Ibn al-Qayyim (in *Ẓād al-Ma'ād*, vol. 3 p. 233) criticises the opinion that Allah will exact punishment without any reason at all.

84 Abū Ya'la, *al-'Uddah*, vol. 5 pp. 1540–1541, Abū 'l-Khaṭṭāb, *al-Tamhīd*, vol. 4 pp. 307–310, Ibn Qudāmah, *al-Rawḍah*, vol. 2 p. 356, Ṣafī al-Dīn, *Qawā'id*, pp. 102–103.

85 Ibn Taymiyyah, *Fatāwā*, vol. 20 pp. 33–36, vol. 19 pp. 206–207, *Minhāj*, vol. 5 pp. 239–240. In *Minhāj al-Sunnah*, Ibn Taymiyyah states that a *mujtahid* whose intention is to adhere to what the Lawgiver decreed cannot be accused of unbelief (*kufr*), nor of transgression (*fisq*), if he practised independent reasoning and failed to ascertain the correct ruling. Ibn Taymiyyah attributes this opinion to the majority of scholars on issues of *furū'*. On issues of creed, however, most of the scholars accused the *mujtahid* who did not determine the correct opinion of unbelief (*kufr*) or transgression (*fisq*). Ibn Taymiyyah asserts that, although this opinion was widespread amongst scholars, it was not known amongst the companions, their followers, nor any of the Imams. He claims the people of innovation (*bida'*) are responsible for the creation of this opinion. According to Ibn Taymiyyah, their objective in creating such an opinion was to charge with unbelief anyone who did not agree with their innovations in the field of creed. See, *Minhāj*, vol. 5 pp. 239–240.

86 Ibn Taymiyyah, *Fatāwā*, vol. 19 p. 207.

87 Ibid.

88 Ibid.

89 See Ibn Taymiyyah's discussion of this issue in *Minhāj al-Sunnah*, vol. 5 pp. 99–125.

90 Ibn Taymiyyah, *Minhāj al-Sunnah*, vol. 5 pp. 99–100. According to Ibn Taymiyyah, what can be understood from the Qur'an and the *sunnah* with regard to the unbelievers in this world is that they are divided into two categories. The first are those who knew about Islam and rejected it and the second are those who did not hear about Islam. Ibn Taymiyyah asserts that the texts indicate that those who did not hear about Islam will be given another chance in the Hereafter. See, Ibn Taymiyyah, *Fatāwā*, vol. 31 pp. 308–310.

91 Al-Saffārīnī, *Lawāmi'*, vol. 1 p. 4, Ibn Taymiyyah, *Fatāwā*, vol. 23 p. 346. This division of the *sharī'ah* into two parts can be found in all of the published Ḥanbalī sources on *fiqh* (which is widely known as *al-furū'*) and its principles (*al-uṣūl*).
92 Ibn Taymiyyah, *Minhāj*, vol. 5 pp. 87–88, al-Ba'lī, *Mukhtaṣar*, p. 68. This claim by Ibn Taymiyyah is problematic as references to this division can be found in the works of some of the predecessors and the Imams, such as al-Shāfi'ī, Ibn Abi Ḥātim (d. 327/937), al-Dārimī (d. 280/893) and Ibn Baṭṭah (d. 387/997). See: al-Shathrī, *al-Tafrīq*, vol. 1 pp. 173–177.
93 Ibn Taymiyyah, *Minhāj*, vol. 5 p. 88, al-Ba'lī, *Mukhtaṣar*, p. 68.
94 Ibid.
95 Ibn Taymiyyah, *Minhāj*, vol. 5 pp. 88–89, al-Ba'lī, *Mukhtaṣar*, p. 68.
96 Ibn Taymiyyah, *Minhāj*, vol. 5 p. 89.
97 Ibid., p. 89, al-Ba'lī, *Mukhtaṣar*, p. 68.
98 Ibid., p. 89.
99 Ibid., pp. 89–90.
100 Ibn Taymiyyah, *Fatāwā*, vol. 5 p. 91. Ibn Kathīr mentions that there are two narrations regarding the response of Allah to this supplication, in the first Allah says 'Yes' and in the second He says 'I have done'. Ibn Kathīr, *Tafsīr*, vol. 1 p. 513.
101 Ibn Taymiyyah, *Fatāwā*, vol. 19 p. 210, *Manhāj*, vol. 5 p. 91.
102 Ibid.
103 Ibn Taymiyyah, *Fatāwā*, vol. 19 p. 211, *Minhāj*, vol. 4 p. 91.
104 Ibid.
105 Ibn Taymiyyah, *Minhāj*, vol. 4 p. 92, *Fatāwā*, vol. 19 p. 212.
106 Ibn Taymiyyah discussed this point on several occasions. See for example *Fatāwā*, vol. 5 pp. 5–12, 155–156, vol. 4 pp. 141–143, vol. 16 pp. 439–440.
107 Ibn Taymiyyah, *Fatāwā*, vol. 3 pp. 306–307, vol. 12 pp. 113–114.
108 Ibid., p. 307. The division of the *sharī'ah* into *uṣūl* and *furū'* is also discussed briefly by Ibn Taymiyyah in *al-Tafsīr al-Kabīr*, vol. 1 pp. 231–232.
109 Ibn Taymiyyah, *Fatāwā*, vol. 22 p. 331, vol. 19 p. 280.
110 Ibn Taymiyyah, *Fatāwā*, vol. 19 p. 281, al-Ṭūfī, *Sharḥ*, vol. 3 p. 229, Abū 'l-Khaṭṭāb, *al-Tamhīd*, vol. 3 pp. 435–436.
111 Ibn Taymiyyah, *Fatāwā*, vol. 19 p. 281.
112 Ibid. Also, Ibn Taymiyyah, *Minhāj*, vol. 6 pp. 411–412.
113 Ibid., pp. 281–283.
114 When the cause is neither stated nor alluded to in the text, then the only way to identify it is through independent reasoning. There are three methods used for this:

1 *Takhrīj al-manāṭ* (extracting the cause): This method is the starting point in an inquiry concerning the identification of the cause. The effective cause is extracted by looking at the relevant possible causes. The jurist may identify more than one cause. Then he moves to the next stage.
2 *Tanqīḥ al-manāṭ* (isolating the cause): The jurist takes into consideration the attributes of the original case, and only that attribute which is considered to be relevant (*munāsib*) is identified as the cause.

The difference between these two stages is that in *takhrīj al-manāṭ*, the jurist is dealing with a situation no cause has been identified, whereas in *tanqīḥ al-manāḥ*, more than one cause has been identified and his task to select the proper cause.

3 *Taḥqīq al-mamāt* (ascertaining the present of a cause in individual cases): See, Ṣafi al-Dīn, *Qawā'id*, pp. 82–83, al-Ṭūfī, *Sharḥ*, vol. 3 pp. 233–245, al-Zarkashī, *al-Baḥr al-Muḥīṭ*, vol. 5 pp. 255–258, al-Shawkānī, *Irshād*, pp. 363, 375–376, Ibn Taymiyyah, *Minhāj*, vol. 2 pp. 474–475, Kamali, *Principles*, pp. 213–214.

115 Ibn Taymiyyah, *Fatāwā*, vol. 19 pp. 281–282. It may appear that it makes no difference whether a ruling is obtained through the use of the source text or is determined by analogy but in reality it is of great importance. For if a ruling is based upon a text itself, it must be adhered to by all scholars. This is founded upon the principle that the text is accepted as the first source of law for all the schools of law. If, however, the ruling is founded upon analogy, it can be rejected by those who do not recognise analogy as a source of law. In the event that it is not rejected completely, it can be criticised as being doubtful or as an incorrect analogy.
116 Ibid., p. 289.
117 Ibid., p. 288.
118 Ibid., pp. 7–8, 285–289, vol. 20 pp. 504–505, vol. 21 p. 540, vol. 34 p. 210.
119 Ibn Taymiyyah, *Fatāwā*, vol. 20 p. 505.
120 Ibid., vol. 20 p. 505.
121 Ibid.
122 Ibid.
123 Ibn Taymiyyah, *Fatāwā*, vol. 20 p. 505.
124 It appears that the vast majority of Ḥanbalī scholars subscribe to this claim; Ibn al-Laḥḥām, the author *of al-Qawāʿid al-Uṣūliyyah*, mentions that this opinion was held by '*aṣḥābunā*' (i.e. our fellow Ḥanbalī scholars) and others and he attributed the opposite opinion to Ibn Taymiyyah alone. See, Ibn al-Laḥḥām, *al-Qawāʿid*, p. 163. Also, al-Mardāwī conveys this statement of Ibn al-Laḥḥām without commenting on it. See, *al-Inṣāf*, vol. 6 p. 3. There are various rulings claimed by various Ḥanbalī scholars to be in opposition to analogy. See, Ibn al-Bannā, *al-Muqniʿ*, vol. 1 p. 238, Ibn Mufliḥ, *al-Furūʿ*, vol. 4 p. 420, al-Buhūtī, *Sharḥ*, vol. 2 p. 351, *al-Inṣāf*, vol. 6 p. 3, Ibn al-Najjār, *Muntahā*, vol. 1 p. 357, al-Karmī, *Ghāyat*, vol. 2 p. 186. Ibn al-Qayyim studies several legal rulings claimed by some scholars, such as Abū Yaʿla, Abū 'l-Khaṭṭāb, and Ibn Qudāmah, to be in contradiction with analogy in *al-Iʿlām* vol. 1 pp. 472–521, vol. 2 pp. 5–37. Ibn al-Qayyim says that in his discussion of this issue he benefited from what he learned from his sheikh Ibn Taymiyyah. Ibn al-Qayyim, *Iʿlām*, vol. 1 p. 472.
125 Ibn Taymiyyah, *Fatāwā*, vol. 20 pp. 567–568.
126 Ibid.
127 Ibid.
128 Ibid., pp. 506–508.
129 Ibid., p. 509.
130 Ibid.
131 Ibid.
132 Ibid., pp. 509–510.
133 Ibid., pp. 555–583.
134 Ibn Taymiyyah, *Fatāwā*, vol. 19 p. 18.
135 This opinion is a narration in the Ḥanbalī School and was also held by several leading Ḥanbalī scholars, such as al-Khiraqī, al-Sharīf Abū Jaʿfar, Ibn ʿAqīl and al-Shirāzī. Furthermore, it was the preferred opinion of Ibn Qudāmah and Ibn Razīn. See: Al-Majd, *al-Muḥarrar*, vol. 2 p. 172, al-Mardāwī, *al-Inṣāf*, vol. 4 p. 131, *Taṣḥīḥ*, vol. 6 pp. 213–214, al-Maqdisī, *al-ʿUddah*, p. 590, Ibn Mufliḥ, *al-Furūʿ*, vol. 6 pp. 213–214, al-Zarkashī, *Sharḥ*, vol. 6 pp. 468–470.
136 Ibn Taymiyyah, *Fatāwā*, vol. 19 p. 18.
137 Ibid., p. 19.
138 Ibid., It is important to note that some of the later Ḥanbalī sources have mentioned only this opinion in relation to this issue, and have not mentioned the predominant opinion of the Ḥanbalī School. For instance, Ibn al-Najjār, *al-Muntaha*, vol. 1 p. 231, al-Buhūtī, *Sharḥ*, vol. 2 pp. 98–99.

139 This is the predominant opinion in the Ḥanbalī School according to al-Mardāwī in *al-Inṣāf* vol. 4 p. 217. Also, this opinion is mentioned by other Ḥanbalī scholars, such as Al-Khiraqī, *Mukhtaṣar*, p. 252, al-Majd, *al-Muḥarrar*, vol. 2 p. 182, Ibn al-Bannā, *al-Muqni'*, vol. 3 p. 1158, al-Maqdisī, *al-'Uddah*, pp. 614–615, Ibn al-Qayyim, *Aḥkām*, vol. 1 p. 3, Ibn Mufliḥ, *al-Furū'*, vol. 6 p. 259, al-Zarkashī, *Sharḥ*, vol. 6 pp. 448–449, Ibn al-Najjār, *al-Muntaha*, and al-Buhūtī, *Sharḥ*, vol. 2 pp. 128–129.

140 Ibn Taymiyyah, *Fatāwā*, vol. 19 pp. 19–23. Ibn al-Qayyim supports the stance of his sheikh. See Ibn al-Qayyim, *Aḥkām*, vol. 1 pp. 6, 9.

141 Al-Buhūtī, *al-Rawḍ*, p. 477, Ibn Qāsim, *Ḥāshiyat*, vol. 7 p. 424, Ibn Mufliḥ, *al-Furū'*, vol. 6 p. 296.

142 See, al-Mardāwī, *al-Inṣāf*, vol. 10 p. 357.

143 Ibn Taymiyyah, *Fatāwā*, vol. 19, pp. 24–26. Ibn Taymiyyah's opinion has been cited by several Ḥanbalī scholars, such as Ibn Mufliḥ, *al-Furū'*, vol. 6 p. 297, al-Mardāwī, *al-Inṣāf*, vol. 10 p. 357, Ibn Qāsim, *Hāshiyat*, vol. 7 p. 424, and al-'Anqirī, vol. 3 p. 347. In most of these sources, Ibn Taymiyyah is cited as asserting that the correct position of Aḥmad and the former Ḥanbalī scholars is that the views of the Arabs have no effect on the permissibility and prohibition of an act. He also states that the first Ḥanbalī scholar who is known to have established this rule is al-Khiraqī. According to Ibn Taymiyyah, this scholar restricted this rule to the consumption of animals that eat carrion. Ibn Taymiyyah also mentions that al-Khiraqī followed al-Shāfi'ī in this rule. Ibn Taymiyyah's statement contradicts the clear and general statement of al-Khiraqī in *al-Mukhtaṣar* (p. 257), where he says: 'what the Arabs described as good is considered lawful, and what they described as foul is considered forbidden.'

144 Al-Majd, *al-Muḥarrar*, vol. 1 p. 108, Ibn Mufliḥ, *al-Furū'*, vol. 2 pp. 4–5, al-Mardāwī, *al-Inṣāf*, vol. 2 pp. 245–246, al-Zarkashī, *Sharḥ*, vol. 2 p. 82, al-Najjār, *al-Muntaha*, vol. 1 p. 86, al-Buhūtī, *Sharḥ*, vol. 1 p. 255, *Kashshāf*, vol. 1 p. 472, al-Karmī, *Ghāyat*, vol. 1 p. 190, Ibn 'Atīq, *Nayl*, p. 49. There are some differences within the Ḥanbalī School concerning who is the most deserving to lead the prayer. Those individuals who have the right to lead the prayer are mentioned in the following statement of al-Khiraqī:

> The best reciter of the Qur'an amongst the congregation leads the prayer. If the followers are as correct as the imam in the recitation of the Qur'an, the most learned of them concerning *fiqh* leads the prayer. If the followers are as knowledgeable as the Imam in relation to *fiqh*, the oldest one amongst them leads. If they are all of the same age, the *ashraf* (the most noble) of them leads. If they are all on the same level of *sharaf* (nobility), the individual who performed the *hijrah* the earliest leads the prayer.
>
> (Al-Khiraqī, *al-Mukhtaṣar*, p. 51)

As mentioned earlier, the Ḥanbalī scholars have differed about the correct arrangement for selecting the Imam for prayer. In addition, they have differed about the exact meaning of the term '*ashraf*,' whether it refers to the tribe of the Quraysh, or applies to all people of nobility. Ibn Qudāmah, *al-Mughnī*, vol. 2 p. 447, Ibn Mufliḥ, *al-Nukat*, vol. 1 p. 109, al-Zarkashī, *Sharḥ*, vol. 2 p. 85. According to both of these opinions, the Arabs are given precedence over non-Arabs in leading the prayer.

145 This *ḥadīth* is narrated by Muslim in his *Ṣaḥīḥ* (on the section about who is more deserving to be the Imam), vol. I pp. 326–327. It should be pointed out that in most narrations of this *ḥadīth*, precedence is given to the older over the younger. Muslim, vol. i pp. 326–327, Abū Dawūd, Section on who is more deserving to be the Imam, vol. 1 pp. 390–391, al-Tirmidhī, Section on who is more deserving to be the Imam, vol. 2 pp. 458–459. Ibn Taymiyyah, however, in *al-Fatāwā* mentions that what is meant here is the one who embraced Islam first and not the one older in age. This

view of Ibn Taymiyyah seems to be based on the narration mentioned earlier of this *ḥadīth*. This position is also taken by Ibn Qudāmah, who asserts the existence of a narration supporting his opinion in which the Prophet says: 'If they are equal in relation to the emigration, then the one who embraced Islam first.' See Ibn Qudāmah, *al-Mughnī*, vol. 2 p. 447.

146 Ibn Taymiyyah, *Fatāwā*, vol. 19 p. 26.

147 Ibid., p. 27.

148 Ibid., Ibn Taymiyyah's opinion asserting that the Arabs have no precedence in leading the prayer has been mentioned by several leading Ḥanbalī scholars, such as Ibn Mufliḥ in *al-Furū'*, vol. 2 p. 5, and al-Mardāwī in *al-Inṣāf*, vol. 2 p. 246.

149 There are two narrations within the Ḥanbalī School on the condition of equality between the man and woman in marriage. The first narration states that equality between the man and woman is a condition for a marital contract to be binding; this is the opinion of several leading Ḥanbalī scholars, such as al-Khiraqī and al-Zarkashī. The second narration states that equality is a condition only for the correctness of the contract. This second narration is adopted by several eminent Ḥanbalī scholars, such as al-Majd, Ibn Mufliḥ, Ibn Qudāmah and al-Mardāwī. Certain other Ḥanbalī scholars state that if a woman accepts a man, even though he is not equal to her, the marriage will be considered valid. They based their opinion upon the principle that it is the woman's right to ask for the condition of equality. Therefore, if she abandons it, the marriage is nevertheless considered legitimate. The outcome of this dispute is that, according to the first narration, which states that the condition of equality is a condition for the contract of marriage to be binding, the aspect of equality is a right for the woman and her *awliyā'* (guardians). Therefore, if this condition is absent, the validity of the contract will be based upon the consent of the woman and her *awliyā'*. However, according to the second narration, the condition of equality is the right of Allah, the woman and her *awlayā'*. The consent of Allah cannot be known and therefore the contract is invalid. Al-Majd, *al-Muḥarrar*, vol. 2 pp. 18–19, Ibn Qudāmah, *al-Muqni'*, vol. 3 p. 29, Ibn Taymiyyah, *Fatāwā*, vol. 19 p. 28, vol. 32 pp. 56–57, Ibn Mufliḥ, *al-Furū'*, vol. 5 p. 189, al-Mardāwī, *al-Inṣāf*, vol. 8 pp. 105–107, al-Zarkashī, *Sharḥ*, vol. 5 pp. 59–62, Ibn 'Asbaslar, *al-Tashīl*, p. 152, al-Najjār, *al-Muntaha*, al-Buhūtī, *Sharḥ*, vol. 3 pp. 26–27.

150 Ibn Taymiyyah, *Fatāwā*, vol. 19 pp. 28–29.

151 Ibid., pp. 29–30.

152 Ibid., p. 30.

153 Ibid., pp. 30–31.

154 āl-Taymiyyah, *al-Musawwadah*, p. 450.

155 Ibn Qudāmah, *al-Rawḍah*, vol. 1 pp. 340–341, Ibn al-Najjār, *Sharḥ*, vol. 4 p. 433.

156 Ibn Qudāmah, *al-Rawḍah*, vol. 1 pp. 341–342.

157 Ibid., vol. 1 pp. 341–342.

158 Al-Turkī, *Uṣūl*, p. 478.

159 Ibn Taymiyyah, *Fatāwā*, vol. 11 pp. 342–343.

160 Ibid., p. 345.

161 Ibid.

162 Ibid.

163 Ibid., vol. 3 p. 371.

164 Ibid., vol. 13 p. 345.

165 Ibn Mufliḥ, *al-Furū'*, vol. 6 pp. 101, 115–116.

166 Ibid., vol. 13 pp. 96–97.

167 Ibid., p. 344.

168 Ibid., p. 345.

169 Ibid., p. 343.

170 Ibn Taymiyyah, *Kubrā*, vol. 6 p. 145.
171 Ibid.
172 Ibid.
173 Ibn Taymiyyah, *Fatāwā*, vol. 19 pp. 199–200.
174 Ibn al-Qayyim, *I'lām*, vol. 1 pp. 103–104.
175 Ibn Taymiyyah, *Fatāwā*, vol. 19 pp. 228–234.
176 Ibn Taymiyyah authored a treatise entitled *Dar' Ta'ārḍ al-'Aql wa 'l-Naql* which was devoted to refuting the claim of some of the philosophers that there is sometimes a contradiction between a text and reason. They state that when this conflict exists, 'reason' will be given precedence over the text, which should then be reinterpreted or suspended. Ibn Taymiyyah asserts this claim is incorrect as correct reasoning always agrees with correct text. The late scholar Muhammad Rashād Sālim, who edited this treatise, obtained his PhD in 1958 from Cambridge University on his work entitled 'The agreement of reason and revelation in Ibn Taimiya.'
177 Abū Ya'la, *al-'Uddah*, vol. 3 p. 724, Ibn Qudāmah, *al-Rawḍah*, vol. 2 p. 50, āl-Taymiyyah, *al-Musawwadah*, p. 181, al-Ṭūfī, *Sharḥ*, vol. 2 p. 688, Ibn Badrān, *al-Madkhal*, p. 270.
178 Āl-Taymiyyah, *al-Musawwadah*, p. 181, Ibn Qudāmah, *al-Rawḍah*, vol. 2 p. 50. Some of these scholars point out that those who permit the legislation of a ruling which cannot be practised and also permit the postponement of clarifications of rulings even though they are needed. See: Ibn Badrān, *Nuzhat*, vol. 2 p. 51, and al-Ṭūfī, *Sharḥ*, vol. 2 p. 688.
179 Āl-Taymiyyah, *al-Musawwadah*, pp. 181–182.
180 Ibn Taymiyyah, *Fatāwā*, vol. 20, pp. 50–51.
181 Ibid., p. 57.
182 Ibid., pp. 58–59.
183 Ibid., p. 59.
184 Ibid.
185 Ibid.
186 Ibid., p. 60.
187 Ibid., pp. 60–61.
188 Abū Ya'la, *al-'Uddah*, vol. 4 pp. 1217–1218, Abū 'l-Khaṭṭāb, *al-Tamhīd*, vol. 4 pp. 396–398, Ibn Qudāmah, *al-Rawḍah*, vol. 2 p. 388, āl-Taymiyyah, *al-Musawwadah*, p. 458, al-Ṭūfī, *Sharḥ*, vol. 3 pp. 656–657, Ibn Badrān, *al-Madkhal*, p. 389.
189 Abū 'l-Khaṭṭāb, *al-Tamhīd*, vol. 4 p. 396, āl-Taymiyyah, *al-Musawwadah*, p. 461, al-Ṭūfī, *Sharḥ*, vol. 3 p. 656, Ibn Badrān, *al-Madkhal*, p. 389. Ibn Taymiyyah defines 'Necessary knowledge' as 'knowledge which is inseparable from a person's soul', *Fatāwā*, vol. 2 pp. 76–77, vol. 4 pp. 43–44. For a discussion of the definition and limits of 'Necessary knowledge' see, Abū Ya'la, *al-'Uddah*, vol. 1 pp. 80–82, Abū 'l-Khaṭṭāb, *al-Tamhīd*, vol. 1 pp. 42–43. Ibn al-Laḥḥām, *al-Mukhtaṣar*, p. 36, al-Juwaynī, *al-Waraqāt*, p. 28, Ibn Mufliḥ, *Uṣūl*, vol. 1 pp. 31–32, Also, see: Abrahamov, 'Necessary knowledge in Islamic theology', in *British Journal of Middle Eastern Studies*, vol. 20 no. 1 1993 pp. 20–32. This article is confined, as its author clarifies, to the Mu'tazilte and Ash'arite sources. One of the definitions mentioned in this article is that of al-Baghdadī (d. 428/1037) in which he defines 'Necessary knowledge' as 'occurring without man's having power to produce and prove it'.
190 Abū Ya'la, *al-'Uddah*, vol. 4 pp. 1225–1226, Abū 'l-Khaṭṭāb, *al-Tamhīd*, vol. 4 p. 399, Ibn Qudāmah, *al-Rawḍah*, vol. 2 p. 389, āl-Taymiyyah, *al-Musawwadah*, pp. 458–459, al-Ṭūfī, *Sharḥ*, vol. 3 pp. 652–653, Ibn Badrān, *al-Madkhal*, p. 389.
191 Abū Ya'la, *al-'Uddah*, vol. 4 p. 1229, Abū 'l-Khaṭṭāb, *al-Tamhīd*, vol. 4 p. 408, Ibn Qudāmah, *al-Rawḍah*, vol. 2 p. 376, āl-Taymiyyah, *al-Musawwadah*, p. 468, Ṣafī al-Dīn, *Qawā'id*, p. 104, al-Ṭūfī, *Sharḥ*, vol. 3 pp. 629–632, Ibn Badrān, *al-Madkhal*, p. 389. Some scholars, such as, Ibn Badrān, *Nuzhat*, pp. 376–377, claim there is an agreement that a *mujtahid* is not permitted to imitate another scholar. This, however, is problematic

as conflicting opinions can be found in various sources of *uṣūl al-fiqh*, including some of the references cited earlier. It should be pointed out that if what is meant here by agreement is the agreement of the Ḥanbalī scholars, this will be possible, as it does not seem that there is a dispute within the School on this issue. It is clear also that scholars agree that when a scholar has reached a conclusion on any matter based on his own independent reasoning regarding an issue, he is not allowed to imitate another scholar. See Ibn Qudāmah, *al-Rawḍah*, vol. 2 p. 376.

192 Al-Shirāzī, *al-Luma'*, p. 119, *Sharḥ al-Luma'*, vol. 2 p. 1013. The attribution of this opinion to Ahmad by al-Shirāzī is mentioned by several Ḥanbalī scholars. See Abū 'l-Khaṭṭāb, *al-Tamhīd*, vol. 4 p. 409, āl-Taymiyyah, *al-Musawwadah*, p. 469, Ibn Badrān, *al-Madkhal*, p. 389. Al-Ṭūfī conveys this opinion from al-Āmidī (and not from al-Shirāzī). See, *Sharḥ*, vol. 3 pp. 629–632. It appears that the majority of Ḥanbalī scholars who transmit this opinion from al-Shirāzī did so because he attributed it to Aḥmad before al-Āmidī. It can be said that al-Āmidī was quoting al-Shirāzī's words when he attributed this opinion to Aḥmad. Some Ḥanbalī scholars, however, such as Ibn Mufliḥ in *Uṣūl*, vol. 4 p. 1516, state that some of the Ḥanbalis mention this view as an opinion in the School.

193 Ibn Taymiyyah, *Fatāwā*, vol. 20 p. 202.

194 Ibid., pp. 202–203.

195 Ibid., pp. 203–204.

196 Ibid., p. 204.

197 Ibn Taymiyyah, *Fatāwā*, vol. 20 pp. 212–213.

198 Ibid., p. 213.

199 Bukhārī in his *Ṣaḥiḥ* vol. IX pp. 289–290, Muslim in his *Ṣaḥiḥ*, vol. IV pp. 1256–1257.

200 Ibn Taymiyyah, *Fatāwā*, vol. 20 pp. 213–214.

201 Ibid., vol. 20 pp. 215–216.

202 Ibn Taymiyyah, *Minhāj*, vol. 2 p. 244, *Fatāwā*, vol. 20 pp. 225–226. Ibn Taymiyyah instead mentions that this opinion is attributed to the Ḥanafī scholar Muhammad b. al-Ḥasan. See, *Fatāwā*, vol. 19 p. 261. It is clear also that several Ḥanbalī scholars reject the attribution of this opinion to Aḥmad. See, for instance, Abū'l-Khaṭṭāb, *al-Tamhīd*, vol. 4 pp. 409–410, āl-Taymiyyah, *al-Musawwadah*, p. 468, al-Ṭūfī, *Sharḥ*, vol. 3 p. 631. It seems that there are two possible reasons for the attribution of this opinion to Aḥmad by al-Shirāzī. The first is that Abū Ḥāmid, according to *al-Musawwadah* (p. 468), attributed this opinion to some of the Ḥanbalīs. The second possible reason relates to a statement of Abū Ya'la in *al-'Uddah*. He mentions that Abū Ḥanīfah and Muhammad [Ibn al-Ḥasan] were of the opinion that it is permissible for a scholar to imitate (*yqallid*) another scholar. Abū Ya'la states that this opinion was narrated by Abū Sufyān in his *Masā'il* 'from him' (*'anhu*). After consulting the books of Ḥanbalī *Tabaqāt* (Abū Ya'la, *Ṭabaqāt*, vol. 1 p. 396, Ibn Mufliḥ, *al-Maqṣad*, vol. 3 p. 72), we find that one of Aḥmad's students, who narrated some *Masā'il* from him, was called Abū Sufyān. Abū Sufyān was a narrator of Aḥmad's opinions and he was not known to narrate Abū Ḥanifah's or Muḥammad b. al-Ḥasan's. Therefore, if Abū Ya'la was narrating the opinion of these two scholars rather than that of Aḥmad, he would have expressly referred to the sources of these two scholars. The narrator from Aḥmad, who was known to ask him about the opinions held by Abū Ḥanifah and his student was Ismā'īl b. al-Shalinjī (d. 230/) not Abū Sufyān. See, Ibn Taymiyyah, *Fatāwā*, vol. 34 p. 114, Ibn Mufliḥ, of *al-Maqṣad*, vol. 1 p. 261. It ought to be noted, however, that Abū Ya'la in several places of *al-'Uddah* attributes opinions to some scholars based on the authority of Abū Sufyān al-Sarkhasī al-Ḥanafī. Abū Ya'la, *al-'Uddah* vol. 2 pp. 349, 591, vol. 3 pp. 737, 766, 887, 918, 969, 983, vol. 4 pp. 1106, 1119, 1159, 1171, 1209, vol. 5 pp. 1433, 1548. Therefore, it seems that the attribution of this opinion to Aḥmad is based on a misunderstanding as to which Abū Sufyān was mentioned by Abū Ya'la. This assumption can be supported by the following points.

First, Abū Sufyān al-Sarkhasī al-Ḥanafī had his own *Masā'il.* Abū Ya'la, *al-'Uddah* vol. 2 p. 528; second, we find in *al-Musawwadah* that the aforementioned opinion is narrated 'from both of them' (*'anhumā*). This indicates that this opinion is attributed by Abū Sufyān to Abū Ḥanifah and Muhammad Ibn al-Ḥasan and not to Aḥmad. Note that the word (*'anhumā*) is placed between two brackets like this [ ] which indicates, according to the editor of the book, that this word was not clear, at least in one of the book's manuscripts.

203 Ibn Taymiyyah, *Fatāwā*, vol. 20 p. 226.
204 Ibid., p. 210.
205 Ibid., p. 9.
206 Ibid., pp. 224–225.
207 Ibid., pp. 208–209.
208 Ibid., p. 209.
209 Ibid., p. 222.
210 Ibn Taymiyyah, *Fatāwā*, vol. 22 p. 248, vol. 35 pp. 366–367.
211 Ibid., vol. 20 p. 208.
212 Ibid., pp. 211–212.
213 Ibid., pp. 220–226.
214 Ibid., pp. 8–9.
215 Ibn Taymiyyah was asked by a questioner whether it was permissible for the followers of the four schools to pray behind one another. He responded that it was permissible and that this was the practice of the predecessors and the early followers of the four schools. Ibn Taymiyyah asserts that anyone who rejected this would be considered a *mubtadi'* (innovator) as his opinion is against the Qur'an, *sunnah* and the consensus of the predecessors and imams. Ibn Taymiyyah, *Fatāwā*, vol. 23 pp. 373–374.
216 Ibid., vol. 22 pp. 254–255.
217 Ibid., vol. 20 pp. 220–221.
218 Ibid., vol. 22 p. 254.
219 Abū Ya'la, *al-'Uddah*, vol. 4 pp. 1142–1151.
220 Abū'l-Khaṭṭāb, *al-Tamhīd*, vol. 3 pp. 273–277.
221 Ibn Qudāmah, *al-Rawḍah*, vol. 2 pp. 298–300.
222 Āl-Taymiyyah, *al-Musawwadah*, pp. 331–333.
223 Ibn Mufliḥ, *Uṣūl*, vol. 2 pp. 410–411.
224 Ibn al-Laḥḥām, *al-Mukhtaṣar*, p. 76.
225 Ibn al-Najjār, *Sharḥ al-Kawkab*, vol. 2 p. 237.
226 Ibn Badrān, *al-Madkhal*, p. 283.
227 Ibn Qudāmah, *al-Rawḍah*, vol. 2 p. 300.
228 Āl-Taymiyyah, *al-Musawwadah*, pp. 332–333, Ibn Mufliḥ, *Uṣūl*, vol. 2 p. 411. It appears that Ibn 'Aqīl's opinion was influenced by the view of certain Mālikī scholars who subscribe to the same opinion. Al-Majd in *al-Musawwadah* describes this opinion as an attempt to evade the real issue at hand (ibid., p. 332). Some later Ḥanbalī scholars who came after the time of Ibn Taymiyyah such as al-Jurā'ī (*Sharḥ al-Mukhtaṣar*, vol. 2 pp. 477–480) and al-Mardāwī (*al-Taḥbīr*, part 2 vol. 1 pp. 62–67), provided some clarifications of the consensus of Ahl al-Madīnah, but often failed to clarify the School's position on this issue.
229 Ibn Taymiyyah, *Fatāwā*, vol. 20 pp. 303–304.
230 Ibid., p. 304. Dutton comments on Ibn Taymiyyah's statement regarding this first category of *'amal*,

> However, in view of the fact that differences remained between the *madhhabs* as to how, for example, the *adhān* should be done, or whether or not the *basmala* should be recited at the beginning of the prayer, this claim

of Ibn Taymiyyah's is, as 'Iyāḍ's comments on the non-Madinans preferring to follow their own local traditions plainly indicate, not wholly correct. (Dutton, *The Origins of Islamic Law*, p. 36)

231 Ibn Taymiyyah, *Fatāwā*, vol. 20 p. 304.
232 Ibid., p. 308.
233 Ibid., pp. 309–310.
234 Ibid., vol. 20 p. 310.
235 Ibid., pp. 310–311. For a study and discussion of the authority of Ahl al-Madīnah's consensus and *'amal*, see: al-Qarāfī, *Sharḥ Tanqiḥ al-Fuṣūl*, p. 334, Ibn Juzayy, *Taqrīb al-Wuṣūl*, p. 132, Ibn al-Laḥḥām, *al-Mukhtaṣar*, p. 76, al-Sarkhasī, *Uṣūl*, vol. 1 p. 314, al-Aṣfahānī, *Sharḥ al-Minhāj*, vol. 2 pp. 595–596, Badshāh, *Taysīr, al-Taḥrīr*, vol. 3 pp. 244–245, al-Juwaynī, *al-Burhān*, vol. 1 p. 720. For a comprehensive study of this issue and the difference between *ḥadīth* and *sunnah*, see: Dutton, *The Origins of Islamic Law: the Qur'ān, the Muwaṭṭa' and Madinan 'Amal*, pp. 33–52, 157–177.

4 RECONSTRUCTION: IBN TAYMIYYAH AND ḤANBALĪ JURISPRUDENCE

1 Ibn 'Abd al- Hādī, *al-'Uqūd*, p. 2, al-Bazzār, *al-A'lām*, p. 33, al-Karmī, *al-Kawākib*, p. 52.
2 Ibn Taymiyyah, *Fatāwā*, vol. 31 p. 36.
3 Ibn Taymiyyah, *Iqtiḍā'*, vol. 2 p. 584. Ibn Taymiyyah's insistence on this criterion for determining whether an act can be considered as an innovation or not is clear. It would not be correct for the criterion to be whether or not the action was considered permissible by some scholars. For scholars occasionally hold opinions which are contrary to the sources of Islamic law.
4 Ibn Taymiyyah, *Minhāj*, vol. 1 p. 306.
5 Ibn Taymiyyah, *Fatāwā*, vol. 11 pp. 345–346, *Iqtiḍā*, vol. 2 p. 594.
6 Ibn Taymiyyah, *Fatāwā*, vol. 13 pp. 67–68
7 Ibid., vol. 7 p. 392.
8 Ibid., vol. 10 p. 367.
9 Ibn Taymiyyah, *Fatāwā*, vol. 20 pp. 184–186.
10 Safiullah, *'Wahhabism*, pp. 68–69.
11 Safiullah, *'Wahhabism*, p. 68.
12 Memon, *Ibn Taymiyyah's Struggle*, pp. 229–230.
13 Ibid., p. 230.
14 Ibn Taymiyyah, *Iqtiḍā'*, vol. 2 p. 584, Muhammad, *Ibn Taymiyyah's Struggle*, p. 231.
15 Ibn Taymiyyah, *Fatāwā*, vol. 22 pp. 306–307.
16 Ibn Taymiyyah, *al-Nubuwwāt*, p. 154.
17 It can be determined that most of the innovations mentioned by Ibn Taymiyyah in the Ḥanbalī School of law pertain to the subject of worship. For Ibn Taymiyyah's explanation of the fact that innovations (*bida'*) exist in worship more than in any other subject, see *Fatāwā*, vol. 19 pp. 274–277.
18 Ibn Taymiyyah, *Fatāwā*, vol. 20 pp. 186–187. Ibn Taymiyyah points out that the beliefs of Ahl al-Sunnah are usually attributed to Aḥmad, not because he invented them but because he affirmed them during a period of widespread innovation (*bida'*). See Ibn Taymiyyah, *Fatāwā*, vol. 6 pp. 214–215.
19 Ibn Rushd, *Bidāyat al-Mujtahid*, vol. 1 p. 3, Ibn 'Uthaymīn, *An Explanation of Riyadh al-Saliheen*, part 1 p. 7. It should be pointed out that although scholars agreed on the stipulation of the intention for acts of worship, they differed on whether intention is a condition for the validity of ablution. For details, see Ibn Rushd, *Bidāyat al-Mujtahid*,

vol. 1 pp. 3–4. Also, al-Sadlān mentions that the scholars differed in three types of deeds. For details, see al-Sadlān, *al-Niyyah*, pp. 281–291.

20 Al-Bukhārī, *Ṣaḥīḥ* , Arabic–English, vol. I p. 1, vol. III p. 1056.

21 Ibn Taymiyyah, *Fatāwā*, vol. 22 pp. 231, 233, 238.

22 Ibid., vol. 22 p. 246, al-Ba'lī, *Mukhtaṣar*, p. 9. A group of well-known Ḥanbalī scholars were of the opinion that the utterance of intention in the prayer is recommended. These included Ibn al-Jawzī and al-Buhūtī. Ibn Mufliḥ al-Mu'arrikh mentions this opinion but does not comment on it. See, Ibn Mufliḥ al-Mu'arrikh, *al-Mubdi'*, vol. 1 p. 414, al-Buhūtī, *Kashshāf*, vol. 1 p. 314. Several Ḥanbalī scholars, such as Ibn Mufliḥ al-Mu'arrikh in *al-Mubdi'*, vol. 1 p. 414, and al-Buhūtī in *al-Rawḍ*, p. 65, state that utterance of intention is not a condition for the validity of prayer. According to Ibn Qāsim in his book *Ḥāshyat*, vol. 1 p. 563, this statement means that the utterance of the intention of prayer is recommended.

23 Ibn Taymiyyah, *Fatāwā*, vol. 22 p. 221.

24 Ibid., vol. 22 pp. 218, 223.

25 Ibid., vol. 22 pp. 217–246, al-Ba'lī, *Mukhtaṣar*, p. 9, al-Ba'lī, *al-Ikhtiyārāt*, p. 11.

26 Al-Ba'lī, *Mukhtaṣar*, p. 9, Ibn Taymiyyah, *Fatāwā*, vol. 22 pp. 221–222, 218, 223, 231, 233.

27 Ibn Taymiyyah, *Fatāwā*, vol. 22 pp. 245–246.

28 Ibid., vol. 22 p. 221. It should be pointed out that the Ḥanbalī scholars agree on the stipulation of intention for the validity of the prayer. See, al-Majd, *al-Muḥarrar*, vol. 1 p. 52, Ibn al-Bannā, *al-Muqni'*, vol. 1 p. 345, Ibn Mufliḥ, *al-Furū'*, vol. 1 p. 390, al-Mardāwī, *al-Inṣāf*, vol. 2 p. 19, al-Zarkashī, *Sharḥ*, vol. 1 p. 539, Ibn Mufliḥ al-Mu'arrikh, *al-Mubdi'*, vol. 1 p. 414, al-Ḥajjāwī, *al-Iqnā'*, vol. 1 p. 106, al-Karmī, *Ghāyat*, vol. 1 p. 124, al-Buhūtī, *Kashshāf*, vol. 1 p. 313, al-'Anqirī, *Ḥāshyat*, vol. 1 p. 160, Ibn Qāsim, *Ḥāshyat*, vol. 1 p. 562, Ibn Rushd, *Bidayat*, vol. 1 p. 132.

29 Ibn Taymiyyah, *Fatāwā*, vol. 22 p. 242, Ibn al-Qayyim in *al-Zād* seems to benefit from his sheikh's discussion on this issue as we find great similarity between them. See, Ibn al-Qayyim, *al-Zād*, vol. 1 p. 201.

30 There are various *ḥadīths* that contain this meaning, including the *ḥadīth* narrated by Muslim in his *Ṣaḥīḥ*, in the book of *janā'iz* vol. II p. 463, Aḥmad in his *Musnad*, vol. 2 p. 297. In addition, the practice of the Prophet testifies to this ruling. See for instance al-Bukhārī, *Ṣaḥīḥ*, vol. ii p. 208, and Muslim, *Ṣaḥīḥ*, vol. ii pp. 461–462.

31 See the section entitled 'Ibn Taymiyyah's detention' in Chapter 1 of this work. Some of these un-Islamic practices existed in various eras after the generation of the predecessors. For example, this was found at the time of the leading Ḥanbalī scholar Ibn 'Aqīl whom we find declaring himself free from these practices. For further details, see, Makdisi, *Ibn 'Aqīl*, pp. 210–213.

32 This nickname and *nasab* amongst the Ḥanbalīs is used to refer to two leading Ḥanbalī scholars: the first is al-Ḥāfiẓ 'Abd al-Ghanī al-Jamā'īlī (541–600/1146–1204), the second is 'Abd Allah b. Aḥmad Ibn Qudāmah (541–620/1146–1224). Most of the treatises discussing the issue of travelling to visit graves do not indicate to which of these two scholars this opinion was attributed. The ambiguity in the sources resulted in confusion for some researchers, such as the editor of Ibn Taymiyyah's treatise *Iqtiḍā' al-Ṣirāṭ al-Mustaqīm*, who declared in the footnote of his book (vol. 2 p. 666) that he could not find anything to clarify this point. This problem could be solved by referring to the *fatwā* of Ibn Taymiyyah on this issue in other treatises where he clearly states that this opinion is attributed to several scholars. Amongst those whom he mentions is Abū Muhammad al-Maqdisī and here he adds 'Ibn Qudāmah'. See the *fatwā* of Ibn Taymiyyah on this issue in the following sources: Ibn Taymiyyah, *Fatāwā*, vol. 27 p. 185, Ibn 'Abd al-Hādī, *al-'Uqūd*, p. 333, al-Karmī, *al-Kawākib*, p. 150. Moreover, some Ḥanbalī scholars attributed this opinion to Ibn Qudāmah. See for instance al-Buhūtī, *Sharḥ Muntahā*, vol. 1 p. 466.

33 Ibn Taymiyyah, *Fatāwā*, vol. 27 pp. 27–28, 185, 215, 226, *Iqtiḍā'*, vol. 2 p. 666, Ibn 'Abd al-Hādī, *al-Ṣārim*, p. 26. Ibn 'Abdūs is 'Ali b. 'Umar b. Aḥmad b. 'Abdūs al-Harānī a Ḥanbalī jurist and preacher of the sixth century (d. 559/1164). He produced various books, including his treatise entitled *al-Mudhahhab* and also compiled a large treatise on the interpretation of the Qur'an. See, Ibn Rajab, *Dhayl*, vol. 1 pp. 241–242. It is interesting that Fakhr al-Dīn Ibn Taymiyyah, the uncle of Ibn Taymiyyah's grandfather and also the uncle of Ibn 'Abdūs, studied, during his initial search for knowledge under Ibn 'Abdūs. See, Ibn Rajab, *Dhayl*, vol. 1 p. 241. This opinion also appears to have been held by scholars in the tenth century, such as al-Ḥajjāwī, *al-Iqnā'*, vol. 1 p. 179.

34 See note 30 of this chapter.

35 This tradition is an agreed upon *ḥadīth* narrated by al-Bukhārī in his *Ṣaḥīḥ* vol. III p. 51, and Muslim in his *Ṣaḥīḥ* vol. II p. 699. It should be pointed out that the exception in this *ḥadīth* is of the kind of *al-istithnā' al-mufarragh* in which the general term is not expressed. Therefore, we find that the scholars, who prohibit journeys to the grave of the Prophet and to minor sanctuaries, assert that the intended meaning of this *ḥadīth* is that 'do not set out for any place (for worship) except for the three mosques'. In contrast, scholars who approve of such pilgrimages argued that the meaning of the phrase was 'do not set out for any mosque except for the three mosques'. Kister, *Studies*, XIII, pp. 174–175.

36 See these proofs, and others, cited by Ibn Taymiyyah's opponents in the following sources: Ibn Taymiyyah, *Fatāwā*, vol. 27 pp. 27–28, 184–189, 215–219, 226, *Iqtiḍā'*, vol. 2 p. 666, Ibn 'Abd al-Hādī, *al-Ṣārim*, p. 26.

37 Ibn Taymiyyah, *Fatāwā*, vol. 27 pp. 334–335.

38 Ibid., vol. 27 pp. 185, 188. The chains and contexts of these *ḥadīths* were studied and criticised by the leading scholar Ibn 'Abd al-Hādī, one of Ibn Taymiyyah's eminent students who had great knowledge of *ḥadīth*, in his book entitled '*al-Ṣārim al-Munkī Fī al-Radd 'ala al-Subkī*'.

39 Ibn Taymiyyah, *Fatāwā*, vol. 27 p. 187. Ibn Taymiyyah in *al-Jawāb al-Bāhir* (*Fatāwā* vol. 27 p. 314) asserts that whoever disagrees with this fact is basing his opinion on mere speculation and has no evidence from the *sunnah*, the companions, their followers or the Imams. In this book, he also challenges his opponents to present any recognised source written by any of the Imams to support their claim. Ibn Taymiyyah suggests that his opponents appear to be ignorant about the actual practice of the companions on this issue.

40 Ibn Taymiyyah, *al-Jawāb al-Bāhir*, p. 11.

41 Ibn Taymiyyah, *Fatāwā*, vol. 27 p. 221.

42 Ibid., vol. 27 pp. 221–222. There is an interesting discussion of this point by Ibn Taymiyyah in *al-Fatāwā* where he differentiates between what is prohibited in Islamic law for the right of Allah and what is prohibited for the right of the people. According to Ibn Taymiyyah, the first is invalid whereas the second is invalid if it is not acceptable to the one who was cheated. For further details of this point, see: Ibn Taymiyyah, *Fatāwā*, vol. 29 pp. 281–292.

43 For detailed discussion of this point, see *Fatāwā* vol. 27 pp. 216–219.

44 Ibid., p. 335.

45 For examples of the various twists of Ibn Taymiyyah's answer on this point, see *Fatāwā*, vol. 27 pp. 225–313.

46 Ibid., vol. 27 pp. 182, 225.

47 Ibid., vol. 30 p. 187.

48 Ibid., pp. 187–188.

49 Ibid.

50 Al-Khiraqī, *Mukhtaṣar*, tran., p. 133, Ibn Qudāmah, *al-Mughnī*, vol. 7 p. 346.

51 Ibid., p. 344.

52 This is evident through Ibn Taymiyyah's treatise entitled *Kitāb Iqāmat al-Dalīl fi Ibṭāl al-Taḥlīl* in which he paid particular attention to the problem of *ḥiyal*. This book is included in *al-Fatāwā al-Kubrā* vol. 6 pp. 3–320.
53 Ibn Taymiyyah, *Kubrā*, vol. 6 p. 17.
54 Ibid., vol. 6 p. 79.
55 Ibid., p. 82.
56 Abū 'l-Khaṭṭāb was one of those Ḥanbalī scholars who validated some types of *ḥiyal*. See Al-Ṭūfī, *Sharḥ*, vol. 3 p. 214.
57 Ibn Taymiyyah, *Kubrā*, p. 143. There are several works by Ḥanafī jurists dealing with the subject of *ḥiyal*, including the book of al-Shaybānī, *Kitab al-Makhārij fi 'l-Ḥiyal*, and al-Khaṣṣāf, *Kitāb al-Ḥiyal wa 'l-Makhārij*. Schacht, *An Introduction*, p. 81, Nurbain, *Ibn Qayyim*, p. 50.
58 Ibn Taymiyyah *Kubrā*, vol. 6 pp. 146–147.
59 Ibid., p. 148. Schacht states that there are certain differences of degree in the attitudes of the schools of law towards *ḥiyal*. The Ḥanafis are the most favourably inclined. *An Introduction*, p. 81.
60 Ibn Taymiyyah, *Kubrā*, vol. 6 pp. 18, 88.
61 Ibid., p. 85.
62 Ibid., pp. 85, 95. All of the four Imams are reported to have declared that their opinions must be compared to what is in the Qur'an and *sunnah*. See, for some reports in this regard, Ibn Taymiyyah, *Fatāwā*, vol. 20 pp. 211–212.
63 Ibn Taymiyyah, *Kubrā*, p. 86.
64 Ibid., pp. 95–96.
65 Ibid., p. 21.
66 Ibid., p. 22.
67 Al-Bukhārī, *Ṣaḥīḥ* Arabic–English, vol. I p. 1.
68 Ibn Taymiyyah, *Kubrā*, pp. 162–163.
69 Ibid., p. 54. Several examples of this point are given by Ibn Taymiyyah. See, for instance p. 55.
70 Ibid., p. 181.
71 Ibid., p. 155.
72 Ibid., p. 157.
73 Al-Khiraqī, *al-Mukhtaṣar*, p. 174, Ibn Qudāmah, *al-'Umdah*, p. 387, al-Buhūtī, *Sharḥ*, vol. 3 pp. 41–42, *al-Rawḍ*, pp. 370–372, Ibn Qāsim, *Ḥāshyat*, vol. 6 pp. 320–321.
74 Ibn Taymiyyah, Ibid., p. 13, al-Maqdisī, *Sharḥ*, p. 387, Ibn Qāsim, *Ḥāshyat*, vol. 6 pp. 320–321.
75 Al-Mardāwī, *al-Inṣāf*, vol. 8 p. 161, al-Zarkashī, *Sharḥ*, vol. 5 pp. 233–234.
76 Ibn Taymiyyah, *Kubrā*, vol. 6 p. 11, al-Mardāwī, *al-Inṣāf*, vol. 8 p. 161, al-Buhūtī, *Sharḥ*, vol. 3 p. 42, Ibn Qāsim, *Ḥāshyat*, vol. 6 pp. 320–321.
77 Ibn Taymiyyah, Ibid., p. 12, al-Mardāwī, *al-Inṣāf*, vol. 8 p. 161, Ibn Mufliḥ, *al-Furū'*, vol. 5 p. 215.
78 Ibn Taymiyyah, Ibid., al-Zarkashī, *Sharḥ*, vol. 5 p. 234, Ibn Mufliḥ, *al-Furū'*, vol. 5 p. 215.
79 Ibid., It is worth mentioning that Ibn al-Bannā in his book *al-Muqni'* (vol. 3 p. 922) supports the opinion invalidating this contract.
80 Ibn Taymiyyah, Ibid., al-Zarkashī, *Sharḥ*, vol. 5 pp. 233–234.
81 Ibn Taymiyyah, Ibid., p. 13.
82 Ibn Taymiyyah, Ibid., pp. 12–13, Ibn Mufliḥ, *al-Furū'*, vol. 5 p. 215. The first point is mentioned by al-Zarkashī, *Sharḥ*, vol. 5 p. 234.
83 Ibn Taymiyyah, Ibid., p. 13. I could not find this narration in the published version of *Masā'il Abū Dawūd*.
84 Ibid., Ibn Taymiyyah clarifies that the contract of *mut'ah* is less significant in relation to the prohibition than the contract of *taḥlīl*. He offers ten arguments to support his

statement, two of which are that: the contract of *mut'ah* is a repealed law whereas the *taḥlīl* was never revealed as a law and there was a disagreement amongst the companions regarding *mut'ah*, whereas there is no disagreement regarding *taḥlīl*. Ibn al-Qayyim mentions these aspects and attributes them to his sheikh and he also adds two other aspects in his book *Ighāthat al-Lahfān*, vol. 1 pp. 417–422.

85 Ibn Taymiyyah, *Kubrā*, vol. 6 p. 273.

86 The name of this narrator as mentioned in *Kubrā* vol. 6 p. 273, is Mūsā b. Muṭayn. Having referred to the books of *rijāl*, such as *Lisān al-Mizān* by Ibn Ḥajar vol. 6 pp. 153–154, *al-Kāmil* by Ibn 'Adī vol. 8 pp. 51–53, and *al-Ḍu'afā'* by al-'Uqailī, vol. 4 pp. 163–164, the researcher found that the name Muṭayn is incorrect and is a misprint as the source books of *rijāl* mention the name as Muṭayr. This narrator is known also as Mūsā al-Hilālī. See, Ibn Ḥajar, *Lisān al-Mizān*, vol. 6 p. 154. Furthermore, it is clear that he was from al-Kufah as we find al-'Uqailī (Ibn Ḥajar, *Lisān*, vol. 6 p. 154, al-'Uqailī, *al-Ḍu'afā'*, vol. 4 p. 163) describes him as Kūfī.

87 Ibn Taymiyyah, *Kubrā*, vol. 6 p. 273. There are several scholars of the science of *rijāl* who agree with Ibn Taymiyyah in his opinion with regard to this narrator and his narrations. For details, see Ibn Ḥajar, *Lisān*, vol. 6 pp. 153–154.

88 Ibn Taymiyyah, *Kubrā*, vol. 6 p. 273. Ibn Ma'īn's description of Mūsā b. Muṭayr as a liar can also be found in Ibn Ḥajar's *Lisān* vol. 6 p. 153.

89 Ibn Taymiyyah, *Kubrā*, vol. 6 p. 273. Ibn Ḥajar attributes this statement to Abū Ḥātim as well as to other scholars, including al-Nasā'ī. See Ibn Ḥajar's *Lisān* vol. 6 p. 153.

90 Ibn Taymiyyah, *Kubrā*, vol. 6 p. 273. Also, Ibn Ḥibbān describes this narrator as 'a narrator of unheard-of things and unacknowledged narrations which whoever hears them knows to be fabricated'. See, Ibn Ḥajar, *Lisān*, vol. 6 p. 153.

91 Ibn Taymiyyah, *Kubrā*, vol. 6 p. 273.

92 Ibid. It is not clear who was this anonymous author to whom Ibn Taymiyyah was referring. Furthermore, after consulting some of the reference of the science of *rijāl*, we did not find any scholars who described this narrator as reliable (*thiqah*). Aḥmad, al-'Uqailī and al-Daraquṭnī (Ibn Ḥajar, *Lisān*, vol. 6 p. 154, al-'Uqailī, *al-Ḍu'afā'*, vol. 4 p. 163) describe this narrator as weak. Aḥmad points out that the narration of Mūsā b. Muṭayr was abandoned by the people (of *ḥadīth*) and al-'Uqailī asserts that Mūsā b. Muṭayr was not reliable. For some details regarding the relation between the grading of scholars and its impact upon the grading of *ḥadīths*, see: Azami, *Studies in ḥadīth methodology and literature*, pp. 58–67.

93 Ibn Taymiyyah, *Kubrā*, p. 13, al-Maqdisī, *Sharḥ*, p. 387.

94 Ibn Taymiyyah, *Kubrā*, p. 14, al-Bannā, *al-Muqni'*, vol. 3 p. 922, al-Zarkshī, *Sharḥ*, vol. 5 pp. 230–233, al-Maqdisī, *Sharḥ*, p. 387, al-Buhūtī, *Sharḥ*, vol. 3 p. 42.

95 Ibn Taymiyyah, *Kubrā*, p. 15, al-Zarkashī, *Sharḥ*, vol. 5 p. 233.

96 Ibn Taymiyyah, *Kubrā*, p. 15.

97 Ibid., p. 15.

98 Ibid.

99 Ibn al-Qayyim, *Ighāthat*, vol. 1 p. 255, *al-Rūḥ*, p. 334.

100 Ibn Taymiyyah, *Fatāwā*, vol. 25 p. 100.

101 Ibid., p. 110, vol. 26 p. 54.

102 Ibid., vol. 26 p. 54.

103 Ibid., vol. 21 pp. 62–63.

104 Ibid., p. 62.

105 Ibid., vol. 22 pp. 335–355.

106 Ibid., p. 336.

107 Ibid., vol. 21 p. 62.

108 Ibid., p. 273.

109 Ibid., vol. 23 pp. 186–187.

110 Ibn Taymiyyah, *Fatāwā*, vol. 21 p. 23.
111 For examples, see *Fatāwā*, vol. 21 p. 363, 622, vol. 25 p. 268, vol. 26 p. 244.
112 This opinion is the most famous opinion in the School. It is held by the majority of Ḥanbalī scholars. See, al-Zarkashī, *Sharḥ*, vol. 2 p. 553, al-Mardāwī, *al-Inṣāf*, vol. 3 p. 269.
113 See the discussion of the Ḥanbalī scholars in relation to this issue in the following sources: Al-Khiraqī, *Mukhtaṣar*, tran. p. 81, Ibn Qudāmah, *al-'Umdah*, p. 148, Ibn al-Bannā, *al-Muqni'*, vol. 2 p. 555, al-Majd, *al-Muḥarrar*, vol. 1 p. 227, Ibn Mufliḥ, *al-Furū'*, vol. 3 pp. 125–126, al-Zarkashī, *Sharḥ*, vol. 2 p. 553, al-Mardāwī, *al-Inṣāf*, vol. 3 pp. 269–270, al-Buhūtī, *Sharḥ*, vol. 1 p. 438, *al-Rawḍ*, p. 172, al-'Anqirī, *Sharḥ*, vol. 1 p. 411, Ibn Taymiyyah, *Fatāwā*, vol. 25 p. 122. Ibn Taymiyyah, in his book *Sharḥ al-'Umdah* (Book of Fasting, vol. 1 pp. 75–131), studies this issue in detail and discusses the evidence cited by the conflicting opinions. He concludes that the most correct opinion is the majority opinion of the School, that fasting on this day is obligatory.
114 Ibn Taymiyyah, *Fatāwā*, vol. 25 pp. 122–123.
115 Ibid., This opinion, according to al-Mardāwī, is the predominant opinion in the Ḥanbalī School and is supported by several Ḥanbalī scholars. In addition, they claim that it is the opinion of Aḥmad. Al-Mardāwī, *al-Inṣāf*, vol. 3 p. 269.
116 Ibn Taymiyyah, *Fatāwā*, vol. 25 p. 124. There is some confusion in certain Ḥanbalī sources about Ibn Taymiyyah's opinion concerning the fast on the day of doubt. Some sources, such as *al-Fā'iq* (*al-Inṣāf*, vol. 3 p. 270), state that Ibn Taymiyyah's opinion is that it is permissible to fast on that day. Other sources, such as al-Zarkashī in his *Sharḥ* (vol. 2 pp. 560–561), mention that the preferred opinion of this scholar is that fasting is recommended. Al-Ba'lī in his treatise *al-Ikhtyārāt* (p. 107), mentions that Ibn Taymiyyah's final opinion is that fasting is not recommended. It appears that this last opinion is the one most likely to have been adopted by Ibn Taymiyyah, as it agrees with the methodology he usually applied when deciding on a jurisprudential ruling; he would base his opinion on textual evidences or draw an analogy from them. In this issue, it is clear that the opinion that fasting on the day of doubt is obligatory or recommended is not founded upon correct clear evidence. On the contrary, the evidences appear to support the opinion that the Lawgiver has prohibited fasting during that time. It should be pointed out that Ibn Qāḍī al-Jabal in *al-Fā'iq* followed Ibn Taymiyyah and criticises the Ḥanbalī scholars' position basing most of his argument on Ibn Taymiyyah's discussion. See, Ibn Mufliḥ, *al-Furū'*, vol. 3 pp. 6–11, al-Mardāwī, *al-Inṣāf*, vol. 3 pp. 269–270.
117 Ibn Taymiyyah, *Fatāwā*, vol. 21 p. 56.
118 Al-Khallāl narrated in his book entitled *al-Wara'* various narrations from Aḥmad dealing with *wara'*.
119 Ibn Taymiyyah, *Fatāwā*, vol. 29 p. 311.
120 Ibid., p. 312.
121 Ibid.
122 For examples of these narrations see, *Fatāwā*, vol. 29 p. 313.
123 Ibn Taymiyyah, *Fatāwā*, vol. 29 p. 315. This *ḥadīth* is narrated by al-Bukhārī, *Ṣaḥīḥ*, vol. I p. 44, Muslim, *Ṣaḥīḥ*, vol. III p. 840.
124 Ibn Taymiyyah, *Fatāwā*, vol. 10 p. 617.
125 Ibid., vol. 20 p. 138.
126 Ibid., vol. 20 pp. 138–139.
127 Ibid., vol. 10 pp. 511–514, 644, vol. 20 p. 138.
128 Ibid., vol. 20 p. 138.
129 Ibid.
130 Ibid., pp. 315–316.
131 Ibid., p. 318.
132 Ibid., vol. 29 p. 320.

133 Ibid., pp. 320–321.
134 Ibid., pp. 322–323.
135 Ibid., vol. 4 p. 168, vol. 11 p. 137, vol. 24 pp. 50–52.
136 Ibid., vol. 27 p. 304. Ibn Taymiyyah asserts that all of the schools of law have opinions that are not opinions of the Imams of these schools. Furthermore, these opinions in most cases are not consistent with the general principles of the Imams. Ibid., Ibn al-Qayyim agrees with his sheikh and asserts that most of the opinions attributed to the Imams are in fact in opposition to the true opinions of these Imams. See, Ibn al-Qāsim, *Ḥāshiyat*, vol. 1 p. 18.
137 Ibn Taymiyyah, *Fatāwā*, vol. 10 p. 367.
138 Ibn Taymiyyah, *Majmūʿ*, vol. 2 p. 412. Ibn al-Qayyim agrees with his sheikh in this point and clarifies that Abū Yaʿla abandoned most of his opinions in his treatise *al-Muḥarrar*. See: Ibn al-Qayyim, *Aḥkām*, vol. 1 p. 279.
139 Ibn Taymiyyah, *al-Ikhtiyārāt*, p. 7.
140 Ibid., vol. 24 p. 50.
141 Ibn Taymiyyah, *al-Qawāʿid*, pp. 132–133.
142 Ibn al-Qayyim (in his book *al-Iʿlām*, vol. 4 pp. 298–299) relates the existence of some incorrect opinions within Islamic schools of law, including the Ḥanbalī School, to the fact that there are various opinions of the Imams which were abandoned by them in favour of new opinions. The scholars of the Schools, however, continued to attribute these opinions to the Imams.
143 For example, when Ibn Taymiyyah discusses the issue of whether it is allowed to pay the value of an item as *zakāt* instead of paying the thing itself, Ibn Taymiyyah mentions that there are various conflicting narrations from Aḥmad on this issue. Ibn Taymiyyah asserts that there are two approaches amongst the Ḥanbalī scholars in determining the exact position of Aḥmad. The first party acknowledge and accept the various opinions and assert that they are dealing with different issues. The second party insist that these conflicting opinions are conflicting narrations from Aḥmad. It is clear that Ibn Taymiyyah supports the first approach. Ibn Taymiyyah, *Fatāwā*, vol. 25 pp. 82–83. For other examples mentioned by Ibn Taymiyyah, see: Ibn Taymiyyah, *al-Qawāʿid*, p. 64, *Fatāwā*, vol. 21 pp. 139–140. Also, additional examples can be obtained in the treatises of Ibn al-Qayyim. See, for instance, *Aḥkām*, vol. 2 pp. 800–801. In this last example, Ibn al-Qayyim supports the opinion of his sheikh. Ibid., pp. 801–805.
144 Ibn Taymiyyah, *Kubrā*, vol. 6 p. 11.
145 This point can be illustrated by the issue of what type of *ḥajj* the Prophet performed. For details, see Ibn Taymiyyah, *al-Qawāʿid*, p. 69. Ibn al-Qayyim cites his sheikh sorting out this problem resulting from the misunderstanding of some terms in the *ḥadīths* dealing with this issue. See: Ibn al-Qayyim, *Zād*, vol. 2 pp. 118–122.
146 An example of this is mentioned by Ibn Taymiyyah through the narration of his student Ibn al-Qayyim in *Aḥkām Ahl al-Dhimmah*, vol. 2 pp. 623, 626–627.
147 Ibn Taymiyyah, *Fatāwā*, vol. 20 p. 497.
148 For instance, see Ibn Taymiyyah, *Ikhtiyārāt*, pp. 43–44.
149 Ibid., vol. 20 pp. 227–228.
150 Ibid., vol. 20 pp. 228–231.
151 This ruling is in conformity with the predominant opinion of the Ḥanbalī School. It is important to note that there is a narration from Imam Aḥmad that mentions that praying in a cemetery is only disliked and not prohibited. In addition, Ḥanbalī scholars disagreed as to whether the prayer of a person in a cemetery is correct or not. Ibn Qudāmah (*al-ʿUmdah* p. 69) Ibn Mufliḥ (*al-Furūʿ*, vol. 1 p. 371) and al-Mardāwī (*al-Inṣāf*, vol. 1 p. 489) in addition to others assert that the correct ruling in the School is that the prayer is incorrect. Other Ḥanbalī scholars suggest that if the individual concerned is aware of the prohibition of performing the prayer in the cemetery, his

prayer is incorrect. If he is ignorant of the prohibition, his prayer will be considered valid. Others were of the opinion that the prayer in a cemetery is prohibited, but they validated it when it occurred. Others permitted praying at cemeteries when necessary. See Ibn Mufliḥ, *al-Furūʿ*, vol. 1 pp. 371–372, al-Mardāwī, *al-Inṣāf*, vol. 1 p. 489. Ibn Taymiyyah mentions that certain jurists thought that the reason for the prayer being reprehensible in a cemetery is that the ground of the cemetery might be contaminated by the buried bodies. Therefore, these scholars differentiate between new and old cemeteries and state that it is allowed in the first and not in the second. Ibn Taymiyyah criticises this opinion, clarifying that the texts contain unambiguous indications of the fact that the prohibition of prayer in cemeteries is based on the danger that it can lead to polytheism. See, Ibn Taymiyyah, *Iqtiḍāʾ*, vol. 2 pp. 672–676. *Fatāwā*, vol. 21 pp. 321–323.

152 Several Ḥanbalī scholars were of this opinion and al-Mardāwī states that it is the correct opinion in the School. Ibn Mufliḥ, *al-Furūʿ*, vol. 1 p. 374–375, al-Mardāwī, *al-Inṣāf*, vol. 1 p. 490, al-Ḥajjāwī, *al-Iqnāʿ*, vol. 1 p. 97, Ibn al-Najjār, *Muntahā*, vol. 1 p. 54, al-Buhūtī, *Sharḥ*, vol. 1 p. 155, al-Karmī, *Ghāyat al-Muntahā*, vol. 1 p. 115, al-Buhūtī, *al-Rawḍ*, p. 63, *Kashshāf*, vol. 1 p. 294, al-Buhūtī, *Sharḥ al-Muntahā*, vol. 1 p. 155, al-Shaybānī, *Nayl*, vol. 1 p. 128.

153 Al-Baʿlī, *Ikhtiyārāt*, p. 44. This opinion of Ibn Taymiyyah is also mentioned by some Ḥanbalī scholars such as Ibn Mufliḥ who preferred this opinion (*al-Furūʿ*, vol. 1 p. 375) and al-Mardāwī in his book *al-Inṣāf* vol. 1 p. 490 and al-Buhūtī in his treatise *Kashshāf* vol. 1 p. 294.

154 For further details of this point see, al-Maqdisī, *al-ʿUddah*, p. 136, al-Majd, *al-Muḥarrar*, vol. 1 p. 139, Ibn Mufliḥ, *al-Furūʿ*, vol. 2 p. 467, *al-Nukat*, with *al-Muḥarrar*, vol. 1 pp. 139–142, al-Mardāwī, *al-Inṣāf*, vol. 3 pp. 148–149, al-Buhūtī, *Sharḥ*, vol. 1 pp. 405–407, *al-Rawḍ*, pp. 158–159.

155 Ibn Taymiyyah, *Fatāwā*, vol. 25 pp. 63–65, Ibn Mufliḥ, *al-Furūʿ*, vol. 2 p. 467, *al-Nukat*, with *al-Muḥarrar*, vol. 1 pp. 139–140 al-Mardāwī, *al-Inṣāf*, vol. 3 p. 149.

156 Ibn Mufliḥ, *al-Furūʿ*, vol. 2 pp. 468–473, *al-Nukat*, with *al-Muḥarrar*, vol. 1 pp. 139–140.

157 Al-Maqdisī, *al-ʿUddah*, pp. 611–612, al-Mardāwī, *al-Inṣāf*, vol. 4 p. 211, al-Buhūtī, *Sharḥ*, vol. 2 p. 125, *al-Rawḍ*, p. 224, al-ʿAnqirī, *Sharḥ*, vol. 2 p. 14.

158 For further details on this point see, al-Maqdisī, *al-ʿUddah*, p. 612, al-Majd, *al-Muḥarrar*, vol. 2 p. 182, Ibn Mufliḥ, *al-Furūʿ*, vol. 6 p. 253, al-Mardāwī, *al-Inṣāf*, vol. 4 pp. 212–213, Ibn Taymiyyah, *Fatāwā*, vol. 32 pp. 15–61, al-Buhūtī, *Sharḥ*, vol. 2 pp. 125–126, *al-Rawḍ*, p. 224, al-ʿAnqirī, *Sharḥ*, vol. 2 pp. 13–14.

159 Al-Mardāwī, *al-Inṣāf*, vol. 4 p. 212.

160 In Dhi al-Qiʿdah 6/628, the Prophet led a group of about 1400–1500 men, intending to perform the pilgrimage at Makkah, but he was prevented from doing so. After a series of negotiations, a truce was drawn up at Hudaybiyah (a place near the city of Makkah). Ibn al-Qayyim, *Zād*, vol. 3 pp. 286–355, *The History of al-Ṭabarī*, vol. III pp. 67–71, Rahman, *A Chronology*, p. 23.

161 Scholars disagree on the actual time period of the truce of the *Hudaybiyah*. Whereas some scholars state that it was for ten years, others assert that it was for four years and others say three years. See Ibn Rushid, *Bidayat*, vol. 2 p. 464.

162 Al-Yahya, *Ibn Qudāmah*, p. 210. Furrukh Ali in his article entitled '*Al-Hudaybiya*: an alternative version' suggests that what happened in that event is that in the year 6/628 the Prophet and the Muslims with him at *al-Hudaybiyah*, instead of being forced to return to Medinah and then return in the following year to perform 'Umra, were actually allowed to make it in 6 AH. Furthermore, Ali maintains that the period of truce was not for ten years, as is the standard view, but only for the three days of the 'Umra. Watt strongly disagrees with this opinion and refutes Ali's claim, on which his previous opinion is based, that '... the Prophet's action at *al-Hudaybiya* fell short of

the standards of honour, valour, and adherence to principles that one would expect from a Prophet of God imbued with a divine mission'. For more details on this point see, W. Watt, 'The Expedition of *al-Hudaybiya* Reconsidered' in *Hamdard Islamicus* vol. VIII/ No.1 Spring 1985.

163 See footnote 158.

164 Al-Mardāwī, *al-Inṣāf*, vol. 4 p. 212.

165 Ibn al-Qayyim, *Aḥkām*, vol. 2 p. 477.

166 Ibn Taymiyyah, *Fatāwā*, vol. 29 p. 140, *Ikhtiyārāt*, p. 315, al-Mardāwī, *al-Inṣāf*, vol. 4 pp. 212–213.

167 Ibn Taymiyyah, *Fatāwā*, vol. 29 pp. 145–146. It is important to point out that Ibn Taymiyyah is of the opinion that either signatory to the contract of truce has the right to dissolve it after notifying the other party. See: Ibn Taymiyyah, *Fatāwā*, vol. 29 p. 140.

168 For further details of these conditions and others, see, al-Khiraqī, *Mukhtaṣar*, tran. pp. 167–172, Ibn al-Bannā, *al-Muqnī'*, vol. 3 pp. 880–898, al-Majd, *al-Muḥarrar*, vol. 2 pp. 15–19, Ibn Mufliḥ, *al-Furū'*, vol. 5 pp. 169–193, al-Mardāwī, *al-Inṣāf*, vol. 8 pp. 50–112, Ibn Taymiyyah, *Fatāwā*, vol. 32 pp. 15–61, *al-Buhūtī*, *Sharḥ*, vol. 3 pp. 13–27, *al-Rawḍ*, pp. 363–366, al-'Anqirī, *Sharḥ*, vol. 3 pp. 68–78.

169 For further details of this point see, al-Khiraqī, *Mukhtaṣar*, tran. pp. 167–172, Ibn Qudāmah, *al-'Umdah*, pp. 386–387, Ibn al-Bannā, *al-Muqni'*, vol. 3 pp. 899–901, al-Majd, *al-Muḥarrar*, vol. 2 pp. 23–27, Ibn Mufliḥ, *al-Furū'*, vol. 5 pp. 211–227, al-Mardāwī, *al-Inṣāf*, vol. 8 pp. 154–205, Ibn Taymiyyah, *Fatāwā*, vol. 32 pp. 15–61, al-Buhūtī, *Sharḥ*, vol. 3 pp. 39–46, *al-Rawḍ*, pp. 370–372, al-'Anqirī, *Sharḥ*, vol. 3 pp. 86–93.

170 Ibn Taymiyyah, *Fatāwā*, vol. 29 p. 175. The majority of Ḥanbalī sources do not mention the rulings on the stipulation of these conditions by the wife in the marital contract. Some sources do, however, comment upon the stipulations of the wife in the event that they were not fulfilled. They state that she has no right to ask for the dissolution of the contract except in one specific condition: if she stipulated that her husband must be a free man and later discovered that he was in fact a slave. It is interesting to note that amongst those scholars who held this opinion was al-Majd, the grandfather of Ibn Taymiyyah. In addition, it is noteworthy that the majority of Ḥanbalī sources only concentrate on the rulings related to the conditions stipulated by the husband. They mention that there are two opinions amongst the Ḥanbalī scholars with regard to this issue. The first states that if the conditions stipulated by the husband are not fulfilled, he assumes the right to accept the marriage or dissolve it. The second opinion is that the husband has no right to cancel the contract of marriage. Al-Majd, *al-Muḥarrar*, vol. 2 p. 24, Ibn Mufliḥ, *al-Furū'*, vol. 5 pp. 219–220, al-Mardāwī, *al-Inṣāf*, vol. 8 p. 168, *Taṣḥīḥ*, vol. 5 p. 220, al-Buhūtī, *Sharḥ*, vol. 3 p. 46.

171 Ibn Taymiyyah, *Fatāwā*, vol. 29 p. 175. This is also supported by a narration from Imam Aḥmad, in which he clarifies that the two parties have the right to dissolve the contract of marriage if their conditions are not fulfilled. See, Ibn Taymiyyah, *Fatāwā*, vol. 29 p. 135, *al-Qawā'id*, p. 132.

172 This is narrated by several scholars of *Ḥādīth*, such as al-Tirmidhī in his *Sunan*, Book of Sales vol. 3 p. 534, Abū Dawūd in his *Sunan*, Book of Sales, vol. 2 p. 490, Ibn Mājah in his *Sunan*, vol. 2 p. 737, al-Nasā'ī in his *Sunan*, Book of Sales, vol. 7 p. 289.

173 Ibn Taymiyyah, *Fatāwā*, vol. 20 p. 529.

174 Ibn Taymiyyah, *Fatāwā*, vol. 20 pp. 529–530, 542–543, vol. 29 pp. 22, 24–26, 31, 47–51, *Tafsīr Āyāt*, vol. 2 pp. 689–703. Also, Ibn Taymiyyah's position with regard to this issue is mentioned by Ibn Mufliḥ, *al-Furū'*, vol. 4 p. 22.

175 Al-Zarkashī, *Sharḥ*, vol. 4 p. 288, *al-Inṣāf*, vol. 7, p. 100, *al-'Uddah*, p. 282, *al-Rawḍ*, p. 325, *Ḥāshīyat*, vol. 5 p. 564.

176 Al-Majd, *al-Muḥarrar*, vol. 1 pp. 370–371.

177 Ibn Qudāmah, *al-'Uddah*, p. 282.

178 Ibn Qudāmah, *al-Mughnī*, vol. 7 p. 608.

179 Al-Zarkashī, *Sharḥ*, vol. 4 p. 290.
180 Al-Mardāwī, *al-Inṣāf*, vol. 7, pp. 100–101.
181 Al-Buhūtī, *al-Rawḍ*, p. 325.
182 Ibn Qāsim, *Ḥāshīyat*, vol. 5 p. 564.
183 Ibn Mufliḥ, *al-Furū'*, vol. 4 p. 622.
184 See Ibn Taymiyyah's discussion of this issue in *Fatāwā* vol. 31 pp. 212–253.
185 Al-Mardāwī, *al-Inṣāf*, vol. 7 p. 101.
186 Ibid., Ibn Kathīr in *al-Bidāyah* mentions some details of the confrontation between the judge Ibn Qāḍī al-Jabal and other Ḥanbalī scholars, among whom was the chief judge of the Ḥanbalī School, Jamāl al-Dīn al-Mardāwī. Ibn Kathīr says that this event took place in the year 757/1356, when several meetings were held to discuss the judgement of Ibn Qāḍī al-Jabal. The Ḥanbalī scholars asserted that what is in the Ḥanbalī jurisprudence is that an endowment can be replaced with another one in a state of necessity and if an endowment becomes unfruitful and nothing is yielded from it, but not where it is merely anticipated that greater benefit will arise from the new endowment. Ibn Kathīr, *al-Bidāyah*, vol. 14 p. 272.
187 Al-Mardāwī, *al-Inṣāf*, vol. 7 p. 101.
188 Ibid. Having searched in *al-Furū'* by Ibn Mufliḥ, the researcher finds that this scholar refers to his sheikh's opinion (*al-Furū'*, vol. 4 pp. 622–623) without expressing any indication of his alleged agreement with Jamāl al-Dīn al-Mardāwī's criticism of Ibn Qāḍī al-Jabal.
189 Al-Mardāwī, *al-Inṣāf*, vol. 7, p. 101. In his book *al-Inṣāf*, al-Mardāwī asserts that these scholars followed Ibn Taymiyyah in relation to this issue. Al-Mardāwī *al-Inṣāf*, vol. 7, p. 101.
190 See, for instance, *al-Inṣāf*, vol. 7, p. 101, Ibn Mufliḥ, *al-Furū'*, vol. 4 pp. 622–623.
191 Ṣāliḥ, *Masā'il*, vol. 3 p. 60, Abū Dawūd, *Masā'il*, p. 227, al-Khiraqī, *Ḥāshīyat*, p. 208, tran., p. 219, Ibn al-Bannā, al-*Muqni'* vol. 3 p. 1051, Ibn Mufliḥ, *al-Furū'*, vol. 5 p. 638, al-Zarkashī, *Sharḥ*, vol. 6 pp. 68–70, al-Mardāwī, *al-Inṣāf*, vol. 9 p. 469, Ibn al-Najjār, *Muntahā*, vol. 2 p. 261, al-Buhūtī, *Sharḥ*, vol. 3 p. 279, al-Shaybānī, *Nayl*, vol. 2 p. 318.
192 Ibn Taymiyyah, *Fatāwā*, vol. 14 p. 85, *al-Tafsīr al-Kabīr*, vol. 3 pp. 51, 52, al-Mardāwī, *al-Inṣāf*, vol. 9 p. 469.
193 Ibn Taymiyyah, *Fatāwā*, vol. 14 p. 85, al-Mardāwī, *al-Inṣāf*, vol. 9 p. 469.
194 Ibn Taymiyyah cites a *ḥādīth* in which the Prophet is reported to have said: 'whosoever kills his slave, we will kill him'. This *ḥādīth* is related by Abū Dawūd in his *Sunan*, in the Book of *Diyāt*, vol. 4 pp. 652–654, al-Nasā'ī, *Sunan*, vol. 8 pp. 20–21, and al-Tirmidhī, vol. 4 p. 26.
195 Ibn Taymiyyah, *Fatāwā*, vol. 14 pp. 85–86, *al-Tafsīr al-Kabīr*, vol. 3 p. 51.
196 Ibid., p. 86, *al-Tafsīr al-Kabīr*, vol. 3 p. 51.
197 Ibid.
198 Ibn Taymiyyah, *Fatāwā*, vol. 14 p. 86, *al-Tafsīr al-Kabīr*, vol. 3 pp. 51–52.
199 Ibid., *al-Tafsīr al-Kabīr*, vol. 4 p. 52.
200 Ibn Taymiyyah, *Fatāwā*, vol. 14 p. 87 *al-Tafsīr al-Kabīr*, vol. 3 p. 52. This *ḥadīth* is narrated by Abū Dawūd in his *Sunan*, vol. 4 p. 667, al-Nasā'ī, *Sunan*, vol. 8 p. 19, and Ibn Mājah, *Sunan*, vol. 2 p. 895.
201 Al-Mardāwī, *al-Inṣāf*, vol. 9 p. 469.
202 Ibn Taymiyyah, *Fatāwā*, vol. 19 pp. 235–236, *Sharḥ*, Book of *Ṭahārah* (purification), p. 474. The same criterion is also mentioned by Ibn al-Qayyim in *I'lām* vol. 1 pp. 337–338. Ibn Mufliḥ, *al-Furū'*, vol. 5 p. 169, and al-Mardāwī, *al-Inṣāf*, vol. 8 p. 45. It should be pointed out that some Ḥanbalī scholars mention this same rule, but they contradict it in various legal issues. See, for instance, Ibn al-Bannā, *al-Muqni'*, vol. 1 p. 280, Ibn Mufliḥ al-Muarrikh, *al-Mubdi'*, vol. 1 p. 269.
203 Ibn Taymiyyah, *Fatāwā*, vol. 19 p. 236.

204 See, for example, al-Bukhārī, *Ṣaḥīḥ*, the Book of Drinks, vol. vii pp. 338, 339–340, vol. viii pp. 503–508, Muslim, *Ṣaḥīḥ*, vol. iii pp. 923–924, 1095, 1100, 1107.
205 Al-Mardāwī, *al-Inṣāf*, vol. 10 p. 228.
206 Ibid., vol. 10 p. 229.
207 Muslim, *Ṣaḥīḥ*, vol. iii pp. 1107–1109.
208 Ibn Taymiyyah, *Fatāwā*, vol. 19 p. 236.
209 Al-Mardāwī, *al-Inṣāf*, vol. 10 p. 229, al-Zarkashī, *Sharḥ*, vol. 6 p. 387.
210 Al-Mardāwī, *al-Inṣāf*, vol. 10 p. 229. Ibn Taymiyyah differentiates between *ḥashīshah* and henbane (*hyoscyamus niger*) on the basis that the first is desirable and sought after, as in the case of *khamr*, whereas this is not true with regard to *hyoscyamus niger*. See: al-Mardāwī, *al-Inṣāf*, vol. 8 pp. 438–439.
211 For details concerning the minimum and maximum period of menstruation mentioned by Ḥanbalī scholars see: al-Khiraqī, *Mukhtaṣar*, tran. pp. 29–31, Ibn Qudāmah, *al-'Umdah*, pp. 54–55, Ibn al-Bannā, al-*Muqni'*, vol. 1 pp. 279–280, al-Majd, *al-Muḥarrar*, vol. 1 p. 24, Ibn Mufliḥ, *al-Furū'*, vol. 1 pp. 267–268, al-Zarkashī, *Sharḥ*, vol. 1 pp. 406–410, al-Mardāwī, *al-Inṣāf*, vol. 1 p. 358, al-Buhūtī, *Sharḥ*, vol. 1 p. 108, Ibn Qāsim, *Ḥāshīyat*, vol. 1 pp. 374–375.
212 Ibn Taymiyyah, *Fatāwā*, vol. 19 pp. 237–238, *Sharḥ*, Book of *Ṭahārah*, pp. 474–476.
213 Ibn Taymiyyah, *Fatāwā*, vol. 19 p. 241.
214 Ibid. Al-Zarkashī mentions that the textual evidences cited by the Ḥanbalī scholars as proofs for the existence of a minimum period of menstruation are either plain but not authentic or authentic but not plain. Al-Zarkashī, *Sharḥ*, vol. 1 p. 408.
215 Ibn Taymiyyah, *Fatāwā*, vol. 19 p. 241.
216 Ibid., 239–240. This opinion of Ibn Taymiyyah regarding the period of postnatal bleeding also opposes the predominant opinion within the Ḥanbalī School, which fixes a certain period for it. For details see: al-Khiraqī, *Mukhtaṣar*, tran. p. 31, Ibn Qudāmah, *al-'Umdah*, pp. 57–58, Ibn *al-Bannā*, *al-Muqni'*, vol. 1 pp. 289, al-Majd, *al-Muḥarrar*, vol. 1 p. 27, Ibn Mufliḥ, *al-Furū'*, vol. 1 p. 282, al-Mardāwī, *al-Inṣāf*, vol. 1 pp. 383–384, al-Buhūtī, *Sharḥ*, vol. 1 p. 116, *al-Rawḍ*, p. 49, Ibn Qāsim, *Ḥāshī*yat, vol. 1 pp. 402–404.
217 For further details of this point see, al-Khiraqī, *Mukhtaṣar*, tran. pp. 53–54, Ibn Qudāmah, *al-'Umdah*, pp. 101–103, Ibn *al-Bannā*, *al-Muqni'*, vol. 1 pp. 428–437, al-Majd, *al-Muḥarrar*, vol. 1 pp. 129–133, Ibn Mufliḥ, *al-Furū'*, vol. 1 pp. 54–67, al-Mardāwī, *al-Inṣāf*, vol. 2 pp. 314–347, al-Buhūtī, *Sharḥ*, vol. 1 pp. 274–283, *al-Rawḍ*, pp. 109–110, al-'Anqirī, *Sharḥ*, vol. 1 pp. 271–281.
218 Ibn Taymiyyah, *Fatāwā*, vol. 19 p. 243
219 This *ḥādīth* is narrated by several scholars. See: al-Bayhaqī, *al-Sunan al-Kubrā*, vol. 3 p. 137, al-Dāraquṭnī, vol. 1 p. 387. The *barid* is four *farsakh* and the *farsakh* is three miles. Therefore, four *barids* are equal to 48 miles. See: al-Zarkashī, *Sharḥ* vol. 2 pp. 137–140, al-Mardāwī, *al-Inṣāf*, vol. 2 pp. 318–319.
220 Ibn Taymiyyah's criticism of the chain of this *ḥadīth* can be further supported by Ibn Ḥajar's statement that this *ḥādīth* is weak. He bases his ruling on the fact that one of the narrators of this *hādīth* was *matrūk* and another narrator was weak in his narrations from Ahl al-Ḥijāz. Ibn Ḥajar asserts that this *ḥādīth* is in fact a statement made by Ibn 'Abbās. Ibn Ḥajar, *al-Talkhīs*, vol. 2 p. 46.
221 Ibn Taymiyyah, *Majmū'*, vol. 2 p. 247.
222 Ibid., pp. 243–245, *Fatāwā*, vol. 19 p. 243.
223 Al-Khiraqī, *Mukhtaṣar*, tran. pp. 189–192, Ibn Qudāmah, *al-'Umdah*, pp. 406–408, Ibn *al-Bannā*, al-*Muqni'*, vol. 3 pp. 952–953, al-Majd, *al-Muḥarrar*, vol. 2 p. 44, Ibn Mufliḥ, *al-Furū'*, vol. 5 p. 343, al-Zarkashī, *Sharḥ*, vol. 5 pp. 355–361, al-Mardāwī, *al-Inṣāf*, vol. 8 p. 382, al-Buhūtī, *Sharḥ*, vol. 3 p. 107, *al-Rawḍ*, pp. 388–389, al-'Anqirī, *Sharḥ*, vol. 3 pp. 136–138.

224 Al-Mardāwī, *al-Inṣāf*, vol. 8 pp. 392–393.
225 Ibn Taymiyyah, *Fatāwā*, vol. 33 pp. 153–154. Ibn Mufliḥ (*al-Furū'*, vol. 5 pp. 345–346), al-Ba'lī in *Ikhtiyārāt*, p. 73 and al-Mardāwī (*al-Inṣāf*, vol. 8 p. 393) narrate this opinion of Ibn Taymiyyah.
226 For further details on this point see, al-Khiraqī, *Mukhtaṣar*, tran. pp. 224–226, Ibn Qudāmah, *al-'Umdah*, pp. 521–526, Ibn al-Bannā, *al-Muqni'*, vol. 3 pp. 1068–1073, al-Majd, *al-Muḥarrar*, vol. 2 pp. 148–150, Ibn Mufliḥ, *al-Furū'*, vol. 6 pp. 39–43, al-Zarkashī, *Sharḥ*, vol. 6 pp. 126–136, al-Mardāwī, *al-Inṣāf*, vol. 10 pp. 119–120, al-Buhūtī, *Sharḥ*, vol. 3 pp. 298–300
227 Al-Khiraqī, *Mukhtaṣar*, tran. p. 224, Ibn Mufliḥ, *al-Furū'*, vol. 6 pp. 39–40, al-Mardāwī, *al-Inṣāf*, vol. 10 pp. 119–120.
228 Ibn Taymiyyah, *Fatāwā*, vol. 19 pp. 255–256.
229 Ibid., vol. 19 p. 256.
230 See this definition in al-Mohideb, *Criminal Procedures*, p. 99.
231 Ibn Taymiyyah, *Fatāwā*, vol. 4 p. 133, vol. 34 pp. 206–207.
232 Ibn Taymiyyah, *al-Tafsīr*, vol. 1 p. 107.
233 Ibn Taymiyyah, *Fatāwā*, vol. 19 pp. 280–285, vol. 22 pp. 331–333.
234 Al-Maymān, *al-Qawā'id*, pp. 152–153. Ibn Taymiyyah states that if anyone claims that a rule is correct without basing the rule on text or consensus, his claim will be rejected. Ibn Taymiyyah, *Fatāwā*, vol. 21 p. 75.
235 Ibn Taymiyyah refers to this rule on numerous occasions. See, for instance, *Fatāwā*, vol. 21 p. 25. This rule is also mentioned and attributed to Ibn Taymiyyah in several Ḥanbalī sources, such as al-Ba'lī in *al-Ikhtiyārāt*, p. 73, Ibn Mufliḥ, *al-Furū'*, vol. 1 pp. 267–268, and al-Sa'dī, *Ṭarīq*, p. 147.
236 Ibn Taymiyyah, *Fatāwā*, vol. 21 pp. 27, 28–29.
237 For additional examples of issues that can be included under this rule used by Ibn Taymiyyah, see: Ibn Taymiyyah, *Fatāwā*, vol. 19 pp. 235–259. Other examples are also mentioned by Ibn Mufliḥ in *al-Furū'*, vol. 1 p. 268.
238 Ibn Taymiyyah, *Fatāwā*, vol. 21 p. 25.
239 Al-Ba'lī, *Mukhtaṣar*, pp. 13–14. Note that Ibn Taymiyyah once held the opinion that water is divided into three types. See, Ibn Taymiyyah, *Sharḥ al-'Umdah*, Book of *Ṭahārah* (purification) pp. 71–81, 84.
240 For further details, see, al-Khiraqī, *Mukhtaṣar*, tran. p. 20, Ibn Qudāmah, *al-'Umdah*, pp. 22–26, Ibn al-Bannā, al-*Muqni'*, vol. 1 p. 192, al-Majd, *al-Muḥarrar*, vol. 1 p. 2, Ibn Mufliḥ, *al-Furū'*, vol. 1 pp. 72–96, al-Zarkashī, *Sharḥ*, vol. 1 p. 114, al-Mardāwī, *al-Inṣāf*, vol. 1 pp. 21–22, al-Buhūtī, *Sharḥ*, vol. 1 pp. 10–16, *al-Rawḍ*, vol. 1 pp. 13–14, al-'Anqirī, *Sharḥ*, vol. 1 p. 15.
241 There are four views among Ḥanbalī scholars as to the classification of water: (1) The majority of Ḥanbalī scholars were of the aforementioned opinion, stating that water is classified into *ṭahūr* (absolute pure water), *ṭāhir* (pure water) and *najis* (impure water). (2) Some Ḥanbalī scholars classified water into two types (a) *Ṭāhir* (b) *Najis* and they further divided the *ṭāhir* into two types: (a) *ṭāhir* and *ṭahūr* (b) *ṭāhir* not *ṭahūr*. It appears that there is no real difference between this opinion and the one preceding it. (3) Ibn Taymiyyah asserts that water can be classified into only two types: (a) *ṭahūr* (b) *najis*. (4) The Ḥanbalī scholar Ibn Razīn was of the opinion that there are four types of water: (a) *ṭahūr* (b) *ṭāhir* (c) *najis* (d) *mashkūk fīh* (doubtful). See, al-Mardāwī, *al-Inṣāf*, vol. 1 p. 22.
242 Ibn Taymiyyah, *Fatāwā*, vol. 21 p. 25.
243 Ibid.
244 Ibid., p. 28.
245 Al-Khiraqī, *Mukhtaṣar*, tran. pp. 28–29, Ibn Qudāmah, *al-'Umdah*, pp. 40–41, Ibn *al-Bannā*, *al-Muqni'*, vol. 1 pp. 268–270, al-Majd, *al-Muḥarrar*, vol. 1 pp. 12–13, Ibn Mufliḥ, *al-Furū'*, vol. 1 pp. 158–159, al-Zarkashī, *Sharḥ*, vol. 1 pp. 391–392,

al-Mardāwī, *al-Inṣāf*, vol. 1 pp. 179–184, al-Buhūtī, *Sharḥ*, vol. 1 pp. 60–61, *al-Rawḍ*, vol. 1 pp. 30–32, al-'Anqirī, *Sharḥ*, vol. 1 pp. 59–63.

246 Ibn Taymiyyah, *Fatāwā*, vol. 19 p. 242, vol. 21 p. 173.

247 Ibid., vol. 21 p. 175.

248 Ibid., vol. 21 p. 173. Ibn Taymiyyah's opinion on this issue is mentioned in the treatises of a group of Ḥanbalī scholars, such as al-Mardāwī in his treatise *al-Inṣāf*, vol. 1 pp. 179, 182. Al-Mardāwī (*al-Inṣāf*, vol. 1 p. 183) and al-Zarkashī (*Sharḥ*, vol. 1 p. 392) mention Ibn Taymiyyah's opinion with regard to the issue of the excessively torn *Khuf*: a person should wipe over the remaining part of the *khuf* and wash the area uncovered by the tear. Al-Zarkashī comments on this view and states that it is in disorder. See, al-Zarkashī, *Sharḥ*, vol. 1 p. 392.

249 See these two opinions in Ibn Taymiyyah, *Fatāwā*, vol. 29 pp. 5–6, Ibn Mufliḥ, *al-Furū'*, vol. 5 pp. 168–169, al-Mardāwī, *al-Inṣāf*, vol. 8 pp. 45–50.

250 Ibn Taymiyyah, *Fatāwā*, vol. 29 pp. 7–21.

251 Ibid., pp. 8–9.

252 Ibid., p. 10

253 Ibid., pp. 12–13.

254 Ibn Taymiyyah, *Fatāwā*, vol. 29 pp. 5–21. Ibn Taymiyyah's opinion has been cited by several Ḥanbalī scholars, such as Ibn Mufliḥ, *al-Furū'*, vol. 5 p. 169, and al-Mardāwī, *al-Inṣāf*, vol. 8 p. 45.

255 Ibn Taymiyyah, *Fatāwā*, vol. 25 pp. 106–113, al-Sa'dī, *al-Mukhtārāt*, p. 60, Ibn al-Laḥḥām, *al-Qawā'id*, p. 126.

256 Ibn Taymiyyah, *Fatāwā*, vol. 10 p. 363. For other examples of rules used by Ibn Taymiyyah which had various ramifications for Ḥanbalī jurisprudence, see: Ibn al-Laḥḥām, *al-Qawā'id*, pp. 197–198.

257 This rule has been mentioned by some Ḥanbalī scholars, such as Ibn Mufliḥ, *al-Furū'*, vol. 1 p. 293, al-Mardāwī, *al-Inṣāf*, vol. 1 pp. 398–400, Ibn al-Najjār, *Muntahā*, vol. 1 p. 43, al-Buhūtī, *Sharḥ*, vol. 1 p. 120, *al-Rawḍ*, p. 52, *Kashshāf*, vol. 1 p. 226, al-Hajjāwī, *Zād*, with *al-Sharḥ* by Ibn 'Uthaymīn, vol. 2 pp. 22–23.

258 Ibn Taymiyyah, *Ikhtiyārāt*, p. 33.

259 Ibid., al-Ba'lī, *Mukhtaṣar*, p. 35.

260 Ibid.

261 Ibn Taymiyyah, *Fatāwā*, vol. 22 pp. 57–58. Ibn Taymiyyah's opinion is narrated by some Ḥanbalī scholars, such as Ibn Mufliḥ, *al-Furū'*, vol. 1 p. 293. It interesting to note that Ibn Munjja (d. 695/1296), who was one of Ibn Taymiyyah's teachers in *fiqh*, clarifies that the Ḥanbalī rule permitting postponement of the prayer for the purpose of fulfilling a condition of the prayer is problematic in two respects: first, this rule was not mentioned by any Ḥanbalī scholar before it was articulated by the leading Ḥanbalī scholar Ibn Qudāmah. On the contrary, it was known that Ḥanbalī scholars did not permit this delay except where the individual intends to combine two prayers. Second, this general permission might excuse the individual who deliberately delayed the prayer until before the end of the time. According to this rule, it would be allowed for him to postpone the prayer until he fulfils its conditions, without taking into consideration that he is the one who is responsible for this delay. The criticism of this Ḥanbalī rule has also been mentioned by Ibn 'Ubaydān. See, al-Mardāwī, *al-Inṣāf*, vol. 1 pp. 399–400.

262 Ibn Taymiyyah, *al-Qawā'id*, p. 128.

263 Ibid., p. 131.

264 Ibid., p. 150.

265 Ibid., p. 131.

266 Ibid., p. 137.

267 Ibn Taymiyyah, *Fatāwā*, vol. 31 pp. 47–48. Ibn Taymiyyah's clarification is also mentioned by several Ḥanbalī scholars. See for instance, al-Ba'lī, *Ikhtiyārāt*, p. 176,

al-Mardāwī, *al-Inṣāf*, vol. 7 p. 56, Ibn Mufliḥ, *al-Furū'*, vol. 4 pp. 600–601, al-Ḥajjāwī, *al-Iqnā'*, vol. 3 pp. 11–12.

268 Ibn Mufliḥ, *al-Furū'*, vol. 2 p. 8.

269 Ibn al-Bannā, *al-Muqni'*, vol. 3 pp. 1141–1142, Ibn Mufliḥ, *al-Furū'*, vol. 6 p. 101, al-Zarkashī, *Sharḥ*, vol. 6 pp. 378–383, al-Mardāwī, *al-Inṣāf*, vol. 10 pp. 229–230, al-Buhūtī, *Sharḥ*, vol. 3 p. 358.

270 Al-Mardāwī, *al-Inṣāf*, vol. 10 p. 230, al-Ba'lī, *al-Ikhtiyārāt*, p. 299. For another example of a narration attributed incorrectly by the leading Ḥanbalī scholars to Aḥmad, according to Ibn Taymiyyah, see: al-Mardāwī, *al-Inṣāf*, vol. 8 pp. 124–125.

271 Al-Zarkashī, *Sharḥ*, vol. 6 pp. 378–381, al-Mardāwī, *al-Inṣāf*, vol. 10 p. 230.

272 Ibn Taymiyyah, *Fatāwā*, vol. 21 pp. 139–140, al-Mardāwī, *al-Inṣāf*, vol. 8 pp. 50–51.

273 Ibn Taymiyyah, *Fatāwā*, vol. 21 p. 140, al-Mardāwī, *al-Inṣāf*, vol. 8 p. 51. For other examples, see: Ibn Taymiyyah, *Fatāwā*, vol. 22 p. 338, 406, 438, al-Mardāwī, *al-Inṣāf*, vol. 9 pp. 124–125. Ibn Taymiyyah occasionally agrees with the correctness of certain narrations, but then asserts that something else is commonly known from Ibn Ḥanbal. For an example, see: al-Mardāwī, *al-Inṣāf*, vol. 9 p. 28.

274 Al-Mardāwī, *al-Inṣāf*, vol. 1 p. 211.

275 Al-Mardāwī, *al-Inṣāf*, vol. 1 p. 211.

276 Ibid.

277 Ibn Taymiyyah, *Fatāwā*, vol. 21 pp. 233–235.

278 Al-Khiraqī, *Mukhtaṣar*, tran. p. 168, Ibn Qudāmah, *al-'Umdah*, p. 364, Ibn al-Bannā, *al-Muqni'*, vol. 3 pp. 887–888, al-Majd, *al-Muḥarrar*, vol. 2 p. 15, 16, Ibn Mufliḥ, *al-Furū'*, vol. 5 p. 172, al-Zarkashī, *Sharḥ*, vol. 5 pp. 79–80, al-Mardāwī, *al-Inṣāf*, vol. 8 p. 55, al-Buhūtī, *Sharḥ*, vol. 3 p. 14, *al-Rawḍ*, p. 363, al-'Anqirī, *Sharḥ*, vol. 3 pp. 70–71.

279 Al-Mardāwī, *al-Inṣāf*, vol. 8 p. 55.

280 Al-Bukhārī, *Ṣaḥīḥ*, vol. vii pp. 51–52.

281 Ibn Taymiyyah, *Fatāwā*, vol. 32 pp. 24–25.

282 Ibid., pp. 23, 25.

283 Ibid., pp. 25–26, 28.

284 Ibid., p. 23.

5 THE LEGACY: THE INFLUENCE OF IBN TAYMIYYAH ON ḤANBALĪ JURISTS

1 Ibn al-'Imād, *Shadharāt*, vol. 8 p. 147, Ibn Rajab, *Dhayl*, vol. 2 p. 395. This scholar's relationship with the different sectors of society can be seen clearly through the study of his life from various sources, such as *al-I'lām*, by al-Bazzār and *Dhayl*, by Ibn Rajab vol. 2 pp. 387–408.

2 Al-Bazzār, *al-I'lām*, p. 31, Ibn Rajab, *Dhayl*, vol. 2 p. 408.

3 Ibn Kathīr, *al-Bidāyah*, vol. 14 p. 111. Ibn Kathīr mentions that this *Amīr* was inseparable from Ibn Taymiyyah.

4 Ibid., vol. 14 p. 272. Ibn Kathīr describes this *Amīr* as 'one of the most devoted students of Ibn Taymiyyah (*min akbar aṣḥāb al-sheikh taqī al-dīn*)'.

5 Ibid., vol. 14 p. 229.

6 Ibid, p. 214.

7 Al-Karmī, *al-Kawākib*, pp. 133, 134–135. Chamberlain remarks: 'A great teacher might just as well work with students in jail as did Ibn Taymiyyah in Alexandria.' Chamberlain, *Knowledge*, p. 78.

8 Some sources mention that al-Dhahabī compiled a treatise entitled *al-Qabbān* in which he gathered the names of the disciples of Ibn Taymiyyah. See, al-Sakhāwī, *al-I'lān*, p. 307. Other scholars assert that no attempt has been made to gather all of Ibn Taymiyyah's students. See, for instance, al-Bazzār, *al-A'lām*, p. 31.

9 Al-Bazzār, *al-A'lām*, p. 31.
10 Ibn Nāṣir, *al-Radd*, pp. 65–73, Ibn al-'Imād, *Shadharāt*, vol. 8 pp. 264–268, 397–399, Ibn 'Abd al-Hādī, *al-Jawhar*, pp. 112–114 and al-Shaṭī, *Mukhtaṣar*, p. 68.
11 See the biography of this scholar in Ibn Rajab, *Dhayl*, vol. 2 pp. 434–435, Ibn Mufliḥ, *al-Maqṣad*, vol. 1 p. 215, Ibn al-'Imād, *Shadharāt*, vol. 8 p. 227, al-Ḥusaynī, *Dhuyūl*, vol. 4 p. 122.
12 *Al-Durar*, vol. 1 p. 16.
13 The theological tendency of al-Ṭūfī is problematic. Several scholars, such as al-Dhahabī, Ibn Rajab and al-Būṭī, were of the opinion that he was a shī'ī. Some contemporary scholars, such as al-Turkī and Zayd, assert that he was a Sunni. See: al-Dhahabī, *Dhuyūl al-'Ibar*, vol. 4 p. 44, Ibn Rajab, *Dhayl*, vol. 2 pp. 368–370, al-Turkī, in his introduction to *Sharḥ al-Rawḍah*, vol. 1 pp. 33–38, Zayd, *al-Maṣlaḥah*, pp. 74–88, al-Būṭī, *Ḍawābiṭ*, pp. 202–206.
14 Several scholars have affirmed that the creed as explained by this scholar, is very clear in comparison with other methods. See, for instance, Ibn Ḥāmid, *Risālah*, pp. 12–14, al-Wāsiṭī, *al-Tadhkirah*, Ibn Rajab, *Dhayl*, vol. 2 p. 393 and Ibn Nāṣir, *al-Radd*, p. 125.
15 Ibn Taymiyyah, in the narration of al-Bazzār, unveils the reason for the considerable attention he attached to the science of creed. He saw a state of confusion amongst the majority of people, caused by various incorrect opinions circulated by the scholars, who were described by him as 'the people of innovation'. He saw it as his duty to devote most of his efforts to correcting the mistakes emanating from the contributions of the scholars to this field. See: al-Bazzār, *al-I'lām*, pp. 35–37.
16 Al-Raḥmānī, preface to *Da'wah* by Aḥmad, pp. 19–20.
17 Ibid., p. 25. Some contemporary writers seem to suggest that Ibn 'Abd al-Wahhāb was the one who later successfully put Ibn Taymiyyah's ideas into practice. See, Safiullah, *Wahhābism*, p. 80. Woodward asserts that Ibn 'Abd al-Wahhāb was a reformer who turned Ibn Taymiyyah's theology into political action far more successfully than Ibn Taymiyyah had been able to do. Martin, *Defenders of Reason*, p. 126.
18 Ibn Kathīr, *al-Bidāyah*, vol. 14 p. 128, *Dhuyūl al-'Ibar*, vol. 4 p. 72.
19 Ibn Kathīr, *al-Bidāyah*, vol. 14 pp. 120–121.
20 Another scholar who was subjected to detention due to his support of Ibn Taymiyyah was the leading scholar of *Ḥadīth*, al-Mizzī. He was imprisoned and then was released by Ibn Taymiyyah himself. See, Ibn Kathīr, *al-Bidāyah*, vol. 14 p. 41.
21 Ibn Rajab, *Dhayl*, vol. 2 p. 448. At some stages, Ibn al-Qayyim did not mention whether his *fatwā* was in agreement with that of his sheikh. Nevertheless, he faced severe opposition from his contemporaries. For an example of this, see Ibn Kathīr, *al-Bidāyah*, vol. 14 p. 233. Ibn Kathīr was also detained for issuing *fatāwā* which agreed with the opinions of Ibn Taymiyyah. See, Ibn al-'Imād, *Shadharāt*, vol. 8 p. 399. Some of Ibn Taymiyyah's students, such as 'Abd al-Raḥmān (Ibn Taymiyyah's brother), accepted imprisonment with their sheikh in order to serve him. See, Ibn Kathīr, *al-Bidāyah*, vol. 14 p. 135.
22 Ibn Mufliḥ, *al-Maqṣad*, vol. 1 p. 93. For another example, see Ibn Nāṣir, *al-Radd*, p. 87.
23 Ibn al-'Imād, *Shadharāt*, vol. 8 p. 245, Ibn Rajab, *Dhayl*, vol. 2 pp. 436–439, Ibn Mufliḥ, *al-Maqṣad*, vol. 2 p. 360, Ibn Nāṣir, *al-Radd*, pp. 62–64.
24 Ibid., vol. 8 p. 227, Ibn Rajab, *Dhayl*, vol. 2 pp. 434–435, Ibn Mufliḥ, *al-Maqṣad*, vol. 1 p. 215.
25 Ibn Ḥajar, *al-Durar*, vol. 1 p. 25.
26 Ibn Nāṣir, *al-Radd*, p. 132, Ibn Rajab, *Dhayl*, vol. 2 p. 393, Ibn al-'Imād *Shadharāt*, vol. 8 p. 376.
27 Ibn al-'Imād, *Shadharāt*, vol. 8 p. 247.
28 Ibn Nāṣir, *al-Radd*, pp. 169–170.
29 Ibid., p. 87.

30 Ibn Rajab, *Dhayl*, vol. 2 pp. 361–362.

31 Ibn Kathīr, *al-Bidāyah*, vol. 14 p. 127. The means by which this influence was transferred to these students were Ibn Taymiyyah's lectures, treatises and *fatāwā*. The treatises and *fatāwā* were written by his students. One of them was Ibn Rushayq, who worked for him as a secretary. On some occasions, Ibn Taymiyyah used to ask him to read his manuscripts. For this reason, he was known for being very well acquainted with Ibn Taymiyyah's works. Ibn Kathīr, *al-Bidāyah*, vol. 14 p. 247, Ibn 'Abd al-Hādī, *al-Uqūd*, p. 27.

32 Ibn al-'Imād narrates a statement from al-Dhahabī in *Shadharāt*, vol. 8 p. 247, concerning the events of the year 745/1344, the year in which al-Ḥarānī died, which can provide an answer to this question. He mentions that this scholar studied with him and under him. Also, Ibn al-'Imād mentions the death of al-Harānī amongst the events of the year 745/1344. This means that when Ibn Taymiyyah died, al-Ḥarānī was 26 years old, and was living in Damascus and seeking knowledge in this city with his sheikh and companion, al-Dhahabī. Therefore, it is unlikely that this scholar did not study under Ibn Taymiyyah. 'Abd al-Ḥamīd, in the introduction of *al-Musawwadah*, p. 3. This can be further supported by the fact that one of al-Ḥarānī's most important works was his compilation of a clean copy of (*bayyaḍa*) al-*Musawwadah*. Ibn Mufliḥ, *al-Maqṣad.*, vol. 1 p. 178. It can be noted throughout *al-Musawwadah* that, when he categorises the opinions of these three scholars, al-Ḥarānī identifies the opinion of Ibn Taymiyyah by starting the sentences with the term *shaykhunā* (our sheikh). This affirms that he was one of his disciples.

33 This can be evidenced through the numerous Ḥanbalī scholars and schools that existed in this city at the time of Ibn Taymiyyah. Al-Nu'aymī mentions in his book '*al-Dāris fi Tārīkh al-Madāris*' the various schools, including the Ḥanbalī scholars and *madāris*, present in Damascus from the fifth to the eighth Islamic century. Ibn Ṭūlūn mentions in his book '*I'lām al-Warā*' some aspects of the educational life of Damascus.

34 This scholar was known as Ibn al-Qayyim or Ibn Qayyim al-Jawziyyah because his father was the Qayyim (superintendent) of the school known as 'al-Jawziyyah'. See Ibn Kathīr, *al-Bidāyah*, vol. 14 p. 252.

35 Ibn Mufliḥ, *al-Maqṣad*, vol. 2 p. 385.

36 Abū Zayd, *al-Taqrīb*, p. 145.

37 See the biography of this scholar in the following: al-Dhahabī, *Dhuyūl al-'Ibar*, vol. 4 pp. 126–127, Ibn al-'Imād, *Shadharāt*, vol. 8 pp. 236–237.

38 Abū Zayd, *al-Taqrīb*, pp. 47–48.

39 Ibn Rajab (*Dhayl*, vol. 2 p. 449) describes those who studied under Ibn al-Qayyim as being great in number (*khalqun kathīr*).

40 These two books have been published several times.

41 In another study of Ibn al-Qayyim, Sharaf al-Dīn declares that Ibn al-Qayyim was a Ḥanbalī scholar but was not a fanatic follower of this School, instead he followed what he thought to be the right opinion based upon his own *ijtihād*. Sharaf al-Dīn, *Ibn al-Qayyim*, p. 99.

42 Abū Zayd, *Ibn al-Qayyim*, p. 44.

43 Nurbain, *Ibn al-Qayyim's Reformation*, p. 94.

44 Al-Ḥusaynī, *Dhuyūl al-'Ibar*, vol. 4 p. 155.

45 Ibn Rajab, *Dhayl*, vol. 2 p. 448, Ibn Mufliḥ, *al-Maqṣad*, vol. 2 p. 385, Ibn Shaṭī, *Mukhtaṣar*, p. 68.

46 Ibn Kathīr, *al-Bidāyah*, vol. 14 p. 117, 202; Sharaf al-Dīn, *Ibn al-Qayyim*, p. 73; Abū Zayd, *al-Taqrīb*, pp. 110, 140. This is problematic as Ibn Rajab (in his book *al-Dhayl* vol. 2 p. 448) mentions that Ibn al-Qayyim was imprisoned in a separate cell in the citadel of Damascus. This imprisonment lasted for two-and-a-half years.

47 See, for instance, Ibn al-Qayyim *Zād*, vol. 1 pp. 71, 264, 319, 324, 375, 499, vol. 5 p. 730, *I'lām*, vol. 4 pp. 223, 264, 295.
48 See, for instance, Ibn al-Qayyim *Zād*, vol. 1 p. 407, *I'lām*, vol. 4 p. 203.
49 *I'lām*, vol. 4 pp. 147–148.
50 See, for instance, *I'lām*, vol. 4 pp. 203, 219, 226, 264, 272, 295, 319, 322.
51 The benefit Ibn al-Qayyim derived from Ibn Taymiyyah is acknowledged in various places; see for instance, *Zād al-Ma'ād*, vol. 2 pp. 21, 22, 118–122, 127, 141, 148–150, 209–210, 231, 333, vol. 5 pp. 811–816. In addition, he cites the words and opinions of his sheikh in various places in his book *Ighāthat al-Lahfān*. for instance, see vol. 1 pp. 410, 412, 417–422, 469–470, 501, 508–509, 550–555, vol. 2 pp. 8–9, 48, 55, 62, 74, 123, 133, 152. Also, he cites and quotes his sheikh in other treatises, such as *Aḥkām Ahl al-Dhimmah*, vol. 1 pp. 51–54, 189, 280, 281–282, 286–290, 342, 360, 380, vol. 2 pp. 462–467, 474, 481–482, 492, 495, 541–543, 567–568, 570, 571, 578–580, 582–583, 592–593, 593–594, 594–596, 601–602, 626–627, 629, 677–707, 800–801, 816–818, 831, 833–865, 865–870. Ibn al-Qayyim benefited from his sheikh during the writing of a large part of his book *al-I'lām*. There is clearly a great similarity between the comments made by Ibn al-Qayyim in this book and the opinions of Ibn Taymiyyah. Ibn al-Qayyim himself acknowledges that he benefited from his sheikh a great deal. This can be evidenced through his discussion concerning the conflict between analogy and text that commences at vol. 1 p. 472. Here he states that the following section is based on what he learnt from his sheikh. The citation appears to continue up to vol. 2 p. 365, where he again states that he acquired the information mentioned on the issue in question from Ibn Taymiyyah. There are many other sections displaying a noticeable similarity between Ibn Taymiyyah's and Ibn al-Qayyim's opinions concerning various issues, for example: the consensus of Ahl al-Madīnah vol. 2 pp. 412–430; stipulation of purity for the performing of *ṭawāf*, vol. 3 pp. 19–39; the triple divorce, vol. 3 pp. 40–54; the marriage of *al-taḥlīl*, vol. 3 pp. 54–66; his discussion of legal devices (*ḥiyal*) vol. 3 pp. 224–502.
52 See, for examples, Ibn al-Qayyim, *Ighāthat*, vol. 1 p. 553.
53 Ibn al-Qayyim, *Zād*, vol. 2 pp. 21, 22.
54 See, for examples, Ibn al-Qayyim, *Zād*, vol. 1 p. 434, vol. 3 p. 37.
55 Ibn al-Qayyim, *I'lām*, vol. 3 pp. 358–359. In support of his opinion on this issue, Ibn al-Qayyim cites the words of Ibn Taymiyyah. Ibid, p. 360.
56 Ibn al-Qayyim, *I'lām*, vol. 1 pp. 337–403, vol. 2 p. 48.
57 Ibid., vol. 3 p. 77.
58 Ibn al-Qayyim, *Zād*, vol. 2 pp. 209–210.
59 Ibid., vol. 2 p. 141.
60 Ibid., vol. 1 p. 440.
61 Ibid., vol. 2 p. 88.
62 Ibid., p. 593.
63 Ibid., vol. 5 p. 415.
64 Ibid., vol. 1 pp. 136–137.
65 Ibn al-Qayyim, *I'lām*, vol. 3 p. 96.
66 Ibid., vol. 4 pp. 144–145.
67 Ibid., p. 144.
68 See, for instance, *Ighāthat*, vol. 2 p. 55, *Aḥkām*, vol. 2 pp. 831–870, *Zād*, vol. 1 p. 311, vol. 2 pp. 118–122, 127, 148–150.
69 See, for instance, Ibn al-Qayyim, *Zād* vol. 1 pp. 276, 438, 464, 465, 472.
70 Ibid., vol. 5 pp. 155, 215.
71 Ibid., p. 730.
72 Ibn al-Qayyim, *I'lām*, vol. 4 p. 334.
73 Ibn al-Qayyim, *al-Nūniyyah*, vol. 2 pp. 72–73.

74 Ibn Rajab, *Dhayl*, vol. 2 p. 448, Ibn Kathīr, *al-Bidāyah*, vol. 14 p. 253.
75 Abū Zayd, *Ibn Qayyim*, pp. 83–85.
76 Ibn Ḥajar, *al-Durar*, vol. 4 p. 21.
77 Ibid, pp. 44–45. Ibn al-Qayyim in *I'lām al-Muwaqqi'īn* declares that he frequently found issues where the right opinion was not in conformity with the position of the Ḥanbalī School. He did not hesitate to declare the other opinions as being correct. Ibn al-Qayyim, *I'lām al-Muwaqqi'īn*, vol. 4 p. 225.
78 See, for instance, *Zād*, vol. 2 p. 193.
79 Ibn al-Qayyim, *Zād*, vol. 5 p. 673.
80 Sharaf al-Dīn, *Ibn al-Qayyim*, pp. 90–93, Abū Zayd, *Ibn Qayyim*, pp. 91–93.
81 Al-Naḥlawī, *Ibn Qayyim*, pp. 25–28.
82 Abū Zayd, *Ibn Qayyim*, pp. 36–37, 89.
83 Ibn Rajab, *Dhayl*, vol. 2 p. 449, Ibn Kathīr, *al-Bidāyah*, vol. 14 p. 203.
84 Abū Zayd, *al-Taqrīb*, pp. 138–151.
85 See, for example, Ibn al-Qayyim, *I'lām*, vol. 2 pp. 149–151.
86 See, for example, footnote no. 51.
87 Abū Zayd, *Taqrīb*, p. 9.
88 Ibn al-Qayyim upheld his sheikh's knowledge by conveying his sheikh's various opinions and by supporting most of his sheikh's opinions, in many instances providing additional evidences.
89 See for instance *Zād al-Ma'ād*, vol. 2 pp. 21, 22, 118–122, 127, 141, 148–150, 209–210, 231, 333 and *al-I'lām*, vol. 1 pp. 137, 520, vol. 2 pp. 5, 8, 9.
90 Al-Shawkānī, *al-Badr*, vol. 2 pp. 144–145.
91 Ibn Ḥajar, *Taqrīẓ*, p. 15, Ibn Nāṣir, *al-Radd*, p. 231.
92 Al-Sa'dī, *Ṭarīq*, p. 303.
93 There are different narrations concerning this scholar's date of birth. For details see, Ibn Mufliḥ, *al-Maqṣad*, vol. 2 p. 520. There is also a disagreement about his age upon his death. Only some scholars, such as Ibn al-'Imād, *Shadharāt*, vol. 8 p. 341, and Ibn Mufliḥ, *al-Maqṣad*, vol. 2 p. 520, say that Ibn Mufliḥ's age when he died was *biḍ' wa khamsūn* (i.e. between 53 and 59 years old)
94 Ibn Mufliḥ, *al-Maqṣad*, vol. 2 pp. 518–519.
95 Ibid., p. 519.
96 Ibid.
97 Ibid., p. 518, *al-Jawhar*, p. 112.
98 Ibn Mufliḥ, *al-Maqṣad*, vol. 2 p. 518.
99 Ibid., p. 520, *al-Jawhar*, p. 113.
100 Ibid.
101 Ibn Mufliḥ, *al-Maqṣad*, vol. 2 p. 519.
102 Ibid., p. 385.
103 Ibn 'Abd al-Hādī, *al-Jawhar* p. 114.
104 Al-Mardāwī mentions this statement in the introduction to *Taṣḥīḥ al-Furū'*, vol. 1 p. 22.
105 Ibn Mufliḥ, for instance, mentions Ibn Taymiyyah's treatises *Sharḥ al-'Umdah*, in *al-Furū'* (vol. 1 pp. 87, 118, 154, 222) *Iqtiḍā'* (vol. 2 p. 440), *Minhāj* (vol. 3 p. 138), *al-Ajwibah al-Maṣriyyah* (vol. 1 p. 460), *al-Ṣārim al-Maslūl* (vol. 1 p. 576), *al-Fatāwā al-Miṣriyyah*, (vol. 2 p. 603).
106 See, for instance, *al-Furū'*, vol. 1 p. 206, vol. 2 p. 185. On some issues, Ibn Mufliḥ draws an analogy from rulings issued by his sheikh to other similar cases. See, for instance, *al-Furū'*, vol. 6 p. 543.
107 For examples of opinions toward which Ibn Taymiyyah appears to have a leaning, see *al-Furū'*, vol. 1 p. 246. For examples of opinions in regard to which Ibn Mufliḥ mentions that his sheikh has reservations or hesitate, see: *al-Furū'*, vol. 2 p. 591, vol. 6 p. 395.

108 See, for instance, *al-Furū'*, vol. 2 pp. 315, 651.
109 There are other signs of the importance Ibn Mufliḥ attached to Ibn Taymiyyah's opinions: On several occasions, Ibn Mufliḥ mentions that his sheikh's opinion concerning certain issues will be mentioned in a coming section or chapter; he also occasionally points out that he has already mentioned his sheikh's opinion in a previous section or chapter. For the first type, see *al-Furū'*, vol. 2 p. 339, vol. 3 pp. 125, 226 and for the second type the same source vol. 3 pp. 137, 145.
110 See, for instance, *al-Furū'*, vol. 1 pp. 128–129, 139, 458, vol. 2 pp. 311, 498–500.
111 Ibid., vol. 3 p. 7.
112 Ibn al-Najjār, *Sharḥ*, vol. 4 p. 250.
113 See, for instance, *al-Furū'*, vol. 1 pp. 244, 258, 306, 547, 577, 587, vol. 2 pp. 118, 130, 155, 249, 287, 445, 537, 619, vol. 3 pp. 4, 50, 65, 66, vol. 4 pp. 38, 162, 187, 202, 411, 435, 474, vol. 5 pp. 154, 187, 205, 215, 293, 491, 506, vol. 6 pp. 68, 76, 256, 313, 550, 599. Also, Ibn Mufliḥ mentions various ruling derivations (*takhrījāt*) drawn by Ibn Taymiyyah. See, for instance, *al-Furū'*, vol. 5 pp. 217, 239, 308, 474, 492, 660, vol. 6 p. 498.
114 See, for instance, *al-Furū'*, vol. 1 pp. 134, 139, 208, vol. 4 pp. 64, 97, 137, 138, 160, 404, 406, vol. 5 p. 363, vol. 6 pp. 287, 455, 499, 527.
115 See, for instance, *al-Furū'*, vol. 3 p. 112.
116 Ibid., vol. 2 p. 440.
117 Ibid., vol. 1 p. 587.
118 Ibid., vol. 4 p. 138.
119 Ibid., p. 265.
120 See, for instance, al-Mardāwī's criticism of Ibn Mufliḥ in *Taṣḥīḥ al-Furū'* (vol. 1 p. 547). He mentions, in *al-Furū'* (vol. 1 pp. 547–548), the existence of two narrations within the Ḥanbalī School regarding a jurisprudential issue which are both based upon the words of Ibn Taymiyyah.
121 See, for instance, *al-Furū'*, vol. 2 pp. 130, 210, 273.
122 See, for instance, for claiming consensus *al-Furū'*, vol. 1 pp. 128, 255, vol. 2 pp. 264, 273, 305, 443, vol. 3 pp. 227, 289, vol. 4 pp. 51, 289, 538, vol. 5 p. 418, 432, vol. 6 pp. 106, 159, 273, 303, 423, 492, 533 and for the claim that some rulings are the opinions of the Predecessors, *al-Furū'*, vol. 2 pp. 651–652, 666.
123 See, for instance, *al-Furū'*, vol. 4 pp. 285–286.
124 Ibid., vol. 1 p. 430, vol. 3 pp. 24, 123–124, 167–168, vol. 5 pp. 162, 367.
125 See, for instance, *al-Furū'*, vol. 2 pp. 251–252, 445–446. On several occasions, Ibn Taymiyyah insists that his opinions, which were in opposition to the opinions of leading Ḥanbalī scholars, were in fact the opinions of Aḥmad and the early Ḥanbalī scholars. See, for instance, *al-Furū'*, vol. 2 p. 304, vol. 3 p. 301.
126 See, for instance, *al-Furū'*, vol. 1 p. 467.
127 Ibid., pp. 101, 118, 547, 584, vol. 2 pp. 160, 264, 265, 273, 305, 311, 312–313, vol. 3 pp. 107–108.
128 See, for instance, *al-Furū'*, vol. 1 pp. 224, 266, 375, 428, 442, vol. 2 pp. 58, 89, 91, 277, 437–438, vol. 3 pp. 390, 492, vol. 5 pp. 11, 304, 515, vol. 6 p. 55. On one occasion, Ibn Mufliḥ prefers the opinion held by Ibn Taymiyyah to that of Aḥmad as he sees the evidence to be in support of his sheikh. *Al-Furū'*, vol. 6 p. 320. In some cases, Ibn Mufliḥ mentions some evidence which can back his sheikh, but does not disclose his own opinions. See, for instance, *al-Furū'*, vol. 5 p. 640. Sometimes, Ibn Mufliḥ mentions some scholars who hold similar opinions to his sheikh, *al-Furū'*, vol. 5 p. 606, vol. 6 pp. 120, 480.
129 See, for instance, *al-Furū'*, vol. 2 pp. 314, 592, 602, vol. 3 pp. 204–205. Ibn Mufliḥ mentions that he could not find the legal evidence for one narration preferred by Ibn Taymiyyah. *Al-Furū'*, vol. 6 p. 588.

130 See, for instance, *al-Furū'*, vol. 2 pp. 402–403, vol. 6 p. 340, vol. 4 p. 92.
131 Ibid., vol. 2 pp. 118, 440, *al-Inṣāf*, vol. 3 p. 115.
132 Ibid., vol. 1 pp. 198, vol. 6 pp. 491, 570.
133 Ibid., vol. 2 pp. 314–315, 602, vol. 4 p. 285, vol. 6 p. 508. Ibn Mufliḥ asserts that the apparent meaning of some texts supports the opinion of his sheikh's opponents, but in some of these issues it seems that there is a clear contradiction in the words of Ibn Mufliḥ. See, for instance, *al-Furū'*, vol. 2 pp. 314–315.
134 See, for instance, *al-Furū'*, vol. 1 p. 460.
135 Ibid., vol. 5 p. 506.
136 Ibid., vol. 2 p. 592.
137 Ibid., vol. 1 p. 123.
138 Ibid., vol. 2 pp. 651–652.
139 An example is an issue mentioned by al-Mardāwī in *al-Inṣāf*. Ibn Abi al-Majd, one of Ibn Taymiyyah's disciples, narrated that the opinion of his sheikh on the issue of the reversal of *khul'* (divorce at the instance of the wife) is that it is permissible to reverse the *khul'* and the compensation paid for it, because this contract takes the status of the contract of sale which can be legally reversed. Al-Mardāwī mentions that it is narrated that Ibn Mufliḥ said to Ibn Abi al-Majd, while the two scholars where debating this issue, 'your narration of this opinion from our sheikh is wrong'. Al-Mardāwī, *al-Inṣāf*, vol. 8 p. 395.
140 See, for instance, *al-Furū'*, vol. 3 p. 50.
141 An example is the issue of the importance of the eve of the middle of Sha'bān. Ibn Mufliḥ mentions (*al-Furū'*, vol. 3 p. 118) that Ibn Taymiyyah holds the opinion that this eve has a special virtue (*faḍīlah*) according to what is narrated from Aḥmad and others. When referring to source works of Ibn Taymiyyah's opinions (such as *al-Ikhtyārāt*, p. 65, *Fatāwā*, vol. 23 p. 131), one finds that the opinion mentioned by Ibn Mufliḥ is, in fact, only a part of Ibn Taymiyyah's opinion. The remainder of Ibn Taymiyyah's opinion states that gathering in mosques for this prayer is an innovation (*bid'ah*).
142 Al-Sakhāwī, *al-Ḍaw'*, vol. 11 p. 32, al-Zaraklī, *al-A'lām*, vol. 2 p. 37.
143 The Sultan of the time was al-Ashraf Barsibāī who was in power from the year 825/1422 till his death in the year 841/1437. The era of this Sultan was a time of political stability. See, *al-Nujūm*, vol. 14 p. 242, *Khiṭaṭ*, vol. 2 p. 188.
144 Al-Sakhāwī, *al-Ḍaw'*, vol. 11 p. 32, al-'Ulaymī, *al-Dur*, vol. 2 pp. 679–680, al-Shaṭī, *Mukhtaṣar*, p. 74.
145 Al-Sakhāwī, *al-Ḍaw'*, vol. 11 p. 32, *Shadharāt*, vol. 9 p. 505.
146 Al-Sakhāwī, *al-Ḍaw'*, vol. 11 p. 32.
147 Ibid.
148 Al-Jurā'ī, *Ghāyat*, p. 56b.
149 Ibid., p. 61b.
150 Ibid., p. 137a.
151 Ibid., p. 71a.
152 Ibid., pp. 187b, 222a.
153 Ibid., p. 155a.
154 Ibid., pp. 41a–b.
155 Ibid., pp. 79a, 209a.
156 Al-Thaqafī, *Muṣṭalaḥāt*, p. 205.
157 Al-Jurā'ī, *Ghāyat*, p. 2a.
158 See, for instance, *Ghāyat*, pp. 148b, 186a.
159 Ibn 'Abd al-Hādī, *al-Jawhar*, p. 62, Ibn Mufliḥ, *al-Maqṣad*, vol. 2 p. 91.
160 Al-Jurā'ī, *Ghāyat*, pp. 40b.
161 Ibid., p. 77a.

162 Ibn 'Abd al-Hādī, *al-Jawhar*, p. 99.
163 Al-Thaqafī, *Muṣtalaḥāt*, p. 207.
164 Ibn 'Abd al-Hādī, *al-Jawhar*, p. 100.
165 Most of the biographical accounts written about al-Mardāwī mention that he compiled the book '*Taṣḥīḥ al-Furū'*' After searching in various indices of manuscripts, we found that one index mentions the existence of a work by this scholar concerning *al-Furū'*. This book is entitled '*Mukhtaṣar al-Furū'* ', and a copy exists in a library in Iraq. It appears that these two works are two different treatises. This can be further supported by the statement of al-Sakhāwī (*al-Ḍaw'* vol. 5 p. 226) that al-Mardāwī made a summary of *al-Furū'* and also made additions to it.
166 See, for instance, *al-Inṣāf*, vol. 1 pp. 38, 43, 67, 77, 79, 81, 292, vol. 3 pp. 177, 179, vol. 4 pp. 44, 221, 234, 235, 463.
167 Ibid., vol. 1 p. 399.
168 Ibid., p. 57, vol. 2 p. 39.
169 Ibid., pp. 54–55.
170 Ibid., vol. 3 p. 235.
171 Ibid., vol. 9 p. 317.
172 Ibid., vol. 3 p. 270.
173 Ibid., vol. 11 p. 117.
174 Ibid., vol. 1 pp. 16–17.
175 Ibid., p. 18.
176 Ibid., vol. 2 p. 181, vol. 4 pp. 52, 57, 66, vol. 8 p. 449, vol. 10 p. 383.
177 Ibid., vol. 7 p. 475.
178 Ibid., vol. 8 p. 64
179 Ibid., vol. 2 p. 189.
180 Ibid., p. 234, vol. 8 pp. 40, 66, 90, 108, 110, 125, 126, 137, 271, 319, 410, 436.
181 See, for instance, ibid., vol. 7 p. 306. Al-Mardāwī sometimes cites and agrees with the criticism made by some Ḥanbalī scholars of some of Ibn Taymiyyah's pronouncements in the field of *ḥadīth*. See, for instance, ibid., vol. 2 p. 78.
182 See, for instance, ibid., vol. 1 p. 84, vol. 4 p. 80, vol. 371, vol. 8 pp. 3–4, 315.
183 See, for instance, ibid., vol. 3 pp. 182, 234, 269, 387, vol. 4 pp. 397, 405, vol. 5 pp. 68, 130, 484, vol. 6 pp. 46, 112, vol. 7 pp. 68, 88, 101, vol. 9 p. 202, vol. 10 pp. 171, 244, vol. 11 p. 18. On some issues, al-Mardāwī cites some Ḥanbalī scholars who assert that the ruling found within the School is in fact related to an issue other than that stated by Ibn Taymiyyah. See, for instance, ibid, vol. 5 p. 237.
184 See, for instance, ibid., vol. 4 pp. 462, 463, 469, vol. 5 pp. 264, 276, 404, vol. 9 pp. 71, 268, vol. 10 pp. 201, 241, 370. In some of these issues where Ibn Taymiyyah claims the existence of consensus, al-Mardāwī cities statements asserting the existence of disputes among scholars. See, for instance, ibid, vol. 5 p. 261.
185 See, for instance, ibid., vol. 1 p. 376, vol. 9 p. 341. Some of these opinions are known in the Ḥanbalī School as opinions and not as narrations from Aḥmad. See, for example, ibid, vol. 9 p. 202.
186 See, for instance, ibid., vol. 1 pp. 47, 59, 60, 82, 87, 114, 128, 155, vol. 3 pp. 22, 434, vol. 4 pp. 351, 461, vol. 5 pp. 34, 271, 339, 372, 375, 425, vol. 6 pp. 36, 37, 202, vol. 7 pp. 31, 117, 137, 370, vol. 8 pp. 10, 64, 160, 387, vol. 9 p. 145, vol. 10 pp. 327, 371, vol. 11 pp. 125, 221.
187 Ibid., vol. 1 p. 405.
188 Ibid., p. 423.
189 Ibid., p. 8, vol. 5 pp. 420, 425, 471 vol. 7 p. 446, vol. 8 p. 101.
190 Ibid., vol. 5 p. 483, vol. 6 p. 179, vol. 7 pp. 156, 231, 349, 423, vol. 8 pp. 69, 80, 120, 201, 255, 289, 362, vol. 9 pp. 5, 483, vol. 10 p. 7, 154, vol. 11 p. 323.

191 See, for instance, ibid., vol. 5 pp. 149, 203, 216, 234, 261, 271, 324, 420, 426–427, vol. 6 p. 82, vol. 8 p. 153, vol. 10 pp. 34, 327, vol. 12 p. 62.
192 See, for instance, ibid., vol. 1 pp. 357, 359, vol. 2 pp. 74, 88, 212, 231, 247, 362, vol. 3 pp. 39, 301, 315, vol. 4 pp. 31, 38, 107, 189, 327, 378, vol. 5 pp. 32, 76, 130, 255, 282, 324, 327, 332, vol. 7 pp. 209, 306, vol. 8 pp. 137, 154, 329, vol. 10 pp. 67, 140, vol. 12 pp. 151, 197.
193 See, for instance, ibid., vol. 2 pp. 47, 290, 567, vol. 3 pp. 218, 286, vol. 4 pp. 185, 339, 373, 398, 459, vol. 5 pp. 204, 322, 324, 373, 440, vol. 6 pp. 117, 132, 219, 376–377, vol. 7 pp. 45, 78, 155, 354, vol. 8 pp. 330, 441, vol. 10 pp. 3, 404, vol. 11 pp. 12, 231, vol. 12 p. 9.
194 Ibid., vol. 1 p. 405.
195 Ibid., vol. 2 p. 47.
196 Ibid., p. 44, vol. 8 p. 6.
197 Ibid., p. 567.
198 Ibid., vol. 5 p. 255.
199 Ibid., vol. 4 p. 38.
200 Ibid., vol. 5 p. 274. Al-Mardāwī occasionally cites rules in the Ḥanbalī School that support the position of Ibn Taymiyyah. See, for instance, *al-Inṣāf*, vol. 5 pp. 274, 324. He also cites some similar rulings within the School to support rulings held by Ibn Taymiyyah. See, for example, ibid., vol. 5 p. 277.
201 See, for instance, ibid., vol. 6 p. 84, vol. 8 p. 58.
202 See, for instance, ibid., vol. 7 p. 49, vol. 9 p. 107. As an aside, in his book entitled '*Sharḥ al-Taḥrīr*', al-Mardāwī studied the position of Ibn Mufliḥ that it is not permissible for a mufti to answer a question at length if he can make the answer shorter. Al-Mardāwī comments upon Ibn Mufliḥ's statement saying that this utterance is problematic for it is well known that scholars would give answers which covered more than the point in question. The end result is that an answer may be comprised of one volume or more. He mentioned the example of Ibn Taymiyyah. Ibn al-Najjār, *Sharḥ al-Kawkab al-Munīr* vol. 4 pp. 596–597. Al-Mardāwī also studied two statements regarding the existence of *mujtahīds*. The first is al-Nawawī's statement, which says that there were no *mujtahids* in his time nor in many eras before. The second statement is made by al-Rāfi'ī, in which he states that the people of his time appear to agree that there was no absolute *mujtahid* during his era. Al-Mardāwī comments that there were in fact some scholars who reached the status of *mujtahid* and again gives Ibn Taymiyyah as an example. Ibn al-Najjār, *Sharḥ al-Kawkab al-Munīr* vol. 4 pp. 569–570.
203 See, for instance, *al-Insāf*, vol. 3 pp. 149, 301, 315, 495, vol. 4 p. 185, vol. 5 p. 274, vol. 9 p. 491.
204 See, for instance, ibid., vol. 2 p. 234, vol. 4 pp. 149, 160, 367, vol. 5 pp. 368, 373, vol. 6 pp. 43, 326, vol. 7 pp. 326, 475, vol. 8 pp. 40, 45, 58, 66, 90, 108, 109–110, 125, 126, 137, 161, 200, 218, 249, 298, 303, 319, 325, 382, 436, vol. 10 pp. 355, 356, 357, 398, vol. 11 pp. 156, vol. 12 pp. 38, 122, 122–123, 145.
205 Ibid., vol. 1 pp. 401–402.
206 Ibid., vol. 5 p. 327.
207 Ibid., vol. 7 p. 53.
208 Ibid., vol. 8 p. 198. On some issues, al-Mardāwī mentions that several Ḥanbalī scholars assert that the opinion claimed by Ibn Taymiyyah to be that of Aḥmad is in fact an old opinion, which was later retracted by Aḥmad. See, for instance, ibid., vol. 2 p. 558.
209 See, for instance, ibid., vol. 2 p. 280, vol. 4 p. 209, vol. 8 p. 362, vol. 9 p. 442.
210 Ibid, vol. 1 pp. 186, 199, 201, vol. 2 p. 451, vol. 7 p. 61. In some issues, al-Mardāwī does not label Ibn Taymiyyah's ruling as incorrect but he asserts that it is in opposition to the apparent meaning of many statements issued by Ḥanbalī scholars. See, for

instance, *al-Inṣāf*, vol. 4 p. 464. Also, al-Mardāwī cites Ibn Mufliḥ in various issues where it seems that he has some reservations or criticism of Ibn Taymiyyah's opinions. See, for instance, ibid, vol. 1 pp. 110, 441, vol. 2 p. 230, vol. 3 pp. 179, 257, 302, 453, vol. 4 pp. 66–67.

211 Ibid., vol. 2 p. 78, vol. 5 p. 261.
212 Ibid., vol. 6 p. 41.
213 Ibid., vol. 1 pp. 355, 357, 361, 383, vol. 3 pp. 299, 300, 332, 432, 434, vol. 4 pp. 57, 217, 301, vol. 5 pp. 23, 33, 125, 168, 210, 238, 281, 344, 440, vol. 6 pp. 13, 29, 30, 44, 93 twice, 94, vol. 7 pp. 9, 10, 11, 12, 21, 22, 23, 25, 101, 112, 116, 133, 134, 311, 323, 348, 352, 405, vol. 8 pp. 45, 122, 152, 213, 248, 271, 318, 347, 354, 424, 448, vol. 9 pp. 55, 64, 95, 150, 233, 316, 334, 371, 383, 395, 406, 469, vol. 10 pp. 67, 140, 150, 154, 199, 285, 295, 312, 342, 357, 408, vol. 11 pp. 165, 237, 271, vol. 12 pp. 108, 122, 211.
214 Ibid., vol. 7 p. 303.
215 Ibid., p. 415.
216 Ibid., vol. 1 pp. 389–390, vol. 2 pp. 263, 365, vol. 3 pp. 65, 85, vol. 4 p. 295.
217 Ibid., vol. 1 pp. 389–390, vol. 2 p. 263.
218 Ibid., vol. 2 p. 192.
219 Ibid., vol. 10 p. 168.
220 Ibid., vol. 8 p. 317, vol. 11 p. 385.
221 Ibid., vol. 1 pp. 62, 88, 215.
222 Ibid., p. 109, vol. 8 p. 90.
223 Ibid., vol. 3 p. 114.
224 Ibid., pp. 86, 389, vol. 7 p. 66.
225 Ibid., vol. 7 p. 304.
226 Ibid., pp. 25, 26, vol. 8 pp. 25, 218, 371.
227 Ibid., vol. 10 pp. 177, 241.
228 Ibid., vol. 1 p. 14.
229 Ibid., p. 441, vol. 3 p. 273, vol. 5 pp. 16, 80.
230 Ibid., vol. 7 p. 46.
231 Ibid., vol. 2 p. 229.
232 Ibid., vol. 1 p. 409.
233 Ibid., p. 92, vol. 3 pp. 270, 303, 447, vol. 4 pp. 29, 89, 348, 356, 374, vol. 4 pp. 415, 473, vol. 5 pp. 69, 80, 154, 167, 205, 215, 269, 327, vol. 6 pp. 146, 155, 168, 286, vol. 8 p. 46. Ibn Qāḍī al-Jabal in his book *al-Fā'iq* adopts the opinions of his sheikh in various issues. See, for instance, ibid, vol. 1 p. 397, vol. 2 p. 289, vol. 3 pp. 179, 286, 294, 303, 312, vol. 4 pp. 295, 302, 374, vol. 5 pp. 34, 210, 249, 438, vol. 6 pp. 255, 414, vol. 8 p. 46.
234 Ibid., vol. 1 p. 24.
235 Ibid., vol. 5 p. 47.
236 Ibn 'Abd al-Hādī, *al-Jawhar*, p. 100.
237 Consult the biography of al-Ḥajjāwī in the following sources: Ibn Shaṭī, *Mukhtaṣar*, pp. 93–94, al-Ghizzī, *al-Na't*, pp. 124–125, al-Kawākib *al-Sā'irah*, vol. 3 pp. 215–216, al-Zaraklī, *al-A'lām*, vol. 8 p. 267, Ibn al-'Imād, *Shadharāt*, vol. 10 p. 472.
238 For the citation of Ibn Taymiyyah's opinions by this scholar in his book *al-Iqnā'* see the tables at the end of this section.
239 See, for instance, *al-Iqnā'*, vol. 1 pp. 77–78, 103, 111, 169.
240 Ibid., vol. 2 p. 397, vol. 3 p. 5.
241 Ibid., vol. 1 p. 32.
242 Ibid., p. 42.
243 Al-Ḥajjāwī, ibid., vol. 1 pp. 2–3.
244 Ibn Badrān, *al-Madkhal*, p. 410, al-Ḥajjāwī, *al-Iqnā'*, vol. 1 p. 3.
245 See, for instance, *al-Iqnā'*, vol. 1 pp. 160, 231, 233, 237, 398.

246 See, for instance, ibid., vol. 1 p. 20. Cf. al-Baʿlī, *al-Ikhtiyārāt*, p. 10. Several Ḥanbalī scholars attribute this ruling to Ibn Taymiyyah rather than to the Ḥanbalī School, see for instance, al-Mardāwī, *al-Inṣāf*, vol. 1 p. 121, al-Buhūtī, *Kashshāf*, vol. 1 p. 75. Another example can be found in *al-Iqnāʿ*, vol. 1 p. 24. Cf. Ibn Taymiyyah, *Fatāwā*, vol. 18 pp. 263–264, vol. 20 pp. 358–359, vol. 22, pp. 218–219, 221, 228, 230, 231, 232, 235–242, 245, 246.
247 See, for instance, *al-Iqnāʿ*, vol. 1 pp. 59, 95. Also, see *Kashshāf*, vol. 1 p. 287.
248 Ibid., vol. 1 p. 303, vol. 2 pp. 24, 39, 48, vol. 3 p. 167.
249 See, for instance, ibid., vol. 2 p. 54, vol. 3 p. 163.
250 Ibid., vol. 1 pp. 4, 19, 79, vol. 3 p. 11.
251 Ibid., pp. 74, 398, vol. 2 p. 92, vol. 3 pp. 11, 35.
252 Ibid., vol. 2 pp. 48, 301, vol. 3 pp. 34–35, 232.
253 Ibid., vol. 1 p. 111.
254 Ibid., p. 149, vol. 2 p. 76.
255 Ibid., p. 160.
256 Ibid., p. 334, vol. 2 p. 209.
257 Ibid., pp. 199, 396 vol. 2 pp. 44, 47, 201, 202, 204.
258 Ibid., vol. 2 p. 55, vol. 3 pp. 190, 229.
259 Ibid., vol. 1 pp. 232, 346.
260 Ibid., pp. 19, 24, 55, 205.
261 Ibid., p. 303.
262 Ibid., p. 149.
263 Ibid., p. 55. It is clear that the reason for this is that *al-Iqnāʿ* is based primarily on al-Mardāwī's works.
264 It ought to be noted that in some rulings al-Ḥajjāwī adopts Ibn Taymiyyah's opinion without explicit reference to him. See, for example, al-Buhūtī, *Kashshāf*, vol. 1 p. 87.
265 An example is the issue of the divisions of water for the purpose of ablution; al-Ḥajjāwī is of the opinion that water is divided into three types. Al-Ḥajjāwī, *al-Iqnīʿ*, vol. 1 p. 97. This opinion agrees with the stance of the predominant opinion in the Ḥanbalī School. For further details of this point see, al-Khiraqī, *al-Mukhtaṣar*, tran. p. 20, Ibn Qudāmah, *al-ʿUmdah*, pp. 22–26, Ibn al-Bannā, *al-Muqniʿ*, vol. 1 p. 192, al-Majd, *al-Muḥarrar*, vol. 1 p. 2, Ibn Mufliḥ, *al-Furūʿ*, vol. 1 pp. 72–96, al-Zarkashī, *Sharḥ*, vol. 1 p. 114, al-Mardāwī, *al-Inṣāf*, vol. 1 pp. 21–22, al-Buhūtī, *Sharḥ*, vol. 1 pp. 10–16, *al-Rawḍ*, vol. 1 pp. 13–14, al-ʿAnqirī, *Sharḥ*, vol. 1 p. 15. This contradicts the opinion of Ibn Taymiyyah. Ibn Taymiyyah, *Fatāwā*, vol. 21 p. 25, al-Baʿlī, *Mukhtaṣar*, pp. 13–14. For other examples, see al-Ḥajjāwī, *al-Iqnāʿ*, vol. 1 pp. 3–8, 12, 16, 17, 30, 32, 40, 52, 57, 65, 72, 87, 89, 97, 165, 179, 184, 192, 308, 321, 323, 395. Some of these opinions are considered to be innovations by Ibn Taymiyyah. See, al-Ḥajjāwī, *al-Iqnāʿ*, vol. 1 pp. 16, 179.
266 Al-Ḥajjāwī, *al-Iqnāʿ*, vol. 1 pp. 2–3.
267 See al-Karmī's introduction to his book *Ghāyat al-Muntahā* vol. 1 pp. 3–4.
268 Abū Zayd, *al-Madkhal*, vol. 2 p. 787.
269 See for the biography of this scholar al-Ghizzī, *al-Naʿt*, pp. 113–116, *al-Kawākib al-Sāʾirah*, vol. 2 p. 112, Ibn Shaṭī, *Mukhtaṣar*, pp. 91–92.
270 Al-Ghizzī, *al-Naʿt*, pp. 141–142, Ibn Shaṭī, *Mukhtaṣar*, pp. 96–97.
271 See for the biography of this scholar al-Ghizzī, *al-Naʿt*, pp. 141–142, al-Zaraklī, *al-Aʿlām*, vol. 6 p. 233, Ibn Shaṭī, *Mukhtaṣar*, pp. 96–97.
272 For instance Ibn al-Najjār, like al-Ḥajjāwī, agrees with the widely recognised opinion within the Ḥanbalī School of law that water is divided into three types for ablution. See, Ibn al-Najjār, *Muntahā*, vol. 1 pp. 11–12, al-Buhūtī, *Sharḥ*, vol. 1 pp. 10–19. For other examples where opinions disagreeing with Ibn Taymiyyah's position are held by

this scholar see Ibn al-Najjār, *Muntahā*, vol. 1 pp. 16, 17, 19, 22, 23, 39, 41, 54, 86, 101, 102, 108, 162, 184, 216, 237, 247, 248, vol. 2 pp. 82–83, 94, 144, 342, al-Buhūtī, *Sharḥ*, vol. 1 pp. 20, 23, 24, 38, 43, 44, 60, 108, 116, 120, 124, 142, 155, 213, 255, 275, 294, 361–362, 405–406, 438. Again, some of these opinions are considered to be innovations by Ibn Taymiyyah. See, Ibn al-Najjār, *Muntahā* with al-Buhūtī, *Sharḥ*, vol. 1 pp. 33, 49, 459.

273 Ibn al-Najjār, *Muntahā*, vol. 1 p. 9, al-Buhūtī, *Sharḥ al-Muntahā*, vol. 1 p. 7.

274 Ibid.

275 Ibn al-Najjār, *Muntahā*, vol. 1 p. 9, al-Buhūtī, *Sharḥ al-Muntahā*, vol. 1 pp. 7–8.

276 This is further supported by the fact that in the science of the general principles of jurisprudence, we notice various references to Ibn Taymiyyah's opinions made by this scholar. The main reason behind this is that this scholar's book *Sharḥ al-Kawkab al-Munīr* is in fact based on al-Mardāwī's work *'Taḥrīr al-Manqūl'*. *Taḥrīr al-Manqūl* is also based on the work of Ibn Mufliḥ entitled *'Kitāb fi Uṣūl al-Fiqh'*. For further clarifications of the history of this book, see Ibn Badrān, *al-Madkhal*, p. 461, Abū Zayd, *al-Madkhal*, vol. 2 pp. 950, 953–954. As clarified in this chapter there is large presence of Ibn Taymiyyah's opinions in the works of both Ibn Mufliḥ and al-Mardāwī. Some of the quotations of Ibn Taymiyyah's opinions used by Ibn al-Najjār, are clearly stated to have been taken from Ibn Mufliḥ. See, for instance, Ibn al-Najjār, *Sharḥ al-Kawkab*, vol. 4 pp. 95, 96, 250. The opinions of Ibn Taymiyyah have been cited by Ibn al-Najjār in *Sharḥ al-Kawkab al-Munīr*. For example in volume 4 he cited Ibn Taymiyyah in the following pages: 95, 96, 222, 223, 225, 250, 264, 291, 413, 414, 532, 543, 570, 575, 577, 597, 613, 625, 651, 673.

277 See, for instance, Ibn al-Najjār, *Ma'ūnat ulī al-Nuhā*, vol. 1 pp. 177, 231, 240, 245–246, 294, 315, 317, 320, 344, 274, 693, 715–715, 752.

278 See, for instance, Ibn al-Najjār, *Ma'ūnat*, vol. 1 pp. 201, 224.

279 See, for instance, ibid., vol. 1 pp. 223, 250, 409, 715–716.

280 Ibid., pp. 281–282, 432–433, 772.

281 Ibid., pp. 387, 432–433.

282 Ibid., pp. 199, 326.

283 Ibid., pp. 204, 294, 344, 413.

284 Ibid., pp. 177, 183, 199, 201, 203, 204, 205, 208, 223, 224, 237, 240, 245–246, 247, 249, 250, 281–282, 315, 326, 344, 378, 382, 409, 492, 502, 587, 608, 693, 701, 711, 769, 772.

285 See, for instance, ibid., vol. 1 pp. 223, 281, 294, 306, 316, 318, 320, 357, 358, 364, 374, 387, 413, 432, 686, 715–716, 752.

286 It is interesting to note that Ibn al-Najjār in the first volume of *Ma'ūnat ulī al-Nuhā*, does not refer to any of Ibn Taymiyyah's books except in four places where he cites *Sharḥ al-'Umdah*. See, Ibn al-Najjār, *Ma'ūnat ulī al-Nuhā*, vol. 1 pp. 183, 245, 357, 680. On three of these occasions (pp. 183, 245, 357) he mentioned this book through the narration of either Ibn Mufliḥ or al-Mardāwī. In the same volume (p. 316), Ibn al-Najjār refers only once to Ibn Taymiyyah's treatise *al-Ikhtiyārāt*. On this occasion also, this reference is in fact based on the narration of al-Mardāwī.

287 See, for instance, Ibn al-Najjār, *Ma'ūnat*, vol. 1 pp. 281, 432, 715.

288 Ibid., vol. 1 p. 608.

289 Ibid., p. 318.

290 For the biography of this scholar see, al-Ghizzī, *al-Na't*, pp. 189–190, Ibn Shaṭī, *Mukhtaṣar*, p. 108 al-Zaraklī, *al-A'lām*, vol. 8 p. 88.

291 Al-Ghizzī, *al-Na't*, p. 191, Ibn Shaṭī, *Mukhtaṣar*, pp. 108–109.

292 Ibid., p. 109.

293 The book compiled by al-Karmī is entitled *'al-Kawākib al-Durriyyah fi manāqib al-Mujtahid Ibn Taymiyyah'*. This book has been published several times. It is evident

that this scholar commanded a particular knowledge of Ibn Taymiyyah's opinions and preferences, for we find him identifying some of his opinions which were cited by some Ḥanbalī scholars without attributing them to Ibn Taymiyyah. See, for instance, *Kashshāf*, vol. 1 pp. 75, 110, 187, *Sharḥ Muntahā*, vol. 1 p. 465.

294 Al-Karmī states clearly in his introduction to *Ghāyat al-Muntahā* that whenever he uses the term '*al-Sheikh*', he means Ibn Taymiyyah. *Ghāyat al-Muntahā*, vol. 1 p. 5. Note that when al-Buhūtī attributes opinions to Ibn Taymiyyah, he adds to al-Sheikh the nickname Taqī al-Dīn.

295 See, for instance, *Kashshāf*, vol. 1 pp. 75, 110, 187, *Sharḥ Muntahā*, vol. 1 p. 465.

296 See, for instance, al-Karmī, *Ghāyat*, vol. 2 pp. 61, 121.

297 See, for instance, ibid., vol. 1 pp. 19, 29–30, 172, 183, 270, 277, 279, *Kashshīf*, vol. 1 pp. 24, 67.

298 See, for instance, *Kashshāf*, vol. 1 pp. 201, 279, 287, *Ghāyat al-Muntahā*, vol. 1 pp. 113, 180, 254, 301, 386, 404, 459, vol. 2 pp. 11, 52, 82, 101, 190, 245, 291, 305. Also, in some issues the opinions of Ibn Taymiyyah were cited in opposition to the opinions of the Imam Aḥmad. For example, see, al-Buhūtī, Sharḥ *al-Muntahā*, vol. 1 p. 92.

299 See, for instance, *Kashshāf*, vol. 1 pp. 256, 294, *Ghāyat al-Muntahā*, vol. 1 pp. 29–30, 177.

300 For example of Ibn Taymiyyah's explanations of Ḥanbalī statements, see al-Buhūtī, *Sharḥ Muntahā*, vol. 1 pp. 13, 19–20, 26, 27, 37, *Ghāyat al-Muntahā*, vol. 1 p. 357, vol. 2 pp. 299–300. For examples of Ibn Taymiyyah's classifications of Ḥanbalī opinions, see, *Ghāyat al-Muntahā*, vol. 1 pp. 269, 489, 509.

301 See, for instance, al-Buhūtī, *Sharḥ Muntahā*, vol. 1 p. 425, *Ghāyat al-Muntahā*, vol. 1 pp. 331, 332, 357, 453.

302 See, for instance, *Kashshāf*, vol. 1 p. 173. Also, on some issues, al-Karmī mentions scholars supporting the position taken by Ibn Taymiyyah. See, for example, *Ghāyat al-Muntahā*, vol. 2 p. 31. In some cases, al-Karmī placed conditions on the acceptance of Ibn Taymiyyah's opinion. See, for example, *Ghāyat al-Muntahā*, vol. 1 pp. 493–494.

303 See, for instance, *Kashshāf*, vol. 1 pp. 35, 54, 67.

304 Ibid., p. 413.

305 Ibid., pp. 183, 506. The editor of *Ghāyat al-Muntahā* also identifies some unattributed opinions as being from *Ikhtiyārāt*. See, for example, vol. 1 pp. 29–30.

306 *Kashshāf*, vol. 1 p. 149. In other places of his treatises, al-Karmī cites, without specifying the source, Ibn Mufliḥ narrating some of the opinions of Ibn Taymiyyah. See *Kashshāf*, vol. 1 pp. 120, 149, 437, *Ghāyat al-Muntahā*, vol. 1 p. 473.

307 Al-Ghizzī, *al-Na't*, pp. 210–213, al-Zaraklī, *al-A'lām*, vol. 8 p. 249, Ibn Shaṭī, *Mukhtaṣar*, p. 115.

308 Each of these works has been published several times.

309 See, for instance, *Kashshāf*, vol. 1 pp. 75, 110, 187, *Sharḥ Muntahā*, vol. 1 p. 465.

310 Note that when al-Buhūtī attributes opinions to Ibn Taymiyyah, he adds the nickname 'Taqī al-Dīn' to '*al-sheikh*'.

311 See, for instance, *Kashshāf*, vol. 1 pp. 35, 54, 67.

312 See, for instance, ibid., vol. 1 p. 413.

313 Al-Buhūtī, ibid., vol. 1 pp. 176, 183, 232, 244, 270, 294, 299, 506.

314 Ibid., p. 149. Sometimes al-Buhūtī cites Ibn Mufliḥ without mentioning the source, see, for instance, ibid, vol. 1 pp. 120, 149, 437.

315 Al-Buhūtī, ibid., vol. 1 p. 212.

316 Ibid., pp. 201, 279, 287. In some issues the opinions of Ibn Taymiyyah oppose Aḥmad himself. For example, see, al-Buhūtī, *Sharḥ al-Muntahā*, vol. 1 p. 92.

317 See, for instance, *Kashshāf*, vol. 1 pp. 256, 294.

318 See, for instance, al-Buhūtī, *Sharḥ Muntahā*, vol. 1 p. 425.

319 For explanations given by Ibn Taymiyyah of Ḥanbalī statements, see footnote 300.

320 Al-Buhūtī, *Kashshāf*, vol. 1 pp. 159, 232, 359.

321 See, for instance, ibid., vol. 1 pp. 24, 67.
322 Al-Buhūtī, ibid., vol. 1 p. 173.
323 See, for instance, al-Buhūtī, *Sharḥ al-Muntahā*, vol. 3 p. 513.
324 Al-Buhūtī, *Kashshāf*, vol. 1 p. 71.
325 Ibid., vol. 1 p. 54.
326 Ibid., p. 158.
327 Ibid., p. 222.
328 Ibid., p. 470.
329 See, for instance, al-Buhūtī, *Sharḥ al-Muntahā*, vol. 1 pp. 61–62, vol. 2 pp. 427, 511.
330 Al-Buhūtī, *Kashshāf*, vol. 1 p. 35.
331 For examples, see the following: *al-Iqnāʿ*, vol. 1 p. 17 and compare to *Kashshāf*, vol. 1 p. 67, and for an example where al-Karmī gives preference to Ibn Taymiyyah's opinion in clear disagreement with al-Ḥajjāwī in *Muntahā*. See, al-Karmī, *Ghāyat*, vol. 1 p. 404.
332 See for example, al-Karmī, *Ghāyat*, vol. 1 pp. 6–10, 17, 19, al-Buhūtī, *al-Rawḍ*, p. 21, *Kashshāf*, vol. 1 p. 65, 314, *Sharḥ Muntahā*, vol. 1 pp. 274, 459. Al-Karmī holds that it is permissible to set out on a journey to visit graves. Al-Karmī, *Ghāyat*, vol. 1 p. 277. It is clear that this opinion is in agreement with the position taken by Abū Muhammad Ibn Qudāmah At the same time, it is in opposition to the position of Ibn Taymiyyah who declares this practice to be an innovation only invented by some later scholars. See the section entitled 'innovation in Ḥanbalī *fiqh*' in Chapter 4 of this work.
333 See, for example, the ruling concerning stroking the wall of the Prophet's room (*tamassuḥ bi al-ḥujrah*) *al-Rawḍ*, p. 213, and the duration of a truce in *al-Rawḍ*, p. 224, the terms used to ratify the contract of marriage also in *al-Rawḍ*, pp. 362–363, and the types of water in al-Karmī, *Ghāyat*, vol. 1 pp. 6–10.
334 Al-Buhūtī, *Kashshāf*, vol. 1 p. 35.
335 Ibn ʿAbd al-Wahhāb, *Arbaʿ Qawāʿid*, p. 14.
336 See al-Karmī's introduction to his treatise entitled *Ghāyat al-Muntahā*, vol. 1 pp. 4–5, and al-Buhūtī in *Kashshāf al-Qināʿ* vol. 1 p. 10, and in *al-Rawḍ*, p. 9.
337 There is a disagreement amongst some contemporary scholars regarding the extent of ignorance and polytheism that existed at the time of Ibn ʿAbd al-Wahhāb. For further details, see al-ʿUbūd, *ʿAqidat al-Sheikh*, vol. 1 pp. 37–105.
338 There are several treatises dealing with the personal, educational and political life of Ibn ʿAbd al-Wahhāb. See, for instance, al-Mukhtār, *Tārīkh*, pp. 35–57, Ḍahīr, *al-Daʿwah al-Wahhābiyyah*, al-Freih, *The Historical Background of the Emergence of Muhammad Ibn Abd al-Wahhāb and his Movement* and Nasri, *Ibn Abd al-Wahhāb's Philosophy of Society*.
339 There are various references that mention the influence of Ibn Taymiyyah upon Ibn ʿAbd al-Wahhāb. See, for instance, Nicholson, *A History*, pp. 463, 465, ¨alas, *ʿAṣr*, p. 21, Ḍahīr, *al-Daʿwah*, pp. 44–45 (in this book, the writer refers to several scholars who state that Ibn Taymiyyah influenced Ibn ʿAbd al-Wahhāb), Safiullah, *Wahhābsim*, pp. 69–70, Fazlur Rahman, *Islam*, pp. 114, 196–201, Makdisi, *Ibn ʿAqil*, p. 209, Lambton, *State and Government*, p. 151, Kucukcan, *Some Reflections*, pp. 68–69, Kutty, *Muhammad Ibn ʿAbdul Wahhāb*, pp. 43–44, 47–48, ʿAbd al-Ḥamīd, *Tajdīd*, p. 99. Some writers appear to suggest that Ibn ʿAbd al-Wahhāb used the widespread influence of Ibn Taymiyyah, rather than that he was influenced by him. Safiullah, *Wahhābism*, p. 67.
340 Nasri, *Ibn ʿAbdul Wahhāb's Philosophy*, p. 11.
341 Ibn ʿAbd al-Wahhāb, *Arbaʿ Qawāʿid*, p. 14.
342 An example of this is that the editors of the book of purification by Ibn ʿAbd al-Wahhāb, one of whom is the contemporary scholar Sheikh Ṣāliḥ al-Aṭram, write that amongst the reasons affirming that this book was compiled by Ibn ʿAbd al-Wahhāb is that it is in complete agreement with this scholar's way of writing. One characteristic feature is the repeated citation and quotation of the opinions of Ibn Taymiyyah. See the introduction to the book of *al-Ṭahārah* by Ibn ʿAbd al-Wahhāb.

343 Ibn ʿAbd al-Wahhāb, *Arbaʿ Qawāʿid*, p. 14.
344 Ibid., pp. 3–4.
345 For further details of Ibn ʿAbd al-Wahhāb's opinions regarding these issues and others, see: Ibn ʿAbd al-Wahhāb, *Kitāb al-Tawhīd*, al-ʿUbūd, *ʿAqīdat al-Sheikh Muhammad b. ʿAbd al-Wahhāb*, vol. 1 pp. 247–687, vol. 2.
346 Martin, *Defenders*, p. 127.
347 See, for instance, Ibn ʿAbd al-Wahhāb *Arbaʿ Qawāʿid*, pp. 5, 8–10, 11.
348 Ibn ʿAbd al-Ṭahāb, *Kitāb al-ahārah*, p. 7.
349 Ibid., pp. 22–23.
350 Ibid., p. 33.
351 Ibn ʿAbd al-Wahhāb, *Arbaʿ Qawāʿid*, p. 14.
352 Esposito, *Woman*, pp. 104–105.
353 Ibn ʿAbd al-Wahhāb, *Kitāb al-Ṭahārah*, p. 13, *Mukhtaṣar*, pp. 26, 74, 204, 225, 342.
354 Schacht remarks: 'From the eighth/fourteenth century onwards the Ḥanbalī school declined and seemed on the verge of extinction, when the puritanical movement of the Wahhābis of the twelfth/eighteenth century, and especially the Wahhābī revival in the present century, gave it a new lease of life. The religious founder of this movement, Muhammad Ibn ʿAbd al-Wahhāb (d. 1201/1787), was influenced by the works of Ibn Taymiyyah', Schacht, *An Introduction*, 66. The study and analysis of some of the treatises of the following two selected Ḥanbalī scholars, al-Saʿdī and Ibn ʿUthaymīn, proves the growing influence of Ibn Taymiyyah on contemporary Ḥanbalī scholars. Moreover, we find that the Ḥanbalī scholars in *al-Durar al-Najdiyyah* cited Ibn Taymiyyah's jurisprudential opinions on many issues, see *al-Durar al-Najdiyyah*, vol. 4 pp. 11, 12, 24 twice, 31, 34 thrice, 37, 38 thrice, 39, 53, 68, 70 twice, 94, 99, 100, 114, 143, 144, 160, 161, 166, 167, 169, 172, 173, 181, 183, 186, 187, 188, 190, 194, 196, 197, 199, 241, 252, 254, 259 twice, 264, 281, 307, 309, 312, 315, 316 twice, 317, 318 twice, 336, 344, 351, 357, 359, 360, 365, 366, 370–371, 373, 378, 385, 390, 391 twice, 392, 397, 406, 407, 408, 415, 423, 425 twice, 427, 434, 436, vol. 5 pp. 8, 17, 24, 40, 44, 50, 54, 57, 68, 82, 84, 99, 102, 108, 135, 145, 160, 162, 174, 204, 210, 212, 215, 238, 259, 260 twice, 161, 275, 276 twice, 277 twice, 283, 284, 294 twice, 295, 299, 301, 309, 310, 312, 314 thrice, 316, 317, 334, 335, 352 twice, 353, 354, 355, 356, 357, 364, 373, 376, 384, 385, 395, 397 twice, 398, 401, 403, 414, vol. 6 pp. 5, 25, 30, 31, 35, 36, 46 twice, 53, 55 twice, 56, 59, 67, 80, 104, 106, 108, 109, 122, 124 twice, 125 twice, 126, 129, 132, 135, 136, 137, 140, 141 twice, 142, 144, 149, 150, 157, 159, 171, 180, 181, 182 twice, 184, 186 twice, 188–190, 194 twice, 195, 197, 205 twice, 206 thrice, 207, 208, 210 thrice, 248, 250, 253, 258, 259, 260, 261, 263, 273, 274 twice, 278, 284, 285, 292, 293–294, 306, 308, 310, 312, 320 twice, 322 twice, 324, 325, 333, 336, 337, 338, 347, 349, 358, 370, 371 twice, 371, 372, 382, 384, 385, 390, 391, 392, 394 twice, 395 twice, 399 twice, 409, 418, 419, 426, 427, 428, 430, 459, vol. 8 pp. 174, 179, 182,183, 187, 189, 213, 219, 221, 224, 241, 244, 246, 317, 336, 340, 345, 361, 365, 377, 442, 450, 473, 484, 485, 487, 489, vol. 9 pp. 90, 115, 117, 124, 138, 159, 162, 165, 189, 191, 209, 232 twice, 234, 246, 248, 255, 294, 305 twice, 311, 322, 401–402, vol. 10 p. 17 twice, 19, 63, 69, 70, 71, 73, 81, 88, 93, 118 twice, 119, 144, 164–167, 167–168, 169, 175–177, 178, 179–180, 181, 189, 192, 194, 232 twice, 233, 249 twice, 331, 354–355, 356, 357, 360–375, 376, 377, 378, 380, 381, 386, 393, 401, 403.
355 Al-Mohideb, *Criminal*, p. 22.
356 Al-Ṭurafī, *Tārīkh*, p. 138.
357 For example, *Ḥāshiyat al-Rawḍ al-Murbiʿ* is taught in the *sharīʿah* faculties affiliated with the Imam University. This treatise is written by the contemporary Ḥanbalī scholar, Ibn al-Qāsim (1392/1972) who states (*Ḥāshiyat* vol. 1 p. 164) that Islam and the Muslim world since the time of Ibn Taymiyyah up to his era had not been

granted a scholar more knowledgeable than Ibn Taymiyyah in the texts, reason and the disputes amongst the scholars. He mentions that the title '*al-sheikh*' was initially associated with Ibn Qudāmah until the appearance of Ibn Taymiyyah. Now this title has become more associated with Ibn Taymiyyah. Ibn al-Qāsim also admits that in most cases he prefers the opinions of Ibn Taymiyyah as these opinions, according to him, are based upon correct evidences. He stresses however that Ibn Taymiyyah was not infallible (*Ḥāshiyat*, vol. 1 p. 164). This scholar, who also gathered the *fatāwā* of Ibn Taymiyyah, mentions (*Ḥāshiyat*, vol. 1 p. 9) that the treatises of Ibn Taymiyyah and Ibn al-Qayyim provided some of the sources on which he based his *Ḥāshiyat*. In the footnotes of this book, Ibn al-Qāsim cites various opinions of Ibn Taymiyyah which disagree with the opinion, or the predominant opinion, of the Ḥanbalī School. For examples see: vol. 1 pp. 59, 63, 73, 76, 79, 82, 88, 89, 96–97, 99, 110, 113, 127, 131, 139, 151, 159, 174, 183, 187, 192, 217, 219, 231, 233, 236, 241.

358 See, for instance, Ibn 'Abd al-Wahhāb, *Kitāb al-Ṭahārah*, p. 2, where he cites *Sharḥ al-'Umdah*, and *Ikhtiyārāt*, p. 9.

359 Al-'Ubūd, *'Aqidat*, vol. 1 pp. 206, 217.

360 See, for instance, Ibn 'Abd al-Wahhāb, *Kitāb al-Ṭahārah*, p. 6.

361 Ibn 'Abd al-Wahhāb mentions a vast number of Ibn Taymiyyah's opinions in his treatise entitled '*Mukhtaṣar al-Inṣāf wa al-Sharḥ al-Kabīr*' which runs to around 800 pages, It is clear, however, that Ibn 'Abd al-Wahhāb cites these opinions from the original work, *al-Inṣāf*. For details of this point see the table at the end of this section.

362 *Tarjamat*, with *al-Ikhtiyārāt* p. 305, al-'Abbād, *al-Sheikh* p. 14, al-Ṭayyār, *Fiqh*, vol. 1 p. 18.

363 *Tarjamat*, with *al-Ikhtiyārāt* p. 305, al-'Abbād, *al-Sheikh* pp. 25–26, al-Ṭayyār, *Fiqh*, vol. 1 pp. 83–84.

364 Al-Sa'dī was behind the founding of the Waṭaniyyah library in the city of 'Unazah which contains a large number of sources and references. Later on, this library became a place where al-Sa'dī's students studied under his supervision. See: al-'Abbād, *al-Sheikh*, p. 18, al-Ṭayyār, *Fiqh*, vol. 1 pp. 23–24.

365 *Tarjamat*, with *al-Ikhtiyārāt* p. 306, al-'Abbād, *al-Sheikh* p. 18, al-Ṭayyār, *Fiqh*, vol. 1 pp. 24–25.

366 Al-'Abbād, *al-Sheikh* p. 18, al-Ṭayyār, *Fiqh*, vol. 1 p. 24.

367 Although this book critically studies the book *al-Rawḍ al-Murbi'* by al-Buhūtī in particular, it is clear as al-Sa'dī also points out in *al-Mukhtārāt* pp. 3–4, that the corrections made by him can be applied to the other Ḥanbalī sources as some of these opinions can be found in them.

368 Quoted by al-Ṭayyār, *Fiqh*, vol. 1 p. 89.

369 Quoted by al-'Abbād, *al-Sheikh*, p. 29.

370 Quoted by al-Ṭayyār, *Fiqh*, vol. 1 p. 94.

371 Al-'Abbād, *al-Sheikh*, p. 59, al-Ṭayyār, *Fiqh*, vol. 1 p. 75. This is also asserted by one of al-Sa'dī's students. See, *Tarjamat*, with *al-Ikhtiyārāt*, p. 306.

372 Al-Ṭayyār, *Fiqh* vol. 1 p. 50.

373 Al-Sa'dī, *Ṭarīq al-Wuṣūl*, p. 3.

374 Ibid.

375 Quoted by al-'Abbād, *al-Sheikh*, p. 30.

376 Ibid.

377 Quoted by al-'Abbād, *al-Sheikh*, p. 30. Al-Sa'dī has a poem in which he praises Ibn Taymiyyah and Ibn al-Qayyim and their scholarly heritage. See, al-Sa'dī, *al-Fatāwā*, pp. 673–675.

378 See, for instance, al-Sa'dī, *al-Fatāwā*, pp. 241–242, 286, 329, 472–474, 476–478, 512.

379 See, for instance, al-Sa'dī, ibid., p. 517.

380 Al-'Abbād, *al-Sheikh*, p. 8.

381 This is also mentioned by al-Ṭayyār in his book *Fiqh al-Sheikh Ibn Sa'dī*, vol. 1 p. 100.
382 Al-Sa'dī, *Ṭarīq*, p. 4.
383 This published treatise is entitled *Ṭarīq al-Wuṣūl ila al-'Ilm al-Ma'mūl.*
384 This is mentioned by Ibn 'Uthaymīn. Al-Badrānī, *'Ulamā'una*, p. 8. Al-Ṭayyār reached the same conclusion after he studied the *fiqh* of al-Sa'dī. He clarifies that, during the first stage of his scholarly life, al-Sa'dī confined himself to the Ḥanbalī School of law. Later on, and especially after his extensive study of the works of Ibn Taymiyyah and his student Ibn al-Qayyim, he resorted to the evidences of the *sharī'ah* rather than the opinions of the Ḥanbalī School of law. Nevertheless when there is no clear evidence in support of any of the conflicting opinions, al-Sa'dī imitates Aḥmad's opinion. Al-Ṭayyār, *Fiqh*, vol. 1 pp. 90, 96, 113.
385 Al-Ṭayyār, *Fiqh*, vol. 2 p. 200.
386 On some occasions, al-Sa'dī mentions the opinions of the Ḥanbalī School and Ibn Taymiyyah without making a preference. For instance, see al-Sa'dī, *al-Qawā'id*, pp. 146–147.
387 For instance, al-Sa'dī, *al-Qawā'id*, pp. 146–147, al-Ṭayyār, *Fiqh*, vol. 2 p. 246.
388 For instance, al-Sa'dī, *al-Muhktārāt*, pp. 60–61. In some of these issues, al-Sa'dī mentions that Ibn Taymiyyah supports his opinions with a large number of evidences. He argues that whosoever encounters them would have no option but to follow Ibn Taymiyyah's opinions. Al-Sa'dī, *al-Muhktārāt*, pp. 108–109.
389 Al-Sa'dī, *al-Fatāwā*, p. 286.
390 Ibid., pp. 528, 570, 598. On one of these issues, al-Sa'dī mentions that precaution should be employed to avoid the disagreement between Ibn Taymiyyah and the Ḥanbalī scholars. Ibid., p. 528.
391 Ibid, pp. 155, 576. On one of these issues, al-Sa'dī is not sure if he should adopt the way of precaution or to support the opinion hold by Ibn Taymiyyah. Ibid, p. 155.
392 Ibid., p. 144.
393 Ibid., p. 183.
394 Ibid., p. 295.
395 This can be seen clearly in *al-Mukhtārāt al-Jaliyyah* where al-Sa'dī clearly attributes only some of the opinions to Ibn Taymiyyah.
396 In this treatise, which is entitled *al-Muhktārāt al-Jaliyyah min al-Masā'il al-Fiqhiyyah*, al-Sa'dī critically studies *al-Rawḍ al-Murbi'* by al-Buhūtī which is a commentary on *Zād al-Mustaqni'* by al-Ḥajjāwī. Al-Sa'dī states that he chose this book for study because it was the most ubiquitous book amongst the students of his time. These corrections, as al-Sa'dī asserts, can be also applied to other Ḥanbalī treatises where similar incorrect opinions are found. Al-Sa'dī, *al-Mukhtārāt*, pp. 3–4.
397 Al-Sa'dī, *Bahjat*, p. 134.
398 This scholar has left a large number of treatises, around 40 of which have been published. For further details of the treatises of this scholar see: *Tarjamat*, pp. 307–308, al-'Abbād, *al-Sheikh*, pp. 43–58.
399 For examples, see, *Tarjamat*, pp. 306–307, al-'Abbād, *al-Sheikh*, p. 35–37, al-Ṭayyār, *Fiqh*, vol. 1 pp. 51–68.
400 A biography of Ibn 'Uthaymīn has been written by al-Ṭayyār who is one of his students and is a professor at al-Imam University. See al-Ṭayyār, *Fiqh al-Sheikh Ibn Sa'dī*, vol. 1 p. 63. Another biography can be found in Ibn 'Uthaymīn's work entitled '*al-Khilāf bayn al-'Ulamā': asbābuhu wa mauqifuna minhu*' (Differences of opinions amongst the scholars; their causes and our position towards them), English edition pp. 6–8.
401 For an example, see Ibn 'Uthaymīn's explanation of the term '*al-'Umūm al-Ma'nawī*', which is used by Ibn Taymiyyah, Ibn 'Uthaymīn, *al-Sharḥ*, vol. 1 p. 126.

402 Ibn ʻUthaymīn, *al-Sharḥ*, vol. 7 p. 284.
403 Ibid., vol. 1 pp. 302, 357, vol. 7 pp. 45, 70, vol. 8 pp. 100, 289, 374, 394.
404 Ibid., pp. 291–292, vol. 5 p. 258, vol. 7 p. 519.
405 Ibid., vol. 8 p. 63.
406 Ibid., vol. 7 pp. 484–485.
407 Ibid., vol. 8 p. 114.
408 Ibid., p. 222.
409 Ibid., p. 53.
410 Ibid., p. 265.
411 Ibid., vol. 7 p. 91.
412 Ibid., vol. 8 p. 83, 187, 189.
413 Ibid., pp. 195, 215, vol. 8 p. 418.
414 Ibid., vol. 8 pp. 37–38.
415 Ibid., pp. 203, 234, vol. 7 p. 53, vol. 8 p. 400.
416 Ibid., vol. 7 p. 91.
417 See, for instance, *al-Sharḥ*, vol. 3 p. 538, vol. 7 p. 506.
418 See, for instance, ibid., vol. 7 p. 9, 375.
419 See, for instance, ibid., vol. 7 p. 10, vol. 8 pp. 189, 366.
420 Ibid., vol. 8 pp. 232–233.
421 Ibid., vol. 7 pp. 193–194.
422 Ibid., vol. 2 p. 157. Ibn ʻUthaymīn states that when a *mujtahid* cannot reach a conclusion on an issue, he must not issue a *fatwā* and it is permissible for him to imitate another scholar out of necessity. Ibn ʻUthaymīn, *Mujmūʻ*, vol. 4 p. 81.
423 Ibn ʻUthaymīn, *al-Sharḥ*, vol. 7 p. 300.
424 Ibid., vol. 2 pp. 39–40, 51–52, 132–135, 235, 285, vol. 3 pp. 296, 469, 494, 510, 517, vol. 7 pp. 79, 153, 174–175, 150, 327, vol. 8 pp. 63, 152, 168, 174, 206, 236, 260, 284, 304, 404–405, 447.
425 Ibid., vol. 2 p. 34.
426 Ibid., vol. 2 p. 158.
427 See, for instance, ibid., vol. 3 p. 471, vol. 8 p. 133.
428 See, for instance, ibid., vol. 7 p. 79.
429 Ibn ʻUthaymīn, ibid., vol. 2 p. 52, 60, vol. 3 p. 323.
430 Ibn ʻUthaymīn, *al-Khilāf*, p. 6.
431 Ibid., pp. 6–7.
432 Ibid., p. 7.
433 Ibid., p. 7.
434 Eight volumes of *al-Sharḥ al-Mumtiʻ* by Ibn ʻUthaymīn have been published since 1994. Seven volumes concern jurisprudential issues related to worship and, as a consequence, most of the issues cited by the researcher relate to this topic.
435 See the section entitled ʻRules used by Ibn Taymiyyah and certain aspects of their implications for Ḥanbalī jurisprudenceʼ in Chapter 4 of this work.
436 Ibid.
437 Ibn ʻUthaymīn, *al-Sharḥ*, vol. 1 p. 44.
438 Al-Majd, *al-Muḥarrar*, vol. 1 p. 2, Ibn al-Bannā, *al-Muqniʻ*, vol. 1 p. 189, Ibn Mufliḥ, *al-Furūʻ*, vol. 1 p. 84, al-Mardāwī, *al-Inṣāf*, vol. 1 pp. 55–56, al-Zarkashī, *Sharḥ*, vol. 1 pp. 129–130, Ibn Mufliḥ al-Mu'arrikh, *al-Mubdiʻ*, vol. 1 p. 52, al-Ḥajjāwī, *al-Iqnāʻ*, vol. 1 p. 8, al-Karmī, *Ghāyat*, vol. 1 p. 10, al-Buhūtī, *Kashshāf*, vol. 1 p. 36, al-ʻAnqirī, *Ḥāshiyat*, vol. 1 p. 24, Ibn Qāsim, *Ḥāshiyat*, vol. 1 p. 89.
439 Ibn Taymiyyah, *Fatāwā*, vol. 21 p. 32.
440 Ibn ʻUthaymīn, *al-Sharḥ*, vol. 1 p. 32.
441 Al-Majd, *al-Muḥarrar*, vol. 1 p. 11, Ibn al-Bannā, *al-Muqniʻ*, vol. 1 p. 199, Ibn Mufliḥ, *al-Furūʻ*, vol. 1 p. 125, al-Mardāwī, *al-Inṣāf*, vol. 1 pp. 117–118, al-Zarkashī, *Sharḥ*,

vol. 1 p. 166, Ibn Mufliḥ al- Mu'arrikh, *al-Mubdi'*, vol. 1 p. 99, al-Ḥajjāwī, *al-Iqnā'*, vol. 1 p. 19, al-Karmī, *Ghāyat*, vol. 1 p. 21, al-Buhūtī, *Kashshāf*, vol. 1 p. 72, al-'Anqirī, *Ḥāshiyat*, vol. 1 p. 42, Ibn Qāsim, *Ḥāshiyat*, vol. 1 p. 150.

442 Ibn Taymiyyah, *al-Ikhtiyārāt*, p. 10. Ibn Mufliḥ *al-Furū'*, vol. 1 p. 125, al-Zarkashī *Sharḥ*, vol. 1 p. 166, al-Ḥajjāwī, *al-Iqnā'*, vol. 1 p. 19, al-Buhūtī, *Kashshāf*, vol. 1 p. 72, Ibn Qāsim, *Ḥāshiyat*, vol. 1 p. 151. These scholars state that the opinion that the *siwāk* is permitted for a fasting person in the afternoon is *aẓhar*. All of these scholars were either students of Ibn Taymiyyah or came after his era and most of them refer to Ibn Taymiyyah's opinion regarding this issue.

443 Ibn 'Uthaymīn, *al-Sharḥ*, vol. 1 pp. 122–124.

444 According to another view in the School, the utterance can be audible. Ibn 'Uthaymīn asserts that this opinion is even weaker than that the utterance is recommended and the worshipper says it silently. Ibn 'Uthaymīn, *al-Sharḥ*, vol. 1 p. 159.

445 Ibn Taymiyyah, *Fatāwā*, vol. 22 pp. 218, 223.

446 Ibn 'Uthaymīn, *al-Sharḥ*, vol. 1 p. 159.

447 Al-Khiraqī, *al-Mukhtaṣar*, tran. pp. 28–29, Ibn Qudāmah, *al-'Umdah*, pp. 40–41, Ibn al-Bannā, *al-Muqni'*, vol. 1 pp. 268–270, al-Majd, *al-Muḥarrar*, vol. 1 pp. 12–13, Ibn Mufliḥ, *al-Furū'*, vol. 1 pp. 158–159, al-Zarkashī, *Sharḥ*, vol. 1 pp. 391–392, al-Mardāwī, *al-Inṣāf*, vol. 1 pp. 179–184, al-Buhūtī, *Sharḥ*, vol. 1 pp. 60–61, *al-Rawḍ*, vol. 1 pp. 30–32, al-'Anqirī, *Sharḥ*, vol. 1 pp. 59–63.

448 Ibn Taymiyyah, *Fatāwā*, vol. 19 p. 242, vol. 21 p. 173, *al-Ikhtiyārāt*, p. 14.

449 Ibn 'Uthaymīn, *al-Sharḥ*, vol. 1 pp. 190–192.

450 Al-Mardāwī, *al-Inṣāf*, vol. 1 pp. 182–183, al-Majd, *al-Muḥarrar*, vol. 1 p. 13, al-Zarkashī states that this opinion has been specified by Aḥmad and the Ḥanbalī scholars assert it authoritatively to the extent that al-Majd mentions it as an agreed upon ruling. Al-Zarkashī, *Sharḥ*, vol. 1 p. 395.

451 Ibn Taymiyyah, *Ikhtiyārāt*, p. 13.

452 Ibn 'Uthaymīn, *al-Sharḥ*, vol. 1 p. 208.

453 Ibn Mufliḥ, *al-Furū'*, vol. 1 pp. 260–261, al-Mardāwī, *al-Inṣāf*, vol. 2 pp. 222–223, 348.

454 Ibn Taymiyyah, *Ikhtiyārāt*, p. 27, Ibn Mufliḥ, *al-Furū'*, vol. 1 p. 261.

455 Ibn 'Uthaymīn, *al-Sharḥ*, vol. 1 p. 275.

456 Al-Mardāwī, *al-Inṣāf*, vol. 1 p. 260.

457 Ibid., vol. 1 p. 260.

458 Ibn 'Uthaymīn, *al-Sharḥ*, 308.

459 Al-Mardāwī, *al-Inṣāf*, vol. 2 pp. 355–356.

460 Ibn Taymiyyah, *Ikhtiyārāt*, p. 28.

461 Ibn 'Uthaymīn, *al-Sharḥ*, vol. 1 p. 410.

462 Al-Mardāwī, *al-Inṣāf*, vol. 5 p. 482.

463 Ibn Taymiyyah, *Ikhtiyārāt*, p. 151, al-Mardāwī, *al-Inṣāf*, vol. 5 p. 482.

464 Ibn 'Uthaymīn, *al-Sharḥ*, vol. 6 pp. 89–90.

465 Al-Mardāwī, *al-Inṣāf*, vol. 3 p. 299.

466 Ibn Taymiyyah, *Ikhtiyārāt*, p. 108.

467 Ibn 'Uthaymīn, *al-Sharḥ*, vol. 6 pp. 380–381.

468 Al-Mardāwī, *al-Inṣāf*, vol. 3 p. 302.

469 Ibn Taymiyyah, *Ikhtiyārāt*, p. 108.

470 Ibn 'Uthaymīn, *al-Sharḥ*, vol. 6 pp. 395–396. For further examples of issues in *al-Sharḥ al-Mumti'* where Ibn 'Uthaymīn refers to Ibn Taymiyyah's opinions and agrees with him, see: vol. 1 pp. 88–89, 216–218, 226, 323, 382, 402, 410, vol. 2 23, 27, 34, 113, 117, 128, 147, 153, 157, 158, 160, 165, 192, 192–193, 204, 315, vol. 3 pp. 11, 53, 61, 339, 392, 468, 520, 534, 536, vol. 5 pp. 208, 258, 479, vol. 7 pp. 77, 80–81, 89, 91, 188–189, 260, 396, 456, 485, 502, vol. 8 pp. 53, 369, 391, 418.

471 See *al-Durar al-Najdiyyah*, vol. 8 pp. 188–190.

6 A CASE OF CONFLICT? THE INTENDED TRIPLE DIVORCE REVISITED

1 The *fatwā* of Ibn Taymiyyah regarding the triple divorce as a single pronouncement and the stated number having no effect resulted in his interrogation. See, Ibn 'Abd al-Hādī, *al-'Uqūd*, p. 324, al-Karmī, *al-Kawākib*, p. 145.

2 This issue was of great interest to Ibn Taymiyyah. This is evident from his thorough study and discussion of this matter. Ibn 'Abd al-Hādī mentions that Ibn Taymiyyah wrote approximately twenty volumes concerning the issues of divorce and the dissolution of marriage, and other related points. See, Ibn 'Abd al-Hādī, *al-'Uqūd*, p. 38.

3 Ibn Mufliḥ, *al-Furū'*, vol. 5 p. 370, al-Mardāwī, *al-Inṣāf*, vol. 8 pp. 448–449, al-Zarkashī, *Sharḥ*, vol. 5 pp. 371–381, al-Buhūtī, *Sharḥ*, vol. 3 pp. 123–126, *al-Rawḍ*, pp. 394–395. There are some types of divorce which are a source of disagreement amongst the scholars in relation to whether they are *sunni* or *bid'ī*. An example is a divorce which takes place during the wife's period of purity after sexual intercourse has occurred, resulting in known pregnancy. Ibn Taymiyyah, however, maintains that this disagreement amongst the scholars is fruitless. Ibn Taymiyyah, *Fatāwā*, vol. 33 p. 7.

4 In the revocable divorce the husband can return to his wife without the need to enter into a new contract of marriage. This is because the two parties are still considered by law as husband and wife. In the irrevocable divorce they are considered to be complete strangers to one another and in order to return to a state of marriage, there is a need for the following: First, if the irrevocable divorce was the result of one pronouncement of divorce, followed by its complete waiting period without retraction from the husband, a new contract of marriage is required. This means that the husband will be considered as a complete stranger, whose proposal can be accepted or rejected. Second, if the irrevocable divorce was a result of a triple repudiation, a return to the state of marriage is not allowed except if the wife was to marry another man and then divorce him. This is dependent upon the condition that the second marriage was not performed solely in order to make the wife eligible to return to her former husband.

5 Al-Mardāwī, *al-Inṣāf*, vol. 8 p. 453.

6 Al-Zarkashī, *Sharḥ*, vol. 5 p. 373, Ibn al-Mubarrid, *Sayr*, pp. 211–218, al-Mardāwī, *al-Inṣāf* vol. 8 pp. 451–452, Ibn Mufliḥ, *al-Furū'*, vol. 5 pp. 371–372, Ibn al-Bannā, *al-Muqni'*, vol. 3 pp. 959–960, al-Maqdisī, *al-'Uddah*, p. 411, al-Majd, *al-Muḥarrar*, vol. 2 p. 51, al-Buhūtī, *al-Rawḍ*, p. 394.

7 Most of the Ḥanbalī sources mention two narrations from Ibn Ḥanbal regarding the ruling on triple divorce. See, for example, Al-Zarkashī, *Sharḥ*, vol. 5 p. 373, Ibn al-Bannā, *al-Muqni'*, vol. 3 pp. 959–960, al-Maqdisī, *al-'Uddah*, p. 411. Other sources mention more than this number, such as *al-Muḥarrar*, by al-Majd vol. 2 p. 51, and *al-Furū'* by Ibn Mufliḥ vol. 5 pp. 371–372, who mention the existence of three narrations and al-Mardāwī in *al-Inṣāf*, vol. 8 pp. 451–452, and Ibn al-Mubarrid in *Sayr al-Ḥāth*, pp. 211–218, who say that there are four narrations from Aḥmad regarding this issue. It appears that this discrepancy is based on the various methods of classification adopted by some of these scholars rather than a contradiction between narrations related from Aḥmad. For an example, see the narrations on this issue mentioned by al-Zarkashī, *Sharḥ*, vol. 5 p. 373.

8 Ibn Qudāmah, *al-'Umdah*, pp. 411–412, al-Majd, *al-Muḥarrar*, vol. 2 p. 51, al-Zarkashī, *Sharḥ*, vol. 5 p. 373, Ibn al-Mubarrid, *Sayr* p. 211, al-Mardāwī, *al-Inṣāf*, vol. 8 p. 451, Ibn Mufliḥ, *al-Furū'*, vol. 5 p. 371, al-Maqdisī, *al-'Uddah*, p. 411, al-Buhūtī, al-*Rawḍ*, p. 394. Ibn Mufliḥ mentions that this was the position of most of the Ḥanbalī scholars and al-Mardāwī labels it as the predominant opinion in the School, adopted by the vast majority of Ḥanbalī scholars. Ibn Mufliḥ, *al-Furū'*, vol. 5 p. 371, al-Mardāwī, *al-Inṣāf*, vol. 8 p. 451.

9 Ibn Taymiyyah, *Fatāwā*, vol. 33 pp. 70–71, 72–73, 76–81.
10 Ibid., vol. 33 p. 87.
11 Ibid.
12 Al-Mardāwī, *al-Inṣāf*, vol. 8 p. 453, Abū Ya'la, *Riwāyatayn*, vol. 2 p. 145, Ibn Qudāmah, *al-Kāfī* vol. 2 p. 785, *al-Muqni'*, vol. 3 p. 138, *al-Furū'*, vol. 5 p. 371, Ibn al-Bannā, *al-Muqni'*, vol. 3 p. 959, al-Buhūtī, *Sharḥ*, vol. 3 pp. 136–138. This is the general ruling concerning this issue. It should be noted that according to the Ḥanbalī scholars, if the triple divorce is pronounced triply in one word (i.e. *thalāthan*) the ruling differs depending on whether the woman is *madkhūlan biha* (the marriage has been consummated) or not. If the divorcee is not *madkhūlan biha*, she will be considered divorced by a first divorce and then if they agree to marry again, they will have two divorces left, but if the divorcee is *madkhulan biha*, she will be divorced thrice. Al-Mardāwī, *al-Inṣāf*, vol. 9 pp. 22–25.
13 Ibn Taymiyyah, *Fatāwā*, vol. 33 p. 8.
14 Ibid., pp. 7–8.
15 Muslim, *Ṣaḥīḥ*, vol. 2 p. 759, Aḥmad, *al-Musnad*, vol. 4 p. 314.
16 Aḥmad, *al-Musnad*, vol. 4 p. 123. Aḥmad Shākir stated that this *ḥadīth* is authentic. For a counter-argument by the opponents of Ibn Taymiyyah to these textual evidences, see: Ibn Taymiyyah, *Fatāwā*, vol. 33 pp. 14–15, al-Zarkashī, *Sharḥ*, vol. 5 pp. 373–376, Ibn al-Mubarrid, *Sayr*, pp. 123–141.
17 Ibn Taymiyyah, *Fatāwā*, vol. 33 pp. 12–13.
18 Ibid., pp. 17–18, 24.
19 Ibid., p. 24.
20 Ibid., p. 25.
21 Ibid., pp. 15–16.
22 Ibid., p. 16.
23 Ibid., pp. 16–17.
24 Muslim, *Ṣaḥīḥ*, vol. 2 pp. 769–773.
25 Bukhari, *Ṣaḥīḥ*, Arabic and English edition, vol. VII p. 136.
26 Al-Bukharī, *Ṣaḥīḥ*, Arabic and English edition, vol. VII p. 135, 173–174, Muslim, *Ṣaḥīḥ* vol. 2 pp. 778–779.
27 Al-Zarkashī, *Sharḥ*, vol. 5 p. 373.
28 Ibn Taymiyyah, *Fatāwā*, vol. 33 p. 77.
29 Ibid., pp. 77–78.
30 Ibid., pp. 38–40.
31 Al-Mardāwī, *al-Inṣāf*, vol. 8 p. 453, Abū Ya'la, *Riwāyatayn*, vol. 2 p. 145, Ibn Qudāmah, *al-Kāfī*, vol. 2 p. 785, *al-Muqni'*, vol. 3 p. 138, *al-Furū'*, vol. 5 p. 371, Ibn al-Bannā, *al-Muqni'*, vol. 3 p. 959, al-Buhūtī, *Sharḥ*, vol. 3 pp. 136–138.
32 Ibn Taymiyyah, *Fatāwā*, vol. 33 p. 8.
33 'Abd Allah, *Masā'il*, vol. 3 pp. 1109–1110, Abū Dawūd, *Masā'il*, p. 173, Ṣāliḥ, *Masā'il*, vol. 1 p. 441, vol. 3 p. 220. It is clear that in these narrations, Ibn Ḥanbal differentiates between whether the divorcee is *madkhulan biha* or not if the form of triple divorce was by the use of one word (*thalāthan*). In a similar manner, he earlier clarified the statement of the Ḥanbalī scholars that explains the origin of the existence of this differentiation in the School.
34 Al-Khiraqī, *al-Mukhtaṣar*, p. 185. Al-Khiraqī's statement appears to suggest that in the Ḥanbalī School triple divorce is regarded as a Sunni type of divorce without a reference to any other opinion within the School regarding this type of divorce as a *bid'ī* (innovation). This statement could be al-Khiraqī's own opinion or may be due to the fact that al-Khiraqī intended that his book be a summary of Ḥanbalī jurisprudence, as he mentioned in the introduction of his *Mukhtaṣar*, English translation p. 19.
35 Ibn al-Bannā, *al-Muqni'*, vol. 3 pp. 959–960, 966, 969, 970–971, 972–973, 974–975. Ibn al-Bannā mentions the same stance of the Ḥanbalī School in which there is a

differentiation between a *madkhulan bihā* divorcee (where the marriage has been consummated) and a divorcee who was not *madkhulan bihā.*

36 Ibn Qudāmah, *al-'Umdah*, pp. 411, 419–420.

37 Al-Maqdisī, *al-'Uddah*, with *al-'Umdah*, pp. 411, 419–420.

38 Al-Majd, *al-Muḥarrar*, vol. 2 pp. 51, 56.

39 This scholar was a jurist, teacher, judge and a mufti and became the sheikh of the School. He commanded an extensive knowledge of Ḥanbalī jurisprudence and his treatises in this science have become reliable references in the School. See: Ibn al-Mubarrid, *al-Jawhar*, pp. 99–101. For further details about this scholar and his knowledge, see the section entitled 'al-Mardāwī' in Chapter 5 of this work.

40 Ibn Mufliḥ, *al-Maqṣad*, vol. 2 pp. 517–520. For further details about this scholar and his knowledge, see the section entitled 'Ibn Mufliḥ' in Chapter 5 of this work.

41 Al-Mardāwī, *al-Inṣāf*, vol. 8 p. 453.

42 Ibid., pp. 453–454.

43 Ibn Mufliḥ, *al-Furū'*, vol. 5 pp. 371–372. It is important to note that Ibn Mufliḥ, like al-Mardāwī, mentions that Ibn Taymiyyah attributes this opinion to his grandfather al-Majd as well.

44 Ibn al-Mubarrid asserts that it is incorrect to claim that the opinion that triple divorce takes the effect of a single divorce was a narration from Aḥmad. Rather, it is an opinion attributed to the School by some scholars, such as Ibn al-Qayyim and Ibn Mufliḥ. Ibn al-Mubarrid, *Sayr al-Ḥāth*, p. 111.

45 Ibn Taymiyyah, *Fatāwā*, v33 p. 87.

46 Ibid.

47 Ibid., p. 35.

48 Ibn al-Qayyim, *Ighāthat*, vol. 1 p. 484.

49 Ibid., pp. 438–439.

50 Ibid., p. 436.

51 Ibn Qudāmah, *al-Mughnī*, vol. 10 pp. 96–97, al-Shirāzī, *al-Muhadhdhab*, vol. 4 pp. 287–288, al-Ma'allimī, *al-Ḥukm al-Mashrū'*, pp. 9–10, Ibn Ḥazm, *al-Muḥalla*, vol. 10 pp. 203–211, al-Dusūqī, *Hāshiyat*, 2 pp. 361–362, al-Shawkānī, *Nayl*, vol. 8 pp. 19–20.

52 *Abḥāth Hay'at*, vol. 1 p. 392.

53 Al-Marwazī, *Ikhtilāf al-Fuqahā'*, p. 134. It should be pointed out that al-Marwazī restricts the consensus of scholars to the triple divorce of a *madkhulan biha* divorcee only (where the marriage has been consummated).

54 Ibn al-Qayyim, *Ighāthat*, vol. 1 p. 478, *Abḥāth Hay'at*, vol. 1 p. 392.

55 Ibn al-'Arabī, *Aḥkām*, vol. 1 pp. 190–191, Ibn al-Qayyim, *Ighāthat*, vol. 1 p. 478, *Abḥāth Hay'at*, vol. 1 p. 392.

56 *Abḥāth Hay'at*, vol. 1 p. 392.

57 Ibn al-Mubarrid, *Sayr al-Ḥāth*, p. 107, *Abḥāth Hay'at*, vol. 1 p. 392.

58 Ibn 'Abd al-Barr, *al-Kāfī*, vol. 2 pp. 572–573, al-Dusūqī, *Ḥāshiyat*, 2 p. 362. It should be pointed out that there is an opinion in Mālikī jurisprudence also, which differentiates between a *madkhulan biha* divorcee (where the marriage has been consummated) and a divorcee who was not *madkhulan biha*. See, al-Azharī, *Jawāhir*, vol. 1 pp. 338–339, al-Zurqānī, *Sharḥ*, vol. 4 p. 83.

59 Ibn Ḥajar, *Fatḥ*, vol. 11 p. 278.

60 Ibn Ḥajar al-Haythamī, *Tuḥfat al-Muḥtāj*, vol. 8 p. 83, al-Ramlī, *Nihāyat al-Muḥtāj*, vol. 7 p. 8.

61 Ibn Ḥajar al-Haythamī, *Tuḥfat al-Muḥtāj*, vol. 8 p. 83.

62 Al-Dusūqī, *Hāshiyat*, vol. 2 p. 362.

63 Note however that Ibn al-Mubarrid states that Ibn al-Mundhir' statement regarding this issue is not explicit. Ibn al-Mubarrid, *Sayr al-Ḥāth*, p. 77. Ibn al-Qayyim cites Ibn al-Mundhir narrating the existence of a dispute amongst the scholars on this issue.

Ibn al-Qayyim, *Ighāthat* vol. 1 pp. 435–436. This confusion seems to stem from what appear to be conflicting statements made by Ibn al-Mundhir in *al-Ijmā‘*, pp. 113, 114, 115, and *al-Ishrāf*, vol. 1 pp. 143–144.

64 Al-Sarkhasī, *al-Mabsūṭ*, vol. 6 p. 57.

65 Ibn Taymiyyah and Ibn al-Qayyim both mention this accusation and attribute it to 'some scholars'. Ibn Taymiyyah, *Fatāwā*, vol. 33 pp. 30–34, Ibn al-Qayyim, *Ighāthat*, vol. 1 p. 474. Ibn al-Qayyim asserts that some of the scholars who claimed a consensus on this issue did so as a last resort because of the weakness of their other proofs. Ibn al-Qayyim, *Ighāthat*, vol. 1 p. 474.

66 Ibn Taymiyyah, *Fatāwā*, vol. 33 p. 91.

67 Ibid., vol. 33 p. 93.

68 Ibid., p. 83. This text of Ibn Mughīth is also cited by Ibn al-Qayyim in his *Ighāthat*, vol. 1 p. 482, al-Mardāwī, *al-Inṣāf*, vol. 8 p. 455, Ibn Ḥajar, *Fatḥ*, vol. 11 p. 278, Al-Shawkānī, *Nayl*, vol. 8 p. 20.

69 Ibn Taymiyyah, *Fatāwā*, vol. 33 pp. 83–84.

70 Ibid., vol. 33 p. 83.

71 Ibid., p. 8. See also Ibn al-Qayyim, *Ighāthat*, vol. 1 pp. 435, 482, Ibn al-Mubarrid, *Sayr al-Ḥāth*, p. 157.

72 Ibn Taymiyyah, *Fatāwā*, vol. 33 pp. 30–31.

73 Ibid., vol. 33 p. 91.

74 Ibid., pp. 32–33.

75 Ibn Ḥazm, *al-Muḥalla*, vol. 10 p. 204.

76 Ibn Rushd, *Bidayat*, p. vol. 2 p. 72.

77 Al-Nawawī, *Sharḥ Muslim*, vol. 4 p. 70.

78 Ibn Qudāmah mentions the scholars' disagreement on a triple divorce pronounced by one word (i.e. *anti ṭāliq thalāthan*). *Al-Mughnī*, vol. 10 pp. 96–97. He also mentions the existence of disagreement on triple divorce which is carried out in separate words, in the case of a wife whose husband has not consummated the marriage. Ibn Qudāmah, *al-Mughnī*, vol. 10 pp. 298–301.

79 Ibn al-Qayyim, *Ighāthat* vol. 1 p. 482.

80 Ibid., vol. 1 p. 483.

81 Ibid., p. 484.

82 Ibid., p. 484.

83 Ibn al-Qayyim states that the consensus cited by the opposition is based upon their ignorance of the existence of a dispute amongst the scholars. He made a survey, supported by twenty proofs, in which he proved that the ruling of triple divorce had been the subject of disagreement amongst scholars since the time of the companions up to his time. Ibn al-Qayyim, *Ighāthat*, vol. 1 pp. 478–487.

84 Ibn Ḥajar, *Fatḥ*, vol. 11 pp. 277–278.

85 Al-Shawkānī, *Nayl*, vol. 8 pp. 19–20.

86 Ibn Bāz, *Fatāwā al-Ṭalāq*, pp. 79–81.

87 *Abḥāth Hay'at*, vol. 1 pp. 385–407.

88 Examples are Ibn Ḥajar al-Haythamī, al-Subkī and Ibn Jamā‘ah. See, *Tuḥfat al-Muḥtāj*, vol. 8 pp. 83–84.

89 Ibn Taymiyyah, *Fatāwā*, vol. 33 pp. 93–94.

90 Ibid., p. 17.

91 Ibid., pp. 17–18, 24.

92 Ibn Taymiyyah, *al-Nubuwwāt*, p. 231.

93 Ibn Taymiyyah, *Fatāwā*, vol. 33 p. 29.

94 Muslim, *Ṣaḥīḥ*, Book of *al-Aqḍiyah*, vol. III p. 930.

95 Ibn Taymiyyah, *Fatāwā*, vol. 27 p. 301.

96 Ibid., vol. 33 pp. 40–42.

97 Ibn al-Mubarrid, *Sayr al-Ḥāth*, p. 157.
98 Ibid., pp. 112, 155. This scholar compiled various treatises in defence of Ibn Taymiyyah's opinion on the triple divorce. Ibn al-Mubarrid, *al-Jawhar*, pp. 174–175.
99 This scholar was detained because he issued *fatāwā* in agreement with those of Ibn Taymiyyah in relation to the issue of triple divorce. Ibn al-Mubarrid, *Sayr*, p. 122.
100 Ibn al-Mubarrid, *Sayr*, p. 157. It is interesting that Ibn al-Mubarrid in his book *Sayr al-Ḥāth* does not choose between the conflicting opinions with regard to this issue. He asserts that he only compiled this book to grant equity to both parties of jurists. Ibn al-Mubarrid, *Sayr*, pp. 219–220.
101 Al-Mu'alamī, *al-Ḥukm al-Mashrū'*, p. 13, al-Biṭār, *Ḥayāt*, pp. 59–60, al-Ghandūr, *al-Ṭalāq*, p. 243.
102 Al-Ghandūr, *al-Ṭalāq*, p. 243.
103 Ibn Māni', *Ḥāshiyat Ghāyat al-Muntahā*, vol. 3 p. 122.
104 Al-Ddībānī, *al-Madkhal*, p. 275.
105 Al-Sa'dī, *al-Mukhtārāt*, pp. 108–109. Al-Sa'dī states that whosoever studies the discussion of Ibn Taymiyyah regarding this issue has no option but to follow his opinion. He explains that this is because of the reliability and variety of the evidence cited by him and at the same time the weakness of the opinions cited by his opponents.
106 It should be pointed out that Ibn Bāz agrees with Ibn Taymiyyah concerning divorcing triply in one sentence (i.e. *anti ṭāliqun thalāthan*). He justifies his agreement with the opinion of Ibn Taymiyyah by mentioning evidence cited by him, and also because it is a source of ease for the people. Ibn Bāz agrees with the opinion of the Ḥanbalī School with regard to divorcing triply by three separate sentences connected by conjunction or without the use of conjunction, if the repetition was not intended as a confirmation of the occurrence of divorce. He explains that he disagrees with Ibn Taymiyyah on this point, as he believes that the evidence cited by him only refer to the triple divorce uttered in one sentence and not in more than one. For further details of this point, see the *fatāwā* issued by Ibn Bāz on the issue of divorce gathered and edited by al-Ṭayyār, one of his students, under the title '*Fatāwā al-Ṭalāq*', pp. 73–113. This stance of Ibn Bāz is in fact in opposition to the opinion of the previous *mufti* of Saudi Arabia, the late Muhammad Ibn Ibrahīm. In addition, it is also in opposition to the decision taken on 12/11/1393H by the majority of the Body of Senior Scholars of the Kingdom of Saudi Arabia. This decision appears in *Abḥāth Hay'at*, vol. 1 pp. 408–415.

BIBLIOGRAPHY

Arabic references

Abā al-Khayl, Sulaymān, *Muqadimah fī 'l-Fiqh*, 1st Ed., Dār al-'Āṣimah, Riyadh, 1997.

Al-'Abādī, *Fī Tārīkh al-Ayyubiyyin wa 'l-Mamālik*, Dār al-Nahḍah al-'Arabiyyah, Beirut, 1995.

'Abd al-Ḥamīd, Muḥsin, *Tajdīd al-Fikr al-Islāmī*, al-Ma'had al-'Ālamī li 'l-Fikr al-Islāmī, 1st Ed., 1996.

'Abd al-Qādir, 'Alī, *Naẓrah 'Āmmah fī Tārīkh al-Fiqh al-Islāmī*, 1st Ed., Dār al-Kutub al-Ḥadīthah, Cairo, 1965.

Abd Rahim, Rahimin, 'The concept of *Ijmā'* in Islamic law: A comparative study' in *Hamadred Islamicus* vol. XVII, Summer 1994, no. 2, pp. 91–103.

Abū Dāwūd, *Sunan*, 2nd Ed., Mausū'at al-Sunnah, Dār al-Da'wah and Dār Suḥnūn, 1992.

Abū Zahrah, Muḥammad, *Ibn Taymiyyah*, Dār al-Fikr al-'Arabī, Cairo, 1974.

Abū Zahrah, Muḥammad, *Mālik*, 2nd Ed., Dār al-Fikr al-'Arabī, n.d.

Abū Zahrah, Muḥammad, *Tārīkh al-Madhāhib al-Islāmiyyah*, Dār al-Fikr al-'Arabī, n.d. and another edition by the same publishing house in the year 1989.

Abū Zayd, Bakr, *al-Taqrīb li Fiqh Ibn al-Qayyim*, Maṭābi' Dār al-Hilāl, Riyadh, n.d.

Al-'Ak, Khalid, *al-Uṣūl al-fikriyyah li 'l-Manāhij al-Salafiyyah 'inda sheikh al-Islām*, 1st Ed., al-Maktab al-Islāmī, Beirut, 1995.

'Alī, Muhammad, *Khuṭaṭ al-Shām*, Dār al-'Ilm li 'l-Malayyin, 2nd Ed., Beirut, 1969.

'Alī, Muhammad, *Tarjamat sheikh al-Islām Ibn Taymiyyah*, 3rd Ed., al-Maktab al-Islāmī, Beirut, 1978.

Al-Āmidī, 'Alī, *al-Iḥkām fī Uṣūl al-Aḥkām*, 1st Ed., Dār al-Kutub al-'Imiyyah, Beirut, 1985.

Al-'Amrī, Nādiyah, *al-Ijtihād fī 'l-Islām*, 3rd Ed., Mu'assasat al-Risālah, Beirut, 1986.

Al-'Amrī, Nādiyah, *Ijtihād al-Rasūl*, 4th Ed., Mu'assasat al-Risālah, Beirut, 1987.

Al-'Anqirī, 'Abd Allah, *Ḥāshiyat al-Rawḍ al-Murbi'*, Dār Ibn al-Jawzī, Saudi Arabia, n.d.

Al-Aṣfahānī, Aḥmad, *Ḥilyat al-Awliyā' wa Ṭabaqāt al-Asfiyā'*, Dār al-Kutub al-'llmiyyah, Beirut, n.d.

Al-Aṣfahānī, Maḥmūd, *Sharḥ al-Minhāj li 'l-Bayḍāwī fī 'Ilm al-Uṣūl*, edited by al-Namlah, Maktabat al-Rushd, Riyadh, 1st Ed., 1410.

Al-Ashqar, 'Umar, *Tārīkh al-Fiqh al-Islāmī*, 3rd Ed., Maktabat al-Falāḥ, Kuwait, 1991.

Al-Asnawī, 'Abd al-Raḥīm, *Ṭabaqāt*, 1st Ed., edited by al-Jabūrī, Maṭba'at al-Irshād, Baghdad, 1970.

Al-Azharī, Ṣāliḥ, *Jawāhir al-Iklīl*, al-Maktbah al-Thaqāfiyyah, Beirut, n.d.

Badrān, Badrān, *al-Sharī'ah al-Islāmiyyah*, Mu'assasat shabāb al-Jāmi'ah, Alexandria, n.d.

Al-Badrānī, Fahad, and al-Barāk, Fahad, *'Ulamā'unā*, 2nd Ed., Mu'assasat al-Juraysī, 1410.

Al-Baghawī, 'Abd Allah, *Juz' fī Masā'il 'an Abi 'Abd Allah Aḥmad Ibn Ḥanbal*, 1st Ed., Dār al-'Āṣimah, Riyadh, 1407H.

Al-Ba'lī, 'Alī, *al-Mukhtaṣar fī Uṣūl al-Fiqh 'alā Madhhab al-Imām Aḥmad Ibn Ḥanbal*, edited by Baqa, Jāmi'at Umm al-Qura, 1980.

Al-Ba'lī, 'Alī, *al-Qawā'id*, 1st Ed., Dār al-Ḥadīth, Cairo, 1994.

Al-Ba'qūbī, Muhammad, *Sharḥ al-'Ibādāt al-Khams*, edited by al-'Ubaykān, 1st Ed., Maktabat al-'Ubaykān, 1995.

Barakah, Ibrāhīm, *Ibn Taymiyyah wa juhūduh fī 'l-Tafsīr*, al-Maktab al-Islāmī, Beirut, 1984.

Al-Bayhaqī, Aḥmad, *al-Sunan al-Kubra*, edited by 'Aṭa, Dār al-Kutub al-'lmiyyah, Beirut, 1st Ed., 1994.

Al-Biṭār, Muhammad, *Ḥayāt Sheikh al-Islām Ibn Taymiyyah*, 3rd Ed., al-Maktab al-Islāmī, Beirut, 1986.

Al-Buhūtī, Manṣūr, *Kashshāf al-Qinā' 'an matn al-Iqnā'*, 'Ālam al-Kutub, Beirut, n.d.

Al-Buhūtī, Manṣūr, *al-Rawḍ al-Murbi'*, 1st Ed., Dār al-Bayān, al-Ṭā'if, Saudi Arabia, 1990.

Al-Buhūtī, Manṣūr, *Sharḥ Muntahā al-Irādāt*, Dār al-Fikr, n.d.

Al-Bukhārī, 'Abd al-'Azīz, *Kashf al-Asrār*, al-Ṣadaf, Pakistan, n.d.

Al-Bukhārī, Ṣafī al-Dīn, *al-Qawl al-Jalī*, 1st Ed., Maktabat līnah, Egypt, n.d.

Al-Būṭī, Muḥammad, *Ḍawābiṭ al-Maṣlaḥah fī 'l-Sharī'ah al-Islamiyyah*, al-Maktabah al-Amawiyyah, Damascus, 1st Ed., 1966.

Al-Dārquṭnī, 'Alī, *Sunan al-Dārquṭnī*, edited by al-Madanī, Dār al-Maḥāsin li 'l-Ṭibā'ah, Cairo, 1966.

Al-Dawūdī, *Ṭabaqāt al-Mufasirīn*, Dār al-Kutub al-'Lmiyyah, 1st Ed., Beirut, 1983.

Al-Ddībānī, 'Abd al-Majid, *al-Madkhal ilā Dirāsat al-Fiqh al-Islāmī*, 1st Ed., Jāmi'at Qar yunis, Libya, 1994.

Al-Dhahabī, Muḥammad, *Dhayl al-'Ibar fī khabar man ghabar*, edited Zaghlūl, Dār al-Kutub al-'Lmiyyah, Beirut, n.d.

Al-Dhahabī, Muḥammad, *Dhayl Tadhkirat al-Huffāẓ*, Dār al-Kutub al-'Lmiyyah, Beirut, n.d.

Al-Dhahabī, Muḥammad, *al-'Ibar fī khabar man ghabar*, edited Zaghlūl, Dār al-Kutub al-'Lmiyyah, Beirut, n.d.

Al-Dhahabī, Muḥammad, *Siyar A'lām al-Nubalā'*, 1st Ed., edited by several researchers under the supervision of al-Arna'ūṭ, Mu'assasat al-Risālah, Beirut, 1982.

Al-Dhahabī, Muḥammad, *Tadhkirat al-Ḥuffhẓ*, Dār al-Kutub al-'Lmiyyah, Beirut, n.d.

Al-Dhahabī, Muḥammad, *Thalāthat Tarājim Nafisah* [part of *Dhayl Tārīkh al-Islām*], edited by al-'Ajmī, 1st Ed., Dār Ibn al-Athīr, Kuwait, 1995.

Dimashqiyyah, 'Abd al-Raḥmān, *al-Maqālāt al-Saniyah*, 1st Ed., Dār al-Muslim, Riyadh, 1998.

Al-Dr'ān, 'Abd Allah, *al-Madkhal li al-Fiqh al-Islāmī*, 1st Ed., Maktabat al-Tawbah, Riyadh, 1993.

Al-Dusūqī, Muḥammad and Amīnah al-Jābir, *Muqadimah fī Dirāsat al-Fiqh al-Islāmī*, 1st Ed., Dār al-Thaqāfah, Qatar, 1990.

Al-Farā', Ibn Abi Ya'la, *Kitāb al-Tamām*, edited by al-Ṭayyār and al-Madd Allah, 1st Ed., Dār al-'Āṣimah, Riyadh, 1414H.

Al-Farrā', Abū Ya'la, *Kitāb al-Riwāyatayn wa 'l-wajhayn* (*al-Masā'il al- al-Fiqhiyyah*), edited by al-Lāḥim, 1st Ed., Maktabat al-Ma'ārif, Riyadh, 1985.

Al-Farrā', Abū Ya'la, *Kitāb al-Riwāyatayn wa 'l-wajhayn* (*al-Masā'il al-Uṣūliyyah*), edited by al-Lāḥim, 1st Ed., Maktabat al-Ma'ārif, Riyadh, 1985.

Al-Farrā', Abū Ya'la, *al-'Uddah fī Uṣūl al-Fiqh*, edited by al-Mubārakī, 2nd Ed., n.d.

Al-Faryawā'ī, 'Abd al-Raḥmān, *Sheikh al-Islām Ibn Taymiyyah wa juhūduh fī al-ḥadīth wa 'Ulūmih*, 1st Ed., Dār al-'Āṣimah, Riyadh, 1996.

Ghanā'im, Muḥammad, *Fī al-Tashrī' al-Islāmī*, 1st Ed., Dār al-Hidāyah, n.d.

Al-Ghandūr, Aḥmad, *al-Ṭalāq fī al-Sharī'ah al-Islamiyyah wa 'l-Qānūn*, 1st Ed., Dār al-Ma'ārif, Cairo, 1967.

Al-Ghazālī, Abū Ḥāmid, *al-Mustaṣfā*, Dār al-Arqam, Beirut, n.d.

Al-Ḥadīthī, Khadijah, *Abū Ḥayyān al-Naḥwī*, 1st, Ed., Maktabat al-Nahḍah, Baghdad, 1966.

Al-Ḥāj, Sāsī, *al-Ẓāhirah al-Istishrāqiyyah wa atharuha fī al-Dirāsāt al-Islāmiyyah*, 1st Ed., Markaz Dirasāt al-'Ālam al-Islāmī, Malta, 1991.

Al-Ḥajjāwī, Mūsa, *al-Iqnā' fī fiqh al-Imām Aḥmad Ibn Ḥanbal*, Maktabat al-Riyadh al-Ḥadīthah, Saudi Arabia, n.d.

Al-Hamadhānī, *al-Buldān*, edited by al-Hādī, 1st Ed., 'Ālam al-Kutub, Beirut, 1996.

Al-Ḥamawī, Yaqūt, *Mu'jam al-Buldān*, edited by al-Jindī, Dār al-Kutub al-'lmiyyah, Beirut, 1st Ed., 1990.

Ḥāmid, 'Abd Allah, *Risālah*, edited by al-Shaybānī, 1st Ed., Maktabat Ibn Taymiyyah, Kuwait, 1988.

Ḥarbī, Muḥammad, *Ibn Taymiyyah wa Mawqifuh min ahm al-Firaq wa 'l-Diyānāt fī 'Aṣrih*, 1st Ed., 'Ālam al-Kutub, Beirut, 1987.

Harrās, Muḥammad, *Ibn Taymiyyah al-Salafī*, 2nd Ed., Maktabat al-ṣaḥābah, Ṭanṭa, Egypt, 1405.

Al-Hāshimī, 'Abd al-Mun'im, *Ibn Taymiyyah*, 1st Ed., Dār Ibn Kathīr, Beirut, 1993.

Ḥassān, Ḥusain, *al-Madkhal li Dirāsat al-Fiqh al-Islāmī*, Maktabat al-Mutanabb', Cairo, n.d.

Al-Haythamī, Aḥmad, *Tahfat al-Muḥtāj bi Sharḥ al-Minhāj*, Dār Iḥyā' al-Turāth al-'Arabī, n.d.

Al-Hazāymih, Muḥammad and Muṣtafā Najīb, *al-Madkhal ilā Dirāsat al-Tashrī' al-Islāmī*, 1st Ed., Dār 'Amar, Jordan, 1991.

Al-Hilālī, Salīm, *Ibn Taymiyyah al-Muftara 'Alayyh*, 1st Ed., al-Maktabah al-Islāmīyyah, Amman, 1984.

Al-Ḥuṣarī, Aḥmad, *Tārīkh al-Fiqh al-Islāmī*, 1st Ed., Dār al-Jīl, Beirut, 1991.

Al-Husaynī, *Dhayl al-'Ibar fī khabar man ghabar*, edited Zaghlūl, Dār al-Kutub al-'Lmiyyah, Beirut, n.d.

Al-Ḥusaynī, *Dhayl Tadhkirat al-Huffāẓ*, Dār al-Kutub al-'Lmiyyah, Beirut, n.d.

Al-Ḥushānī, 'Abd Allah, *Manhaj Ibn Taymiyyah fī al-Da'wah*, 1st Ed., Markaz al-Dirasāt wa 'l-I'lām, Dār Ashbilya, Riyadh, 1996.

Ibn 'Abd al-Hādī, *al-Ṣārm al-Munkī fī 'l-Radd 'alā al-Subkī*, edited by al-Anṣārī, Ismā'īl, 1st Ed., Maktabat Ibn Taymiyyah, Cairo, n.d.

Ibn 'Abd al-Hādī, Muḥammad, *Manāqib al-A'immah al-Arba'ah*, 1st Ed., Dār al-Mua'yyad, Riyadh, 1416.

Ibn 'Abd al-Hādī, Muḥammad, *al-'Uqūd al-Duriyyah, Maktabat al-Mua'yyad*, Riyadh, n.d.

Ibn Abū Ya'la, *Ṭabaqāt al-Ḥanābilah*, Dār al-Ma'rifah, Beirut, n.d.

Ibn al-'Arabī, Muḥammad, *Aḥkām al-Qur'an*, edited by Alī Muhammad al-Byjāwī, Dār al-Ma'rifah, Beirut, n.d.

Ibn Asbasalār, Muḥammad, *al-Tashīl fī al-Fiqh*, edited by al-Ṭayyār and al-Madd Allah, 1st Ed., Dār al-'Āṣimah, Riyadh, 1414.

Ibn al-Athīr, 'Alī, *al-Kāmil fī al-Tārīkh*, Dār Ṣādir, Beirut, 1966.

Ibn 'Atīq, Sa'd, *Nayl al-Murād bi naẓm matn al-Zād*, Dār al-Hidāyah, Riyadh, n.d.

Ibn Badrān, 'Abd al-Qādir, *al-Madkhal ilā Madhhab al-Imām Aḥmad*, 3rd Ed., Mu'assasat al-Risālah, Beirut, 1985.

Ibn Badrān, 'Abd al-Qādir, *Nuzhat al-Khāṭir al-'Āṭir*, 1st Ed., Dār al-Ḥadīth, Beirut, 1991.

Ibn al-Bannā, al-Ḥasan, *al-Muqni' fī Sharḥ Mukhtaṣar al-Khiraqī*, 2nd Ed., Maktabat al-Rushd, Riyadh, 1994.
Ibn Barada, Yūsuf, *al-Manhal al-Ṣāfī*, edited by Muhammad Amīn, al-Hay'ah al-Miṣriyyah li al-Kitāb, 1984.
Ibn Barada, Yūsuf, *al-Nujūm al-Ẓāhirah fī Mulūk Miṣr wa 'l-Qāhirah*, wazārat al-Thaqafah, Egypt, n.d.,
Ibn al-Farrā', Muḥammad, *Kitāb al-Tamām*, 1st Ed., Dār al-'Aṣimah, Riyadh, 1414.
Ibn Ḥabīb, Ṭāhir, *Mukhtaṣar al-Manār*, Maktabat al-Imām al-Shāfi'ī, Riyadh, 2nd Ed., 1410.
Ibn Ḥajar, *Taqrīẓ*, edited by al-Shaybānī, 1st Ed., Maktabat Ibn Taymiyyah, Kuwait, 1988.
Ibn Ḥajar, Aḥmad, *al-Durar al-Kāminah fī a'yān al-Mi'ah al-Thāminah*, edited by Muhammad Jād al-Ḥaq, Dār al-Kutub al-Ḥadīthah, Cairo, n.d.
Ibn Ḥajar, Aḥmad, *Lisān al-Mizān*, 1st Ed., Dār al-Fikr, Beirut, 1987.
Ibn Ḥajar, Aḥmad, *Tahdhīb al-Tahdhīb*, Dār Ṣādir, Beirut, copy of the first edition of Dā'irat al-Ma'ārif, India, 1325.
Ibn Ḥajar, Aḥmad, *Talkhīs al-Ḥabīr fī Takhrīj Aḥādīth al-Rāfi'ī al-Kabīr*, edited by al-Madanī, al-Madīnah al-Munawwarah, 1964.
Ibn Ḥāmid, al-Ḥasan, *Tahdhīb al-Ajwibah*, edited by al-Samarā'ī, 'Ālam al-Kutub, Beirut, 1988.
Ibn Ḥanbal, 'Abd Allah, *Masā'il al-Imām Aḥmad*, 1st Ed., al-Maktab al-Islāmī, Beirut, 1981.
Ibn Ḥanbal, 'Abd Allah, *Masā'il al-Imām Aḥmad*, 1st Ed., Maktabat al-Dār, Madīnah, Saudi, 1986.
Ibn Ḥanbal, Ṣāliḥ, *Masā'il al-Imām Aḥmad Ibn Ḥanbal*, 1st Ed., Dār al-'Lmiyyah, India, 1988.
Ibn Ḥazm, 'Alī, *Marātib al-Ijmā'*, 3rd Ed., Dār al-Āfāq al-Jadīdah, Beirut, 1982.
Ibn Ḥazm, 'Alī, *al-Muḥalla*, Maṭba'at al-Imām, Cairo, n.d.
Ibn al-Jawzī, *al-Muntaḍam fī Tārīkh al-Mulūk wa 'l-Umam*, edited by Muhammad and Muṣtafa 'Aṭa, 1st Ed., Dār al-Kutub al-'Lmiyyah, Beirut, 1992.
Ibn Juzayy, Muḥammad, *Taqrīb al-Wuṣūl ilā ilm al-Uṣūl*, edited by Farkūs, Dār al-Turāth al-Islāmī, Algeria, 1st Ed., 1990.
Ibn Kathīr, *Tafsīr al-Qur'an al-'Aẓīm*, al-Maktabah al-Tijāriyyah, Makkah, 1992.
Ibn Khuldūn, *al-'Ibar wa diwān al-Mubtada' wa 'l-Khabar*, 3rd Ed., Maktabat al-Madrasah wa Dār al-Kutub al-Lubnānī, Beirut, 1967.
Ibn Mājah, *Sunan*, 2nd Ed., Mausū'at al-Sunnah, Dār al-Da'wah and Dār Suḥnūn, 1992.
Ibn Manṣūr, Isḥāq, *Masā'il al-Imām Aḥmad wa Isḥāq Ibn Rahawayh*, edited by al-Mazyad, 1st Ed., Maṭba'at al-Madanī, Cairo, 1994.
Ibn Mufliḥ al-Mua'rrikh, Ibrāhīm, *al-Mubdi' fī Sharḥ al-Muqni'*, al-Maktab al-Islāmī, Beirut, 1980.
Ibn Mufliḥ, Muḥammad, *al-Furū'*, 4th Ed., 'Ālam al-Kutub, 1985.
Ibn Mufliḥ, Muḥammad, *Uṣūl al-Fiqh*, edited by al-Sadḥān, Maktabat al-'Ubaykān, Riyadh, 1st Ed., 1999.
Ibn al-Mundhir, Muḥammad, *al-Ijmā'*, edited by Ḥanīf, 2nd Ed., Maktabat al-Furqān, 'Ajmān, and Maktabat Makkah, Ra's al-Khaymah, UAE, 1999.
Ibn al-Mundhir, Muḥammad, *al-Ishrāf 'alā Madhāhib Ahl al-'Ilm*, edited by al-Bārūdī, al-Maktabah al-Tijāriyyah, Makkah, n.d.
Ibn Nāṣir, Muḥammad, *al-Radd al-wāfir*, edited by al-Shawīsh, 1st Ed., al-Maktab al-Islāmī, Beirut, 1980.
Ibn Qāsim, *Ḥāshiyat al-Rawḍ al-Murbi'*, 2nd Ed., 1403.
Ibn al-Qayyim, *Asmā' muallafāt sheikh al-Islām Ibn Taymiyyah*, 4th Ed., Dār al-Kitāb al-Jadīd, 1983.

Ibn al-Qayyim, *al-Rūḥ*, 1st Ed., edited by al-Ṣabābṭī, Dār al-Ḥadīth, Cairo, 1994.

Ibn al-Qayyim, Muḥammad, *Aḥkām Ahl al-Dhimmah*, edited by al-Ṣāliḥ, 3rd Ed., Dār al-'Lim li 'l-Malayyīn, Beirut, 1983.

Ibn al-Qayyim, Muḥammad, *Ighāthat al-Lahfān fī Maṣāyd al-Shayṭān*, 2nd Ed., al-Maktab al-Islāmī, Beirut, 1989.

Ibn al-Qayyim, Muḥammad, *I'lām al-Muaqqi'īn 'an rab al-'Alamīn*, Maktabat Ibn Taymiyyah, Cairo, n.d.

Ibn al-Qayyim, Muḥammad, *al-Kāfiyah al-Shāfiyah 'al-Nuniyyah'*, published with its commentary *Tawḍīḥ al-Maqāṣid* by Ibn 'Īsa, 3rd Ed., al-Maktab al-Islāmī, Beirut, 1986.

Ibn al-Qayyim, Muḥammad, *al-Ṭuruq al-Ḥukmiyyah fī al-Siyāsah al-Shar'iyyah*, Dār Iḥiyā' al-'Ulūm, Beirut, n.d.

Ibn al-Qayyim, Muḥammad, *Zād al-Ma'ād fī hadi khayr al-'Ibād*, 15th Ed., Mu'assasat al-Risālah, Beirut, 1987.

Ibn Qudāmah, Muḥammad, *al-Kāfī*, edited by Zuhayr al-Shāwīsh, 5th Ed., al-Maktab al-Islāmī, Beirut, 1988.

Ibn Qudāmah, Muḥammad, *al-Mughnī*, edited by al-Saiyyd, Khaṭṭāb and Sādiq, 1st Ed., Dār al-Ḥadīth, Cairo, 1995.

Ibn Qudāmah, Muḥammad, *al-Muqni'*, Maktabat al-Riyadh al-Ḥadīthah, Riyadh, 1980.

Ibn Qudāmah, Muḥammad, *al-'Umdah*, n.d.

Ibn Rajab, *al-Dhayl 'alā Ṭabaqāt al-Ḥanābilah*, Dār al-Ma'rifah, Beirut, n.d.

Ibn Rajab, *Ṭabaqāt al-Ḥanābilah*, Dār al-Ma'rifah, Beirut, n.d.

Ibn al-Ṣalāḥ, *Adab al-Mufti wa 'l-Mustaftī*, published with *Fatāwā wa Rasā'l Ibn al-Ṣalāḥ*, edited by Qal'ajī, Dār al-Ma'rifah, Beirut, 1st Ed., 1986.

Ibn Shaṭī, Muḥammad, *Mukhtaṣar Ṭabaqāt al-Ḥanābilah*, 1st Ed., Dār al-Kitāb al-'Arabī, Beirut, 1986.

Ibn Taymiyyah, 'Abd al-Salām, *al-Muḥarrar*, 2nd Ed., Maktabat al-Ma'ārif, Riyadh, 1984.

Ibn Taymiyyah, Aḥmad, *al-Arba'ūn Ḥadīthan*, edited by al-Sirawān, 1st Ed., Dār al-Qalam Beirut, 1986.

Ibn Taymiyyah, Aḥmad, *Dār' ta'āruḍ al-'Aql wa al-Naql*, edited by A. 'Abd al- Raḥmān, 1st Ed., Dār al-Kutub al-'Lmiyyah, Beirut, 1997.

Ibn Taymiyyah, Aḥmad, *al-Fatāwā al-'Irāqiyyah*, edited by A. al-Muftī, Maṭba'at al-Jāḥiḍ, Baghdad, 1988.

Ibn Taymiyyah, Aḥmad, *al-Fatāwā al-Kubra*, edited by 'Aṭa, Dār al-Kutub al-'Lmiyyah, Beirut, n.d. In this thesis refered to as '*Kubra*'.

Ibn Taymiyyah, Aḥmad, *al-Imān*, edited al-Shawīsh, 4th Ed., al-Maktab al-Islāmī, Beirut, 1993.

Ibn Taymiyyah, Aḥmad, *al-Istiqāmah*, edited by Rashād Sālim, 1st Ed., Jāmi'at al-Imām Muhammad Ibn Sa'ud al-Islāmiyyah, Riyadh, 1983.

Ibn Taymiyyah, Aḥmad, *al-Jawāb al-Bāhir fī zuwwār al-Maqābir*, edited by al-Shabrāwī, 1st Ed., Dār al-Jīl, Beirut, 1997.

Ibn Taymiyyah, Aḥmad, *Iqtiḍā' al-Ṣirāṭ al-Mustaqīm*, edited by al-'Aqīl, 1st Ed., 1404.

Ibn Taymiyyah, Aḥmad, *Majmū' al-Fatāwā*, edited by al-Qāsim, Abd al-Raḥmān, and his son Muhammad, Dār 'Ālam al-Kutub, Riyadh, 1991. In this thesis refered to as '*Fatāwā*'.

Ibn Taymiyyah, Aḥmad, *Majmū'at al-Rasā'il wa 'l-Masā'il*, Dār al-Kutub al-'Lmiyyah, Beirut, n.d.

Ibn Taymiyyah, Aḥmad, *Minhāj al-Sunnah al-Nabawiyyah*, 1st Ed., Jāmi'at al-Imām Muhammad Ibn Sa'ud al-Islāmiyyah, Riyadh, 1986.

Ibn Taymiyyah, Aḥmad, *Naqd al-Manṭiq*, Maktabat al-Sunnah al-Muḥamadiyyah, Cairo, n.d.

Ibn Taymiyyah, Aḥmad, *al-Nubūwāt*, edited by Muhammad 'Awād, Dār al-Kitāb al-'Arabī, Beirut, 1991.

Ibn Taymiyyah, Aḥmad, *al-Qawā'id al-Nuraniyyah al-Fiqhiyyah*, edited by Shāhīn, 1st Ed., Dār al-Kutub al-'Lmiyyah, Beirut, 1994.

Ibn Taymiyyah, Aḥmad, *Raf' al-Malām 'An al-A'immah al-A'lām*, published with *al-Inṣāf* by al-Mardāwī, edited by al-Faqī, 2nd Ed., Mu'assasat al-Tārīkh al-'Arabī, Beirut, n.d.

Ibn Taymiyyah, Aḥmad, *Sharḥ al-'Umdah fī al-Fiqh*, part of *Kitāb al-Ṣalāh*, edited by al-Mushayqiḥ, 1st Ed., Dār al-'Āṣimah, Riyadh, 1997.

Ibn Taymiyyah, Aḥmad, *Sharḥ al-'Umdah fī al-Fiqh, Kitāb al-Ḥajj*, edited by al-Ḥasan, 1st Ed., Maktabat al-Ḥaramayn, Riyadh, 1988.

Ibn Taymiyyah, Aḥmad, *Sharḥ al-'Umdah fī al-Fiqh, Kitāb al-Ṣiyām*, edited by al-Nushairī, 1st Ed., Dār al-Anṣārī, Jeddah, 1996.

Ibn Taymiyyah, Aḥmad, *Sharḥ al-'Umdah fī al-Fiqh, Kitāb al-Ṭahārah*, edited by al-'Uṭayshān, 1st Ed., Maktabat al-'Ubaykān, Riyadh, 1412.

Ibn Taymiyyah, Aḥmad, *al-Siyāsah al-Shar'iyyah fī iṣlāḥ al-Rā'ī wa 'l-Ra'iyyah*, edited by al-Ḥarstānī, 1st Ed., Dār al-Jīl, Beirut, 1993.

Ibn Taymiyyah, Aḥmad, *Tafsīr Ayāt ashkalat 'alā kathīr min al-'Ulamā'*, a published MA thesis, edited by al-Khalīfah, 1st Ed., Maktabat al-Rushd, Riyadh, 1997.

Ibn Ṭūlūn, Muḥammad, *I'lām al-Wara*, edited by Muhammad Dahmān, Wazārat al-Thaqāfah wa 'l-Irshād al-Qawmī, Damascus, 1964.

Ibn Ṭūlūn, Muḥammad, *al-Qalā'id al-Jawhariyyah fī Tārīkh al-Sāliḥiyyah*, 2nd Ed., Maṭbu'āt Majma' al-Lughah al-'Arabiyyah, n.d.

Ibn 'Uthaymīn, Muḥammad, *al-Sharḥ al-Mumti' 'alā Zād al-Mustaqni'*, edited by Abā al-Khayl and al-Mushayqiḥ, 3rd Ed., Mu'assasat Asām, Riyadh, in a series started 1994.

Al-Ibrāhīm, Mūsā, *al-Madkhal ilā Uṣūl al-Fiqh*, 1st Ed., Dār 'Amar, Amman, Jordan, 1989.

Al-Ismā'īl, Muḥammad, *Ḥāshiyat Mukhtaṣar al-Imām Abi al-Qāsim al-Khiraqī*, 1st Ed., Maktabat al-Ma'ārif, Riyadh, 1988.

Ismā'īl, Sha'bān, *al-Tashrī' al-Islāmī*, 2nd Ed., Maktabat al-Nahḍah al-Miṣriyyah, 1985.

Al-Jurā'ī, Abū Bakr, *Sharḥ Mukhtaṣar Uṣūl al-Fiqh, min awwalih ilā masā'il al-Khabar*, edited by al-Qāydī, unpublished MA thesis, al-Jāmi'ah al-Islamiyyah, al-Madīnah, 1407.

Al-Jurjānī, 'Abd Allah, *al-Kāmil fī ḍu'afā' al-Rijāl*, edited by 'Abd al-Mawjūd and Mu'awwaḍ, Dār al-Kutub al-'Lmiyyah, Beirut, 1st Ed., 1997.

Al-Juwaynī, 'Abd al-Malik, *al-Burhān fī Uṣūl al-Fiqh*, edited by al-Dhīb, 1st Ed., published on the expense of the Amir of Qatar, 1399.

Al-Juwaynī, 'Abd al-Malik, *al-Talkhīṣ fī Uṣūl al-Fiqh*, edited by al-Nibālī and al-'Amrī, 1st Ed., Dār al-Bashā'r al-Islāmiyyah, Beirut, 1996.

Al-Juwanyī, 'Abd al-Malik, *al-Waraqāt*, Maktabat al-Imām al-Shāfi'ī, Riyadh, 2nd Ed., 1410.

Kaḥālah, 'Umar, *Mu'jam al-Mualifīn*, maṭba'at al-Taraqī, Damascus, 1959.

Al-Karmī, Mar'ī, *Ghāyat al-Muntahā*, 2nd Ed., al-Mu'asasah al-Sa'idiyyah, Riyadh, n.d.

Al-Karmī, Mar'ī, *al-Kawākib al-Duriyyah fī manāqib al-Mujtahid Ibn Taymiyyah*, 1st Ed., Dār al-Gharb al-Islāmī, Beirut, 1986.

Al-Katbī, Muḥammad, *Fawāt al-Wāfiyyāt*, edited by Iḥsān 'Abbās, Dār Ṣādir, Beirut.

Al-Khabāzī, 'Umar, *al-Mughnī fī Uṣūl al-Fiqh*, edited by Baqa, 1st Ed., Jāmi'at Umm al-Qura, 1403.

Khallāf, 'Abd al-Wahhāb, *Khulāṣat Tārīkh al-Tashrī' al-Islāmī*, Dār al-Anṣār, Cairo, n.d.

Al-Khallāl, Aḥmad, *Aḥkām Ahl al-Milal*, 1st Ed., Dār al-Kutub al-'Lmiyyah, Beirut, 1994.

Al-Khallāl, Aḥmad, *Kitāb al-Wara'*, Dār al-Kitāb al-'Arabī, Beirut, 1988.

Al-Khallāl, Aḥmad, *Kitāb al-Wuqūf*, edited by al-Zayd, 1st Ed., Maktabat al-Ma'ārif, Riyadh, 1989.

Khayāṭ, Fawziyyah, *al-Ahdāf al-Tarbawiyyah al-Sulukiyyah 'inda sheikh al-Islām Ibn Taymiyyah*, 1st Ed., Maktabat al-Manārah, Makkah 1987.

Al-Khiraqī, 'Umar, *Mukhtaṣar*, 1st Ed., Maktabat al-Ma'ārif, Riyadh, 1988.

Al-Khuḍarī bik, Muḥammad, *Tārīkh al-Tashrī' al-Islāmī*, 1st Ed., Dār al-Fikr al-'Arabī, Beirut, 1992.

Al-Kulwadhānī, Abū 'l-Khaṭṭāb, *al-Intiṣār fī al-Masā'il al-Kibār*, edited by al-'Umayr and others, 1st Ed., Maktabat al-'Ubaykān, 1993.

Al-Kulwadhānī, Abū 'l-Khaṭṭāb, *al-Tamhīd fī Uṣūl al-Fiqh*, edited by al-Ibrāhīm and Abū 'Amshah, 1st Ed., Dār al-Madanī, 1985.

Louast, *Naẓariyyāt sheikh al-Islām Ibn Taymiyyah fī al-Siyāsah wa 'l-Ijtimā'*, 1st Ed., Dār al-Anṣār, Cairo, 1977.

Al-Madkhalī, Rabī', *Taqsīm al-Ḥadīth ilā Ṣaḥīḥ wa ḥasan wa ḍa'īf*, Maktabat Dār al-Salām, Riyadh, 1st Ed., 1411.

Madkūr, Muḥammad, *al-Ijtihād fī al-Tashrī' al-Islāmī*, 1st Ed., Dār al-Nahḍah al-'Arabiyyah, Cairo, 1984.

Madkūr, Muḥammad, *al-Madkhal li al-Fiqh al-Islāmī*, 2nd Ed., Dār al-Kitāb al-Ḥadīth, Cairo, 1996.

Al-Maḥmūd, 'Abd al-Raḥmān, *Mawqif Ibn Taymiyyah min al-Ashā'irah*, 1st Ed., Maktabat al-Rushd, Riyadh, 1995.

Maḥmūd, Aḥmad, *Ishām fī Tārīkh al-Madhhab al-Ḥanbalī*, 1st Ed., Dār Qutaybah, Beirut, 1990.

Al-Majd, *al-Muḥarrar fī 'l-Fiqh*, 2nd Ed., Maktabat al-Ma'ārif, Riyadh, 1984.

Al-Manṣūr, Ṣāliḥ, *Ibn Taymiyyah wa Uṣūl al-Fiqh*, 2nd Ed., 1985.

Al-Maqdisī, 'Abd al-Raḥmān, *al-'Uddah Sharḥ al-'Umdah*, n.d.

Al-Maqdisī, Ibn Qudāmah, *Rawḍat al-Nāẓir*, 1st Ed., Dār al-Ḥadīth, Beirut, 1991.

Al-Mardāwī, 'Alī, *al-Inṣāf*, edited by al-Faqī, 2nd Ed., Mu'assasat al-Tārīkh al-'Arabī, Beirut, n.d.

Al-Mardāwī, 'Alī, *al-Taḥbīr bi Sharḥ al-Taḥrīr fī Uṣūl al-Fiqh*, edited by three PhD students: al-Jibrīn, al-Qarnī and al-Sarrāḥ, Jāmi'at al-Imām Muḥammad Ibn Saud, submitted to the Imam University in the academic years 1414, 1415, 1416 H.

Al-Mardāwī, 'Alī, *al-Tanqīḥ al-Mushbi'*, 2nd Ed., al-Maṭba'ah al-Salafiyyah, Cairo, 1406.

Al-Mardāwī, 'Alī, *Taṣḥīḥ al-Furū'*, 4th Ed., 'Ālam al-Kutub, 1985.

Al-Marwazī, Muḥammad, *Ikhtilāf al-Fuqahā'*, edited by al-Samarrā'ī, 2nd Ed., 'Ālam al-Kutub, Beirut, 1986.

Al-Maymān, Nāṣir, *al-Qawā'id wa 'l-Ḍawābiṭ al-Fiqhiyyah 'Ind Ibn Taymiyyah fī Kitābay al-Ṭahārah wa 'l-Ṣalāh*, published MA, Umm al-Qura University, Makkah, 1996.

Muāfī, Aḥmad, *Taysīr al-Fiqh al-Jāmi' li al-Ikhtiyārāt al-Fiqhiyyah li Sheikh al-Islām Ibn Taymiyyah*, 1st Ed., Dār Ibn al-Jawzī, al-Dammām, Saudi, 1993.

Al-Mubarkfūrī, *Tuḥfat al-Aḥwadhī*, edited by 'Abd al-Raḥmān 'Uthmān, 2nd Ed., n.d.

Muhammad, Sa'd, *Sheikh al-Islām Ibn Taymiyyah*, 1st Ed., Dār al-Liwā', Riyadh, 1987.

Al-Mukhtār, Ṣalāḥ al-Dīn, *Tārīkh al-Mamlakah al-'Arabiyyah al-Sa'udiyyah*, Dār Maktabat al-Ḥayāt, n.d.

Al-Munajjid, Ṣalāḥ al-Dīn, introduction of the first volume of *Siyar A'lām al-Nubalā'*, Ma'had al-Makhṭūṭāt al-'Arabiyyah, Cairo, n.d.

Mūsā, Kāmil, *al-Madkhal ilā al-Tashrī' al-Islāmī*, 1st Ed., Mu'assasat al-Risālah, Beirut, 1989.

Mūsā, Muḥammad, *Ibn Taymiyyah*, 2nd Ed., al-'Aṣr al-ḥadīth, Beirut, 1988.

Mūsa, Muḥammad, *Muḥāḍarāt fī Tārīkh al-Fiqh al-Islāmī*, 2nd Ed., 1410.

Al-Naḥlāwī, 'Abd al-Raḥmān, *Ibn Qayyim al-Jawziyyah*, 1st Ed., Dār al-Fikr al-Mu'aṣir, Beirut, 1991.

Al-Naḥlāwī, 'Abd al-Raḥmān, *Ibn Taymiyyah*, 1st Ed., Dār al-Fikr al-Mu'āṣir, Beirut, 1986.

Al-Najjār, Muḥammad, *Sharḥ al-Kawkab al-Munīr*, 1st Ed., University of Umm al-Qurā, 1987.

Al-Nasā'ī, *Sunan*, 2nd Ed., Mausū'at al-Sunnah, Dār al-Da'wah and Dār Suḥnūn, 1992.

Al-Nashrātī, Ḥamzah, Farghali, 'Abd al-Ḥafīz and Mustafa, 'Abd al-Ḥamid, *al-Imām al-Zāhid Aḥmad Ibn Ḥanbal*, Wakālat al-Ahrām, n.d.

Al-Nawawī, Muḥiyy al-Dīn, *al-Majmū'*, edited by al-Muṭī'ī, Maktabat al-Irshād, Jaddah.

Al-Nawawī, Muḥiyy al-Dīn, *Mukhtaṣar Ṭabaqāt al-Fuqahā'*, 1st Ed., Dār al-Fikr, 1995.

Al-Nawawī, Muḥiyy al-Dīn, *Sharḥ Ṣaḥīḥ Muslim*, Dār al-Rayyān li al-Turāth, 1st Ed., Cairo, 1987.

Al-Nu'aymī, 'Abd al-Qādir, *al-Dāris fī Tārīkh al-Madāris*, edited by al-Ḥasanī, maṭba'at al-Taraqī, Damascus, 1948.

Al-Qarāfī, Aḥmad, *Sharḥ Tanqīḥ al-Fuṣūl*, edited by Sa'd, Maktabāt al-Kulliyyāt al-Azhariyyah, Cairo, n.d.

Al-Qaṭṭān, Mannā', *Tārīkh al-Tashrī' al-Islāmī*, 1st Ed., Maktabat al-Ma'ārif, Riyadh, 1992.

Al-Ramlī, Muḥammad, *Nihāyat al-Muḥtāj ilā Sharḥ al-Minhāj*, Dār al-Kutub al-'Ilmiyyah, Beirut, 1993.

Al-Rāzī, Muḥammad, *al-Maḥṣūl fī 'Ilm al-Uṣūl*, edited by al-'Alwānī, 1st Ed., 1979.

Al-Sa'dī, 'Abd al-Raḥmān, *Bahjat Qulūb al-Abrār*, al-Ri'āsah al-'Āmmah li al-Buḥūth wa 'l-Iftā', 1405.

Al-Sa'dī, 'Abd al-Raḥmān, *al-Mukhtārāt al-Jaliyyah min al-Masā'il al-Fiqhiyyah*, al-Mu'assasah al-Sa'idiyyah, Riyadh, n.d.

Al-Sa'dī, 'Abd al-Raḥmān, *al-Qawā'id wa 'l-Uṣūl al-Jāmi'ah*, 1st Ed., Dār Ramadī, Dammām, Saudi Arabia, 1996.

Al-Sa'dī, 'Abd al-Raḥmān, *Ṭarīq al-Wuṣūl ilā al-'Lim al-Ma'mūl*, al-Mu'assasah al-Sa'idiyyah, Riyadh, n.d.

Al-Sadlān, *al-Niyah wa atharha fī al-Aḥkām*, 2nd Ed., Dār 'Ālam al-Kutub, Riyadh, 1993.

Al-Ṣafadī, *al-Wāfī bi al-Wafiyyāt*, edited by Iḥsān 'Abbās, 2nd Ed., Franz, 1982.

Al-Saffārīnī, Muḥammad *Lawāmi' al-Anwār al-Bahiyyah*, al-Maktab al-Islāmī, Beirut, Dar al-Khānī, Riyadh, 3rd Ed., 1991.

Ṣafī al-Dīn, *al-Qawl al-Jalī fī tarjamat al-Sheikh Taqī al-Dīn Ibn Taymiyyah al-Ḥanbalī*, Maktabat Līnah, Egypt, n.d.

Ṣafī al-Dīn, 'Abd al-Mu'min, *Qawā'id al-Uṣūl wa ma'āqid al-Fuṣūl*, edited by al-Ḥakamī, 1st Ed., Jāmi'at Umm al-Qura, 1988.

Al-Sāhī, Shawqī, *al-Madkhal li Dirasat al-Fiqh al-Islāmī*, 1st Ed., Maktabat al-Nahḍah al-Miṣriyyah, Cairo, 1989.

Al-Sakhāwī, Muḥammad, *al-Ḍaw' al-Lāmi' li Ahl al-Qarn al-Tāsi'*, Dār Maktabat al-Hayāt, Beirut, n.d.

Al-Sakhāwī, Muḥammad, *al-I'lān bi al-Tawbīkh li man dhamm al-Tārīkh*, edited by Franz Runthal, Dār al-Kutub al-'lmiyyah, Beirut, n.d.

Salāmah, Muṣtafa, *al-Ta'sīs fī Uṣūl al-Fiqh*, 1st Ed., Maktabat Khalid, Bayt 'Aqabah, n.d.

Al-Sarkhasī, Muḥammad, *al-Mabsūṭ*, Dār al-Fikr, Beirut, 1989.

Al-Sarkhasī, Muḥammad, *Uṣūl al-Sarkhasī*, edited by al-Afghānī, Dār al-Kitāb al-'Arabī, Cairo, 1372.

Shalabī, Muḥammad, *al-Madkhal fī al-Ta'rīf bi al-Fiqh al-Islāmī*, Dār al-Nahḍah al-'Arabiyyah, Beirut, 1985.

Al-Shanqīṭī, Sayyid, *Dirāsāt I'lāmiyyah fī fikr Ibn Taymiyyah*, 1st Ed., Dār al-Muslim, Riyadh, 1996.

Sharaf al-Dīn, 'Abd al-'Aẓīm, *Tārīkh al-Tashrī' al-Islāmī*, 4th Ed., Jāmi'at Qar yunis, Benghazī, Labia, 1993.

Al-Shāshī, Aḥmad, *Uṣūl al-Shāshī*, Dār al-Kitāb al-'Arabī, Beirut, 1982.

Al-Shathrī, Sa'd, *al-Tafrīq bayn al-Uṣūl wa 'l-Furū'*, 1st Ed., Dār al-Muslim, Riyadh, 1997.

Al-Shawkānī, Muḥammad, *al-Badr al-Ṭāli' bi Maḥāsin man ba'd al-Qarn al-Sābi'*, 1st Ed., Maṭba'at al-Sa'ādah, Egypt, 1348.

Al-Shawkānī, Muḥammad, *Irshād al-Fuḥūl ilā taḥqīq 'lim al-Uṣūl*, 1st Ed., Mu'assasat al-Kutub al-Thaqāfiyyah, Beirut, 1992.

Al-Shawkānī, Muḥammad, *Nayl al-Awṭār Sharḥ Muntaqa al-Akhbār*, Maktabat al-Qāhirah, Cairo, 1978.

Al-Shaybānī, 'Abd al-Qādir, *Nayl al-Mā'rib fī Dalīl al-Ṭālib*, edited by al-Ashqar, Maktabat al-Falāḥ, Kuwait, 1st Ed., 1983.

Al-Shaybānī, Muḥammad, *Awrāq Majmū'ah min Ḥayāt Sheikh al-Islām Ibn Taymiyyah*, 1st Ed., Maktabat Ibn Taymiyyah, Kuwait, 1989.

Al-Shaybānī, Muḥammad, *Majmū'at Mualafāt sheikh al-Islām Ibn Taymiyyah*, 1st Ed., Markaz al-Makhṭūṭāt, Kuwait, 1993.

Al-Shaybānī, Muḥammad, *qiṭ'ah min maktūb Ibn Marī*, 1st Ed., Maktabat Ibn Taymiyyah, Kuwait, 1988.

Al-Shaysānī, H., *al-Ḥāfiẓ Shams al-Dīn al-Dhahabī*, 1st Ed., Dār al-Kutub al-'Ilmiyyah, Beirut, 1990.

Al-Shibl, 'Alī, *al-Thabt*, 1st Ed., Dār al-Waṭan, Riyadh, 1417.

Al-Shirāzī, Ibrāhīm, *al-Luma' fī Uṣūl al-Fiqh*, edited by al-Ḥalabī, Dār al-Nadwah al-Islamiyyah, 1988.

Al-Shirāzī, Ibrāhīm, *al-Muhadhdhab fī Fiqh al-Imām al-Shāfi'ī*, edited by Muhammad al-Zuḥaylī, Dār al-Qalam, 1st Ed., Damascus, 1996.

Shukrī, Murād, *Daf' al-Shubah al-Ghawiyyah 'An sheikh al-Islām Ibn Taymiyyah*, 1st Ed., 1994.

Al-Shurī, *al-Ḥāwī fī takhrīj Aḥādīth Majmū' al-Fatāwī*, 1st Ed., Dār al-Kutub al-'Lmiyyah, Beirut, 1995.

Al-Sijistānī, Sulyamān, *Masā'il al-Imām Aḥmad*, Dār al-Ma'rifah, Beirut, n.d.

Al-Subkī, 'Abd al-Wahhāb, *Ṭabaqāt al-Shāfi'iyyah al-Kubrā*, edited by al-Ṭunāḥī and al-Ḥulu, 2nd Ed., Hajar li al-Ṭiba'ah, 1992.

Sulaymān, *al-Fikr al-Fiqhī 'Inda Ibn Taymiyyah*, PhD thesis at the University of Cairo, 1978.

Al-Suyūtī, 'Abd al-Raḥmān, *Dhayl Tadhkirat al-Ḥuffāẓ, Dār al-Kutub al-'Lmiyyah*, Beirut, n.d.

Al-Suyūṭī, 'Abd al-Raḥmān, *Ḥusn al-Muḥāḍarah fī Tārīkh Miṣr wa 'l-Qāhirah*, edited by Ibrahim, 1st Ed., Dār Iḥyā' al-Kutub al-'Arabiyyah, Cairo, 1968.

Al-Ṭabarī, Muhammad, *Ikhtilāf al-Fuqahā'*, Dār al-Kutub al-'Ilmiyyah, Beirut, n.d.

Al-Ṭablāwī, Maḥmūd, *Mawqif Ibn Taymiyyah min falsafat Ibn Rushd*, 1st Ed., Maṭba'at al-Amānah, Cairo, 1989.

Al-Taftazānī, Sa'd al-Dīn, *Sharḥ al-Talwīḥ 'alā al-Tawḍīḥ*, Maktabat Ṣabīḥ, Cairo, n.d.

Ṭalas, Muḥammad, *'Aṣr al-Inbi'āth*, Dār al-Andalus Beirut, 1963.

Al-Ṭanṭāwī, Maḥmūd, *al-Madkhal ilā al-Fiqh al-Islāmī*, 1st Ed., Maktabat Wahbah, Cairo, 1987.

Al-Thaqafī, Sālim, *Mafātīḥ al-Fiqh al-Ḥanbalī*, 1st Ed., Al-Ahrām, Cairo, 1978.

Al-Thaqafī, Sālim, *Muṣṭalaḥāt al-Fiqh al-Ḥanbalī*, 2nd Ed., Dār al-Naṣr li al-Ṭibā'ah al-Islāmiyyah, Cairo, 1981.

Al-Tirmidhī, *Sunan*, 2nd Ed., Mausū'at al-Sunnah, Dār al-Da'wah and Dār Suḥnūn, 1992.

Al-Ṭūfī, Sulaymān, *Sharḥ Mukhtaṣar al-Rawḍah*, 1st Ed., Mu'assasat al-Risālah, Beirut, 1987.

Al-Ṭurayfī, Nāṣir, *Tārīkh al-Fiqh al-Islāmī*, 1st Ed., Sharikat al-'Ubaykān, Riyadh, 1987.

Al-Turkī, 'Abd Allah, *Uṣūl Madhhab al-Imām Aḥmad*, 3rd Ed., Mu'assasat al-Risālah, Beirut, 1990.

Al-'Ulaymī, 'Abd al-Raḥmān, *al-Dūr al-Munaḍḍad fī Dhikr Aṣḥāb al-Imām Aḥmad*, edited by al-'Uthaymīn, 1st Ed., Maktabat al-Tawbah, Riyadh, 1992.

Al-'Ulaymī, 'Abd al-Raḥmān, *al-Na't al-Akmal*, edited by 'Abd al-Ḥamīd, 2nd Ed., 'Ālam al-Kutub, Beirut, 1984.

Al-'Uqaylī, Muḥammad, *Kitāb al-Ḍu'afā' al-Kabīr*, edited by Qal'ajī, Dār al-bāz, Makkah, 1st Ed., n.d.

Al-'Uṭayshān, Sa'ūd, *Manhaj Ibn Taymiyyah fī al-Fiqh*, unpublished PhD thesis submitted to the University of al-Madīnah, 1985.

Al-Wāsiṭī, *al-Tadhkirah*, edited by al-Faryawā'ī, 1st Ed., Dār al-'Āṣimah, Riyadh, 1994.

Al-Zaraklī, Khayr al-Dīn, *al-A'lām*, 3rd Ed., n.d.

Al-Zarkashī, Muḥammad, *al-Baḥr al-Muḥīṭ fī Uṣūl al-Fiqh*, edited by Abū Ghuddah, 2nd Ed., Wazārat al-Awqāf wa 'l-Shu'ūn al-Islāmiyyah, 1992.

Al-Zarkashī, Muḥammad, *Salāsil al-Dhahab*, edited by al-Shanqīṭī, 1st Ed., 1990.

Al-Zarkashī, Muḥammad, *Sharḥ al-Zarkashī*, 1st Ed., Maktabat al-'Ubaykān, Riyadh, 1991.

Al-Zarqā', Muṣṭafā, *al-Fiqh al-Islāmī*, 1st Ed., Dār al-Qalam, Damascus, 1995.

Zayd, Muṣṭafā, *al-Maṣlaḥah fī al-Tashrī' al-Islāmī wa Najm al-Dīn al-Ṭūfī*, 2nd Ed., Dār al-Fikr al-'Arabī, 1964.

Zaydān, 'Abd al-Karīm, *al-Madkhal li Dirāsat al-Sharī'ah al-Islāmiyyah*, 11th Ed., Mu'assasat al-Risalah, Beirut, 1990.

Al-Zurqānī, 'Abd al-Bāqī, *Sharḥ al-Zurqānī 'alā Mukhtaṣar sīdī Khalīl*, Dār al-Fikr al-'Arabī, n.d.

English references

Abd Rahim, Rahimin, 'The concept of *Ijmā'* in Islamic law: a comparative study' *Hamadred Islamicus* vol. XVII, Summer 1994, no. 2, pp. 91–103.

Abrahamopv, 'Necessary knowledge in Islamic theology' *British Journal of Middle Eastern Studies*, vol. 20, no. 1, 1993, p. 20–32.

Alhomaid, Abdullah, *Authority of the Text and the Limits of Religious Toleration in Islamic Political Thought: The Case of Ahmad Ibn Taymiyah*, a dissertation presented to the faculty of the graduate school, University of Southern California, 1996.

Al-'Alwani, Taha, *Uṣūl al-Fiqh al-Islamī*, 1st Ed., the international institute of Islamic thought, Virginia, 1990.

Amital-Preiss, R.A., *Mongols and Mamluks*, Cambridge University Press, Cambridge, 1995.

Arnaldez, R., Grammaire et théologie chez Ibn Hazm de Cordoue, Paris, 1956.

Ashtor, E., *A Social and Economic History of the Near East in the Middle Ages*, Collins, London, 1976.

Ayalon, David, 'Some remarks on the Economic decline of the Mamluk Sultanate' pp. 108–124 in *Jerusalem Studies in Arabic and Islam*, vol. 16, 1993.

Azami, *Studies in Hadith Methodology and Literature*, 2nd Ed., American Trust publications, Indianapolis, IN, 1992.

Berkey, J., *The Transmission of Knowledge In Medieval Cairo*, Princeton University Press, Princeton, NJ, 1992.

Bosworth, C.E., 'The Qur'anic Prophet Shu'aib and Ibn Taymiyya's Epistle concerning him,' pp. 425–440, *Medieval Arabic Culture and Administration*, Variorum Reprints, London, 1982.

Burton, John, *An introduction to the Ḥadīth*, Edinburgh University Press, Edinburgh, 1994.

Chamberlain, M., *Knowledge And Social Practice In Medieval Damascus*, 1190–1350, Cambridge University Press, Cambridge, 1994.

Dutton, Yasin, *The Origins of Islamic Law, the Qur'an, the Muwaṭṭa' and the Madinan 'Amal*, 1st Ed., Curzon press, Surrey, UK, 1999.

Esposito, John, *Woman in Muslim family law*, 1st Ed., Syracuse University Press, Syracuse, NY, 1982.

Al-Freih, *The Historical Background of the Emergence of Muhammad Ibn Abd Al-Wahhab and his Movement*, unpublished PhD thesis, University of California, Los Angeles, 1990.

Hallaq, Wael, *Ibn, Taymiyya Against the Greek Logicians*, Clarendon press, Oxford, 1993.

Haque, 'Ahmad Ibn Hanbal: the saint-scholar of Baghdad', p. 68, *Hamadard Islamicus*, vol. VIII/ November 3 /Autumn 1985.

Heinrichs, W., 'Contacts between scriptural hermeneutics and literary theory in Islam: the case of majaz', Zeitschrift fuer Geschichte der Arabisch-Islamischen Wissenschaften/ Majallat Tarikh al-'Ulum al-'Arabiya wa 'l-Islamiya, no. 7, pp. 253–284, 1992.

Heinrichs, W., 'On the Genesis of the Haqıqa-Majaz Dichotomy', *Studia Islamica*, vol. 59, 1984, pp. 111–140.

Holt, P.M., *The Age of the Crusades*, Longman, London, 1986.

Ibn Khallikan, *Biographical Dictionary*, trans. by Slane, Librairie Du Liban, Beirut, 1970.

Ibn Rushd, Muhammad, *Bidāyat al-Mujtahid*, trans. by Nyazee, 1st Ed., the centre for Muslim contribution to civilisation, Garent Publishing Limited, Reading, 1994–1996.

Ibn Taymiyya, *Public Duties in Islam*, trans. Holland, Islamic Foundation, Leicester, UK, 1982.

Ibn Taymiyyah, Aḥmad, *Ibn Taymiyya on Public and Private Law in Islam*, trans. by Farrukh, 1st Ed., Khayat, Beirut, 1966.

Irwin, Robert, *The Middle East in the Middle Ages*, Southern Ciliinois University Press, Carbondale, 1986.

Islahi, A., *Economic Concepts of Ibn Tayimiyah*, The Islamic Foundation, Leicester, UK. 1988.

Jokisch, B., '*Ijtihad* in Ibn Taymiyya's *fatawa*', in *Islamic Law, Theory and Practice*, edited by Gleave, R. and Kermeli, E., I.B. Tauris Publishers, London, 1996.

Kamali, Muhammad, *Principles of Islamic Jurisprudence*, Islamic Texts Society, Cambridge, 1991.

Khalid, Anas, *The 'Mukhtaṣar' of Al-Khiraqi: A Tenth century work on Islamic Jurisprudence*, unpublished PhD thesis submitted to the University of New York, October 1992.

Khan, Qamarudin, *The Political Thought of Ibn Taymiyya*, 2nd Ed., Adam publisher and distributors, Delhi, 1992.

Kucukcan, Talip, 'Some reflections on the Wahhabiyyah' in *Hamadred Islamicus*, vol. XVIII, Summer 1995, no. 2, pp. 67–82.

Kutty, Bilal, 'Muhammad Ibn 'Abdul Wahhab and his reform movement' in *Hamadred Islamicus*, vol. XX/ April–June 1997, no. 2, p. 43.

Lambton, Ann, *State and Government in Medieval Islamic Political theory*, Oxford University Press, Oxford, 1981.

Lane-Poole, Stanley, *The Mohammadan Dynasties*, Khayats, Beirut, 1966.

Little, Donald, 'The Historical and historiographical significance of the detention of Ibn Taymiyya' in *The International Journal of Middle East Studies*, vol. 4, 1973, pp. 311–327.

Loucel, H., 'L'Origine du langage d'après les grammairiens arabes', Arabica 10, 1963, pp. 188–208 and pp. 253–81; Arabica 11, 1964, pp. 57–72 and pp. 157–187.

Makdisi, George, *Ibn 'Aqil*, Edinburgh University Press, Edinburgh, 1997.

Makdisi, George, 'Ibn Taymiyya's autograph manuscript on Istihsan: material for the study of Islamic legal thought', *Arabic and Islamic studies in honour of H.A.R. Gibb* 1965, pp. 446–479.

Makdisi, George, *The Rise of Colleges*, Edinburgh University Press, Edinburgh, 1981.

Martin, Richard and Woodward with Atmaja others, *Defenders of Reason in Islam*, Oneworld publications, Oxford, 1997.

Melchert, Christopher, *The Formation of the Sunni Schools of Law, 9th–10th centuries* CE, Brill, Leiden, New York, 1997.

Memon, *Ibn Taymiyya's Struggle against Popular Religion*, Mouton the Hague, Paris, 1976.

Al-Mohideb, AbdulRahman, *Criminal Procedures relevant to crimes of killing in the Kingdom of Saudi Arabia*, unpublished PhD thesis submitted to the University of Glasgow, June 1996.

Mughni, Syafiq, *Hanbali Movement in Baghdad from Abū Muhammad al-Barahari to Abū Ja'far al-Hāshimī*, unpublished PhD thesis submitted to the University of California, Los Angeles, 1990.

Nasri, Hani, *Ibn Abd al-Wahhab's Philosophy of Society: An Alternative to the Tribal Mentality*, unpublished PhD thesis, Fordham University, Bronx, NY, 1978.

Netton, Ian, *A Popular Dictionary of Islam*, 1st Ed., Curzon Press Ltd., London, UK, 1992.

Netton, Ian, *Allah Transcendent: Studies in the Structure and Semiotics of Islamic Philosophy, Theology and Cosmology*, 1st Ed., Routledge, London, and New York, 1989.

Nimrdo, Hurvitz, *Ahmad Ibn Hanbal and the formation of Islamic orthodoxy*, unpublished PhD thesis submitted to the University of Princeton, 1994.

Philips, Abū Ameenah, *The Evolution of Fiqh*, 3rd Ed., International Islamic publishing house, Riyadh, 1995.

Ridgeon, Lioyd, *Nothing but the Truth*, unpublished PhD thesis, Leeds University, 1996.

Safiullah, M., 'Wahhabism: a conceptual relationship between Muhammad Ibn 'Abdul Wahhab and Taqiyy al-Din Ahmad Ibn Taymiyya' in *Hamadard Islamicus*, vol. X, no. 1, Spring 1987, pp. 67–83.

Schacht, Joseph, *An Introduction to Islamic law*, Oxford University Press, Oxford, 1994.

Al-Shāfi'ī, Muhammad, al-Shāfi'ī's *Risāla*, trans. Khadduri, 2nd Ed., the Islamic texts society, Cambridge, MA, 1987.

Shah, M., 'The philological endeavours of the early Arabic linguists: theological implications of the tawqıf-istilah antithesis and the majaz controversy (parts I and II)', *Journal of Quranic Studies*, vol. 1, no. 1, 1999, pp. 27–46, and vol. 2, no. 1, 2000, pp. 44–66.

Sourdel, D., *Medieval Islam*, Routledge and Kegan Paul, London, 1983.

Al-Tabari, *The History of al-Tabari* (*Tārīkh al-Rusul wa 'l-Mulūk*), trans. and published by State University of New York Press, Albany, 1985.

The Encyclopaedia of Islam, new edition, Brill, Leiden, Luzac and Co., London, 1961–1971.

Watt, W.M., *Islamic Philosophy and Theology*, Edinburgh University Press, Edinburgh, 1962.

Watt, W.M., 'The expedition of *al-Hudaybiya* reconsidered', in *Hamadard Islamicus*, vol. VIII, no. 1, Spring 1985.

Weeramantry, C.G., *Islamic Jurisprudence: An International Perspective*, Macmillan, Basingstoke, 1988.

Weiss, B.G., 'Medieval muslim Discussions of the origin of language', Zeitschrift der deutschen morgenlndischen Gesellschaft, Wiesbaden, vol. 125, 1974, pp. 33–41.

Al-Yahya, Nasser, *Ibn Qudamah's methodology and his approach to certain aspects of the Islamic law of international relations in the Ḥanbalī juristic tradition*, unpublished PhD thesis submitted to the University of Manchester, 1992.

Yusuf, Aremu, *The Theory of Istihsan*, unpublished PhD thesis, the University of MacGill, Canada 1992.

INDEX